EMPLOYMENT LAW IN SCOTLAND

EMPLOYMENT LAW IN SCOTLAND

Second Edition

Victor Craig
Solicitor
Professor of Employment Law
Heriot-Watt University

Kenneth Miller
Professor of Law
University of Strathclyde

T&T CLARK
EDINBURGH
1996

T&T CLARK LTD
59 GEORGE STREET
EDINBURGH EH2 2LQ
SCOTLAND

First published 1991
Reprinted 1993
Second Edition 1996

British Library Cataloguing-in-Publication Data
A catalogue record for this book is
available from the British Library

ISBN 0 567 00510 0

Typeset by Fakenham Photosetting Ltd, Norfolk
Printed and bound in Great Britain by Bell & Bain Ltd, Glasgow

CONTENTS

CONTENTS

PREFACE TO THE SECOND EDITION

Although there have been many changes to the substantive law since July 1991 the authors have sought to retain the structure of the first edition by integrating the relevant developments where appropriate. It should not be thought however that such changes as have occurred are marginal or insignificant. That is not the case — and for that reason alone this edition might have been regarded as overdue.

Employment law in Scotland continues to reflect a mixture of specialist tribunals and ordinary courts. Even where the underlying legal provisions are the same Scots lawyers can still arrive at different conclusions — witness the different approaches taken regarding jurisdiction and time limits for enforcing European employment rights. Where the common law is concerned, the attitude of Scots law to important questions like illegal contracts and restrictive covenants continues to require mention, as does the circumstances in which the Court of Session will entertain an application for judicial review — an area of law where Scots law has developed its own rules — and the novel matter of when a trade union in a representative capacity may bring judicial review proceedings. The Scottish appeal in *Brown v. Rentokil Ltd* dealing with the important question of dismissal for absence during pregnancy has been referred to the European Court of Justice.

In addition to legislation consolidating the law regarding trade unions and collective labour relations, individual employment rights and industrial tribunals, since the first edition legislation has virtually eliminated the concept of continuous employment, extended the law regarding unfair dismissal, removed the arbitrary restrictions on compensation for acts of sexual discrimination while shifting the focus away from the trade union as the collective agent where negotiation and consultation are concerned. Material changes to the law regarding industrial action and trade union government and membership were introduced in 1993 and the Disability Discrimination Act 1995 will become effective as far as employment is concerned on December 2, 1996. Although legislation is expected soon to transpose Directives on Working Time and Children and Young Persons and the government has published a draft Bill on Employment Rights Dispute Resolution, at the time of writing there are no major legislative proposals currently before Parliament. A second edition seemed necessary and timely.

Completing this edition would not have been possible without support at work and understanding at home. T&T Clark, to whom the first drafts were submitted before the Parliamentary timetable for the Employment Rights Act 1996 and the Industrial Tribunals Act 1996 was known, dealt with obscure manuscript and innumerable textual alterations with an ever-cheerful disposition for which we record our thanks. The authors alone are responsible for any errors or omissions which remain and have sought to state the law as at August 22, 1996.

Vic Craig & Kenny Miller
Edinburgh and Glasgow
September 1, 1996

TABLE OF CASES

TABLE OF STATUTES

1

STATUTORY INSTRUMENTS

ABBREVIATIONS

Statutes

CPPA 1875	Conspiracy and Protection of Property Act 1875
DDA 1995	Disability Discrimination Act 1995
EA 1980	Employment Act 1980
EA 1982	Employment Act 1982
EA 1988	Employment Act 1988
EA 1989	Employment Act 1989
EA 1990	Employment Act 1990
EPA 1975	Employment Protection Act 1975
EPCA 1978	Employment Protection (Consolidation) Act 1978
ERA 1996	Employment Rights Act 1996
EqPA 1979	Equal Pay Act 1970
IRA 1971	Industrial Relations Act 1971
ITA 1996	Industrial Tribunals Act 1996
RRA 1976	Race Relations Act 1976
SDA 1975	Sex Discrimination Act 1975
SDA 1986	Sex Discrimination Act 1986
TDA 1906	Trade Disputes Act 1906
TUA 1871	Trade Union Act 1871
TUA 1913	Trade Union Act 1913
TUA 1984	Trade Union Act 1984
TULRA 1974	Trade Union and Labour Relations Act 1974
TULR(A)A 1976	Trade Union and Labour Relations (Amendment) Act 1976
TULRCA 1992	Trade Union and Labour Relations (Consolidation) Act 1992
TULERA 1993	Trade Union Reform and Employment Rights Act 1993
WA 1986	Wages Act 1986

Institutions

ACAS	Advisory, Conciliation and Arbitration Service
CA	Court of Appeal
CAC	Central Arbitration Committee
CBI	Confederation of British Industry
CIR	Commission on Industrial Relations
CO	Certification Officer
CRE	Commission for Racial Equality
CROTUM	Commissioner for the Rights of Trade Union Members
DE	Department of Employment
EAT	Employment Appeal Tribunal
EC	European Communities
ECJ	European Court of Justice
EOC	Equal Opportunities Commission
HC	High Court of Justice
HL	House of Lords
IH	Inner House of the Court of Session
IT	Industrial Tribunal
JIC	Joint Industrial Council
NDC	National Disability Council
NICA	Northern Ireland Court of Appeal

NIRC	National Industrial Relations Court
OH	Outer House of the Court of Session
TUC	Trades Union Congress
STUC	Scottish Trades Union Congress
WC	Wages Council

Law Reports and Journals

AC	Appeal Cases
All ER	All England Reports
BJIR	British Journal of Industrial Relations
Ch	Chancery Cases
CLJ	Cambridge Law Journal
GWD	Green's Weekly Digest
ICR	Industrial Cases Reports
ILJ	Industrial Law Journal
IRLR	Industrial Relations Law Reports
IRRR	Industrial Relations Review and Report
ITR	Industrial Tribunals Reports
JC	Justiciary Cases
JR	Juridical Review
KIR	Knight's Industrial Reports
LQR	Law Quarterly Review
MLR	Modern Law Review
QB	Queen's Bench Reports
SC	Session Cases
SCLR	Scottish Civil Law Reports
SLT	Scots Law Times
WLR	Weekly Law Reports

Other Abbreviations

GOQ	Genuine Occupational Qualification
LOST	Lay Off or Short Time
UMA	Union Membership Agreement or Arrangement

Chapter One

DEVELOPMENT OF MODERN LABOUR LAW

1.1 The early law of master and servant

Before the last century, the relationship of master and servant was, in Scotland as in England, primarily a matter of status rather than consensual agreement. This did not mean that service entailed a servile or even quasi-servile role, though this was the case in a few exceptional occupations such as collier or salter,[1] where workers were *adscriptae glebae* and were conveyed along with the lands on which they worked. The category of servants which Erskine[2] describes as "necessary" (and contrasts with "voluntary") were also required by law to take work when it was offered to them. Stair, however, distinguishes between the position of the bondsman and that of the hired labourer, and observes[3] "Servants with us, which now retain that name, are judged free persons, and have but hired their labour and work to their masters for a time, which is a kind of contract betwixt them." The state of slavery itself was described as incompatible with the law of Scotland in *Knight v. Wedderburn.*[4] But while it is true that a degree of freedom was seen as existing from Stair's time both with regard to the decision to enter into employment and the terms and conditions that applied when this was done, the content of the employment relationship itself was largely determined in advance of it being entered into. It was shaped not only by the custom and practice of the particular trade, but also by legislation which fixed, through rules of criminal law, wage rates and penalised unauthorised absences on the part of employees. It was only in the nineteenth century, when it became accepted practice to explain reciprocal obligations through the medium of consensual agreement and a philosophy of individualism[5] that the contract of employment began to take on the central role which it still has today. "[T]he Victorian era witnessed a radical change in this as in many other matters. The contract of service is the result of a purely voluntary consent on both sides. It may contain such terms as the parties thereto agree upon. The obligations which it imposes are strictly mutual."[6] However, the movement from a kind of status to contract was not necessarily associated with social reform or improvements in legal protections for the weaker party to the relationship. In *Bartonshill Coal Co. v. Reid,*[7] for example, the House of Lords imposed in the Scottish courts the doctrine of common employment, by

---

[1] For an account of the special features of certain early employment relationships in Scotland, see J. R. Philip, "Early Labour in Scotland" (1934) 46 JR 121; Erskine, *Principles*, I, VII, 60. See, generally, O. Kahn-Freund, "Blackstone's Neglected Child: the Contract of Employment" (1977) 93 LQR 508.

[2] *Principles* I, VII, 61.

[3] *Institutions* I.3.15.

[4] (1778) Mor 14545.

[5] P. S. Atiyah, *The Rise and Fall of Freedom of Contract* (1979), pp. 226–237.

[6] Umpherston, *The Law of Master and Servant* (1904), p. v.

[7] (1858) 3 Macqueen 266.

which a servant was deemed to have agreed, as an implied term of his contract of employment, that he would not sue his master to recover damages for injuries caused by the negligence of a fellow-servant. Prior to that decision the Scottish courts had had no truck with the doctrine, "a principle as distasteful as it was alien to Scottish jurisprudence"[8]; after it, the Scottish courts were obliged to operate this fictional agreement within the contract as a means of limiting delictual liability.[9]

1.2 The spread of contract

Apart from being influenced by the general enthusiasm for contract as a basis for the ordering of society, the rise of the contract of employment as a legal device was also attributable to its usefulness to the parliamentary draftsmen of the late nineteenth and early twentieth centuries who had the task of defining the scope of legislation. This was important as statute law in the area of employment was introduced on a large scale to complement the older common law rules.[10] For example, the early provision made for industrial injury under the Workmen's Compensation Act 1906 applied generally only to those who were employed under a contract of service or apprenticeship,[11] and similarly the National Insurance Act 1911, which first made general provision for unemployment and sickness insurance and so can be described as one of the precursors of the welfare state, applied only to persons in this category. The increase in legislation dealing with welfare and employment thus contributed to the success of the contract of employment (or service) as a technical legal advice. The result was the unification of working relationships so that, in legal theory, the great majority of working people, whatever the content of the jobs they did, came to be seen as working under the same legal framework. It was this tendency (which was further developed in the course of the present century) which led Kahn-Freund to make his famous judgment that the contract of employment is the "cornerstone" of British labour law.[12] But it is worth remembering that this unity was not always a feature of the law. One may point by way of contrast to Bell's treatment of the employment relationship and note the distinctions he draws between the rules applied to hiring of domestic servants, managers, ordinary labour and skilled labour. For each of these categories there are a separate set of legal rules to be applied.[13] In modern times and even after increased statutory intervention the contract of employment continues to play an important, though not exclusive, role in defining employment rights. The significance of satisfying the rules regarding continuity of employment[14] as the means of accessing statutory employment rights has been greatly reduced by the passage of the Employment Protection (Part-time Employees)

---

[8] *Radcliffe v. Ribble Motor Services Ltd* [1939] AC 215 at p. 235 *per* Lord MacMillan; *Dixon v. Rankin* (1852) 14 D 420. For a fuller discussion of the doctrine of common employment see V. Craig and K. Miller, *Introduction to the Law of Health and Safety at Work in Scotland* (1994), pp. 25–28.

[9] See Fraser, *Master and Servant* (2nd edn, 1872), pp. 198–229; A. C. Gibb, *Law from Over the Border* (1950), pp. 99–100.

[10] Fraser, *Master and Servant*, p. 243.

[11] Section 13. Some of the early decisions made under this legislation are still of practical importance. See, e.g. the reliance placed on *Simmons v. Heath Laundry Co.* [1910] 1 KB 543, CA by Sir John Donaldson MR in *O'Kelly v. Trusthouse Forte plc* [1983] IRLR 369, CA [1983] ICR 728, CA.

[12] A. D. Flanders and H. A. Clegg (eds), *The System of Industrial Relations in Great Britain* (1954), p. 45.

[13] *Principles* s. 190.

[14] See para. 3.2.

Regulations 1995[15] which provide that a week counts towards a period of continuous employment provided in that week there exists a contract of employment[16]; and the significance of a qualifying period of continuous employment may be reduced further depending on the legislature's reaction to the decision of the Court of Appeal in *R. v. Secretary of State for Employment, ex parte Seymour-Smith and Perez*[17] that in respect of entitlement to claim unfair dismissal imposing a two year qualifying period may be indirect sexual discrimination. However, while the courts and tribunals continue to develop implied terms[18] and more significant changes result from statutes whose application in the main is confined to the relationship contained in the contract of employment, it is necessary to note (i) that some important statutes apply to contractual relationships which are not strictly those of employment[19]; (ii) the willingness of the courts to look behind the stated form of a relationship[20]; and (iii) many European Directives apply to the "employment relationship" rather than merely to the technical concept of the contract of employment and particularly where domestic law has been enacted to implement such a Directive any domestic provision which seeks to define its application by reference to a contractual relationship will have to reflect the Directive wherever possible.[21]

1.3 Collective labour relations

The growth of industrial employment in the nineteenth century led directly to the formation of trade unions, which sought to regulate relations between employers and employed by means of collective bargaining. In the course of the century both the nature and functions of trade unionism radically altered. Originally the descendants of organisations which had brought together skilled workmen in selected professions, the unions by the end of the century had extended to cover also large sections of the unskilled workforce, and in so doing had become a powerful political force. It has been remarked that, despite periods of oppression and difficulty, trade unions had, by the end of the Victorian period, become an integrated part of the economic and political life of society.[22] But this acceptance of trade unions by society at large was perhaps less evident in Scotland than elsewhere in the United Kingdom, where an industrial system founded on cheap labour in manufacturing industries bred a class consciousness and class hostility that was to prove long-lasting and divisive.[23] In any event, the gradual assimilation of unions within British society was a movement not reflected in the attitudes of the common law. Throughout the century, the judges (at first with the active

---

[15] SI 1995 No. 31.

[16] ERA, s. 212.

[17] [1995] IRLR 464, CA.

[18] See, for example, *W. A. Goold (Pearmark) Ltd, v. McConnell* [1995] IRLR 516 (employer's duty to promptly afford a reasonable opportunity to employees to obtain redress of grievances) and *Whitbread plc t/a Thresher v. Gullyes* (EAT Case No. 478/92) (duty of employer to provide adequate support staff to enable employee to carry out tasks).

[19] See, for example, the Sex Discrimination Act 1975, s. 83(1), the Race Relations Act 1976, s. 78(1), the Disability Discrimination Act 1995, s. 68(1) and the Employment Rights Act 1996, s. 230(3); and see *B. P. Chemicals v. Gillick* [1995] IRLR 28, EAT.

[20] See, for example, *McMeechan v. Secretary of State for Employment* [1995] IRLR 461, EAT (temporary worker has contract with employment agency).

[21] See, for example, *Leighton v. Michael and Charalambous* [1996] IRLR 67, EAT (effect of Equal Treatment Directive on interpreting s. 83 of the Sex Discrimination Act 1975). And see Directive 77/187 (Acquired Rights in Transfers of Undertakings), Art. 3(1).

[22] H. Phelps-Brown, *The Origins of Trade Union Power* (1983), Ch. I.

[23] T. C. Smout, *A Century of the Scottish People, 1830–1950* (1986), p. 4.

assistance of Parliament, later in opposition to the prevailing tendency of legislation) developed and extended forms of liabilities, both civil and criminal, which restricted the activities of unions in general, and in the organisation of strikes and picketing in particular. The legislative milestones in this period of development were the reform of the Combination Acts in 1824, the statutes of 1871 and 1875[24] which granted immunities from judge-made liabilities. But of equal importance to these direct reforms were the acts which in 1832, 1867 and 1884 extended the Parliamentary franchise. The liberalising measures of the 1870s were directly attributable to the new political power wielded by the working class, manifested in the Trades Union Congress, which first met in 1868. The reforming measures of 1871 and 1875 introduced immunities in respect of conspiracy (criminal and civil), and allowed the unions some freedom of action in the organisation of their affairs, internal and external. But as late as 1901 the House of Lords was able to deliver a crippling blow to union activity in the *Taff Vale* decision,[25] by holding that unions could be sued for damages in respect of wrongs committed by its officials. This decision required legislative reversal, which came in the shape of the great ''settlement'' of the Trade Disputes Act 1906. This statute set, for more than 60 years, the framework within which unions enjoyed a freedom — always relative, and varying according to the attitudes taken by the judiciary at different times — sufficient to allow them to operate without perpetual legal opposition; in common with the legal systems of Western Europe, organised labour in Britain may be said to have passed through an environment first of legal repression, then toleration, followed by recognition.[26] The hostility which the movement met from the judiciary during its formative period contributed, however, to a distrust on the part of unions of legislation which had to be applied by the courts[27] and to the tradition of ''absentionism'' (i.e. the exclusion of the law from relations between employers and unions) which characterised British labour law until the 1970s.

1.4 Acceptance of the legitimacy and desirability of trade unions within the general social fabric was, however, a feature of successive governments, Conservative and Labour, throughout most of the present century. This acceptance was marked by several features: the acceptance of international standards demonstrating a commitment to freedom of association,[28] the acceptance of collective bargaining, conducted through representative unions, by government, in its capacity as employer, and by a commitment to collective bargaining as the preferred method for settling disputes over terms and conditions of employment in different industries. In the years since 1970, however, collective labour law has undergone a series of transformations. The Royal Commission on Trades Unions and Employers Associations (the Donovan Commission), which reported in 1968, recommended major changes in collective bargaining, but argued for the preservation of the voluntarist traditions. However, the Conservative government of 1971 tried, through the Industrial Relations Act 1971, to effect a reform of industrial relations posited on a new framework of legal controls on trades unions. And the

---

[24] Trade Union Act 1871; Conspiracy and Protection of Property Act 1875.
[25] *Taff Vale Railway Co. v. Amalgamated Society of Railway Servants* [1901] AC 426. See Chapter Eleven.
[26] A. Jacobs in *The Making of Labour Law in Europe* (Bob Hepple (ed.), 1986), pp. 194 ff.
[27] P. Davies and M. R. Freedland (eds), *Kahn-Freund's Labour and the Law* (3rd edn, 1986), p. 53.
[28] E.g. International Labour Organisation, Conventions Nos 87, 98.

1980s and 1990s have seen an even more profound attack on unionism, by a government which sees unions as responsible for many of the inadequacies of the labour market, and has accordingly drastically reduced the statutory immunities which allowed trade unions to operate free of legal intervention. Since 1980 the principle of legal support for collective bargaining has been progressively and seriously eroded,[29] and it is no longer possible to identify positive governmental support for this activity. Indeed it may be argued that in some cases recent legislative action has undermined existing trade union positions. Thus in 1993 to combat decisions of the Court of Appeal[30] legislation was enacted[31] so that a tribunal, when faced with evidence that the purposes of an employer in taking action (awarding a pay increase only to those employees who agreed to personal (as opposed to collective) negotiation) were to further a change in his relationship with his employees — a lawful purpose — and to deter or penalise union membership — an unlawful purpose — was, irrespective of what might be described as the dominant purpose, in effect required to disregard the latter unlawful purpose. The clear signal was to fortify employers who may have been considering abandoning collective bargaining. A similar attitude to recognised trade unions is seen when one considers the legislation introduced to comply with the European Union Directives dealing with Collective Redundancies and the Transfer of Undertakings.[32] While the relevant statutory instrument[33] requires all employers to consult prior to dismissal on grounds of redundancy or the transfer of an undertaking where an employer already recognises a trade union the employer may choose to consult with the worker representatives to the exclusion of the trade union representatives.[34]

1.5 Contract and statute

We have seen that in the nineteenth century the contract of employment achieved its pivotal position in explaining the relationship between employer and employee. Important though the contract of employment is, however, it must be considered alongside the various statutes which also regulate employment terms and conditions. Statutory intervention designed to protect the interests of employees has a long history. The Truck Acts 1831–96 for over 150 years stood to protect full payment of wages without unauthorised deductions to persons engaged in manual labour until their repeal in 1986.[35] In the field of health and safety at work too, statutory regulation dates back to the nineteenth century. Yet these early legislative incursions into the content of the employment relationship are often viewed as the exception rather than the rule in a system which we have said was characterised by legal "abstentionism".[36] In the last 30 years, however, there are indications that a

---

[29] See Chapters Nine and Eleven. See also R. Lewis, "The Role of the Law in Employment Relations" in R. Lewis (ed.), *Labour Law in Britain* (1986), pp. 7–8.

[30] *Associated British Ports v. Palmer* [1993] IRLR 336; *Associated Newspapers v. Wilson* [1992] IRLR 440. In fact the Court of Appeal was overturned by the House of Lords: [1995] IRLR 258 but the legislation had been introduced before the House of Lords heard the appeals.

[31] TURERA, s. 13.

[32] Directive 75/129 and Directive 77/187.

[33] The Collective Redundancies and Transfer of Undertakings (Protection of Employment) (Amendment) Regulations 1995, SI 1995 No. 2587.

[34] See Chapter Nine, para. 9.48.

[35] Wages Act 1986. See para. 3.29.

[36] See, e.g., R. Lewis, "The Historical Development of Labour Law" (1976) *British Journal of Industrial Relations*, Vol. XIV, No. 1, 1, 7.

new approach towards legislation has become established. Whereas in the period 1950 to 1959 there were five general Acts of Parliament regulating employment, the total increased to 16 in 1960 to 1969 and 30 in the period 1970 to 1979.[37] The reasons for this proliferation of statute law are diverse. In part it can be explained by the entry of the United Kingdom into the European Economic Community, which brought with it the continuing obligation to amend and reform our law to comply with the requirements of the Treaty of Rome and the Directives made under it. In part it is to be attributed to the politicisation of employment law which took place in the 1970s following the enactment of the Industrial Relations Act 1971. It has also happened (as in the case of the Health and Safety at Work etc. Act 1974) that statutory reform of out-dated legislation has occurred at a time when other events were taking place. Thus employment legislation has been used by governments in recent years as a means of promoting particular economic policies. A good example is the Redundancy Payments Act 1965 which, by offering financial compensation to individuals whose jobs disappeared, was intended to encourage the adoption of new technology and a corresponding rise in productive efficiency.[38] But state intervention in the fixing of terms and conditions of employment may proceed from less obvious sources. The consensus among politicians of the 1960s that there was a need to reform the voluntarist system of collective bargaining in order to control inflation, led directly to the imposition of prices and incomes policies which interfered with the operation of free collective bargaining in the setting of rates of pay. Furthermore, when a different and more combative strategy of controlling the power of trades unions was tried by a Conservative government in 1971 with the passing of the Industrial Relations Act, concessions in the shape of the introduction of statutory protection for individuals against unfair dismissal were made by the government, arguably in order to make the total package of reforms more acceptable to the union movement. The use of labour law reform as an inducement to obtain political co-operation from interest groups within society is not the prerogative of any one political party. Many rights for individuals were introduced in the Employment Protection Act 1975, legislation which the Labour government of the day hoped would be instrumental in securing the support of the trade union movement for its policies as part of its incomes policy, which went by the name of a "social contract".[39] All these provide reasons for the large-scale reform of individual employment law through statute which took place between 1963 and 1979.

1.6 Deregulation of employment law

The period since 1979 has been typified by the tension produced by the determination of the United Kingdom government to reduce or deregulate the labour market and its obligation to introduce such measures as are necessary to give effect to those tenets of the European Union's social policy relating to non-discrimination, worker consultation and employment conditions. Thus the qualifying period for claiming unfair dismissal having been increased from six months to

[37] B. Hepple, "Individual Labour Law", in G. S. Bain (ed.), *Industrial Relations in Britain* (1983).

[38] P. Lewis, *Twenty Years of Statutory Redundancy Payments in Great Britain*, Universities of Leeds and Nottingham, Occasional Papers in *Industrial Relations* No. 8, 1985.

[39] See H. Phelps-Brown, *The Origin of Trade Union Power*, 1983, Ch. XI; P. Davies and M. R. Freedland, "Labour Law and the Public Interest — Collective Bargaining and Economic Policy" in Wedderburn and Murphy (eds), *Labour Law and the Community: Perspectives for the 1980s* (1983).

one year in 1979[40] was further increased to its current period of two years in 1982.[41] Similarly the duty to give employees written particulars of disciplinary procedures was relaxed,[42] the qualifying period for entitlement to receive written reasons for dismissal was increased to two years[43] and, with a view to reducing groundless but time-consuming complaints, pre-hearing reviews — which could result in the industrial tribunal requiring a complainant to lodge a deposit not exceeding £150.00 in order to be able to continue the proceedings — were introduced.[44] Other "liberalising" methods included at first the restriction of the powers of the Wages Council to employees 21 years of age and over[45] and eventually their abolition[46] and in 1983 the Fair Wages Resolution of the House of Commons was revoked. More recently still, the drive towards deregulation has resulted in the enactment of the eponymous Deregulation and Contracting Out Act 1994 which itself repeals[47] that provision which declared unfair a dismissal for redundancy without resort to collective procedures[48] and allows for repeal by statutory instrument of legislation which is seen to be unreasonably cumbersome and outmoded.[49] The purpose and motivation for these measures was to remove or ease the impediments to taking on workers or taking up work, a policy which was first mooted in *Employment: The Challenge for the Nation*[50] then developed in 1985 by the Department of Trade and Industry's *Burdens on Business* and in 1986 by the Department of Employment's Green Paper *Building Business, Not Barriers*. The theory was that lifting the burden of legislation from employers, particularly small employers, would create a climate of enterprise and job creation[51] although it has been questioned whether employment legislation was so burdensome as to discourage employment.[52]

In order to implement some of its policies it has been necessary for the United Kingdom to withdraw from and denounce certain international standards[53] and it is ironic therefore that membership of the European Union has in some areas at least thwarted the reduction in employment rights. Thus the effect of the rules regarding continuous employment which provide access to protection against dismissal and entitlement to redundancy payments have been found to be discriminatory and required to be changed[54] and arguably the two-year qualifying period itself offends against the Equal Treatment Directive and Article 119 of the Treaty of Rome.[55]

---

[40]   Unfair Dismissal (Variation of Qualifying Period) Order 1979 (SI 1979 No. 959).
[41]   Employment Act 1982, Sch. 2, para. 5.
[42]   Employment Act 1989, s. 13.
[43]   *Ibid.* s. 15.
[44]   *Ibid.* s. 20; and see the Industrial Tribunals (Constitution and Rules of Procedure) (Scotland) Regulations 1993 (SI 1993 No. 2688).
[45]   Wages Act 1986, s. 12(3).
[46]   TURERA, s. 35.
[47]   Deregulation and Contracting Out Act 1994, s. 81; Sch. 17.
[48]   EPCA, s. 59(1)(b).
[49]   See, for example, the use made of the powers in s. 37 of the 1994 Act to repeal some outdated health and safety and other measures.
[50]   Cmnd. 9474, p. 11.
[51]   *Building Business, Not Barriers*, para. 22. And see G. Standing, *Unemployment and Labour Market Flexibility: the United Kingdom* (1986).
[52]   See Daniel, *The Impact of Employment Laws* (1978).
[53]   See, for example, ILO Convention No. 95 on Protection of Wages.
[54]   See the Employment Protection (Part-time Employees) Regulations 1995 (SI 1995 No. 31) passed following the decision of the House of Lords in *R. v. Secretary of State for Employment, ex parte EOC* [1994] IRLR 176.
[55]   See *R. v. Secretary of State for Employment, ex parte Seymour-Smith and Perez* [1995] IRLR 464, CA.

Much of the Trade Union Reform and Employment Rights Act 1993 was enacted to give effect to European Union requirements while the recently-made regulations requiring consultation with workers' representatives in the event of transfers of undertakings or large-scale redundancies make only a minimalist — and perhaps inadequate — response to the decision of the European Court of Justice.[56] The prospect of having to implement the Working Time Directive[57] which restricts the working week (including overtime) led the United Kingdom to challenge the legality of the Directive in the European Court of Justice.[58]

INTERACTION WITH INDUSTRIAL RELATIONS

1.7 General characteristics

The British system of industrial relations is traditionally characterised by a combination of features: (1) a high level of union membership, (2) extensive reliance on free collective bargaining as the principal method of settling terms and conditions of employment, (3) the non-interventionist, or "abstention" of the law in the day-to-day management of industrial affairs. The continuation of these characteristics in any description of the system is now, however, open to question in the light of the changes which in recent years have altered the shape of British industrial relations.

1.8 Union membership and the closed shop

Trade union membership reached a peak of 13.2 million in 1979, but by 1993 had fallen to 8.7 million and in 1994 was just over 7 million — a drop of around 46%.[59] Increasing unemployment, of course, leads to a fall in union numbers, but the effects of economic depression on the unions has been exacerbated by structural changes in the economy. Many of the jobs which have gone have been in the manufacturing sector, where traditionally unions were strongly represented. Unions have proved more successful in retaining high membership levels in the public sector than they have in the private. Present indications are that new employment growth, where it occurs, is increasingly to be found in the area of self-employment and part-time work, areas where unions find recruitment difficult. Many unions have taken steps to try to increase membership by seeking to recruit from sections of the working population — especially women and ethnic minorities — where previously they have had relatively little impact.[60] It is uncertain whether such new strategies will be successful in bringing the period of declining membership to an end and proper significance must be attached to the fact that in the new computing industry union membership is only 4% and that while 86% of public sector workers are employed by employers who recognise trade unions the equivalent figure for the private sector is 34%.

---

[56] The Collective Redundancies and the Transfer of Undertakings (Protection of Employment) (Amendment) Regulations 1995 (SI 1995 No. 2578); these are discussed in Chapter Ten. At the time of writing the legality and adequacy of the regulations has been confirmed by the High Court: *R v. Secretary of State for Trade and Industry, ex parte UNISON* [1996] IRLR 438.

[57] Council Directive 93/104/EC.

[58] In the opinion of the Advocate General (March 12, 1996) the Directive is valid.

[59] *Employment Gazette*, May 1995, p. 205; Labour Force Survey, *Employment Gazette*, May 1995, p. 191.

[60] M. Stevens and A. Waking, "Union density and workforce composition", *Employment Gazette*, August 1990.

With this decline in membership there has also been a dramatic decline of the importance of the "closed shop",[61] under which the holding of union membership is accepted by both union and employer as a prerequisite for continued employment. The institution of the closed shop raises in sharp focus the conflict between individual and collective values in industrial relations, and its entrenched status in Britain has long been a thorn in the flesh for Conservative governments.

The decline in the closed shop during the 1980s was undoubtedly hastened by the new legal rules which progressively increased the legal obstacles surrounding its implementation.[62] Since 1979 the government has expressed its opposition to the practice on both moral and economic grounds.[63] The weakening of the institution has had the consequence of inhibiting the power of unions to conduct industrial action, for the controlling discipline which the closed shop gives to a union over its members is an important part of the union's industrial strength. In 1986 the official figures for working days lost due to industrial disputes were at their lowest for over twenty years and while those figures had doubled by 1989 the number of stoppages begun has continued to fall and the number of workers involved has not significantly increased.[64] Since 1989 the trend has continued inexorably so that in 1994 0.28 million days were lost due to stoppages — the lowest since records began in 1891.[65]

Government policy, the changing structure of the work force and the effects of the economic recession have resulted in only 33% of employees being union members,[66] a figure which is lower than the equivalent figure for the 1950s and 1960s.[67]

1.9 Collective bargaining[68]

Collective bargaining was first extensively developed within British industry in the nineteenth century, and has continued since then to occupy a central role in the regulation of terms and conditions of employment in both public and private sectors. In the 1970s (following the reforms set in train as a consequence of the recommendations made by the Donovan Commission) there were various formal attempts to reform the structure of collective bargaining. Assistance by the state for the improvement and extension of collective bargaining was forthcoming, first through the short-lived Commission on Industrial Relations (CIR), latterly through the Advisory Conciliation and Arbitration Service (ACAS). By statute[69] ACAS was originally charged not just with the general duty to promote the improvement of industrial relations, but also to encourage the extension of collective bargaining and the development and reform of collective bargaining machinery. Also in the period 1976–1980 ACAS had central responsibility for a scheme which undoubtedly had the effect of extending and supporting collective

---

[61] See M. Stevens, N. Millward and D. Smart, "Trade Union Membership and the Closed Shop in 1989", *Employment Gazette*, November 1989.

[62] As to the present position see paras 5.67.

[63] "The Government's view of the closed shop is clear: it is opposed to the principles underlying it. That people should be required to join a union as a condition of getting or holding a job runs contrary to the general traditions of personal liberty in this country." *Trade Union Immunities* (Cmnd 8128, 1981), p. 66.

[64] Labour Market Data, *Employment Gazette*, 1989.

[65] See D. Bird and J. Davies, "Labour Disputes in 1994", *Employment Gazette*, July 1995.

[66] *Ibid.*

[67] See note 60 above.

[68] See Chapter Nine.

[69] Employment Protection Act 1975, s. 1, repealed and re-enacted in part by TULRCA, s. 209.

negotiation by creating a statutory procedure – admittedly somewhat cumbersome and indirect — whereby employers could be required to recognise a trade union for collective bargaining.[70] That part of its jurisdiction was removed with the repeal of the relevant legislation by the Employment Act 1980 and in 1992 the change in the attitude of the State to collective bargaining was seen in the repeal of ACAS's statutory duty to encourage the extension of collective bargaining and development and reform of collective machinery.[71] In recent years the structure and content of collective bargaining has undergone considerable change, so that now greater emphasis is placed on factory-level agreements and less on industry-wide national bargaining. The moves towards decentralisation of bargaining are particularly prevalent in the private sector, although the government has indicated it would like to see similar movement in public sector collective bargaining too.[72] However, as noted earlier, in 1994 less than half of all workers had their terms and conditions of employment negotiated collectively.

One relatively recent innovation in bargaining is the "single-union agreement", where recognition is given by management to a single union for all or most of the workers employed in an undertaking, irrespective of different job functions amongst the workforce. These arrangements are most frequently found in connection with the establishment of new manufacturing operations, and are particularly associated with job flexibility, acceptance of arbitration as a means of settling disputes and, most controversially, undertakings on the union side not to have recourse to strikes. These agreements have been and are a cause of great controversy within the union movement, and have highlighted the differences between traditional left-wing unions with a continuing commitment to socialist values, and the new "business" unions (such as the E.E.P.T.U.) which have prospered in the 1980s and are primarily concerned with achieving the best possible terms of employment for their members, with far fewer political scruples about how this is done.

1.10 Legal abstentionism

Although it was true until the 1960s, it can no longer be seriously argued that the law in the form of legislation now abstains from attempting to regulate the substance as well as the procedures of the employment relationship. Certainly until the passage of the Industrial Relations Act in 1971 legislative intervention was best described as *ad hoc*. Leaving aside statutes which were concerned with the safety of the workplace the only legislation of any significance was the Truck Acts 1831–96 (and the associated Payment of Wages Act 1960), the Contracts of Employment Act 1963 (which, strictly, dealt only marginally with the *contract* of employment) and the Redundancy Payments Act 1965. While the Industrial Relations Act 1971 envisaged a legal infrastructure which would permit the management of collective relations it did, crucially, introduce into individual employment law protection against unfair dismissal. The effect of this was not merely to require employers to substantiate their decisions to terminate the employment contract; it also resulted in the examination of the entire employment relationship by industrial tribunals. Arguably this itself prompted employers to

---

[70] Employment Protection Act 1975, ss. 11–16.
[71] TULRCA, s. 209.
[72] See e.g. B. C. Roberts, "Recent trends in collective bargaining in the United Kingdom", *International Labour Review*, vol. 123, May–June 1984, p. 287. Advisory Conciliation and Arbitration Service, *Collective Bargaining in Britain: its Extent and Level*, Discussion Paper No. 2, February 1983.

reconsider and clarify or reformulate the terms of the employment relationship and to devise supplementary but non-contractual rule systems to support or fortify dismissals for indiscipline or misconduct. Additionally, although the protection against unfair dismissal was exclusively statutory, paradoxically, elements of that protection required consideration of issues which were purely contractual[73] and this intermixture of statutory rules and contractual theory has remained the hallmark of the United Kingdom system of employment protection.

However, the 1970s saw the first legislative intervention into the substance of the employment relationship with the passage of the Employment Protection Act 1975. This Act created a platform of individual employment rights in some respects improved and refined by the Trade Union Reform and Employment Rights Act 1993 and now contained in the Employment Rights Act 1996. Legislative interventionism had arrived by 1975 and is now here to stay. Unlike Continental systems the United Kingdom system attaches little if any significance to collective agreements; they lack any normative effect.[74] Accordingly fundamental and strategic change to the terms of the employment relationship depends on statutory intervention. Although somewhat ironically the advent of statutory employment law saw the spawning of implied contractual terms introducing flexible duties not to damage trust and confidence or render performance very difficult and to show serious concern for genuine grievances, it is impossible to comprehend how the law of the contract of employment could have coped with the elimination of sexual or racial discrimination or the automatic transference of the employment contract to the employer who acquires a business or, in ''Eurospeak'', a ''stable economic entity''.[75] The legislation which was designed to achieve these objectives by, in the first instance, restricting the right to determine with whom one should enter a contract and, in the second instance, creating a contract between two parties even where one of them does not agree to its creation is anathema to the very roots of the Scots law of contract.

In collective matters it is equally clear that legislation plays a major, if restricting, role. Since the Industrial Relations Act 1971 collective industrial relations have continued to attract legislative intervention although since 1980 that intervention has generally had the effect of limiting the role of the trade union as the representative collective agent. Thus the Employment Act of that year deprived a trade union of the legal procedures designed to ensure an employer would recognise it for collective bargaining.[76] Legislation throughout the 1980s and 1990s has incrementally yet persistently narrowed the opportunities for lawful industrial action. On the other hand the common law of delict could have coped with the perceived need to control trade union power — the law of delict if not tempered by legislative immunities would have outlawed virtually all effective industrial action.[77] However, once it is accepted that not all industrial action should be regarded as illegal the role of legislation becomes very much sensitive to, and influenced by, the political complexion allied with the economic policies of the

---

[73] Consider, for example, the questions of (a) capability for the job the employee is *employed to do*, (b) the test for constructive dismissal, (c) the role of the implied contractual duty in cases of dismissal for conduct involving disclosure of employer's trade secrets and (d) whether there has been a deduction from wages under the Wages Act 1986.

[74] The provisions of Schedule 11 to the Employment Protection Act 1975 which permitted the extension of collectively agreed terms to workers where employers had not participated in the negotiations were repealed by the Employment Act 1980, s. 10.

[75] See Chapter Five, para. 5.76.

[76] Employment Act 1980, s. 19.

[77] See Chapter Eleven.

government of the day. While there may be debate about the extent of legislative intervention in the field of industrial action, standing the common law rules of delict not even trade unionists would contend that the law in the shape of Parliamentary intervention should abstain. On the other hand the same could not be said regarding the statutory regulation of the internal government of trade unions.[78] Arguably such a matter could be left to the members or the unions themselves which, especially after the demise of the closed shop, may now be more accurately described as voluntary organisations.

PARTICULAR LEGAL DEVELOPMENTS

1.11 The incrementally pervasive intervention of legislation in the employment relationship and in the field of industrial relations has brought with it certain special features which require special mention, namely, (i) codes of practice and other official guidance, (ii) the judicial freedom to consider government statements made in the course of the legislative process and (iii) the influence of the law of the European Community.

1.12 Codes of practice

Although not the invariable rule, much of contemporary employment law requires consideration of the standard of reasonableness. Thus unfair dismissal law itself eventually requires the industrial tribunal to decide whether the employer's dismissal fell within the "bands of reasonable" responses and had been preceded by a reasonable procedure[79] while the statutory entitlement to time-off is couched in terms of reasonableness.[80] It would be inimical to a system of rules which requires to be sensitive to the varied circumstances of each case for statute to attempt to set down rigidly precise rules of universal application. It is also useful, if not necessary, for legislation which is radical and ground-breaking to be accompanied by an official statement of what would normally be acceptable standards of behaviour practice. Undoubtedly the approach of legislation in the 1970s was to make use of codes of practice promulgated and issued by expert bodies to facilitate the translation of vague standards or new concepts into meaningful and more concrete actions. The Code of Practice issues by ACAS on Disciplinary Practices and Procedure and those issued by the Equal Opportunities Commission (EOC) and the Commission for Racial Equality (CRE) dealing with the elimination of discrimination in employment are obvious examples of such codes of practice.[81] However, more recently the government has seized the opportunity of influencing the texture and effect of legislative ideas by issuing codes of practice dealing with Picketing and Industrial Action[82] and while ACAS has the power to issue codes of practice containing such practical guidance as it thinks fit for the purpose of promoting the improvement of industrial relations,[83]

---

[78] See Chapter Ten.
[79] See Chapter Five, para. 5.36.
[80] See Chapter Three, and Chapter Nine, para. 9.62 ff.
[81] And see the codes of practice issued by the Health and Safety Executive dealing with safety representatives and the codes or guidance issued in 1992 to supplement the health and safety regulations issued to give effect to the European Community's Health and Safety Directives. For a detailed coverage see V. Craig and K. Miller, *Introduction to the Law of Health and Safety at Work* (1995).
[82] See Chapter Eleven, para. 11.75.
[83] Employment Protection Act 1975, s. 6(1).

the Employment Act 1980 confers on the Secretary of State for Employment an identical power.[84] Following the Secretary of State's refusal to endorse ACAS's revision of its Code of Practice on Disciplinary Practices and Procedures,[85] it is perhaps not surprising that the power to issue codes of practice under the Disability Discrimination Act 1995[86] is conferred on the Secretary of State and not the National Disability Council; indeed, although it would be unthinkable for him to do so, while the Secretary of State is required to consult various bodies before issuing a code of practice he is not expressly required to consult the National Disability Council itself.[87]

1.13 The legal status of codes of practice

Codes of practice may be best described as semi-obligatory in that the usual rule is that a failure on the part of any person to observe any provision of a code of practice shall not of itself render him liable to any proceedings but the provisions of a code of practice shall be admissible in evidence.[88] The practical effect of codes of practice is well illustrated by judicial decisions dealing with a variety of issues.[89]

There are other sources of official guidance but the legal status to be attributed to these varies. As indicated earlier, the booklet issued by ACAS ("Discipline at Work"), while a source of useful information and guidance on contemporary good practice in the area, does not have the status of a code of practice issued under the Employment Protection Act 1975. Its status would appear to be similar to the Code of Good Practice on the employment of disabled people issued in 1984 by the Manpower Services Commission. However, this code will be superseded by the code of practice to be issued by the Secretary of State in exercise of the powers conferred by the Disability Discrimination Act 1995 which will, like the "guidance" to be issued under that Act, be admissible in industrial tribunals and courts.[90] On the other hand, although strictly not possessing the status of a code of practice issued in reliance on statutory powers, the European Commission's Code of Practice on Sexual Harassment is relied upon by industrial tribunals.[91]

1.14 The law of the European Community

The new legal order instituted by the treaties which establish and regulate the European Communities has resulted in the creation of legal rights which in certain

---

[84] Employment Act 1980, s. 3(1).

[85] ACAS eventually issued a non-statutory booklet giving general guidance on discipline at work but this lacks the legal status of a code of practice issued under its statutory powers: see para. 5.35.

[86] Disability Discrimination Act 1995, s. 53.

[87] *Ibid.* s. 54(1).

[88] Codes of practice issued by ACAS, the EOC and the CRE are admissible only in proceedings before industrial tribunals although those issued by ACAS are also admissible in proceedings before the Central Arbitration Committee; codes issued by the Secretary of State may be taken into account in tribunal and court proceedings. (Employment Protection Act 1975, s. 6(1); Sex Discrimination Act 1975, s. 56A(10); Race Relations Act 1976, s. 47(1); Disability Discrimination Act 1995, s. 53(5); Employment Act 1980, s. 3(B)). For the effect of Health and Safety Executive codes of practice see the Health and Safety at Work etc. Act 1974, s. 17.

[89] See, for example, *West Midlands Passenger Transport Executive v. Singh* [1988] IRLR 186, EAT (race relations); *Robinson v. Ulster Carpet Mill Ltd* [1991] IRLR 348, NICA (redundancy selection); *Thomas v. N.U.M.* [1985] IRLR 136 (picketing).

[90] Sections 3(3), 53(4)–(6).

[91] See *Wadman v. Carpenter Farrer Partnership* [1993] IRLR 374, EAT.

cases are enforceable at the instance of the individual and to an unusual extent employment law has provided the setting for considering the issues which are involved in the translation of European rights into domestic law. In addition to the direct applicability of Regulations[92] this (the creation of rights for individuals) may come about in three ways. First, certain Treaty Articles are sufficiently precise and unconditional to be enforceable by the courts or tribunals of Member States. Second, although Directives are addressed to Member States[93] it is now clear individuals may rely on them in the domestic tribunals and courts. Third, in the event that a Member State fails to implement a Directive it will be liable at the instance of an individual who has suffered loss as a result of that failure — the *Francovich* doctrine. The issues raised by these are dealt with in detail where the relevant substantive law is considered later[94] and at this stage it is intended to deal only with the relationship between domestic and European law.

1.15 Treaty articles

Provided the wording of an article is sufficiently precise and unconditional to be justiciable, that is to say capable of being enforced by a court or tribunal, it is of direct effect and may be relied on by an individual in an issue with another individual or organisation or the State.[95] Thus Article 48 (free movement of workers) is of direct effect[96] as is Article 119 (equal pay).[97] The latter with its interpretative Directive[98] has had an inestimable effect on the domestic employment law. It required the introduction by legislation of a right to equal pay on the grounds that the work of the man and the woman was of equal value[99] — a major development of equal pay law — and reference to it ensured that domestic law could not be applied in such a way as to allow employers to defeat the equal pay claims of women by the technique of employing a "token man".[100] In *Macarthys Ltd v. Smith*[101] it was held that Article 119, unlike the domestic Equal Pay Act 1970,[102] was not restricted to making comparisons between men and women employed contemporaneously so that a woman could claim equal pay with a man whom she had replaced; on the same basis the Employment Appeal Tribunal has admitted a claim by a woman who was replaced by a man who was paid considerably more.[103] Although the Equal Pay Act 1970 applies to any inequality in contractual terms it clearly did not extend to pension benefits,[104] redundancy payments or compensation for unfair dismissal[105] and perhaps the greatest impact

---

[92] EC Treaty, Art. 189; for an example of the direct application of a regulation, see *Brown v. Secretary of State for Scotland* 1989 SLT 402, ECJ.

[93] EC Treaty, Art. 189.

[94] See particularly Chapter Five, para. 5.76 and Chapter Seven, para. 7.13.

[95] *Van Gend en Loos v. Nederlandse Administratie der Belastingen* [1963] ECR 1, ECJ.

[96] See *Van Duyn v. The Home Office* [1974] ECR 1337; and see *Union Royale Belge des Sociétés de Football Association ASBL v. Bosman, The Times*, January 2, 1996, ECJ (Case C-415/93) discussed in (1996) 41 JLSS, p. 71 (Spink, J.) and (1995) 3 *Sport and the Law Journal*, p. 17 (Farrell, R.).

[97] *Defrenne v. SABENA SA* [1976] ECR 455; [1976] ICR 547, ECJ.

[98] Directive 75/117.

[99] Equal Pay (Amendment) Regulations 1983 (SI 1983 No. 1794).

[100] See *Pickstone v. Freemans plc* [1988] IRLR 357, HL.

[101] [1980] ICR 672, ECJ & CA.

[102] See the decision to that effect of the Court of Appeal reported at [1979] ICR 672.

[103] *Diocese of Hallam Trustee v. Connaughton* (EAT, 1128/95), *The Times*, June 11, 1996.

[104] Equal Pay Act 1970, s. 6(1A).

[105] Such payments were statutory and clearly not covered by "terms of a contract" (EqPA 1970, s. 1(2)).

of Article 119 has been to extend its broad principle of equal pay to eliminate discrimination with regard to pension benefits and access, redundancy payments and compensation for unfair dismissal. These developments are discussed later.[106] Issues which remain are the mechanisms and procedures (including time limits) for the enforcement of such individual rights as are created by Article 119. In this respect the Scottish EAT (which in this context requires to be distinguished from the EAT sitting in Scotland) has undertaken the relaxed view that individual tribunals have jurisdiction to entertain claims based exclusively on Article 119 — referred to sometimes as "free-standing" claims — provided these claims are brought within a reasonable period.[107] On the other hand, the English EAT and the Court of Appeal inclines to the view that industrial tribunals being creatures of statute may only give effect to Article 119 through the medium of domestic law including its time limits. The result of this is to exclude claims which became arguable following decisions of the European Court of Justice which are regarded as being no more than declaratory of the law contained in Article 119.[108]

1.16 Directives

As indicated earlier because directives do not have direct effect individuals generally do not derive any legal rights from them which can be relied on in an issue with a private individual or organisation; unlike regulations and certain articles of the treaties directives do not have horizontal legal effect — they require to be translated into the United Kingdom's legal system by legislation. However, this general rule is subject to two important reservations. First, as is vividly illustrated by the decision of the European Court of Justice in *Marshall v. Southampton and South West Hampshire Area Health Authority (Teaching)*,[109] where the issue is not between two private individuals or organisations but between an individual (or organisation) and the state or an emanation of the state, provided the directive is sufficiently clear to be enforced by a court or a tribunal, an individual may rely on it in a domestic tribunal.[110] The theory is that neither the state nor any of its agencies is entitled to plead in its defence its own failure to implement a directive in accordance with its treaty obligations.

The right of an individual to rely on a directive in an issue with the state is illustrated in relation to cases of the many female members of the armed forces who were discharged on becoming pregnant. The policy previously operated by the Ministry of Defence was to require females who became pregnant either to elect to have the pregnancy terminated or to be discharged from the service. The Ministry of Defence believed this obviously discriminatory stance was justified by the Sex Discrimination Act 1975, s. 85(4) which excluded "naval, military or air forces of the Crown". However, EC Directive 76/207 which forbids discrimina-

---

[106] See Chapter Seven. And see V. Craig, "The implications of *Seymour-Smith*", *Employment Law* (1995) Issue 10, pp. 9 ff and V. Craig, "Article 119 and Retrospective Pension Rights", *Employment Law* (1996) Issue 11, pp. 7 ff.

[107] See *Rankin v. British Coal Corporation* [1993] IRLR 69, EAT and *Methilhill Bowling Club v. Hunter* [1995] IRLR 232, EAT.

[108] See *Biggs v. Somerset County Council* [1996] IRLR 203, CA. And see *Barber v. Staffordshire County Council* [1996] IRLR 209, CA. And see the interesting comment on the decision of the EAT by B. Napier, "Time Limits and Procedural Questions after *Biggs*", *Employment Law* (1995) Issue 8, pp. 2 ff.

[109] [1986] IRLR 140, ECJ; [1986] ICR 335, ECJ; and see *Marshall v. Southampton and South West Hampshire Area Health Authority (No. 2)* [1993] IRLR 445, ECJ; [1993] ICR 893, ECJ.

[110] *Cf Duke v. GEC Reliance* [1988] IRLR 118, HL.

tion on grounds of pregnancy[111] contains no such exclusion and was held to render unlawful the policy operated by the Ministry of Defence.[112] As a result many hundreds of female service personnel were able to obtain substantial amounts of compensation for their unlawful discharge. With effect from February 1, 1995 s. 85(4) was amended so that discrimination may only be practised for the purpose of ensuring "combat effectiveness".[113] More recently it has been held by an industrial tribunal that a servicewoman who refrained from pregnancy to protect her service career is now entitled to compensation for injury to her feelings.[114] There is an important corollary to the right to rely on a directive, namely, that the time limit for instituting proceedings which are founded on a directive does not begin to run until the domestic legal system has introduced such legislation as is necessary to properly implement the directive.[115] The crucial result is that employees who are fortunate enough to be employed by the state (or one of its emanations)[116] are able to rely on directives in direct contradiction of domestic law; those employed by private sector employers require to await the introduction of legislation before their Community rights can be enforced against such employers[117] — although it may be only a matter of time. Thus the decision of the European Court in *Marshall*[118] was given on February 26, 1986 and by November 7, 1987 the remedial provision of the Sex Discrimination Act 1986 had become effective, while in *Marshall (No. 2)*[119] the decision of the European Court was given on August 2, 1993 and by November 22, 1993 the necessary subordinate legislation[120] was in force.[121] Of course, where a directive is insufficiently precise to permit enforcement against the state a determination of whether and to what extent a state has failed to take the necessary implementing measures may result in the European Commission instituting legal proceedings against a recalcitrant member state in the European Court of Justice. Invariably this will result in appropriate domestic legislation being introduced. Thus only after the European Court of Justice had found that the United Kingdom had failed to implement those parts of the Directives on Collective Redundancies and Transfers of Undertakings[122] was the necessary legislation introduced.[123]

However, directives are capable of influencing domestic law in another way.

---

[111] *Dekker v. Stichting Vormingscentrum voor Jonge Volwassenen Plus* [1991] IRLR 27, ECJ.

[112] *R. v. Secretary of State for Defence, ex parte EOC and Others* [1992] COD 276, DC.

[113] See the Sex Discrimination Act 1975 (Application to Armed Forces etc.) Regulations 1994 (SI 1994 No. 3276).

[114] *O'Hare v. Ministry of Defence*, COIT 13491/95. And see *Ministry of Defence v. Lowe, The Times*, June 27, 1996, EAT (compensation for injury to feelings following abortion).

[115] See *Emmott v. Minister for Social Welfare and Attorney General* [1991] IRLR 387, ECJ.

[116] See the discussion of what the concept of an emanation of the State involves in *Foster v. British Gas plc* [1990] IRLR 353, ECJ; [1991] IRLR 268, HL. And see the rules in application in *Fidge and Others v. Governing Body of St Mary's Church of England Aided Junior School and Others, The Times*, November 19, 1994, EAT.

[117] But see para. 1.17 regarding the *Francovich* doctrine which may allow an action by an individual against the state.

[118] [1986] IRLR 140, ECJ; [1986] ICR 335, ECJ.

[119] [1993] IRLR 445, ECJ; [1993] ICR 893, ECJ.

[120] Sex Discrimination and Equal Pay (Remedies) Regulations 1993 (SI 1993 No. 2798).

[121] Similarly the decision of the High Court in *R. v. Secretary of State for Defence, ex parte EOC and Others*, above, was given on December 17, 1991 and while the (remedial) legislation did not become effective until February 1, 1995, the policy was discontinued earlier.

[122] Directive 75/129 and Directive 77/187. And see *EC Commission v. United Kingdom* [1994] IRLR 392 at p. 412, ECJ.

[123] See the Collective Redundancies and Transfer of Undertakings (Protection of Employment) (Amendment) Regulations 1995 (SI 1995 No. 2587).

This comes about through a judicial awareness of the need to give effect to the purpose of a directive in circumstances in which the domestic legislation is ambiguous and capable of sustaining different meanings, one of which is consonant with the purpose of the relevant directive. Such a purposive approach to interpretation is favoured by the European Court of Justice[124] and is no doubt encouraged by the decision of the House of Lords in *Pepper v. Hart*[125] permitting resort to Hansard to resolve an ambiguity. Perhaps the most striking approach to such a purposive approach is seen in *Litster v. Forth Dry Dock and Engineering Co. Ltd*[126] in which the House of Lords felt entitled to introduce words into the Transfer of Undertakings (Protection of Employment) Regulations 1981, words which Parliament had not inserted, in order to ensure that employer/transferors did not defeat the protective purpose of the Regulations when considered in light of the Directive.[127] While such judicial enthusiasm for giving effect, where possible, to European directives in this way is to be welcomed, it should not be regarded by the government as an alternative to legislation.[128]

1.17 The Francovich Doctrine

In *Francovich v. Italian Republic*[129] the European Court of Justice established the principle that members states were obliged to make good damage caused to individuals by breaches of Community law attributable to the state and that principle holds good whatever the organ of the state (including the legislative) whose act or omission was responsible for the breach, and exemplary damages could be awarded against the state for claims based on breaches of Community law if they could be awarded in similar claims based on domestic law.[130] Significantly the Court of Justice has held that reparation of loss or damage could not be made conditional on fault on the part of the organ of the state responsible for the breach, beyond that of a sufficiently significant breach of Community law, and the obligation to make good loss or damage could not be limited to damage sustained after the delivery of the judgment of the European Court.[131] However while the doctrine would clearly encompass employment rights an industrial tribunal has no jurisdiction to entertain such a claim.[132]

---

[124] See, for example, *Katsikas v. Konstantinidis* [1993] IRLR 179, ECJ.
[125] [1993] IRLR 33, HL.
[126] [1989] IRLR 161, HL; [1989] ICR 341, HL; 1989 SC (HL) 96. And see *Pickstone v. Freemans plc* [1988] IRLR 357, HL and *Webb v. EMO Air Cargo (UK) Ltd* [1995] IRLR 645, HL.
[127] See Chapter Five, para. 5.76.
[128] Consider the attempt of the House of Lords to interpret the Sex Discrimination Act 1975 in such a way as to give effect to the Equal Treatment Directive in *Webb v. EMO Air Cargo (UK) Ltd* [1995] IRLR 645, HL and whether an amendment of the Act itself might not have been more appropriate.
[129] [1992] IRLR 84, ECJ.
[130] *Brasserie du Pêcheur SA v. Federal Republic of Germany; R. v. Secretary of State for Transport, ex parte Factortame Ltd and Others (No. 3)* [1996] IRLR, 267, ECJ.
[131] *Ibid.*
[132] *Secretary of State for Employment v. Mann* [1996] IRLR 4, EAT.

Chapter Two

THE CONTRACT OF EMPLOYMENT AND ITS CONSTITUTION

2.1 The contract of employment

The contract of employment (or contract of service) has to be distinguished from the contract for services[1] and is of central importance to modern employment law. Perhaps strangely, this is so not because the rights of employees and employers are determined directly by the terms of the contract in contract law actions but for four distinct but related reasons.

(1) Many strategically significant employment rights and duties are created by statutes which are, in the main, applicable only where the work relationship takes the form of a contract of employment. The best example of such a statute is the Employment Rights Act 1996 which almost exclusively applies only to employees.[2] Although other statutes are of wider application — and the significance of the value of this must not be underestimated[3] — it is clear that they also, and most frequently, apply to the contract of employment.[4] Thus the contract of employment is the main medium through which access to modern substantive employment rights is achieved.

(2) Furthermore once access to the various statutory codes has been achieved it quickly becomes apparent that although the rights are intrinsically statutory their application and adjudication involve an appreciation of contract law issues. The close connection between statutory rights and contract law can be illustrated by reference to statutory provisions relating to (a) unfair dismissal, (b) redundancy and (c) deductions from wages. In the law of unfair dismissal[5] whether an employee has been ''constructively dismissed''[6] depends essentially on whether the conduct of the employer which causes the employee to leave is either a repudiation or an anticipatory breach of the contract of employment and not merely conduct on the part of the employer which may be characterised as unreasonable.[7] Whether the statutory definition of redundancy[8] is satisfied depends to a large extent on whether the needs of a business for employees to carry out ''work of a particular kind'' in ''the place where the employee was employed''

---

[1] See paras 1.2, 2.2.
[2] Section 230(1) defines an employee as ''an individual who has entered into or works under a contract of employment''.
[3] See, for example, *BP Chemicals v. Gillick* [1995] IRLR 128, EAT and *Hill Samuel Investment Services Group Ltd v. Nwauzu* EAT Case No. 87/94.
[4] See, for example, the Equal Pay Act 1970, s. 6(1), the Sex Discrimination Act 1975, s. 82(1) and the Employment Rights Act 1996, s. 230(3).
[5] See Chapter Five.
[6] See Chapter Five, para. 5.17.
[7] *Western Excavating (ECC) Ltd v. Sharp* [1978] IRLR 27, CA.
[8] ERA, s. 139(1) and see Chapter Six.

have reduced.[9] Both issues of "work of a particular kind" and "the place where the employee was employed" are to be determined by reference to the terms of the contract of employment (although not those relating to the transfer from one place to another[10]) and not merely by a test of actuality.[11] Although the definition of "wages" in the Employment Rights Act 1996[12] is wide enough to include non-contractual payments[13] many complaints brought under that Act require consideration of the contractual provisions regarding remuneration, hours of work and shift-patterns.[14] Indeed a complaint regarding deduction from wages, although strictly statutory, must now be regarded as an attractive alternative to a breach of contract action.[15]

(3) Because the contract of employment is a specific type of contract in the absence of express provisions being agreed by the parties the law implies into the contract various terms. As will be seen later in this chapter the contract of employment can often be validly constituted orally or by implication with little more than a bare agreement to do certain work for wages.[16] However once it is clear that the contract is one of employment the relationship between the employer and employee is regulated not just by the express term but by a complex range of additional terms implied by law into each contract of employment.[17] Two examples suffice. There is implied into the contract of employment an obligation that the employer will not act in such a way as is likely to damage the trust and confidence on which the employment contract is based.[18] Also implied into the contract is an obligation that the employee will execute his duties with reasonable care.[19] However if the contract is not one of employment such terms are not implied automatically.

(4) When a contract of employment is created the employer becomes vicariously liable for the negligence of his employee while acting in the scope of his employment[20] whereas if the contract is for services then, generally,[21] the employer or person who agrees with the contractor that the work should be done will have no

---

[9]   ERA, s. 139(1).
[10] *Bass Leisure Ltd v. Thomas* [1994] IRLR 104, EAT.
[11] *Nelson v. BBC* [1977] ICR 649; [1977] IRLR 148, CA; *United Kingdom Atomic Energy Authority v. Claydon* [1974] IRLR 6, NIRC; [1974] ICR 128, NIRC.
[12] See Chapter Three, para. 3.21.
[13] Section 27(1); and see *MacRuary v. Washington Irvine Ltd.* (IDS Brief 518, 1994, EAT).
[14] See, for example, *Yemm v. British Steel plc* [1994] IRLR 117, EAT.
[15] See, for example, *MacRuary v. Washington Irvine Ltd* (IDS Brief 518, 1994, EAT; and see K. Miller, "Unilateral Variation of Contract and the Recovery of Wages", *Scottish Law Gazette*, 1994, Vol. 62, p. 137.
[16] In Scots law express agreement regarding wages is not essential since it is presumed that services are performed in return for wages (*Thomson v. Thomson's Tr* (1889) 16 R 333).
[17] But note express terms may have the effect of creating a relationship other than a contract of employment. See paras 2.2, 2.3.
[18] *Courtaulds Northern Textiles Ltd v. Andrew* [1979] IRLR 84, EAT; *Woods v. W M Car Services (Peterborough) Ltd* [1981] ICR 666, EAT; [1982] ICR 693, CA; [1982] IRLR 413, CA.
[19] *Clydesdale Bank Ltd v. Beatson* (1882) 10 R 88. And para 3.38.
[20] On vicarious liability in the course of employment see Gloag and Henderson, *The Law of Scotland* (10th edn), para. 33.6.
[21] The exceptions would be where the contractor is subject to the control of the employer and where the contractor contracts with the Crown (Crown Proceedings Act 1947, ss. 2 and 38(2)).

liability for the negligence of the contractor or his employees in carrying out the contract.[22]

NATURE OF THE CONTRACT

2.2 Identifying the contract of employment

Being able to identify the contract of employment or contract of service, and to distinguish it from other working relationships — particularly the contract under which the independent contractor provides services to another, the contract for services — is therefore not merely of academic interest. It has important legal and practical consequences. The modern distinction between the contract of employment and the contract for services reflects the distinction in Roman law between *locatio conductio operis* and *locatio conductio operarum*[23] and modern law makes no distinction between contracts of employment for ordinary as distinguished from skilled work or labour.[24] Although previous courts attached much significance to the control — either actual or potential — exercisable by one party (the employer) over the other (the employee)[25] it soon became apparent that control, although continuing to be a relevant criterion was too restrictive to be regarded as the absolute one[26] and the test which now finds judicial favour includes control only as one of many and varied factors.[27] Even in cases of vicarious liability where it could be logically argued that ''control'' remain as an essential condition the Scottish courts have adopted ''a broad overhead view''[28] and the test now generally[29] applied to differentiate the contract of employment from the contract for services is one which, by examining a range of factors, seeks to determine the substance or economic reality of the relationship.[30] It is frequently referred to as the ''multiple and variable test'' because it permits consideration of a multiplicity of factors with different factors possibly receiving greater or less weight according to the circumstances of the employment.[31] There is no exclusive list of relevant factors but many of the factors which will fall for consideration are listed in *Market*

---

[22] *Stephen v. Thurso Police Commissioners* (1876) 3 R 535; and see *Marshall v. William Sharp and Sons* 1991 SLT 114, IH.

[23] *Cf* Lord Fraser, *Master and Servant* (3rd edn) ch. 1.

[24] *Cassidy v. Minister of Health* [1951] 2 KB 343, CA, whereas the distinction is emphasised by Bell (*Principles*, ss. 146–152) and is reflected in *Sim v. Rotherham B.C.* [1986] IRLR 391.

[25] See for example *Performing Right Society Ltd v. Mitchell and Booker (Palais de Danse) Ltd* [1924] 1 KB 762, CA; *Stagecraft Ltd v. Minister of National Insurance* 1952 SC 288; *Cassidy v. Minister of Health* [1951] 2 KB 343, CA.

[26] *AEU v. Minister of Pensions* [1963] 1 All ER 864 in which Megaw J stated ''the question of the control of an employee is an important element in deciding whether the contract is one of service, but it is a test or criterion that is far from being an absolute one. The nature of the control which is required to bring the employment within the scope of a contract of service varies almost infinitely with the general nature of the duties involved.''

[27] In *Argent v. Minister of Social Security* [1968] 3 All ER 208 Roskill J neatly summarises the change in emphasis from control, through integration into a business, to ''what in modern parlance is called economic reality.''

[28] *Per* Lord President Cooper in *Kilboy v. South Eastern Fire Area Joint Committee* 1952 SLT 332 at p. 335; and see *Marshall v. William Sharp & Sons Ltd* 1991 SLT 114, IH; *United Wholesale Grocers Ltd v. Sher* 1993 SLT 284 OH.

[29] In cases of secondment of employees or employment *pro hac vice* the authority to control the work objective and method is still of critical importance. See para. 2.4(a).

[30] *E.g. Global Plant Ltd v. Secretary of State for Health and Social Security* [1972] 1 QB 139. And see *Andrews v. King* [1991] ICR 846 (agricultural ganger).

[31] *Hall v. Lorimer* [1994] IRLR 171, CA (freelance TV technician).

Investigations Ltd v. Minister of Social Security.[32] In particular circumstances other factors would include whether the work is performed as part of a business or merely ancillary to it[33] and, especially where the work is performed on a casual basis or as an outworker, the respective extents to which the employer is required to provide work and the employee is required to perform work when it is available.[34]

2.3 Whether or not a contract of employment exists is a question of law;[35] however, answering that question involves an appreciation and evaluation of questions of fact and degree[36]; even where the contract is to be found in a comprehensive written document the construction of the contract has to take place in its "factual matrix".[37] Since the existence of relevant factors may be a matter of inference for the tribunal of fact it may be difficult to challenge the decision of a tribunal of first instance unless it can be shown that no reasonable tribunal acting judicially could have arrived at that decision. Thus in *Nethermere (St Neots) Ltd v. Taverna*[38] the existence of "the irreducible minimum of obligation on each side"[39] (to provide work and to do it when provided) was entirely a matter of inference; although the evidence before the industrial tribunal was "tenuous"[40] there was sufficient to allow the tribunal to find that the relationship between Nethermere Ltd and the homeworkers could be described as an "umbrella" or "global" contract thus satisfying the need to have an irreducible minimum of mutual obligation.[41] The scope entrusted to tribunals of fact is illustrated by contrasting *Hellyer Brothers Ltd v. McLeod*[42] with *Boyd Line Ltd v. Pitts.*[43] Both cases involved the redundancy of trawlermen and in each case the question arose as to whether during the periods between various voyages undertaken by McLeod and Pitts there was sufficient mutuality of obligation for these periods to be covered by a contract of employment. In the latter case the Employment Appeal Tribunal held there was evidence on which the industrial tribunal *could*[44] find there was a "global" or

---

[32] [1968] 3 All ER 732. "The most that can be said is that control will no doubt have to be considered, although it can no longer be regarded as the sole determining factor; and factors which may be of importance are such matters as whether he who performs the services provides his own tools and equipment, whether he hires his own helpers, what degree of financial risk he takes, what degree of responsibility for investment and management he has and whether and how far he has the opportunity of profiting from sound management in the performance of the task" *per* Cooke J.

[33] *Stevenson Jordan and Harrison Ltd. v. McDonald and Evans* [1952] TLR 101, CA; *Whittaker v. Minister of Pensions and National Insurance* [1967] 1 QB 156.

[34] *O'Kelly v. Trusthouse Forte plc* [1983] IRLR 369, CA; [1983] ICR 728, CA; *Nethermere (St Neots) Ltd v. Taverna* [1984] IRLR 240, CA; [1984] ICR 612, CA. And contrast *Hellyer Brothers Ltd v. McLeod* [1987] ICR 526, CA with *Boyd Line Ltd v. Pitts* [1986] ICR 244, EAT.

[35] *Davies v. Presbyterian Church of Wales* [1986] ICR 280, HL.

[36] *O'Kelly v. Trusthouse Forte plc,* above; *Sidey v. Phillips (Inspector of Taxes)* (1987) 131 SJ 76; *The Times* December 12, 1986; *Lee v. Chung* [1990] IRLR 236, PC.

[37] *McMeechan v. Secretary of State for Employment* [1995] IRLR 461, EAT.

[38] [1984] IRLR 240, CA; [1984] ICR 612, CA.

[39] *Ibid., per* Stephenson LJ.

[40] *Ibid.*

[41] Stephenson LJ could "not see why well founded expectations of continuing homework should not be hardened or refined into enforceable contracts by regular giving and taking of work for periods of a year or more ... ".

[42] [1987] ICR 526, CA.

[43] [1986] ICR 244, EAT.

[44] EAT's emphasis.

"umbrella" contract whereas in the former the findings of the majority of the industrial tribunal precluded the Employment Appeal Tribunal and the Court of Appeal arriving at a similar conclusion.[45]

What type of contract the parties intend to create is also a relevant factor.[46] However, because the contract of employment is a legal concept there are several limitations on the freedom of the parties purporting to create a contract of employment. Thus a contract of employment under which the parties agree not to make deductions for income tax and national insurance contributions is likely to be illegal and void[47] but this may not affect an employee's ability to present a statutory complaint.[48] In *Salvesen v. Simons*[49] the EAT, sitting in Scotland, reviewed the law relating to contracts *ex turpi causa* in relation to employment contracts and concluded that the rule applied to render the contract unenforceable provided the party seeking to found a claim on an illegal contract knew what was being done whether or not he knew it was illegal, adding the salutary caution that "it is not inequitable that those who seek to take advantage of the tax system ... should not be entitled to be treated as if they were employed under a normal contract of employment".[50] Where A and B enter a contract by which one of them is to work exclusively for C the contract is one *sui generis*[51] and until recently tribunals have refused to "lift the veil" and bring within employment protection legislation agency workers who are excluded by the simple expedient of the interposition of the third party agency.[52] In *McMeechan v. Secretary of State for Employment*[53] however the Employment Appeal Tribunal has emphasised that the nature of the relationship is to be determined by an analysis and construction of the terms and conditions rather than by looking at previous cases dealing with agency workers, and having considered the terms of the contract between Mr McMeechan and the employment agency the Employment Appeal Tribunal concluded that it was a contract of employment. While an express declaration that the contract is to be one of employment will not *per se* ensure the contract is of the same type as the label of description given to it by the parties[54] the court will recognise the clearly stated genuine intentions of the parties provided the other terms of the contract are

---

[45] In *Hellyer* the industrial tribunal's findings, reported in the decision of the EAT ([1986] ICR 122), included "(3) any trawlerman was free to work for an owner other than the one for whom he had just sailed, if he wished. .... (6) Owners had the right, if they wished, not to re-engage any trawlerman after completion of a particular voyage, and that right continued for as long as the shipowner might wish."

[46] *Per* Lord Dunpark in *Marshall v. William Sharp & Sons Ltd* 1991 SLT 114, IH at p. 125; *Massey v. Crown Life Insurance Co.* [1978] IRLR 31, CA.

[47] *Tomlinson v. Dick Evans "U" Drive Ltd* [1978] IRLR 77, EAT; [1978] ICR 639, EAT. *Cf Lightfoot v. D&J Sporting Ltd* [1996] IRLR 64, EAT.

[48] *Leighton v. Michael and Charalambous* [1996] IRLR 67, EAT.

[49] [1994] IRLR 52, EAT.

[50] *Cf Annandale Engineering v. Samson* [1994] IRLR 59 EAT in which the unhelpful distinction between repeated and regular payments and small, occasional and irregular payments was made, so that knowledge that the latter were made without deduction of tax did not render the contract illegal. *Sed quaere*. Also it is unfortunate that there was a considerable conflict in the evidence regarding the vital matters of size and regularity of the payments.

[51] *Construction Industry Training Board v. Labour Force Ltd* [1970] IX KIR 269.

[52] See *Wickens v. Champion Employment* [1984] ICR 365, EAT. *Pertemps v. Nixon*, EAT Case No. 496/91.

[53] [1995] IRLR 461, EAT.

[54] The Scottish courts had recognised at an early stage the need to examine labels and nomenclature – *Nisbett v. Dixon & Co.* (1852) 14 D 973; and see *Ferguson v. John Dawson & Partners (Contractors) Ltd* [1976] IRLR 346, CA; *Young & Woods Ltd v. West* [1980] IRLR 201, CA.

not inconsistent with that type of contract especially where the other factors are not conclusive of the matter.[55] Particularly where the parties seek to alter an existing relationship by entering into a written contract will tribunals wish to be satisfied that the change has been more than a paper or formal one.[56]

2.4 Special cases

Some employment types and situations deserve special mention.

(a) Pro hac vice. The normal rule is that because the contract of employment is based on the notion of *delectus personae*[57] the rights under the contract cannot be assigned without the parties' consent.[58] Thus an employer cannot unilaterally transfer an employee to another employer without the employee's consent.[59] However this rule does not prevent an employer from instructing his employee to provide his services for another.[60] Where this occurs although there is no change in the responsibilities of employer or employee under the contract of employment there arises the question of who is vicariously liable for the negligence of the employee when he is performing his contract of employment for the purposes of the other person; is he still the employee of his employer or has he become the employee *pro hac vice* of the other person?[61] If the employee (A) of X has become the employee of Y *pro hac vice* the latter is liable to third parties injured as a result of his negligence. However the onus of proving that A has become the *pro hac vice* employee of Y rests on X, the original employer,[62] and, although all the facts and circumstances have to be taken into account, which of the two employers has the authority to direct not merely the use made of the plant etc. but also the manner in which it is operated is often the critical factor.[63] In *Mersey Docks & Harbour*

---

[55] *Massey v. Crown Life Insurance Co.* [1978] IRLR 31, CA; *BSM (1257) v. Secretary of State for Social Services* [1978] ICR 894, QBD. Cf *Global Plant Ltd v. Secretary of State for Health and Social Security* [1971] 3 WLR 269; [1972] 1 QB 139; *Narich Pty Ltd v. Commissioner of Pay-roll Tax* [1984] ICR 286, PC.

[56] See *Massey v. Crown Life Insurance Co.* [1978] IRLR 31, CA; *Catamaran Cruisers Ltd v. Williams* [1994] IRLR 386.

[57] A contract is said to involve *delectus personae* when the personal and other individual characteristics of the contracting parties are material considerations in determining whether and on what terms to enter the contract. For a full description of *delectus personae* see Gloag on *Contracts* (2nd edn 1929), pp. 416–421.

[58] Even the Transfer of Undertakings (Protection of Employment) Regulations 1981, as amended by the Trade Union Reform and Employment Rights Act 1993, s. 33, recognises the employee's right to resist the transfer of his contract of employment (Reg. 5(4A)).

[59] *Nokes v. Doncaster Amalgamated Collieries Ltd* [1940] AC 1014. Also it would be a material breach for an employer to tell his employee who enquires about payment of his wages to look to another employer for whom work has been performed.

[60] Frequently but not necessarily this will involve operating a vehicle, plant or equipment owned by the employee's employer for the purpose of another, typically a person who has entered into a contract of hire with the employee's employer; the contract of hire will often include the services of an operative, an employee of the owner of the vehicle, etc.

[61] Such a question only arises in cases of liability to a third party injured as a result of the employer's negligence (*County Plant Hire Ltd v. Jackson* [1970] VIII KIR 989, CA per Denning MR). And see *Savory v. Holland & Hannen & Cubitts* [1964] 1 WLR 1158, CA at p. 1165.

[62] *Malley v. LMS Railway Co.* 1944 SC 129; *Mersey Docks and Harbour Board v. Coggins & Griffith (Liverpool) Ltd* [1947] AC 1.

[63] *Mersey Docks and Harbour Board v. Coggins & Griffith (Liverpool) Ltd*, above; *McGregor v. J. S. Duthie & Sons & Co Ltd* 1966 SLT 133; *Kerr v. Hailes (Plant) Ltd* 1974 SLT (Notes) 31, OH. While in practice the location of the authority to exercise detailed control over the method of the work is the most influential factor, as indicated by the approach of LJ-C Cooper in *Malley v. LMS Railway Co.* 1944 SC 129, the matter is more complex.

Board v. Coggins & Griffith (Liverpool) Ltd[64] the board hired out to Coggins & Griffith, a firm of stevedores, a crane with a driver. On whether the driver had become their employee, *pro hac vice* Lord Macmillan stated "*Prima facie* he (the driver) was the Board's employee. But it is always open to an employer to show that he has for a particular purpose temporarily transferred the services of one of his general servants to another so as to constitute him *pro hac vice* the servant of that other party. The burden is on the general employer to establish such transference has been effected. The stevedores were entitled to tell him what parcels to pick up, where to go etc., that is to say they could direct him as to what they wanted him to do; but they had no authority to tell him how to handle his crane in doing the work." However in *McGregor v. J. S. Duthie & Sons & Co Ltd*[65] the general employer was able to show that his employee was acting *pro hac vice* the employee of another (J. S. Duthie Ltd) whose lorry their employee was driving at the time two passengers were injured as a result of his negligence.[66] Who has the right to exercise control of the manner of the work is what is important and not who had *de facto* control[67] and a provision in a commercial contract for the liability of the contracting parties *inter se* will not affect the question of whether an employee has become *pro hac vice* the employee of another.[68]

(b) Apprentices. While the contract of apprenticeship attracts the benefits of modern employment legislation[69] there are important differences between it and the contract of employment in that the former must involve an obligation to instruct the apprentice on the master's or employer's part.[70] As a result of the Age of Legal Capacity (Scotland) Act 1991 and the Requirements of Writing (Scotland) Act 1995 respectively, questions regarding the need for a curator's consent and that the contract of apprenticeship requires writing for its constitution and proof no longer arise. Also, unlike the contract of employment[71] there is probably no right to terminate the apprenticeship contract by merely paying wages in lieu of notice because the apprentice is entitled to be so instructed in his trade or profession that his wages or salary on completion will reflect his completed

---

[64] [1947] AC 1.

[65] 1966 SLT 133. Transfer *pro hac vice* also occurred in *Gibb v. United Steel Companies Ltd* [1957] 1 WLR 668.

[66] The negligent driver was in the general employment of a partnership which had entered a commercial contract with J. S. Duthie Ltd for sawing timber but it was agreed that he would drive one of Duthie's lorries when required and his general employers would be reimbursed his wages — "There is no doubt that from the time he left Kingairloch until he reached Fort William he (the driver) was engaged on Duthie's business and acting in accordance with instructions they had a right to give. I do not think the partnership (the general employers) would have had any right to instruct (the driver) ... when he was driving their lorry, it was Duthie and Duthie alone who had the right to control the work he did" (*McGregor v. J. S. Duthie & Sons & Co Ltd* 1966 SLT 133, *per* LJ-C Grant). And see *Bowie v. Shenkin* 1934 SC 459, IH.

[67] This is emphasised by the fact that the presence of one of the partners in the lorry at the time of the accident was regarded by LJ-C Grant as irrelevant – he was "a mere hitchhiker". And see *McAllister v. Oban Transport and Trading Co. Ltd* 1971 SLT (Notes) 51.

[68] *Arthur White (Contractors) Ltd v. Tarmac Civil Engineering Ltd* [1967] 1 WLR 1508; *Kerr v. Hailes (Plant) Ltd* 1974 SLT (Notes) 31, OH.

[69] ERA, s. 230(2); Eq PA, s. 1(6)(a); SDA, s. 82(1); RRA, s. 78(1); TULRCA, s. 295(1).

[70] *Gardner v. Smith* (1775) Mor 593; *Royce v. Greig* 1902, 2 SLT 298. Equally a perverse or determined refusal to learn would be a breach on the part of the apprentice (*Butler v. Dillon* [1952] 87 *Irish Law Times Reports* 95). And see *Daley v. Allied Suppliers* [1983] IRLR 14, EAT.

[71] See para. 4.2.

training and instruction.[72] Although it has been doubted whether Scots law would follow English law that the obligations in the apprenticeship contract are so independent that misconduct by the apprentice does not justify his dismissal,[73] there is no doubt that in the context of statutory unfair dismissal law[74] apprentices are required to be treated more leniently than mature, qualified employees.[75]

(c) Directors. Because a limited company has a legal personality distinct from its shareholders and officers[76] it is quite logical for a director also to have a contract of employment (or "service agreement" as it is often called) with the company.[77] Where a service agreement is entered into between a company and a director a copy of such agreement or a written memorandum of its terms must be kept at the registered office or the principal place of business of the company[78] and service agreements for five years or more require approval by shareholders.[79] As previously stated, whether a contract of employment exists is a question of law involving a detailed evaluation of matters of fact[80] and such a process is particularly important in determining the true status of a company director. Equally, the size of a director's shareholding is not conclusive;[81] what matters is what functions the director actually carried out and the extent to which he was subject to the control of the company.[82] Each case will depend on its own facts and evidence is required to establish that a director is employed by a company.[83] While it is not possible to lay down firm rules the following issues will often be influential. (1) Is the director required to devote his whole time to the affairs of the company and is he employed on terms that his employment may be terminated by notice? (2) Is he subject to control by the company? (3) Does he draw a weekly wage or salary? (4) Is there a written service agreement or a board minute or memorandum?[84]

---

[72] Lyle v. Service (1863) 2 Macq 115; Dunk v. George Waller & Son Ltd [1970] 2 QB 163, CA.

[73] See the comments on Waterman v. Fryer [1922] 1 KB 499 in Gloag on Contract (2nd edn), p. 593; and see the English decisions of Maloney v. St Helens Industrial Co-operative Society Ltd [1933] 1 KB 293, CA to the effect that illness will not justify dismissal of an apprentice and Newell v. Gillingham Corporation [1941] 1 All ER 552.

[74] See Chapter Five.

[75] See, for example, Stanton v. Wolfendens Cranes Ltd [1972] IRLR 82, IT.

[76] Lee v. Lee's Air Farming Ltd [1961] AC 12, PC.

[77] For an interesting discussion of the possible "duality" of a director's tenure see R. R. Pennington, Company Law (7th edn), p. 737.

[78] Companies Act 1985, s. 318. However the failure to preserve such a copy or to reduce the agreement to writing will not prevent the conclusion that the relationship between director and company is one of employment (Folami v. Nigerline (UK) Ltd [1978] ICR 277, EAT).

[79] Companies Act 1985, s. 319(1). But note the exception regarding successive contracts where the second contract is entered into in the 6 months before the expiry of the first contract (s. 319(2)).

[80] See para 2.2.

[81] Road Transport Industry Training Board v. Readers Garage Ltd [1969] VI KIR 137.

[82] "The issue would depend exactly what Mr Reader did. If for instance his main work was that of director, and he only occasionally stepped into the shoes of a workman that might be one thing; but if, on the other hand, he kept regular hours at the petrol pumps and only worked for a short period on the administrative side ... there might be a different conclusion." Ibid. per Lord Parker of Waddington CJ, at p. 141.

[83] McMillan v. Guest [1942] AC 561; Trussed Steel Concrete Co. Ltd v. Green [1946] Ch 115; Robinson v. George Sorby Ltd [1967] 2 ITR 148; Eaton v. Robert Eaton Ltd [1988] IRLR 83, EAT.

[84] Parsons (A. J.) & Sons Ltd v. Parsons [1979] IRLR 117, CA; Eaton v. Robert Eaton Ltd, above.

(d) Public employment. Although the employment of many employees who work for public or government agencies is regulated by the terms of their contracts of employment as supplemented by statutory provisions contained in legislation, principally the Employment Rights Act 1996, some in public employment (especially those who occupy senior positions or hold particular offices) have their relationships regulated not only by their contracts of employment — supplemented in the way mentioned — but by certain rules of public law. A distinction must be made between public employees whose employment merely has a "statutory flavour" and those whose employment is truly regulated by public law or statute. The former are in no different a position than employees who work in the private sector of industry and commerce[85]; the latter however derive additional protection *via* the medium of public law.[86] Although, for the purposes of determining the scope of the supervisory jurisdiction of the Court of Session[87] Scots law has not sought to develop the popular English distinction between "private" and "public" law[88] it is generally the case that the tripartite relationship required for the exercise of that jurisdiction[89] will most frequently be met in what may for convenience be described as public employment. Where an application to the supervisory jurisdiction is competent the court's powers of interdict, declarator and reduction can with considerable despatch achieve something neither the law of contract nor employment protection legislation can generally[90] achieve — they may declare a purported dismissal "invalid" thus depriving it of legal effect. Where such a declaration of invalidity occurs no question of reinstatement arises because there has never been a lawful dismissal.[91]

Employment in the public sector by the state (or an employer which may be described as emanation of the state) is of considerable significance in permitting an employee to rely directly on European Directives which are sufficiently precise and unconditional to enable their application by the courts of a member state.[92] The most notable example of this may be seen in *Marshall v. Southampton and South West Hampshire Area Health Authority (Teaching)*[93] in which Mrs Marshall, who was employed by the Health Authority which was regarded as an emanation of the state, was able to rely on the provisions of the European Equal Treatment Directive[94] to override the Sex Discrimination Act 1975 and invalidate the

---

[85] See for example *Vidyodaya University of Ceylon v. Silva* [1965] 1 WLR 77, PC; *Tehrani v. Argyll & Clyde Health Board (No. 2)* 1990 SLT 118. *Cf R. v. Visitor of the University of Hull, The Times*, April 2, 1991; *R. v. Lord Chancellor's Department* [1991] ICR 743, DC.

[86] See, for example, *Vine v. National Dock Labour Board* [1957] AC 488; *Malloch v. Aberdeen Corporation* 1973 SC 227.

[87] Rules of Court 1994, rule 58 (the successor to rule 260B).

[88] For an insight into the English provisions see I. T. Smith and J. C. Wood, *Industrial Law* (5th edn.), pp. 275 ff. and for a recent illustration of the English courts' pre-occupation with whether the issue involves public law see *R. v. Crown Prosecution Service, ex parte Hogg, The Times* April 14, 1994, CA.

[89] *West v. Secretary of State for Scotland* 1992 SLT 636, IH. And see para. 3.64.

[90] It is true that, exceptionally, the effect of a dismissal potentially unfair by virtue of ss. 100, 102 and 103 of ERA can be postponed (ERA, s. 128(5)) and that the English courts are more prepared to grant injunctions to restrain a dismissal in breach of contract where the relationship between employer and employee has not broken down; see para. 3.59.

[91] Thus in *Malloch v. Aberdeen Corporation* 1973 SC 227; [1971] 1 WLR 1578; 1974 SLT 253 the effect of the order was to reduce Malloch's purported dismissal to a legal nullity with the result that he continued to be entitled to his salary.

[92] See Chapter Seven, para. 7.13.

[93] [1986] IRLR 140, ECJ; [1986] ICR 335, ECJ.

[94] Directive 76/207.

discriminatory retirement rule applied by her employers. Such a remedy is not available to an employee whose employer is in the private sector[95] although the private sector employee who has suffered a loss may be able to sue his own state for failing to implement a Directive.[96]

Certain groups of public employees require special mention. Holders of public offices (*munera publica*) derive their tenure and its incidents from the fact of their office-holding as protected by the common law.[97] Consideration of the relationship between the Crown and the civil servant[98] involves two apparently conflicting schools of thought. The first, exemplified by *Riordan v. War Office*[99] is to the effect that as the Crown cannot effectively fetter its future executive action by contract[100] the relationship between the Crown and the civil servant, being terminable at the pleasure of the Crown, cannot sensibly be described as contractual; this has led to the wife of a civil servant being unable to arrest her husband's salary,[100] although the right to dismiss at pleasure can be lawfully restricted by legislation.[101] The second school of thought is typified by *Kodeeswaran v. Attorney-General of Ceylon*[103] in which Lord Diplock reviewed the law and concluded that prior to *Mulvenna v. The Admiralty*[104] the arrears of salary of a civil servant were recoverable in England, the right to determine a contract at will being not inconsistent with the existence of a contract until so terminated. This school of thought recognises the need and the right of the Crown to terminate at pleasure the employment of the civil servant while preventing the abuse of such a power to dictate changes in contractual terms unilaterally.[105] Although it has been recognised that there is nothing unconstitutional about civil servants being employed under contracts of employment, whether or not the relationship is to be regarded as contractual has in England been resolved by considering whether there was evidence that the parties intended that such a relationship should be created.[106] More recently that approach has not been followed[107] and it is doubtful whether such a strict approach would operate in Scotland.[108] On appointment a police

---

[95] *Duke v. GEC Reliance Systems Ltd* [1988] ICR 339, HL.

[96] *Francovich v. Italian Republic* [1992] IRLR 84, ECJ; and see *Secretary of State for Employment v. Mann* [1996] IRLR 4, EAT.

[97] *Hastie v. McMurtie* (1883) 16 R 715; *Rothesay Magistrates v. Carse* (1903) 5 F 383; *Mackay and Esslemont v. Lord Advocate* 1937 SC 860.

[98] The Civil Service has been described as "A body of officials in the service of the Crown, who discharge duties belonging to the exercise of the Queen's executive powers, but not being members of Her Majesty's naval, military or air forces, and not being the holders of political offices" (Mustoe, *The Law and Organisation of the British Civil Service*, p. 26).

[99] [1960] 3 All ER 774n, CA; [1961] 1 WLR 210, CA.

[100] *Rederiaktiebolaget Amphitrite v. R.* [1921] 3 KB 500.

[101] *Mulvenna v. The Admiralty* 1926 SC 842, disapproved in *Kodeeswaraan v. Attorney-General of Ceylon* [1970] 2 WLR 456, PC.

[102] *Gould v. Stuart* [1896] AC 575, PC; *Reilly v. R.* [1934] AC 176, PC.

[103] [1970] 2 WLR 456, PC. And see *Cameron v. Lord Advocate* 1952 SC 165.

[104] 1926 SC 842.

[105] *Kodeeswaran v. Attorney-General of Ceylon*, above. And see *Attorney-General for Guyana v. Nobrega* [1969] 3 All ER 1604, PC.

[106] *R. v. Civil Service Appeal Board, ex p Bruce* [1988] ICR 649, QBD. One important practical effect of *ex p Bruce* is TULCRA, s. 273(1) which, for the purposes of the law of industrial conflict, deems the relationship between the Crown and the civil servant to be contractual. And note ERA, s. 191 which has a similar effect for individual employment protection law.

[107] *R. v. Chancellor's Department, ex parte Nangle* [1991] ICR 743, DC where it was stated that the relationship of employment "must of its very nature involve an intention to create legal relations".

[108] See para. 2.9.

constable affirms that he will "faithfully discharge the duties of the office of constable"[109]; a police constable does not have a contract of employment[110] and this has not been altered by the statutory provision[111] which makes the chief constable liable in reparation in respect of any wrongful act or omission on the part of a constable under his general direction "as a master is ... liable in respect of a wrongful act or omission on the part of a servant in the course of [his] employment."[112] While a police authority may enter into contracts of employment with officers (not being constables) for the assistance of constables,[113] a police cadet is not employed under a contract of employment and is therefore unable to claim unfair dismissal[114] and in England it has been held that a special constable is not employed under a contract because there was no intention to enter into a contractual relationship.[115] However although a police constable's legal status deprives him of the protection afforded to those who have contracts of employment[116] in England the official or public law element involved will permit application for judicial review.[117]

FORMATION

2.5 The constitution of the contract of employment

Although the usual rules about the constitution and proof of contracts generally apply equally to the contract of employment, the coincidence of different factors distinguishes it from other contracts. First the terms of the contract of employment are very often not the subject of direct negotiation between the parties (they are invariably imposed by the more powerful of the two as individuals — the employer) or are the result, at least in part, of negotiations between a trade union and an employer or an association of employers. Secondly, even if the terms on which the employment contract is initially agreed can be clearly ascertained — although this is likely to involve an expedition through letters of appointment, statutory statements of particulars of employment, works' rulebooks, notices on display on the office wall and collective agreements both local and national — by

---

[109] The Police (Scotland) Regulations 1976, reg. 10.

[110] *Young v. Magistrates and Town Council of Glasgow* (1891) 18 R 825; *Girdwood v. Standing Joint Committee of Midlothian* (1894) 22 R 11; *Yates v. Lancashire C.C.* [1975] ITR 20. And see *Ridge v. Baldwin* [1964] AC 40.

[111] Police (Scotland) Act 1967, s. 39. And see s. 8 (2) regarding police cadets.

[112] *Robertson v. Bell* 1969 SLT 119, OH. Section 39 is a procedural device and does not alter the substance of the officer's relationship with the chief constable.

[113] Police (Scotland) Act 1967, s. 9. And see *R. v. Derbyshire County Council, ex p Noble* [1990] IRLR 332, CA (refusal of judicial review because police surgeon was appointed under ordinary contract for services).

[114] *Wiltshire Police Authority v. Wynn* [1980] ICR 649, CA.

[115] *Sheikh v. Anderton, The Times,* July 18, 1988, EAT. But see para. 2.9.

[116] The most significant exclusion is ERA, s. 280. And see *Yates v. Lancashire C.C.* [1975] ITR 20. Other legislation (e.g. Sex Discrimination Act 1975, s. 17) treats holding the office of constable as employment. *Cf Sheikh v. Anderton,* above (special constable could not bring a complaint under the Race Relations Act 1976 because he did not have a contract).

[117] *R. v. Chief Constable of South Wales, ex p Thornhill* [1987] IRLR 313, CA; *R. v. Chief Constable of Thames Valley Police, ex p Stevenson, The Times,* April 22, 1987, QBD. However, in a disciplinary matter an investigating officer does not owe a common law duty of care towards the officers under investigation and neither legislation nor regulations create a private law right of action for breach of statutory duty thus excluding any claim for damages (*Calveley v. Chief Constable of Merseyside Police, The Times,* July 9, 1988, CA).

the time any issue or dispute arises it is likely that the original agreement will have been the subject of variation or modification, often the subject of some remote negotiations, or just not observed or applied. Few, if any, contracts entered into by the ordinary person, without professional representation or advice, can rival the contract of employment for its informality and fluidity and it is these factors together which sometimes suggest that the contract of employment is not an ideal subject for the application of the usual rules of contract. However, few provisions special to the contract of employment have been developed and this, no doubt, is why statute has enacted modest provisions to ensure minimum formalities will accompany many, but not all, employment relationships.[118]

2.6 Thus the constitution of a valid contract of employment or apprenticeship requires that the parties have adequate capacity and that the contract is not illegal. Formerly the contractual capacity of those under the age of majority (fixed at 18 years by the Age of Majority (Scotland) Act 1969) was regulated by the common law which distinguished pupillarity (boys aged less than 14 and girls less than 12) from minority (boys between 14 and 18 years of age and girls between 12 and 18 years of age). Generally pupils had no legal capacity[119] while the capacity of minors depended on (a) whether they were forisfamiliated or had a curator who was either absent or abroad and (b) the type of contract.[120] The contractual capacity of those who have not yet reached the age of majority is now regulated by the Age of Legal Capacity (Scotland) Act 1991.[121] Generally boys and girls under 16 years of age have no contractual capacity while those over that age have full contractual capacity[122] and where a person under 16 purports to enter into a contract for which he has no legal capacity the contract shall be void.[123] However, while the Act has no legal effect on any enactment which lays down an age limit expressed in years,[124] for employment law purposes it is important to note the exception that a person under 16 years has full legal capacity to enter into a contract of a kind commonly entered into by persons of his age and circumstances on terms which are not unreasonable.[125] By introducing notions of ''commonness'' and ''reasonableness'' the legislation ensures sufficient flexibility to reflect future social and cultural changes and would seem to confer on, say, 15-year-old school children the capacity to enter into contracts for (casual/part time) employment. However the rule which allows a person under 21 years of age to have a ''prejudicial'' transaction set aside by the court applies only to such transactions or contracts entered into while he/she was between 16 and 18 years of age,[126] a prejudicial transaction being (a) one which an adult, exercising reasonable prudence, would not have entered in the circumstances which prevailed at the time the 16- to

---

[118] See e.g. ERA, ss. 1–7 requiring the issue of written particulars of terms of employment.
[119] Bell, *Principles*, s. 2067.
[120] See Bell, *Commentaries*, I, 129; *M'Feetridge v. Stewarts & Lloyds Ltd* 1913 SC 773; *O'Donnell v. Brownieside Coal Co. Ltd* 1934 SC 534. For a general discussion of this area of the law see the report of the Scottish Law Commission on *Legal Capacity and Responsibility of Minors and Pupils* (1987).
[121] The Act became effective on September 25, 1991.
[122] Age of Legal Capacity (Scotland) Act 1991, s. 1(1).
[123] *Ibid*. s. 2(5).
[124] *Ibid*. s. 1(2)(d).
[125] *Ibid*. s. 2(1).
[126] *Ibid*. s. 3(1).

18-year-old entered into the contract and (b) which is likely to cause substantial prejudice to him.[127] However, employment lawyers should note that this rule itself is subject to the qualification that it does not apply to transactions or contracts (i) in the course of the applicant's trade, business or profession,[128] (ii) ratified by the applicant after reaching 18 years of age in the knowledge that he could have applied to the court to have the transaction set aside,[129] or (iii) ratified by the court.[130]

2.7 Assuming adequate contractual capacity, contracts of all types including those of employment and apprenticeship are enforceable only insofar as they are not illegal nor offend against public policy.[131] Of particular significance are the provisions of the Children and Young Persons (Scotland) Act 1937[132] to the effect that, subject to local authority bye-laws, no child shall be employed so long as he is under the age of 13 years.[133] However this area of the law is soon likely to receive legislative attention in order to comply with the EU Directive on the Protection of Young People at Work.[134] The Directive seeks to prohibit the employment of children under the compulsory school leaving age and to ensure that the working conditions of those under 18 are carefully regulated.[135] However Member States are allowed to make exceptions for employment of children in cultural, artistic, sporting or advertising activities[136] and children under 14 may be permitted to work under combined work/training schemes and those 13 or over may be employed on light work in certain circumstances.[137] The Directive also requires that employers disclose specific risks to health and safety of employees under 18 years of age and make detailed provision for the regulation of working time, night work, daily and weekly rest breaks and holidays for young workers.[138] More generally a contract of employment for an illegal or immoral purpose will not be

---

[127] *Ibid.* s. 2.

[128] *Ibid.* s. 3(3)(f).

[129] *Ibid.* s. 3(3)(h).

[130] This can occur where a 16- to 18-year-old is proposing to enter into a contract which could subsequently be set aside on his application; on the joint application of all of those to be involved in the transaction the court may, unless satisfied that an adult exercising reasonable prudence in similar circumstances would not enter the transaction, ratify the transaction which then becomes unchallengeable on grounds of prejudice (*ibid.* s. 3(3)(j)).

[131] See W. W. McBryde, *The Law of Contract in Scotland*, pp. 628–632. Examples of statutory illegality include an alien failing to obtain the permission of the Secretary of State before changing his employment (*Rastegarnia v. Richmond Designs*, unreported, 4 COIT 765/38), a barmaid under 18 years of age being employed contrary to licensing laws (*Lay v. Hamilton*, unreported, COIT, 1394/211).

[132] Section 28 as amended by Children and Young Persons Act 1963, ss. 34, 64 and the Children Act 1972, s. 1. Note the Employment of Children Act 1973 has not yet been brought into force.

[133] On other restrictions on employment of minors see Chapter Three, paras. 3.27 ff.

[134] Directive 94/33. At the time of writing the Scottish Office has issued a model draft bye-law which, if adopted by local authorities, would make the changes necessary to implement the Directive.

[135] Article 1.

[136] Article 5.

[137] Articles 3 and 4.

[138] Article 8. These provisions do not require implementation before the year 2000.

enforced[139] and cannot establish a period of continuous employment for the purpose of asserting a statutory right.[140] However it seems that if only part of the contract is tainted with illegality then it does not necessarily follow that the entire contract is unenforceable,[141] and where a contract is illegal only in its method of performance a party who is ignorant of the illegality will be able to enforce the contract.[142] Further as the rule *ex turpi causa non oritur actio* is based on public policy it has to be applied flexibly and pragmatically and not rigidly and automatically[143] but what matters is whether the party seeking to found on the contract knew what was being done, it not being necessary to show that he knew it was illegal.[144] Most contracts which purport to reduce or exclude statutory employment rights, although not strictly illegal, are declared to be void[145] and such statutory avoidance of a contract is in addition to rules of common law which may also affect its validity.[146]

2.8 Formalities

Generally the contract of employment can be created without the need for any formal writing. Thus it can be constituted orally, by implication,[147] or by a written contract, or indeed by a mixture of these methods. However, at common law a contract of employment for a period of more than one year and a contract of

---

[139] In *Coral Leisure Group Ltd v. Barnett* [1981] ICR 503, EAT, while it was affirmed that a contract for immoral purposes was illegal and could not form the basis of a claim for unfair dismissal, that had to be distinguished from a contract whose terms and purpose were not illegal although immoral acts (procuration of prostitutes) were committed in the course of his employment. And see *R. v. Salford Health Authority, ex parte Janaway* [1989] AC 537, HL, and s. 4 of the Abortion Act 1967: "no person shall be under any duty ... by contract ... to participate in any treatment ... to which he has a conscientious objection."

[140] *Tomlinson v. Dick Evans "U" Drive Ltd* [1978] IRLR 77, EAT; [1978] ICR 639, EAT; *Hyland v. J. H. Barker (North West) Ltd* [1985] ICR 861, EAT; [1985] IRLR 403, EAT. Both cases involved illegal tax-free payments to the employee and although in *Hyland* the tax-free allowance did not render the entire contract unenforceable, because it occurred during the period of continuous employment necessary to qualify for unfair dismissal protection — a period ending with the date of dismissal — no unfair dismissal right accrued. But see *Wilkinson v. Lugg* [1990] ICR 599, EAT and *Leighton v. Michael and Charalambous* [1996] IRLR 67, in which the EAT has held that a complaint under the Sex Discrimination Act is not precluded by the illegality of the contract of employment. *Cf Lightfoot v. D&J Sporting Ltd* [1996] IRLR 64, EAT (legitimate tax avoidance).

[141] W. W. McBryde, *The Law of Contract in Scotland*, para. 26–29. *Cf Napier v. National Business Agency Ltd* [1951] 2 All ER 264, CA.

[142] *Newland v. Simons & Willer (Hairdressers Ltd* [1981] IRLR 359, EAT.

[143] Contrast *Salvesen v. Simons* [1994] IRLR 52, EAT with *Annandale Engineering v. Samson* [1994] IRLR 69, EAT.

[144] *Salvesen v. Simons* [1994] IRLR 52, EAT.

[145] See, for example, EPCA, s. 140, SDA 1975, s. 77 and ERA, s. 203(1).

[146] *Hennessy v. Craigmyle & Co Ltd* [1986] ICR 461 in which the Court of Appeal held that a contract settling an unfair dismissal complaint even although arrived under the auspices of a Conciliation Officer could nevertheless be avoided on a successful plea of duress (force and fear).

[147] A good example can be seen in *Taylor v. Furness, Withy and Co. Ltd* [1969] VI KIR 488 in which the existence of the contract was implied from the issue of a letter welcoming T. as an employee of the company and an identity card.

apprenticeship[148] require to be constituted by probative writing[149] and cannot be proved by parole.[150] Improbative writings followed by *rei interventus*[151] will perfect the agreement for the whole of the period agreed upon.[152] Thus provided the improbative writing is the writ of at least one of the parties[153] *rei interventus* (but not homologation) may not merely perfect the informal writing; it can also provide consent to an agreement where an element of consent would otherwise be lacking.[154] Also, although there was no strict rule, contracts which had special or unusual terms may have required written evidence of their terms.[155] However for contracts of employment or apprenticeship entered into on or after August 1, 1995 these common law requirements are abolished by the Requirements of Writing (Scotland) Act 1995. The effect is that the validity of contracts of employment for a fixed period of more than one year and contracts of apprenticeship entered into up to and including July 31, 1995 is to be determined having regard to the common law rules and thus require either formal writing (or informal writing followed by *rei interventus*) while those entered into after that date may be created and proved orally, in writing, by implication or indeed by a mixture of these.[156] However notwithstanding the Requirements of Writing (Scotland) Act some statutes still require certain formalities to be observed when employment contracts are entered.[157] Although in the ordinary case the contract can be created without

---

[148] *Grant v. Ramage & Ferguson Ltd* (1897) 25 R 35.

[149] Bell, *Principles*, ss. 173, 190; *Nisbet v. Percy* 1951 SC 350. For an explanation of the origin of this rule see Fraser, *Master and Servant* (3rd edn.), p. 28. *Cf Walker v. Greenock and District Hospital Board* 1951 SLT 329. Similarly where employment for more than one year is contained in a contract dealing with other matters writing is required (*Cook v. Grubb* 1963 SC 1).

[150] But see the interesting observations in the Scottish Law Commission's Consultative Memorandum No. 66 (1985) paras. 2.17–2.19.

[151] According to Bell (*Principles*, s. 26) "*Rei interventus* is inferred from any proceedings not unimportant on the part of the obligee, known to and permitted by the obligor to take place on the faith of the contract as if it were perfect; provided they are unequivocally referable to the agreement, and productive of alteration of circumstances, loss or inconvenience, though not unretrievable." And see *Tojeiro v. McKettrick-Agnew & Co Ltd* 1967 SLT (Notes) 11, OH, in which the failure to aver facts unequivocally referable to a contract for more than a year was fatal and *Heneaghan v. Aero Technologies Ltd* 1990 GWD 13-692 in which it was held there was no agreement on which *rei interventus* could operate in spite of the existence of a draft. And see para. 2.10.

[152] *Campbell v. Baird* (1827) 5 S 335.

[153] In *Nisbet v. Percy* 1951 SC 350 the statement that the position was for three years in the trade union rule book was held not to be improbative writing of either party and in *Gow v. D. McEwan & Son* (1901) 8 SLT 484, an unsigned handwritten memorandum showing a name, starting date and a scale of wages was too vague to found *rei interventus* because the deficiencies were of substance, not merely of form. And see *Heneaghan v. Aero Technologies Ltd* 1990 GWD 13–692.

[154] *Law v. Thomson* 1978 SLT 250; *Rutterford Ltd v. Allied Breweries Ltd* 1990 SLT, 249, OH.

[155] See, for example, *Davies v. City of Glasgow Friendly Society* 1935 SC 224. "I have grave doubt whether a contract of service with such exceptional conditions (that the employee should receive increments related to sales volume generated by him) can be competently be established by parole evidence ..." *per* Lord Murray, *obiter*. See now the Requirements of Writing (Scotland) Act 1995, s. 11.

[156] For a detailed account of the legislation see D. Cusine and R. Rennie, *The Requirements of Writing (Scotland) Act 1995.*

[157] Thus the Merchant Shipping Act 1974, s. 1, provides "... an agreement in writing shall be made between each person employed as a seaman on a ship registered in the UK and the persons employing him and shall be signed by both him and by or on behalf of them." And see para. 2.4(c) regarding service contracts of directors.

writing, the current practice — no doubt stimulated by provisions originally contained in the Contracts of Employment Act 1963[158] — is to set out the elements of the contract in writing, either in a single comprehensive document or, more usually in respect of employees in large workforces, in a series of documents, for example collective agreements, which frequently are tied into the contract of employment by adoption or incorporation.[159] When the contract is created orally or by implication difficulties arise in proving the terms of the contract.[160]

2.9 Contractual intention

The contract of employment is no exception to the rule that the purpose of the parties must be to oblige each other by seriously consenting to their respective obligations; it has been suggested that this state of mind falls short of the doctrine of English law that agreements are not binding as a contract if they are made without the intention of creating legal relations.[161] Nevertheless, although a serious agreement defective in form (for example an unwritten contract of employment for more than a year) is not a legally enforceable contract, in the context of business or commerce it is difficult to show that an agreement was not intended to create legal relations.[162] Thus where an employer enters an agreement — frequently in some form of writing and signed or at least acknowledged by the parties — in which he undertakes to make payment (and perform other obligations) and the worker agrees to obey his directions[163] it is improbable that it would be held that there is no contract because of the absence of a serious consent or purpose. However difficulties can arise where parties to a contract of employment, which, as already observed, is subject to periodic, informal and remote modifications,[164] alter their standards of performance. Are such modifications accompanied by the ''serious consent'' necessary to vary the original contract or are they merely forms of non-binding extra-contractual agreements, arrangements or tolerance? The problem arises particularly where the contract of employment is in practice relaxed or departed from (and is intensified by the rule that the conclusion of a collective agreement does not automatically alter terms of the individual contract in the industry or undertaking concerned[165]) and a distinction is to be made between proper cases of consensual variation of the contract[166] and those cases in which an

---

[158] Sections 4, 5. The equivalent current provisions are now in ERA, ss. 1–7; see para. 2.10.

[159] See paras 2.14, 2.15.

[160] See M. R. Freedland, *The Contract of Employment*, p. 19. However some terms will be implied by law into such informal or incompleted contracts.

[161] See W. W. McBryde, *The Law of Contract in Scotland*, pp. 51–54.

[162] *Edwards v. Skyways Ltd* [1964] 1 All ER 494; *Regina v. Lord Chancellor's Department, ex parte Nangle* [1991] IRLR 343, QBD to the effect that the relationship of employment must by its very nature be one that involves the intention to create legal relations unless such intention is excluded either expressly or by necessary implication, and note the opinion of Lord President Clyde in *R. and J. Dempster Ltd v. Motherwell Bridge and Engineering Co Ltd* 1964 SC 308 at p. 328 that ''the essence of commerce is making bargains, and unenforceable arrangements are the exception and not the rule.''

[163] It is not being suggested that these are the essentials of a contract of employment merely that there is usually some agreements about these matters.

[164] See para. 2.1.

[165] See para. 2.14.

[166] See, for example, *Armstrong Whitworth Rolls Ltd v. Mustard* [1971] ITR 79 QBD, in which the term regarding the normal working week incorporated from a collective agreement was consensually varied by Mustard's working 60 hours a week for a period of 7 years when the collective agreement provided for 40 hours a week only. The inference was that the parties must have intended to alter the contract.

element of flexibility is introduced without any change in the legal obligations contained in the contract. Thus the English courts have held that a relaxation of the contract was to be attributed to a gesture of co-operation by the employee[167] or the assumption of obligations by the employer *ex gratia*[168] and in Scotland it has been held that the employer's representative lacked the authority to make the contract the employee argued existed.[169] Similarly it is unsafe to assume that absence of dissent means assent so that sending new terms and conditions of employment to employees did not have the effect of extending or incorporating a mobility clause[170]; indeed even the signing of a document (by an employee) may not itself be sufficient to indicate assent to a unilateral variation of an existing contract.[171] Similarly, whether a policy adopted by management unilaterally has become a term of the employee's contract by custom and practice requires consideration of many factors including whether it has been drawn to the attention of employees or followed without exception for a substantial period.[171a]

2.10 The statutory written statement of particulars

It is also necessary to distinguish the contract of employment from the written statement of particulars of terms of employment which employers are required to give[172] all qualifying employees[173] not later than two months after employment begins.[174] In *Robertson v. British Gas Corporation*[175] the Court of Appeal reiterated the Employment Appeal Tribunal in *System Floors (UK) Ltd v. Daniel*[176] that "the status of the written statement is this. It provides very strong *prima facie* evidence of what were the terms of the contract between the parties but it does not constitute a written contract between the parties. Nor are the statements of the terms conclusive."[177] Unlike a contract it is essentially a unilateral statement given

---

[167] See *Turriff Construction v. Bryant* [1967] II KIR 659 and *Saxton v. NCB* [1970] ITR 196; in *Bryant* local site negotiations which altered the working hours were regarded as "co-operation not contract" while in *Saxton* Lord Parker CJ stated "Here was a man who was being called upon to co-operate to help his employers to run down this colliery, and one would think that in those circumstances it was difficult to say that he was working as he did otherwise than without prejudice ... I do not think, in these circumstances, one can possibly say that there has been a consensual variation of the terms of his contract of employment."

[168] *Longman v. Merseyside Transport Services Ltd* [1968] 3 ITR 108, QBD. And see K. W. Wedderburn *The Legal Force of Plant Bargains*, 1969, 32 MLR 99.

[169] *Hoogerbeets v. British Coal Corporation* 1991 GWD 2-113, OH. Contrast with *Hawker Siddeley Power Engineering Ltd v. Rump* [1979] IRLR 425, EAT that oral undertaking by employer's representative was unaffected by employee signing contradictory contract.

[170] *Anglia Regional Co-operative Society v. O'Donnell* EAT Case No. 655/91. And see *Aparau v. Iceland Frozen Foods plc* [1996] IRLR 119, EAT (urging great caution before implying consent from continuing in employment without objection).

[171] *Hawker Siddeley Power Engineering v. Rump* [1979] IRLR 425, EAT.

[171a] *Quinn v. Calder Industrial Materials Ltd* [1996] IRLR 126, EAT.

[172] The current provisions were enacted by TURERA s. 26, Sch. 4 to comply with EC Directive 91/533 on information concerning employment conditions.

[173] Qualifying employees are those who have been employed for at least one month (ERA, s. 198). For other exclusions see ERA, ss. 196, 199.

[174] ERA, s. 1. Where an employee is required to work he must receive his written statement before he leaves and an employee whose employment terminates before 2 months is still entitled to receive a written statement (ERA, s. 2(5)(b)).

[175] [1983] ICR 351, CA.

[176] [1982] ICR 54, EAT.

[177] And see *Turriff Construction v. Bryant* [1967] II KIR 659 and *Greater Glasgow Health Board v. Pate* 1983 SLT 90, in which a job title was not to be regarded as conclusive of Pate's contractual duties.

to the employee by the employer showing what he (the employer) believes the terms of employment to be,[178] and no doubt it is designed to compensate for the position at common law whereby no written contract is generally required and to eliminate disputes between employer and employees.[179] However, it is clear that the employer's written statement when construed as an offer of employment on the stated terms can be converted into a contract by acceptance by the employee. Thus in *Gascol Conversions v. Mercer*[180] the employee, by signing a statement in the following terms "I confirm receipt of a new Contract of Employment ... which sets out, as required by [the Act] the terms and conditions of my employment", had converted a unilateral statement into a binding bilateral written contract which excluded extraneous evidence. If the written statement can be expressly accepted as the contract presumably it can also become such by acquiescence[181]; and it would seem that a written statement showing the period of employment to be for a fixed period of more than one year[182] could, say, in the event of the employee not completing the necessary formality of probative acceptance, be the basis for *rei interventus*.[183] The provisions regarding the form and content of the written statement were amended by the Trade Union Reform and Employment Rights Act 1993[184] enacted to give effect to Directive 91/533. The written statement, which may now be given by instalments,[185] must contain particulars of (1) the names of the employer and employee, (2) the date when the employment began and (3) the date on which the employee's period of continuous employment[186] began (taking into account any employment with a previous employer which counts towards that period).[187] The statement must also contain particulars[188] of:

(a)   the scale or rate of remuneration or method of calculating it and the intervals at which it is to be paid[189];

(b)   any terms and conditions relating to hours of work (including any relating to normal working hours);

(c)   any terms and conditions relating to (i) entitlement to holidays including

---

[178] And see J. T. Cameron, *The Contract of Employment Act 1963*, 1963 SLT (News) 203.

[179] See *Cole v. Midland Display Ltd* [1973] IRLR 62, NIRC.

[180] [1974] IRLR 155, CA.

[181] See *Davies v. City of Glasgow Friendly Society* 1935 SC 224. But *cf Evenden v. Guildford City Association Football Club Ltd* [1975] ICR 367, CA, and *Jones v. Associated Tunnelling Co Ltd* [1981] IRLR 477, EAT.

[182] ERA, s. 1(4)(g).

[183] Even an unsigned document, provided it contains all the essentials of a contract, may be the basis for a plea of *rei interventus — Bell v. Goodall* (1883) 10 R 905 *per* LP. Inglis at p. 908; *Wares v. Duff-Dunbar's Trs* 1920 SC 5. *Cf Gow v. D. McEwan & Son* (1901) 8 SLT 484, OH; *Nisbet v. Percy* 1951 SC 350; *Heneaghan v. Aero Technologies Ltd* 1990 GWD 13-692.

[184] Section 26, Sch. 4.

[185] ERA, s. 1(1). But note that particulars about certain matters must be given in a single document known as the "principal statement" (s. 1(4)).

[186] Whether or not employment is continuous depends on compliance with a set of statutory rules contained in ERA, ss. 210–219 and where qualification for a statutory right is concerned what matters is compliance with these rules and not what is in the written statement; and see paras 3.2–3.6.

[187] ERA, s. 1(2).

[188] These must reflect the particulars of employment at a specified date not more than 7 days before the statement (or the instalment) is given (ERA, s. 1(4)).

[189] As to degree of particularity, see *Owens v. Multilux Ltd* [1974] IRLR 113, NIRC. And as to what would be covered by "remuneration", see in a different context *Chapman v. Aberdeen Construction Group Ltd* 412 IRLIB, OH (use of company car).

public holidays and holiday pay[190], (ii) incapacity for work due to sickness or injury including any provision for sick pay and (iii) pensions and pension schemes[191];

(d) length of notice required to be given by either party to terminate the contract of employment;

(e) job title or brief description of the work the employee is employed to do[192];

(f) where the employment is not intended to be permanent, the period for which it is expected to continue or, if it is for a fixed term the date when it is to end;

(g) the place of work, or where the employee is required or permitted to work at various places, an indication of that and of the address of the employer;

(h) any collective agreements which directly affect the terms and conditions of employment including, where the employer is not a party, the persons by whom they were made; and

(i) where the employee is required to work outside the United Kingdom for more than one month (i) the period for which he is to work outside the UK, (ii) the currency of his remuneration during that period, (iii) any additional remuneration or benefits to be provided by reason of his being required to work outside the UK and (iv) any terms relating to his return.[193]

In view of the attempts to differentiate "mandatory" from "non-mandatory" particulars[194] and the fact that the relevant statutory provisions were intended to supply a simple system whereby an employee and an employer should each have a clear statement in writing of the terms and conditions of employment agreed between them and a simple remedy if there was a dispute, the Trade Union Reform and Employment Rights Act 1993 did little to address the difficulties of interpretation and application these provisions have raised[195] and still provides that if there are no particulars to be entered under any of the items (1)–(3) or (a)–(i) above that fact shall be stated.[196]

By virtue of the amendments introduced by the Trade Union Reform and Employment Rights Act 1993 the opportunities for employers to convey the information in the written statement by reference to other documents is greatly reduced. Thus, provided always that the employee has a reasonable opportunity of reading it in the course of his employment or it is reasonably accessibly to him in some other way, the statement may refer the employee to some other document to give particulars of the matters covered in (c)(ii) and (iii) above and may refer to the

---

[190] While the particulars must enable the employee's entitlement to accrued holiday pay on termination to be precisely calculated this does no more than recognise that a contract can contain a provision about entitlement to accrued holiday on termination and if it does the written statement must contain particulars of it (*Morley v. Heritage plc* [1993] IRLR 400, CA).

[191] There is an exception for pension schemes established by or under an Act of Parliament (ERA, s. 1(5)).

[192] Either a title or description must be given and while the latter will be more detailed tribunals will be likely to construe the former to include ancillary duties (*Churcher v. Weyside Engineering (1926) Ltd* [1976] IRLR 402, IT; *Glitz v. Watford Electric Co Ltd* [1979] IRLR 89, EAT; *Greater Glasgow Health Board v. Pate* 1983 SLT 90).

[193] ERA, s. 1(4).

[194] See, for example, *Mears v. Safecar Security Ltd* [1982] ICR 626, CA at p. 641D–E and *Eagland v. British Telecommunications plc* [1990] ICR 248, EAT; [1992] IRLR 323, CA.

[195] However, ERA, s. 11(1) (formerly EPCA, s. 11(1), as amended), codifies the preferred interpretation of Stephenson LJ in *Mears v. Safecar Security Ltd* [1982] ICR 626 at p. 642B.

[196] ERA, s. 2(1).

law or a collective agreement to give particulars of the length of notice required[197] and although the written statement may be issued in instalments, particulars regarding the matters covered in (a), (b), (c)(i), (e) and (g) above must all be contained in a single document.[198] In addition to these particulars of employment, normally[199] the statement must specify or refer to any disciplinary rules applicable to the employee as well as indicating initial and subsequent procedures for redressing disciplinary and other grievances except those relating to health and safety and state whether there is a contracting-out certificate in force.[200]

Where a change in the particulars occurs, not later than one month after the change the employer shall give the employee a statement containing particulars of the change, and the employer may refer the employee to some other document only insofar as reference to another document is permitted when the initial statement is given.[201] Where the change is merely to the name of the employer or the identity of the employer without any break in the continuity of the employee's employment the new employer is not required to give a statement of particulars *de novo* but is required to intimate the change to the employee.[202]

2.11 Where an employer fails to comply with his obligations to give a statement or notify changes in terms of employment, an employee may refer the matter to an industrial tribunal[203] which may determine the particulars which ought to have been included or confirm, amend of substitute particulars.[204] However, the industrial tribunal is unable to determine the meaning of a term or indicate what might be reasonable notice for termination of the contract[205]; and the guidance in *Mears v. Safecar Security Ltd*[206] that an industrial tribunal had power to "invent" a term, in the sense of determining either what term should have been agreed or what term would have been reasonable has been criticised and should not be followed.[207] The tribunal treats "the application as one for the determination of the conditions of the employee's ... employment, leaving the applicant to make such use of [the] determination as he thinks fit."[208] Thus because of the somewhat inconclusive nature of the tribunal procedure when considered in isolation, applications for a determination of particulars are more usefully combined with

---

[197] ERA, s. 2(2).

[198] ERA, s. 2(4).

[199] An exception exists for employers who employed fewer than 20 employees at the date of the commencement of an employee's employment (ERA, s. 3(3)).

[200] ERA, s. 3.

[201] ERA, s. 4(4).

[202] ERA, s. 4(6).

[203] ERA, s. 11. In some cases an employer can also apply to an industrial tribunal (s. 11(2)). No reference may be entertained more than three months after employment has ceased, unless not reasonably practicable (s. 11(4)).

[204] ERA, s. 12(1), (2). The procedures by which a reference may be made seem unnecessarily complicated especially in view of the limited effect of the tribunal's determination; see *Mears v. Safecar Security Ltd* [1982] ICR 626, CA.

[205] *Owens v. Multilux Ltd* [1974] IRLR 113, NIRC; *Cuthbertson v. A.M.L. Distributors* [1975] IRLR 228, IT; and see *Simmons v. Tom Garner Motors Ltd* [1972] ITR 246. *Cf Eagland v. British Telecommunications plc* [1992] IRLR 323, CA to effect that the industrial tribunal, where nothing is stated regarding notice, would have power to conclude there must be reasonable notice and what it would be.

[206] [1982] ICR 626, CA.

[207] *Eagland v. British Telecommunications plc* [1992] IRLR 323, CA; and see *Morley v. Heritage plc* [1993] IRLR 400.

[208] *Mackay v. W. B. Henderson Ltd* [1967] ITR 98, IT; and see *Eagland v. British Telecommunications plc* [1990] ICR 248, EAT; [1992] IRLR 323, CA.

applications relating to unfair dismissal, redundancy payments, unlawful deductions from wages and breach of contract actions, and, although there is no penalty that an industrial tribunal can impose for an employer's failure to comply with his obligation to give a written statement,[209] the real advantage for the employer is the knowledge that his workforce are in no doubt as to the terms of their employment along with the corresponding industrial relations benefits.

CONTRACTUAL TERMS

2.12 The terms of the contract — express and implied

The terms of the contract of employment, like those of many other nominate or innominate contracts, can be express or implied. An express term will often be written in what may be described as primary contractual documents like letters of appointment and acceptance or in formal contracts themselves but equally can be found in secondary sources like collective agreements or works notices or handbooks. However, an express term does not have to be written; in an oral contract of employment it is perfectly possible for the parties to be express about particular issues or terms — an express term merely describes the situation in which the contracting parties (or one of them) having considered a matter relevant to their dealings, consciously and deliberately give(s) expression to their agreement by specific writings or words.[210] Where terms are express and questions of interpretation[211] and construction arise for the performance of the contract,[212] the normal rules of construction will apply, although the Employment Appeal Tribunal has been reluctant to apply the *contra proferentem* rule[213] or the extrinsic evidence rule[214] in relation to the contract of employment.[215] Indeed the Scottish Law Commission has recently proposed that the existing rule that extrinsic evidence to prove an additional term of a contract be replaced by the rebuttable presumption that where the terms of a contract are embodied in one or more documents which appear to contain all the express terms of the contract it shall be presumed that the document(s) contains all the express terms of the contract,

---

[209] Strictly an employer can refuse to issue any statements leaving industrial tribunals to do the work instead.

[210] Express terms may be found in advertisements (*Tayside Regional Council v. McIntosh* [1982] IRLR 272, EAT; *Deeley v. British Rail Engineering* [1980] IRLR 147, CA), notices (*Petrie v. MacFisheries* [1940] 1 KB 258, CA), works rules (*Murray v. Robert Rome & Son Ltd* 1968 SLT (Notes) 90), collective agreements etc. (*NCB v. Galley* [1958] 1 WLR 16, CA; [1958] 1 All ER 91, CA).

[211] See, for example, *Associated British Ports v. TGWU* [1989] IRLR 399, HL; *Burroughs Machines Ltd v. Timmoney* 1977 SC 393, IH.

[212] On the construction and interpretation of contracts see W. W. McBryde, *The Law of Contract in Scotland*, Ch. 19.

[213] The effect of this rule is that ambiguous terms of contract are to be construed against the party pleading or founding on them.

[214] The effect of this is that normally (there are various exceptions) once a contract has been reduced to writing it is incompetent to contradict its terms by parole evidence. See Gloag and Henderson, *The Law of Scotland* (10th ed), para. 6.7 ff.

[215] *Tayside Regional Council v. McIntosh* [1982] IRLR 272, EAT — reducing the contract to writing did not exclude evidence of the obligation to possess a driving licence which was stated in the newspaper advertisement in response to which the job was obtained but to which no reference occurred in the written contract. And see *Pederson v. Camden London Borough Council* [1981] ICR 674, CA. Cf *Gascol Conversions v. Mercer* [1974] IRLR 155, CA. And see Bell, *Principles*, s. 136; *Pollock v. McAndrew* (1828) 7 S 189.

although extrinsic evidence, oral or documentary, shall be admissible to prove the contract includes additional express terms[216] thus approving the approach adopted by Sheriff Principal Nicholson in *Porteous v. British Coal Staff Superannuation Scheme Trs Ltd.*[217] Porteous sought a declarator that he was entitled to be credited with an additional 5 years' service for calculating his pension entitlement under British Coal's pension scheme on the ground that he had entered into a contract with British Coal Staff Superannuation Scheme Trs Ltd (B.C.) notwithstanding his redundancy within about one year of entering the contract. Porteous appealed against the sheriff's sustaining B.C.'s plea to the relevancy arguing that the sheriff was wrong to take account of the background context of the letters. However, the Sheriff Principal rejected Porteous's appeal holding that the prior communings rule did not preclude consideration of surrounding circumstances when the question was whether a particular document was part of a contract at all. B.C.'s offer-letter was written against the background of, and in terms of, the scheme which provided for an actuarially reduced added pension in Porteous's circumstances. Similarly the circumstances surrounding the nomenclature used in a contract and the intentions of the parties to a collective agreement which is incorporated into a contract of employment are admissible in construing the contract provided the words which require to be construed are not ambiguous.[218] However, although there may be a dispute about the meaning of express terms, they have the advantage that generally[219] they cannot be contradicted by implied terms.[220] On the other hand, the express words used by the contracting parties may be too vague in meaning to be enforced[221] and where they have the effect of conferring a discretion on one party it is legitimate for a court or tribunal to imply a term requiring the discretion to be exercised reasonably[222] or not in such a way as to prevent the employee from being able to carry out his part of the contract.[223]

2.13 Implied terms

Broadly, implied terms can fall into two categories — (1) those terms which may be implied into the contract having regard to the facts and circumstances of the particular contract and (2) those terms which are implied by law (common law or statute). In the first category, although terms may also be implied by the custom of a trade and from a course of dealing, perhaps the most significant method of implying a term is a positive desire on the part of courts and tribunals to give a

---

[216] Discussion Paper No. 97, April 1994.

[217] 1993 GWD 19–1196.

[218] *Greater Glasgow Health Board v. Pate* 1983 SLT 90; *Adams v. British Airways plc, The Times*, May 5, 1996, CA.

[219] In *Johnstone v. Bloomsbury Health Authority* [1991] IRLR 118, CA the Court of Appeal accepted that an express term regarding hours of work could be overridden by the employer's implied duty to take reasonable care for the employee's safety.

[220] *Cummings v. Charles Connell & Co (Shipbuilders) Ltd* 1968 SC 305; *McWhirter v. Longmuir* 1948 SC 577.

[221] In *Cook v. Grubb* 1963 SC 1, the phrase "permanent employment" was too vague to be enforced and in *Jaques v. Lloyd D. George & Partners Ltd* [1968] 2 All ER 187, CA the words "should you be instrumental in introducing a person willing to sign a document capable of becoming a contract to purchase" were similarly treated. *Cf Lawrie v. Brown & Co Ltd* 1908 SC 705 ("regular employment"); *NCB v. Galley* [1958] 1 WLR 16, CA ("to work such days or part days in each week as may be reasonably required by the management").

[222] *BBC v. Beckett* [1983] IRLR 43, EAT.

[223] *United Bank v. Akhtar* [1989] IRLR 507, EAT, explained in *White v. Reflecting Roadstuds Ltd* [1991] IRLR 331, EAT. And see *St Budeaux Royal Legion Club Ltd v. Cropper*, unreported, case no. 39/94, EAT.

contract business efficacy.[224] In relation to the contract of employment the following are examples of terms being implied from the circumstances — *Sagar v. Ridehalgh & Son Ltd*[225] (implied term regarding deductions from wages for poor performance), *Bristol Garage (Brighton) Ltd v. Lowen*[226] (implied term limiting employee's liability to make good financial loss), *Murco Petroleum Ltd v. Forge*[227] (implied term entitling employee to wage increase), *Bliss v. South East Thames Regional Health Authority*[228] (no implied term that employer could require Bliss to submit to psychiatric examination), *Sim v. Rotherham Metropolitan B.C.*[229] (implied term that schoolteacher will comply with administrative arrangements (covering for absent colleagues for running school)) and *Sybron Corporation v. Rochem Ltd*[230] (implied term that employee had duty to disclose misconduct of fellow employee). Many terms are implied into the contract of employment from collective agreements which are treated separately.[231]

Because the contract of employment is a nominate or specific contract the second category comprises certain terms implied as part of the general law. Thus common law implies into the contract of employment various terms: for example, that the employee will carry out his duties with reasonable care[232] and will serve his employer with good faith and fidelity[233] and that an employer will not conduct himself in a manner likely to seriously damage the relationship of trust and confidence on which the employment relationship is based.[234] The substance of these and other implied terms is discussed later.[235] The significance of these legally implied terms is that in the absence of express terms dealing with the matter they are incorporated automatically into every contract of employment. Thus although the parties to a contract of employment may only express terms dealing with, say, wages and hours of work, their complete contractual relationship is to be judged not only according to these express terms but according to such terms as supplemented by such additional terms that the law implies. Accordingly, a positive response to the following question brings into play a whole range of contractual rights and duties — "Will you work as my employee for 38 hours each week at £3.50 per hour?" Occasionally statute implies terms into the contract of employment. However, although this is relatively unusual — most modern employment rights are statutory and do not depend on actual or fictional

---

[224] Perhaps the best-known *dictum* on the business efficacy method of implying a term is that of Bowen LJ in *The Moorcock* (1889) 14 PD 64, CA. And see *McWhirter v. Longmuir* 1948 SC 577 at p. 589. *Cf Gallagher v. Post Office* [1970] 3 All ER 714. Another similar method of implying a term is to refer to what an "officious bystander" would have agreed (*Shirlaw v. Southern Foundries (1926) Ltd* [1939] 2 KB 206, CA).

[225] [1931] 1 Ch 310, CA.

[226] [1979] IRLR 86, EAT.

[227] [1987] ICR 282, EAT; [1987] IRLR 50, EAT.

[228] [1985] IRLR 308, CA; [1987] ICR 700, CA.

[229] [1986] ICR 897; [1986] IRLR 391, Ch D.

[230] [1983] IRLR 253, CA; [1983] ICR 801, CA.

[231] See para. 2.14.

[232] *Lister v. Romford Ice and Cold Storage Co Ltd* [1957] AC 555.

[233] *Graham v. R. & S. Paton Ltd* 1917 SC 302; *Hivan Ltd v. Park Royal Scientific Instruments Ltd* [1946] Ch 169, CA.

[234] *Courtaulds Northern Textiles Ltd v. Andrew* [1979] IRLR 84, EAT; *Woods v. W. M. Car Services (Peterborough) Ltd* [1981] ICR 666, EAT.

[235] See Chapter Three.

contractual provisions[236] — the following statutorily implied contractual terms may be noted. (1) By the Equal Pay Act 1970[237] the terms of a contract of employment[238] shall be deemed to include an "equality clause" whereby men and women doing particular work[239] are entitled to equal pay. Because the clause is essentially contractual, claims based on it may be raised in either the ordinary courts or in industrial tribunals. (2) Quite oddly the final steps to enforce an employer's obligation to disclose information to a trade union for collective bargaining are achieved by implying into individual contracts of employment the terms of an award of the Central Arbitration Committee.[240]

2.14 Collective agreements

Collective agreements[241] lead a "Jekyll and Hyde" existence in employment law, for although an argument can be made for collective agreements to be legally enforceable in Scots law,[242] current practice is reflected by the statutory provision[243] that collective agreements will generally not be treated as legally enforceable contracts.[244] However, this provision relates only to the status of the collective agreement between the trade union(s) and the employer(s) and does not prevent the terms of a collective agreement — itself not an enforceable contract — being productive of legally binding rights and duties when incorporated expressly or by implication into a contract of employment.[245] When such incorporation occurs the legal quality of the collectively agreed terms derives not from the collective agreement but from the individual contract of employment of which it has become a part. The general principles to be applied in determining whether a collective agreement is incorporated into individual contracts of employment are

---

[236] Also most statutes expressly prohibit contractual interference with or exclusion of their respective statutory rights. See, for example, ERA, s. 203, SDA 1975, s. 77 (as applied by SDA 1986, s. 6).

[237] EqPA 1970, s. 1(1).

[238] The Equal Pay Act also applies to contracts of apprenticeship and contracts to personally execute work (EqPA, s. 1(6)(a)).

[239] For detailed coverage of equal pay see Chapter Seven.

[240] The Trade Union and Labour Relations (Consolidation) Act 1992, s. 185. And see Chapter Nine.

[241] The Trade Union and Labour Relations (Consolidation) Act 1992, s. 178(1) defines a collective agreement as any agreement or arrangement made by or on behalf of one or more trade unions and one or more employers or employer's associations relating to the matters referred to in s. 178(2) of that Act. And see Chapter Eleven.

[242] See J. Casey, "Collective Agreements: Some Scottish Footnotes" 1973 JR 22 and R. L. C. Hunter "Collective Agreement Fair Wages Clause and the Employment Relationship in Scots Law" 1975 JR 47.

[243] The Trade Union and Labour Relations (Consolidation) Act 1992, s. 179 provides that any collective agreement "shall be conclusively presumed not to have been intended by the parties to be a legally enforceable contract unless the agreement — (a) is in writing and (b) contains a provision which (however expressed) — states that the parties intended that the agreement shall be a legally enforceable contract" but that where conditions (a) and (b) are satisfied the agreement is conclusively presumed to have been intended to be a legally enforceable contract. And see *NCB v. NUM* [1986] ICR 736 in which a statement in a collective agreement that the parties were to "be bound by this agreement" did not satisfy condition (b) above.

[244] According to W. W. McBryde, *The Law of Contract in Scotland*, Scots law does not require that contracts be preceded by this degree of *animus* or intention. See para. 2.9.

[245] See in this respect the important decision of the Court of Appeal in *Marley v. Forward Trust Group Ltd* [1986] IRLR 369, CA overturning the Employment Appeal Tribunal [1986] IRLR 43, that a term in a collective agreement stated to be binding in honour only was not binding even if incorporated into the contract of employment.

succinctly set out in *Alexander v. Standard Telephones & Cables (No 2) Ltd*[246] thus:

(1)   it is the contractual intention of the employer and the employee that is important;

(2)   the fact that another document (*e.g.* collective agreement) is not itself contractual does not prevent incorporation;

(3)   where general reference to a document occurs it is necessary to consider whether a particular part of it is apt for incorporation; and

(4)   in a case of implied incorporation the character of the document or the relevant part of it and whether it is apt for inclusion in an individual contract are critical factors.

However, a collective agreement may be incorporated into a contract of employment either expressly or by implication[247] whether or not the employee is a member of the relevant trade union or the employer is represented at the collective negotiations.[248] And the Court of Appeal has rejected as quite untenable the proposition that where a closed shop agreement was in force rules of the trade union were implied into the contract of employment of every employee covered by the closed shop agreement.[249] Express corporation occurs where in the contract of employment there is a clear reference to a specific collective agreement[250] or where there is a more general reference to "such national and county (collective) agreements as are in force."[251] The words of reference may be specific resulting in the incorporation of only particular provisions of a collective agreement[252] or they may be couched in more general terms in which case all appropriate provisions in the collective agreement will become part of the individual's contract of employment.[253] Where such general reference occurs an employee will not be able to resist the incorporation of a collective term of which he does not approve.[254]

In the absence of express incorporation a collectively agreed term may nevertheless become part of the individual employee's contract of employment by implication. However, it is wrong to assume that collectively agreed terms (or, for that matter, terms set out in some other document to which no express reference is

---

[246] [1991] IRLR 286, HCt.

[247] It is necessary to note that the process of incorporation is not restricted to collective agreements; contracting parties are generally free to agree that their terms of contract are to be found in or determined by an extraneous document or source, but by far the most common document to be incorporated is the collective agreement.

[248] *Cf* Patents Act 1977, s. 40.

[249] *Associated Newspaper Group v. Wade* [1979] IRLR 201.

[250] The following is an example of express incorporation — "The terms of your employment are subject to the Agreement on Wages and Conditions of Employment dated 1973 made between the Hawick Knitwear Manufacturers' Association and the GMBATU ...".

[251] *NCB v. Galley* [1958] 1 WLR 16, CA.

[252] See, for example, *Pearson v. William Jones Ltd* [1967] 1 WLR 1140 where the collective agreement was referred to only for overtime working.

[253] An individual's contract of employment may require him to work under, for example, "the terms of the national agreement" or "such terms as may be negotiated from time to time with the recognised trade unions".

[254] *NCB v. Galley*, above; *Callison v. Ford Motor Co Ltd* [1969] ITR 74. In *Galley* the employee's situation was exacerbated by his union agreeing to a term of which Galley (and others) did not approve but also by the loose wording of the term incorporated — "to work such days or part days ... as may be reasonably required by management". And see *Lombard Tricity Finance Ltd v. Paton*, The Times, October 31, 1988 to effect that although it was unusual a contract could provide for its terms to be varied unilaterally by one party in his absolute discretion to the detriment of the other party; and *Lee v. GEC Plessey Telecommunications* [1993] IRLR 383, QBD.

made in the contract of employment itself) will automatically become incorporated into contracts of employment[255] because whether or not the collectively agreed term is to be implied into the contract will depend on whether the implication satisfied one or more methods which, by the principles of contract law, permit such an implication. In essence, therefore, whether a collective agreement (or part of it), can, in the absence of an express reference, be implied into the contract of employment, depends on whether implication of the term(s) is justified in the particular circumstances[256] or to give the contract "business efficacy" and, where there have been previous employments, a course of dealing. Thus merely because an employer observes the terms of a collective agreement does not *per se* mean it is incorporated into the contract of employment because "the application of the collective agreement . . . was equally consistent with the view that [the employers] did so as policy, not necessarily because they were bound to do"[257]; although membership of an employer's association may require the introduction of collective agreements into contracts of employment entered into by associated employers.[258]

However, the potential for express or implied incorporation of collective agreements is subject to the term being suitable or appropriate for incorporation into an individual's contract of employment and a special statutory provision regarding what may be briefly described as a "no-strike clause". Collective agreements, particularly industry-wide or national agreements, frequently cover a wide range of matters of interest to the parties — trade unions and employers. Many of these matters are primarily concerned with negotiating machinery and institutions and long-term strategy — essentially collective issues relevant to the industry or parties. Equally, however, the agreements will include more mundane issues like pay rates, sick leave entitlement, redundancy compensation packages, job mobility/transfer schemes etc. — issues which readily translate into terms of individual contracts of employment. The significance of this distinction is reflected by a judicial reluctance to incorporate "collective" provisions into individual contracts of employment.[259] Thus a provision in a collective agreement which involved interviewing potentially redundant employees prior to the preparation of a list showing which employees preferred retraining to redundancy was regarded as a long-term plan regarding the policy of redundancy implementation rather than the rights of individual employees.[260] Similarly parts of the collective agreement

---

[255] Thus in *Singh v. BSC* [1974] IRLR 131, IT the conclusion of a new collective agreement with the recognised trade unions *per se* had no effect on Singh's contract of employment. And see *Rodwell v. Thomas* [1944] 1 KB 596.

[256] An example of circumstantial incorporation is seen in *Joel v. Cammell Laird (Ship-Repairers) Ltd* [1969] ITR 206 in which the industrial tribunal specified satisfaction of the following three conditions before implied incorporation could take place: (1) specific knowledge of the collective term by the party alleged to be bound; (2) conduct on the part of that person which indicated he accepted the collective agreement; and (3) clarity of the mechanics of incorporation. And see *Maclea v. Essex Line Ltd* [1933] 45 Lloyd's Rep. 254, KBD, in which the terms and conditions of the National Maritime Board were implied into the contract between Maclea and the Essex Line Ltd; however, from the judgement of Lord Acton it is obvious that the Board conditions could have been implied on the basis of custom of the trade or a previous course of dealing.

[257] *Young v. Canadian Northern Railway Co.* [1931] AC 83, PC *per* Lord Russell of Killowen. And see *Hamilton v. Futura Floors Ltd* [1990] IRLR 478, OH; *Littlejohn v. Clyde Port Authority* 1995 GWD 31–1611.

[258] *Hamilton v. Futura Floors Ltd* [1990] IRLR 478, OH.

[259] *Burroughs Machines v. Timmoney* 1977 SC 393.

[260] *British Leyland (UK) Ltd v. McQuilken* [1978] IRLR 245, EAT.

arrived at in 1946 between the National Coal Board and the National Union of Mineworkers which created a National Reference Tribunal (a tribunal to deal with disputes) was intended to resolve disputes between employer and trade union and was not intended to be enforceable between the board and its individual employees[261]; and, because a statutory written statement of employment particulars is not required to deal with redundancy a clause therein that an employee's "basic terms and conditions of employment" were subject to a collective agreement was not expressly incorporated into his contract of employment; nor was it impliedly incorporated because none of the other clauses of this collective agreement was apt for inclusion in an individual contract of employment.[262] On the other hand, a collective provision dealing with transferring employees from one type of work to another has been held to be incorporated into the contract of employment,[263] as have terms which provided that employees who accepted significantly different alternative employment would have six months to assess the suitability of the new job without prejudice to enhanced redundancy benefits.[264] However, it is respectfully suggested that care needs to be taken when deciding whether a collectively agreed term — especially one that is referred to expressly — is suitable or appropriate for incorporation into a contract of employment. Provided a collectively agreed term is neither too vague nor too indefinite to be enforced,[265] the fact that the parties to the collective agreement did not envisage that a term of that agreement would be incorporated into an individual's contract of employment is of limited importance in the face of evidence that the contracting parties (the employer and the employee) themselves intended that it be so incorporated.[266] However, this suggestion is subject to the statutory provision[267] that no term of a collective agreement which prohibits or restricts (or has the effect of prohibiting or restricting) the right[268] of workers[269] to engage in a strike or other industrial action shall not either expressly or by implication form part of the contract between the worker and his employer unless the collective agreement satisfies certain conditions which cannot be overridden by the collective agreement or the contract of employment.[270] Arguably a collective agreement would restrict the right to take industrial action if, say, as part of a dispute procedure it is provided that there will be no resort to industrial action until the procedure has been exhausted but given that the circumstances which led to the enactment of the original statutory

---

[261] *NCB v. NUM* [1986] ICR 736, Ch D.

[262] *Alexander v. Standard Telephones & Cables Ltd (No. 2)* [1991] IRLR 286, HCt.

[263] *Joel v. Cammell Laird (Ship-Repairers) Ltd* [1969] ITR 206.

[264] *Marley v. Forward Trust Ltd* [1986] IRLR 369, CA.

[265] On the question of contracts being void from uncertainty see W. W. McBryde, *The Law of Contract in Scotland*, paras 4–18 ff.

[266] And see *Marley v. Forward Trust Ltd*, above.

[267] TULRCA, s. 180.

[268] It is debatable whether British workers have a "right" to engage in industrial action; most workers who take industrial action — whether or not supported by a majority in a ballot — will break their contracts of employment and if dismissed may not have a right to claim unfair dismissal. See Chapters Three and Five.

[269] Strictly s. 180 is not limited to those who have contracts of employment (TULRCA, s. 296(1)).

[270] These conditions are (i) the collective agreement is in writing, (ii) it expressly provides the "no-strike" clause may be incorporated into a contract of employment, (iii) it is reasonably accessible to, and available for consultation by, the worker during his working hours, and (iv) the trade union(s) which is (are) parties to the collective agreement are independent trade unions (TULRCA, s. 180(2)).

provision are unlikely to be repeated,[271] that it applies only to incorporation of terms from collective agreements and that the industrial action itself is likely to be a breach of contract the provision of section 180 of the Trade Union and Labour Relations (Consolidation) Act 1992 should not be overemphasised because it is by no means certain such "no strike" clauses would have been regarded as appropriate for inclusion in individual contacts.[272]

2.15 The effect of incorporation

Once the collective term is incorporated into the contract of employment it becomes, like any other term of the contract, removable or alterable only with the consent of the parties.[273] Also, in the absence of a clear provision to the effect, courts are reluctant to render the application of a collectively agreed term dependent on the unilateral decision of the employer. Thus in *Dalgleish v. Lothian and Borders Police Board*[274] the court rejected the employer's argument that the collective term, although agreed with employees' representatives, required the Board's approval before it could be incorporated into employment contracts. Similarly in *Davies v. Hotpoint Ltd*[275] the collectively agreed term which guaranteed a 39-hour week was subject to the condition that the guarantee would be reduced proportionately where "approved" short time working was worked as an alternative to redundancy and the employers argued that "approval" merely meant approval by the employers. However, this was rejected on the grounds that "approved" indicated a requirement of the consent or agreement of someone other than the person making the decision to be approved and if the guarantee was to have any substance it could not have been the intention that it should depend solely on the unilateral decision of the employer. Furthermore the fact that the employer terminates the collective agreement or leaves the employer's organisation which concluded the agreement, will have no effect on the term as incorporated into the contract of employment.[276] Thus where an employee's contract of employment was subject to the condition that "wages and conditions of service shall be in accordance with national or local agreements for the time being in force", by which employees became entitled to a guaranteed weekly payment, the employee's right to such a payment was unaffected by the employer's decision to terminate the relevant collective agreement.[277] However where a benefit is not the

---

[271] It is generally believed s. 180 (in its original form of TULRA, s. 18) was enacted to prevent the recurrence of the concession made in *Rookes v. Barnard* [1964] AC 1129 that a "no strike" clause in a collective agreement was incorporated into individual contracts of employment. See Chapter Eleven.

[272] On the other hand trade unions can now include "no strike" clauses in collective agreements in the knowledge that they need not be translated into contractual duties at the level of the individual. Where they are incorporated it could be argued that provided, say, the dispute procedure was exhausted first the industrial action would not be a breach of contract.

[273] *Lee v. GEC Plessey Communications* [1993] IRLR 383, QBD.

[274] 1992 SLT 721, OH. *Cf Cadoux v. Central Regional Council* 1986 SLT 117, OH.

[275] *The Times*, July 29, 1994, EAT.

[276] *Burroughs Machines Ltd v. Timmoney* 1977 SC 393; *Robertson v. British Gas Corporation* [1983] ICR 351, CA. And see *Hamilton v. Futura Floors Ltd* [1990] IRLR 478, OH.

[277] *Gibbons v. Associated British Ports* [1985] IRLR 376, QBD. The position is summarised neatly by Kerr LJ in *Robertson v. British Gas Corporation* [1983] ICR 351, CA thus "The terms of an individual contract are in part to be found in the agreed collective agreements as they exist from time to time, and if these cease to exist as collective agreements, then the terms as expressly varied between the individual and the employer will remain as they were by reference to the last agreed collective agreement incorporated into the individual contracts."

product of (a collective) agreement it may be withdrawn by a unilateral decision of the employer. Thus where an employee's terms provided that the "post is subject to the conditions of service laid down by the National Joint Council (for local authority staff) and as supplemented by the Authorities' Rules and as amended from time to time" the employers were entitled to withdraw a non-contributory life assurance scheme by amending their own rules because "the reference to the authorities' rules as amended from time to time shows that it was in the contemplation of the parties that the (employers') rules might be altered ... and the clear inference from the fact that they are the employers' rules is that the employers have power to alter them." [278]

2.16 Custom and agency

Terms of the contract of employment may also originate in custom through an intermediary or agent. Where a custom or trade practice is well-known and well-settled in a trade or industry, is not contrary to a rule of law and is reasonable in the circumstances, it will, in the absence of a contrary term, become a term of the contract without proof of its express communication to the contracting party when the contract is entered into.[279] Thus, where no express term regarding remuneration was made, the customary wage rate for the locality was implied into the contract[280] and where merchant seamen were engaged "simply by being told to join a ship without anything more, it is always assumed on both sides that the engagement is upon the terms and conditions of the National Maritime Board".[281] Also while acceptance of employment on terms known to include the provisions of rule books, notices etc. will result in those terms being implied into the contract,[282] a policy adopted by management unilaterally cannot become a term of employees' contracts on the grounds that it is an established practice unless it is at least shown that the policy has been drawn to the attention of the employees or has been followed without exception for a substantial period.[283] Although there is no insurmountable legal impediment to a trade union becoming the duly authorised agent of those members it represents in collective bargaining,[284] the present position would seem to be that generally trade union members neither expressly nor impliedly confer any authority on the trade union or its negotiators so as to ensure that the collective agreement when made — or at least those parts of it which create legal obligations — will form a set of legal rights and duties between on the one hand the member and those employers represented at the collective negotiations and on the other hand the union (agent) and its members (principals). Of course, while many trade unions are authorised at the commencement of collective negotiations to achieve a particular target, such authorisation seldom emanates from individual members but almost universally from a representative

---

[278] Per L. Ross, *Cadoux v. Central Regional Council* 1986 SLT 117 at p. 120.

[279] *Hogarth & Sons v. Leith Cotton Seed Co. Ltd* 1909 SC 955.

[280] *Stuart v. McLeod* (1901) 9 SLT 192.

[281] *Maclea v. Essex Line* [1933] 45 Lloyd's Reps 254, KBD.

[282] See D. M. Walker, *The Law of Contracts and Related Obligations in Scotland* (3rd edn), para. 22.11 and the cases referred to.

[283] *Duke v. Reliance Systems Ltd* [1982] ICR 449, EAT. And see *Quinn v. Calder Industrial Materials Ltd* [1996] IRLR 126, EAT.

[284] Because of the number of principals likely to be involved, it would be a case of acting on behalf of principals whose identities were undisclosed; new members could be dealt with by the application of the rules of ratification although a question might arise about whether the principal was in existence at the time of the collective negotiations. On Agency, see Gloag and Henderson, *The Law of Scotland* (10th edn).

conference or committee. Furthermore the result of the now customary membership ballots indicates that proof of the negotiators' authority to act as agent for all members would be elusive. The current legal position — although there are *dicta* to the contrary[285] — is that in the absence of special circumstances[286] a trade union negotiating a collective agreement does not act as the duly authorised agent of its members so that they are bound as principals.[287] Until there is a radical change in the attitudes of unions, their members or the legislature, the impact of collective agreements on employment terms of employer and employee — whether members of trade union or employers' organisations — will continue to depend on incorporation into the contract of employment.

---

[285] See the observations of Denning MR in *Chappell v. Times Newspapers Ltd* [1975] IRLR 90, CA.

[286] See, for example, *Edwards v. Skyways Ltd* [1964] 1 All ER 494; *Sutherland v. Montrose Fishing Co. Ltd* (1921) 37 Sh. Ct Rep. 239.

[287] *Holland v. London Society of Compositors* [1924] 40 TLR 440, KBD; *Rodwell v. Thomas* [1944] 1 KB 596; *Burton Group Ltd v. Smith* [1977] IRLR 351, EAT; *Gray Dunn & Co Ltd v. Edwards* [1980] IRLR 23, EAT; *Lee v. GEC Plessey Telecommunications* [1993] IRLR 383.

Chapter Three

RIGHTS AND DUTIES ARISING DURING THE CONTRACT OF EMPLOYMENT

3.1 Introduction

Once the contract of employment has been created different types of legal rights and duties come into play. The relationship between employer and employee is sufficiently close to bring into operation the "neighbour" principle of the law of reparation so that an employer must take reasonable care to ensure the safety of his employees. Obviously contractual rights and duties will also come into play. Rights and duties which arise from the law of reparation and the law of contract have their origins in the common law. Especially since the 1960s, however, many employment law rights and duties have been created by statute, for example, (1) redundancy payments,[1] (2) unfair dismissal[2] and (3) sexual and racial discrimination.[3] However, statutory employment rights can be distinguished from those which are based on the common law in at least two ways. First, nearly all statutory employment rights are enforced through the medium of the industrial tribunals[4] whereas rights in the employment field which originate in the law of delict or contract generally are enforced through the ordinary courts.[5] Secondly, many[6] statutory employment rights are conferred only on those employees who have accumulated the relevant period of continuous employment.[7] Accordingly whether or not an employee possesses a period of continuous employment must be considered as a prelude to the operation of the statutory rules relating to the substance of the statutory right claimed.

CONTINUOUS EMPLOYMENT

3.2 General

Whether employment is continuous depends on a set of statutory rules[8] contained

---

[1]   See Chapter Six.
[2]   See Chapter Five.
[3]   See Chapter Seven.
[4]   Chapter Eight.
[5]   The only circumstance in which an industrial tribunal can entertain an action for breach of contract is where the claim arises or is outstanding on the termination of the employee's employment (Industrial Tribunals Extension of Jurisdiction (Scotland) Order 1994 (SI 1994 No. 1624)); and see Chapter Eight.
[6]   The main exceptions are rights relating to sexual and racial discrimination and the parts of unfair dismissal law dealing with union membership, pregnancy, health and safety, and assertion of statutory rights.
[7]   Usually it has to be continuous employment with the employer against whom the claim is being made but there are special rules permitting employment with other employers to be considered. See para. 3.5.
[8]   The rules are mandatory and cannot be altered by agreement (*Secretary of State for Employment v. Globe Elastic Thread Co. Ltd* [1979] ICR 706, HL; *Hanson v. Fashion Industries (Hartlepool) Ltd* [1980] IRLR 393, EAT).

in the Employment Rights Act 1996[9] but irrespective of these rules no period of employment can be counted if it took place under an illegal contract of employment.[10] Although the length of a period of continuous employment is calculated in calendar months or years the basic unit is the week.[11] Thus to determine whether or not an employee has, say, two years' continuous employment it is necessary to apply the statutory rules to each of the weeks in that two year period. Normally[12] a week which cannot be taken into account also interrupts any period of continuous employment already accumulated as does the receipt of a redundancy payment[13] and the employee will have to recommence the qualifying process. Except for redundancy payments (for which employment below 18 years of age is ignored[14]), an employee's period of continuous employment begins with the day on which he starts work[15] and ends with the day by reference to which the period has to be ascertained[16] and, unless the contrary is proved, employment with one employer[17] is presumed to have been continuous.[18]

3.3 Which weeks count towards continuous employment?

In *R. v. Secretary of State for Employment, ex p EOC*[19] the House of Lords held that the qualifying conditions for redundancy payments and compensation for unfair dismissal infringed European Union provisions requiring equal pay and treatment. The offending conditions were those provisions of the Employment Protection (Consolidation) Act 1978 which, in computing a period of qualifying service, disregarded weeks in which the employee worked fewer than 16 hours or, where he had been employed for 5 years, weeks in which he worked fewer than 8 hours. To remove these discriminatory provisions the Employment Protection (Part-time Employees) Regulations 1995[20] were introduced. The Regulations amend the statutory provisions regarding continuity of employment so that, with effect from February 6, 1995, whether a week counts towards continuous employment is no longer determined by the number of hours actually worked or the number of hours of employment a contract of employment normally involves.[21] The question now is simply whether the week is one in which the employee's

---

9   Sections 210–219.
10 *Hyland v. J. H. Barker (North West) Ltd* [1985] ICR 861, EAT; *Salvesen v. Simons* [1994] IRLR 52, EAT; *Annandale Engineering Ltd v. Samson* [1994] IRLR 59, EAT. *Cf Wilkinson v. Lugg* [1990] ICR 599, EAT.
11 ERA, s. 210.
12 The exception is a week during which the employee takes part in a strike or is locked out (ERA, s. 216).
13 ERA, s. 214.
14 ERA, s. 211(2).
15 As to "starts work" see *Salvation Army General v. Dewsbury* [1984] IRLR 222, EAT.
16 ERA, s. 211(1). A week is deemed to end on a Saturday (ERA, s. 235(1)).
17 *Secretary of State for Employment v. Cohen and Beaupress Ltd* [1987] IRLR 169, EAT. And see *Tipper v. Roofdec Ltd* [1989] IRLR 419, EAT to effect that where there are successive periods of employment with one employer the reason for the termination of the earlier one is of no significance.
18 ERA, 210(5).
19 [1994] IRLR 176, HL.
20 SI 1995 No. 31.
21 *Ibid.* reg. 4 which repeals EPCA, Sch 13, paras. 3, 5–8 and amends para. 4. The Regulations were revoked by ERA, Sch 3, which re-enacts identical provisions (ERA, s. 212(1)).

relations with the employer are governed by a contract.[22] In addition, however, the following weeks also count towards a period of continuous employment:

(a)   A week in which the employee is, for part of or the whole of the week, incapable of working because of illness, pregnancy or childbirth,[23] or is absent on account of a temporary cessation of work, or an arrangement or custom whereby continuity of employment is to be preserved.[24] However, it is not necessary that the employee be incapable of doing any work. What matters is whether he is incapable of the work on which he was engaged prior to that which is in question as a possible interruption of the continuity of his employment, so that weeks during which an employee took light work with another employer, when he was incapable of working under his original contract, counted towards his continuous employment when he subsequently returned to work for that (original) employer.[25] What constitutes a "temporary cessation of work" has produced much litigation which has resulted in support for the following propositions — (i) a temporary cessation of work can occur between two (or more) fixed term contracts,[26] (ii) the provision relates to temporary cessation of paid work,[27] (iii) the amount of work has to cease and no longer be available for the employer to give to the employee.[28] Whether a temporary cessation of work has occurred is a question of fact and degree including the whole history of the employment and although it is possible to compare periods when work continues with periods when it has ceased such a "mathematical" approach is not appropriate where the pattern of work and cessation of work is irregular.[29] In *Sillars v. Charringtons Fuels Ltd*[30] although the lay members of the EAT approved of the broad approach set out in *Fitzgerald* and *Flack* because the "mathematical" approach might result in unfairness, the industrial tribunal had been correct to apply the "mathematical" approach in the circumstances.

(b)   A week of absence because of pregnancy where a woman has exercised her statutory right to return to work.[31]

(c)   A week which is covered by the statutory provision[32] which postpones the

[22]   ERA, s. 212(1); and note Crown employees are deemed to have contracts (ERA, s. 191).

[23]   ERA, s. 212(3). The maximum permitted absence for illness and pregnancy under this provision is 26 weeks (ERA, s. 212(4)).

[24]   *Ibid.* In *Letheby & Christopher Ltd v. Bond* [1988] ICR 480, EAT it was held that the tribunal was required to determine whether the parties regarded the employment as continuing and that the use of separate contracts (for each spell of work) suggested they did not regard it as continuing.

[25]   *Donnelly v. Kelvin International Services Ltd* [1992] IRLR 496, EAT; *Pearson v. Kent County Council* [1993] IRLR 165, CA.

[26]   *Ford v. Warwickshire County Council* [1983] IRLR 126, HL. Cf *Moncrieff v. Tayside Regional Council* 1983 SLT 378, IH.

[27]   *University of Aston in Birmingham v. Malik* [1984] ICR 492, EAT.

[28]   *Byrne v. Birmingham District Council* [1987] IRLR 191, CA. (Allocating work to employees in a pool of workers does not mean there is a temporary cessation of work in respect of those employees to whom work is periodically not offered.)

[29]   *Fitzgerald v. Hall Russell & Co. Ltd* 1970 SC (HL) 1; *Flack v. Kodak Ltd* [1986] ICR 775, CA.

[30]   [1988] IRLR 180, EAT; affirmed [1989] IRLR 152, CA. And see *Berwick Salmon Fisheries Ltd v. Rutherford* [1991] IRLR 203, EAT.

[31]   ERA, s. 212(2).

[32]   ERA, ss. 92(7), 97(2), 145(5).

effective date of termination[33] or is between dismissal for redundancy and a renewal or re-engagement.[34]

3.4 Strikes and lock-outs

However, even if a week falls into one of the paragraphs (a)–(c) above it will not count if, during that week the employee takes part in a strike or is locked out.[35] "Strike" is defined to mean "the cessation of work by a body of persons employed acting in combination, or a concerted refusal or a refusal under a common understanding or any number of persons employed to continue to work for an employer in consequence of a dispute, done as a means of compelling their employer or any person or body of persons employed, to accept or not to accept terms or conditions of or affecting employment"[36] and "lock-out" means "(a) the closing of a place of employment; (b) the suspension of work, or (c) the refusal by an employer to continue to employ any number of persons employed by him in consequence of a dispute, done with a view to compelling persons employed by the employer, or to aid another employer in compelling persons employed by him, to accept terms or conditions of or affecting employment".[37] It must be emphasised that these definitions are provided for dealing with questions of continuity of employment although they may be of assistance when the meaning of "strike" or "lock-out" arises in relation to other questions (for example where an employer claims an employee has been dismissed during a strike or lock-out).[38] However, the rule that weeks on strike or when locked out do not count is tempered by the further provisions that (i) in calculating the *length* of a period of continuous employment the beginning of that period is postponed only by the days of strike or lock-out[39] and (ii) continuity of employment is not fractured by a strike or lock-out.[40] The latter provision is of great significance because without it employees would be extremely vulnerable and greatly inhibited from taking strike action.[41]

3.5 Different employers

Normally the rules of continuous employment permit consideration of employment with a particular employer; each time an employee changes his employer he has to start afresh to accumulate continuous employment.[42] However, in the following situations it is permitted to have regard to employment with more than one employer —

(a)　where a trade, business or undertaking is transferred a period of employment with the transferor counts as a period of employment with the transferee (the new owner) in respect of any employee who is employed by the transferor at the time of the transfer.[43] Whether a business has been transferred is a mixed question of fact and law and it is important to distinguish between the transfer of a business

---

[33]　See para. 5.27.
[34]　ERA, s. 213.
[35]　ERA, s. 216.
[36]　ERA, s. 235(4), (5).
[37]　*Ibid.*
[38]　See Chapter Eight.
[39]　ERA, s. 216.
[40]　*Ibid.* s. 216(2), (3).
[41]　*Cf* TULRCA, s. 237 regarding employees who take part in unofficial action.
[42]　ERA, s. 218. And see *Secretary of State for Employment v. Cohen and Beaupress Ltd* [1987] IRLR 169, EAT. *Cf Donnelly v. Kelvin International Services Ltd* [1992] IRLR 496, EAT.
[43]　ERA, s. 218(2).

as a going concern and the mere transfer of the assets of the business.[44] Thus in *Melon v. Hector Powe Ltd*[45] where a factory which made suits was transferred there was no transfer of a business because the new owners made suits not merely for their own retail outlets but for sale to any retail outlets which wished to sell them. As Lord Fraser of Tullybelton remarked in *Melon v. Hector Powe Ltd* "individual employees may continue to do the same work in the same environment and they may not appreciate that they are working in a different business".[46] The above provisions apply to the transfer of any trade, business or undertaking whether private or public and this latter category includes the functions of ministers and government departments.[47] However, it is necessary to have regard to the provisions of the Transfer of Undertakings (Protection of Employment) Regulations 1981[48] which apply to the transfer of an economic unit[49] and provide that after the transfer, contracts of employees in the undertaking at the time of the transfer and those who but for their unfair dismissal would have been employed at that time[50] continue to have effect as if they were made between such employees and the transferee, and all the rights and liabilities of the transferor under or in connection with the contract of employment attach to the transferee.[51] Thus in a situation to which these regulations apply an employee whose contract of employment subsists at the time of the transfer can, after the transfer, exercise any rights against the transferee on the basis of his employment with both transferor and transferee in so far as the other rules regarding continuity are met. The phrase "at the time of the transfer"[52] is to receive a liberal construction so that it is not to be regarded as applying to the particular moment in time when the transfer takes place.[53] Thus an employee has been held to be employed at the time of the transfer even although there was a gap between the end of his employment with the transferor and commencing with the transferee[54] and where he remained in the employment of the transferor for a short period after the transfer;[55]

(b)   where by Act of Parliament one body corporate is substituted for another in a contract of employment, employment with both bodies counts towards continuous employment;[56]

(c)   where after the death of an employer employment is continued by trustees or representatives of the deceased employer, employment before and after the employer's death counts towards continuous employment;[57]

(d)   where an employee transfers to an employer who is an associated employer

---

[44] *Bailey's Exrs v. Co-operative Wholesale Society Ltd* 1976 SLT 92, OH. And see *Rastill v. Automated Refreshment Services Ltd* [1978] ICR 289, EAT; *Mannin Management Services v. Ward* IDS Brief 393, CA.

[45] [1980] IRLR 477, HL. *Cf Gibson v. Motortune Ltd* [1990] ICR 740, EAT.

[46] *Ibid.* If employees have cause to doubt that the business has been transferred they should consider making claims against the transferor before the relevant time limits expire.

[47] ERA, s. 191(4).

[48] SI 1981 No. 1794.

[49] *Workman & Birchley v. Servisystem Ltd* 1994, IRLIB 507, p. 7. And see Chapter Five.

[50] *Litster v. Forth Dry Dock & Engineering Co Ltd* [1989] IRLR 161, HL.

[51] Transfer of Undertakings (Protection of Employment) Regulations 1981, reg. 3.

[52] ERA, s. 218(2).

[53] *Macer v. Abafast Ltd* [1990] IRLR 137, EAT.

[54] *Justfern Ltd v. D'Ingerthorpe* [1994] IRLR 165, EAT.

[55] *A & G Truck Ltd v. Bartlett* [1994] IRLR 162, EAT.

[56] ERA, s. 218(3).

[57] *Ibid.* s. 218(4). And see the similar provision relating to the change in the composition of a partnership or trustees (s. 218(5)) and *Jeetle v. Elster* [1985] IRLR 227, EAT.

of the other employer employment with both employers counts towards continuous employment.[58]

3.6 Re-engagement

Where, following a complaint of unfair dismissal (or action taken by a conciliation officer[59]) an employee is re-instated or re-engaged the period between dismissal and re-employment counts towards continuous employment.[60] Continuity is also preserved where an employee is re-employed before the complaint of unfair dismissal is heard[61] or where no complaint at all is made and re-employment results from a settlement or arrangement.[62] Also, where a liquidator re-engages employees whose contracts have been terminated by the winding up of the company for which the employees had worked, the liquidator is regarded as continuing their employment "for and on behalf of the company".[63]

REMUNERATION

3.7 Introduction

The rights and duties if the employer and employee relating to remuneration are regulated both by contractual provisions and statutory rules. Thus, whether wages are due during periods of sickness[64] and whether they can be withheld during industrial action are matters to be determined by the contract, while entitlement to medical suspension pay, guarantee and redundancy payments are regulated by statute,[65] as are deductions from wages.[66] It has been observed that "remuneration" can connote a *quid pro quo* for services rendered including payment in kind[67] or more specifically a monetary payment[68] depending on the circumstances.[69] Arguably, though, the concept of "remuneration" is narrower than

---

[58] ERA, s. 218(6). Employers are "associated" if "(a) one is a company of which the other (directly or indirectly) has control, or (b) both are companies of which a third person (directly or indirectly) has control" (ERA, s. 231). This definition is exhaustive and must embrace at least one limited company — *Gardiner v. Merton London Borough Council* [1980] IRLR 472, CA. "Control" means control by a majority of votes attaching to shares exercised in a general meeting and not *de facto* managerial control; however, evidence might show that one person in practice controls the voting powers attaching to the shares of another so that he controls his own shares as well as those of the other person — *South West Launderettes Ltd v. Laidler* [1986] IRLR 305, CA — or that one person holds shares as a nominee of another — *Payne v. Secretary of State for Employment* [1989] IRLR 352, CA. And note the alertness of the EAT when confronted with companies forming a partnership or joint venture: *Pinkney v. Sandpiper Drilling Ltd* [1989] IRLR 425, EAT. The company may be registered abroad: *Hancill v. Marcon Engineering Ltd* [1990] IRLR 51, EAT.
[59] See para. 5.9.
[60] The Employment Protection (Continuity of Employment) Regulations 1993 (SI 1993 No. 2165); and see ERA, Sch. 2, para. 2.
[61] *Smith v. Carlisle City Council* 1983, unreported EAT.
[62] ERA, s. 212(3)(c); *Ingram v. Foxon* [1985] IRLR 5, EAT.
[63] *Smith v. Lord Advocate* 1978 SC 259.
[64] This must be distinguished from statutory sick pay which is paid by employers on behalf of the Department of Social Security; see para. 3.17.
[65] See ERA, ss 64, 28, 135; and see paras 3.15, 3.16 and Chapter Six.
[66] See ERA, ss. 13, 14; and see para. 3.21.
[67] E.g. *R v. Postmaster General* [1876] 1 QBD 658.
[68] E.g. *S & U Stores Ltd v. Wilkes* [1974] 3 All ER 401, NIRC.
[69] *Chapman v. Aberdeen Construction Group plc* 1990 GWD 18-1012 (reversed on another point, 1993 SLT 1205).

"pay" as understood by Article 119 of the European Economic Community Treaty.[70]

3.8 The contractual terms

Wages. Contractual terms regarding the payment of wages or salary are usually express.[71] However, in the absence of an express term there is a rebuttable presumption that services are given for payment.[72] While by a clear contractual term it is permissible to leave for future determination the precise amount of wages due[73] such a power of determination will not justify withholding all wages.[74] Where there is neither an express nor implied term regarding the amount of remuneration to be paid the parties can have resort to the equitable principle of *quantum meruit*.[75] Where performance ceases between two payment dates the question whether an employee has a right to accrued wages may arise. Where the contract is indivisible it seems that no right to wages for part performance will arise unless it is due to the employee's death or illness.[76] In contracts which may be terminated by notice whether wages accrue in respect of past performance and the rate of accrual may be implied from the terms of the contract and the practice of the contracting parties.[77] Although the Apportionment Act 1870 allocates on a *per diem* basis annuities including salaries[78] it has been doubted whether the Act applies to payments made under a contract of employment.[79] What may be of more practical significance is (1) failure to perform his duties under the contract will deprive him of the opportunity of compelling the employer to pay wages and will bring into play the principles of compensation where the employer has suffered

[70] Thus ERA, s. 71(2) refers to "remuneration". *Cf* the Trade Union Reform and Employment Rights Bill, cl. 20.

[71] Although it is not a contract the written statement required to be issued under ERA, s. 1 has to specify particulars of "the scale or rate of remuneration, or the method of calculating remuneration" and "the intervals at which remuneration is paid (that is, weekly, monthly or other specified intervals)."

[72] *Thomson v. Thomson's Tr* (1889) 16 R 333. *Cf* Lord Fraser, *Master and Servant* (3rd edn, 1881), pp. 39 ff where many of the cases discussed feature services by near relatives; also in some of the older cases the issue was whether wages were due in addition to board and/or accommodation.

[73] *Re Richmond Gate Property Co. Ltd* [1964] 3 All ER 936.

[74] Lord Fraser, *Master and Servant*, p. 135. In *Richmond Gate* the board's power to determine the salary of the managing director was superseded by the company's liquidation. *Cf Avintair v. Ryder Airline Services* 1993 SLT 1339, OH.

[75] *Mackenzie v. Baird's Trustees* 1907 SC 838; *Powell v. Braun* [1954] 1 All ER 484, CA. *Cf McNaughtan v. Brunton* (1882) 10 R 111.

[76] Bell, *Principles*, 179; Erskine, *Institutes* III, 3, 16. *Cf Douglas v. Argyle* (1736) Mor 11102 and *Cutter v. Powell* (1795) 6 Term Rep. 320 in which entitlement to wages seems to have been conditioned on completion of the voyage.

[77] *Macgill v. Park* (1829) 2 F 272; and see *Buchanan v. Strathclyde Regional Council* 1981, OH (unreported). Merely because there is a right to terminate by notice to expire on a date before the next payment of wages/salary is due will not necessarily mean that payments will have accrued for the period up to the expiry of the notice (*Diamond v. English Sewing Cotton Co. Ltd* [1922] WN 237, CA).

[78] Apportionment Act 1870, ss. 2, 5.

[79] Contrast *Macgill v. Park*, above, with *Inman v. Ackroyd Best Ltd* [1901] 1 QB 613, CA. In *Sim v. Rotherham Metropolitan Borough Council* [1986] ICR 897, Scott J was prepared to hold that the Apportionment Act 1870 applied to the salary of a school teacher and in *In re BCCI* [1994] IRLR 282 the Act was used to determine arrears of salary due to senior managers. And see *Thames Water Utilities v. Reynolds* [1996] IRLR 186, EAT (apportionment of accrued holiday pay by calendar and not working days) and Mathews, "Salaries in the Apportionment Act 1870" (1982) 2 *Legal Studies* 302.

damage[80] and (2) where wages are not paid an employee does not have a lien over his employer's moveables.[81]

3.9 *Withholding wages.* In accordance with the rule of mutual contracts where either party to the contract of employment is in material breach he is unable to compel performance by the other party.[82] Thus a ship's engineer failed in an action for payment of salary when his employer pleaded he was relieved of his duty of paying salary because of the pursuer's continued misconduct and neglect of duty.[83] The same rule applies to an employee who takes industrial action which is in breach of contract[84]; he cannot enforce a contractual right to wages withheld by his employer in respect of the period during which the industrial action occurred.[85] And the employer faced with a breach by the employee is not required to rescind the contract before he is entitled to withhold wages (or other performance).[86] However, it is doubtful whether an insignificant breach justifies the withholding of wages[87] although it would seem that, provided the breach does justify withholding remuneration, the amount withheld cannot be challenged.[88] However, it is arguable that the conduct of the employer towards an employee in breach may indicate acceptance of partial performance and justify a finding that the employer has

[80] Erskine, *Institutes* III, 3, 16; *Scottish North-Eastern Railway Co. v. Napier* (1859) 21 D 700; *Pegler v. Northern Agricultural Implement Co.* (1877) 4 R 435. And see G. H. L. Fridman, *Modern Law of Employment* (1963), p. 484.

[81] Bell, *Principles* s. 1412; *Barnton Hotel Co Ltd. v. Cook* (1899) 1 F 1190. According to W. M. Gloag, *The Law of Contract* (2nd edn), p. 632, *Findlay v. Waddell* 1910 SC 670 indicates the distinction between an employee who is merely a custodier of his employer's moveables and others who obtain, for example, books and papers for a particular piece of work; the former has "custody only on which no right of retention can be founded" whereas the latter have "possession and a right to retain".

[82] *Turnbull v. McLean & Co* (1874) 1 R 730; *Graham & Co. v. United Turkey Red Co. Ltd* 1922 SC 533.

[83] *Sharp v. Rettie* (1884) 11 R 745. Lord President Inglis stated "The defence to the action is not a challenge of the amount said to be due ... but an averment that the pursuer has committed a breach of contract and is therefore not entitled to sue on the contract ... It is always competent when one party sues upon a contract ... for the latter to say — You broke the contract and instead of my being in debt to you, you are in debt to me. This form of defence amounts in substance to an action in damages and is in fact an action for damages for real injury done by the pursuer to ... the defender ...".

[84] Industrial action does not always involve a breach of contract by the employee (*Power-Packing Casemakers Ltd v. Faust* [1983] IRLR 117, EAT) nor does a lock-out always involve a breach of contract by the employer (*Express & Star Ltd v. Bunday* [1988] IRC 379, CA). And see para. 5.70.

[85] *Buchanan v. Strathclyde Regional Council* 1981, OH (unreported); *Laurie v. British Steel Corporation* 1988 SLT 17, OH. See also *Miles v. Wakefield Metropolitan District Council* [1987] IRLR 193, HL; *Wiluszynski v. London Borough of Tower Hamlets* [1989] IRLR 259, CA. And see para. 3.42.

[86] *Laurie v. British Steel Corporation* 1988 SLT 17, OH; *Cresswell v. Board of Inland Revenue* [1984] IRLR 190, Ch D.

[87] See W. M. Gloag, *Law of Contract* (2nd edn), p. 623 "... a failure in the performance of a contract may not be so material as to justify the rescission of the contract, yet may be sufficiently material to entitle the other party to withhold counter-performance." *Cf Sim v. Rotherham Metropolitan Borough Council* [1986] IRLR 391 Ch D in which it was held that a teacher's failure to cover for an absent colleague for one period of 35 minutes was sufficient "to impeach the plaintiff's title to his full contractual salary." Also in *Wiluszynski v. London Borough of Tower Hamlets*, above, all the employee failed to do was to deal with enquiries from councillors of which there were only 2 or 3 *per* week.

[88] See note 87 above. This, together with the exceptional provisions in TULRCA ss. 267, 268 places an employee who takes industrial action in a vulnerable situation.

affirmed the contract.[89] Thus where a local government employee's breach of contract was confined to a refusal to deal with enquiries from councillors the employer's right to withhold wages was not defeated by permitting the employee to attend and perform his other duties because it had been made clear to the employee on his arrival each day for work that he was not required to work except in full compliance with his contract and that any work he did would be voluntary and unpaid,[90] although giving the employee directions to work would have resulted in a finding of affirmation of part performance of the contract and could not have been accompanied by a withholding of all wages.[91] Also, to be entitled to his full contractual wages an employee must be prepared to work in accordance with his employer's lawful instructions.[92] Although the Employment Rights Act 1996 regulates deductions from wages or salary it does not apply to any deduction from a worker's wages made on account of his having taken part in industrial action[93]; indeed on the view that wages are payable if they are legally required to be paid[94] it is arguable that since, by virtue of the worker's breach of contract, wages are not "payable"[95] the Act has no application at all to instances of withholding of wages.[96]

3.10 *Suspension, lay-off and late payment.* Although statutory provision is now made to protect — in a very modest way — income of employees whose employer does not, for certain reasons, provide work,[97] employees whose remuneration is paid on a time basis (by the hour/day etc.) are entitled to be paid at the appropriate rate for the contracted number of hours and paying less than the agreed rate, laying off or suspending the employee without pay will, in the absence of a clear contractual term entitling the employer so to act, be a material breach of contract entitling the employee to rescind and/or damages.[98] However, where the contract gives an employer the right to lay off an employee without pay in the event of a reduction of work, the employer will not be in breach merely by continuing to lay off for a long time.[99] On the other hand, where the reason for the suspension without pay relates to a disciplinary matter it has been held that a contractual provision which entitled the employer to suspend without pay had to be construed so that the employer would not act unreasonably in suspending the employee and

---

[89]   *Royle v. Trafford Borough Council* [1984] IRLR 184, QBD; *MacPherson v. London Borough of Lambeth* [1988] IRLR 470.

[90]   *Wiluszynski v. London Borough of Tower Hamlets,* above.

[91]   *Ibid.*

[92]   In *Cresswell v. Board of Inland Revenue* above, it was held that withholding all remuneration was justified for the period during which the employee was not prepared to operate new technology even though he was prepared to do the same task manually. And see *MacPherson v. London Borough of Lambeth,* above.

[93]   ERA, s. 14(5).

[94]   See *Secretary of State for Employment v. Crane* [1988] IRLR 238, EAT.

[95]   By ERA, s. 27(1) wages mean "any sums *payable* to the worker in connection with his employment . . ."; and s. 13(3) provides that "where the total amount of wages paid . . . is less than total amount of the wages *properly payable* . . . on that occasion . . . the amount of the deficiency shall be treated . . . as a deduction."

[96]   *Bird v. British Celanese Ltd* [1945] KB 336, CA.

[97]   ERA, s. 28. And see para. 3.15.

[98]   *McKenzie (D & J) Ltd v. Smith* 1976 SLT 216, OH; *Burroughs Machines Ltd v. Timmoney* 1977 SC 393.

[99]   *McRae (Kenneth) & Co Ltd v. Dawson* [1984] IRLR 5, EAT. And see the interesting article by K. Miller, "Unilateral Variation of Contract and Recovery of Wages" (1994) SLG Vol. 62, 137, commenting on *MacRuary v. Washington Irvine Ltd* (1994 IDS Brief 518).

would only continue the suspension while there were reasonable grounds for doing so.[100] Where the remuneration is related to the amount of work done, an employer is required to provide a steady supply of work while the contract exists[101] although an established custom may provide that in certain circumstances the obligation to pay wages may be suspended.[102] Where wages are not paid on time it is arguable that the employee is entitled to interest on the amount unpaid[103] but late payment will only be regarded as a material breach of contract if it indicates an intention no longer to be bound by the contract.[104]

3.11 *Wages during illness of employee.* Although the income of an employee unable to work during periods because of incapacity for work is now protected by the introduction of statutory sick pay (SSP)[105] a question may still arise regarding an employee's contractual entitlement to receive wages during illness. In the absence of an express provision[106] it has been held in England[107] that a doubt may be resolved by resorting to "the presumption that the wage is to be paid till the employment is ended".[108] However, where a contractual term regarding sick pay[109] exists then, in the absence of an express provision, the employer's obligation to pay sick pay continues only for such a period as is reasonable.[110] The position in Scotland has not been the subject of recent judicial pronouncement but it is arguable that where the contract is for a fixed period the employer must continue to pay wages during short periods of illness[111] whereas in other contracts an employee's right to wages depends on a term being implied from the facts or circumstances because there is no Scots authority reflecting the English rule that where no term about sick pay can be implied there is a presumption that wages will be payable until the contract is determined.[112] Of course whether the contract be for a fixed period or terminable by notice the incapacity of the employee may be such as to frustrate the contract.[113]

---

[100] *McLory v. Post Office* [1992] ICR 758, Ch.

[101] Bell, *Principles* sec. 192; *Cowdenbeath Coal Co v. Drylie* (1886) 3 Sh. Ct Rep. 3.

[102] *Devonald v. Rosser & Sons* [1906] 2 KB 728, CA.

[103] Lord Fraser, *Master and Servant* (3rd edn), p. 138; F. A. Umpherston, *The Law of Master and Servant*, p. 61; *Mansfield v. Scott* (1831) 9 S 780. Cf *Wallace v. Geddes* (1821) 1 Sh. App. 42.

[104] *Hanlon v. Allied Breweries (UK) Ltd* [1975] IRLR 321, IT; *Adams v. Charles Zub Associates Ltd* [1978] IRLR 551, EAT.

[105] See para. 3.17.

[106] Sick pay, may take the form of a loan which becomes repayable in the event of an award of compensation: *Franklin v. British Railways Board* [1993] IRLR 441, CA.

[107] *Mears v. Safecar Security Ltd* [1982] ICR 626, CA, above, disapproving *Orman v. Saville Sportswear Ltd* [1960] 1 WLR 1055. Although the Court of Appeal has in *Eagland v. British Telecommunications plc* [1992] IRLR 323 overruled *Mears*, the decision in *Eagland* relates to the powers of an industrial tribunal under EPCA, s. 11 (written statement of particulars) (see now ERA, ss. 11, 12).

[108] *Mears v. Safecar Security Ltd*, above, at 651 *per* Stephenson LJ.

[109] In *Howman & Sons v. Blyth* [1983] ICR 416 the EAT emphasised the distinction between sick pay and wages.

[110] *Howman & Sons v. Blyth*, above.

[111] Stair, *Institutions*, I, 15, 2; Bell, *Principles*, s. 179. Cf *White v. Baillie* (1794) Mor 10147.

[112] Lord Fraser, *Master and Servant* (3rd edn), p. 141; V. Craig, "*Wages during Sickness in Scotland*" 1982 SLT (News) 252.

[113] See para. 4.6.

3.12 Remuneration and statute

Although in most cases an entitlement to receive, and an obligation to pay, wages are settled by reference to the terms of the contract various statutory provisions seek to protect the income of employees in a variety of measures relating to: (1) guarantee payments, (2) medical suspension pay, (3) pay during notice, (4) itemised pay statements, (5) deductions from wages and (6) wages councils orders, and these are dealt with here. However, statute also enacts rights to redundancy payments,[114] maternity pay[115] and equal pay for men and women[116] and these are dealt with elsewhere as indicated.

Week's pay. The statutory concept of a week's pay is relevant to various issues in modern employment law like, for example, the computation of a redundancy payment and the basic award of unfair dismissal; statute determines the amount of these (and other) statutory payments by reference to the week's pay of the relevant employee. The rules for computing a week's pay are set out in the Employment Rights Act 1996, ss. 220–229 and vary depending on whether the employee has, or has not, normal working hours.[117] Before summarising these rules it is necessary to note that although "week's pay" means the gross amount due to the employee by virtue of the contract[118] it does not include expenses,[119] tips[120] or travelling or subsistence allowances[121]; overtime earnings are included in a week's pay only if the employer has a duty to provide it and the employee a duty to work it when provided.[122] However, for the purposes of calculating some statutory payments, for example a redundancy payment and the basic award of compensation for unfair dismissal,[123] statute prescribes the maximum amount that may be taken into account.[124] However, where there is a statutory minimum wage, that should be used as the basis for calculation even if the employee is receiving less, provided of course the weekly maximum is not exceeded.[125] Broadly, where the employee has normal working hours his week's pay is:

(a)   where pay does not vary according to the work done (i.e. time rates) the amount payable by the employer under the contract if the employee works throughout his normal working hours in a week[126];

(b)   in other cases (i.e. piecework and work paid by commission) the average

---

[114] See Chapter Six.

[115] See para. 3.18.

[116] See Chapter Seven.

[117] Particulars of normal working hours should be contained in the written statement issued under ERA, s. 1 (see para. 2.10) and generally exclude hours paid at overtime rates unless the minimum contractual hours include some hours paid at overtime rates in which case the normal working hours are the minimum contractual hours (ERA, s. 234).

[118] *Secretary of State for Employment v. John Woodrow & Sons (Builders) Ltd* [1983] ICR 582, EAT; *Murphy Telecommunications (Systems) Ltd v. Henderson* [1973] ICR 581, NIRC. It may also include commission (*Bickley (J & S) Ltd v. Washer* [1977] ICR 425, EAT).

[119] *S & U Stores Ltd v. Wilkes* [1974] ICR 645, NIRC.

[120] *Palmanor Ltd v. Cedron* [1978] ICR 1008, EAT.

[121] *Carmichael (A. M.) Ltd v. Laing* [1972] ITR 1, QBD.

[122] *Tarmac Roadstone Holdings Ltd v. Peacock* [1973] ICR 273, CA. And see *Marcusfield (A. B.) Ltd v. Melhuish* [1977] IRLR 484, EAT regarding bonus payments.

[123] *Cf* the special award payable only where a dismissal is unfair under TULRCA, s. 152 (union membership/activities) or ERA, s. 100 (health and safety). See paras 5.68, 5.79.

[124] ERA, s. 227. The maximum is presently £210.

[125] *Cooner v. Doal & Sons* [1988] IRLR 338; *Reid v. Camphill Engravers* [1990] IRLR 268, EAT.

[126] ERA, s. 221.

hourly rate calculated over the 12-week period before the calculation date[127] — in effect the total pay divided by the total hours over 12 weeks multiplied by the normal working hours;[128] or

(c) where the normal working hours vary from week to week (e.g. shiftwork) the average week's pay over 12 weeks prior to calculation date.[129]

Where the employee has no normal working hours his week's pay is the average week's pay over the 12 weeks prior to the calculation date.[130]

3.13 *Wages councils.* Although there is no general minimum wage legislation in the United Kingdom the wage rates of workers in particular industries have been the subject of statutory control since 1909[131] through various instruments, notably[132] wages councils,[133] independent but official arbitration machinery[134] and the Fair Wages Resolutions of the House of Commons.[135] The main reasons for such official interventions into the area of wage rates were (1) to protect the income of workers in industries where worker organisation was poor or non-existent with the result that collective bargaining was ineffective, and (2) to ensure that competition for lucrative contracts awarded by central or local government did not result in payment of unfairly low wages. Since 1980 the trend has been to remove or limit such statutory or official attempts to maintain wages rates. Thus Schedule 11 to the Employment Protection Act 1975 has been repealed[136] and in 1982 the United Kingdom denounced I.L.O. Convention No. 94 and the House of Commons voted to revoke the Fair Wages Resolution. Most significantly, however, the Wages Act 1986, although leaving the wages council system intact,[137] repealed[138] the Wages Councils Act 1979,[139] reduced the powers of existing wages councils[140] and made new provisions for the abolition of, or variation of the scope of, wages councils.[141]

---

[127] As to the meaning of "calculation date" see ERA, s. 225.

[128] See *British Coal Corpn v. Cheesbrough* [1990] IRLR 148, HL.

[129] ERA, ss. 221, 222; weeks in which no work is done and weeks in which no remuneration is payable are disregarded (s. 223). Whether remuneration is "payable" see *Secretary of State for Employment v. Crane* [1988] IRLR 238, EAT. And note the effect of *British Coal Corpn v. Cheesbrough*, above, that by s. 223(1) the average is to be arrived at by taking account of all hours (basic and overtime) and all remuneration with any overtime premium stripped out — workers who worked overtime may receive a smaller redundancy payment.

[130] ERA, s. 224; again weeks in which no remuneration is paid are disregarded (*ibid.*) And see special provisions in s. 228 for employees employed for a period so short that averaging is difficult.

[131] Trade Boards Act 1909, now repealed.

[132] See also the Agricultural Wages (Scotland) Act 1949, the Road Haulage Wages Act 1938 repealed by EA 1980, s. 19(c).

[133] Wages Councils Acts 1948, 1979, also repealed.

[134] See the Terms and Conditions of Employment Act 1959 repealed and superseded by EPA 1975, s. 98, Sch.11, now also repealed by EA 1980, s. 19.

[135] The Fair Wages Resolution of 1891 was superseded by a similar Resolution of 1946.

[136] EA 1980, s. 19(c).

[137] About 2.7 million workers were covered by 24 wages councils.

[138] Section 12; Sch. 5, Pt. II.

[139] Thus no new wages council can be established except by exercise by the Secretary of State of the power given by the Wages Act 1986, s. 13(4) to bring workers previously under one wages council under another one.

[140] Sections 12, 14–18.

[141] Section 13.

3.14 *Abolition of Wages Councils.* In keeping with the legislative attitude displayed since 1980 Wages Councils, whose competences had been previously reduced, were abolished in 1993 by the Trade Union Reform and Employment Rights Act 1993[142] which repealed Part II of the Wages Act 1986 with effect from August 30, 1993. Prior to their abolition approximately 2.5 million people had their pay rates regulated by Wages Councils but the government was of the view that their abolition would have little impact on wage levels. However, in the survey "What Price Abolition?"[143] it was established that of the jobs surveyed 18.1% were now paying below the previous Wages Council rate.[144]

3.15 *Guarantee payments.* A system of guaranteeing an employee's income when his employer is unable to employ him throughout a day was first introduced by the Employment Protection Act 1975[145] but the current provisions are now contained in the Employment Rights Act 1996.[146] However, the provisions are modest and are dependent on the employee satisfying various conditions. Unless excluded,[147] an employee with one month's continuous employment[148] is entitled to a guarantee payment for a day throughout which he is not provided with work.[149] However, a payment is only due in respect of a day during any part of which the employee would normally be required to work in accordance with his contract of employment.[150] Thus no payment is due for holidays or rest days[151] or for days on which the employee has agreed not to work.[152] Also the reasons for the employer's failure to provide work must be because of a diminution in the requirements of the business for the kind of work the employee is employed to do or "any other occurrence affecting the normal working of the employer's business".[153] However, the fact that the failure to provide work is due to a trade dispute will only disentitle the employee to a payment if the dispute results in a strike, lock-out or other industrial action involving an employee of the laying-off employer or an

---

[142] Section 35.
[143] "What Price Abolition?" published by Greater Manchester Low Pay Unit. And see "After the Safety Net", published by Low Pay Network (1994).
[144] Particularly in the retail sector large "underpayments" were found; in hairdressing an underpayment of 22.6% was found.
[145] Sections 22–28.
[146] ERA, ss. 28–35.
[147] Exclusions cover share fishermen (ERA, s. 199(2)), employees who ordinarily work outside Great Britain (ERA, s. 196(2)) and employees who are employed under a contract for a fixed term of three months or less or for a specific task which is not expected to last for more than three months unless his continuous employment actually exceeds three months (ERA, s. 29(2)).
[148] ERA, s. 29(1); and see paras. 3.2 ff.
[149] ERA, s. 28(1).
[150] *Mailway (Southern) Ltd v. Willsher* [1978] IRLR 322, EAT.
[151] In *North v. Pavleigh Ltd* [1979] IRLR 461, IT, the employers gave employees two days of "unpaid holidays" but as the contract contained no provision for such they were days on which the employees were normally required to work.
[152] *Clemens v. Peter Richards Ltd* [1977] IRLR 332, IT; *Daley v. Strathclyde Regional Council* [1977] IRLR 414, IT. *Cf Robinson v. Claxton & Garland (Teesside) Ltd* [1977] IRLR 159, IT, in which it was held that a day on which an employee was suspended without pay was still a day he was normally required to work in accordance with his contract. And see ERA, s. 31(6).
[153] ERA, s. 28(1)(b). This phrase is extremely wide and would cover an employer's inability to heat the workplace to the correct temperature (*Meadows v. Faithfull Overalls Ltd* [1977] IRLR 330, IT), a machine breakdown, a failure of supplies or power, etc.

associated employer.[154] However, an employee will lose the right to a guarantee payment by unreasonably refusing to carry out suitable alternative work (which may be outside the terms of the existing contract of employment)[155] or by failing to comply with reasonable requirements to ensure the availability of his services.[156] Employers will also be excluded from receiving guarantee payments as such if the Secretary of State has made an order exempting the industry from the application of the general statutory rules.[157] However, guarantee payments are put into perspective by the provision[158] which limits the daily rate of a guarantee payment to £14.50[159] and the number of days in respect of which entitlement to a guarantee payment may arise to five in any period of three months[160] and that which permits setting off any liability to pay a statutory guarantee payment against any contractual right to receive remuneration for workless days.[161] In the event of an employer failing to pay a guarantee payment the employee's remedy is by way of a complaint to an industrial tribunal which can order the payment to be made.[162]

3.16 *Medical suspension pay.* An employee who has been continuously employed[163] for one month, provided he is not incapable of work by reason of disease or bodily or mental disablement, is entitled to be paid remuneration by his employer during periods when he is suspended from work[164] on medical grounds in consequence of — (1) any requirement imposed by or under any provision of any legislation[165] or (2) any recommendation in any provision of a code of practice issued or approved under the Health and Safety at Work etc. Act 1974.[166] For each week in which suspension occurs an employee is entitled to a week's pay[167] for up to a maximum of twenty-six weeks[168] but any contractual remuneration paid for any period goes toward discharging an employer's liability to pay medical suspension pay and *vice versa.*[169] However, an employee who is employed under a

---

[154] ERA, s. 29(3). *Cf Garvey v. J. & J. Maybank (Oldham) Ltd* [1979] IRLR 408, IT, which illustrates the width of the exclusion prior to amendment. As to "associated employer" see para. 3.5, n. 58.

[155] See, for example, *Purdy v. Willowbrook International Ltd* [1977] IRLR 388, IT.

[156] ERA, s. 29(5). In *Meadows v. Faithfull Overalls Ltd*, above, an industrial tribunal held that an employee who declined her employer's offer of refreshments in the canteen and went home pending the arrival of heating oil failed to comply with reasonable requirements to ensure the availability of her services.

[157] ERA, s. 35 permits an order to be made where a collective agreement or a wages order already guarantees remuneration and provides for disputes to be resolved by independent arbitration or adjudication or by an industrial tribunal.

[158] ERA, s. 31(1).

[159] This figure is subject to an annual review (ERA, s. 208).

[160] ERA, s. 31(2), (3).

[161] ERA, s. 32. This also results in entitlement to contractual remuneration for five days in a period of three months preventing entitlement to a guarantee payment for additional workless days in the same three month period (*Cartwright v. G. Clancey Ltd* [1983] ICR 552, EAT).

[162] ERA, s. 34. A complaint must be presented within three months although the tribunal has a discretion to accept late complaints.

[163] ERA, s. 29(1); and see paras 3.2 ff.

[164] An employee is regarded as suspended from work only while he continues to be employed by his employer but is not provided with work or does not perform the work he normally performed (ERA, s. 64(5)).

[165] Both primary and delegated legislations are included.

[166] ERA, s. 64.

[167] "Week's pay" is defined in ERA, ss. 220–229.

[168] ERA, ss. 64, 69. If in any week remuneration is payable only in respect of part of a week the amount of a week's pay shall be reduced accordingly.

[169] ERA, s. 69(3).

fixed term contract of three months or less or under a contract for a specific task not expected to last more than three months (unless it does result in more than three months' continuous employment), who unreasonably declines his employer's offer of suitable alternative work (which need not fall within the work he has contracted to do) or who fails to comply with his employer's reasonable requirements to ensure the availability of his services, is not entitled to medical suspension pay.[170] In the event of an employer failing to pay medical suspension pay the employee's remedy is by presenting (within three months or such further period as the tribunal considers reasonable) a complaint to an industrial tribunal which can order payment of the appropriate amount.[171] The purpose of these provisions is to protect the income of an employee who is capable of work but who is suspended from work on medical grounds, for example, the need to avoid the employee's (continued) exposure to a health hazard. The provisions do not themselves entitle an employer to suspend work or pay or both and any suspension to comply with a requirement or recommendation referred to in the Employment Rights Act 1996, s. 64(1), (2) for which the employer does not have a contractual right would in most instances support a claim of constructive dismissal and it has to be noted that such a constructive dismissal will found an unfair dismissal complaint after only four weeks' continuous employment.[172]

3.17 *Statutory sick pay.* Statutory Sick Pay (SSP) was introduced by the Social Security and Housing Benefits Act 1982[173] whose provisions relating to SSP are now contained in the Social Security Contributions and Benefits Act 1992, Part XI.[174] SSP was introduced essentially to simplify the system of income maintenance for those who were unable to work for short periods because of sickness[175] and had been heralded by the introduction of "self-certification" for claiming the first week of Sickness Benefit.[176] Although with effect from April 5, 1995 Sickness and Invalidity Benefit have been replaced by Incapacity Benefit, the introduction of Incapacity Benefit has no effect on entitlement to SSP. The effect of the scheme is to require employers to pay for a maximum of 28 weeks[177] to incapacitated employees an amount equivalent to what would have been paid by way of state benefit.[178] Thus subject to the employee meeting certain qualifying conditions[179] an employer is liable to pay to the employee, for a day of incapacity for work in relation to his contract of service, a payment (to be known as "statutory sick pay")

---

[170] ERA, s. 65.
[171] ERA, s. 70.
[172] ERA, s. 108(2). Of course the dismissal may be fair; alternatively the contract might have become frustrated (supervening illegality) in which case there would be no dismissal. And see para. 5.25. *Cf Johnstone v. Bloomsbury Health Authority* [1991] IRLR 118, CA.
[173] Sections 1–27.
[174] And see the Statutory Sick Pay (General) Regulations 1982 (SI 1982 No. 894).
[175] See the White Paper "Income During Initial Sickness" Cmnd. 7864 (1980).
[176] Social Security (Medical Evidence, Claims and Payments) Amendment Regulations 1982, SI 1982 No. 699.
[177] Social Security Contributions and Benefits Act 1992, s. 155.
[178] For a detailed coverage of SSP, see D. Bonner *et al*, *Non-Means Tested Benefits: The Legislation* (1995 edn), pp. 831 ff. and Ogus & Barendt *The Law of Social Security* (3rd edn.), pp. 229–230.
[179] Briefly, the day for which payment is made (1) must form part of a "period of incapacity for work" which itself means a period of at least four consecutive days, (2) must fall within a period of entitlement and (3) must be a day on which employee would normally be expected to work (a qualifying day) (SSCBA, ss. 152–154).

in respect of that day.[180] However, certain employees are excluded — (1) those over pensionable age, (2) those with contracts for a specified period of not more than three months, (3) those who have not yet started work, (4) those who fall sick while there is a trade dispute,[181] (5) those who have received SSP for the maximum period of entitlement in respect of the employer (28 weeks) and (6) those who are pregnant in respect of any days after the beginning of the eleventh week before the expected week of confinement.[182] Entitlement to SSP is in addition to any contractual rights and cannot be limited or excluded by agreement.[183] The amount of SSP is subject to review by the Secretary of State[184] and is now payable at a single rate.[185] Disputes about entitlement to SSP are dealt with by Adjudication Officers and Social Security Appeal Tribunals.[186]

3.18 *Statutory maternity pay.* The right to statutory pay complements the right not to be dismissed because of pregnancy,[187] the right to Maternity Leave Period (MLP),[188] the right to return to work after pregnancy[189] and the right to time-off for ante-natal care.[190] A statutory right to receive payment during maternity leave was first introduced in 1975[191] and until April 1987 the right to such a payment (which was granted only to employees who had at least two years' continuous employment) operated in addition to the right to receive state maternity allowance payable by the Department of Social Security.[192] However, this was a cumbersome and unnecessarily complicated procedure[193] and by Part V of the Social Security Act 1986 Statutory Maternity Pay (SMP) was introduced.[194] In order to implement the provisions of the Pregnant Workers' Directive,[195] which gives every pregnant employee the right to 14 weeks' Maternity Leave Period (MLP) and the right to an adequate allowance during MLP, it was necessary to amend by regulation[196] the

---

[180] SSCBA, s. 151(1).
[181] Unless the employee proves he did not participate in nor have a direct interest in the trade dispute.
[182] SSCBA, Sch. 11, paras 2(a)–(h). Note also employees, to be eligible at all, must earn more than the minimum earnings on which national insurance contributions are paid (*ibid*).
[183] SSCBA, s. 151(2).
[184] SSCBA, s. 157(2).
[185] For employees whose earnings exceed the minimum rate on which NI contributions become payable (£61.00 per week) the rate is £54.55 per week (Social Security Benefits Uprating Order 1996 (SI 1996 No. 599)).
[186] Social Security Administration Act 1992, s. 22.
[187] See para. 5.62.
[188] ERA, ss. 71–78.
[189] See para. 5.62.
[190] See para. 3.25.
[191] Employment Protection Act 1975, s. 36.
[192] For detailed coverage of SMP see Ogus and Barendt, *The Law of Social Security* (3rd edn.), pp. 229–232; and see D. Bonner *et al.*, *Non-means Tested Benefits: the Legislation* (1994), pp. 283 ff.
[193] Any state maternity allowance was deducted from maternity pay (EPCA, s. 35(1)) and the employer received a rebate from the Maternity Pay Fund (EPCA, s. 39(1)).
[194] The current provisions are contained in SSCBA, ss. 164–171. And see Statutory Maternity Pay (General) Regulations 1986 (SI 1986 No. 1960), Maternity Allowance and Statutory Maternity Pay Regulations 1994 (SI 1994 No. 1230) and Social Security Maternity Benefits and Statutory Sick Pay (Amendment) Regulations 1994 (SI 1994 No. 1367).
[195] Directive 92/85 EEC.
[196] Maternity Allowance and Statutory Maternity Pay Regulations 1994 (SI 1994 No. 1230), Social Security Maternity Benefits and Statutory Sick Pay (Amendment) Regulations 1994 (SI 1994 No. 1367).

law regarding SMP to ensure that it was not less than SSP. The effect of the amending regulations is that employed earners who (i) have been continuously employed for 26 weeks by the beginning of the fifteenth week before the expected week of confinement and (ii) have earnings above the lower earnings limit for National Insurance Contributions are entitled to 18 weeks' SMP, the first six weeks of which are payable at the higher rate of 90% of normal earnings and the remaining 12 weeks at the rate for SSP.[197] In addition the woman must give (a) medical evidence of pregnancy and (b) at least three weeks' notice of leaving work.[198] In effect the employer is being cast in the role of an agent for the Department of Social Security and in addition to being entitled to recover 92% of payments made[199] he is entitled to deduct 5.5% to compensate for the extra National Insurance contributions that are paid on SMP.[200] To further emphasise the employer's role as social security agent, disputes regarding entitlement to SMP lie to an Adjudication Officer with rights of appeal to a Social Security Appeal Tribunal.

3.19 *Pay during notice.* Where an employee has been given contractual notice he will have a contractual right to receive his remuneration for the period of notice. Alternatively where his contract is, in the absence of his repudiating his contract, terminated without notice, he is entitled to payment in lieu of notice.[201] Whether such a payment should be gross or net of deductions like income tax would seem to depend on whether the payment is viewed as damages for breach or merely a payment due under the contract. In England it has been held that where an employer has an obligation to pay wages in lieu it is truly a payment of damages and therefore to be net of deductions.[202] In Scotland the employer has an implied right to end the contract without notice provided wages and other emoluments are paid in lieu[203]; arguably such a payment should be gross being the amount due under the contract. If the payment is regarded as an emolument it is chargeable to income tax under the Income and Corporation Taxes Act 1988, s. 19; if it is made in connection with the termination of employment the first £30000 is exempt.[204] In addition, however, to complement the statutory right to minimum periods of notice[205] legislative provision[206] exists to protect the wages of an employee during the period of notice required by statute[207] who gives or receives notice and, in the event of an employer failing to give the statutory notice, an employee's right to

---

[197] In 1996 £54.55.

[198] SSCBA, s. 164.

[199] This is done by adjusting the amount of his contribution to the National Insurance Fund.

[200] Statutory Maternity Pay (Compensation of Employers) Amendment Regulations 1996 (SI 1996 No. 668).

[201] See paras 4.2 ff.

[202] *Foster Wheeler (London) Ltd v. Jackson* [1990] IRLR 412, EAT. Cf *Gothard v. Mirror Group Newspapers Ltd* [1988] IRLR 396, CA.

[203] See Chapter Four, para. 4.2.

[204] Income and Corporation Taxes Act 1988, s. 188. And see *Mairs v. Haughey* [1993] STC 569.

[205] ERA, s. 86. Although the minimum periods of notice are prescribed by statute the remedy is an action of damages for breach of contract and could now be pursued as an unlawful deduction (*Westwood v. Secretary of State for Employment* [1985] ICR 209, HL). And see para. 4.3.

[206] ERA, s. 87. The provision does not extend to those employees who are entitled to receive notice of termination which is at least one week more than the minimum prescribed by ERA, s. 86 (ERA, s. 87(4)).

[207] ERA, s. 86.

receive his remuneration during the period of that notice shall be taken into account in assessing liability for breach of contract.[208] The extent to which an employee's remuneration is protected during notice largely depends on whether or not the employee has "normal working hours".[209] Where an employee has normal working hours he is entitled to be paid during the period of notice at his normal hourly rate[210] if during the period in question (1) he is ready and willing to work but work is not provided, (2) he is incapable of work because of sickness or injury or (3) he is absent from work in accordance with the terms of his employment relating to holidays.[211] Where the employee does not have normal working hours the employer is required to pay not less than a week's pay for each week of notice and this obligation operates while the employee is incapable of work through sickness or injury or is on contractual holiday leave although at other times it is conditional on the employee's readiness and willingness to do enough work to earn a week's pay.[212] However, where notice of termination is given by the employee liability to make payment is postponed until the notice expires[213] and no liability at all arises under these provisions[214] where the employee has requested and has been granted time off[215] or takes part in a strike during the notice period.[216]

3.20 *Itemised pay statements.* Every employee[217] has the right to be given by his employer a written itemised pay statement containing particulars of (1) the gross wage or salary,[218] (2) variable or fixed deductions and the purposes for which they are made,[219] (3) the net wage or salary and (4) where different parts of the net amount are paid in different ways, the amount and method of payment of each part payment.[220] Where a dispute arises as to what particulars ought to have been included in such an itemised statement or where an employer fails to give such a statement application may be made to an industrial tribunal[221] which can (1) confirm, amend or substitute particulars or (2) where an employer fails to give any statement or gives an incomplete statement, make a declaration to that effect and

---

[208] ERA, s. 91(5).

[209] ERA, ss. 88, 89; "normal working hours" are defined by ERA, s. 234.

[210] The normal hourly rate is arrived at by dividing his week's pay by his normal working hours (ERA, s. 88(1)).

[211] ERA, s. 88. Other payments (SSP, holiday pay etc.) go towards meeting the employer's liability (*ibid.*). And see s. 90 (incapacity benefit and industrial injuries) and s. 91 (breach during notice period).

[212] ERA, s. 89. Again other payments go towards meeting the employer's liability. And see s. 91 (breach during notice) and s. 90 (incapacity benefit).

[213] ERA, ss. 88(3), 89(5).

[214] Of course a liability might arise from any agreement.

[215] ERA, s. 91(1).

[216] ERA, s. 91(2).

[217] ERA, s. 8.

[218] But this excludes "tips" because they are not monies paid by the employer under the contract of employment (*Cofone v. Spaghetti House Ltd* [1980] ICR 155, EAT).

[219] ERA, s. 9 permits the omission of particulars of fixed deductions provided the statement contains an aggregate amount of fixed deductions and there has been given to the employee before the issue of the particular pay statement a written standing statement of fixed deduction which gives details of how the aggregate is comprised; standing statements have to be re-issued at intervals of not more than 12 months.

[220] ERA, s. 8.

[221] Where the employment has ceased the reference must occur within three months of it ceasing (ERA, s. 11(4)).

order payment of the aggregate of unnotified deductions made during the thirteen weeks prior to the reference.[222]

3.21 *Deductions from wages and methods of payment.* The law regarding deductions from wages and methods of payment was overhauled by the Wages Act 1986 which repealed the Truck Acts 1831–1940 and the Payment of Wages Act 1960 as well as other legislation dealing with deductions from wages in particular industries.[223] The Truck Acts had provided for the wages of manual workers to be paid only in cash[224] and had imposed strict conditions on deductions from the wages of such workers.[225] However, by the 1980s it was debatable whether the tenets of the Truck Acts where in keeping with modern conditions[226] and the Wages Act 1986 removed the special protections conferred on manual workers.[226a] Now all workers[227] may be paid in whatever way the parties to the contract choose and most contracts now include an express term[228]; where there is no express term it may be arguable that there is an implied right to be paid in a particular way. In this context "wages" means any sums payable in connection with the worker's employment including emoluments referable to his employment whether payable under the contract of employment or otherwise.[229] While they therefore include non-contractual payments[230] they do not include a payment of wages in lieu of notice because such a payment relates to the period after the termination of employment and falls to be distinguished from a payment during "garden leave".[231] Where the total amount of wages that are paid on any occasion by an employer to a worker is less than the total amount of the wages that are properly payable on that occasion (after deductions) then except in so far as the deficiency is attributable to an error of computation the amount of the deficiency shall be treated as a deduction from wages on that occasion[232] so that there is a deduction from wages where an employer wrongly believes he is entitled to demote the employee

---

[222] ERA, s. 12(4). The tribunal may make a penal award (*Scott v. Creager* [1979] IRLR 162, EAT). And note that where a deduction is unlawful under Part II of ERA the aggregate payments ordered may not exceed the amount of the deduction (ERA, s. 26).

[223] Wages Act 1986, s. 32(2). The particular legislation and the extent to which it was repealed is set out in Sch. 5, Pt. III.

[224] Although by the Payment of Wages Act 1960 workers could agree to be paid other than in cash they were free to revoke such agreements at any time.

[225] For an interesting survey of the truck system see G. W. Hilton, *The Truck System* (1960).

[226] Ironically, in the years leading up to the repeal of the Truck Acts several cases suggested that a measure of protection was still required. See *Riley v. Joseph Frisby Ltd* [1982] IRLR 479, IT; *Bristow v. City Petroleum Ltd* [1985] IRLR 459, QB; *Sealand Petroleum Ltd v. Barratt* [1986] ICR 423. And see "Deductions from Pay and Repeal of the Truck Acts", 1983 ILJ 236.

[226a] The relevant provisions of the Wages Act 1986 have been repealed and re-enacted in ERA, Part II.

[227] "Worker" is defined to mean those who work under contracts of service and apprenticeship and other contracts under which an individual undertakes to perform personally any work or services for another party who is not a client or customer of a business carried on by the individual (ERA, s. 230(3)).

[228] Where an express term is used it may be advisable to provide for a degree of flexibility.

[229] ERA, s. 27. Also payments under ss. 114, 115, 128 and 184(2) and SSP and SMP fall within the meaning of "wages" while other payments are expressly excluded: a loan or advance of wages, expenses in carrying out employment, retirement/compensation for loss of office, redundancy monies and monies paid otherwise than in the capacity of worker.

[230] *Kent Management Services Ltd. v. Butterfield* [1992] IRLR 394, EAT.

[231] *Delaney v. Staples* [1992] IRLR 191, HL. And see paras 3.23 and 3.60.

[232] ERA, s. 13(3).

with a consequent reduction in salary and such a deduction is not attributable to an error of computation,[233] there is also a deduction where an employer of a waiter whose contract of employment entitled him to a specified rate "plus service" took a share of the service charge because what is properly payable to those who give service is that which is paid for service notwithstanding that the distribution of the sum collected among the various employees is a matter for the employer's discretion.[234] With regard to deductions[235] although additional provision is made in respect of retail workers, the basic rules which now apply to all workers (retail and non-retail) provide that no deduction from wages may be made unless (1) it is required or authorised by statute[236] or a relevant provision of the worker's contract, or (2) the worker has previously consented to it in writing.[237] A provision is a relevant provision if: (1) it is in a written contract of which a copy has been given to the worker before the deduction is made, or (2) whether the contract is in writing or not and whether the term(s) is (are) express or implied the worker has received written notice of the existence of the term(s) and its (their) effect prior to the deduction being made.[238] The effect of these provisions is that, statutorily authorised deductions excepted, deductions from wages must be consented to by the worker and must be preceded by written notice of the term(s). A failure to comply with these requirements will render the deduction (or payment) unlawful unless covered by one of the following six exceptions relating to deductions (or payments): (1) for reimbursing overpayments of wages or expenses, (2) in consequence of disciplinary proceedings held by virtue of any statutory provisions, (3) the employer is required by statute to make a pay over to a public authority, (4) of sums (typically trade union dues under a check-off agreement)[239] for onward payment to a third person; it should be noted, however, that this exception is conditional on the worker having consented in writing and the third person (the trade union, in relation to a check-off agreement) notifying the employer of the amounts to be deducted,[240] (5) where the worker has taken part in a strike or other

---

[233] *Morgan v. West Glamorgan County Council* [1995] IRLR 68, EAT; and see *Bruce v. Wiggins Teape (Stationery) Ltd* [1994] IRLR 536, EAT. *Cf Thames Water Utilities v. Reynolds* [1996] IRLR 186, EAT (proportion of accrued holiday pay).

[234] *Saavedra v. Aceground Ltd* [1995] IRLR 198, EAT. And regarding tips added to credit card and cheque payments see *Nerva v. RL & G Ltd* [1995] IRLR 200, QB, [1996] IRLR 461, CA.

[235] The same rules apply to payments by workers (ERA, s. 15); and see *Merchiston Hearts Social Club v. Nicholson* 1995 GWD 24-1293.

[236] For example, legislation regarding national insurance contributions, income tax; and see *Slater v. Grampian Regional Council* 1991 SLT (Sh Ct) 72, *Reynolds v. Cornwall CC*, EAT Case No. 1189/95 and the Debtors (Scotland) Act 1987, s. 71 which brings the fee of an employer arrester within ERA, s. 13(1). ERA, s. 13(7) preserves statutory provisions regulating deductions from payments other than wages.

[237] ERA, s. 13(1).

[238] ERA, s. 13(2); by s. 13(5) where the contract is varied or consent is given to permit a deduction no retrospective effect is possible. However, it is not necessary for a collective agreement which introduced the variation to be in writing but the effect of the new collectively agreed term must be notified in writing to the worker (*York City & District Travel Ltd v. Smith* [1990] ICR 344, EAT).

[239] A check-off agreement is an agreement or understanding between an employer and a trade union whereby the employer agrees (usually as part of a recognition agreement) to deduct union subscriptions from employees who are union members and pay the aggregate amount to the union.

[240] And note the provisions introduced by TURERA, s. 15 inserting a new s. 68 into TULRCA regarding the renewal of consent to the deduction of union dues; see para. 3.23.

industrial action and the deduction is made on that account,[241] (6) for satisfying a court or tribunal order requiring payment to be made by the worker to the employer provided the worker has consented in writing.[242] Where a deduction falls within one of these exceptions it is not necessary for the industrial tribunal to consider whether the deduction is otherwise lawful.[243] Thus where a deduction is to recover an overpayment or in respect of the employee's participation in industrial action the jurisdiction of the tribunal is excluded without the need to examine the legality of the employer's right to recover the money.[244] Where a deduction (or payment) falls within one of the above exceptions whether it is lawful depends on the common law or other legislation dealing with deductions.[245] So, for example, where an overpayment has been made whether it can be recovered will depend on whether the payment falls within the *conditio indebiti*[246] and, on the assumption that it can be recovered, whether recovery can take place *via* deduction would turn on whether a contractual term to that effect can be supported by the evidence, and these contractual issues would be for the ordinary courts. On the other hand where a deduction (or payment) does not fall within one of the exceptions its legality is determined by reference to the Employment Rights Act 1996, unless the worker is in retail employment in respect of which special provisions are made.

3.22 *Retail workers.* It must be noted that these special provisions are in addition to the general rules about the legality of deductions (and payments) already discussed.[247] Where the worker is employed in retail employment[248] then, except in respect of the final instalment of wages,[249] the maximum deduction (or payment required to the employer by the worker) that may be made on account of one or more cash shortages[250] or stock deficiencies[251] must not exceed one-tenth of the

---

[241] The need for such an exception is arguable because where a worker fails to perform his contract by taking industrial action it is doubtful whether wages are "payable". See ERA, s. 27(1) and para. 3.9.

[242] ERA, s. 14(6).

[243] *Sunderland Polytechnic v. Evans* [1993] IRLR 196, EAT rejecting the approach in *Home Office v. Ayres* [1992] IRLR 59, EAT; and see *SIP Industrial Products v. Swinn* [1994] ICR 473, EAT.

[244] See note 243 above.

[245] E.g. ERA, ss. 8–12; TULRCA, s. 68.

[246] A remedy for recovering money paid under the mistaken belief that it was due; see Gloag & Henderson *The Law of Scotland* (10th edn.), paras 29.4 ff. But note the recent decision of the Court of Session sitting as a court of 5 judges that money paid under error of law is recoverable and that previous cases to the contrary were wrongly decided (*Morgan Guaranty Trust Co. v. Lothian Regional Council, The Times*, January 19, 1995).

[247] Thus ERA, s. 18(1) provides "Where (in accordance with section 13) the employer ... makes a deduction ...".

[248] By ERA, s. 18(2) this means employment (regular or casual) involving (1) carrying out by the worker of retail transactions (*viz.* the sale or supply of goods or services) directly with members of the public or with fellow workers or other individuals in their personal capacities or (2) collection by the worker of amounts payable in connection with retail transactions (*viz.* the sale or supply of goods or services) carried out by other persons directly with members of the public or with fellow workers or other individuals in their personal capacities.

[249] ERA, s, 22(2); final instalment of wages means (1) the wages payable in respect of the last period he is employed prior to termination of his contract excluding any wages referable to an earlier period (for example "lying time" or holiday pay) or (2) pay in lieu of notice if paid after amounts paid in (1) (ERA, s. 22(1)).

[250] *Viz.* "a deficit arising in relation to amounts received in connection with retail transactions" (ERA, s. 17(1)).

[251] *Viz.* "a stock deficiency arising in the course of retail transactions" (ERA, s. 17(1)).

gross wages payable on any occasion.[252] This provision is to protect retail workers who were required to accept a contractual term to the effect that they would suffer a deduction from wages to cover any cash or stock shortages occurring during their employment often whether or not due to their own fault. According to some contractual terms the entire amount of the shortage could be deducted from a single wage payment thereby upsetting the worker's budget and expenditure arrangements. Deductions (and payments) on account of a cash shortage or stock deficiency include those made on account of: (1) the worker's dishonesty or conduct, or (2) any other event in respect of which he (alone or with others) has contractual liability and this is so whether or not the amount reflects the exact shortage or deficiency[253] and special provision is made to avoid the employer pleading that what has occurred is not a deduction from the retail worker's wages but merely part of the method of calculating wages.[254] Also, even if all the other provisions are complied with, no deduction (or first deduction) from wages of a retail worker may be lawfully made later than 12 months after the date the shortage or deficiency was established.[255] On the assumption that the general rules[256] have been complied with, the propriety of a retail worker's employer receiving payment for a cash shortage or stock deficiency depends on him satisfying the following conditions — (1) prior written notice to the worker of his total liability in respect of the particular shortage or deficiency, (2) issuing to the worker a written demand for payment on one of his pay days and (3) not demanding payment before the first pay day following a day the worker is notified of his total liability or later than the end of the period of 12 months beginning with the employer establishing the shortage or deficiency.[257]

3.23 *Remedy for unlawful deductions and payments, wages in lieu of notice and check-off.* The remedy of a worker in respect of unlawful deductions and payments is by way of a complaint to an industrial tribunal "and not otherwise".[258] There has been disagreement regarding whether a "non-payment" of wages can properly be treated as a deduction to allow a complaint to be lodged. Thus the Court of Appeal has held[259] that a dispute about commission payable was a simple common law claim in contract and therefore outside the jurisdiction of the industrial tribunal. On the other hand, however, the EAT sitting in Scotland had held that there is no distinction between an undisputed deduction and one which is in dispute[260] and that approach is undoubtedly correct so that if necessary a tribunal must consider the relative contractual provisions to determine what is properly payable.[261] Thus a complaint is competent where an employer unilaterally altered an employee's shift pattern so that the employee received less pay than before the

---

[252] ERA, s. 18(1).
[253] ERA, s. 17(4).
[254] ERA, s. 19.
[255] ERA, s. 18(3); and in respect of payments by a retail worker to his employer see ERA, s. 20(3) which has similar effect and s. 20(5) that no legal proceedings to recover a cash shortage or stock deficiency may be commenced after the period of 12 months referred to in s. 20(3)(b) unless a demand for payment has been made before the expiry of that period.
[256] As contained in ERA, s. 13(1).
[257] ERA, s. 20(1)–(3); s. 21(2) permits an employer to discount amounts for which a demand has been made but not paid in calculating the amount that can be lawfully demanded on subsequent pay days.
[258] ERA, s. 205(2).
[259] *Rickard v. P B Glass Supplies Ltd*, April 10, 1989, unreported.
[260] *Kournavous v. J. R. Masterton & Sons (Demolition) Ltd* [1990] IRLR 119, EAT.
[261] *Fairfield Ltd v. Skinner* [1993] IRLR 4, EAT.

alteration[262] and any non-payment or reduction in wages properly payable, other than a shortfall in payment caused by an error of computation, allows a complaint to be made.[263] The result of "deduction" having such a wide meaning is to allow the employee whose employer breaks a contractual term regarding wages or one which results in a reduction in the amount of wages payable an alternative to a contractual action for debt or rescission.[264] Like other disputes concerning statutory employment rights a complaint under Part II of the Employment Rights Act may be conclusively settled by agreement arrived at under the auspices of a Conciliation Officer or by a compromise agreement, but any other agreement which purports to exclude or limit the operation of the Act is void.[265] The following may be the subject of a complaint to an industrial tribunal[266] — (1) deductions from the wages of a worker which are unlawful by virtue of s. 13(1) or s. 18(2), (2) payments received from a worker which are unlawful by virtue of s. 15(1) or s. 20(1), (3) deduction from the wages of retail workers exceeding one-tenth of the gross wages payable and (4) payments received from a retail worker which exceed one tenth of the gross wages payable on the relevant day.[267] Where a tribunal upholds a complaint it shall issue a declaration to that effect and, depending on the nature of the employer's unlawful action, order payment or repayment of such amounts as have been deducted or paid in contravention of the Employment Rights Act 1996[268] and although there is no scope for a punitive award of compensation, where a tribunal has ordered payment or repayment by an employer provision is made to prevent the employer recovering the amount of such payments of repayments by raising an action in the civil courts.[269]

There has been some dispute whether wages in lieu of notice are "wages" for the purposes of Part II of the Employment Rights Act 1996. It had been argued that where an employer terminated the contract summarily, when not entitled to do so by virtue of the employee's repudiation, without paying in lieu of the notice, there had been a deduction from wages. In Scotland there is authority for the view that an employer who terminates the contract is not in breach provided he pays money or wages in lieu of notice[270] and arguably a failure to make such a payment would

---

[262] *Yemin v. British Steel plc* [1994] IRLR 117, EAT.

[263] *Bruce v. Wiggins Teape (Stationery) Ltd* [1994] IRLR 536, EAT.

[264] See K. Miller, "Unilateral Variation of Contract and Recovery of Wages" 1994 SLG Vol. 62, p. 137; *McCree v. Tower Hamlets* [1992] IRLR 56.

[265] ERA, s. 203.

[266] A complaint must be presented within three months of the deduction or payment although the tribunal may extend this period if timeous presentation was not reasonably practicable (ERA, s. 23(4)).

[267] ERA, s. 23(1). Note that by s. 20(4) and (5) the employer's demand for payment need be restricted to one-tenth of the gross wage only where the demand is made "on any pay day". Thus, it seems, no such restriction operates to demands made on other days. But where a court orders payment to recover a cash shortage or stock deficiency (provided the employer has complied with the requirements of s. 13(1)(a) or (b)) it shall ensure payment is made at a rate not more than that set out in s. 20 (one-tenth of gross wage) unless payment is ordered after the worker has received his final instalment of wages (ERA, s. 22(4)).

[268] ERA, s. 24. And see s. 25 which requires a tribunal to take account of (1) the employer complying with either s. 13(1)(a) or (b) but only with regard to some of the deductions or payments and (2) any monies already paid or repaid to the worker.

[269] ERA, s. 25(4), (5). Clearly such civil proceedings would be possible where the employer had a contractual right to receive a payment but in respect of which he has not complied with the relevant provisions of the Act. However, a contractual term entitling a payment to be received (without complying with the relevant provisions of the Act) would be void by s. 203(1).

[270] *Cooper v. Henderson* (1825) 3 S 619; and see para. 4.2.

support an action of debt[271] for payment of monies due under the contract. In England such a payment was, it appears, more properly to be seen as damages and until the amount due had been quantified there was no sum payable.[272] In *Delaney v. Staples*[273] the House of Lords concluded that whether the wages in lieu were contractually payable or not, because they were payments in respect of the termination of employment and as wages were payments in respect of the rendering of services they were excluded from the definition of "wages" in s. 27 of the Act, payments in respect of termination only being included where the Act expressly provided. However, payments in respect of "garden leave", being advance payments of wages due under a subsisting contract, are "wages" for the purpose of s. 27[274] and could be recovered using the Act. However, in view of the extension of the industrial tribunal's jurisdiction to entertain breach of contract claims[275] the distinction is now largely academic.

Whether the deduction at source of a worker's trade union subscription is lawful depends on the provisions of the Employment Rights Act 1996 and TULRCA, s. 68.[276] As indicated, the former (which applies to any deduction paid over to a third party) excludes the application of the general rules[277] provided the worker has consented in writing to the deduction and the trade union notifies the employer of the amount to be deducted.[278] However, once such consent had been given the worker had no unilateral right of revocation and it was to ensure that consents were still current that s. 68 now provides that, for the lawful deduction of trade union membership subscriptions, the employer shall ensure that deductions are authorised and do not exceed the permitted amount. To be authorised a deduction must be preceded by a document signed and dated by the worker and the deduction must take place within three years of the document being executed by the worker.[279] The worker can withdraw his authorisation at any time by giving a written notice to that effect to his employer and it will not be lawful to deduct any increased amount unless at least a month before the deduction of the increased amount the employer gives the worker written notice stating (i) the amount of the increase (ii) the new (increased) subscription and (iii) that the worker can withdraw his consent to deductions by giving written notice to his employer.[280] Where a deduction of a union subscription is made in contravention of these provisions the worker may complain to an industrial tribunal which, if the complaint is well founded, shall order payment of any amounts unlawfully deducted.[281]

3.24 *Wages and other payments in event of employer's insolvency.*[282] Special statutory provisions exist to protect sums due to an employee in the event of his employer's insolvency; the provisions do two things — (1) treat as preferred debts certain payments due by the employer to the employee,[283] (2) require the Secretary

---

[271] *Ibid.*
[272] *Foster Wheeler v. Jackson* [1990] IRLR 412, EAT.
[273] [1992] ICR 483, HL.
[274] *Ibid.*
[275] See para. 3.61.
[276] Inserted by TURERA, s. 15.
[277] ERA, s. 13(1).
[278] ERA, s. 14(4).
[279] TULRCA, s. 68(1), (2), (3).
[280] TULRCA, s. 68(3), (4).
[281] TULRCA, s. 68A.
[282] And see Chapter Four, para. 4.9.
[283] Bankruptcy (Scotland) Act 1985, s. 51(1)(e), Sch. 3, paras 5, 6.

of State for Employment to make payment out of the Redundancy Fund[284] certain payments due to an employee by an insolvent employer.[285]

(1) A preferred debt is an unsecured debt which ranks before all other secured debts in bankruptcy or winding up.[286] Subject to a statutory maximum[287] the following are treated as preferred debts: (a) remuneration (including commission) payable in respect of the period of four months before the relevant date,[288] (b) accrued holiday pay,[289] (c) guarantee payment,[290] (d) medical suspension pay,[291] (e) pay during certain time-off,[292] (f) statutory sick pay[293] and (g) pay due during a protective award.[294] Contributions (payable by employer or employee) to the National Insurance Fund and to certain occupational pensions schemes also rank as preferred debts.[295]

(2) Although the above debts are preferred the employer's financial position may prevent any payments being made and it is to protect employees[296] against such an eventuality that the Secretary of State for Employment is required to make in respect of employees whose employment had been terminated[297] the following payments[298] out of the National Insurance Fund — (a) arrears of pay (including the payments specified in the Employment Rights Act 1996[299] in respect of up to eight weeks,[300] (b) pay in respect of statutory notice,[301] (c) up to six weeks' holiday pay,[302] (d) basic award of unfair dismissal compensation[303] and (e) a reasonable sum payable as reimbursement of a fee or premium paid by an apprentice or

---

[284] The Employment Act 1990 merges this with the National Insurance Fund.

[285] For purposes of ERA, ss. 182–190 an employer is insolvent if (a) sequestration is awarded, he executes a trust deed for creditors or enters a composition contract; (b) he has died and a judicial factor is required by Judicial Factors (Scotland) Act 1889, s. 11A to divide insolvent's estate among his creditors or (c) a winding up order is made or a resolution for a voluntary winding up is passed or a receiver is appointed (ERA, s. 184(4)).

[286] As to priority among preferred debts, see Bankruptcy (Scotland) Act 1985, s. 51(4).

[287] Bankruptcy (Scotland) Act 1985, Sch. 3, paras 5, 6; Insolvency Act 1986, Sch. 6, paras 9, 12.

[288] Bankruptcy (Scotland) Act 1985, Sch. 3, para. 5(1); Insolvency Act 1986, Sch. 6, para. 9. "Relevancy date" is defined to mean (a) date of sequestration or date of death (Bankruptcy (Scotland) Act 1985, Sch. 3, para. 7); (b) date of administration order (Insolvency Act 1986, s. 387(3)(a)); (c) date of appointment of provisional liquidator or the date of winding up order; (d) date of voluntary winding up resolution and (e) date of appointment of a receiver (s. 387(3)(b), (c)).

[289] Bankruptcy (Scotland) Act 1985, Sch. 3, para. 5; Insolvency Act 1986, Sch. 6, para. 10.

[290] Bankruptcy (Scotland) Act 1985, Sch. 3, para. 9(2); Insolvency Act 1986, Sch. 6, para. 13(2) and see para. 3.15.

[291] Ibid.; and see para. 3.16.

[292] Ibid.; and see para. 3.30.

[293] Ibid.; and see para. 3.17.

[294] Ibid.; and see Chapter Nine, paras 9.34 ff.

[295] Bankruptcy (Scotland) Act 1985, s. 55(1)(e), (2); Insolvency Act 1986, s. 386.

[296] Certain employees are excluded. See ERA, ss. 196(7), 197(3), (5).

[297] ERA, s. 182(b).

[298] Note that the extent to which a debt is preferred may not be the extent to which it can be claimed from the Secretary of State. Compare ERA, s. 184(1) with Bankruptcy (Scotland) Act 1985, Sch. 3, paras 5, 9.

[299] ERA, s. 184.

[300] ERA, s. 184(1)(a).

[301] ERA, s. 184(1)(b).

[302] ERA, s. 184(1)(c). Holiday pay is defined by ERA, s. 184(3).

[303] ERA, s. 184(1)(e).

articled clerk.[304] However, the total amount payable in respect of any such debt where the amount is referable to a period of time is subject to a maximum weekly limit[305] and on making a payment the Secretary of State is subrogated to any rights the employee has directly against his employer.[306] To receive a payment from the National Insurance Fund a written application must be made to the Secretary of State for Employment who may require a written statement (from the person responsible for the insolvency procedures) of the amount which remains unpaid[307] with a right of complaint to an industrial tribunal in the event of the application being unsuccessful or met only in part.[308]

HOURS OF WORK AND TIME-OFF

3.25 Hours of work — general

Apart from statute providing that an employer must give certain employees written particulars of any terms or conditions of employment relating to hours of work,[309] generally, settling of terms of employment including hours of work is left to the contracting parties. However, a contractual right to require an employee to work a specified number of hours per week may itself be subordinate to the employer's duty to take reasonable care for the safety of his employees.[310] Such restrictions as legislation imposes are selective and, frequently, subject to extension or modification by the appropriate authority where the circumstances justify a departure from the normal rules. Some restrictions on working hours are to protect the workforce[311] while others are primarily for the protection of the public[312] and breaches of the restrictions attract criminal penalties in some cases for the employee as well as the employer.[313] The extent and effect of such restrictions as do exist vary according to the nature of the work, where it is done and the age of the employees or a combination of these. Most of the statutory restrictions on the employment of females 18 years and over have been removed by the Sex Discrimination Act 1986 but note that any legislation for the protection of women (as regards (a) pregnancy or maternity or (b) other risks specifically affecting women) continues to have

---

[304] *Ibid.* And see the provisions in EPCA, s. 123 for payment by the Secretary of State of unpaid contributions to occupational pension schemes.

[305] ERA, s. 186(1). Currently, by Employment Rights Act 1996, s. 227, the weekly limit is £210.00 making a maximum entitlement of arrears of wages of £1680.00 (8 × £210.00); and see *Morris v. Secretary of State for Employment* [1985] ICR 492, EAT (weekly limit to be applied before deductions of income tax and national insurance).

[306] ERA, s. 189(1).

[307] ERA, s. 187(2), (3).

[308] ERA, s. 188(1); the complaint must be submitted within three months of the Secretary of State's decision.

[309] ERA, s. 1.

[310] See *Johnstone v. Bloomsbury Health Authority* [1991] IRLR 118, CA.

[311] See, for example, the Factories Act 1961, s. 86 (limits on the hours of work of young persons while employed in a factory) and the Coal Mines Regulation Act 1908, s. 1 (limits on the time spent underground by a miner).

[312] See, for example, the Transport Act 1968, Part VI (limits on hours of work of drivers of goods and certain public service vehicles).

[313] See the Coal Mines Regulation Act 1908, s. 7 as amended by the Mines and Quarries Act 1954, s. 187. And see *Anklagemyndigheden v. Hansen & Son*, *The Times*, August 14, 1990, ECJ.

effect.[314] The statutory provisions affecting hours of work are varied and detailed but the following general rules may be stated.

3.26 *Adults — male and female.* There are presently[315] very few restrictions on the working hours of adults.[316] In the event of the European Court of Justice upholding the validity of the Working Time Directive (Dir. 93/104) member states will be required to give effect to its provisions by November 23, 1996 or, in the case of annual leave entitlement, November 23, 1999. The main requirements of the Directive are as follows:

(1)   A minimum daily rest period of 11 consecutive hours in each 24 hour period.

(2)   A rest break where the working day exceeds six hours.

(3)   A minimum uninterrupted weekly rest period of 24 hours.

(4)   At least four weeks paid annual leave.

(5)   Restrictions on night work, including an average limit of eight hours in 24 hours.

(6)   Organisation of work patterns to take account of health and safety requirements and the adaptation of work to the worker.

(7)   An average working limit of 48 hours over each seven day period calculated over a reference period of four months.

However, much scope is allowed for derogations, either through collective agreements or the decisions of member state governments but no derogation is permitted in respect of the four weeks' paid annual leave (although its full implementation may be delayed until 1999) or the 48 hour week (although this limit itself may be avoided provided the worker's consent has been obtained and no worker is subjected to a detriment for withholding his consent). Undoubtedly implementation of the Directive will require introduction of the appropriate legislation, but even in the absence of such employees of the state or an emanation of the state will, provided the Directive is sufficiently precise to create an enforceable right, be able to rely on the Directive in their employment relationship.

The main exceptions at the time of writing are in relation to miners and certain drivers. Although this is subject to suspension or exception in respect of, *inter alia*, emergencies, national danger or economic disturbance due to the demand for coal,[317] no miner[318] may spend more than seven hours a day (including time going to and from his work station) below ground.[319]

The hours of work of drivers engaged in the carriage of passengers or goods by road are subject to different restrictions depending on whether the driving is regulated only by domestic legislation or domestic legislation as amended to

---

[314] SDA 1975, s. 51 as substituted by EA 1989, s. 3(3). And note the legislation in EA 1989, Sch. 1 is expressly continued presumably because it is for the protection of women as regards pregnancy etc.

[315] Although the Council of Ministers has adopted the Working Time Directive (Dir 93/104/EC) the validity of the Directive passed by qualified majority voting is challenged by the UK.

[316] Adults are those 18 years of age and over.

[317] In mines of ironstone, shale or fireclay the limits are slightly longer: Coal Mines Regulation Act 1908, s. 1(1), (7).

[318] For others (deputy, pump-minder, fan-worker, etc.) the period is eight hours a day: Coal Mines Regulation Act 1908, s. 1(7) proviso (a), as amended.

[319] Coal Mines Regulation Act 1908, s. 1(1); the daily limit may be extended by up to 30 minutes at the mine manager's discretion (s. 3).

accord with EC rules.[320] Whether the hours of work are regulated by EC rules depends on a variety of factors including the number of passengers a vehicle carries, its maximum weight when fully laden, the length of its regular route and whether the driver works only in Britain or in Britain as well as abroad.[321] Where the matter is regulated by domestic law a driver shall not drive[322] certain vehicles[323] on any working day[324] for more than 10 hours and, when he has been on duty[325] for $5\frac{1}{2}$ hours without having had a break of at least 30 minutes, he must have such a break unless the expiry of the spell of $5\frac{1}{2}$ hours coincides with the end of his working day[326] and the working day of a driver shall not exceed 11 hours although that limit may be increased to $12\frac{1}{2}$ hours provided the driver has been off duty for a period(s) of not less than the period by which his working day exceeds 11 hours.[327] The driver's working week[328] must not require him to be on duty[329] for more than 60 hours and in each working week he must be off duty for a period of at least 24 hours.[330]

Where EC rules apply to the vehicle the hours of drivers are also restricted.[331] Thus for goods vehicles[332] the maximum spell of driving shall not exceed $4\frac{1}{2}$ hours without a rest break of at least 45 minutes[333] and the driving period must not normally exceed 9 hours a day nor 90 in 2 consecutive weeks.[334] There must be a daily rest period of (normally) 11 consecutive hours during the 24 hours preceding the spell of driving or at work, although these rules differ if the rest is taken at the crew's base or elsewhere and where a bunk is provided.[335] There must be a weekly rest period of 45 hours, reducible in some circumstances to 24 hours.[336]

Persons who are employed on successive shift systems in a necessarily

---

[320] Transport Act 1968, Part VI (as amended).

[321] See EC Council Regulation 3820/85 and the Community Road Transport Rules (Exemptions) Regulations 1978 (SI 1978 No. 1158) as amended. For a specialist text reference may be made to Kitchin's *Road Transport Law* (28th edn, 1992).

[322] Driving is defined to mean "being at the driving controls of the vehicle for the purpose of controlling its movement whether it is in motion or stationary with the engine running": Transport Act 1968, s. 103(3).

[323] The restrictions relate to driving of vehicles to which Part VI of the Transport Act 1968 relates; these are public services vehicles, vehicles constructed or adapted to carry more than 12 passengers, locomotives, motor tractors or articulated drawing units, or vehicles constructed or adapted to carry goods other than the effects of passengers: Transport Act 1968, s. 98(2).

[324] Transport Act 1968, s. 103(1). And see *Carter v. Walton* [1985] RTR 378.

[325] Transport Act 1968, s. 103(4).

[326] *Ibid.* s. 96(2)(b).

[327] *Ibid.* s. 96(3). The working day of the driver of an express or contract carriage (defined in s. 159(1)) may be extended to 14 hours: s. 96(3)(c).

[328] *Ibid.* s. 103(1).

[329] *Ibid.* s. 103(4).

[330] *Ibid.* s. 96(5), (6).

[331] A provision of domestic law which imposes strict liability on the employer of a driver who breaks EC rules is not unlawful: *Anklagemyndigheden v. Hansen & Son, The Times* August 14, 1990, ECJ.

[332] The permitted hours of work for drivers of passenger vehicles vary slightly.

[333] Council Regulation 3280/85. The requirement for a 45 minute break is modified where breaks are permitted during the $4\frac{1}{2}$ hour spell and on vehicles over 20,000 kgs. the rest periods are longer.

[334] Reg. 3280/85. There is no weekly maximum but a weekly rest must be taken after not more than six days of driving.

[335] Reg. 3280/85.

[336] Reg. 3280/85. As to the timing of the rest period see *Kelly v. Shulman* [1988] IRLR 478, DC.

continuous process in the sheet glass industry have their shift period limited to 8 hours, and their weekly hours limited to not more than 42 hours with a compulsory interval of 16 hours between shift.[337] The Baking Industry (Hours of Work) Act 1954 which regulated employment in night bakeries has been repealed.[338]

3.27 *Women, young persons and children.* As noted previously the law regarding the employment of women has been radically altered by the Sex Discrimination Act 1986 and the Employment Act 1989. The former[339] removed the restrictions on the employment of women contained in (i) the Hours of Employment (Conventions) Act 1936, s. 1 (employment of women by night in industrial undertakings), (ii) the Mines and Quarries Act 1954, ss. 126, 128, 131 (hours of work of women at a mine) and (iii) the Factories Act 1961 ss. 86, 88–102, 106–115 (hours of employment of women in factories), while the latter[340] (i) removed the restrictions on women being employed below ground in a working mine and from being employed on certain work in relation to mining and (ii) amended the Factories Act 1961, s. 20 (prohibition of cleaning machinery by a woman) and the Offices, Shops and Railway Premises Act 1963, s. 17 (fencing of exposed machinery). The Employment Act 1989 also enacts two mutually dependent provisions — (i) any provision of an Act passed before the Sex Discrimination Act 1975[341] (or an instrument made thereunder) is of no effect if it requires an act which would be unlawful by virtue, *inter alia* of Part II of the Sex Discrimination Act 1975[342] but (ii) nothing in, *inter alia*, Part II of the Sex Discrimination Act 1975 shall render unlawful an act done to comply with a statutory provision concerning the protection of women as regards pregnancy, maternity or other risks specifically affecting women.[343] However, a prohibition on night work by women is contrary to the Equal Treatment Directive[344] when no similar provision applies to men.[345] Although the special provisions for young persons employed as shop assistants have been repealed[346] certain general provisions relating to all shop assistants still remain. Thus shop assistants are entitled to have at least one half day off each week[347]; their meal times are regulated by statute[348] and seats have to be provided for female shop assistants.[349] The prohibition against opening a shop on a Sunday[350] did not apply to Scotland[351] but shop workers in England and Wales who, when the Sunday Trading Act 1994 became effective, could not be required to work on Sundays have special rights regarding Sunday work.[352]

---

[337] Hours of Employment (Conventions) Act 1936, s. 3.
[338] SDA 1986, s. 6.
[339] SDA 1986, ss. 7, 9.
[340] EA 1989, s. 9.
[341] Acts passed between the SDA 1975 and EA 1989 may be amended or repealed by order of the Secretary of State (EA 1989, s. 2).
[342] EA 1989, s. 1.
[343] SDA 1975, s. 51 as substituted by EA 1989, s. 3. And note the provisions in EA 1989, Sch. 1 which are, in effect, deemed to be for protection of women.
[344] Directive 76/207.
[345] *Stoeckel v. Ministère Public* [1991] ECR 4097.
[346] See EA 1989, s. 10, Sch. 3.
[347] Shops Act 1950, s. 17(1).
[348] *Ibid.* s. 19, Third Schedule. As to the application of the rules regarding meal breaks see *Hutchinson v. Cumming* 1926 JC 110.
[349] Shops Act 1950, s. 37.
[350] *Ibid.* s. 47, repealed by the Sunday Trading Act 1994, s. 5.
[351] Shops Act 1950, s. 66.
[352] Sunday Trading Act 1994, Sch. 4. See now ERA, Part IV.

At the time of writing the employment of children and young persons is regulated by domestic law. However, the UK has recently agreed to a Council Directive on the Protection of Young People at Work[353] which will require domestic legislation, in some areas, by June 1996.[353a] The main provisions of the Directive are set out below.[354] In keeping with the Government's desire to remove restrictions on recruitment and employment[355] many of the restrictions on the employment of young persons (those over compulsory school leaving age[356] but under 18 years of age) have been removed,[357] while others have been amended so as generally not to apply to persons over school leaving age.[358]

The employment of children is strictly regulated to prevent their exploitation, to ensure their safety and to avoid jeopardising their education. Thus a child[359] must not be employed in any factory or at any mine or quarry,[360] and generally the employment of a child under the age of thirteen is forbidden.[361] The hours of work and the type of employment of children over thirteen are also regulated by enactment[362] and local bye-laws.[363] No child may be employed during school hours on any school day or for more than two hours on any school day or Sunday.[364] However, these general restrictions are invariably supplemented by local legislation which may prohibit totally the employment of children in certain specified employments, require the employer of children to observe other conditions in relation to their employment or even raise the age below which children generally

---

[353] Directive 94/33/EC (OJ 1994 L216).

[353a] At the time of writing the government is considering representations made following the publication of model bye-laws which are intended to give effect to the Directive.

[354] See para. 3.28.

[355] See "Building Businesses ... not Barriers", Chapter Seven (Cmnd. 9794) and the Wages Act 1986, Part II.

[356] Education (Scotland) Act 1980, s. 135.

[357] See EA 1989, s. 10 and Sch. 3 which repeal many provisions including Employment of Women, Young Persons and Children Act 1920, s. 1(3) (employment of young persons at night in industrial undertakings), Children and Young Persons (Scotland) Act 1937, s. 29 (power to make bye-laws for persons (not children) under 18), the Shops Act 1950, ss. 18, 20, 24–36, 68, 72 (holidays, meal times and hours of employment of young persons), the Mines and Quarries Act 1954, ss. 125–128, 130, 132 (hours of young persons) and the Factories Act 1961, ss. 86–94, 96–109, 112–115, 138, 140 (hours, holidays, occupation of young persons).

[358] See EA 1989, Sch. 3, Pts II and III.

[359] For the purpose of the education legislation "child" means a person who is not over school age (Education (Scotland) Act 1962, s. 145(12); Education (Scotland) Act 1980, s. 135(1)). For the purpose of any enactment relating to the prohibition or regulation of the employment of children, any person who is not over school age for the purpose of the Education (Scotland) Act 1980 is deemed to be a child within the meaning of that other enactment (Education (Scotland) Act 1980, s. 125)).

[360] Education (Scotland) Act 1962, s. 136.

[361] Children and Young Persons (Scotland) Act 1937, s. 28(1)(a) (substituted by the Children Act 1972, s. 1(2)). Education authority byelaws may, however, authorise such children to be employed by their parents or guardians in light agricultural or horticultural work and a child may take part in a performance under a licence (ibid).

[362] See the Children and Young Persons (Scotland) Act 1937, Part III (ss. 28–38). The Shops Act 1950, s. 27 was repealed by EA 1989, s. 29(4).

[363] Byelaws may be made by education authorities under the Children and Young Persons (Scotland) Act 1937, s. 28(2). These are in addition to any restrictions contained in s. 28(1).

[364] Ibid., s. 28(1)(b), (d), (e). Nor may he be employed before 7 am or after 7 pm on any day: s. 28(1)(c) (substituted by the Children and Young Persons Act 1963, s. 34). He must not be required to lift, carry or move anything so heavy as to be likely to injure him: Children and Young Persons (Scotland) Act 1837, s. 28(1)(f).

may not be employed.[365] Although legislation has been passed which will transfer to the Secretary of State the power to make regulations for the employment of children,[366] such legislation remains inoperative, the matter being still regulated by bye-laws.

3.28 *Directive on the Protection of Young People at Work.* With the exception of Arts 8(1)(b), 8(2), 9(1)(b) and 9(2), implementation of which may be delayed by the United Kingdom until June 22, 2000, Directive 94/33 becomes effective on June 22, 1996. The purposes of the Directive are (i) to prohibit work by children[367] and ensure that the minimum working age is not lower than compulsory school age, (ii) to ensure that work by adolescents[368] is strictly regulated and (iii) to ensure that employers guarantee that young people[369] have working conditions which suit their age and that they are protected against economic exploitation and any work likely to harm their health and safety, moral or social development or to jeopardise their education.[370]

The Directive applies to any person under 18 years of age in employment although there are derogations for occasional or short-term domestic work in a private household or work regarded as not being harmful in a family undertaking.[371] However, work by children is prohibited except (i) light work[372] where the child is at least 13 years of age and (ii) work for the purposes of performance in cultural, artistic, sports or advertising activities.

The employer's general obligations to protect the safety and health of young people is underpinned by obligations to (1) conduct an assessment of the occupational hazards to young people before the work begins or where a major change in working conditions occurs and, should the assessment disclose a risk, to provide free health monitoring, (2) disclose possible risks to young people and the parents/guardians of children[373] and (3) refrain from employing young people for certain types of work including, for example, work which is beyond their physical or psychological capacity and work involving the risk of accidents which cannot be recognised or avoided by young people owing to their insufficient attention to safety or their lack of experience or training.[374]

Article 8 imposes limits on the working time[375] of children of (a) eight hours a day (40 hours a week) for training and work experience schemes, (b) during school terms two hours a school day but outside school hours and no more than seven hours a day for non-school days, (c) outside school terms, seven hours a day and

---

[365] *Ibid.*, s. 28(2)(b), (c). For example, the Lothian Region Byelaws provided that no child is to be employed until the education authority had issued an employment certificate to the effect that the proposed employment was not likely to be prejudicial to the child's wellbeing or to render him unfit to obtain the full benefit of education.

[366] See the Employment of Children Act 1973, s. 1(3), Sch. 1, Pt I, para. 5, Pt II. The Act received the royal assent on May 23, 1973, but no commencement order had been made under s. 3(4).

[367] A child is a young person who is less than compulsory school age (Art. 3).

[368] An adolescent is a young person between compulsory school leaving age and 18 years of age (Art. 3).

[369] A young person is a person under 18 years of age (Art. 3).

[370] Article 1.

[371] Article 2.

[372] Defined as not harmful to health or attendance at school (Art. 3).

[373] Article 6.

[374] Article 7. Work involving exposure to the agents and processes in the Annex to the Directive is work which is likely to entail risks to young people.

[375] Defined to mean any period the person is at the employer's disposal (Art. 3(e)).

35 hours a week and (d) seven hours a day and 35 hours a week for light work provided the child is above compulsory school age.[376] Where adolescents are concerned the working day is limited to eight hours and the working week to 40 hours with working time with several employers being cumulative.[377]

Night work by children is prohibited between 8 pm and 6 am and by adolescents between 10 pm (11 pm) and 6 am (7 am) although the limit for adolescents may be avoided where supervision by an adult takes place and special exemption may operate for shipping, fisheries, armed forces or police, hospitals and cultural, sporting or advertising activities.[378] Children are entitled to a rest period of 14 consecutive hours and adolescents a rest period of 12 consecutive hours for each period of 24 hours and two consecutive rest days although it is possible for these limits to be reduced by national legislation on objective grounds in the types of employment mentioned above but with the addition of agricultural, tourism and the hotel, café or restaurant sector[379] subject always to the overriding purposes set out in Article 1 of the Directive. Also where the daily working time is more than four-and-a-half hours young people are entitled to a break of at least 30 minutes, consecutive if possible.[380]

3.29 Time off — General

Whether an employee is entitled to time off work is generally to be settled by the contracting parties although there are several situations in which statutory rights to time off work operate.[381] However, before considering these statutory rights it is necessary to observe that an employee who takes unauthorised time off will be in breach of this contract as will an employee who fails to return to work after a period of authorised time off. However, an agreement to the effect that an employee's failure to return to work timeously is to be treated as an automatic termination of the contract of employment may be void.[382]

3.30 *Statutory time off rights.* The right to time off for carrying out or participating in trade union duties or activities is dealt with elsewhere.[383] The following other time off rights have been created:

(1)   An employer must permit employees[384] who hold certain public offices or who are members of certain public bodies to take time off, without pay, to perform their public duties.[385] This provision embraces Justices of the Peace, members of (1) a local authority,[386] (2) a statutory tribunal, (3) a National Health Service Trust or Health Board, (4) a school board, school or college governing body or further education corporation or board of management of a college of further education

---

[376] Since a child is by definition a young person who is under compulsory school age the impact of this is not entirely obvious.

[377] Article 8(2).

[378] Article 9.

[379] Article 10.

[380] Article 12.

[381] And note at common law the right of certain workers to time off for finding work at the end of a term (*Alexander v. Gardner* (1863) 1 Guthrie's Sh. Ct. Cases 369.

[382] Compare *Igbo v. Johnson Matthey Chemicals Ltd* [1986] IRLR 215, CA with *Logan Salton v. Durham C.C.* [1989] IRLR 99, EAT.

[383] See Chapter Nine.

[384] The right is no longer applicable only to employees who work for 16 hours or more per week (SI 1995 No. 31).

[385] ERA, s. 50.

[386] And see *Ratcliffe v. Dorset C.C.* [1978] IRLR 191, IT; *R. v. Eden D.C. ex p Moffat, The Times*, November 24, 1988, CA.

and (5) the Scottish Environment Protection Agency.[387] The amount of time off to be allowed is whatever is reasonable in the circumstances[388] and although membership of a local authority working party is not to be equated with membership of one of its committees or sub-committees,[389] it is a breach of an employee's right merely to re-time the classes of a lecturer whereby he does the same amount of work.[390]

(2)   An employee who is called for jury service commits an offence if he fails to attend unless he is disqualified, ineligible or excused.[391] Jurors are entitled to receive allowances at rates determined by the Secretary of State.[392]

(3)   An employee who has received notice of dismissal by reason of redundancy and who has sufficient continuous employment[393] to receive a redundancy payment by the time the notice expires is entitled to reasonable time off with pay to look for new work or make arrangements for training for future employment.[394] Although no limit is imposed on the amount of time off to be allowed an employer may not be required to pay more than two fifths of a week's pay in respect of the notice period.[395]

(4)   Safety representatives are entitled to time off with pay for performing certain functions[396] and for undergoing reasonable training having regard to the code of practice approved by the Health and Safety Commission.[397] Payments made under the contract of employment and for time off for trade union duties go towards discharging any liability to make payment to safety representatives.[398]

(5)   A pregnant employee is entitled not to be reasonably refused[399] time off for an ante-natal care appointment made on the advice of a doctor, midwife or health visitor.[400] For appointments other than the first the employee must if requested by her employer produce a certificate of pregnancy and an appointment card or similar document.[401] Where an employee is permitted to take time off she is entitled to be paid at the appropriate hourly rate which is to be determined according to statutory rules.[402]

(6)   Trustees of an employer's occupational pension scheme are entitled to reasonable paid time off for the purpose of performing their duties as a trustee or undergoing relevant training.[402a]

---

[387] ERA, s. 50.

[388] ERA, s. 50(4). And see the Local Government and Housing Act 1989, s. 10 which limits local authorities who choose to pay employees who take time off for public duties.

[389] *R. v. Eden D.C. ex p Moffat*, above.

[390] *Ratcliffe v. Dorset C.C.*, above.

[391] Criminal Procedure (Scotland) Act 1975, s. 99(1) as amended by the Law Reform (Miscellaneous Provisions) (Scotland) Act 1980, s. 2(3).

[392] Juries Act 1949 s. 24 as substituted by the Law Reform (Miscellaneous Provisions) (Scotland) Act 1980, s. 28, Sch. 2.

[393] Note that with effect from February 5, 1995, s. 52 is no longer applicable only to those who work 16 hours per week or more (SI 1995 No. 31).

[394] ERA, s. 52; and see *Dutton v. Hawker Siddeley Aviation Ltd* [1978] ICR 1057, EAT.

[395] ERA, s. 53(5). Contractual and statutory payments are set-off (ERA, s. 53(7)).

[396] The functions are set out in Safety Representatives and Safety Committees Regulations 1977 (SI 1977 No. 500), which also define "safety representatives" and contain provisions regarding their appointment.

[397] Safety Representatives and Safety Committees Regulations 1977, reg. 4.

[398] *Ibid.*

[399] See *Gregory v. Tudsbury Ltd* [1982] IRLR 267, IT.

[400] ERA, s. 55.

[401] *Ibid.*

[402] ERA, s. 56(1), (2).

[402a] ERA, s. 58.

(7)   Until recently an employer who was proposing to dismiss employees as redundant, or an employer who was about to transfer or acquire a business, was not required to consult representatives of employees unless he recognised a trade union in respect of the relevant category of employees. The obligations to consult were not triggered unless the employer chose to recognise a trade union. However this failed to comply with Directives 75/129 and 77/187 and the law has been changed so that employers must now consult representatives (either trade union appointed or worker elected) and such representatives are entitled to reasonable paid time off to perform their functions or to stand as a candidate.[402b]

The remedy of an employee who is denied any of these rights is to complain within three months to an industrial tribunal[403] which may make a declaratory order and an order requiring the employer to pay the employee the appropriate amount.[404]

SAFETY

3.31 The nature of the employer's duty[405]

The law of delict imposes on employers a duty to promulgate and operate a reasonably safe system of work. However, a similar duty may be implied into the contract of employment[406] in that an employee is entitled to terminate the contract on being required to do work — within the scope of the contract — if in the circumstances he would be exposed to undue personal risk or danger[407] and in the law of unfair dismissal industrial tribunals are used to accepting that a failure to take reasonable care for the safety of an employee may be a breach of the contract sufficiently material to found a constructive dismissal.[408] This is the result of the decision of the Court of Appeal in *Western Excavating (ECC) Ltd v. Sharp*[409] that for a constructive dismissal the employee must leave because the employer has broken the contract in a material way or has indicated he no longer intends to be bound by it.[410] However, while aspects of an employer's duty of devising and

---

[402b] ERA, s. 61. And see Chapter Nine.

[403] ERA, ss. 51(2), 54, 60, 63; Safety Representatives and Safety Committees Regulations 1977, reg. 11(2).

[404] ERA, ss. 51(3), 54(3), 60(3); Safety Representatives and Safety Committees Regulations 1977, reg. 11(3), (4).

[405] For a more detailed coverage of the employer's duty of safety see V. Craig and K. Miller, *Introduction to the Law of Health and Safety at Work in Scotland.*

[406] *McKeating v. Frame* 1921 SC 382. In *Matthews v. Kuwait Bechtel Corpn* [1959] 2 QB 57, CA the Court of Appeal allowed an employee injured in the course of his employment to sue for damages on the footing that the employer was in breach of an implied contractual term to take care for the employee's safety. And see *Johnstone v. Bloomsbury Health Authority* [1991] IRLR 118, CA.

[407] See F. A. Umpherston, *The Law of Master and Servant* (1904) p. 48 and *Knight v. Barra Shipping*, 1992, unreported, case no. 187/92, EAT. *Cf MacKinnon v. Iberia Shipping Co Ltd* 1955 SC 20.

[408] See para. 5.17.

[409] [1978] IRLR 27, CA; [1978] ICR 221, CA.

[410] Instances of industrial tribunals holding that unsafe work practices have justified rescission by the employee are — *British Aircraft Corporation Ltd v. Austin* [1978] IRLR 332, EAT; *Keys v. Shoefayre Ltd* [1978] IRLR 476, IT; *Graham Oxley Tool Steels Ltd v. Firth* [1980] IRLR 135, EAT; *Dutton & Clarke Ltd v. Daly* [1985] IRLR 363, EAT; and *Knight v. Barra Shipping* 1992, unreported, case no. 187/92, EAT. *Cf Jagdeo v. Smiths Industries Ltd* [1982] ICR 47, EAT.

maintaining a reasonably safe system of work may thus be capable of expression as an implied term of the contract of employment, it is well established that in its delictual form the duty is personal to the employer and cannot be discharged merely by delegating its performance to a third person, for example another employee.[411] In *McDermid v. Nash Dredging Reclamation Co. Ltd*[412] McDermid was required to work under a tugboat captain who was employed by a subsidiary company of McDermid's employer. He was injured when the tugboat captain failed to operate the system he had devised for McDermid's safety. In holding McDermid's employer personally liable Lord Brandon stated:

"An employer owed his employee a duty to exercise reasonable care to ensure that the system of work provided for him was a safe one ... The duty has been described as a personal or non-delegable one, which meant that if it was not performed, it was no defence for the employer to show that he had delegated its performance to a person, whether his servant or not, whom he had reasonably believed to be competent to perform it ... I cannot accept that (the captain's) negligence was negligence in failing to operate the system that he had devised but rather casual negligence in the course of operating the system for which the employers, since (the captain) was not their servant, were not liable. (The captain's) negligence had not been casual but central. It had involved abandoning the safe system and operating in its place a manifestly unsafe system. In the result there had been a failure by the employers in operating a safe system of work."

Similarly where two employers entered into a contract whereby one employer agreed to supply labour to another employer, the first employer was liable for the injuries of an employee caused by inadequate instruction and training of the employee even although the second employer could tell the employee what to do and how to do it.[413] It is also necessary to note that the common law duties relating to a reasonably safe system of work are distinct from and in addition to the many duties imposed by legislation on employers, occupiers of factories and others. Much protective legislation imposes duties which are enforced by criminal penalties. Thus the general duties of the Health and Safety at Work etc. Act 1974 imposed on employers (and others) have no effect on civil law rights and duties[414] whereas certain provisions of other protective legislation may confer civil law rights on the intended beneficiaries of the legislation.[415]

3.32 The scope of the duty

While the duty is framed in general terms — to take care for the safety of employees — it does not extend to a general duty of care to take all reasonable steps to protect an employee's economic welfare while acting in the course of his employment by insuring an employee against special risks or advising of the

---

[411] *Davie v. New Merton Board Mills Ltd* [1958] 1 QB 210 at p. 238 *per* Parker LJ citing *Bain v. Fife Coal Co Ltd* 1935 SC 681. For a detailed textbook on the delictual duty see D. M. Walker, *Delict*.

[412] [1987] ICR 917, HL.

[413] *Morris v. Breaveglen Ltd* [1993] ICR 766, CA. However, in England, relying on the Civil Liability (Contribution) Act 1978, which has no application in Scotland, the first employer has been held entitled to a complete indemnity against the second employer: *Nelhams v. Sandells Maintenance Ltd, The Times*, June 15, 1995, CA.

[414] Health and Safety at Work etc. Act 1974, s. 47(1).

[415] *Atkinson v. Newcastle Waterworks* (1877) 2 Ex D 411; *Grant v. NCB* 1956 SC (HL) 48. And see Gloag and Henderson, *The Law of Scotland* (10th edn) para. 31.3.

existence of the risk so that the employee himself may effect appropriate insurance. Thus the employer of an employee, who, while acting in the course of his employment while abroad, was injured due to the negligence of a third party/ driver who could not be traced, was not liable because (1) it would be inappropriate for the common law to devise such a duty which Parliament could have — but had not — imposed and (2) in the absence of a contractual term the employer's duty was limited to protecting the employee against physical harm or disease.[416] However, such a view might now be regarded as too cautious in that more recently an employer has settled a claim brought by a junior hospital doctor for psychological injury claimed to have been caused by requiring him to work excessively long continuous periods without adequate provision for rest periods[417] while another employer has been held liable for the nervous breakdown and associated psychological injuries sustained by a social work employee on his return to work where appropriate steps to reduce and monitor his workload were set up but not followed in practice[418] and yet another has been held to be in breach of an implied term of the contract by failing to inform employees of the existence of a time limit for applying for a financial benefit.[419] The duty also extends to ensuring an employee is not exposed to fellow employees' cigarette smoke[420] and repetitive strain injuries.[421] The duty to take reasonable care for an employee's safety may be conveniently studied by considering it in relation to the following headings —

(a) Safe system of work. Before requiring an employee to carry out work an employer must consider his operations and promulgate a reasonably safe system whereby his commercial objectives may be obtained[422] and where his employee has to work with employees of another employer or self-employed workers the system must embrace the co-ordination of the work.[423] Whether a safe system of work exists is a question of fact which will be influenced by the circumstances of each case, and is determined by having regard to the standard of reasonable foresight.[424] It may include prohibiting certain methods of performance[425] and

---

[416] Reid v. Rush and Tompkins Group plc [1989] IRLR 265, CA; and see Rutherford v. Radio Rentals Ltd 1990 GWD 28-1612, OH. Note that by the Employers' Liability (Compulsory Insurance) Act 1969 an employer is required to maintain insurance against liability for bodily injury and disease sustained by his employees rising out of and in the course of their employment in Great Britain; see para. 3.33.

[417] See Johnstone v. Bloomsbury Health Authority [1991] IRLR 118, CA. And consider also the possibility of health care workers being exposed to injury by contact with patients infected with HIV unless reasonable precautions are taken. For a full account of exposure to HIV see Southam and Howard, Aids and Employment Law (1988).

[418] Walker v. Northumberland County Council [1995] IRLR 35; and see H. Collins (1992) 55 MLR 556.

[419] Scally v. Southern Health and Social Services Board [1991] IRLR 522, HL.

[420] Bland v. Stockport Metropolitan Council, The Times, January 28, 1993; Roe v. Stockport Metropolitan Council, The Scotsman, July 1995.

[421] Mountenay v. Bernard Matthews plc (unreported, 1994); Lodge & McSherry v. British Telecom (unreported, 1993); Victor Hunter v. Clyde Shaw plc, unreported, September 2, 1994, OH.

[422] Sword v. Cameron (1839) 1 D 493; English v. Wilsons and Clyde Coal Co. Ltd 1937 SC (HL) 46.

[423] McArdle v. Andmac Roofing Co [1967] 1 WLR 356, CA; McDermid v. Nash Dredging & Reclamation Co. Ltd [1987] ICR 917, HL.

[424] Paris v. Stepney Borough Council [1951] AC 367.

[425] King v. Smith [1995] ICR 339, CA reviewing views expressed in General Cleaning Contractors Ltd v. Christmas [1953] AC 180, HL.

guarding against risk of injury by criminals.[426] While the decision in *Paris v. Stepney Borough Council*[427] is authority for the rule that the special risk of serious injury resulting from, for example, the known disabilities of a particular employee, is a relevant consideration in determining the precautions which an employer should take in the fulfilment of the duty of care which he owes to an employee, it has been stated that that decision was about the provision of plant and equipment rather than a system case.[428] However, to perform this aspect of his duty an employer need not employ specialist consultants[429] although in some circumstances obtaining sufficient information to appraise the risks an operation might involve could require specialist help.

(b) Competent staff. The personal duty of an employer to select competent staff or co-workers[430] is separate from his vicarious liability for a negligent employee acting in the course of his employment. Thus, although an employee impliedly warrants his competence to do the job he accepts,[431] in an issue with another employee it would seem an employer could not rely on such a warranty. Also, the duty to select competent staff extends to the dismissal of employees who behave in an unsafe way[432] and it has been held to be fair to dismiss an employee whose medical condition was such that a failure on his part could expose his fellow employees to toxic substances.[433]

(c) Plant, equipment and materials. An employer must provide such plant, equipment and materials as are necessary to ensure the employee's safety and to operate a system of maintenance and monitoring to detect failures.[434] However, an employer who supplies defective plant, equipment or materials will only be liable for any resulting injury if he knew or ought to have known of the defect[435] and an employee's knowledge of the defect will not necessarily be imputed to the employer,[436] much depending on the responsibilities exercised by the employee. While at common law an employer is not liable for a latent defect which could not be revealed by reasonable inspection, by the Employers' Liability (Defective Equipment) Act 1969 where a defect in equipment, plant, machinery or materials[437] is attributable to the fault[438] of a third party the employer is liable for any resultant personal injury to an employee whether or not the defect could have been detected by the employer. Liability under the Act cannot be excluded by contract,

---

[426] *Williams v. Grimshaw and Others* [1967] III KIR 610; *Houghton v. Hackney Borough Council* [1967] III KIR 615.

[427] [1951] AC 367, HL.

[428] *Forsyth v. Lothian Regional Council* (unreported, December 13, 1994, OH).

[429] *Charlton v. Forrest Printing Ink Co. Ltd* [1980] IRLR 331, CA.

[430] *Bett v. Dalmeny Oil Co Ltd* (1905) 7 F 787. And see *Tossa Marine Co. Ltd v. Alfred C. Toepfer Schiffahrtsgesellschaft GmbH* [1985] 2 Lloyd's Rep. 325 (Court of Appeal while agreeing that the warranty of seaworthiness also required the provision of adequate and competent crew, held it did not require that the employment conditions of the crew complied with the standards of the ITF).

[431] *Pinkerton v. Hollis Bros* 1989 SLT 165, OH.

[432] *Hudson v. Ridge Manufacturing Co. Ltd* [1957] 2 QB 348, *per* Streatfield J.

[433] *Singh-Deu v. Chloride Metals Ltd* [1976] IRLR 56, IT.

[434] *English v. Wilsons and Clyde Coal Co. Ltd* 1937 SC (HL) 46.

[435] *Davie v. New Merton Board Mills* [1958] 1 QB 210, CA; [1959] AC 604, HL.

[436] *Maclean v. Forestry Commission* 1970 SLT 265.

[437] The reasoning in *Knowles v. Liverpool City Council* [1993] IRLR 6, CA and *Ralston v. Greater Glasgow Health Board* 1987 SLT 386, OH seems preferable to *Loch v. British Leyland (UK) Ltd* 1975 SLT (Notes) 67.

[438] ''Fault'' means negligence, breach of statutory duty or other act or omission which gives rise to liability in damages in Scotland (Employers' Liability (Defective Equipment) Act 1969, s. 1(3)).

and to the above liabilities in respect of plant, equipment and materials have been added recently enacted provisions relating to product liability.[439]

(d) Safe place of work. The place of work together with access to and from it must be reasonably safe[440] but the standard of care may vary depending on, for example, whether the work is done outside or inside and whether special clothing is provided[441] and although the fact that the employee works on premises which are outwith his employer's control may affect the standard of care the employer will be expected to attain, it will not absolve him from all responsibility.[442] While it may not be practicable for the employer of a window cleaner to inspect every house where the employee will work the same would not apply to the employer of an employee sent to work at a fairground.[443] Some statutes expressly require employers to provide places for employees to leave clothing not worn during working hours[444] and particular provisions may be interpreted as conferring civil law rights.[445] With regard to clothing the position is now regulated by the Workplace (Health, Safety and Welfare) Regulations 1992[446] which require that suitable and sufficient accommodation be provided for any person at work's own clothing which is not worn during working hours and for special clothing which is worn by any person at work but which is not taken home.[447] However, in the absence of such statutory provisions an employer's duty does not require that he protects the employee's property against theft[448] although where an employer provides places for storage and safe-keeping of employees' property he may be regarded as a (gratuitous) depository[449] with an obligation to take reasonable care.[450]

3.33 Employer's liability insurance

A system of rules and obligations to protect the employee would be pointless if a defender was unable to pay the sum awarded to the employee in damages. To

---

[439] Consumer Protection Act 1987, Sch. 3; and see J. Blaikie, "Injured Workers and the Consumer Protection Act 1987'', 1993 SLT (News) 2.

[440] *Brydon v. Stewart* (1855) 2 Macq. 30, HL. *Cf Ramsay v. George Wimpey & Co. Ltd* 1951 SC 692.

[441] *Bradford v. Robinsons Rentals Ltd* [1967] 1 WLR 337.

[442] *McQuilter v. Goulandris Bros ltd* 1951 SLT (Notes) 75, OH.

[443] Compare *Wilson v. Tyneside Window Cleaning Co* [1978] 2 QB 110, CA with *McDowell v. FMC (Meat) Ltd* [1968] III KIR 595; and see now *King v. Smith* [1995] ICR 339, CA.

[444] See, for example, Factories Act 1961, s. 59 and Offices, Shops and Railway Premises Act 1963, s. 12. In *McCarthy v. Daily Mirror Newspapers Ltd* [1949] 1 All ER 801, CA, it was held that the forerunner of s. 59 required protection against risk of theft.

[445] Thus in *Barr v. Cruickshank & Co. Ltd* 1959 SLT (Sh. Ct) 9, the forerunner of s. 59 of Factories Act 1961 was held to confer a civil law action.

[446] SI 1992 No. 3004; the Regulations became effective for existing workplaces on January 1, 1993 and apply to all workplaces from January 1, 1996. Breach of the Regulations gives rise to an action for breach of statutory duty.

[447] *Ibid.* reg. 23.

[448] *Deyong v. Shenburn* [1946] KB 227, CA; *Edwards v. West Herts Group Hospital Management Committee* [1957] 1 WLR 415, CA.

[449] The deposit may be proved *prout de jure: Walter v. Scottish & Newcastle Breweries* 1970 SLT (Sh. Ct) 21.

[450] Bell, *Principles*, ss. 212–218; *Copland v. Brogan* 1916 SC 277 in which it was held that the onus is on the depositary to explain the loss of an item deposited while in his custody or to show he had exercised reasonable care.

obviate such a result the Employers' Liability (Compulsory Insurance) Act 1969[451] requires every employer[452] who conducts business in Great Britain to maintain approved insurance with an authorised insurer for liability for bodily injury[453] or disease sustained by an employee arising out of, and in the course of, his employment in Great Britain. Thus, except in so far as specifically provided by regulations,[454] the legislation does not extend to injury or diseases suffered or contracted outside Great Britain[455] and this, when combined with a judicial reluctance to extend the duty of care to employees working abroad,[456] dictates that employees who are dispatched abroad require to be satisfied in advance about the extent of their employer's liabilities and insurance therefor. Although an employee who is required to work outside the United Kingdom for more than a month is now entitled to certain written information before he leaves this does not include information about insurance against the risk of injury while abroad.[457] Additionally it has to be emphasised that the 1969 Act merely requires the maintenance of approved insurance cover upon which the employer may call in the event of his liability for the employee's injury or disease being established in accordance with the rules discussed earlier. The policy or policies must provide cover of £2 million in respect of claims relating to any one or more of the employer's employees arising out of any one occurrence.[458] For a policy to be "approved" it must not contain any condition that there shall be no liability (on the part of the insurer) in the event of (a) some specified thing being done, or omitted to be done, after the happening of the event which gave rise to the claim; (b) the policy-holder failing to take reasonable care to protect his employees against risk of bodily injury or disease in the course of their employment; (c) the policy-holder failing to comply with any enactment for the protection of employees against such a risk in the course of their employment or (d) the policy-holder failing to keep specified records or provide the insurer with certain information; however, a term or condition which requires the policy-holder to pay to the insurer sums the latter has, under the policy, paid out in respect of employees is permitted. Similarly, and rather oddly, there is nothing in the legislation to prevent an insurer inserting particular exclusions which may result in an injured employee's claim being defeated. Thus an approved policy may legitimately exclude cover for liability for silicosis, asbestosis and pneumoconiosis and it has been suggested[459] that the effect

---

[451] The legislation is currently under review following the consultation document entitled "Review of Employers' Liability (Compulsory Insurance) Act 1969 and related legislation". For a detailed critical analysis of the 1969 Act see R. Hasson, "The Employers' Liability (Compulsory Insurance) Act 1969 — A Broken Reed" (1974) 3 ILJ 79.

[452] Many public employers are exempt from the Act's provisions: Employers' Liability (Compulsory Insurance) Act 1969, s. 3, Employers' Liability (Compulsory Insurance) Exemption Regulations 1971 (SI 1971 No. 1933).

[453] In England the Court of Appeal has held in a criminal case that as a person's body included his nervous system bodily injury might include injury to any of these parts of his body responsible for his mental and other faculties and that "actual bodily harm" could include psychiatric injury (R. v. Chan-Fook [1994] 1 WLR 689, CA).

[454] See the Offshore Installations (Application of Employers' Liability (Compulsory Insurance) Act 1969) Regulations 1975 (SI 1975 No. 1289).

[455] Employers' Liability (Compulsory Insurance) Act 1969, s. 1.

[456] Reid v. Rush & Tompkins Group plc [1990] ICR 61, CA; Square D Ltd v. Cook [1992] IRLR 35, CA.

[457] ERA, s. 1.

[458] Employers' Liability (Compulsory Insurance) General Regulations 1971, reg. 3 (SI 1971 No. 1117).

[459] See R. Hasson, above.

of the legislation is to permit an approved policy to contain terms which free the insurer of liability to indemnify the insured in the event of recklessness or gross negligence on the part of the insured or in the event of the insured failing to advise the insurers of an increase in risk. By agreement with the Department of Employment the Health and Safety Commission has accepted responsibility for the enforcement of the 1969 Act. Failure to effect and maintain insurance as required by the 1969 Act is itself a criminal offence punishable by a fine for each day of the failure[460] but does not give rise to liability for breach of statutory duty.[461] Accordingly, since the contract of insurance is a contract based on the utmost good faith, where an employer misrepresents or fails to disclose a material fact when effecting or renewing a policy not only does he run the risk of the insurer reducing the contract but, also, he will be liable to a fine for failing to maintain an approved policy. An insurer who enters into an approved policy is required, within 30 days of commencement or renewal, to issue a Certificate of Insurance in statutory form and it is an offence for an employer, to whom such a certificate(s) has been issued to fail to display or produce it (them); similarly it is an offence for an employer who has entered into a contract of insurance in accordance with the 1969 Act not to permit its inspection by an inspector authorised by the Secretary of State.[462]

PROVIDING WORK

3.34 The employer's contractual duties[463]

Although it may seem purely academic, in certain situations there has arisen the question of whether an employee is entitled to have the opportunity of actually carrying out his work or whether his employer is merely required to pay him his wages and other contractual benefits while denying him the opportunity of working. However, the question has a practical dimension. For example in *Langston v. Chrysler (UK) Ltd*[464] because a dispute had arisen between Langston and the Amalgamated Union of Engineering Workers, Chrysler (UK) Ltd suspended him with pay for several months while Langston maintained he had a right not just to contractual benefits but also to do his work. However, in spite of dicta which seek to elevate the notion of "a right to work"[465] into a legal principle the courts have to date been much more cautious[466] although there is support for the following propositions. (1) An employee who is paid on a piece-work basis is entitled to receive a constant supply of work until the contract is terminated[467] or to be paid wages as if he was given normal work.[468] (2) In other cases provided the employer pays the wages the employee would have earned under the contract he is not bound to provide work[469] unless from the nature and circumstances of the

---

[460] Employers' Liability (Compulsory Insurance) Act 1969, s. 5.
[461] *Richardson v. Pitt-Stanley* [1995] ICR 303, CA; Employers' Liability (Compulsory Insurance) Act 1969, s. 5.
[462] Employers' Liability (Compulsory Insurance) Act 1969, s. 4. Employers' Liability (Compulsory Insurance) General Regulations, regs. 5–8.
[463] Regarding statutory duties see para. 3.15.
[464] [1974] ICR 180.
[465] See, for example, the judgment of Lord Denning MR in *Langston*, above.
[466] And see Kahn-Freund's comment that the "right to work" theory in its present inchoate form is unlikely to be of practical application: [1974] ILJ 186 at p. 197.
[467] Bell, *Principles*, s. 192; *Cowdenbeath Coal Co v. Drylie* (1886) 3 Sh. Ct Rep 3.
[468] *Devonald v. Rosser & Sons* [1906] 2 KB 728, CA.
[469] *Turner v. Sawdon & Co.* [1901] 2 KB 653, CA.

employment a term to provide work may be implied.[470] Thus in contracts involving public appearances by the employee a term has been implied that the employer's obligation includes allowing the employee to make public appearances and thereby achieve the enhancement of his reputation which the contract envisaged.[471] Similarly, where an employee would quickly lose his expertise or contacts if no opportunity to practise and maintain these were allowed, a duty to secure such an opportunity by providing work could be implied.[472] Although it has been held in the context of a disciplinary procedure that there may be cases in which there will be implied a term that an employer's right to suspend would contine only so long as these were reasonable grounds for doing so.[473] (3) The fact that statute now provides, in a very modest way, for the protection of income during periods when no work is available[474] has not resulted in the general implication of a right to lay off when no work is available.[475] However, although an employer may breach the contract by denying an employee the opportunity of doing his work the employee's remedies would not extend to an order of specific implement.[476]

RESPECT

3.35 The employer's contractual duty

Even the older law while implying into the employment relationship obedience, submission and respect on the part of the employee recognised the employer's duty of "gentleness and moderation in his bearing towards his servant".[477] Thus habitual use of intemperate language or spiteful withholding of privileges or benefits from one employee could allow him to rescind[478]; young employees and females particularly were entitled to proper treatment by their employer and an early attempt to protect female workers against sexual harassment is seen in the rule entitling a female employee to rescind her contract should her employer attempt her honour.[479] Modern law regards the relationship of employer and employee as one in which each owes the other a duty of "mutual respect"[480] and the content of such a duty will be largely influenced by the nature of the employment, the status of the employee[481] and contemporary values. Although there is no implied term to the effect that an employer is not entitled to make a decision without first informing the employee the decision is to be made,[482] courts and tribunals have been prepared to imply into the modern contract of employment terms to the effect that (1) an employer will not, without proper cause, conduct

---

[470] Collier v. Sunday Referee Publishing Co. Ltd [1940] 2 KB 647.
[471] Herbert Clayton and Jack Waller Ltd v. Oliver [1930] AC 209.
[472] Breach v. Epsylon Industries Ltd [1976] ICR 316, EAT. And see Bosworth v. Angus Jowett & Co. Ltd [1977] IRLR 374, IT (employee entitled to be provided with work until the end of his fixed term contract); Hemmings v. International Computers Ltd [1976] IRLR 37, IT (circumstances in which a term to provide work were summarised); Euro Brokers Ltd v. Rabey [1995] IRLR 206, Ch (money broker losing "cutting edge" during notice).
[473] McClory v. Post Office [1993] IRLR 159.
[474] See para. 3.15.
[475] Namyslo v. Secretary of State for Employment [1979] IRLR 450, IT.
[476] See para. 3.57, 3.58.
[477] Lord Fraser, Master and Servant (3rd edn), p. 120.
[478] Ibid. pp. 120, 121.
[479] Ibid. p. 126; McLean v. Miller (1832) 5 Deas Rep. 270.
[480] Wilson v. Racher [1974] ICR 428, CA; Palmanor Ltd v. Cedron [1978] ICR 1008, EAT.
[481] Lord Fraser, Master and Servant (3rd edn), p. 125.
[482] McClory v. Post Office [1993] IRLR 159.

himself in a manner likely seriously to damage the relationship of trust and confidence on which the employment relationship is based,[483] (2) a senior employee is entitled to his employer's support for his authority and status[484] and (3) an employer must not exercise a contractual disciplinary power harshly or unreasonably.[485] However, although there is no implied term that an employer shall treat his employees fairly or reasonably[486] or that he may not carry out efficiency or work-study tests[487] it has recently been held that it is an implied term of the employment contract that employers will reasonably and promptly afford a reasonable opportunity to their employees to obtain redress of a grievance otherwise Parliament would not have required that the statutory written statement contain information about this.[488] However, to these implied contractual terms there have to be added certain statutory rights which are also concerned with a failure to show proper respect towards employees. Thus an employer who sexually or racially harasses an employee will thereby subject the employee to a detriment.[489]

REFERENCES

3.36 The nature of the employer's duties

Until the House of Lords reviewed the law regarding employment references in *Spring v. Guardian Assurances plc*,[490] unless the matter was the subject of an express term of the contract,[491] an employer was not required to give a reference or "character" on completion of employment[492] and if he chose to do so would be protected by qualified privilege whether the reference was given to the servant directly or to a third party[493] and where a job applicant is offered employment subject to "satisfactory references" it has been held that that does not denote the application of an objective standard but allows the prospective employer to decide

---

[483] *Courtaulds Northern Textiles Ltd v. Andrew* [1979] IRLR 84, EAT; *Woods v. W M Car Services (Peterborough) Ltd* [1981] ICR 666, EAT. And see *Bliss v. South East Thames Regional Health Authority* [1985] IRLR 308 in which the Court of Appeal held that requiring an employee to undergo a psychiatric examination when there was nothing more than a breakdown of relationships between Bliss and other employees was a breach of the implied duty not to damage trust and confidence.

[484] *Associated Tyre Specialists (Eastern) Ltd v. Waterhouse* [1976] IRLR 386, EAT; *Wigan Borough Council v. Davies* [1979] ICR 411, EAT; *Whitbread plc v. Gullyes* unreported, case no. 478/92, EAT.

[485] *BBC v. Beckett* [1983] IRLR 43, EAT; *Cawley v. South Wales Electricity Board* [1985] IRLR 89, EAT.

[486] *Post Office v. Roberts* [1980] IRLR 347, EAT; *McClory v. Post Office*, above.

[487] *Davies v. Richard Johnson & Nephew Ltd* [1934] 51 TLR 115, ChD.

[488] *W. A. Goold (Pearmark) Ltd, v. McConnell* [1995] IRLR 516, EAT.

[489] *Porcelli v. Strathclyde Regional Council* [1986] ICR 564, IH; *De Souza v. Automobile Association* [1986] ICR 514, CA. And see Chapter Seven.

[490] [1994] IRLR 460, HL.

[491] *Grant v. Ramage & Ferguson Ltd* (1897) 25 R 35, *per* Lord Young at p. 39.

[492] Lord Fraser, *Master and Servant* (3rd edn), p. 128.

[493] Bell, *Principles*, s. 188; *McGillivray v. Davidson* 1934 SLT 45. *Cf Bryant v. Edgar* 1909 SC 1080.

the questions subjectively.[494] Following an earlier English development[495] the House of Lords has now held (Lord Keith of Kinkel dissenting)[496] that an employer who provides a reference concerning an employee or former employee to a prospective employer owes to that employee a duty of care[497] and may be held liable to him in damages for any economic loss suffered as result of a negligent statement. The law of defamation was an inadequate protection and in any event dealt with untrue or inaccurate terms of the reference itself whereas the action for negligence is based on the lack of care of the author of the reference. The employer's duty is to take reasonable care when compiling or giving the reference and in verifying the information on which it is based. Contrary to the opinion expressed by a Scottish court[498] Lord Woolf, relying on Lord Bridge of Harwich in *Scally v. Southern Health and Social Services Board*[499] concluded that there are circumstances in which it is necessary to imply a term into the contract of employment that the employer will provide the employee with a reference at the request of a prospective employer and that such a reference will be based on facts revealed after making reasonably careful enquiries and that these circumstances were met where (1) there was a contract of employment (2) the contract related to a class of employee where it is the normal practice to require a reference from a previous employer before employment is offered and (3) the employee cannot be expected to enter that class of employment except on the basis that his employer will, on the request of another employer made not later than a reasonable time after the termination of employment, provide a full and frank reference as to the employee.[500] Also where an employee's record is kept by computer the Data Protection Act 1984 permits an employee (or ex-employee) to have access to the information as well as compensation for any inaccuracies.[501] However, the Act does not apply to personal data which consist exclusively of an indication of an employer's intention as opposed to an expression of opinion.[502] Thus whether or not the Act entitles an employee to its remedies might turn on whether the employer's statement is regarded as an indication of intention or the expression of an opinion. It should also be noted that while the Rehabilitation of Offenders Act 1974[503] excuses the non-disclosure of a "spent" conviction it seems that if a spent conviction is disclosed, for example in a reference, the employer can plead *veritas*[504] in an action of defamation unless malice is proved.[505]

---

[494] *Wishart v. National Association of Citizens Advice Bureaux Ltd, The Times*, June 25, 1990, CA.

[495] *Lawton v. BOC Transhield Ltd* [1987] ICR 7, QBD.

[496] *Spring v. Guardian Assurance plc* [1994] IRLR 460.

[497] The House of Lords also held that alternatively the obligation may be a term implied into the contract of employment.

[498] *Grant v. Ramage & Ferguson Ltd,* above, *per* Lord Young at p. 39.

[499] [1991] IRLR 522, HL.

[500] [1994] IRLR 460 at p. 481. In this respect it is important to note that in accordance with the rules of LAUTRO members companies are required to obtain and provide "full and frank" references for potential representatives and that Spring was seeking employment as such.

[501] Data Protection Act 1984, ss. 21–24.

[502] *Ibid.* s. 1(3).

[503] Section 4(2), (3).

[504] To be defamatory a statement must be untrue and a plea of *veritas* is simply that the allegedly defamatory statement is true.

[505] Rehabilitation of Offenders Act 1974, s. 8(5); and see *Herbage v. Pressdram* [1984] 1 WLR 1160. However the law is currently under review: "On the Record: The Government's Proposals for Access to Criminal Records for Employment etc in England and Wales" (CM 3308).

COMPETENCE AND CAREFUL PERFORMANCE

3.37 Competence

Although there would seem to be a distinction between a competent employee performing his duties carelessly and an incompetent employee performing carefully[506] the distinction has not been developed. Indeed in England the employee's implied duty to perform his work with reasonable care is founded on a case in which the point at issue was whether an employee warranted his competence to perform the work he had undertaken[507] and more recently it has been held in Scotland that the employee's duty of careful performance subsumes capability or competence to perform carefully at his particular job.[508] While most employers today seek to satisfy themselves that employees have the necessary competence for the relevant work, for example by obtaining references and examining qualifications and in some cases requiring job applicants to undergo selection tests, it is implied that the employee has the ordinary skill and competence to perform the job.[509] Thus the employer would be entitled to rescind the contract of a manager if it could be established that he lacked the competence necessary for performing the managerial tasks required by his contract.[510] However where the employer wishes to employ an expert or an employee with "superior skill" it is up to the employer to satisfy himself that the employee comes up to that higher standard.[511]

3.38 Reasonable care

It is equally clear that an employee must perform his duties with reasonable care.[512] Thus a bank teller who carelessly gave out £1,000 instead of £100 had to account to his employers for the difference.[513] In England it has been held in *Lister v. Romford Ice and Cold Storage Co. Ltd*[514] that an employee who carries out his contractual duties negligently may be required to indemnify his employer against claims by a third party injured as a result of the employee's negligence. Following a claim by a fellow employee injured as a result of Lister's negligent driving,

---

[506] Compare, for example, *Gunn v. Ramsay* (1801) Hume 384 in which it was held that an employer was not entitled to dismiss for incompetence a (careful) cook who had expressly qualified her cooking skills with *Clydesdale Bank v. Beatson* (1882) 10 R 88 in which an otherwise competent bank teller, through want of reasonable care, handed over the wrong denomination of bank notes and was held liable for the employer's loss (£900).

[507] Although in *Lister v. Romford Ice and Cold Storage Co. Ltd* [1957] AC 555 the House of Lords confirmed it was an implied term that an employee would perform the contract carefully, considerable reliance was placed on *Harmer v. Cornelius* (1858) 5 CBNS 236 which was concerned with the implication of a warranty of competence.

[508] *Pinkerton v. Hollis Bros* 1989 SLT 165, OH.

[509] Bell, *Commentaries* I, 489; Bell, *Principles*, ss. 152–154, 178–189; *Gunn v. Ramsay*, above. But note that in *Heddel v. Duncan*, 5 June 1810 FC, 681 it was held the employer could not expect of a 17-year-old the prudence of a man where the employee had acted in good faith.

[510] *Pinkerton v. Hollis Bros* 1989 SLT 165, OH.

[511] Bell, *Principles*, s. 153. *Gunn v. Ramsay*, above; *McNally v. Welltrade International Ltd* [1978] IRLR 497, QBD.

[512] Lord Fraser, *Master and Servant* (3rd edn), pp. 68, 69.

[513] *Clydesdale Bank v. Beatson* (1882) 10 R 88. And see *Janata Bank v. Ahmed* [1981] ICR 791, CA (bank employee allowed unsecured overdraft facilities without making adequate checks on the credit-worthiness of the borrower).

[514] [1957] AC 555, HL.

Lister's employer's insurers relying on their right of subrogation[515] insisted that Lister's employers sue him for breach of contract, namely, his failure to perform his duties with reasonable care. In partial mollification of this decision British insurance companies have, in a "gentleman's agreement", undertaken not to exercise subrogation rights against employees.[516] However, where insurance contracts are not involved the ruling in *Lister*[517] highlights the vulnerability of an employee whose employer (or liquidator) chooses to exercise his right of indemnity[518] and probably for this reason the English courts have attempted to curtail its impact.[519] Thus in *Harvey v. R. G. O'Dell Ltd*[520] the decision in *Lister* was distinguished on somewhat transparent grounds while in *Morris v. Ford Motor Co. Ltd*[521] it was not regarded as just and equitable to force Ford Motor Co. Ltd to allow their employee to be sued in their name and, in the industrial setting of the case, there was an implied term which excluded the exercise of subrogation rights against employee.[522] How the Scottish courts would react to circumstances similar to those in *Lister* or *Morris* is a matter of conjecture; while the underlying principles are similar[523] whether the attitudes demonstrated by *Morris* and *Harvey v. R. G. O'Dell*[524] would be reflected in Scotland must await further decision.

RESPECT AND OBEDIENCE

3.39 The attitude of the older law

The older law, perhaps because many employees worked in and around their employer's home, stressed the employee's duty of respectful behaviour towards his employer and family. Thus writing in 1882 Lord Fraser stated, "It is the duty of the servant at all times to conduct himself towards his master or mistress in a

---

[515] This is a right almost invariably found in contracts of insurance, indemnity and guarantee to the effect that, in the case of an insurance contract, the insurer is entitled to exercise any rights available to the insured to recover monies paid out under the insurance contract.

[516] There is the proviso that there is no wilful misconduct or collusion and the gentleman's agreement relates only to personal injury claims. See Glanville Williams, "Vicarious Liability and the Master's Indemnity" (1952) 20 MLR 220, 437; G. Gardiner "Reports of Committees" (1959) 22 MLR 652.

[517] By a majority of 3 to 2 their Lordships rejected the plea that if such a right of indemnity existed it was accompanied by the duty that the employer should maintain insurance to cover the employee's potential liability.

[518] See *Janata Bank v. Ahmed*, above.

[519] Arguably such an exercise should be undertaken by the legislature.

[520] [1958] 2 QB 78. And see *Vandyke v. Fender* [1970] 2 QB 292, CA, *per* Denning MR at p. 303.

[521] [1973] QB 792, CA.

[522] M was injured as a result of the negligence of an employee of Ford Motor Co. Ltd; however by the commercial (cleaning) contract between Ford and M's employer (the cleaning contractors) the latter undertook to indemnify Ford against all claims by their own employees even if caused by the negligence of employees of Ford. M recovered damages from Ford which, on the basis of the indemnity, M's employers were required to meet, but the Court of Appeal refused to allow M's employers to subrogate themselves to the right of Ford and thereby recover the award of damages directly from the negligent employee.

[523] There is no Scottish equivalent to the English Civil Liability (Contribution) Act 1978 by which a vicariously liable employer can recover a contribution from the negligent employee. The employer and employee are not jointly and severally liable, so s. 3(2) of the Law Reform (Miscellaneous Provisions) (Scotland) Act 1940 does not apply. But see D. M. Walker, *Delict* (2nd edn), pp. 125–126.

[524] [1958] 2 QB 78.

respectful manner; and there is no ground which the courts of law have been so uniform in holding a valid reason of dismissal as insolence on the part of the servant.''[525] And while it was always accepted that the degree of respect required to be exhibited by the employee would depend much on the employer's station and the nature of the work the employee was employed to do, employees have been lawfully dismissed for disrespect in the form of laughing and sneering at their employer's instructions[526] and for demonstrating a ''saucy and impertinent manner unbecoming the relative positions of the parties''.[527]

3.40 The modern law

Modern employment law having been developed by statutory provisions which seek to redress the inequality often inherent in the contract of employment, for example by enacting laws protecting against unfair dismissal and discrimination, now implies into the contract of employment the duty of ''mutual respect''[528] and an obligation not to do anything likely to undermine the trust and confidence on which the employment relationship is based.[529] Thus the extent to which an employee is contractually required to exhibit respect for his employer and other (senior) employees is to be determined having regard to these implied obligations giving weight to the status of the employee involved[530] with the proviso that an isolated, occasional or provoked outburst of anger or disrespectful language will seldom entitle an employer to rescind the contract and dismiss without notice.[531] However, today the extent to which an employee's disrespect justifies termination of his employment more commonly occurs in the context of unfair dismissal law[532] which permits the fair dismissal of an employee where the reason for his dismissal relates to his conduct[533] or is for some other substantial reason.[534]

3.41 Obedience

The obligation of an employee to carry out his employer's instructions also straddles contract and unfair dismissal law and it is worth noting that although in an unfair dismissal complaint the essence of the matter is whether the employer acted fairly in dismissing the employee the extent of the employee's contractual duties will be relevant.[535] However, it is trite law that an employee who deliberately refuses to carry out his employer's clearly communicated[536] and

---

[525] *Master and Servant* (3rd edn), p. 70.

[526] *Ibid.* p. 71.

[527] *Ibid.*

[528] *Wilson v. Racher* [1974] ICR 428, CA; and see para. 3.35.

[529] See para. 3.35. The implication of such a duty is often relied on by an employee to challenge the action of his employer (usually in the context of constructive dismissal).

[530] See Lord Fraser, *Master and Servant* (3rd edn), p. 71.

[531] *Ibid.*; and see *Wilson v. Racher*, above. *Cf Pepper v. Webb* [1969] 1 WLR 514, CA.

[532] See Chapter Five. In a contractual context any doubt as to whether the perceived lack of respect justifies termination can be avoided by either giving notice or wages in lieu of notice.

[533] ERA, s. 98(2)(b). See *Whitlow v. Alkanet Construction Ltd* [1975] IRLR 321, IT (employee engaging in sexual activity with managing director's wife).

[534] ERA, s. 98(1)(b). See *Boychuk v. H. J. Symons Holdings Ltd* [1977] IRLR 395, EAT (employer entitled to order the removal of lapel badges displaying the slogan ''Lesbians Ignite'' as potentially offensive to customers and fellow employees).

[535] *Wicks v. Charles A. Smethurst Ltd* [1973] IRLR 327, IT.

[536] *Thomson v. Douglas* (1807) Hume 392.

lawful instructions will be in material breach of his contract[537] and where an employer has issued rules or instructions whose purpose is to secure the efficient operation of his undertaking it will be a breach of the employee's implied duty if he sets about interpreting them in an unreasonable manner designed to defeat that purpose. Thus in *Secretary of State for Employment v. ASLEF (No. 2)*[538] when members of the trade union ASLEF engaged in industrial action which took the form of a rigid adherence to the British Railways Board Rule Book, which contained 239 rules, they were held to breach the implied term of their contracts that they would "not, in obeying ... lawful instructions, seek to obey them in a wholly unreasonable way which has the effect of disrupting the system, the efficient running of which (they are) employed to ensure."[539] Similarly, control of the work method is the prerogative of the employer subject to the proviso that any alteration of the work method must not fundamentally change the nature of the employee's job. Thus in *Cresswell v. Board of Inland Revenue*[540] employees who refused to use a computer to do their work which previously had been done manually using pen, paper and pocket calculator were acting in breach of contract by not observing their employer's instructions regarding how their tasks should be accomplished.[541]

3.42 Industrial action

In *Secretary of State for Employment v. ASLEF (No. 2)*[542] the industrial action which occurred can be described as a "work-to-rule". However, most other forms of industrial action are likely to involve a breach of contract with the possible exception of a "work-to-contract" whereby employees deliberately restrict their performance to that which can be required by reference to the express terms of their contract. What must not be overlooked, however, is the ability of courts to supplement contracts by interpretation or implication of terms so that what employees regard as the limits of their contractual obligations are extended. Examples of this may be seen in *Sim v. Rotherham Metropolitan Borough Council*[543] and *British Telecommunications v. Ticehurst*.[544] In the former school-teachers refused to fill in for absent colleagues believing, in the absence of an express contractual term, they had no obligation to do so. It was held, however, that Sim, as a secondary schoolteacher had an implied obligation to stand in for absent colleagues on the basis that the contracts of professional employees could not normally be expected to detail the duties of the employee under the contract; the contractual obligations are largely defined by the nature of their professions and teachers have a professional obligation to co-operate in the running of the school in accordance with the timetable and other reasonable administrative

---

[537] Lord Fraser, *Master and Servant* (3rd edn), pp. 70–73; *Thomson v. Stewart* (1888) 15 R 806.

[538] [1972] 2 QB 455, CA.

[539] *Ibid. per* Roskill LJ. Alternatively by seeking to interpret the employer's instructions in an unreasonable way the employees could have been in breach of their implied duty of faithful service. See in particular the judgment of Buckley LJ.

[540] [1984] IRLR 190, ChD.

[541] Note, however, the reservation of Walton J that the employer must provide any necessary training but that "it can hardly be considered that to ask an employee to acquire basic skills as to retrieving information from a computer or feeding such information into a computer is something in the slightest esoteric or ... unusual".

[542] [1972] 1 QB 455, CA.

[543] [1986] ICR 897.

[544] [1992] ICR 383, CA.

arrangements. In the latter Ticehurst was employed as a manager by British Telecommunications (BT) who were in dispute with her trade union which resulted in it calling on members including Ticehurst to take strike action and generally withdraw goodwill in their dealings with BT. Ticehurst, after taking strike action, refused to sign an undertaking that she would thenceforth ''work normally in accordance with the terms of my contract,'' because it implied she had not been prepared to do so sooner and was held to be in breach of the implied term in the contract of employment that an employee, entrusted with responsibility and discretion in supervising other employees, would not participate in an act such as a concerted withdrawal of goodwill where that was done not in an honest exercise of discretion but to cause maximum inconvenience.[545] A strike is a breach of contract,[546] as is ''blacking'', whereby employees refuse to do particular duties usually as a result of a refusal to handle goods which, for example, have originated from an enterprise involved in a trade dispute[547] and, arguably, a ''go-slow''.[548]

3.43 General limits

Industrial action by employees aside, it is clear that an employer's right to insist that employees carry out his instructions is subject to the following limitations:
(1)   Generally an employee is not required to carry out an instruction which would require him to do work outside the scope of his contract[549]; exceptionally in an emergency an employee is required to accommodate the urgent and necessary requirements of his employer's business.[550] In many cases the parameters of the scope of the contract will be contained in a job description which, either expressly or by implication, will have been imported into the contract of employment. In such a case whether a particular function or task falls within the scope of the contract is a matter of interpretation but generally courts will be reluctant to extend an expressed range of specific duties or responsibilities. On the other hand where there is imported into the contract a brief job title or a general description of a particular post an extension to include related duties not previously performed will be relatively easy. Thus where an employee's job title was ''clerk/typist'' that was wide enough to include an obligation to do photocopying.[551] However, it is important to note that in determining the scope of the contract it is necessary to take into account the circumstances surrounding the nomenclature of the job title. Thus in deciding whether an employee whose letter of appointment included the job title ''assistant speech therapist'' and who had always worked with school children could be required to work with geriatric patients and do a wide range of clerical and other duties, it was necessary to take account of (a) the fact that the

---

[545] See also *Miles v. Wakefield Metropolitan District Council* [1987] ICR 368, HL; *Wiluszynski v. London Borough of Tower Hamlets* [1989] ICR 493, CA.

[546] *Simmons v. Hoover Ltd* [1977] ICR 61, EAT. And see paras 2.14, 3.9.

[547] See, for example, *Hadmor Productions Ltd v. Hamilton* [1982] IRLR 102, HL.

[548] Kahn-Freund maintains in *Labour and the Law* (2nd edn), p. 265 that a ''go-slow'' would be a breach of the implied obligation to work at a reasonable speed.

[549] *Moffat v. Boothby* (1894) 11 R 501; *London Borough of Redbridge v. Fishman* [1978] ICR 569, EAT.

[550] *Wilson v. Simson* (1844) 6 D 1256; *Sim v. Rotherham Metropolitan Borough Council*, above. And note the unreported decision of the NIRC (1972) in *Smith v. St Andrew's Scottish Ambulance Service* to the effect that it was fair to dismiss an employee who refused to pick up a seriously ill child because the journey could not have been completed before the end of his contractual working hours.

[551] *Glitz v. Watford Electric Co. Ltd* [1979] IRLR 89, EAT; *Churcher v. Weyside Engineering (1926) Ltd* [1976] IRLR 402, IT.

employee's initial appointment was in the department of the director of education to whom the employee was responsible, (b) the subsequent actings of the employee and her employers and (c) the type of work the employee had actually done prior to the attempted change of duties.[552]

(2)   An employee is not required to carry out an instruction which would involve him committing an illegal act.[553] Thus an employee cannot be required to falsify a record that his employer requires him to keep.[554] However, it has been held that it is not immoral to require employees to participate in broadcasts to a country which operates a policy of apartheid[555]; nor is a medical secretary who was required to type a letter arranging a patient's referral to a consultant to enable the formation of an opinion as to whether the patient's pregnancy should be terminated under the Abortion Act 1967 being required to "participate in any treatment" authorised by that Act.[556] Similarly while every prison officer has the powers of a constable[557] there was no implied term in his contract of employment entitling him to refuse to obey instructions to admit prisoners even when he genuinely feared that the prison was so overcrowded that there was a danger of a breach of the peace occurring because while the contractual duty of the prison officer was only to carry out lawful orders, an order of a prison governor did not become unlawful simply because a prison officer took the view that compliance with it would lead to a breach of the peace.[558]

(3)   An employee is entitled to refuse to carry out an instruction which would expose him to an unreasonable risk which the employment did not contemplate. Thus the crew of a merchant vessel were entitled to refuse to sail the ship to Nagasaki in Japan even although that was within the articles the crew had signed because the ship's cargo (coal) had been declared contraband in the war between Russia and Japan; according to Lord Stormonth-Darling ''... it had been held that in view of the proximity of belligerent ships, special risks, not covered by the crew's agreements did exist. It is therefore plain that the whole question turned ... on whether the crew having signed an agreement to service on an ordinary commercial voyage subject only to the perils of the sea, were justified in refusing to serve after the agreement had been broken by the shipowner requiring them to serve on a voyage, which although within the geographical limits of the articles, was attended with risks not contemplated by these articles.''[559] Similarly requiring a seaman to work in a small area within 8–10 feet of the stern of the vessel in severe weather conditions with winds of force 7–8, rough seas and a swell in which the seaman was momentarily submerged by a breaking sea and feared he could be swept overboard could breach ''an important term of the contract of employment that an employer would not require an employee to work in conditions which are intolerable and that conditions which present a danger to life

---

[552] *Greater Glasgow Health Board v. Pate* [1983] SLT 90; *Dunbar v. Baillie (Contractors) Ltd* 1990 GWD 26-1487. *Cf London Borough of Redbridge v. Fishman*, above.

[553] Lord Fraser, *Master and Servant* (3rd edn), p. 27.

[554] *Morrish v. Henlys (Folkstone) Ltd* [1973] ICR 482, NIRC.

[555] *BBC v. Hearn* [1977] ICR 685, CA. But consider the legislation preventing trade with certain foreign countries.

[556] *R. v. Salford Health Authority, ex p Janaway* [1989] AC 537, HL.

[557] Prisons Act 1952, s. 8.

[558] *Secretary of State for the Home Department v. Barnes, The Times*, December 12, 1994, QB.

[559] *Lang v. St Enoch Shipping Co. Ltd* 1908 SC 103; and see *Burton v. Pinkerton* (1867) LR 2 Ex 340; *Ferrie v. Western No. 3 District Council* [1973] IRLR 162, IT. Also contrast *Ottoman Bank v. Chakarian* [1930] AC 277, PC with *Bouzourou v. Ottoman Bank* [1930] AC 271, PC and *Walmsley (F. G.) v. Udec Refrigeration Ltd* [1972] IRLR 80, IT.

can properly be regarded as intolerable''[560]; and even where an employee's employment contract designated Ireland as part of his area he could have been justified in refusing to go to Belfast (but not Wexford) since that would have involved a serious risk not contemplated at the time of the formation of the contract.[561]

FIDELITY

3.44 Introduction

While it does not involve *uberrima fides* (utmost good faith) and, generally, there is no duty on the employee to disclose his own misconduct or that of a fellow employee[562] there is no doubt that there is implied into the contract of employment an obligation of fidelity or loyalty on the employee's part. However, as has been observed[563] this branch of the law of Scotland is ''somewhat obscure and not fully developed''. Perhaps because the limits of the implied obligation are unclear most employers seek to protect themselves against the risk of employees and ex-employees harming their businesses by requiring the employee to agree to an express contractual term — a restrictive covenant — by which such a risk may be eliminated or reduced. Such covenants are treated separately[564] and while, if properly drawn, they are generally more effective than relying on the implied term it is nevertheless necessary to consider the latter which will be of considerable significance where no express clause exists.[565]

3.45 The implied duty

Although the implied duty is couched in general terms of loyal service, litigation tends to relate to (1) restraints on an employee acting in competition with his employer, (2) protection of trade secrets and confidential information against misuse by employees, and (3) the rights of an employee to engage in spare-time work or to obtain earnings from secondary employment.[566] However, before dealing with these issues it has been stated as a general principle that the loyal employee must, within the sphere of his employment, use all reasonable means to advance his employer's business and refrain from any activity which would injure that business[567] or in slightly different language that the employee has a duty to serve with good faith and fidelity[568] so that where a conflict arises he must place his employer's interests before his own[569] for example by informing his employer that one of his (major) clients is dissatisfied instead of saying nothing and accepting the

---

[560] *Knight v. Barra Shipping Co. Ltd*, unreported, case no. 187/92, EAT.

[561] *Walmsley (F. G.) v. Udec Refrigeration Ltd*, above.

[562] *Sybron Corporation v. Rochem Ltd* [1983] IRLR 253, CA.

[563] *Chill Foods (Scotland) Ltd v. Cool Foods Ltd* 1977 SLT 38 at p. 40, *per* Lord Maxwell.

[564] See para. 3.50.

[565] While there is no direct authority it seems that the implied term and the express covenant can co-exist and the former can be relied on in the event of the latter being unenforceable: *Roger Bullivant Ltd v. Ellis* [1987] IRLR 491, CA.

[566] And see the political restrictions on certain local government employees: Local Government and Housing Act 1989, ss. 1–3.

[567] *Malloch v. Duffy* (1882) 19 SLR 697, OH; *Graham v. R. & S. Paton Ltd* 1917 1 SLT 66, IH, *per* Lord McKenzie at p. 69.

[568] *Hivac Ltd v. Park Royal Scientific Instruments Ltd* [1946] Ch 169, CA; *Faccenda Chicken Ltd v. Fowler* [1986] ICR 297, CA.

[569] *Boston Deep Sea Fishing & Ice Co. Ltd v. Ansell* (1888) 39 Ch D 339, CA.

client's offer of employment.[570] However, while it must be stressed that these are general principles whose effect and impact are largely influenced by the facts and circumstances of the employment[571] an employer is not entitled to require an employee to produce any document in his possession which relates to the employer's business and which the employer has a legitimate interest in seeing because, although an employee owes duties of good faith to his employer and must comply with all reasonable requests which are lawful and within the scope of his employment, in this case the documents were transcripts of interviews between the employee and a liquidator who had obtained an order for his examination under the Insolvency Act 1986 and were not created or obtained[572] by the employee in the course of his employment.

3.46 *Competition.* The implied duty of fidelity does not prevent an employee from purchasing commodities in which his employer deals[573] nor from working as an unskilled employee for a competitor of his employer.[574] However, it is important to distinguish the employee who during his contract of employment but in his own time forms an intention to compete with his employer in the future (even although he writes to suppliers and declares his intention to them) from a managing director who forms a scheme with another manager to set up in competition in order to take away the business of the employer's best client and an employee who tenders for work currently carried out by his employer or one who, during his notice period, seeks an order from one of his employer's customers. The actions of the first employee are not a breach of the implied duty while those of the others are[575] and, while it is a delictual wrong knowingly and without justification to induce a fellow employee to break his contract of employment, for example by leaving without proper notice or disclosing confidential information, it is also a breach of the implied duty of fidelity for an employee who proposes to set up in competition with his employer to offer employment to a fellow employee.[576] Although much will depend on the nature of the employment and the type of work in which the employee is engaged[577] it seems logical that the implied term should not enable the employer to prohibit all employment for a competitor in his spare time during the currency of the contract when such an objective cannot be obtained by an express term after the contract has ended and those decisions which relate the right to work for a competitor to the nature of the employment and the type of work[578] are to be

---

[570] *Sanders v. Parry* [1967] 1 WLR 753.

[571] *Faccenda Chicken Ltd v. Fowler,* above, per Neill LJ at p. 309.

[572] *Macmillan Incorporated v. Bishopgate Investment Trust plc* [1993] IRLR 393, Ch D.

[573] *Graham v. R. & S. Paton Ltd,* above, in which Lord President Strathclyde seemed prepared to allow an employee to purchase commodities in which his employer dealt even if he knew this would prejudice the employer.

[574] *Nova Plastics Ltd v. Froggatt* [1982] IRLR 146, EAT.

[575] Contrast *Laughton & Hawley v. Bapp Industrial Supplies Ltd* [1986] IRLR 245, EAT and *Balston v. Headline Filters* [1990] FSR 385 with *Marshall v. Industrial Systems and Control Ltd* [1992] IRLR 294, EAT and *Adamson v. B & L Cleaning Services Ltd* [1995] IRLR 193, EAT.

[576] *Balston v. Headline Filters Ltd,* above. *Cf Hanover Insurance Brokers v. Schapiro* [1994] IRLR 82, CA.

[577] See particularly the judgment of Lord Greene MR in *Hivac Ltd v. Park Royal Scientific Instruments Ltd* [1946] Ch 169, CA.

[578] *Hivac Ltd v. Park Royal Scientific Instruments Ltd,* above; *Harris & Russell Ltd v. Slingsby* [1973] IRLR 221, NIRC; *United Sterling Corporation Ltd v. Felton* [1974] IRLR 314, Ch; *Nova Plastics Ltd v. Froggatt,* above.

preferred to those which suggest the implied term necessarily precludes any working for a competitor.[579]

3.47 *Confidential information.* Although it is not a crime for an employee dishonestly to exploit his employer's confidential information,[580] unless disclosure can be justified by considering the public interest[581] it is a breach of the employee's implied duty to reveal or misuse his employer's trade secrets or information imparted to him in confidence[582] and an employer to whom an employee (or ex-employee) owed a duty of confidence had a right to protect confidentiality against others (for example other employers) who had received the information with the knowledge that it has originally been communicated in confidence.[583] Clearly whether a duty of confidence exists in respect of information is a question of law[584] and although the limits of the duty will depend on the particular facts of the case it has been observed that " 'confidential' does not merely mean secret ... in this branch of the law the expression 'confidential' relates to information which is the subject of an obligation of confidence".[585] Thus the mere fact that the information has become known to a third party or has been published in some limited way will not *per se* mean that a court will not grant an interdict to prevent further disclosure of confidential information[586] although there must come a stage at which publication has become so widespread that the information can no longer be regarded as confidential.[587] In *Faccenda Chicken Ltd v. Fowler*[588] the Court of Appeal endorsed the rule that after the employment is terminated the implied duty in relation to confidential information — while still in existence – is considerably restricted to the obligation not to misuse or disclose information which is a secret process, design or method or information of a sufficiently high degree of confidentiality to amount to a trade secret unless the information has become part of the ex-employee's own skill or knowledge even though acquired during employment.[589] Where the employment is continuing then the employee must not misuse or disclose (1) information which is imparted to him in confident, or (2) specific trade secrets even though he knows the information by heart.[590] The extent of the duty varies according to the nature of the contract but would be broken by an

---

[579] E.g. *Malloch v. Duffy* (1882) 19 SLR 697, OH.

[580] *Grant v. Allan* 1988 SLT 11.

[581] *Initial Services Ltd v. Putterill* [1958] 1 QB 396, CA; *Lion Laboratories Ltd v. Evans* [1985] QB 526, CA; *In Re A Company's Application* [1989] IRLR 477, Ch D.

[582] Lord Fraser, *Master and Servant* (3rd edn), p. 98; *Robb v. Green* [1985] 2 QB 315, CA in which Lord Esher MR stated "... it is impossible to suppose that an [employer] would have put an [employee] into a confidential position of this kind unless he thought that [he] would be bound to use good faith towards [the employer]; or that [the employee] would not know ... the [employer] would rely on his observance of good faith in the confidential relation between them".

[583] *Lord Advocate v. Scotsman Publications Ltd* 1988 SLT 490, *per* LJ-C Ross at p. 503 where his Lordship also opines that the laws of Scotland and England are to the same effect.

[584] *General Nutritions Ltd v. Yates, The Times,* June 6, 1981.

[585] *Lord Advocate v. Scotsman Publications Ltd* 1988 SLT 490 *per* LJ-C Ross at p. 503.

[586] *Ibid.*; see also *Speed Seal Products Ltd v. Paddington* [1986] 1 All ER 91, CA.

[587] Compare, for example, *Lord Advocate v. Scotsman Publications Ltd*, above, with *Attorney-General v. Guardian Newspapers Ltd (No. 2)* [1988] 2 WLR 805, CA.

[588] [1986] ICR 297, CA.

[589] E.g. *United Sterling Corporation Ltd v. Felton* [1974] IRLR 314, Ch; and see *Cantor Fitzgerald (UK) Ltd v. Wallace* [1992] IRLR 215 and *Balston v. Headline Filters* [1990] FSR 385.

[590] *Faccenda Chicken Ltd v. Fowler*, above; and see *Chill Foods (Scotland) Ltd v. Cool Foods Ltd* 1977 SLT 38, OH. *Cf Balston v. Headline Filters* [1990] FSR 385.

employee copying or memorising a list of his employer's customers for transmission to a third party or for use after his employment ended.[591]

3.48 *Confidential information after the contract ends.* The nature of the restriction regarding confidential information after termination of employment is well illustrated by *Faccenda Chicken Ltd v. Fowler* in which Fowler left his position as sales manager of Faccenda Chicken Ltd to set up business selling fresh chickens from refrigerated vans in the same area as that in which Faccenda Chicken Ltd operated a similar business. However, Faccenda Chicken Ltd alleged that Fowler in his own enterprise was wrongly making use of their "sales information" comprising (1) the names and addresses of Faccenda's customers and their usual requirements, (2) the most convenient routes for the itinerant refrigerated vans as well as the customers' preferred delivery days and times and (3) the price structure used for respective customers which, they maintained, when taken as a whole constituted confidential information. Neill LJ re-stated that while the ex-employee's obligation might cover secret processes of manufacture and other information of a high degree of confidentiality so as to amount to a trade secret it probably did not extend to information which was "confidential" only in that had it been disclosed while the contract of employment was subsisting it would have been a breach of the implied duty of fidelity[592] and in order to determine whether after employment the use or disclosure of information may be restricted he identified the following matters requiring consideration — (1) the nature of the employment, (2) the nature of the information, in particular can it be equated with a trade secret, (3) has the employer stressed to the employee the confidentiality of the information[593] and (4) whether the (confidential) information can be easily isolated from that which the ex-employee is free to use and disclose. In the event the sales information was not regarded as having the degree of confidentiality to prevent its use or disclosure because the information was necessarily acquired by Fowler in his employment, was widely known at junior levels (van drivers and secretaries) and the confidential nature of the information had not been emphasised. The approach adopted in *Fowler* has been followed in Scotland in *Harben Pumps (Scotland) Ltd v. Lafferty.*[594]

3.49 *Spare time working.* Where the contract of employment requires him to be at work the employee must apply himself exclusively to the performance of the contract at the relevant times.[595] Generally, therefore, employees are free to take on employment at other times subject to two provisos: (1) The other (subsidiary) work does not affect his efficient performance of the original (main) contract. So where

---

[591] *Faccenda Chicken Ltd.* And see *Robb v. Green* [1895] 2 QB 315, CA; *Liverpool Victoria Friendly Society v. Houston* (1900) 3 F 42.

[592] And see Cross J in *Printers & Finishers Ltd v. Holloway* [1965] RPC 239 at 253 — "In this connection ... not all information which is given to a servant in confidence and which it would be a breach of his duty for him to disclose to another person during his employment is a trade secret which he can be prevented from using for his own advantage after the employment is over ... It would have been a breach of duty [for Holloway] to divulge any of the [printing instructions handed to him to be used during his employment] to a stranger while he was employed, but many of these instructions are not really 'trade secrets' at all ... but in so far as the instructions cannot be called 'trade secrets' and he carried them in his head, he is entitled to use them for his benefit or for the benefit of a future employer."

[593] But labelling information "confidential" is of no effect: *Mainmet Holdings v. Austin* [1991] FSR 538.

[594] 1989 SLT 752, OH.

[595] *Cameron & Co. v. Gibb* (1867) 3 SLR 282.

a clerk of works engaged for a particular building project took on work for other building contractors and his main employers contended that by doing so he was in breach of his contract Lord Pearson who was unable to accept the contention stated, "of course if the accumulation of other work leads to the inefficient performance of the duties ... the employer has a remedy ... Here no suggestion is made that the pursuer's superintendence was in any sense inefficient. There is no stipulation in the contract as to giving whole time; and ... I do not see my way to reach the conclusion that the remuneration stipulated is so high as to import an obligation to give his full time and take no other job."[596] However, consideration must be given to the possibility of skilled technical, research or senior employees revealing to a competitor, by spare time working, their main employer's technical or manufacturing data in which case a breach of the implied duty is at least arguable[597] whereas other classes of employee will require restrictions on their spare time activity to be the subject of an express clause.[598] (2) Any loss caused to the main employer as a result of subsidiary employment or activity in breach of the implied duty of fidelity is recoverable and secondary earnings or profits have to be accounted for.[599]

3.50 The express covenant

As indicated previously employers frequently seek to protect their interests against the activities of employees and ex-employees by inserting into the contract of employment[600] a clause or covenant which, for example, might restrict the employee's right to work in his spare time or, more commonly, to engage in new employment after termination of a previous contract.[601] Such restrictive covenants are to be construed fairly and in context and it is the duty of a court to give effect to them as expressed and not to correct their errors and supply their omissions.[602] Thus where a covenant prevented an employee/shareholder from "carrying on business in competition with the employer/company or any of its subsidiaries" without preventing him from becoming a director or employee of a competing business the court, emphasising the distinction between an individual carrying on business and a company carrying on business, refused to interdict the employee/shareholder from becoming a director of a competing company[603]; and while it has been queried whether a restrictive covenant is binding in a contract of employment which is the subject of the Transfer of Undertakings (Protection of Employment)

---

[596] *Currie v. Glasgow Central Stores Ltd* 1905, 12 SLT 651, OH.

[597] *Hivac Ltd v. Park Royal Scientific Instruments* [1946] Ch 169, CA.

[598] *Nova Plastics Ltd v. Froggatt* [1982] IRLR 146, EAT.

[599] *Boston Deep Sea Fishing and Ice Co v. Ansell* [1888] 39 Ch D 339, CA. And see *Reading v. Attorney-General* 1951 AC 507, in which a resourceful soldier by accompanying, in uniform, vehicles carrying illicit alcohol received about £20,000 when the vehicles, through his presence, avoided being examined by the police. He had no right to retain the money so earned. *Cf Attorney-General v. Blake, The Times*, April 23, 1996, Ch D.

[600] Typically, restrictive covenants are part of the contract of employment but equally may be contained in subsidiary or *ad hoc* agreements provided they are referable to the contract of employment: *Stenhouse Australia Ltd v. Phillips* [1974] AC 391, PC.

[601] It is also helpful to insert an express clause that on termination the employee will deliver up all papers, property etc. of the employer which may be in his possession.

[602] *Home Counties Dairies v. Skilton* [1970] 1 WLR 526; *Hanover Insurance Brokers v. Schapiro* [1994] IRLR 82, CA. *Cf J. A. Mont (UK) Ltd v. Mills* [1993] IRLR 172, CA.

[603] *WAC Ltd v. Whillock* 1990 SLT 213, IH. Also note the (unanswered) question whether the rights of subsidiaries can be protected by means of a contract between the parent company and its employees/directors.

Regulations 1981[604] the Court of Appeal has preferred to construe the restriction in such a way that the quality of the burden on the employee is not substantially altered. Thus, where the employee had agreed that he would not for a period of one year after ceasing his employment seek to do business with any person or firm which had done business with the employers in the period of the year before the cessation of his employment, it was held that after the employer's business was sold the new owner could enforce the covenant in respect of those who had done business with the seller/employer but not in respect of those who had done business with the purchaser/employer.[605] Although there is no reported Scots authority dealing with the enforceability of a contractual term which prevents an ex-employee from inviting current employees from leaving their employment, the issue has come before the Court of Appeal; unfortunately the decisions seem to contradict each other. In *Hanover Insurance Brokers v. Schapiro*[606] such a contractual term was held to be unenforceable on the ground that an employee has the right to work for whatever employer is willing to employ him although the principle seems to have become confused by considering whether it would apply to all employees, irrespective of seniority and when their employment began. More recently in *Alliance Paper Group plc v. Prestwich*[607] a covenant against poaching existing employees was upheld on the ground that the employer had a legitimate interest in maintaining a stable trained workforce in a highly competitive business. Before a Scottish court was to decide how to approach such a covenant it may be necessary for it to consider the following questions: (a) while for covenants against competition by former employees it is apt to consider whether there exists a legitimate interest which requires protection, is it correct to use the same criteria for anti-poaching covenants bearing in mind that the employer is already in a contractual relationship with his employees whereas that will seldom be the case regarding existing customers; (b) the employer can ensure the services of his employees by appropriate contractual provisions including inserting restrictive covenants into their own contracts; (c) it is not necessarily the case that the value of an employee to an employer has been enhanced by training which the employer has provided and (d) even in the absence of an express term which prohibits employment by a competitor, an employer may always rely on the ex-employee's implied duty to protect confidential information. Further, the issue of the enforceability of an anti-poaching clause must be seen against the background of the employer's existing delictual action to restrain the actions of an ex-employee from inducing the breach of a contract of employment knowingly and without justification.

3.51 *Pacta illicita.* Whether a covenant is in restraint of trade depends on its substance[608] and an employer's right to enforce restrictive covenants is subject to the following two overriding principles: (1) such covenants will be regarded by the courts as *pacta illicita* if the restriction is wider than necessary to protect the legitimate interests of the employer and (2) exclusion of competition *per se* is not a legitimate interest for protection because public policy demands that trade shall be free to everybody.[609] Thus while an employer is not permitted through such a

---

[604] *Initial Services Ltd v. McCall* 1992 SLT 67, OH.
[605] *Morris Angel & Son Ltd v. Hollande* [1993] IRLR 169, CA.
[606] [1994] IRLR 82, CA.
[607] [1996] IRLR 25, CA; and see *Ingham v. ABC Contracts Ltd*, unreported, CA.
[608] *Stenhouse Australia Ltd v. Phillips* [1974] AC 391.
[609] *Scottish Farmers Dairy Co. (Glasgow) Ltd v. McGhee* 1933 SC 148.

covenant to secure for himself an advantage he would not otherwise be able to secure, he is entitled to prevent an ex-employee taking up particular employment if that is necessary to protect the employer's confidential information or trade connections.[610] However, a non-solicitation clause may be all that is necessary to protect the employer's declared interest (the protection of goodwill), in which case a restriction on employment or competition is likely to be regarded as too wide[611] but where there are groups of companies it appears that the Scottish courts are prepared to lift the corporate veil in order to determine the extent of an employer's legitimate interests.[612] Where a restriction applies to protect not just the business of the employing company an employee, before signing the covenant, would be well advised to ascertain roughly the type of work carried out by the other companies in the group although it is always possible for him to argue that the restriction is too wide on the grounds that he had only had dealings with customers of the employing company.[613] In certain special types of employment an employer may not claim a proprietary interest in trade connections built up by the employee as a result of his personal qualities.[614] In certain circumstances the provisions of the Restrictive Trade Practices Act 1976 may operate to invalidate an agreement.[615] However, the Restrictive Trade Practices (Services) (Amendment) Order 1989 now provides that registration of the covenant is not necessary where there is a sale or purchase of 50% or more of the issued share capital of a business or where there is transferred the whole of the vendor's interest in a business and as the 1976 Act only applies where two or more people are carrying on business it follows that no registration is necessary where in the normal case the covenant is between an employee and an employer for only the latter is a person carrying on business.[616]

3.52 *Reasonableness.* Having been satisfied that the employer has a legitimate interest to protect, it is then necessary to consider whether the particular covenant is reasonable as between the parties and in terms of the public interest.[617] This involves a consideration of the geographical area and the duration of the restraint as well as the duties of the ex-employee. Previous decisions are no more than examples of whether a restriction has been regarded as reasonable in the particular circumstances of the case. Thus a restrictive covenant in the contract of employment of a trainee manager employed by a company which manufactured jeans that for a period of two years after the end of his employment he would not perform any services for any person or business entity in competition with his employers has been held to be reasonable even though the restriction was world-wide and it

---

[610] See, for example, *A & D Bedrooms Ltd v. Michael* 1984 SLT 297, OH; *Rentokil Ltd v. Hampton* 1982 SLT 422, OH; *PR Consultants Scotland Ltd v. Mann* [1996] IRLR 188, OH.

[611] *Office Angels Ltd v. Rainer Thomas* [1991] IRLR 214.

[612] See *Group 4 Security Ltd v. Ferrier* 1985 SC 70; *Hinton & Higgs Ltd v. Murphy* 1989 SLT 450, OH and *Hall Advertising Ltd v. Woodward*, unreported, July 1, 1992, OH. *Cf WAC Ltd v. Whillock*, above.

[613] See *Marley Tile Co. Ltd v. Johnson* [1982] IRLR 75; *Hanover Insurance Brokers v. Schapiro*, above.

[614] See, for example, *Cantor Fitzgerald (UK) Ltd v. Wallace* [1992] IRLR 215. *Cf Euro Brokers Ltd v. Rabey* [1995] IRLR 206.

[615] See *Donald Storrie Estate Agency Ltd v. Adams* 1989 SLT 305, OH; *Sterling Financial Services v. Johnson* 1990 SLT 111.

[616] SI 1989 No. 1082. And see *WAC Ltd v. Whillock*, above.

[617] On this latter ground it would seem that individuals who are not parties to an agreement may challenge its validity as it affects them; see *Kores Manufacturing Co. Ltd v. Kolok Manufacturing Co. Ltd* [1959] Ch 108, CA; *Eastham v. Newcastle United FC Ltd* [1964] Ch 413.

prevented him from working not merely in the jeans factories or departments of competitors but from being employed at all by a competitor during the short period of the restriction.[618] On the other hand a covenant that for a period of 18 months an employee would not work for any previous or present client of the pursuer's group of companies was held to be unreasonably wide because on the face of it it was world-wide and even if it were treated as applying only to the UK the restriction was too wide because the employee's areas of operation with his previous employer were both in Scotland.[619] While the facts of each case are obviously of great significance a contractual declaration of the reasonableness of a restrictive covenant is likely to be regarded as an illegitimate attempt to oust the jurisdiction of the court and therefore not conclusive and, generally, the reasonableness of a restriction has to be tested at the time the contract is made.[620] An example of a restriction being unreasonable in the public interest can be seen in *Bull v. Pitney-Bowes Ltd*[621] in which breach of the restraint resulted in a retired employee losing pension rights but the effect was to require a future employer to pay Bull an inflated salary to compensate for loss of his pension with the result that the costs of such a future employer would be artificially high and to that extent against the public interest.[622]

3.53 *Enforcement.* Relying on an English decision to the effect that a restrictive covenant which is phrased so as to operate on the termination of the employment of the employee, however that comes about and whether lawfully or not, is manifestly unreasonable[623] (on the grounds that it would appear to allow an employer to enforce a contractual term where an employee has rescinded following repudiation by the employer), a similarly worded covenant was held unenforceable in the Scottish case of *Living Design (Home Improvements) Ltd v. Davidson*[624] and that decision was applied in *Lux Traffic Control Ltd v. Healey.*[625] More recently, however, the Scottish courts have inclined to apply that approach only to cases in which the restriction had to be read as applying to cases of

---

[618] *Bluebell Apparel Ltd v. Dickinson* 1980 SLT 157.

[619] *Hinton & Higgs (UK) Ltd v. Murphy* 1989 SLT 450, OH; and see *Spencer v. Marchington* [1988] IRLR 393 in which the covenant which prohibited the ex-employee from being engaged in an employment agency or similar business within a radius of 25 miles of her former employer's place of business in Banbury was held to be too wide because the existing customers of the former employer were all, except one, within a 20-mile radius and, in practice, the restriction not only prevented the ex-employee from servicing customers inside the 25-mile radius but also for quite a distance outside because customers outside the area would look to Oxford or Northampton (within the 25-mile radius) and they would be prevented from going to an agency in which the ex-employee was concerned; note the similar approach adopted in *Dallas McMillan & Sinclair v. Simpson* 1989 SLT 464. And compare *Greer v. Sketchley Ltd* [1979] IRLR 445, CA, with *Littlewoods Organisation Ltd v. Harris* [1977] 1 WLR 1472, CA.

[620] *Hinton & Higgs (UK) Ltd v. Murphy*, above.

[621] [1967] 1 WLR 273.

[622] Similarly it was pointed out in *Stenhouse Australia Ltd v. Phillips* [1974] AC 391, PC, that a restraint cannot be disguised by permitting an ex-employee to contact any of his former employer's customers provided he pays a premium for each customer solicited; and similarly *Marshall v. N. M. Financial Management Ltd* [1995] ICR 1042, Ch D.

[623] *Briggs v. Oates* [1990] IRLR 472, Ch; and see *Dairy Crest Ltd v. Wise*, unreported, September 24, 1993, QBD.

[624] [1994] IRLR 69, OH.

[625] 1994 SLT 1153, OH; surprisingly, perhaps, the omission of the words "whether lawful or unlawful" was not regarded as significant.

unlawful termination by the employer.[626] Where a covenant is valid the employer is entitled to prevent an ex-employee from contacting all customers who fall within its scope notwithstanding that some customers no longer wish to patronise the employer.[627] Similarly while an invalid covenant cannot be cured by limiting the extent to which it is to be enforced[628] a covenant which contains several restrictions of which one (or more) is invalid may nevertheless be enforced in its remainder if the invalid restriction(s) can be severed, provided the invalid restriction is capable of removal without adding to or altering what remains and the removal of the invalid parts does not change the character of the contract.[629] Arguably, severance can only occur with regard to a part which is trivial or technical and not part of the substance of the covenant.[630] However, it seems competent for the parties to agree that if part of a restriction is found to be unenforceable it will nevertheless be applied in its amended or reduced state. Thus where the employer and employee agreed that if "a restriction[631] would be valid if some part thereof were deleted or the period of application reduced, such restriction shall apply with such modifications as may be necessary to make them valid or effective" their agreement was applied by the court which distinguished it from a request that the court re-write the contract[632] but it is doubtful whether such an express contractual term allows a court to do anything it could not do otherwise.[633]

PATENTS AND COPYRIGHT

3.54 Employee's inventions

As a result of the Patents Act 1977, notwithstanding any other rule of law, any invention[634] made by an employee, as between himself and his employer, is taken to belong to his employer if (a) the invention was made in the course of his normal duties or such other duties as were specifically assigned to him and an invention might reasonably be expected to result from carrying out those duties[635] or (b) the invention was made in the course of the employee's duties and at the time of making the invention, because of the nature of those duties and the responsibilities arising therefrom, the employee had a special obligation to further the interests of

---

[626] See *NCH (UK) Ltd v. Mair* 1994 GWD 34-1986; *Aramark plc v. Sommerville* 1995 SLT 749, OH; and *PR Consultants Scotland Ltd v. Mann* [1996] IRLR 188, OH.

[627] *John Michael Design plc v. Cooke* [1987] ICR 445, CA.

[628] *Agma Chemical Co. Ltd v. Hart* 1984 SLT 246, IH.

[629] *Sadler v. Imperial Life Assurance Co. of Canada Ltd* [1988] IRLR 388, QBD; and see *Lucas (T.) & Co. Ltd v. Mitchell* [1974] Ch 129, CA; *Rentokil Ltd v. Hampton* 1982 SLT 422, OH, where severance was suggested but rejected.

[630] Contrast *Living Design (Home Improvements) Ltd v. Davidson* [1994] IRLR 69, with *Marshall v. N. M. Financial Management* [1996] IRLR 20, Ch D.

[631] Which is found to be void.

[632] *Hinton & Higgs (UK) Ltd v. Murphy* 1989 SLT 450, OH. And see *WAC Ltd v. Whillock* [1990] IRLR 23, IH.

[633] *Living Design (Home Improvements) Ltd v. Davidson* [1994] IRLR 69.

[634] An invention is patentable only if it is new, involves an inventive step, is capable of industrial application and the grant of a patent is not excluded by the Patents Act 1977, s. 1(2), (3) (Patents Act 1977, s. 1(1)). Certain things are expressly excluded by Patents Act 1977, s. 12; e.g. (1) scientific theories, schemes for playing a game or doing business and (2) literary, dramatic, musical and artistic works as well as computer programs, but those in category (2) are the subject of copyright legislation.

[635] Patents Act 1977, s. 39(1)(a).

his employer's undertaking.[636] However, any other invention belongs to the employee.[637] An example of neither condition (a) nor (b) being satisfied is seen in *Reiss Engineering Co. Ltd v. Harris*[638] in which it was held that when Harris — who was employed as a sales manager in a company whose business involved the sale, but not the design or manufacture, of valves — invented a new kind of valve the invention belonged to him and not his employer, because he did not make the invention in the course of his normal or specially assigned duties and, unlike a managing director, Harris had no special duty to further his employer's interests. However, even though an employer has the right to an invention as a result of either condition (a) or (b) being satisfied he will invalidate the patent if he falsely declares that he and not the employee is the inventor[639] and since the rights of employee and employer to an invention are regulated solely by s. 39 of the 1977 Act no recourse can or need be made to the employee's implied duty of fidelity to determine to whom an invention made by an employee belongs.[640]

3.55 *Reduction of rights and compensation.* Any agreement[641] which purports to reduce an employee's rights to an invention is unenforceable,[642] and it is now provided[643] that where an invention belongs to an employee, nothing done by him in pursuing an application for a patent or performing or working the invention shall be taken to infringe any copyright or design right (in any model or document relating to the invention) to which, as between the employee and his employer, his employer is entitled. This is a useful provision because it attempts to ensure that an employee's rights in his own invention are not sterilised by the exercise of related design rights invested in his employer. Even where an invention of an employee belongs to his employer by virtue of s. 39 of the 1977 Act or where an employee has assigned his rights in an invention to his employer the employee-inventor may apply to the Comptroller-General of Patents, Designs and Trade Marks for an award of compensation under s. 40 of that Act.[644] The amount of the compensation should secure for the employee-inventor ''a fair share of . . . the benefit'' which the employer has derived or may derive.[645] However, an employee's right to apply to the Comptroller-General for compensation is defeated if there is a relevant collective agreement which provides for compensation.[646]

---

[636] *Ibid.* s. 39(1)(b).
[637] *Ibid.* s. 39(2).
[638] [1985] IRLR 232, Ch D.
[639] Patents Act 1977, s. 13(2).
[640] *Reiss Engineering Co. Ltd v. Harris,* above.
[641] Thus it would include contracts other than the contract of employment.
[642] Patents Act 1977, s. 42.
[643] Patents Act 1977, s. 39(3) introduced by the Copyright, Designs and Patents Act 1988, Sch. 5.
[644] For a discussion of the issues which arise under s. 40 see K. R. Wotherspoon, ''Employee Inventions Revisited'' (1993) 22 ILJ 119.
[645] Patents Act 1977, s. 41(1); relevant criteria for determining what is a fair share are set out in s. 41(4).
[646] ''Collective agreement'' has the meaning given by Trade Union and Labour Relations (Consolidation) Act 1992, s. 178 and an agreement is ''relevant'' if it is in force at the time of the invention and is made between a trade union, of which the employee is a member, and his employer or an association of which the employer is a member (Patents Act 1977, s. 40(6)).

3.56 *Copyright.* Although the law regarding copyright[647] has been substantially overhauled by the Copyright, Designs and Patents Act 1988[648] the law in respect of copyright in literary,[649] dramatic, musical or artistic works made by an employee in the course of his employment remains, in principle, as stated in the Copyright Act 1956 with the exception that the complicated provisions contained in s. 4(2) of that Act are now removed.[650] Thus, where an employee makes such a work in the course of his employment, his employer is the first owner of any copyright in the work subject to any agreement[651] to the contrary.[652] Accordingly, unless the work is made in the course of his employment an employee will be the first owner of any copyright in it[653] subject to any assignation of copyright prior to the work's creation.[654] It is worth noting that, unlike the Patents Act 1977, the Copyright, Patents and Designs Act 1988 makes no provision for compensating an employee the copyright in whose work is transferred to his employer, although there would seem no reason why matters like compensation could not be part of a modifying agreement.

BREACH OF CONTRACT

3.57 General

Breach of the contract of employment can take many forms, for example, non-payment of wages or requiring an employee to perform duties which are outwith the scope of the contract on the employer's part and disclosing trade secrets or failing to perform his contractual duties with reasonable care on the employee's part. Equally the breach might result in the contract being brought to an end, for example by wrongful dismissal or resignation. Wrongful dismissal means a dismissal in breach of the contract[655] and is to be contrasted with unfair dismissal which generally means a dismissal which does not conform with a statutory standard of fairness and reasonableness.[656] To determine whether or not a dismissal is unfair regard is had to the relevant statutory provisions, as supplemented by any

---

[647] The advantage of owning the copyright in material is the exclusive right to copy the work, show it to the public, broadcast and alter it (Copyright, Designs and Patents Act 1988, s. 16).

[648] Before any question of copyright can arise there must be a recording "in writing or otherwise" (Copyright, Designs and Patents Act 1988, s. 3(2)).

[649] Note "literary work" explicitly includes a table of compilation and a computer program (Copyright, Designs and Patents Act 1988, s. 3(1)).

[650] The effect is that what matters now is whether there is a contract of employment or not; questions of whether the author was employed by the proprietor of a newspaper etc. no longer arise.

[651] By using the word "agreement" it would seem an employer's right to be first owner can be qualified not only by a contractual term but, for example, a collective agreement or a set of employer's guidelines.

[652] Copyright, Patents and Designs Act 1988, s. 11(2); and see the similar provision in s. 215(3) in respect of a design right. And see *Danowski v. The Henry Moore Foundation, The Times*, March 19, 1996, CA.

[653] *Ibid.* s. 11(1).

[654] *Ibid.* s. 91.

[655] Arguably it also encompasses a dismissal which occurs in breach of special statutory powers although strictly such dismissals are not merely wrongful but "invalid" and therefore of no legal effect; see *Malloch v. Aberdeen Corporation* 1974 SLT 253 and the terminology used therein.

[656] See Chapter Five.

relevant code of practice, and the contract of employment. To determine whether a dismissal is wrongful regard is had to the express and implied terms of the contract. Thus a wrongful dismissal occurs, for example, where an employee's contract is terminated without notice by the employer when the employee's conduct does not justify such an instant or summary dismissal. However, while it is a wrongful dismissal where, absent a breach by the employee, the employer gives insufficient notice, or where the employer prematurely terminates a contract for a fixed period or task, it is not wrongful to dismiss without notice provided wages in lieu are paid.[657]

3.58 Specific performance, interdict and wrongful termination

Because the law regards the contract of employment as one involving a personal relationship based on mutual trust and confidence the full range of contractual remedies is not available. Thus the common law rule that it is inconsistent with personal liberty that contracts which are merely for the performance of work[658] may not be specifically enforced[659] is now endorsed — as far as enforcement against the employee is concerned — by the statutory declaration that "No court shall by way of (a) an order for specific implementation of a contract of employment or (b) an interdict restraining a breach ... of such a contract compel an employee to do any work or attend any place for the doing of any work."[660] The result of the combination of these common law and statutory rules is that where the breach involves, on the employee's part, a refusal to work (for example by a wrongful resignation) or, on the employer's part, a refusal to employ (for example by a wrongful dismissal) generally the courts will not grant any order whose effect would be to compel the continuation of employment[661] or grant an order which prevents the appointment of a replacement[662]; nor is a dismissed employee entitled to treat the contract as subsisting and claim wages, his claim being one for damages.[663]

3.59 *Trust and confidence.* Decisions of the English courts demonstrate that an injunction may[664] be granted to restrain or at least postpone a potentially wrongful dismissal where there is sufficient confidence on the part of the employer in the employee's ability to do the job.[665] Thus in *Hughes v. London Borough of*

---

[657] *Graham v. Thomson* (1822) 1 S 309; *Morrison v. Abernethy School Board* (1876) 3 R 945.

[658] Such contracts are termed *mera factae quae in meris faciendi finibus consistent* — contracts which consist of bare performance — as opposed to those which also involve transfer of property rights.

[659] *Stewart v. Stewart* (1832) 10 S 674; *De Francesco v. Barnum* (1890) 45 Ch D 430; *Skerret v. Oliver* (1896) 23 R 468; *Murray v. Dumbarton CC* 1935 SLT 239, OH.

[660] TULRCA, s. 236. Also although an industrial tribunal may "order" the reinstatement of an unfairly dismissed employee, breach of the order by the employer only permits the tribunal to increase the compensation it would otherwise have been empowered to award — no other penalty can be imposed on the employer (ERA, ss. 112, 117).

[661] *Murray v. Dumbarton CC*, above; and see *Warren v. Mendy* [1989] IRLR 210, CA.

[662] *Page One Records Ltd v. Britton* [1968] 1 WLR 157; *Skerret v. Oliver*, above. *Cf BMA v. Greater Glasgow Health Board* 1989 SLT 493, HL.

[663] *First Edinburgh Building Society v. Munro* (1884) 21 SLR 291; *Marsh v. National Autistic Society* [1993] ICR 453, Ch.

[664] Interdict and injunction are discretionary remedies.

[665] *Hill v. C. A. Parsons & Co. Ltd* [1972] Ch 305, CA; *Powell v. Brent London Borough Council* [1987] IRLR 466, CA.

Southwark[666] an injunction was granted to restrain the transfer of employees in breach of their employment contracts from hospital-based jobs to work in the community because there was no question of their employers having lost confidence in them; the proposed transfer was necessitated by the employer's shortage of funds. Whereas in *Ali v. London Borough of Southwark*[667] the employer's proposal to discipline Ali was not restrained by injunction because "it was plain the employers had lost all confidence in (her) to carry out the duties involved in the caring for others. Although they had not lost that confidence irrevocably ... they had lost it for the moment on reasonable grounds ... ".[668] However, an order which would, in effect, decree specific performance of the contract of employment has been granted even where it was impossible to conclude that a workable situation would arise because there was no question over the competence of the employee who was prepared to give an undertaking that he would work in accordance with his superior's instructions.[669] Similarly, English courts have been prepared to grant injunctions to restrain a dismissal which is wrongful in that it would be in breach of a procedure engrafted on to a contract of employment.[670] Thus in *Irani v. Southampton and South West Hampshire Health Authority*[671] the Health Authority was restrained by injunction from dismissing Irani without using the contractual procedures for resolving disputes between the employer and employees in circumstances in which there was no criticism of Irani's conduct or professional competence because damages would not have been an adequate remedy. Indeed in England as a result of the procedure available under the Rules of the Supreme Court[672] an injunction to restrain a dismissal in breach of a contractual disciplinary procedure has been granted even when the trust and confidence of the relationship might have broken down. In *Jones v. Gwent County Council*,[673] having been satisfied that the employers had failed to follow the contractual procedure for dismissal for misconduct, the court declared the purported letter of dismissal invalid and granted an injunction restraining the employers from dismissing the employee, being content to leave the question of trust and confidence until the trial. There is no equivalent Scottish procedure so that normally and particularly where the essential mutual trust and confidence has been lost the remedy for a wrongful dismissal is damages. Indeed where an employee is dismissed with wages and other contractual benefits paid in lieu of

---

[666] [1988] IRLR 55, QBD; *Cf Gall v. Stirling District Council* 1993 SLT 1256, OH.

[667] [1988] ICR 567, Ch D.

[668] *Per* Millet J at p. 582; and see *Chappell v. Times Newspapers Ltd* [1975] IRLR 90, CA.

[669] *Wadcock v. London Borough of Brent* [1990] IRLR 223, Ch.

[670] *R. v. BBC ex p Lavelle* [1982] IRLR 404, QBD. A similar attitude was displayed in *Dietman v. Brent London Borough Council* [1987] ICR 737, QBD (affirmed [1988] ICR 842, CA) although ultimately Hodgson J would have refused the injunction because the dismissed employee did not make her position clear at an early stage and thereby prevented the employer from adopting the correct contractual procedure. And see *Wadcock v. London Borough of Brent,* above.

[671] [1985] ICR 590, Ch D; and see *Jones v. Lee and Guilding* [1980] IRLR 67, CA.

[672] RSC Order 14A, Rule 1 provides "The Court may ... determine any question of law or construction of any document arising in any cause or matter at any stage of the proceedings where it appears to the Court that (a) such question is suitable for determination without a full trial of the action and (b) such determination will finally determine ... the entire cause or matter or any claim or issue therein."

[673] [1992] IRLR 521, Ch. And see *Boyo v. London Borough of Lambeth* [1995] IRLR 50, CA.

notice no action for damages will lie on the basis that the employer has an implied right to terminate the contract.[674]

3.60 Other breaches of the contract and interdict

Where the breach does not involve a wrongful termination of the contract with the result that the victim of the breach is not seeking to prolong a relationship which has broken down, interdict to restrain the breach of a particular term of the contract will more readily be granted. Accordingly it is common for an employee or ex-employee to be interdicted against working for a competitor in his spare time by virtue of his implied duty of fidelity or after the contract's termination by virtue of a restrictive covenant.[675] However, as a general rule interdict will not be granted to enforce a negative stipulation if it would have the effect of forcing the employee to work for the employer or to starve through being idle.[676] However, although it must not be regarded as a prerequisite,[677] it may be possible to obviate the alternative of enforced idleness by offering to continue to pay the employee his full contractual benefits during the period for which the interdict is sought. Thus in *Evening Standard Ltd v. Henderson*,[678] in which Lawton LJ suggested the law required fresh examination to reflect modern conditions,[679] Henderson was required by his contract to give a year's notice and not to work for any other company without his employer's permission but, having been offered a position with a competing newspaper, he gave his employers only two months' notice. Evening Standard Ltd were granted an injunction which restrained him from taking up his new employment until the expiry of his proper period of notice and the court's decision to grant the injunction was clearly influenced by Henderson's employers' willingness to provide him with all of his contractual benefits until the contract expired without (a) insisting that he performed his contractual obligations or (b) claiming damages for the period during which he did not work for them. More recently in *Warren v. Mendy*[680] the Court of Appeal has re-affirmed the rule that enforcement of negative obligations will not be permitted if its effect will be to compel an employee to perform his positive obligation and has stated whether such compulsion exists is to be decided by having regard to the psychological, material and physical needs of the employee to maintain his skill and talent; the longer the period for which the injunction is sought, the more readily will compulsion be inferred; compulsion may be inferred where the injunction is sought, not against

---

[674] *Graham v. Thomson* (1882) 1 S 309. However, it appears the employee does not have an equivalent right of termination (*Wallace v. Shishart* (1800) Hume 383). In England it seems that unless the contract expressly provides for termination by payment in lieu of notice, what the employee receives is treated as damages for breach of contract — see *Rex Stewart Jeffries Parker Ginsberg Ltd v. Parker* [1988] IRLR 483, CA; *Abrahams v. Performing Rights Society Ltd* [1995] ICR 1028, CA.

[675] See para. 3.35.

[676] *Warner Brothers Pictures Inc v. Nelson* [1937] 1 KB 209.

[677] *Euro Brokers Ltd v. Rabey* [1995] IRLR 206, Ch.

[678] [1987] ICR 588, CA.

[679] At p. 594 Lawton LJ stated "There is a great temptation for employees ... to break their contracts and go to other employers, usually for higher salaries and when they do (assuming there is no question of confidential information), as the law stands at present, they can ... say: 'You cannot obtain an injunction against me which will have the effect of forcing me either to come back and work out my notice or starve, and it is no good you talking ... about damages because in the real world damages are impossible to quantify'. All the risk they are running in this kind of situation is that they will have to pay the costs of any legal proceedings ... It is time that some court examined the matter fully."

[680] [1989] IRLR 210, CA.

the employee, but a third party (another employer); and an employee's claim that he will be compelled to perform the contract's positive obligations should be examined sceptically, but once satisfied such compulsion exists, the court should refuse the employer's application for an injunction. Although it is competent for the Court of Session to make the equivalent of an "Anton Piller" order[681] caution has been urged in the use of such orders in the context of employment.[682]

3.61 Damages

Industrial tribunals and damages for breach of contract. Although an enabling provision had been enacted in 1975[683] it was not until 1994 that an order was made extending the jurisdiction of industrial tribunals to entertain claims based simply on the contract of employment.[684] Until then,[685] unless the contractual claim could also be framed as a statutory one for which the industrial tribunal had jurisdiction,[686] a breach of the contract by either the employer or the employee could be the subject of litigation only in the ordinary courts. Although the enactment of the Wages Act 1986 enabled employees to formulate claims which were essentially contractual actions for payments as complaints of unlawful deductions from wages for which the informal industrial tribunals had jurisdiction, following the meaning given to the term "wages" in *Delaney v. Staples*[687] (contractual) claims for wages in lieu of notice still required to be pursued in the more formal ordinary courts. One effect of extending the jurisdiction of industrial tribunals to deal with employees' claims based on the contract of employment is that claims for unpaid wages in lieu of notice may now be pursued in industrial tribunals. However, the jurisdiction of the industrial tribunals to entertain claims for breach of the contract of employment is still limited. First, only employees may initiate claims[688]; secondly, the remedy is limited to the recovery of damages or other sums[689]; thirdly, and most significantly, the claim must arise or be outstanding on the termination of the employee's contract of employment[690]; and finally the maximum payment that may be ordered by an industrial tribunal in respect of one or more claims relating to the same contract of employment is £25,000.[691] Gen-

---

[681] See Macphail on *Evidence* (1987), para. 25.07.

[682] *Lock International plc v. Beswick* [1989] IRLR 481.

[683] Employment Protection Act 1975, s. 109. Section 109 was repealed but substantially re-enacted by EPCA, s. 131 which in turn was amended by TURERA, s. 38. The provision is now in the Industrial Tribunals Act 1996, s. 3.

[684] The Industrial Tribunals Extension of Jurisdiction (Scotland) Order 1994 (SI 1994 No. 1624).

[685] The Order became effective on July 12, 1994.

[686] For example breach of an equality clause may be pursued by a contractual action or a complaint to an industrial tribunal under the Equal Pay Act 1970 (see Chapter Seven) and a failure to pay wages which are contractually due may be contested by an ordinary (contractual) action for payment or a complaint to an industrial tribunal under the Wages Act 1986 (see para. 3.21).

[687] [1992] IRLR 191, HL.

[688] Article 8 of the Industrial Tribunals Extension of Jurisdiction (Scotland) Order 1994 limits an employer to counter-claiming by permitting a tribunal to entertain a complaint brought by an employer only if there is already before the tribunal a complaint brought by an employee which has not been settled or withdrawn.

[689] Claims for damages or other sums due in respect of personal injuries are excluded and still have to be pursued in the ordinary courts (Art. 4).

[690] Generally complaints must be lodged within three months of the effective date of termination (Art. 7).

[691] Articles 3(c), 10. Article 5 excludes claims relating to contractual terms about the following: (a) living accommodation for the employee, (b) intellectual property, (c) duty of confidence and (d) restraint of trade.

erally,[692] any breach of the contract will sound in damages; at the very least, nominal damages will be due.[693] An action for damages may be combined with the remedies of rescission, where the breach is so serious as to amount to a repudiation of the contract,[694] lien and retention[695] and, where the action is brought in the ordinary courts, interdict, or may be brought as a separate independent action. At common law it is an implied term of the contract of employment that the employer is entitled to dismiss without notice provided he pays wages and other contractual benefits due to the employee in lieu of notice.[696] Accordingly, in the ordinary case,[697] no action for damages will lie because no breach will have occurred.[698] Also, while a contractual provision may restrict or exclude liability in respect of breach of contract such a provision may be rendered void by the Unfair Contract Terms Act 1977. Thus where rule 6(7) of a company director's share option scheme provided that in the event of dismissal from employment the employee/director shall not be entitled to any damages or compensation or any additional compensation or damages by reason of the alteration of his rights or expectations under the scheme it was held that the pursuer's averments regarding loss of rights under the scheme consequent on his dismissal were nevertheless relevant because the rule purported to restrict the employer's liability to pay damages arising from the breach of the pursuer's employment contract and that, being a secondary contract,[699] it might be struck at by s. 23(a) of the Act.[700]

3.62 *Measure of damages.* Where damages are due the amount or measure of damages is determined according to the normal rules of ordinary and special damages.[701] The result of the application of those rules is that where the breach takes the form of a wrongful dismissal, damages will normally be the wages and other emoluments the employee would have received had the contract been

---

[692] The main exception is in relation to late payment of money (Bell, *Principles*, s. 32); but see para. 3.10, n. 103.

[693] *Webster & Co v. Cramond Iron Co.* (1875) 2 R 752; *Fife Coal Co. Ltd v. MacBain* 1936 SLT (Sh. Ct) 6.

[694] See Chapter Four.

[695] See para. 3.8.

[696] See para. 3.59 and consider to what extent such an implied term is consistent with ERA, s. 86(3) which on the one hand overrides contractual provisions for periods shorter than those set out in s. 86(1) and on the other hand expressly preserves an employee's right of "*accepting* a payment in lieu of notice." See the interesting arguments canvassed by M. R. Freedland, *The Contract of Employment*, pp. 185–189. And see *Trotter v. Forth Ports Authority* 1991 GWD 17-1045, OH that s. 49(1) — the forerunner of s. 86(3) — does not prevent waiving right to pay in lieu of notice as distinct from waiving right to notice itself.

[697] *Cf Dunk v. George Waller & Son Ltd* [1970] 2 QB 163, CA (contract of apprenticeship), *Herbert Clayton and Jack Waller Ltd v. Oliver* [1930] AC 209 (contract involving an element of publicity that would enhance the employee's reputation).

[698] *Graham v. Thomson* (1822) 1 S 309.

[699] Had it been contained in the contract of employment itself, s. 17 of the Unfair Contract Terms Act 1977 would have applied rendering it void if not fair and reasonable.

[700] *Chapman v. Aberdeen Construction Group plc* 1993 SLT 1205, IH. But see *Micklefield v. SAC Technology Ltd* [1990] IRLR 218, Ch in which the equivalent but different English provision of the 1977 Act produced a different result.

[701] For a concise statement of these rules see Gloag and Henderson *The Law of Scotland* (10th edn), para. 13.28.

performed in the least burdensome way by the employer.[702] Therefore, where a contract of employment can be terminated by giving notice, the employee's damages will not exceed what he could have earned during the period of notice to which he was contractually entitled.[703] Where the contract is for a fixed period with no provision for termination by notice before the expiry of the fixed term, damages will reflect the wages or salary and other parts of a remuneration package the employee would have received had the contract been allowed to run its full course, subject always to the employee's duty to mitigate his loss.[704] Damages will include all the parts of a remuneration package to which the employee was contractually entitled[705] and have been held to include the loss of (1) a subscription to a private health insurance scheme, (2) the free use of a car,[706] (3) pension and insurance benefits, (4) rent-free accommodation and an entitlement to a share in profits.[707] However, damages will include neither the loss of a pay rise awarded after a wrongful dismissal because the dismissed employee would not have had a contractual right to it,[708] nor the expenses of submitting an unfair dismissal complaint,[709] on the ground that it could not be reasonably foreseen at the time of contracting. Similarly while a breach of contract — particularly a wrongful dismissal — may cause the innocent party to suffer injury to his feelings and reduce future job prospects, the current view is that damages for breach of the contract of employment will not reflect such injury.[710] An attempt to avoid the limitations of the decision of the House of Lords in *Addis v. Gramophone Co. Ltd*[711] by contending that there was an implied term in the contract of employment of senior bank employees that their employer would not, without reasonable or proper cause, conduct his business with his customers so that employees will by reason of such conduct be put at a disadvantage in the employment market in the

---

[702] *Baird v. Banff District Lunacy Board* (1914) 1 SLT 284; *British Guiana Credit Corpn v. da Silva* [1965] 1 WLR 248, PC. *Cf Rigby v. Ferodo Ltd* [1988] ICR 29, HL that limitation of damages to the notice period does not apply where the employee has not been dismissed and has chosen not to rescind in face of breach by the employer.

[703] And note the equivalent statutory provision in ERA, s. 87 (in respect of employees covered by it) that damages for breach of contract will take into account the rights conferred by ERA, s. 86. In England it has been held that to the earnings during notice there should be added earnings during the period it would take to complete a contractual disciplinary procedure: see *Boyo v. London Borough of Lambeth* [1995] IRLR 50, CA; *sed quaere.*

[704] See, for example, *Yetton v. Eastwoods Froy Ltd* [1967] 1 WLR 104.

[705] However, they will not include unpaid employee contributions to a pension scheme on the basis that being obliged to make the contributions they would not have formed part of his disposable income (*Dews v. NCB* [1987] IRLR 330, HL).

[706] Regarding damages for loss of car see *Cull v. Oilfield Inspection Services Group plc* 1990 SLT 205, OH.

[707] *Baird v. Banff and District Lunacy Board*, above; *Re Rubel Bronze and Metal Co. Ltd and Vos* [1918] 1 KB 315; *Lindsay v. Queen's Hotel Co. Ltd* [1919] 1 KB 212; *Shove v. Downs Surgical plc* [1984] ICR 532, QB.

[708] *Lavarack v. Woods of Colchester Ltd* [1967] 1 QB 278, CA. *Cf Cull v. Oilfield Inspection Group plc*, above, in which the pursuer failed to prove "a real likelihood" of salary increase.

[709] *Blyth v. Scottish Liberal Club* 1983 SLT 260, IH.

[710] *Addis v. Gramophone Co. Ltd* [1909] AC 488. In *Bliss v. South East Thames Regional Health Authority* [1987] ICR 700, CA, Dillon LJ disapproved of *Cox v. Philips Industries Ltd* [1976] ICR 138, QB and affirmed that standing the decision in *Addis* it was not possible for damages for breach of the contract of employment to include an award in respect of distress, vexation, frustration and consequent ill-health which were the result of the breach. See too *O'Laoire v. Jackel International Ltd* [1991] IRLR 170, CA. *Cf Diesen v. Samson* 1971 SLT (Sh Ct) 49; *Heywood v. Wellers* [1976] QB 446. And note the contrary view expressed by Lord Fraser, *Master and Servant* (3rd edn), p. 135.

[711] [1909] AC 488, HL.

event that their employment is terminated was rejected on the ground that it was not part of the employment contract to prepare an employee for employment with future employers and the contracting parties could not be assumed to have agreed to the inclusion of such a term when the contract was made.[712] On the other hand damages will be awarded for the loss of statutory rights which are conditional on a period of continuous employment which was interrupted by a wrongful dismissal.[713]

Where the employee is in breach of contract whether a loss sustained by the employer will sound in damages depends on whether, taking account of the circumstances, it arose naturally from the breach or whether it could have been contemplated by the parties at the time of contracting.[714] Thus where an employee, without whose presence other employees are not permitted to work, refuses to work a shift the employer's loss will not be restricted to the cost of hiring a replacement but may extend to the loss of profit which the shift would have produced.[715] Where an employee receives the benefits of a training course at his employer's expense, to ensure he (the employer) derives some value from the employee's attendance at the course, he may require him to repay a proportion of the training or college fees in the event of his leaving his employment in breach of contract provided the obligation to repay is not regarded as a penalty.[716] Furthermore unless it is part of a clause of liquidated damages[717] the withholding of wages will not preclude recovery of additional losses by way of damages[718] although any wages or other contractual entitlements so withheld will be set off against the employer's loss arising from breach of the contract.[719]

3.63 Mitigation, taxation and receipt of benefits

The amount of damages recoverable, however, is also influenced by (1) the principle of mitigation of loss, (2) the incidence of taxation and (3) the receipt by the victim of the breach of benefits which arise as a consequence of the breach.

(a) Mitigation of loss. The victim of a breach of any contract is able to recover in damages only such losses which he could not reasonably avoid.[720] As has been

---

[712] *Malik v. BCCI* [1995] IRLR 375, CA: thus the dismissed employees' claim for "stigma" damages failed when, shortly after their dismissal for redundancy, the company went into compulsory liquidation amid allegations of corruption and dishonesty in which, the employees contended, they would be seen to be involved.

[713] *Basnett v. J. & A. Jackson Ltd* [1976] ICR 63.

[714] *NCB v. Galley* [1958] 1 WLR 16, CA.

[715] *Ibid.*

[716] *Strathclyde Regional Council v. Neil* 1983 SLT (Sh Ct) 89; applied in *Electronic Data Systems Ltd v. Hubble, Financial Times,* February 4, 1987 in which H's undertaking that if he left his employment within 2 years of completing a training course he would pay them £4,500 was enforced; it was not a penalty as it represented only a fraction of the real cost of the training programme.

[717] Contracting parties are free to stipulate that breach of contract will require a specified amount to be paid by way of liquidated damages; such stipulations will be enforced provided they are not construed as penalties. On penalty clause and liquidated damages, see generally Gloag and Henderson *The Law of Scotland* (10th edn.), paras. 13.21–13.24.

[718] *Dingwall v. Burnett* 1912 SC 1097; *Gaumont-British Picture Corp Ltd v. Alexander* [1936] 2 All ER 1686.

[719] Lord Fraser, *Master and Servant* (3rd edn.), p. 113.

[720] *Ross v. McFarlane* (1894) 21 R 396; *Yetton v. Eastwoods Froy Ltd* [1967] 1 WLR 104. But note that conduct of the victim prior to the breach is irrelevant: *Prestwick Circuits Ltd v. McAndrew* [1990] IRLR 191, IH.

remarked[721] it is inaccurate to talk of the victim of the breach as having a "duty" to mitigate his loss; strictly, an employee who is dismissed in breach of his contract is entitled to remain idle and not seek other employment provided he recognises that by failing to take reasonable steps to obtain other employment he accepts that any award of damages he receives will be reduced accordingly.[722] What steps are reasonable depends on the circumstances of each case[723] but generally an employer's damages will be reduced if he fails to seek a replacement employee just as the employee's damages will be reduced if he fails to seek other employment. Thus where an employee was wrongfully dismissed and a question arose whether he should have accepted alternative employment with the dismissing employers Crichton J opined "The test is this — Did the plaintiff act unreasonably in not taking up this lower-paid and lower-grade job? I have come to the conclusion that he did not. It was not incumbent upon him, having been a works manager, at the age of 59, to have to take a much humbler and less well-rewarded job especially with the defendants themselves and working with people who had been junior to him and would now be senior. I find he was not unreasonable."[724] However, it is submitted that in the case of a contract for a fixed term, although during the period soon after the breach the dismissed employee will be able to reject employment on terms less favourable than those of the contract unlawfully terminated, eventually he may be reasonably expected to consider less well rewarded positions[725]; he will not necessarily act unreasonably by taking an extended holiday to take stock and consider his future employment prospects.[726] Similarly, a dismissed employee might reasonably be expected to claim any statutory benefits to which he is entitled.[727]

 (b) Incidence of taxation. Since the purpose of an award of damages is to compensate it is necessary to take into account, in the case where the employee is prevented from performing the contract, the income tax he would have had to pay on his earnings had the contract been allowed to run its course; if such taxation was not taken into account clearly a dismissed employee would on receipt of an award of damages be in a better position than if he had earned the money.[728] However, although it is settled that taxation has to be taken into account, until recently the methods adopted have varied due principally to the provisions of the Income and Corporation Taxes Act 1988,[729] which requires that awards of compensation for loss of employment in excess of £30,000 be taxed. Thus, where the award of damages exceeds that figure the court will require to take account of the income tax the employee would have paid if his contract had not been broken and the tax on the award of damages itself for which he will have to account to the Inland Revenue.

---

[721] W. W. McBryde, *The Law of Contract in Scotland*, paras. 20–28, 20–29.

[722] In fairness to L J-C McDonald with whom McBryde disagrees (*ibid.*) a complete quotation leaves the reader in no doubt. Thus while his lordship did say an employee "was not entitled to sit idle and make no effort to find suitable employment" he adds in the next sentence "He must fairly and reasonably exert himself to earn his living, and can only come against the defender for the loss he sustains from his inability to secure a position as good as that which he (lost)".

[723] *Ross v. McFarlane*, above.

[724] *Basnett v. J. & A. Jackson* [1976] ICR 63.

[725] *Ibid.*; and see *Yetton v. Eastwoods Froy*, above.

[726] *Cull v. Oilfield Inspection Services Group plc* 1990 SLT 205, OH.

[727] *Parsons v. BNM Laboratories Ltd* [1964] 1 QB 95, CA (unemployment benefit); *Basnett v. J. & A. Jackson Ltd*, above (supplementary benefit).

[728] *British Transport Commission v. Gourley* [1956] AC 185; *Spencer v. Macmillan's Trs* 1958 SC 300; *Stewart v. Glentaggart Ltd* 1963 SLT 119, OH.

[729] Sections 148, 188.

The method adopted in Scotland is exemplified by *Stewart v. Glentaggart Ltd*[730] in which Lord Hunter, having arrived at a figure to compensate for the employee's loss, deducted therefrom an estimate of the income tax the employee would have had to pay had the contract not been unlawfully terminated, then observed that that figure would then have been subject to taxation as an award of damages so that after such taxation had been recovered by the Inland Revenue the victim of the breach would have been left with less than the figure required to compensate him for his loss and to avoid such a situation his lordship proceeded to add on to the sum left after deducting income tax such sum as the recipient would have to pay by way of tax on the award itself. For example, assume an employee's loss is £60,000.

Stage 1	
Loss of earnings	£60,000
Stage 2	
Deduct Income Tax, say	£20,000
	£40,000
Stage 3	
Since net awards exceeds £30,000, add	
estimate of tax on damages, say	£ 4,000
Total award	£44,000

Although this method involves a fair amount of estimate and prediction these are the hallmarks of many awards of compensation.[731]

(c) Benefits arising on the breach. Where the victim of a breach of the contract receives a payment or benefit in respect of the period to which the damages relate, the question arises should such payments or benefits be deducted in arriving at the net award of damages. Similar questions arise in delictual actions for personal injuries[732] and the principles applicable in those cases are generally[733] the same as those which require to be taken into account where the damages result from a breach of contract. Thus in *Redpath v. Belfast and County Down Rly*[734] Andrews CJ opined in a statement approved by Lord Reid in *Parry v. Cleaver*[735] "[A]dmittedly the present case differs from *British Westinghouse Electric and Manufacturing Co. Ltd v. Underground Electric Railways Co. of London Ltd*[736] ... in one important respect, namely, that it was an action for breach of contract whilst in the present case we are concerned with the measure of damages in an action of tort; but I am unable to appreciate why any different principles should apply. The important consideration common to all cases, is that the circumstance relied upon in mitigation of damages arose independently of the cause of action, and was not naturally attributable to it. The defendants' wrongful act may in each case have been a *causa sine qua*

---

730 1963 SLT 119. And see *Cull v. Oilfield Inspection Services Group plc*, above, in which it was held that the effect of ss. 148, 188 rendered the application of a multiplier (1.5) to Cull's salary inappropriate for calculating damages for breach of contract.

731 A similar method has been adopted in England: *Shove v. Downs Surgical plc* [1984] ICR 532, QB.

732 See, for example, *Parry v. Cleaver* [1970] AC 1; *Wilson v. NCB* 1981 SLT 67, HL; *Hodgson v. Trapp, The Times*, November 14, 1988, HL. On the need to take account of mitigating benefits or payments see A. S. Burrows, *Remedies for Torts and Breach of Contract* (1987), pp. 106–115.

733 *Cf* Law Reform (Personal Injuries) Act 1948, s. 2; Administration of Justice Act 1982, s. 10.

734 [1947] NI 167 at p. 187.

735 [1970] AC 1 at p. 14.

736 [1912] AC 673.

non but in no true sense was it the *causa causans* of the circumstance relied on in mitigation of damages.'' The operation of the above principle can be seen in *Lavarack v. Woods of Colchester Ltd*[737] in which, as a result of Lavarack's wrongful dismissal he was released from a restrictive covenant in his contract of employment. This enabled him to take up employment with a company named Martindale in which he acquired shares. He also acquired shares in another company (Ventilation) and the value of both holdings increased. Clearly, while the salary he received by working for Martindale had to be taken into account, the Court of Appeal held that only the increased value of the shares in Martindale had to be deducted from the loss occasioned by the wrongful dismissal.[738] Where the victim of the breach receives incidental payments or benefits it is the net gain of which account must be taken. Thus in *Westwood v. Secretary of State for Employment*[739] W. was dismissed without notice or pay in lieu thereof when his contract entitled him to receive 12 weeks' notice of termination. He became entitled to unemployment benefit for one year, followed, on exhaustion, by supplementary benefit at a lower rate and the House of Lords held that there should be deducted from damages in respect of the 12 weeks for which he received neither notice nor pay in lieu his net gain, namely, not what W. actually received by way of unemployment benefit but the lesser sum he received by way of supplementary benefit after the premature exhaustion of his unemployment benefit. Similarly where an employer is freed from his obligation to pay wages because of a breach by the employee his loss is reduced *pro tanto*.[740] The following receipts[741] must be taken into account when calculating compensation — unpaid national insurance contributions,[742] unemployment benefit,[743] supplementary benefit,[744] family income supplement,[745] statutory sick pay,[746] attendance and mobility allowances[747] and presumably disability living allowance. There are conflicting decisions whether a statutory redundancy payment should be deducted from damages for a wrongful dismissal.[748] However, while emphasising the peculiar and exceptional circumstances of the case, the House of Lords has held that such a

---

[737] [1967] 1 QB 278, CA.

[738] ''I realise that L was only at liberty to invest in Ventilation because his employment was terminated. But nevertheless the benefit from that investment was not a direct result of his dismissal. It was an entirely collateral benefit ... for which he need not account to his [former] employers ... [but his shareholding in] Martindale stands on a different footing'' *per* Lord Denning at pp. 290–291.

[739] [1985] ICR 209, HL.

[740] Lord Fraser, *Master and Servant* (3rd edn), p. 113.

[741] Where a benefit could have been received but was not (because the victim of the breach did not apply), logically it should still be taken into account.

[742] *Cooper v. Firth Brown Ltd* [1963] 1 WLR 418.

[743] *Parsons v. BNM Laboratories Ltd*, above; *Westwood v. Secretary of State for Employment*, above.

[744] *Westwood v. Secretary of State for Employment*, above.

[745] *Gaskill v. Preston* [1981] 3 All ER 427.

[746] *Palfrey v. Greater London Council* [1985] ICR 437, QB.

[747] *Hodgson v. Trapp* [1989] AC 807, HL, in which the purpose of the allowances was highlighted and Lord Bridge could find no general principle to support the opinion of Lord Reid in *Parry v. Cleaver*, above, that Parliament did not intend statutory benefits to be for the benefit of the wrongdoer; and see *Cunningham v. Camberwell Health Authority* [1990] 2 Med L R 49, CA.

[748] Contrast *Stocks v. Magna Merchants Ltd* [1973] 1 WLR 1505 in which a redundancy payment was deducted, with *Basnett v. J. & A. Jackson Ltd*, above, in which it was not; the approach of *Basnett* was preferred in *Mills v. Hassall* [1983] ICR 330, QB.

payment should be deducted from an award of damages in a delictual action,[749] although Lord Scarman stated[750] that in many cases it would not be reasonable or just to deduct a statutory redundancy payment from damages paid to compensate an employee for loss of future earnings. Certainly no deduction is made in respect of the basic award of compensation for unfair dismissal on the grounds that even if the termination had been lawful, protection against unfair dismissal would have been available[751] and this would seem to support the view that a statutory redundancy payment should not be deducted from damages for wrongful dismissal save in exceptional cases (of which *Wilson* is one) and *a fortiori* where the pursuer would have been redundant in any event irrespective of the wrongful dismissal.[752] In an action in tort monies received under an insurance contract or a pension scheme have recently been considered by the House of Lords in *Smoker v. London Fire Authority*[753] which endorsed the principle that there are to be disregarded in calculating damages, the proceeds of insurance and sums coming to the injured employee by reason of benevolence even where the defendants were employers, insurers and tortfeasors. Thus where a fireman was injured as a result of his employer's negligence or breach of statutory duty, the payments he received under a contributory pension scheme were not deducted from damages; similarly the lump sum received by an employee injured as a result of his employer's negligence under an insurance policy taken out by his employers for the benefit of employees was not to be deducted from damages as that sum was to be regarded as a payment by way of benevolence.[754] In *Hopkins v. Norcross plc*[755] the same rules were applied to a claim for wrongful dismissal in which the employee claimed damages based on the earnings he would have had in the period between the dismissal and reaching the age of 60 years — the age at which he was required to retire — a period in respect of which he received a retirement pension but, relying on *Smoker*,[756] it was held that the pension payments should not be deducted from damages.[757]

[749] *Wilson v. NCB*, above, affirming the decision of the Court of Session (1981 SLT 67) in which Lord President Emslie opined ''Once the intrinsic nature and purpose of redundancy payments are known (to compensate . . . for the loss of an established job . . . whether the recipient will or will not find new employment . . . even if the employee immediately secures another . . . better-paid job) . . . the question whether [a] redundancy payment . . . should . . . be disregarded must be resolved by application of the common law which treats the answer as one depending on justice, reasonableness and public policy . . . in this case I can discover no trace of public policy which could justify the pursuer's claim to receive damages for loss of earnings . . . and at the same time keep the redundancy payments as well . . . [but] I do not wish to be taken to be laying down any general rule.''

[750] *Ibid.* p. 73.

[751] *Shove v. Downs Surgical plc*, above. And see *O'Laoire v. Jackel International Ltd*, above, regarding the compensatory award.

[752] See *Baldwin v. British Coal Corporation* [1995] IRLR 139, QB and *Colledge v. Bass Mitchells & Butlers Ltd, The Times*, December 14, 1987 in which *Wilson v. NCB* 1981 SLT 67, HL was declared to be decided with regard to its particular facts and redolent of policy considerations.

[753] [1991] ICR 449, HL.

[754] *McCamley v. Cammell Laird Shipbuilders Ltd* [1990] 1 WLR 963, CA.

[755] [1992] IRLR 304, QB.

[756] [1991] ICR 449, HL.

[757] The court suggested that the apparent double recovery could be avoided by the pension scheme or the contract of employment providing that a pension would not be payable in the event of a claim being made against the employer as a result of an act which itself gives rise to a pension being payable.

PUBLIC LAW AND EMPLOYMENT

3.64 Judicial review

In Scotland the Court of Session and in England the High Court exercise similar jurisdictions to supervise the decisions of inferior courts, tribunals and administrative bodies by way of judicial review. Thus the Rules of Court provide that an application to the supervisory jurisdiction of the court shall be made by way of an application for judicial review and on such an application the court may make such order as it thinks fit being an order which could be made in any action or petition and including an order for reduction, suspension, declarator, interdict, implement, restitution and payment.[758] One result of these administrative law jurisdictions is that decisions of tribunals or administrative bodies relating to employment matters may be subject to the supervision of the Court of Session. Examples of employees seeking to use this additional and special jurisdiction to redress the effect of decisions relating to employment can be seen in *Nahar v. Strathclyde Regional Council*[759] in which Nahar, a schoolteacher, sought a reduction of the decision of Strathclyde Regional Council to dismiss him on grounds of misconduct and *O'Neill v. Scottish Joint Negotiating Committee for Teaching Staff*[760] in which a schoolteacher sought reduction of a decision of the Committee for Teaching Staff in a question relating to entitlement to full salary during maternity leave.

3.65 *No alternative remedy.* A pre-condition of judicial review is that no alternative statutory remedy is available.[761] While doubt has been expressed on whether this prevents judicial review of a decision which could be the subject of an appeal to the Court of Session but only after passage through a hierarchy of statutory tribunals,[762] where an employee has elected to pursue his grievance by some alternative procedure — for example, complaint to an industrial tribunal — any application for judicial review before the conclusion of the alternative procedure will be incompetent.[763]

3.66 *Public law element.* In England perhaps the most significant restriction on judicial review is the need for a public law element to be involved and the preparedness of courts to hold that such an element is involved will be critical in determining the extent to which judicial review is available as an additional procedure in employment matters. The need for such a public law element was emphasised in *R. v. East Berkshire Health Authority, ex p Walsh*[764] in which Walsh, a senior nursing officer, unsuccessfully sought judicial review of the health authority's decision to dismiss him because he was not trying to enforce a public right but his private contractual rights under his contract of employment. The following

---

[758] Rules of Court 58.3, 58.4. The English equivalent is rule 53 of the Rules of the Supreme Court. The wording of Rule 58.3 makes it clear that it is not the rule itself which describes the limits of judicial review but whether the application falls within the Court of Session's supervisory jurisdiction; and see the observations in *West v. Secretary of State for Scotland* 1991 SCLR 795, OH.

[759] 1986 SLT 570, OH.

[760] 1987 SLT 648, OH.

[761] Rule of Court 58.3(2); and see *British Railways Board v. Glasgow Corporation* 1976 SC 224 and *NUPE v. Lord Advocate, The Times,* May 5, 1993, OH.

[762] *Nahar v. Strathclyde Regional Council,* above, *per* Lord Davidson at pp. 573–574.

[763] *Nahar v. Strathclyde Regional Council,* above.

[764] [1984] ICR 743, CA.

quotation from the judgment of Sir John Donaldson MR encapsulates the distinction between public and private law rights.

"Parliament can underpin the position of public authority employees by directly restricting the freedom of the public authority to dismiss, thus giving the employee 'public law' rights and at least making him a potential candidate for administrative law remedies. Alternatively it can require the authority to contract with its employees on specified terms with a view to the employee acquiring 'private law' rights under the terms of the contract of employment. If the authority fails or refuses to thus create 'private law' rights for the employee, the employee will have 'public law' rights to compel compliance, the remedy being [an order] to require the authority so to contract or a declaration that the employee has those rights. If, however, the authority gives the employee the required contractual protection, a breach of that contract is not a matter of 'public law' and gives rise to no administrative law remedies."[765]

Initially the Scottish courts had adopted a similar approach[766] but in *West v. Secretary of State for Scotland*[767] it was authoritatively stated that the competency of an application for judicial review does not depend on any distinction between public and private law; what is required is (i) the conferring of a decision-making power on a body by statute, agreement or other instrument, (ii) an averment that that body has exceeded, abused or failed to exercise that power and (iii) the existence of a tripartite relationship constituted by the conferring of the decision-making power on a third party. Accordingly it was not competent where the question related to a prison officer's terms of employment.[768] On the other hand, the application was held to be competent where a schoolteacher alleged that her employers had acted unlawfully by departing unilaterally from terms of employment promulgated by a committee set up by the Education (Scotland) Act 1980.[769] However, where judicial review does lie, the Court of Session has at its disposal a range of remedies not available in disputes regulated purely by private law.[770] Thus in *Malloch v. Aberdeen Corporation*[771] the effect of the court order was to reduce Malloch's purported dismissal to a legal nullity with the result that (a) he was required to be treated as never having been dismissed and therefore entitled to his salary and other benefits since his date of dismissal and (b) he was entitled to resume his position as a schoolteacher until his contract of employment was lawfully terminated.

THE CONTRACT OF EMPLOYMENT AND THE CRIMINAL LAW

3.67 Since the Employers and Workmen Act 1875[772] removed the sanction of the criminal law for an employee's failure to perform his obligations under the contract the position is that, generally, a breach of the contract *simpliciter* by either the

---

[765] *Ibid.* p. 753.

[766] See, for example, *Tehrani v. Argyll and Clyde Health Board (No. 2)* 1990 SLT 118, IH and *Criper v. University of Edinburgh* 1991 SLT 129, OH.

[767] 1992 SLT 636, IH.

[768] And see *Blair v. Lochaber District Council* [1995] IRLR 135, OH in which the need for a tripartite relationship was challenged. And note, if a relationship is purely contractual there would be an alternative remedy.

[769] *Watt v. Strathclyde Regional Council* 1992 SLT 324, IH.

[770] The usual private law remedies are an action based on the contract of employment or a complaint of unfair dismissal.

[771] 1971 SC(HL) 85.

[772] Sections 9, 14.

employer or the employee does not bring the criminal law into play. However, special note should be made in respect of the following:

(a) *Health and safety.* As previously explained,[773] it is an implied term of the contract of employment that the employer will take reasonable care for the safety of his employees. However, in many cases the standard of care and provision required of employers is specified by statute, delegated legislation or a code of practice[774] which frequently are enforced through the criminal law. Perhaps of greatest significance is the Health and Safety at Work etc. Act 1974 which combines general duties, cast in terms which are very similar to the employer's implied contractual obligation to take reasonable care, with criminal sanctions. Thus s. 2 of the 1974 Act provides: "it shall be the duty of every employer to ensure, so far as is reasonably practicable, the health, safety and welfare at work of all his employees".[775] The effect of such general provisions is that the same failing on the part of an employer can amount not just to breach of the contract but also to the breach of a prescribed statutory standard with the consequent criminal penalties.[776]

(b) *Breach of contract and intimidation.* Legislation enacted last century is the nearest our law now comes to attaching criminal penalties for breach of the employment contract by providing that it is an offence for any person to wilfully and maliciously break a contract of service or hiring in the knowledge that the breach will probably endanger human life, cause serious bodily injury or expose valuable property to destruction or injury.[777] However, the words "wilfully and maliciously" clearly restrict the operation of the legislation and there is no record of any recent prosecutions.[778]

(c) *Malicious mischief and computer misuse.* At common law it is a crime wilfully and maliciously[779] to destroy or damage the property of another. Accordingly where an employee sets out deliberately to damage property of his employer — which would inevitably be a breach of an employee's implied duty of fidelity or good faith[780] — there is a considerable risk that the employee's conduct will justify a charge of malicious mischief. The risk of such a charge being sustained against an employee seems to have been increased since *H.M. Advocate v. Wilson*[781] in which it was held that physical damage to property is not essential to the crime. Thus, an

---

[773] See para. 3.31.

[774] See, for example, the Factories Act 1961, Control of Substances Hazardous to Health Regulations 1988, Code of Practice for Reducing the Exposure of Employed Persons to Noise.

[775] And see the other general duties imposed by ss. 2–9 mainly on employers. *Cf* ss. 7 and 8 that (1) it shall be the duty of every employee to take reasonable care for the health and safety of himself and others at work and (2) no person shall intentionally or recklessly interfere with anything provided in the interests of health, safety or welfare in pursuance of any relevant statutory provision.

[776] And see, for example, *Armour v. Skeen* 1977 SLT 71 and *Wotherspoon v. HM Advocate* 1978 JC 74 demonstrating that criminal liability can attach to managers etc. as individuals.

[777] Trade Union and Labour Relations (Consolidation) Act 1992, s. 240 re-enacting the Conspiracy and Protection of Property Act 1875, s. 5. Note that s. 4 (as amended by the Electricity Supply Act 1919, s. 31) which related only to workers in the gas, electricity and water industries, has been repealed (Industrial Relations Act 1971, s. 133).

[778] Although many provisions of the Conspiracy and Protection of Property Act 1875 have been repealed it is to be noted that among those not repealed in s. 6 which provides that it is an offence for an employer, in breach of a legal duty to do so, to wilfully or negligently fail to provide food, clothing, accommodation or medical aid with the result that the health of an employee or apprentice is likely to be seriously injured.

[779] It is probably sufficient if there is a deliberate disregard or indifference for the property rights of others (*Ward v. Robertson* 1938 JC 32).

[780] See paras 3.44 ff.

[781] 1984 SLT 117.

employee at a power station who wilfully and maliciously activated an emergency "stop" button with the result that generation of electricity was halted for several hours causing considerable financial loss to his employers committed the crime of malicious mischief. It is an interesting question whether an employee who, for example, deliberately inserted a virus into his employer's computing facility also commits the crime of malicious mischief. On the face of the decision in *H.M. Advocate v. Wilson*[782] those employees who wilfully and maliciously insert metaphorical as well as literal "spanners-in-the-works" would seem to commit the crime. On the other hand, the statutory offence of vandalism[783] requires damage to or the destruction of property of another. However, it is not a crime according to Scots law dishonestly to exploit the confidential information of another. Accordingly a charge that an employee had feloniously and without the authority of his employer made copies of a computer print-out with intent to sell them to his employer's competitors was held to be irrelevant although undoubtedly in breach of contract.[784] The Computer Misuse Act 1990 creates the offences of (1) unauthorised access to computer material and (2) unauthorised modification of computer material and it has been held that a former employee who made an entry on his employer's computer resulting in him obtaining a discount committed an offence under the Act which does not require the use of one computer to gain unauthorised access to another.[785] Accordingly if the facts of *Denco Ltd v. Joinson*[786] were to occur today the employee would risk criminal prosecution as well as fair and instant dismissal, when he was dismissed for unauthorised use of the password of another employee to obtain access to computerised information about a subsidiary company.

(d) Sit-ins. Where employees take control of their employer's premises by a sit-in, work-in or some other form of unauthorised occupation[787] it is likely that such employees are in breach of their contracts of employment in at least two respects — (i) by disobeying their employer's lawful instructions with regard to access and egress to the workplace and (ii) acting in a manner wholly inconsistent with their implied duties of loyal service. However, the occupation would probably support a charge of intimidation[788] on the view that those participating in the work-in or sit-in are, by depriving the employers of their use of the premises, preventing them from doing an act they had a legal right to do, namely to enter and leave the premises.[789] Although the Trespass (Scotland) Act 1865 has been used to prosecute "squatters" and travelling people,[790] that Act has not been used to deal with workplace occupations.[791]

---

[782] *Ibid.*

[783] Criminal Justice (Scotland) Act 1980, s. 78.

[784] *Grant v. Allan* 1987 SLT 11.

[785] *Attorney-General's Reference (No. 1 of 1991)* [1992] 3 WLR 432, CA.

[786] [1991] ICR 172, EAT.

[787] See Chapter Eleven.

[788] TULRCA, s. 241, re-enacting the Conspiracy and Protection of Property Act 1875, s. 7, provides "Every person who, with a view to compel any other person to abstain from doing or to do an act which such other person has a legal right to do or to abstain from doing, wrongfully and without legal authority ... deprives him of or hinders him in the use of such property ... shall, on conviction be liable to ... a penalty ...".

[789] *Galt v. Philp* 1983 SCCR 295 in which it was also held that liability under Conspiracy and Protection of Property Act 1875, s. 7 (now TULRCA, s. 241) was not affected by the civil law immunity contained in TULRA, s. 13, now TULRCA, s. 219.

[790] *Paterson v. Robertson* 1945 SLT 31.

[791] However, those who took part in the occupation in *Galt v. Philp*, above, were originally charged under the Trespass (Scotland) Act 1865.

Chapter Four

TERMINATION OF THE CONTRACT

The contract of employment may be terminated in a variety of ways: (1) by notice, (2) by rescission following repudiation, (3) by frustration, (4) by the dissolution of a partnership, the winding up of a limited company and sequestration and (5) by performance and passage of time, and these are now considered in more detail.

NOTICE

4.1 The rules regarding the termination of the contract of employment are both common law and statutory in nature with some matters, for example the length of notice required for lawful termination of the contract, treated by both common law provisions and statutory provisions, although the latter are conditional on the employee having the necessary period of continuous employment.[1] To determine whether proper notice of termination has been given it is therefore necessary to consider whether the statutory or common law rules apply and in this respect it is important to note that, although any contractual provision which is shorter than that provided for by statute[2] will not have effect,[3] it is possible that the length of notice required by common law will exceed the statutory standard. Accordingly, as a matter of practice it is necessary to consider the following questions: (1) Does a statutory provision apply? (2) What is the statutory notice entitlement? (3) Is there a more beneficial express contractual provision? (4) Where there is no such provision, is there a more beneficial term to be implied from the circumstances or the common law?

4.2 The common law rules

Unless the appointment is *ad vitam aut culpam*[4] or the contract is for a determinate period,[5] where the contract makes no provision regarding the notice required for lawful termination[6] the contract of employment may be terminated by either party giving to the other reasonable notice of termination or, in the case of termination by the employer, payment in lieu of notice.[7] The common law implies a condition

---

[1] See paras 3.2 ff.
[2] ERA, s. 86, and see para. 4.3.
[3] ERA, s. 86(3).
[4] See *Mitchell v. School Board of Elgin* (1883) 10 R 982; *Hastie v. McMurtrie* (1883) 16 R 715.
[5] *Brenan v. Campbell's Trs* (1898) 25 R 423. And see R. Hunter, "Well and Wisely Fixed?" (1979) 24 JLSS 317 on the distinction between a contract for a determinate period and a "fixed term contract" employment protection legislation.
[6] Such a provision may be implied by custom (*Hamilton v. George Outram & Co* (1885) 17 D 798).
[7] *Forsyth v. Heathery Knowe Coal Co* (1880) 7 R 887; *Graham v. Thomson* (1882) 1 S 309.

that when an employer "dispenses with his (the employee's) services without cause ... he (the employee) should be allowed the means of livelihood for a period within which he might reasonably be expected to find another situation".[8] Although the older authorities hold that the employer is not in breach by paying wages and other emoluments in lieu of notice, they do not specifically address the question of the nature of the payment. If there is no breach there can be no damages; if there is a breach what the employer pays is (liquidate) damages. However, in an English appeal Lord Browne-Wilkinson has indicated[9] that while the term "'payment in lieu of notice' may describe many types of payment, the legal analysis of which differs", there are four principal categories: (a) where the employer gives proper notice but tells the employee he need not work during that period, in which case what the employee receives is wages and there is no breach[10]; (b) where the contract expressly provides that it may be terminated summarily on payment of a sum in lieu of notice in which case there is no breach of contract by the employer although the payment is not a payment of wages in the ordinary sense; (c) at the end of the employment the employer and the employee agree that the employment is to terminate forthwith on payment of a sum in lieu of notice which is not strictly wages and there is no breach[11]; and (d) without the employee's agreement the employer terminates summarily and tenders payment in lieu of proper notice in which case the employer breaks the contract and the payment is a payment on account of the employee's claim for damages for breach of contract. The position in Scots law would seem to reflect category (b) except that the term allowing termination by notice or a payment of a sum in lieu thereof is implied and not express[12] but there remains the question of what is the nature of the payment which may affect taxation and the duty to mitigate. According to Lord Browne-Wilkinson the payment is not wages and, as there has been no breach by the employer, it cannot be a payment of liquidate damages. The only remaining alternative would seem to be a payment due under a term of the contract, in which case there would seem to be no duty to mitigate any loss[13] and the full payment would be taxable as an emolument from an office or employment[14] unless it can be

---

[8]   *Morrison v. Abernethy School Board* (1876) 3 R 945, *per* Lord Deas at p. 952. It seems that an employer wishing to terminate a contract by making a payment in lieu of notice is required to pay not merely *wages* in lieu of notice but an amount in respect of other contractual benefits lost too. Thus in *Morrison*, above, Lord Deas said a payment or allowance in lieu of notice could "not ... be ... less than ... a quarter's salary and emoluments (a dwellinghouse and a garden)".

[9]   *Delaney v. Staples* [1992] ICR 483, HL, at p. 488.

[10] It is respectfully submitted that to describe the payment the employee receives as a payment *in lieu* of notice is misleading.

[11] It is difficult to see the difference between this situation and situation (b) in that what the employee agrees to is an alteration of his contractual right to a period of notice. Unless it is seen in this way there must be a breach but the employee has agreed to accept the sum in lieu of notice as extinguishing his claim.

[12] It is not breach of contract for the employer to dismiss summarily provided payment in lieu is made: *Graham v. Thomson* above; *Cooper v. Henderson* (1825) 3 S 619.

[13] *Abrahams v. Performing Rights Society Ltd* [1995] ICR 1028, CA; from the point of view of the duty to mitigate it probably makes no difference whether the payment is one of liquidate damages or a payment due under the contract in some other way.

[14] Income and Corporation Taxes Act 1988, s. 19; the payment would be taxed at the full amount received at the appropriate rate for the employee/taxpayer.

argued[15] that it is a payment in connection with the termination of employment, in which case an exemption is available.[16]

What is reasonable notice depends on the facts and circumstances of each case.[17] Where the contract is for a certain term not exceeding one year, unless there is a custom or usage to the contrary,[18] reasonable notice (of termination) has to be given to prevent the renewal of the contract by tacit relocation for a similar period.[19] However, this rule probably applies only to particular "classes of servants—agricultural, domestic and the like".[20] Where an employee is dismissed without notice the contract is ended when the dismissal is communicated.[21]

4.3 The statutory provisions

Statute[22] provides for minimum periods of notice for certain employees.[23] After one month's continuous employment[24] an employee is entitled to receive one week's notice until he has two years' continuous employment when he becomes entitled to one week's notice for every year of continuous employment up to a maximum entitlement of 12 weeks' notice.[25] An employee who has been continuously employed for one month is required to give one week's notice of termination but his obligation does not increase relative to his period of continuous employment. A term in a contract of employment for a shorter period of notice is void[26] and is superseded by the statutory provisions.[27] However, neither party is prevented from terminating the contract without notice by virtue of the other party's repudiation[28] or from waiving his rights to notice.[29] The employee can also

---

15 According to Lord Woolf in *Mairs v. Haughey* [1993] STC 569, HL not every payment under a contract of employment was an emolument from that employment; it also had to be paid in return for acting as or being an employee.

16 Income and Corporation Taxes Act 1988, ss. 148, 188; s. 188 exempts from taxation the first £30,000.

17 See *Forsyth v. Heathery Knowe Coal Co*, above; *Morrison v. Abernethy School Board*, above; *Wilson v. Anthony* 1958 SLT (Sh Ct) 13; *Currie v. Glasgow Central Stores* (1905) SLT 651; *Hill v. C. A. Parsons & Co. Ltd* [1972] 1 Ch 305, CA.

18 *Morrison v. Allardyce* (1823) 2 S 434.

19 Bell, *Principles*, s. 187; Lord Fraser, *Master and Servant* (3rd edn), p. 58.

20 *Lennox v. Allan and Son* (1880) 8 R 38 *per* LJ-C Moncrieff; *Brenan v. Campbell's Trs*, above. Cf *Stevenson v. N. B. Railway* (1905) 7 F 1106; *Houston v. Calico Printer's Association Ltd* (1903) 10 SLT 532. In England the presumption of yearly hiring has ceased (*Richardson v. Koefod* [1969] 3 All ER 1264, CA).

21 *Octavius Atkinson & Sons Ltd v. Morris* [1989] IRLR 158, CA.

22 ERA, s. 86. Note, however, that the rights conferred by ss. 86 and 87 are contractual and not independent statutory rights (*Westwood v. Secretary of State for Employment* [1985] ICR 209, HL).

23 Employees are excluded if they have not been continuously employed for one month (ERA, s. 198); others excluded are (a) those engaged in work outside Great Britain (ERA, s. 196(1)), (b) those employed on specific task not expected to exceed three months and which does not exceed that time (ERA, s. 86(5)), (c) certain seamen (ERA, s. 199) and (d) police officers (ERA, s. 200).

24 See paras 3.2.

25 ERA, s. 86(1).

26 ERA, s. 203(1)(a). Also an employer's failure to give the statutory notice shall be taken into account in computing damages for breach of contract (ERA, s. 91 (5)).

27 ERA, s. 86(3).

28 ERA, s. 86(6).

29 And see *Baldwin v. British Coal Corporation* [1995] IRLR 139.

waive his right of payment in lieu of notice and there is no inconsistency between waiver of rights and the invalidity of a contractual term for notice shorter than the statutory minimum by interpreting the second part of s. 86(3) of ERA as applying only to an occasion other than the making of the contract itself.[30] Also, neither party is prevented from "accepting a payment in lieu of notice"[31] although the precise significance of these words is the subject of debate. It has been suggested that their effect may be to give an employee the right to insist on working the period of notice[32] but this has been rejected in the case of a contract which gives the employer the option of making a payment in lieu of notice so that where an employee has given notice an employer can terminate the contract at any time before the expiry of the employee's notice by giving payment in lieu on the view that since the contract of employment continues throughout the notice period the employer is entitled to utilise any term of the contract to bring it to an end.[33] However, it is insufficient for one party merely to designate the conduct of the other as "gross misconduct" or repudiation; the facts have to support the existence of the repudiatory conduct before the statutory right to notice may be avoided.[34] Since only contractual terms for shorter periods of notice are invalidated, if common law reasonable notice exceeds the statutory provision the party is entitled to enforcement of the contract on the more beneficial term; if the contract of employment expressly incorporates the periods of notice specified by statute the contract will be enforced on that basis. Whether notice is given by the employer or employee the latter is ensured a minimum income during the period of notice.[35] However, this protective measure disappears if the notice the employer must give to terminate the contract exceeds by at least one week the notice statute requires.[36]

4.4 Requirements of valid notice

While there is no rule that notice of termination must be in writing the contract may expressly require it and it is advisable that it should be so to avoid disputes. However, where the contract stipulates termination in specified ways that will not necessarily prevent the contract being terminated in some other way. Thus, where a contract provided that it could be ended by mutual consent, written notice or given in front of witnesses or total unseaworthiness of the ship, an employee's response to his employer's invitation to collect his "tickets" by signing off the ship's log was not to be regarded as termination by mutual consent but rather

---

[30] *Trotter v. Forth Ports Authority* [1991] IRLR 219, OH.

[31] ERA, s. 86(3).

[32] See M. R. Freedland, *The Contract of Employment* (1976), p. 186.

[33] *Marshall (Cambridge) Ltd v. Hamblin* [1994] IRLR 260. EAT. Where, as in England, there is no implied right to terminate the contract by giving pay in lieu of notice, it may well be argued that ERA, s. 86(3) does indeed permit the employee to insist at least that the contract continues until the end of the period of notice, although he will have no means of compelling the employer to allow him to perform his contractual duties.

[34] *Lanton Leisure Ltd v. White* [1987] IRLR 119, EAT.

[35] ERA, s. 87. The rights conferred by ss. 86 and 87 are contractual and not independent statutory rights (*Westwood v. Secretary of State for Employment* [1985] ICR 209, HL, reversing [1983] ICR 280, CA).

[36] ERA, s. 87(4).

termination by the employer because the crew agreement did not list all the ways in which the agreement could be ended but only those clean break terminations which left neither party with any common law cause of action.[37] Verbal notice does not start to run until the day following the day on which it was given[38] and a notice which does not specify the date or contain material from which the date (of termination) is positively ascertainable has no effect on the contract and an employee who leaves on receipt of such an invalid notice will be deemed to have resigned.[39] Thus informing an employee that he will eventually be dismissed without specifying a date is not giving valid notice[40]; nor is an announcement that a factory is to close down by a specific date combined with an invitation to employees to seek alternative work,[41] or that the employer will depart from a particular term of the contract—for example the rate of wages—from a certain date.[42] On the other hand where a trawlerman, whose employer told him over the telephone that it was decommissioning its fleet and that he should collect his "tickets" from the employer's office, signed off the crew agreement he was held to have been dismissed because the facts allowed the industrial tribunal to conclude that what the employee accepted was not an offer to resign or terminate by mutual consent but the acceptance by the employee of an accomplished fact[43] and where an employee wrote "I am left with no option but to resign and instigate ... proceedings against you. I look forward to hearing from you within seven days" a tribunal was entitled to read the letter as meaning that resignation would take effect, if there was no reply, within seven days.[44] A valid notice once given cannot unilaterally be withdrawn before it expires[45]; it operates to terminate the contract. However, an inadequate notice which is itself a repudiation of the contract needs to be accepted before it can affect the contract and it would seem, therefore, such a notice may be withdrawn at any time until it has been accepted by the other (innocent) party.[46]

---

[37] *Hellyer Bros Ltd v. Atkinson* [1992] IRLR 540, CA.

[38] *West v. Kneels Ltd* [1986] IRLR 430, EAT.

[39] *Morton Sundour Fabrics Ltd v. Shaw* [1967] 2 ITR 84; *Hughes v. Gwynedd Area Health Authority* [1977] IRLR 436. EAT. However, if his resignation followed a repudiation by the employer there will be a constructive dismissal for redundancy and unfair dismissal law. See Chapter Five.

[40] *Haseltine Lake & Co. v. Dowler* [1981] ICR 222, EAT.

[41] *International Computers Ltd v. Kennedy* [1981] IRLR 28, EAT, Also an announcement of closure to trade union officials is not to be construed as notice of termination (*Doble v. Firestone Tyre & Rubber Co. Ltd* [1981] IRLR 300, EAT). But see *Anderson v. Wishart* (1818) 1 Murr 429. Equally in view of the provision of the Transfer of Undertakings (Protection of Employment) Regulations 1981, it is unlikely that informing an employee that the business wil be sold on a specific date will amount to a notice of termination.

[42] *Rigby v. Ferodo Ltd* [1987] IRLR 516, HL.

[43] *Hellyer Bros Ltd v. Atkinson*, above.

[44] *Walmsley v. C. & R. Ferguson Ltd* 1989 SLT 258.

[45] *Riordan v. War Office* [1960] 3 All ER 774n, CA; *Harris & Russell Ltd v. Slingsby* [1973] ICR 545, NIRC.

[46] *Decro-Wall International S.A. v. Practitioners in Marketing Ltd* [1971] I WLR 361, CA, particularly Buckley LJ at p. 235. "A repudiation and a notice of termination are clearly different things. A repudiation may be withdrawn at any time before acceptance: a notice of determination validly given cannot thereafter be withdrawn without agreement". And see *Northwest Holst Group Administration Ltd v. Harrison* [1985] ICR 668, CA.

REPUDIATION

4.5 The normal rule that the repudiation of a contract does not terminate it applies to the contract of employment,[47] and it has been stated[48] that those decisions[49] where the contract of employment was terminated by the repudiation and not by its acceptance (the "automatic termination" theory) were wrongly decided. Thus where an employee never accepted a wage reduction imposed by his employers but continued to work without notice being given or being dismissed his contract never came to an end and he was entitled to receive the wages to which he was contractually entitled.[50] Of course, depending on the form or nature of the repudiatory breach, the victim of the breach may have no practical alternative but to accept the repudiation and bring the contract to an end.[51] Although it has been stated by Lord Oliver in *Rigby v. Ferodo Ltd*[52] that "[t]here was no reason in law or in logic why, leaving aside the extreme cases of outright dismissal or walk-out, a contract of employment should be on any different footing from any other contract regarding the principle that an unaccepted repudiation was a thing writ in water and of no value to anybody," the Court of Appeal has attempted to place the contract of employment in a special category which would deprive the parties of their right to decide whether or not to accept a repudiation so that, where by an unequivocal and unilateral action the employer repudiates his obligations under the contract of employment in a way in which his decision is brought to the attention of the employee, the employee should not have the opportunity of rejecting that repudiation; rather his duty is to mitigate his loss by immediate recognition of the employer's repudiation.[53]

Whether a breach is material depends on the terms of the particular contract and although no general rule can be laid down[54] the nature of the breach itself and its

---

[47] *London Transport Executive v. Clarke* [1981] ICR 355, CA; *Norris v. Southampton County Council* [1982] ICR 177, EAT; *Boston Deep Sea Fishing and Ice Co. Ltd v. Ansell* (1888) 39 Ch D 339, CA. And see *Rasool v. Hepworth Pipe Co. Ltd (No. 1)* [1980] IRLR 88, EAT and the instructive judgment of Megarry V-C in *Thomas Marshall (Exports) Ltd v. Guinle* [1978] IRLR 174, Ch D. For an interesting discussion of, and suggested solutions to, the problems involved see McMullen, "A Synthesis of the Mode of Termination of Contracts of Employment" (1982) 41 CLJ 110.

[48] *London Transport Executive v. Clarke*, above, *per* Dunn LJ at p. 372.

[49] *Gannon v. J. C. Firth Ltd* [1976] IRLR 415, EAT; *Kallinos v. London Electric Wire* [1980] IRLR 11, EAT; *Smith v. Avana Bakeries Ltd* [1979] IRLR 423.

[50] *Rigby v. Ferodo Ltd*, above.

[51] Both Templeman and Dunn LJJ in *London Transport Executive v. Clarke*, above, recognise that the rule may have to suffer some qualification. Thus Templeman L at p. 368 states: "If a worker walks out of his job and does not thereafter claim to be entitled to resume work, then he repudiates his contract and the employer accepts that repudiation by taking no action to affirm the contract. No question of unfair dismissal arises unless the worker claims he was constructively dismissed. If a worker walks out of his job or commits any other breach of contract, repudiatory or otherwise, but at any time he claims he is entitled to resume or continue his work, then his contract of employment is only determined if the employer expressly or impliedly asserts and accepts repudiation on the part of the workers", while at p. 373 Dunn LJ admits there may be cases where the innocent party has no option but to accept the repudiation and terminate the contract. See also Salmon and Sachs LJJ in *Decro-Wall International S.A. v. Practitioners in Marketing Ltd* [1971] 1 WLR 361, CA, and Lord McDonald in *Trust House Forte v. Murphy* [1977] IRLR 186; *Batchelor v. British Railways Board* [1987] IRLR 136, CA.

[52] [1987] IRLR 516, at p. 518.

[53] *Boyo v. London Borough of Lambeth* [1995] IRLR 50, CA; *sed quaere?*

[54] *Woods v. W. M. Car Services (Peterborough) Ltd* [1982] IRLR 413, CA.

impact on the contractual relations of the parties is of importance.[55] The effect of a breach and whether it indicates an intention not to be bound by the contract has to be assessed by reference to the standards of a reasonable person, the actual intentions of the party in breach being irrelevant.[56] Exceptionally the contract of employment may contain distinct severable obligations and a material failure in respect of one obligation may not result in the repudiation of the contract[57] but the cumulative effect of repeated non-material breaches may justify rescission.[58] Examples of material breach of the employment contract by the employer include the sale of business in which the employee works,[59] a failure to take reasonable steps to ensure an employee's safety,[60] oppressive use of a disciplinary power,[61] a failure to give support to a manager or supervisor[62] and a failure to pay the agreed wages.[63] Unjustified summary dismissal is itself a repudiation of the contract which generally leaves the employee with no choice but to rescind.[64] Because of the remedy of unfair dismissal few modern cases turn on questions of contract law but the following are illustrations of material breach by the employee: refusal to carry out a lawful instruction,[65] breach of an obligation, express or implied, protecting trade secrets and confidential information,[66] and engaging in most forms of industrial action.[67]

The repudiation may take the form of an anticipatory breach entitling the victim

---

[55] *Wade v. Waldon* 1909 SC 571, IH; *Millbrook Furnishing Industries Ltd v. McIntosh* [1981] IRLR 309, EAT.

[56] *Forslind v. Bechely-Crundall* 1922 SC (HL) 173; *BBC v. Beckett* [1983] IRLR 43, EAT; *Blyth v. Scottish Liberal Club* 1983 SLT 260, IH; *Millbrook Furnishing Industries Ltd v. McIntosh*, above.

[57] *Land v. West Yorkshire Metropolitan C.C.* [1981] IRLR 87, CA.

[58] See *Pepper v. Webb* [1969] 1 WLR 514; *Hanlon v. Allied Breweries (UK) Ltd* [1975] IRLR 321, IT; *Lewis v. Motorworld Garages Ltd* [1985] IRLR 465, CA. See also Lord Fraser, *Master and Servant* (3rd edn), p. 138; *Mansfield v. Scott* (1831) 9 S 780.

[59] *Ross v. McFarlane* (1894) 21 R 396; *Collier v. Sunday Referee Publishing Co* (1940) 2 KB 647. See also *Trevillion v. Hospital of St John and St Elizabeth* [1973] IRLR 176, NIRC. But note the provisions of the Transfer of Undertakings Regulations 1981 which transfer the contracts of employment of employees employed in the business at the time of the transfer (reg. 5).

[60] *Donovan v. Invicta Airways Ltd* [1970] 1 Lloyd's Rep. 486, CA; *British Aircraft Corporation Ltd v. Austin* [1978] IRLR 332, EAT.

[61] *BBC v. Beckett*, above; *Cawley v. South Wales Electricity Board* [1985] IRLR 89, EAT.

[62] *Associated Tyre Specialists (Eastern) Ltd v. Waterhouse* [1976] IRLR 386, EAT.

[63] *Industrial Rubber Products v. Gillon* [1971] IRLR 389 EAT; *Stokes v. Hampstead Wine Co. Ltd* [1979] IRLR 298, EAT. However, it is the materiality of the breach that is important and not whether it is an alteration in basic pay or an additional payment: *Gillies v. Richard Daniels & Co. Ltd* [1979] IRLR 457, EAT.

[64] *Ross v. Pender* (1874) 1 R 352; *Murray v. Dumbarton C.C.* 1935 SLT 239, OH. *Cf* the special cases of *Hill v. C. A. Parsons & Co. Ltd* [1972] 1 Ch 305; *R v. BBC, ex p Lavelle* [1982] IRLR 404. But note the decision of Hodgson J in *Dietman v. Brent London Borough Council* [1987] ICR 737, QBD (affirmed [1988] ICR 842, CA) that even a repudiatory dismissal requires acceptance for the contract to be terminated—*sed quaere*.

[65] *Pepper v. Webb*, above. In emergencies an employee may be required to perform duties outwith normal contractual provisions: *Wilson v. Simson* (1844) 6 D 1256; *Millbrook Furnishing Industries Ltd v. McIntosh*, above. In certain circumstances refusal to obey may not be material (*Laws v. London Chronicle Ltd* [1959] 1 WLR 698).

[66] *Thomas Marshall (Exports) Ltd v. Guinle* [1978] IRLR 74, Ch D; *Hivac Ltd v. Park Royal Scientific Instruments Ltd* [1946] Ch 169, CA (where only wartime regulations prevented instant dismissal).

[67] Not all forms of industrial action involve breach of the contract as in *Power Packing Casemakers Ltd v. Faust* [1983] IRLR 117, EAT, where overtime could not be required under the contracts.

of the breach to sue at once.[68] However, a party who has committed an anticipatory breach is entitled to withdraw it before the innocent party has elected to accept[69] and it must be clear that a breach is inevitable.[70] Thus, the announcement of the imposition of new terms (to which the employee did not agree) by a certain date justifies immediate termination by the employee[71] as does a proposal to unilaterally vary the contract and to give lawful notice of termination if the employer did not agree.[72] However, a genuine dispute regarding the terms of the contract is not an anticipatory breach[73] and while an employer's genuine though mistaken belief (that an employee would not be returning to work because a settlement had been arrived at) was a relevant factor, determining whether there had been a repudiation (telling customers the employee was no longer employed and appointing a replacement) depended on the circumstances including whether the belief was reasonable and brought about in whole or in part by the conduct of the employee.[74]

Certain conduct may be inconsistent with rescission although it is unlikely mere delay would indicate an affirmation of the contract[75] and, because of the different consequences attaching to affirmation and rescission it is necessary for the position of the innocent party to be clear and unequivocal.[76] Thus, where an employee's contract was repudiated by his employer intimating to him (wrongly) that his contract was frustrated and therefore at an end, it did not in law come to an end until the employee had finally committed himself to a contested hearing of an action for breach of contract because in order to rescind the contract there has to be a conscious acceptance intending to bring the contract to an end.[77] While the circumstances of each case are important, going on strike, continued acceptance of wages and reporting for duty[78] have been held to be inconsistent with rescission. However, continuing to work after clear words showing acceptance (of the new or altered contractual terms) only under protest will not result in affirmation of the

---

68 *Hochester v. De La Tour* (1853) 2 E & B 678.
69 *Norwest Holst Group Administration Ltd v. Harrison* [1985] ICR 668, CA. In fact in *Harrison* the Court of Appeal goes further and permits the withdrawal of the anticipatory breach any time before the innocent victim communicates his election to accept and rescind the contract.
70 *Haseltine Lake & Co. v. Dowler* [1981] IRLR 25, EAT (an employee was told he had no future with the company but no date of dismissal was fixed and EAT held no anticipatory breach because nothing suggested he would be dismissed without proper notice). See also *Morton Sundour Fabrics Ltd v. Shaw* [1967] 2 ITR 84 (announcement of likely redundancy) and *Maher v. Fram Gerrard Ltd* [1974] ICR 31, NIRC (intimation of transfer of employee against his will).
71 *Wellworthy Ltd v. Ellis* (unreported), case no. 915/83, EAT; *Rigby v. Ferodo Ltd* [1987] IRLR 516, HL.
72 *Greenaway Harrison Ltd v. Wiles* [1994] IRLR 380, EAT.
73 *Financial Techniques Ltd v. Hughes* [1981] IRLR 32, CA.
74 *Brown v. JBD Engineering Ltd* [1993] IRLR 568, EAT.
75 *Bashir v. Brillo Manufacturing Co* [1979] IRLR 295, EAT, distinguishing *Western Excavating (ECC) Ltd v. Sharp* [1978] IRLR 27, CA. See also *Ross v. Pender* (1874) 1 R 352. Cf *Fraser v. Laing* (1878) 5 R 596.
76 *Vitol SA v. Noref Ltd* [1996] QB 108, CA.
77 *Boyo v. London Borough of Lambeth* [1995] IRLR 50, CA,
78 *Grant v. Brown & Root Manpower Services* (unreported), case no. 167/84, EAT; *Hunt v. British Railways Board* [1979] IRLR 379, EAT Cf *Bliss v. South East Thames Regional Health Authority* [1985] IRLR 308, CA.

contract.[79] Conversely, a plea that a repudiatory dismissal had not been accepted so as to rescind the contract will not succeed where the victim of the breach (1) chose to fight the case on its merits (instead of pleading there was no termination at all), (2) presented a complaint to an industrial tribunal without stating it was merely to preserve rights, (3) failed to offer to continue working and (4) accepted a job with another employer.[80]

FRUSTRATION

4.6 Circumstances amounting to frustration[81]

The death or inability to perform through illness of either party frustrates the contract.[82] Where illness is concerned the case must be judged according to its own circumstances[83] although the factors identified in *Marshall v. Harland and Wolff Ltd*[84] and *Egg Stores (Stamford Hill) Ltd v. Leibovici*[85] will be relevant.[86] However, in a case of frustration the contract is terminated by operation of law and the fact that the employer has issued a notice of dismissal does not prevent a plea of frustration and although the Employment Appeal Tribunal has cautioned against too easy an application of the doctrine of frustration[87] it is incorrect to hold that in the employment field frustration by illness is normally only relevant where the contract is for a long term which cannot be determined by notice.[88] Although inconsistent with Scots principles,[89] imprisonment of the employee may support a plea of frustration[90] because although the employee's criminal conduct was deliberate it was the act of the judge in imposing the custodial sentence which affected the contract. Conscription or internment[91] and even a short period of legal

---

[79]   *Marriott v. Oxford & District Co-operative Society Ltd (No 2)* [1970] 1 QB 186, CA; *Burdett-Courts v. Hertfordshire C.C.* [1984] IRLR 91, QB; *Rigby v. Ferodo Ltd* [1987] IRLR 516, HL; *Bliss v. South East Thames Regional Health Authority*, above.

[80]   *Dietmann v. Brent London Borough Council* [1987] ICR 737, affirmed [1988] ICR 842, CA.

[81]   And see para. 5.23.

[82]   *Hoey v. MacEwan and Auld* (1867) 5 M 814; *Poussard v. Spiers* [1876] 1 QBD 410; *Condor v. Barron Knights Ltd* [1966] 1 WLR 87; *Ranger v. Brown* [1978] ICR 603, EAT.

[83]   *Westwood v. SMT Co.* 1938 SN 8.

[84]   [1973] 2 All ER 715.

[85]   [1977] ICR 260, EAT.

[86]   These factors include the terms of the contract, nature of the employment, its expected duration where no illness, the nature of the illness and prospects of recovery, period of past employment, was the person a ''key'' employee, the acquisition of statutory rights by the replacement employee, payment of wages during absence, employer's actings (e.g. did he dismiss the employee) and whether a reasonable employer could be expected to wait any longer.

[87]   *Williams v. Watsons Luxury Coaches Ltd* [1990] IRLR 164, EAT.

[88]   *Notcutt v. Universal Equipment Co. (London) Ltd* [1986] ICR 414, CA, disapproving *Harman v. Flexible Lamps Ltd* [1980] IRLR 418, EAT. And see *Hart v. A. R. Marshall & Sons (Bulwell) Ltd* [1977] IRLR 51, EAT.

[89]   Lord Fraser, *Master and Servant*, p. 322 referring to Bell and Pothier. And see *McEwan v. Malcolm* (1867) 5 SLR 62.

[90]   *Shepherd (F. C.) & Co. Ltd v. Jerrom* [1986] IRLR 358, CA, disapproving *Hare v. Murphy Bros Ltd* [1974] ICR 603, CA.

[91]   *Marshall v. Glanvill* [1917] 2 KB 87; *Unger v. Preston Corporation* [1942] 1 All ER 200. However, enlistment would seem to be a repudiation.

disqualification from holding office can frustrate the contract.[92] Thus losing his HGV licence following a heart attack has frustrated the contract of an HGV driver.[93] However, taking account of the Equal Treatment Directive,[94] a national law which forbids pregnant women from working at night will not frustrate a contract of employment which is not for a fixed term because pregnancy only operates to temporarily prevent night working.[95] While parties may expressly provide that a particular event will not frustrate the contract[96] where frustration occurs the contract is valid until then and contractual claims relative to the period prior to frustration are competent.[97] Where the right to payment has not yet accrued at the time of frustration (e.g. holiday pay and pensions) an equitable remedy (on the principles of unjustified enrichment) would be available.[98]

DISSOLUTION OF PARTNERSHIP

4.7 Where the employer is a partnership possessing a legal personality distinct from the personalities of the partners[99] dissolution of the partnership may operate to terminate contracts of employment with the firm and where the dissolution is brought about by the death of a partner the contract will be frustrated[100] although the same might not result where the dissolution is deliberate.[101] However, in a continuing partnership contracts of employment with the firm are not affected by death, resignation or assumption of a partner or partners.[102] In any event continuity of employment is preserved by statute[103] and where the reconstruction of the partnership takes the form of a transfer of a business from an old partnership to a new one the provisions of the Transfer of Undertakings (Protection of Employment) Regulations 1981 would apply so that the contracts of employment of

---

[92] *Tarnesby v. Kensington & Chelsea & Westminster Area Health Authority* [1981] IRLR 369, HL. However, in accordance with Scots principles is it not arguable that Tarnesby's professional misconduct leading to his suspension under the Medical Act 1956 was repudiation?

[93] *Dunbar v. Baillie Bros* 1990 GWD 26-1487.

[94] Dir. 76/207.

[95] *Habermann-Beltermann v. Arbeiterwohlfahrt Bezirksverband* [1994] IRLR 364, ECJ.

[96] D. M. Walker, *The Law of Contracts and Voluntary Obligations in Scotland* (3rd edn) para. 31.53. Whether the contract provides for there to be no frustration on the happening of a particular event will be a question of interpretation and in *Shepherd (F. C.) & Co. Ltd v. Jerrom* [1986] IRLR 358, CA, it was held that imprisonment did frustrate the contract even where the contract included a suspensory power in respect of "willful absence".

[97] Walker, above.

[98] In England claims are dealt with under the Law Reform (Frustrated Contracts) Act 1943.

[99] Partnership Act 1890, s. 4(2).

[100] *Hoey v. MacEwan and Auld* (1867) 5 M 814. Partnership Act 1890, s. 33(1) provides for dissolution by death of any partner in the absence of a term to contrary.

[101] See the judgment of Lord Deas in *Hoey v. MacEwan & Auld*, above and *Harkins v. Smith* (1841) SJ 381, decided on the employee's acceptance of the breach. And see the English decisions of *Phillips v. Alhambra Palace Co* [1901] 1 QB 59; *Tunstall v. Condon* [1980] ICR 786, EAT.

[102] *Campbell v. Baird* (1827) 5 S 335. In *Berlitz School of Languages Ltd v. Duchene* (1903) 6 F 181 it was suggested that an alternative ground of decision was that the contract of employment contained an implied term to accept change in the composition of the partnership. *Cf Garden Haig-Scott & Wallace v. Prudential Approved Society for Women* 1927 SLT 393, OH. Also see *Phillips v. Alhambra Palace Co*, above.

[103] ERA, s. 218(2). And see *Allen & Son v. Coventry* [1979] IRLR 399, EAT.

employees in the firm at the time of the transfer of the business would be automatically transferred to the new firm.[104]

SEQUESTRATION AND WINDING UP

4.8 The bankruptcy or insolvency of an employer is a breach of the contract and permits the employee to rescind the contract and claim damages.[105] The reasoning is that after the bankruptcy or insolvency the employee cannot expect to receive the stipulated wages.[106] A compulsory winding up order operates as a notice of termination of the contracts of employment then subsisting between the company and its employees[107] and where the employee continues his employment it will be under a new contract, express or inferred, entered by the liquidator, but for and on behalf of the company.[108] In such a case the liquidator is personally liable for the wages due under the new contracts.[109]

While a resolution for the voluntary winding up of a company may operate to terminate contracts of employment the effect of the voluntary winding up depends on the facts and circumstances of each case.[110] Thus where the voluntary winding up was coupled with a stated intention to cease business and insolvency there was a breach of contract by the company[111] but where the voluntary winding up was to facilitate a take-over it did not operate so as to repudiate the employee's contract.[112]

Where a receiver is appointed by the holder of a floating charge or by the court on the application of the holder[113] the appointment itself will not affect subsisting contracts of employment with the company.[114] The position seems to be similar to that in England where a receiver appointed by debenture holders acts as the agent of the company and the appointment does not affect contracts of employment[115] unless the continuation of the particular employment contract is incompatible with the role of the receiver[116]; the receiver himself may expressly dismiss employees[117]

---

[104] Transfer of Undertakings (Protection of Employment) Regulations 1981 (SI 1981 No. 1794), reg. 5.

[105] Bell, *Principles*, s. 185; *Day v. Tait* 1900, 8 SLT 40, OH. As the employee's claim is for damages and not wages he ranks as an ordinary creditor.

[106] *Day v. Tait*, above.

[107] *Day v. Tait*, above. However, in view of the fact that inability to pay debts is not the sole ground on which a winding-up order may be made (see the Insolvency Act 1986, s. 122), where there is no insolvency the effect of the winding-up order may be different: see *Laing v. Gowans* 1902, 10 SLT 461, OH.

[108] *Smith v. Lord Advocate* 1979 SLT 233, IH.

[109] *Smith v. Lord Advocate*, above, *per* Lord President Emslie at p. 241.

[110] *Reigate v. Union Manufacturing Co. (Ramsbottom) Ltd* [1918] 1 KB 592, CA; *Ferguson v. Telford Grier and McKay & Co* [1967] ITR 387, IT; *Fox Brothers (Clothes) Ltd v. Bryant* [1979] ICR 64, EAT.

[111] *Reigate v. Union Manufacturing Co. (Ramsbottom) Ltd*, above.

[112] *Midland Counties District Bank Ltd v. Attwood* [1905] 1 Ch 353; *Ferguson v. Telford, Grier, McKay & Co. Ltd* [1967] ITR 387.

[113] Insolvency Act 1986, s. 51(1), (2).

[114] *Ibid.* s. 57(4).

[115] *Re Foster Clark Ltd's Indenture Trusts* [1966] 1 All ER 43; *Re Mack Trucks (Great Britain) Ltd* [1967] 1 WLR 780; *Nicoll v. Cutts* 1985 BCLC 322, CA.

[116] *Griffiths v. Secretary of State for Social Services* [1974] QB 468 where the functions of a manager were assumed by the receiver.

[117] Insolvency Act 1986, s. 55(2), Sch. 2, para. 11.

or by his conduct, for example by selling the business, repudiate existing contracts of employment.[118]

Where existing contracts of employment are continued or adopted by the receiver he is personally liable on such contracts subject to his statutory right of indemnity.[119] However, to encourage receivers in their attempts to secure and subsequently sell any viable businesses or parts thereof, it is also provided that nothing the receiver does during the first 14 days of his appointment is to be taken to amount to the adoption of any contracts of employment[120] and relying on this receivers had issued a letter to employees to the effect that although the receiver was continuing their employment this was not to be taken as the receiver adopting or assuming personal liability for their contracts of employment.[121] The legitimacy of such a practice was re-examined by the Court of Appeal in *Powdrill v. Watson and Others*[122] in which the administrators continued the employment of Watson and other employees of Paramount Airways Ltd for several months after their appointment until their dismissal when the administrators recognised a buyer could not be found. The Court of Appeal and subsequently the House of Lords[123] held that for the purpose of s. 19 (which deals with administrators[124]) and s. 44 (which deals with administrative receivers[125]) of the Insolvency Act 1986 an employee's contract is adopted if he continued in employment for more than 14 days after the appointment of an administrator or receiver and, because adoption was an all or nothing matter involving acceptance or rejection of the contract as a whole, a receiver could not avoid this by unilaterally informing the employee that the adoption was conditional or that he was not adopting the contract. The government responded to the pleas of the insolvency practitioners with unprecedented speed and enacted the Insolvency Act 1994 which has effect in relation to all contracts of employment adopted on or after March 15, 1994. With regard to these contracts the position is that continuing employment after the 14-day period will be regarded as an adoption of the contract but the receiver's liabilities under such contracts are now limited to "qualifying liabilities".[126] A liability is a qualifying liability if (a) it is to pay a sum by way of wages or salary or contribution to an occupational pension scheme, (b) it is incurred while the receiver is in office and (c) it is in respect of services rendered wholly or partly after the adoption of the contract.[127] While wages and salary include sick pay and holiday pay and money payable in lieu of the latter, significantly there is omitted from the list of "qualifying liabilities" wages in lieu of notice or for the unexpired portion of a fixed term contract as are unpaid pension contributions and arrears of wages owed in respect of the period before adoption of the contract.[128] The nearest equivalent provisions in respect of a permanent trustee in bankruptcy provide for the adoption of any

---

[118] *Foster Clark Ltd's Indenture Trusts, Re* [1966] 1 All ER 43.

[119] Insolvency Act 1986, s. 57(3).

[120] Insolvency Act 1986, s. 57(5).

[121] The efficacy of such a letter was endorsed by Harman J in the unreported English decision in *Re Specialised Mouldings* (1987).

[122] [1994] IRLR 295, CA.

[123] *Powdrill and Atkinson v. Watson and Others* [1995] IRLR 269, HL.

[124] Technically, s. 19 being in Part II of the Insolvency Act 1986 applies to Scotland and England although administrators are rare in both jurisdictions.

[125] The equivalent Scots provisions is s. 57 which applies to receivers in Scotland and the decision of the House of Lords applies equally to ss. 44 and 57.

[126] Insolvency Act 1986, s. 57 as amended by the Insolvency Act 1994, s. 3.

[127] Insolvency Act 1986, s. 57(2A), (2B).

[128] Similar provisions are made with regard to administrators by amendments to s. 19 of the 1986 Act.

contract entered into before the sequestration except where adoption is precluded by the express or implied terms of the contract.[129] Assuming that this would not preclude the adoption of a contract of employment[130] the trustee has 28 days from receiving a request that he adopt the contract to decide whether to do so. If he does adopt the contract he becomes personally liable[131] but, unlike the receiver, without being limited to "qualifying liabilities". On the other hand, except in the cases where he has been requested to adopt the contract and replies to that request or does not reply within 28 days (in which case he is deemed to have refused to adopt the contract), whether the trustee has adopted the contract would seem to be a matter of fact.

EMPLOYEE'S RIGHTS IN BANKRUPTCY AND INSOLVENCY

4.9 The rights of an employee in the event of his employer's bankruptcy or insolvency are protected in two ways. First certain payments due to the employee rank as preferential debts.[132] Secondly, where an insolvent[133] employer is liable to make certain payments to an employee whose employment has been terminated the employee may claim directly against the Secretary of State for Employment.[134] Payments falling into the first category of preferred debts include: (a) remuneration[135] of an employee in respect of the whole or any part of the period of four months prior to the relevant date[136] subject to a maximum prescribed by the Secretary of State,[137] (b) any accrued holiday pay of an employee whose employment has been terminated in respect of any period of employment prior to the relevant date,[138] (c) a guarantee payment,[139] (d) medical suspension pay,[140] (e) payments for time off for (i) trade union duties, (ii) looking for work in a

---

[129] Bankruptcy (Scotland) Act 1985, s. 42.

[130] While it is clear that a contract for the personal services of the bankrupt is incapable of adoption (*Anderson v. Hamilton & Co.* (1875) 2 R 355) the same would not necessarily apply to a contract of employment entered into by the bankrupt employer before sequestration; *sed quaere.*

[131] *Dundas v. Morison* (1875) 20 D 255.

[132] In receivership, to have priority over the floating charge, the debts must have been intimated, or otherwise have become known to the receiver, within six months of advertisement by him in the Edinburgh Gazette and a local newspaper (Insolvency Act 1986, s. 59(1), (2)).

[133] An employer is insolvent only if (a) there has been an award of sequestration, a trust deed or composition contract, (b) after death a judicial factor is required to divide his estate among his creditors or (c) there has been a winding up order or resolution, the appointment of a receiver or a voluntary arrangement (ERA, s. 183).

[134] ERA, s. 182.

[135] Remuneration includes wages or salary for time or piecework and commission (Bankruptcy (Scotland) Act 1985, Sch. 3, para. 9(1)(a); Insolvency Act 1986, Sch. 6, paras. 9, 13) but not director's fees (*Hughes (C. W. & A. L.) Ltd, Re* [1966] 1 WLR 1369).

[136] The relevant date is: (a) date of sequestration or death of insolvent debtor (Bankruptcy (Scotland) Act 1985, Sch. 3, para. 7); (b) date of (i) an administration order, (ii) appointment of provisional liquidator or (iii) winding up order (Insolvency Act 1986, s. 387 (3)(a), (b)); (c) date of winding up resolution (Insolvency Act 1986, s. 387(3)(c)); and (d) date of appointment of receiver (Insolvency Act 1986, s. 387(3)(b)).

[137] Bankruptcy (Scotland) Act 1985, Sch. 3, paras 5, 6; Insolvency Act 1986, Sch. 6, paras 9, 12.

[138] Bankruptcy (Scotland) Act 1985, Sch. 3, paras 5, 9; Insolvency Act 1986, Sch. 6, paras 10, 13, 14. Note the definition of holiday pay in Bankruptcy (Scotland) Act 1985, Sch. 3, para. 9(3).

[139] Bankruptcy (Scotland) Act 1985, Sch. 3, para. 9; Insolvency Act 1986, Sch. 6, para. 13.

[140] *Ibid.*

redundancy situation and (iii) ante-natal care,[141] (f) statutory sick pay and statutory maternity pay[142] and (g) remuneration due under a protective award.[143] However, during the period that an administration order is in force no proceedings may be commenced against the company or its property except with the consent of the administrator or with leave of the court[144] and "proceedings" in this respect includes a complaint to an industrial tribunal but a complaint made during the period of an administration order is not null and void.[145] The following payments fall into the second category and, subject to a statutory maximum,[146] may, in the event of the employer's assets being insufficient to meet even preferred debts, on application to the Secretary of State be met out of the National Insurance Fund[147]—(a) up to eight weeks arrears of pay,[148] (b) pay during statutory notice or pay in lieu thereof,[149] (c) up to six weeks' holiday pay[150] in respect of the 12 months prior to the date of insolvency, (d) a basic award of unfair dismissal compensation and (e) an apprenticeship premium.[151] Liability for statutory maternity pay and statutory sick pay after the employer becomes insolvent passes to the Secretary of State[152] and an employee's entitlement to a redundancy payment may be made out of the National Insurance Fund.[153] An employee in respect of whom a protective award[154] has been made is, in the event of the insolvency of his employer, able to recover the amount due from the Secretary of State who is not entitled to deduct sums paid in lieu of statutory notice because the set-off provisions[155] apply only to payments made by an employer and there is nothing in the Insolvency Directive[156] which permits set-off; nor does the Directive render unlawful the maximum weekly liability contained in ERA, s. 186(1).[157] The Secretary of State may also be required to pay into an occupational pension scheme[158] any unpaid contributions due by an insolvent employer either on his

---

[141] *Ibid.*

[142] *Ibid.* And see Bankruptcy (Scotland) Act 1985, Sch. 3, para. 9(4) and Insolvency Act 1986 Sch. 6, para. 15 regarding contractual sick pay.

[143] *Ibid.* See Greene and Fletcher, *The Law and Practice of Receivership in Scotland,* para. 6.13.

[144] Insolvency Act 1986, s. 11(3)(d).

[145] *Carr v. British International Helicopters Ltd (in administration)* [1994] ICR 18, EAT.

[146] ERA, s. 186. The statutory maximum is not affected by the Insolvency Directive (80/987): *Secretary of State for Employment v. Mann* [1996] IRLR 4, EAT.

[147] By EA 1990, s. 11 the Redundancy Fund is wound up and merged with the National Insurance Fund.

[148] These include (1) guarantee payments, (2) medical suspension pay, (3) time-off payments and (4) payments under a protective award (ERA, s. 184(2)). But see *Secretary of State for Employment v. Forster* (unreported), case no. 220/87, EAT regarding loans by employee to employer.

[149] Where the employee had no loss by starting a new job immediately there can be no claim against the fund: *Secretary of State for Employment v. Wilson* [1977] IRLR 483, EAT.

[150] As defined in ERA, s. 184(3).

[151] ERA, s. 184(1)(e).

[152] Statutory Maternity Pay (General) Regulations 1986 (SI 1986 No. 1960), reg. 7(3); Statutory Sick Pay (General) Regulations 1982 (SI 1982 No. 894), reg. 9B.

[153] ERA, ss. 166, 169.

[154] See para. 9.34.

[155] See TULRCA 1992, s. 190(3).

[156] Dir. 80/987.

[157] *Secretary of State for Employment v. Mann* [1996] IRLR 4, EAT.

[158] As defined in Pension Schemes Act 1993, s. 124.

own accord or on behalf of an employee.[159] Employees[160] who apply to the Secretary of State but are partly or totally refused such a payment and those interested in an occupational pension scheme in respect of which the Secretary of State refuses—partly or totally—to make a payment may, within three months, complain to an industrial tribunal which may declare the amount of any payment the Secretary of State should make.[161] The correct approach is to apply the statutory maximum[162] and deduct therefrom, where appropriate, income tax and National Insurance deductions[163] and where the claim relates to a failure to give proper notice the employee must take reasonable steps to mitigate his loss.[164] Also, where the Secretary of State makes a payment to an employee or to an occupational pension fund he becomes entitled to exercise any rights and remedies available to the employee and persons competent to act in respect of the pension scheme.[165]

TERMINATION BY PERFORMANCE AND PASSAGE OF TIME

4.10 Where the contract is to perform a particular and finite piece of work it is brought to an end or discharged when the work is completed.[166] Generally where the contract is for a fixed term it comes to an end when the term expires and strictly neither party is required to give notice of impending expiry.[167] Only in those classes of employment[168] where by well-established custom the contract is renewed for a further similar period is notice of termination necessary to prevent tacit relocation.[169]

SPECIAL EMPLOYMENTS

4.11 In the case of the ordinary relationship of employer and employee there is no obligation at common law either to provide the dismissed employee with a statement of the reasons for his dismissal or to allow the employee the opportunity

---

[159] Pension Schemes Act 1993, ss. 123–125.

[160] Various groups of employees are excluded. See ERA, s. 196(7) (those who ordinarily work outside the territory of the European Communities); s. 199 (share fishermen and merchant seamen); s. 200 (police).

[161] ERA, s. 188.

[162] ERA, s. 186(1).

[163] *Morris v. Secretary of State for Employment* [1985] ICR 492, EAT; *Secretary of State for Employment v. Cooper* [1987] ICR 766, EAT. But note these decisions were on the basis that money paid in lieu of notice was a payment of damages.

[164] *Westwood v. Secretary of State for Employment* [1985] ICR 209, HL; *Munday v. Secretary of State for Employment* (unreported), case no. 618/88, EAT.

[165] ERA, s. 189; Pension Schemes Act 1993, s. 124.

[166] Stair, *Institutions* I. 18. 3. See also *Ryan v. Shipboard Maintenance Ltd* [1980] ICR 88, EAT; *Wiltshire CC v. NATFHE* [1980] ICR 455, CA; *Brown v. Knowsley BC* [1986] IRLR 102, EAT.

[167] *Lennox v. Allan & Son* (1880) 8 R 38; *Brenan v. Campbell's Trs* (1898) 25 R 423. In *Robson v. Hawick School Board* (1900) 2 F 411 the very fact that the contract was for a fixed period was itself notice of dismissal.

[168] *Viz* "agricultural domestic etc." *per* LJ-C Moncrieff, *Lennox v. Allan & Sons*, above. *Cf Campbell v. Fyfe* (1851) 13 D 1041; *Stevenson v. N B Railway Co.* (1905) 7 F 1106.

[169] Bell, *Principles*, s. 187; Lord Fraser, *Master and Servant*, p. 58; W. M. Gloag, *The Law of Contract* (2nd edn), p. 732.

of a hearing before effecting a dismissal.[170] However, the holder of a *munus publicum* is afforded special protection which will include observance of the principles of natural justice.[171] Equally, where the employee enjoys a statutory status a failure to follow the proper procedure or to observe the rules of natural justice will render the dismissal null and invalid.[172] However, neither the fact that the employer is a public body nor that the employer's powers are based on statutes will *per se* restrict the employer's powers of termination by requiring observance of the rules of natural justice,[173] and whether recourse can be had to the Court of Session for judicial review of the termination of an employment depends not on whether there may be a public law element involved but rather on whether the decision-making process has been entrusted to a body other than the employer or the decision has been taken by a public body acting beyond its powers so that an employee is prejudiced.[174]

Where a person holds a statutory status or public office the legal remedies for unlawful removal from office exceed the contractual and statutory remedies normally available with respect to the ordinary employer–employee relationship. Thus the reduction of an invalid *ultra vires* dismissal may in practice operate as reinstatement at least until the correct legal process is carried through.[175]

STATUTORY STATEMENT OF REASONS FOR DISMISSAL

4.12 An employee[176] who, by the effective date of termination, has been continuously employed[177] for a period of not less than two years[178] is entitled, on his dismissal with or without notice or on the expiry of a fixed-term contract which is not renewed, to receive from his employer, within 14 days of requesting[179] it, a

---

[170] Fraser, *Master and Servant*, p. 120; *Vine v. NDLB* [1957] AC 488, HL; *Ridge v. Baldwin* [1964] AC 40, HL; *Vidyodaya University of Ceylon v. Silva* [1965] 1 WLR 77, PC. And see *McClory v. Post Office* [1993] IRLR 159.

[171] *Magistrates of Montrose v. Strachan* (1710) Mor 13118; *Rothesay Magistrates v. Carse* (1903) 5 F 383; *Ridge v. Baldwin* [1964] AC 40.

[172] *Vine v. National Dock Labour Board* [1957] AC 488; *Malloch v. Aberdeen Corporation* 1971 SLT 245, HL. *Cf Barber v. Manchester Regional Hospital Board* [1958] 1 WLR 181.

[173] In *Malloch v. Aberdeen Corporation*, above, Lord Reid distinguished employees in higher grades or offices from others who are in the same position as employees in the private sector.

[174] *Blair v. Lochaber District Council* [1995] IRLR 135, OH applying *West v. Secretary of State for Scotland* 1992 SLT 636, IH. And see para. 3.64.

[175] See, for example, *Malloch v. Aberdeen Corporation*, above; and see paras 3.64ff; where no valid dismissal arises entitlement to arrears of salary or pension contributions may arise. And see para. 2.4(d), *supra*, regarding the ability of an employee of the state to rely on an EU Directive.

[176] Certain employees are excluded from the right to receive a written statement of the reasons for dismissal: see ERA, s. 192(1) (members of the forces), s. 196(2), (3) (employment outside Great Britain), s. 199(2) (share fishermen) and s. 200(1) (police).

[177] See para. 3.2.

[178] ERA, s. 92(3). *Cf* s. 92(4) which entitles a woman dismissed while pregnant or during maternity leave period to receive a statement without two years' employment and without having to request it.

[179] Section 92 cannot be used to correct a statement which an employer has volunteered where no request has been made: *Catherine Haigh Harlequin Hair Design v. Seed* [1990] IRLR 175, EAT.

written statement[180] giving particulars of the reasons for his dismissal.[181] Where an employer (1) unreasonably[182] refuses[183] to provide a written statement, or (2) provides a statement whose particulars the employee alleges are inadequate or untrue,[184] the employee may present a complaint to an industrial tribunal.[185] If the employee's complaint is upheld the tribunal (1) may make a declaration of what were the true reasons for dismissal,[186] and (2) must award the employee two weeks' pay.[187] No special technicalities are required of the employer, and he may refer the employee to another document, already given to the employee, which provides the particulars,[188] but to be adequate the statement must be such that the employee or anyone else who sees it can know from the statement why the employee was dismissed.[189]

---

[180] The statement is admissible in evidence in any proceedings, ERA, s. 92(5).

[181] ERA, s. 92(1). As to the purpose of the statutory entitlement, contrast *Horsley Smith & Sherry Ltd v. Dutton* [1977] ICR 594; [1977] IRLR 172, EAT, with *Charles Lang & Sons Ltd v. Aubrey* [1978] ICR 168, EAT; [1977] IRLR 354, EAT. In the former case Phillips J appreciated the social purpose of finding out the reason for a dismissal, whereas Lord McDonald viewed the provision as penal. In *Harvard Securities plc v. Younghusband* [1990] IRLR 17 the EAT observed the purpose of ERA, s. 92 is to tie down the employer to the reason on which he genuinely relied thus making clear to the employee the case he has to meet.

[182] Whether a refusal is unreasonable is a matter for the industrial tribunal. A tribunal has held that it is unreasonable for employers to refuse a statement just because the police asked them not to answer any correspondence in connection with the offence which led to the dismissal: *Daynecourt Insurance Brokers Ltd v. Iles* [1978] IRLR 335, EAT.

[183] There has to be a refusal: *Lowson v. Percy Main and District Social Club and Institute Ltd* [1979] ICR 568, EAT; [1979] IRLR 227, EAT. However, a prolonged failure to produce the statement may allow the tribunal to conclude that there has been a refusal: *Newland v. Simons & Willer (Hairdressers) Ltd* [1981] ICR 521; [1981] IRLR 359, EAT.

[184] But this does not permit a tribunal to examine the justification for the dismissal: *Harvard Securities plc v. Younghusband*, above.

[185] ERA, s. 93(2). The time for presenting such a complaint is the same as that for making a complaint of unfair dismissal (s. 93(3)). Thus, unless the tribunal deems an earlier complaint not reasonably practicable the time limit will be three months beginning with the effective date of termination (s. 111(2), (3)).

[186] ERA, s. 93(2)(a). This can have important implications for unfair dismissal; see Chapter Five.

[187] ERA, s. 93(2)(b). There is no maximum for s. 92.

[188] *Marchant v. Earley Town Council* [1979] ICR 891, EAT; [1979] IRLR 311, EAT.

[189] *Horsley Smith and Sherry Ltd v. Dutton*, above. The import of the decision is that one single document or statement must contain the essential reasons for the dismissal, although it may refer to other documents for further details. And see *Harvard Securities plc v. Younghusband*, above.

Chapter Five

UNFAIR DISMISSAL

INTRODUCTION

5.1 The law giving employees the right not to be unfairly dismissed was first introduced by the Industrial Relations Act 1971 and became effective on February 28, 1972. The present law on unfair dismissal is regulated by the Employment Rights Act 1996, Part X. In particular, s. 94(1) declares that, subject to certain exceptions, every employee shall have the right not to be unfairly dismissed by his employer. The aim is to create a statutory regime whereby an employee has the right to complain to an industrial tribunal when his contract is terminated and the tribunal will assess the legitimacy of the dismissal on the basis of fairness and reasonableness. This arrangement complies with international standards[1] and fulfils the recommendation of the Donovan Commission in 1968 that statutory machinery should be created which would require the employer to prove that he had a valid reason connected with the capacity or conduct of the worker or based on the operational requirements of the undertaking for any dismissal.[2] The industrial tribunal was selected as the appropriate forum for such complaints because it was an agency which seemed to possess the virtues of relative accessibility, informality, speed and lack of expense[3] — vital requirements for this area of the law.

5.2 It should be noted that the law of unfair dismissal does nothing to remove an employee's common law right to seek damages for wrongful dismissal in the civil courts. Thus an employee may have two remedies in relation to dismissal — one involving a breach of contract claim in a civil court and the other a statute-based complaint before an industrial tribunal. In the former, the outcome will depend largely on the terms of the contract of employment; in the latter, the decision will turn on the tribunal's assessment of the reasonableness or otherwise of the conduct of the employer. In addition, employees now have the right to complain to an industrial tribunal for breach of contract of employment where such a claim arises or is outstanding on the termination of employment. Such a claim is limited to a maximum of £25,000.[4] In most cases, a complaint of unfair dismissal will be the preferable option since it is faster and because it provides at least the possibility of re-employment. However, given the qualifying requirements for unfair dismissal and the practical limitations in terms of remedies, there might still be circum-

---

[1] See International Labour Organisation Recommendation No. 119.
[2] See the Report of the Royal Commission on Trade Unions and Employers' Associations Cmnd 3623 at para. 545.
[3] *Ibid.* para. 572.
[4] See generally the Industrial Tribunals Extension of Jurisdiction (Scotland) Order 1994 (SI 1994 No. 1624).

stances where a wrongful dismissal action is preferable[5] and, indeed, on some occasions it may be the only remedy.

5.3 Qualifying for the right, exclusions and time limits

The basic rule is that before an employee is eligible to complain of unfair dismissal he must, on the effective date of termination of the contract of employment, have been continuously employed[6] by his employer (or any associated employer)[7] for a minimum period of two years.[8] At one time the qualifying period was as low as 26 weeks.[9] The present qualifying period was introduced as part of the Conservative Government's policies aimed at encouraging the recruitment of new staff.[10] The two-year qualifying condition has been the subject of judicial review where it was argued that such a condition amounted to indirect discrimination against women. At first instance the action failed largely because it could not be established that a considerably smaller proportion of women could comply with the service require-ment than men: though the Divisional Court rejected the Government's contention that the condition was also justifiable on social policy grounds.[11] On appeal, however, the Court of Appeal held that the 1985 Order breached the principle of equal treatment enshrined in European law.[12] The court reversed the earlier decision on the impact of the Order and concluded that there was a considerable and persistent difference as regards the percentages of men and women who could satisfy the two-year qualification period. The Court of Appeal agreed with the Divisional Court that the Order was not objectively justifiable since it was neither suitable nor requisite for attaining the aim of increased employment.[13] Clearly, the qualifying period provides a substantial period during which an employer can form a view as to an employee's suitability without the fear of unfair dismissal proceedings being raised against him should he decide to dismiss. However, there are certain special cases where an employee has a right to complain of unfair dismissal without serving any qualifying period. These apply where an employee is dismissed for an automatically unfair reason *viz* because of his wish to join or to take part in the activities of an independent trade union or because of his refusal to become or remain a member of a trade union. Equally, there are now no qualifying requirements where employees claim unfair dismissal on the ground of pregnancy

---

[5] See, for example *Dietman v. Brent London Borough Council* [1987] IRLR 146, CA.

[6] A matter discussed in more detail in Chapter Three, paras 3.2–3.6.

[7] Under ERA, s. 231 any two employers are to be treated as associated if one is a company of which the other (either directly or indirectly) has control, or if both are companies of which a third person (directly or indirectly) has control.

[8] ERA, s. 108(1). For a case where the employer confirmed that the employee had the necessary two years' service when this was not in fact the case, see *Leicester University Students' Union v. Mahomed* [1995] IRLR 292, EAT.

[9] The qualifying period was increased on a number of occasions by the Conservative Government from the 26 week qualifying period which operated when the Conservatives came to power in 1979. The present two year qualifying period was set by the Unfair Dismissal (Variation of Qualifying Period) Order 1985 (SI 1985 No. 782) where the period of continuous employment began on or after June 1, 1985.

[10] This issue has been a constant theme of the Government's industrial and economic policies. See, for example, *Lifting the Burden*, Cmnd 9571, 1985 and *Building Businesses Not Barriers*, Cmnd 9794, 1986.

[11] *R. v. Secretary of State for Employment, ex parte Seymour-Smith and Perez* [1994] IRLR 448.

[12] See, in particular, the Equal Treatment Directive 76/207.

[13] *R. v. Secretary of State for Employment, ex parte Seymour-Smith and Perez* [1995] IRLR 464, CA.

or for a pregnancy-related reason,[14] for asserting a statutory right[15] or for exercising certain health and safety benefits.[16] In these cases a person obtains unfair dismissal protection as soon as employment has commenced.[17] Moreover, where employees are dismissed because of their sex or race a complaint under the Sex Discrimination Act 1975 or Race Relations Act 1976 will be competent because neither of these Acts stipulates a minimum qualifying period.

5.4 There are a number of ways in which a person can be denied the right to complain of unfair dismissal even in circumstances where it appears that the two year qualifying period has been satisfied. First, the right not to be unfairly dismissed only applies to those persons who satisfy the statutory definition of employee.[18] Thus only people who are employed under a contract of employment or a contract of apprenticeship can bring a complaint. A self-employed person working under a contract for services is excluded. Equally, those employed on the basis of non-standard contractual arrangements such as police cadets[19] or ministers of religion[20] are excluded. Despite the uncertainty as to whether or not Crown servants are employed under contracts of employment they do qualify for unfair dismissal rights.[21] However, persons who are employed under contracts of employment can still be denied the right to complain if their contracts have an illegal objective such as a fraud on the Inland Revenue. If a contract is illegal it is considered as being void *ab initio* and, therefore, cannot exist as a means of creating any rights to unfair dismissal.[22] In this area much will depend upon the knowledge of the employee as to the existence of this illegality[23]; although a contract of employment which seeks to defraud the Inland Revenue is illegal and unenforceable even though neither party knew that it was illegal.[24] However, tax avoidance schemes are not *per se* unlawful so as to prevent an unfair dismissal application.[25] Given the consequences for the complainant the tribunals are reluctant to hold that a contract of employment is illegal for this purpose. Thus a contract which appears legal on its face but is performed in an illegal way has been accepted as lawful in unfair dismissal law.[26]

5.5 Exclusions

Also there are a number of exclusions which deny a person a right to complain. First, an employee who is above retirement age is excluded.[27] Thus there is no right

---

[14] ERA, s. 99.

[15] ERA, s. 104.

[16] ERA, s. 100.

[17] TULRCA, s. 152 and s. 154, ERA, s. 108(3).

[18] ERA, s. 230(1). See also Chapter Two, paras 2.2–2.3.

[19] *Wiltshire Police Authority v. Wynn* [1980] ICR 649, CA.

[20] *Methodist Conference President v. Parfitt* [1984] ICR 176, CA; *Davies v. Presbyterian Church of Wales* [1986] ICR 280, HL; *Birmingham Mosque Trust Ltd v. Alavi* [1992] ICR 435, EAT.

[21] There is an equivalent provision for House of Commons Staff in ERA, s. 195.

[22] *Tomlinson v. Dick Evans "U" Drive Ltd* [1978] ICR 639, EAT.

[23] *Tomlinson*, above.

[24] *Salvesen v. Simons* [1994] IRLR 52, EAT. The position may be different in the case of small occasional payments without deduction of tax: *Annandale Engineering v. Samson* [1994] IRLR 59, EAT.

[25] *Lightfoot v. D & J Sporting Ltd* [1996] IRLR 64, EAT.

[26] *Coral Leisure Group Ltd. v. Barnett* [1981] ICR 503, EAT; *Hewcastle Catering Ltd. v. Ahmed* [1991] IRLR 473, EAT.

[27] ERA, s. 109(1).

of complaint if the employee has on or before the effective date of termination attained the following age:

(1) if in the undertaking in which he was employed there was a normal retiring age for an employee holding the position[28] which he held and the age was the same whether the employee holding that position was a man or a woman, that normal retiring age; and

(2) in any other case, the age of sixty-five.[29]

It is clear that if there is a non-discriminatory normal retiring age in the undertaking such an age will apply for the purposes of unfair dismissal law no matter whether this age is above or below normal pensionable age. If there is no such age in the undertaking the appropriate age will be 65 for both men and women.

5.6 Although the concept of a normal retiring age has caused disagreement amongst the judges of the Court of Appeal in the past,[30] it is now clear that there is a presumption that the normal retiring age will be the contractual retirement age applicable to all, or nearly all, the employees holding the position of the employee concerned.[31] "Normal retiring age" involves tribunals discovering what, at the effective date of termination of the applicant's employment, and on the basis of the facts then known, was the age which employees of all ages in the applicant's position could reasonably regard as the normal age of retirement applicable to the group.[32] As already stated, this will usually be ascertained by reference to the contractual retirement age: though it could feature as an aspect of the employer's employment policy.[33] The presumption can be displaced where there is evidence to show that the relevant employees had a reasonable expectation that a higher age of retirement would replace the contractual age.[34] In order to displace the presumption it is not necessary to establish an express abandonment; it is enough if there is evidence that it is regularly departed from in practice.[35] In deciding whether there is such a departure, the tribunal must examine the class of employees to which the dismissed employee belonged. Thus the normal retiring age would not be disturbed when there is an agreement with an individual employee to continue longer in employment since a normal retiring age involves a comparison with other

---

[28] "Position" means the following matters taken as a whole, that is to say, his status as an employee, the nature of his work and his terms and conditions of employment: ERA, s. 235(1). For the meaning of terms and conditions in the context of retirement see *Barber v. Thames Television plc* [1992] IRLR 410, CA.

[29] This provision was substituted by SDA 1986, s. 3(1) in order to comply with the decision of the European Court of Justice in *Marshall v. Southampton and South West Hampshire Area Health Authority (Teaching)* [1986] ICR 335, ECJ. For the position under the earlier law see *Nothman v. London Borough of Barnet* [1979] ICR 111, HL. And see now ERA, s. 109(1).

[30] Cf *Post Office v. Wallser* [1981] IRLR 37, CA and *Howard v. Department for National Savings* [1981] ICR 208, CA.

[31] *Per* Lord Fraser of Tullybelton in *Waite v. Government Communications Headquarters* [1983] ICR 653, HL at p. 662. See also *Highlands and Islands Development Board v. MacGillivray* [1986] IRLR 210, IH.

[32] *Brooks v. British Telecommunications plc* [1992] IRLR 66, CA.

[33] *Secretary of State for Education and Science v. Birchall* [1994] IRLR 630, EAT. But an employer must ensure that any such policy does not breach the contract: *Bratko v. Beloit Walmsley Ltd* [1996] ICR 76, EAT.

[34] *Hughes v. Department of Health and Social Security* [1985] ICR 419, HL.

[35] *Whittle v. Manpower Services Commission* [1987] IRLR 441, EAT; *Secretary of State for Scotland v. Meikle* [1986] IRLR 208, EAT.

employees who hold the same position as the applicant.[36] If the contractual retiring age is not observed in practice and employees retire at a variety of different ages there can be no normal retiring age for that undertaking so that in such a case the age of retirement will be taken to be 65.[37]

5.7 Employees who under their contracts of employment ordinarily work outside Great Britain are excluded from unfair dismissal law.[38] In the past it was thought possible for an employee ordinarily to work both in Britain and abroad.[39] However, it is now clear as a result of the decision of the Court of Appeal in *Wilson v. Maynard Shipbuilding Consultants AB*[40] that an employee must either ordinarily work in or outside Great Britain; he cannot do both at once. As the statutory directions make clear, the starting point for discovering a person's place of work must be the contract of employment. This involves the tribunal looking at the relevant terms of the contract, express or implied, over the whole period of employment. The question cannot be answered simply by reference to what has actually happened during the period of employment before termination took place.[41] The important issue is to consider the part of the employee's employment which relates to the work that he is employed to perform and to ignore the place where he was initially engaged or the place where leave is spent.[42] Frequently, however, the contractual terms will provide little, if any guidance as to the actual place of work. In such a case the correct approach is to examine all the facts in order to discover the employee's "base".[43] This base will usually be considered as the place where the employee ordinarily works even although the employee spends a considerable period of time in other places. Although all the facts should be considered in determining an employee's base, such facts as the place where the employee gets his orders; where the travels involved in his employment begin and end; where his private residence is or is expected to be; where, and in what currency, he is paid; and whether or not he pays British national insurance contributions[44] might be particularly significant.

5.8 Any agreement which limits an employee's statutory rights or denies him the opportunity of complaining to an industrial tribunal is void.[45] In the context of unfair dismissal law this would mean that any contractual term which denied an employee the right to complain to an industrial tribunal would be unenforceable.[46]

---

[36] *Age Concern Scotland v. Hines* [1983] IRLR 477, EAT.
[37] *Waite v. Government Communications Headquarters* [1983] ICR 653, HL. Equally, where the employer seeks to impose a term which the employee resists: *Patel v. Nagesan* [1996] ICR 988, CA.
[38] ERA, s. 196(2). Section 196(5) declares that a person employed to work on board a UK registered ship shall be regarded as ordinarily working in Great Britain unless his employment is wholly outside Great Britain or he is not ordinarily resident here. Discussed in *Wood v. Cunard Line Ltd* [1990] IRLR 281, CA.
[39] *Portec (UK) Ltd v. Mogensen* [1976] ICR 396, EAT.
[40] [1978] ICR 376, CA.
[41] *Wilson*, above.
[42] *Wood v. Cunard Line Ltd*, above.
[43] *Wilson*, above; *Todd v. British Midland Airways Ltd* [1978] ICR 959, CA. But see the judgment of Donaldson LJ in *Janata Bank v. Ahmed* [1981] ICR 791, CA, who pointed out that the base test is only an aid to construction and reminded tribunals that they should adopt a "broad brush approach" when examining the contractual position.
[44] *Per* Megaw LJ in *Wilson v. Maynard Shipbuilding Consultants AB*, above.
[45] ERA, s. 203(1).
[46] For the special position of the fixed term contract see para. 5.10.

Equally, any agreement by a dismissed employee to abandon a complaint of unfair dismissal would be ineffective even where the employer has made a severance payment to that employee consistent with his entitlement to compensation under unfair dismissal law.[47] However, there are some exceptions to this general rule. In particular there can be no complaint to an industrial tribunal where the employee is covered by a "dismissal procedures agreement" for which a relevant order has been made by the Secretary of State after joint application by all the parties to the agreement.[48] Such an agreement must be in writing and must be made by or on behalf of one or more independent trade unions and one or more employers or employers' associations.[49] Before making the order the Secretary of State must be satisfied as to the following:

(1)   the procedures are non-discriminatory;
(2)   the remedies provided by the agreement are on the whole as beneficial as statutory unfair dismissal law;
(3)   there is a right to arbitration or adjudication by some independent body;
(4)   the provisions of the agreement can be determined with reasonable certainty as to whether or not a particular employee is covered by it.[50]

5.9 An employee will also be prevented from pursuing a complaint to an industrial tribunal where a conciliation officer of ACAS has taken action in relation to that complaint by promoting a settlement.[51] In exercising this function a conciliation officer is not obliged to follow any specific formula. An officer would be held to have promoted a settlement where his involvement with the parties was simply to ensure that they had truly reached an agreement.[52] A settlement cannot be challenged because the conciliation officer did not explain the applicant's rights to him — there must be some evidence of bad faith or unfair methods[53]; or perhaps economic duress.[54] Although such settlements are usually recorded on a form provided by ACAS which is signed by the parties, it has been held that an oral agreement reached through the intermediary of an ACAS conciliation officer was to exclude an unfair dismissal application.[55] Despite the fact that the Industrial Tribunals Act 1996, s. 18(1), requires that a complaint be presented to a tribunal before a conciliation officer can become involved, it has been accepted that an officer can act not only where the employee has made a formal or express complaint but also where a claim can be implied from the overt acts or attitudes of the employee.[56] A settlement which is effected by a conciliation officer after the involvement of the applicant's adviser who has been named as his representative before the tribunal is binding upon that applicant whether or not the adviser had actual authority to enter into it.[57]

A complaint of unfair dismissal will also be excluded where there is a

---

[47]   *Council of Engineering Institutions v. Maddison* [1977] ICR 30 EAT.
[48]   ERA, s. 203(2)(c).
[49]   ERA, s. 235(1).
[50]   ERA, s. 110. The only major exempt industry is the Electrical Contracting Industry.
[51]   ERA, s. 203(2)(e), and ITA, ss. 18 and 19.
[52]   *Moore v. Duport Furniture Products Ltd* [1982] IRLR 31, HL.
[53]   *Slack v. Greenham (Plant Hire) Ltd* [1983] ICR 617, EAT.
[54]   *Hennessy v. Craigmyle & Co. Ltd* [1986] ICR 461, CA.
[55]   *Gilbert v. Kembridge Fibres Ltd* [1984] ICR 188, EAT.
[56]   *Moore v. Duport Furniture Products Ltd*, above; and see ITA, s. 18(5).
[57]   *Freeman v. Sovereign Chicken Ltd.* [1991] IRLR 408, EAT.

compromise agreement between the parties.[58] For such an agreement to be effective it must:

(a)   be in writing;

(b)   relate to the particular complaint;

(c)   involve independent[59] legal advice from a qualified lawyer[60] as to the terms and effect of the proposed agreement and, in particular, its effect upon any claim to the tribunal;

(d)   relate to a current policy of insurance covering the risk of a claim by the employee in respect of loss arising in consequence of the advice;

(e)   identify the adviser; and

(f)   state that the conditions regulating compromise agreements under ERA have been satisfied.[61]

5.10 It has already been noted that an agreement is void if it excludes an employee's statutory rights. However, an exception is made for an employee who is employed on a fixed term contract[62] of one year or more. It is not competent to agree a waiver clause in a fixed term contract which is for less than one year even where this contract is the last in a series of fixed contracts which did contain waiver clauses.[63] On the other hand, the original waiver will be effective where the additional period of employment can be genuinely viewed as merely an extension of the original contract so that it is part and parcel of that original contract.[64] An employee employed on a fixed term contract for a year or more can agree in writing before the contract's expiration to waive any rights as to unfair dismissal but only insofar as the dismissal arises from the expiry and non-renewal of the contract. Thus an employee working under a fixed term contract only waives his unfair dismissal rights as far as the non-renewal of that contract is concerned and this is so no matter what is the reason for the dismissal; however, his rights to complain of unfair dismissal in any other circumstance remain unaffected by the agreement. A fixed term contract is a contract where the parties have agreed a definite termination date. However, in *Dixon v. British Broadcasting Corporation*[65] the Court of Appeal held that a contract is for a fixed term even although it provides for termination by notice on either side before the expiry of the term. On the other hand, a contract which is inherently temporary but which is indeterminate in time, such as a contract to work until a particular task is completed, is not a fixed term contract.[66]

5.11 A number of specific employments are excluded from the ambit of unfair dismissal law. Persons employed in the police service are excluded[67]; though members of the armed forces now have protection against unfair dismissal except

---

[58]   ERA, s. 203(2)(f).

[59]   "Independent", in relation to legal advice to the employee, means that it is given by a lawyer who is not acting in the matter for the employer or an associated employer: ERA, s. 203(4).

[60]   "Qualified lawyer" means in Scotland, an advocate, whether in practice as such or employed to give legal advice, or a solicitor who holds a practising certificate: ERA, s. 203(4).

[61]   ERA, s. 203(3).

[62]   ERA, s. 197(1).

[63]   *British Broadcasting Corporation v. Ioannou* [1975] IRLR 184, CA.

[64]   *Mulrine v. University of Ulster* [1993] IRLR 545, NICA.

[65]   [1979] ICR 281.

[66]   See, for example, *Wiltshire CC v. NATFHE* [1985] ICR 455, CA.

[67]   ERA, s. 200.

in the case of health and safety dismissals[68] and trade union membership dismissals.[69] The unfair dismissal provisions also do not apply to employment as a master or as a member of the crew of a fishing vessel where the person is paid by means of a share in the profits or gross earnings of the vessel.[70] Although, as we have seen, civil servants enjoy the advantages of unfair dismissal law this protection can be lost if a certificate issued by a Minister of the Crown is in force excluding that person in order to safeguard national security.[71] At one time there were also exclusions for employed spouses[72] and registered dock workers.[73] Both of these groups of employees can now complain of unfair dismissal.

5.12 Time limits

An employee has three months from the effective date of termination[74] of his contract to complain to an industrial tribunal.[75] The correct way to calculate the period of three months beginning with the effective date of termination is first to find the effective date of termination, take the date before it, and then go forwards three months.[76] This period expires at midnight on the last day of the three months, even when this is a non-working day[77] and runs from the date of dismissal.[78] This is not necessarily the date when the employee is informed that an appeal against dismissal has failed,[79] nor the date when he receives his P45.[80] Where an unfair dismissal application has been posted within the three month period but arrives after that period has expired, the question is whether the applicant could reasonably have expected the application to be delivered in time in the ordinary course of the post. This is a question for the tribunal to determine on the evidence.[81] It is also advisable for the applicant to have some system of checking that the application has been received since there is no presumption that what is posted will be delivered.[82] A failure to present the complaint within this period will render the complaint time-barred.[83] However, the tribunal has the power to extend this period when it is satisfied that it was not reasonably practicable for the

---

[68] ERA, s. 192(1), (2).

[69] TULRCA, s. 274.

[70] ERA, s. 199(2).

[71] ERA, s. 193. See also *Council of Civil Service Unions v. Minister for the Civil Service* [1985] ICR 14, HL. There is also a power to exclude non-civil servants on security grounds: ITA, s. 10(4).

[72] EPCA, s. 146(1) repealed by EA 1982, s. 21(2), Sch. 3, para. 6.

[73] EPCA, s. 145 repealed by Dock Work Act 1989, s. 7(1) and Sch. 1.

[74] See paras 5.27 to 5.29.

[75] ERA, s. 111(2). This period is extended to six months in the case of a selective re-engagement of employees involved in industrial action: TULRCA, s. 239(2).

[76] *Pruden v. Cunard Ellerman Ltd* [1993] IRLR 317, EAT.

[77] *Swainston v. Hetton Victory Club Ltd* [1983] ICR 341, CA.

[78] For the current approach where there is more than one ground of dismissal see *Marley (UK) Ltd v. Anderson* [1994] IRLR 152, EAT.

[79] *Savage v. J. Sainsbury Ltd* [1981] ICR 1, CA.

[80] *London Borough of Newham v. Ward* [1985] IRLR 509, CA.

[81] See generally *St Basil's Centre v. McCrossan* [1991] IRLR 455, EAT.

[82] *Capital Foods Retail Ltd v. Corrigan* [1993] IRLR 430, EAT. The checking system should be contemporaneous: *Camden and Islington Community Services NHS Trust v. Kennedy* [1996] IRLR 381, EAT.

[83] But there is no time limit when it is proposed to add a new or substitute respondent to an originating application which has been lodged timeously: *Gillick v. BP Chemicals Ltd* [1993] IRLR 437, EAT applied by the EAT in England in *Drinkwater Sabey Ltd v. Burnett* [1995] IRLR 238.

complaint to be presented within the three months.[84] The issue of reasonable practicability is essentially a question of fact for the industrial tribunal.[85] It would seem that the correct question for the tribunal is to ask whether it was reasonably feasible for the complaint to be presented in time.[86] This is a test which the courts and tribunals apply strictly. An applicant's ignorance of his rights would not normally be a ground for extending the three month period.[87] Equally, where the delay is the fault of the applicant or a mistake by his adviser[88] in not informing him fully of his rights, there will be no extension of the time limit.[89] But this is not a rule of law and the question is essentially one of fact for the industrial tribunal so that an applicant will not necessarily lose for all time his right to rely on the reasonably practicable defence once he consults his adviser who gives him wrong advice. The defence is most likely to be accepted where the applicant distrusts the advice of his adviser and immediately seeks further advice from another source.[90] An employee may be able to submit a late application where new facts come to light after the expiry of the three month period. Such new facts may create a fresh period of complaint so that there is the possibility of separate complaints on separate grounds submitted at different times.[91] A late application may be allowed where the mistake is reasonable so that there is a just cause and excuse for it.[92] Thus an employee who knew of the time limit but who thought that his complaint for unfair dismissal would be heard by the same tribunal which considered his complaint for unemployment benefit was held entitled to submit a late complaint because his mistake was genuine.[93]

5.13 There are two further problems concerning the three month time limit. First, what is the position of an employee who awaits the outcome of a final internal appeal and then discovers that when this has failed a right to complain to an industrial tribunal has become time-barred? At one time there were conflicting decisions of the Employment Appeal Tribunal on this point.[94] However, the Court of Appeal has now made it clear that the mere fact that an employee has been pursuing an appeal through the employer's internal machinery does not mean that it was not reasonably practicable for the unfair dismissal application to be made in time.[95] Thus an employee in such a position would be well advised to submit an application anyway in order to protect his rights. The other problem concerns the case where material information comes to the employee's attention after the expiry of the three months. In *Machine Tool Industry Research Association v. Simpson*[96]

---

[84] ERA, s. 111(2).
[85] *Palmer v. Southend-on-Sea Borough Council* [1984] ICR 372, CA.
[86] *Palmer*, above.
[87] *Dedman v. British Building and Engineering Appliances Ltd* [1974] ICR 53, CA.
[88] *Riley v. Tesco Stores Ltd* [1980] IRLR 103, CA. This case also makes it clear that an adviser who is a trade union official or CAB worker is to be treated in the same way as a solicitor.
[89] *Dedman*, above; *Walls Meat Co. Ltd v. Khan* [1979] ICR 52 CA; *Riley*, above.
[90] *London International College Ltd v. Sen* [1993] IRLR 333, CA.
[91] *Marley (UK) Ltd v. Anderson* [1996] IRLR 163, CA.
[92] *Khan*, above; *Riley*, above.
[93] *Khan*, above.
[94] *Crown Agents for Overseas Government and Administration v. Lawa* [1979] ICR 103, EAT (good reason for an extension); *Bodha v. Hampshire Area Health Authority* [1982] ICR 200, EAT (no extension).
[95] *Palmer v. Southend-on-Sea Borough Council* [1984] ICR 372. For the position of part-time employees dismissed in the past who now believe that they have a complaint because of the operation of European law see *Biggs v. Somerset County Council* [1996] ICR 364, CA.
[96] [1988] IRLR 212.

the Court of Appeal considered that this would be a circumstance where a late application would be accepted so long as the information was crucial or important and was reasonably unknown to the applicant during the three months so that once it was acquired it gave the applicant a genuine belief that a claim should be brought. This decision has important implications, in particular, for the redundant employee who later discovers that someone has been hired to replace him.

MEANING OF DISMISSAL

5.14 It is crucial for unfair dismissal law that the termination of the employee's contract satisfies the statutory definition of dismissal. Usually, this is not a problem since it is obvious that the employee has been dismissed. However, where this is an issue the onus of proving statutory dismissal rests with the employee. Dismissal is defined to apply in the following four cases:

(a)   where the contract is terminated by the employer with or without notice;

(b)   where under a fixed term contract the term expires without being renewed under the same contract;

(c)   where the employee terminates the contract with or without notice in circumstances entitling him to terminate without notice by reason of the employer's conduct;

(d)   where a woman is refused permission by her employer to return to work after maternity leave.[97]

5.15 Termination by the employer

There will be a dismissal where the employer's words are a clear instruction to the employee that his contract is being terminated with or without notice. However, if the words used are ambiguous, it is necessary to construe them in context. This would entail looking at such factors as the status of the employee and, if the language was verbal, the place and circumstances in which the words were used.[98] Only if the words remain ambiguous after looking at them in their context should the tribunal then consider how these words could reasonably be interpreted and decide whether they were so interpreted by the employee concerned.[99] Problems can sometimes arise when the employer uses unambiguous words of dismissal in the heat of the moment. Such language need not constitute dismissal so long as the words are withdrawn almost immediately.[100] It will be a question of degree as to whether or not a retraction can prevent dismissal. Employers might also be taken to have dismissed when they unilaterally impose radically different terms of employment if, objectively, this can be construed as a removal or withdrawal of the old contract.[100a] Where the employee uses unambiguous language consistent with resignation, the employer is entitled to treat it as such and accept the employee's repudiation of contract at once.[101] A tribunal is entitled to apply the

---

[97]   ERA, ss. 95, 96.

[98]   Problems can sometimes arise as to whether offensive language used by an employer is intended simply to be abusive or meant to terminate the contract. See, for example, *Futty v. D. & D. Brekkes Ltd* [1974] IRLR 130, IT.

[99]   *Stern (J. & J.) v. Simpson* [1983] IRLR 52, EAT.

[100] *Martin v. Yeoman Aggregates Ltd* [1983] ICR 314, EAT.

[100a] *Alcan Extrusions v. Yates* [1996] IRLR 327, EAT, reviewing *Hogg v. Dover College* [1990] ICR 39, EAT.

[101] *Kwik-Fit (GB) Ltd v. Lineham* [1992] IRLR 156, EAT.

natural meaning of the employee's language and accept the fact of the employer's understanding of it without the need to decide how the reasonable employer would have reacted.[102] The only exception to this rule would be where there is something in the context of the exchange or in the circumstances of the employee himself that establishes, that despite appearances, there was no real resignation.[103] These special circumstances may include decisions taken in the heat of the moment, or involving an immature employee,[104] or where the employee is jostled into a decision by the employer.[105] Where there are special circumstances it is important that the employer allow a reasonable period of time of a day or two to elapse before accepting the resignation since during this time facts may arise which cast doubt upon whether the resignation was really intended and can properly be assumed. If the employer does not investigate these facts he runs the risk of the tribunal holding that there was no genuine resignation.[106]

Another area of difficulty is the case where at first sight it may appear that the employee has resigned, but it can be shown that the resignation was forced upon the employee by the employer. It is clear that where the employer issues an ultimatum such as "resign or be sacked" this should be construed as dismissal.[107] The same would apply where the employee is pressurised into resigning because of employer fraud.[108] The crucial test in such cases is to consider who really terminated the contract.[109] However, employer dismissal depends upon there being a causal link between the employer's threat and the employee's resignation. Thus it would not be dismissal for an employer to tell an employee that if he does not find a job elsewhere his employment will eventually be terminated.[110]

5.16 Non-renewal of contract

An employer's non-renewal of a fixed term contract is a dismissal. As already noted, a contract can be for a fixed term even although it contains a notice clause.[111] Problems can still arise with this type of contract. Thus, for example, it would not be a dismissal in law when the contract came to an end and was not renewed because the contract specified that it would last only as long as sufficient funds were provided by sponsors and no further funding was received. In this case the contract came to an end automatically on the happening or non-happening of a future event — there was no need for action by anybody.[112]

5.17 Constructive dismissal

The third type of dismissal is "constructive" dismissal. This arises where, although it is the employee who ends the contract by walking out or giving notice,

---

[102] *Sothern v. Franks, Charlesly & Co.* [1981] IRLR 278, CA.
[103] *Sovereign House Security Services Ltd v. Savage* [1989] IRLR 115, CA.
[104] *Sovereign House Security Services Ltd*, above.
[105] *Barclay v. City of Glasgow District Council* [1983] IRLR 313, EAT. It was also held in this case that there may be occasions (e.g. where an employee is suffering from emotional stress) where the employer is required to take account of the employee's special circumstances before deciding whether to treat the employee as having resigned.
[106] *Kwik-Fit (GB) Ltd v. Lineham*, above.
[107] *East Sussex County Council v. Walker* [1972] 7 ITR 280; *Sheffield v. Oxford Controls Ltd* [1979] IRLR 133, EAT.
[108] *Caledonian Mining Co. Ltd v. Bassett* [1987] ICR 425, EAT.
[109] *Martin v. MBS Fastenings (Glynwed Distribution) Ltd* [1983] ICR 511, CA.
[110] *Haseltine, Lake & Co. v. Dowler* [1981] ICR 222, EAT.
[111] *Dixon v. BBC* [1979] ICR 281, CA.
[112] *Brown v. Knowsley Borough Council* [1986] IRLR 102, EAT.

the real reason for the termination is some prior conduct by the employer. Although there was some confusion in the past, it is now clear that for employee's resignation to constitute a dismissal in law, the act must be in response to a material breach of contract by the employer; it would not be sufficient if the employer had merely acted in an unreasonable manner towards the employee.[113] Thus the present test for constructive dismissal concentrates upon the terms of the contract of employment both express and implied.[114] It enables employers to introduce new work rules so long as they are within the scope of the contract.[115] In order to satisfy this test the employer's conduct must go to the root of the contract so as to indicate that he no longer intends to be bound by it. This intention is judged objectively so that there might still be a material breach even where the employer believes that he has acted in conformity with the contract.[116] Equally, the fact that an employer acts in good faith on a genuine though mistaken belief as to the employee's circumstances is not enough by itself to prevent there being a repudiatory breach of contract.[117] Obvious examples of such a material breach would be a failure to pay wages[118]; a unilateral alteration in duties without contractual authority[119]; a suspension without pay where this is not authorised by the contract[120]; a demotion out of proportion to the offence[121] or a failure to follow the contractual disciplinary rules.[122] Usually a constructive dismissal will arise as a result of a single act of the employer. However, there might be occasions where the right to resign can arise after a series of incidents so that the employee is entitled to rely on their cumulative effect.[123]

5.18 To a large extent each constructive dismissal case will depend upon its own facts with the terms of the contract constituting a critical focus for analysis. Thus, for example, in a case where the employee argues that a change in his place of work constitutes a material breach the tribunal will be required to discover whether or not there is a clear and unambiguous mobility clause giving the employer the power to relocate work[124] and that the employer applied it.[125] An employer will be

---

[113] *Western Excavating (ECC) Ltd v. Sharp* [1978] ICR 221, CA applied in Scotland in *Greater Glasgow Health Board v. Pate* 1983 SLT 90.

[114] See, for example, *Woods v. W M Car Services (Peterborough) Ltd* [1982] ICR 693, CA.

[115] *Dryden v. Greater Glasgow Health Board* [1992] IRLR 469, EAT.

[116] *Lewis v. Motorworld Garages Ltd* [1986] ICR 157, CA. See also *Blyth v. Scottish Liberal Club* 1982 SC 140.

[117] *Brown v. JBD Engineering Ltd* [1993] IRLR 568, EAT.

[118] *Industrial Rubber Products v. Gillon* [1977] IRLR 389, EAT. However, it has been held that where the contract does not provide for regular pay increases, no such term can be implied so that a failure to increase wages would not necessarily be a material breach: *Murco Petroleum Ltd v. Forge* [1987] IRLR 50, EAT. Equally, there is no breach when the employer reduces wages in conformity with the contract even though employees suffer a loss of income: *White v. Reflecting Roadstuds Ltd* [1991] IRLR 331, EAT.

[119] Removal of an employee's important duties leaving him with duties of a humdrum nature is undoubtedly grounds for employee resignation: *Coleman v. S. & W. Baldwin* [1977] IRLR 342, EAT. Even a temporary change of duties could be a material breach: *McNeill v. Charles Crimin (Electrical Contractors) Ltd* [1984] IRLR 179, EAT. See also *Hogg v. Dover College* [1990] ICR 39, EAT.

[120] *McKenzie (D. & J.) Ltd v. Smith* [1976] IRLR 345, OH.

[121] *BBC v. Becket* [1981] IRLR 515, EAT.

[122] *Post Office v. Strange* [1981] IRLR 515, EAT. This would also apply as regards grievance arrangements: *W. A. Goold (Pearmark) Ltd v. McConnell* [1995] IRLR 516, EAT.

[123] *Lewis v. Motorworld Garages Ltd*, above.

[124] *Rank Xerox v. Churchill* [1988] IRLR 280, EAT.

[125] *Curling v. Securicor Ltd* [1992] IRLR 549, EAT.

in breach of contract when he requires an employee to work at a place which does not satisfy the conditions of such a clause.[126] But there is no requirement that a specific contractual power is subject to an implied term that it should be exercised reasonably.[127] However, even where there is no express term in the contract stipulating the employee's place of work, a right to transfer that employee might be implied on the basis of business efficacy.[128] Usually a term will be implied permitting a change in place of work so long as it is within reasonable daily travelling distance of the employee's home.[129] However, insufficient notice of such a change is undoubtedly a material breach.[130] The implied terms of the contract are also important in the sense that an employee may have a ground for resignation where the employer is in breach of one of his implied contractual duties. In particular, a complaint alleging that the employer's conduct has destroyed or seriously damaged the relationship of mutual trust and confidence between the parties is a fruitful means of establishing constructive dismissal.[131] Examples of this type of material breach include employer use of offensive language towards an employee[132]; questioning an employee's competence when this is not a true opinion of his abilities[133]; and denying the employee protection from harassment by fellow employees.[134]

5.19 For a constructive dismissal complaint to succeed it is also necessary that the employee establishes a causal link between the employer's material breach and his decision to leave.[135] An employee who delays his decision to resign might be prevented from successfully arguing constructive dismissal on the basis that he has accepted a variation in the terms of his contract.[136] To avoid this the employee should leave as quickly as possible or, if there are circumstances preventing this, to indicate that he does not accept the employer's conduct and is continuing to work under protest.[137] Thus an employee who makes clear his objection to the employer's conduct, should not be taken to have affirmed the contract by continuing to work and draw pay for a limited period even where this is simply to

---

[126] *Bass Leisure Ltd v. Thomas* [1994] IRLR 104, EAT.
[127] *White v. Reflecting Roadstuds Ltd* [1991] IRLR 331, EAT. *Cf United Bank Ltd v. Akhtar* [1989] IRLR 507, EAT.
[128] *Courtaulds Northern Spinning Ltd v. Sibson* [1988] IRLR 305, CA.
[129] *Sibson*, above; *Jones v. Associated Tunnelling Co. Ltd* [1981] IRLR 477, EAT.
[130] *Prestwick Circuits Ltd v. McAndrew* [1990] IRLR 191, IH.
[131] See, for example, the decision of the Court of Appeal in *Woods v. W M Car Services (Peterborough) Ltd*, above.
[132] *Isle of Wight Tourist Board v. Coombes* [1976] IRLR 413, EAT.
[133] *Courtaulds Northern Textiles Ltd v. Andrew* [1979] IRLR 84, EAT.
[134] *Wigan Borough Council v. Davies* [1979] IRLR 127, EAT. An employer's failure to take seriously an employee's complaint of sexual harassment can be grounds for resignation: *Bracebridge Engineering Ltd v. Darby* [1990] IRLR 3, EAT, as is a failure to implement the procedure: *W. A. Goold (Pearmark) Ltd v. McConnell* [1995] IRLR 516, EAT.
[135] *Walker v. Josiah Wedgwood & Sons Ltd* [1978] ICR 744, EAT.
[136] *Western Excavating (ECC) Ltd v. Sharp* [1978] ICR 221, CA. However, this would not apply where the employer's breach is either a continuing breach or a breach which also involves a breach of statute: *Reid v. Camphill Engravers* [1990] IRLR 268, EAT.
[137] *Cox Toner (W. E.) (International) Ltd v. Crook* [1981] ICR 823, EAT. An employee who performs acts which can only be construed as consistent with the continuation of the contract will lose his right to complain. On the other hand, if the employee is only continuing in order to allow the employer to remedy his breach a complaint of unfair dismissal may still succeed. Equally, mere passage of time does not necessarily imply acceptance: *Aparau v. Iceland Frozen Foods plc* [1996] IRLR 119, EAT.

enable him to find alternative work.[138] There may also be circumstances where the employee can anticipate the employer's breach by resigning before the employer has broken the contract.[139] Once the employee has established constructive dismissal it is still open to the employer to show that the reason for the dismissal was fair,[140] although usually this would be difficult.

5.20 Save for the special case of the employee who is not allowed to return to her old job after confinement, which will be discussed shortly, a complaint of unfair dismissal lies only where termination takes one of these three forms. Thus it is not a relevant form of dismissal where the parties mutually agree to terminate the contract, unless there was some unlawful employer pressure which forced the employee to agree to the termination.[141] In the past the tribunals applied the concept of mutual termination narrowly. For example, it was still a relevant dismissal where the employer dismissed an employee who had volunteered to go or who had no objection to being dismissed.[142] However, this position must now be contrasted with the case where the employee applies for retirement and this is accepted by the employer. In such a case there will be mutual termination, notwithstanding that the retirement was at the employee's request and subject to the employer's approval.[143] The issue is likely to turn on the facts and it does not follow that merely because it is the act of the employee in compliance with the employer's request which marks the termination of the contract that such an act will establish an agreed termination.[144]

5.21 Automatic termination

However, there is one important limitation on the concept of an agreed termination. For example, an employee, in return for being given extended leave, may agree that if he does not return to work on a specific date his contract will have terminated automatically. The legitimacy of this approach was tested and approved by the Employment Appeal Tribunal in *British Leyland (UK) Ltd v. Ashraf*[145] where it was held that in the circumstances there was no dismissal in law. However, this decision has now been reversed by the Court of Appeal in *Igbo v. Johnson Matthey Chemicals Ltd*[146] where the court, concerned about the damaging consequences of this approach for employees,[147] argued that an agreement of this

---

[138] *Marriott v. Oxford & District Co-operative Society (No. 2)* [1970] 1 QB 186. See also *Hogg v. Dover College* [1990] ICR 39, EAT.

[139] *Greenaway Harrison Ltd v. Wiles* [1994] IRLR 380, EAT.

[140] *Berriman v. Delabole Slate Ltd* [1985] ICR 546, CA; *Stephenson & Co. (Oxford) Ltd v. Austin* [1990] ICR 609, EAT. See also the decision of the Second Division in *Greater Glasgow Health Board v. Pate* 1983 SLT 90 but note the dissent of Lord Dunpark who argued that once it had been held that the complainant had been constructively dismissed there was no room for argument that her dismissal had been other than unfair.

[141] *Staffordshire County Council v. Donovan* [1981] IRLR 108, EAT. And see *Logan Salton v. Durham C.C.* [1989] IRLR 99, EAT.

[142] *Burton, Allton & Johnson Ltd v. Peck* [1975] ICR 193, QBD.

[143] *Birch v. University of Liverpool* [1985] ICR 470, CA.

[144] *Hellyer Bros Ltd v. Atkinson and Dickinson* [1992] IRLR 540, EAT.

[145] [1978] ICR 979, EAT.

[146] [1986] ICR 505, CA.

[147] The potential application of the *Ashraf* principle could have been very wide. For example, could it have been used to deal with the employee with a poor attendance record? The absurdities of this approach are discussed by Parker LJ in *Igbo*, above at p. 512.

kind was void[148] because it constituted an attempt to limit the operation of the Act.

5.22 Self-dismissal

One other potential problem area concerns the notion of self-dismissal and its recognition as a form of termination of a contract of employment. This involves arguing that where an employee has committed an act of gross misconduct, that act alone should be taken as terminating the contract without the need for any dismissal by the employer. The acceptance of this argument would also deny a tribunal jurisdiction on the basis that the ending of the contract in such circumstances did not involve a dismissal. The Employment Appeal Tribunal recognised its validity in *Gannon v. J. C. Firth Ltd*[149] where the employees, in the course of a dispute, walked out of the factory without informing the management and left the premises in a dangerous state. It was held that this conduct was repudiatory of the contract and that it also ended the contract so that the employees had not been dismissed and could not complain of unfair dismissal. However, this case has also been overruled by the Court of Appeal. In *London Transport Executive v. Clarke*[150] a majority of that court held that a repudiatory breach does not automatically terminate a contract of employment. Instead, it gives the innocent party the right to elect to terminate the contract or not. It is only once the innocent party has decided to accept the repudiation and terminate the contract that the relationship is ended. In the context of employee misconduct, this means that the employer must dismiss the employee in order to end the contract.[151] Hence, in such circumstances the employee will at least be able to complain to a tribunal, although it is likely that the employer will be able to satisfy the tribunal as to the fairness of this decision.

5.23 Frustration

One circumstance where an employee will be denied the opportunity of complaining to an industrial tribunal is where his contract is terminated by operation of law. It is a general rule applicable to all contracts that a contract will end automatically when there is some frustrating event which renders that contract impossible or illegal to perform or involves performance of a radically different kind from that originally envisaged by the parties. As discussed earlier this doctrine undoubtedly applies to contracts of employment[152] and has special significance in unfair dismissal law for sick employees or those serving prison sentences. Its application to the sick employee was reviewed by the National Industrial Relations Court in *Marshall v. Harland and Wolff Ltd*[153] where it was stated that in considering whether an employee's sickness could frustrate the contract the tribunals should take account of certain factors.[154]

5.24 The reference to contracts of long standing led the Employment Appeal

---

[148] ERA, s. 203.

[149] [1976] IRLR 415, EAT followed in *Kallinos v. London Electric Wire* [1980] IRLR 11, EAT.

[150] [1981] ICR 355, CA (Templeman and Dunn LJJ, Lord Denning MR dissenting). See also *Rasool v. Hepworth Pipe Co. Ltd (No. 1)* [1980] ICR 494, EAT. And see Chapter Four, para. 4.5

[151] See Chapter Four, para. 4.5.

[152] See generally W. W. McBryde *The Law of Contract in Scotland* at paras 15–22 to 15–48.

[153] [1972] ICR 101, NIRC.

[154] See Chapter Four, para. 4.6.

Tribunal to argue in *Egg Stores (Stamford Hill) Ltd v. Leibovici*[155] that frustration would not normally be relevant in the case of short-term periodic contracts terminable at short notice. It was also argued that, although there were a large number of issues which had to be considered before a contract would be treated as frustrated, one critical consideration would be to discover whether the time had come when the employer could no longer be reasonably expected to keep the absent employee's post open for him. The Employment Appeal Tribunal also argued that much may turn on the reason for the employer's inaction (e.g. avoidance of his statutory obligations) should this moment arise and the employer do nothing.[156] Indeed, the Employment Appeal Tribunal has gone so far as to argue in *Harman v. Flexible Lamps Ltd*[157] that the doctrine of frustration should not apply at all to a contract of employment which could be terminated by notice and should therefore be restricted to long-term contracts without notice provisions. This narrow view of the operation of the doctrine has been criticised by the Court of Appeal in *Notcutt v. Universal Equipment Co. (London) Ltd*.[158] In this case it was argued that there was no reason in principle why a periodic contract of employment determinable by relatively short notice should not also be capable of being terminated by frustration. When considering this question it is not necessary to take account of the injustice to the parties of the rules of frustration. The *Notcutt* case undoubtedly ensures that it will be much easier for the employer to argue in the future that the contract of a sick employee has been frustrated.[159] Nonetheless, in *Williams v. Watsons Luxury Coaches Ltd*[160] the Employment Appeal Tribunal counselled tribunals to guard against too easy an application of the doctrine of frustration and reiterated that the tribunal should always consider the factors discussed in *Marshall* and *Liebovici* in order to determine whether a contract of employment has genuinely been frustrated.

5.25 There is no doubt that the serving of a custodial sentence can also be a potentially frustrating event. However, just like the sick employee the circumstances of each case must be considered with due regard for such factors as the employee's position in the business and the expected period of his absence from work.[161] Although usually frustration can only apply where the frustrating event is not the fault of either party, an exception is made for the imprisoned employee. Thus although in some senses it is the employee's fault which creates the circumstances making performance impossible, this would not bar the application of frustration so long as it is the employer who seeks to take advantage of the doctrine.[162]

5.26 Return to work after confinement

The final type of dismissal for unfair dismissal purposes applies in the case of the female employee seeking to return to work after confinement. When an employee

---

[155] [1976] IRLR 376, EAT.
[156] *Hart v. A. R. Marshall & Sons (Bulwell) Ltd* [1977] IRLR 15, EAT.
[157] [1980] IRLR 418, EAT.
[158] [1986] ICR 414.
[159] The *Notcutt* case was actually a claim for damages for contractual sick pay. However, the principles applicable here are the same as for unfair dismissal. In this case, a contract which had run for 27 years and which could be terminated by twelve weeks' notice was held to be frustrated by an eight months' absence.
[160] [1990] IRLR 164, EAT.
[161] *Shepherd (F. C.) & Co. Ltd v. Jerrom* [1985] ICR 552, EAT.
[162] *Shepherd (F. C.) & Co. Ltd v. Jerrom* [1986] ICR 802, CA.

is entitled to return to work and has exercised her right to do so, but is not permitted to return, she should be regarded as being continuously employed until the notified date of her return and treated as dismissed with effect from that day for the reason for which she was not permitted to return.[163]

5.27 Effective date of termination

One further important issue as regards dismissal is the establishment of the employee's effective date of termination (EDT). This is important because it fixes the date upon which the employee's period of continuous employment ends and it starts the three month period during which the employee must submit his complaint of unfair dismissal to the tribunal. Clearly the exact date of this event will vary depending upon the form of dismissal. EDT is defined as follows:

(a)   in the case of an employee whose contract is terminated by notice, whether given by the employer or employee, the EDT will be the date on which that notice expires;

(b)   in the case of an employee whose contract is terminated without notice, the EDT will be the date on which the termination takes effect; and

(c)   in the case of an employee employed under a fixed term contract, where that term expires without being renewed under the same contract, the EDT will be the date on which that term expires.[164]

5.28 It is clear that where dismissal is communicated to an employee in a letter, the contract of employment will not terminate until the employee has actually read the letter or had a reasonable opportunity of reading it. In such a case the EDT is the date when the employee either does read the letter or the date when he reasonably had the opportunity of knowing about it — it is not backdated to the date when the letter was written.[165] A dismissal will terminate the contract once it has been communicated to the employee even although the dismissal is in breach of contract.[166] In England a distinction has been made between a case where an employee is dismissed with notice but is given payment in lieu of working out that notice, and a case where no notice of dismissal is given but a payment is made in lieu of notice. In the former the EDT is the date when the notice expires; in the latter the EDT is the date of receipt of the payment.[167] Much will depend upon the tribunal's construction of the employer's letter in deciding which alternative applies in a given case.[168]

5.29 There are also special statutory rules applying in the case of constructive dismissal. Where the employee gives notice the EDT is the date when the notice expires.[169] In cases where no notice is given the EDT will be the date when the contract would have ended had the employee received the statutory minimum notice period. This date will be calculated as running from the date when the employee ended the contract, or gave notice of termination.[170] However, the position is different where the employee is under notice of termination from the

---

[163] ERA, s. 96(1).

[164] ERA, s. 97(1).

[165] *Brown v. Southall & Knight* [1980] ICR 617, EAT.

[166] *Stapp v. Shaftesbury Society* [1982] IRLR 326, CA; *Batchelor v. British Railways Board* [1987] IRLR 136, CA. But see Chapter Three, para. 3.40 and Chapter Four, para. 4.5.

[167] *Adams v. GKN Sankey Ltd* [1980] IRLR 416, EAT.

[168] *Chapman v. Letheby & Christopher Ltd* [1981] IRLR 440, EAT.

[169] ERA, s. 97(1)(a).

[170] ERA, s. 97(4)(5).

employer and that employee gives counter notice to terminate the contract at an earlier date. In such a case the employee may leave and still be taken as having been dismissed by the employer and the reason for the dismissal will be that of the employer.[171] Ultimately, in cases of difficulty tribunals must ask themselves, "When did the termination take effect?" and there is no universally applicable rule that this will be the date when acceptance of the repudiatory act occurs. The issue really turns on the legal relationship between the parties on the date in question.[172]

REASONS FOR DISMISSAL

5.30 In the normal unfair dismissal case it is for the employee to show on a balance of probabilities that he was dismissed. Thereafter, the burden of proof passes to the employer to show that the reason for the dismissal falls within one of the fair grounds of dismissal as recognised by statute. There are several issues which have to be considered at this point. First an employer is required to give on request a written statement of the reasons for dismissal.[173] Second, an employer is required to prove the reason or, if there is more than one, the principal reason for the dismissal[174] and that it fell within one of the recognised categories of fair dismissal.[175] These are:

(1)   a reason related to the capability or qualifications of the employee for performing work of the kind which he was employed by the employer to do;
(2)   a reason related to the conduct of the employee;
(3)   the reason was the redundancy of the employee;
(4)   the reason was that the employee could not continue to work in the position which he held without contravention (either on his part or on that of his employer) of a statutory duty or restriction[176]; or
(5)   some other substantial reason of a kind such as to justify the dismissal of an employee holding the position which that employee held.[177]

Finally, it is for the tribunal to decide whether in the circumstances (including the size and administrative resources of the employer's undertaking) the employer acted reasonably or unreasonably in treating the reason as a sufficient reason for dismissing the employee; and that question is to be determined in accordance with equity and the substantial merits of the case.[178]

5.31 A reason for dismissal is a set of facts known to the employer or beliefs held by him which cause him to dismiss the employee.[179] An employer is not

---

[171] ERA, s. 95.
[172] *BMK Ltd v. Logue* [1993] IRLR 477, EAT.
[173] See Chapter Four, para. 4.12.
[174] ERA, s. 98(1)(a).
[175] See generally *UCATT v. Brain* [1981] ICR 542, CA.
[176] ERA, s. 98(2)(a)-(d).
[177] ERA, s. 98(1)(b).
[178] ERA, s. 98(4), which "neutralises" the onus of proof and reduces the burden on employers.
[179] *Abernethy v. Mott, Hay & Anderson* [1974] ICR 323, CA. This case permits a tribunal to substitute the correct reason for dismissal for an invalid or misdirected reason given by the employer through misapprehension or mistake. It has been extended by the Court of Appeal to allow for the supply of a reason, which as a consequence of the employer's misapprehension of the true nature of the circumstances, he was unable to treat as such at the time: *Ely v. YKK Fasteners (UK) Ltd* [1993] IRLR 500.

necessarily bound by the reason given to the employee at the time of the dismissal. Thus a wrong label applied by the employer at the time of dismissal need not be fatal to his case.[180] Where there is a discrepancy between the reason given at the time of dismissal and the real reason, the critical question is whether the employee was aware of the real reason, and, therefore, whether the real reason was available to him to challenge in the industrial tribunal proceedings.[181] The real issue is for the employer to lead some evidence before the tribunal which shows that the reason upon which he relied allowed him to form a belief as to the ground for dismissal. However, where the employer adduces one reason as the only reason for the dismissal and that reason proves to be unfounded, the tribunal would be entitled to find the dismissal unfair since the employer has failed to show a potentially valid reason for dismissal.[182] The more difficult case is where the employer puts forward a number of reasons for the dismissal. In such a case, the tribunal is directed to discover the principal reason for that dismissal. It has been held that this direction does not require the tribunal to dissect the employer's reasons in analytical detail.[183] However, an employer must be careful when a number of reasons are put forward and one of these reasons proves unfounded that that specific reason did not form an important part of the principal reason for dismissal. The other reasons must be the more important reasons for the dismissal and constitute the principal reason by themselves for the employer to prove that he had a relevant reason for dismissal.[184]

5.32 There is no doubt that generally the test for identifying the employer's reason for dismissal is subjective so that the tribunal should seek to discover what was in the employer's mind at the time of the dismissal. In this regard, it is a fundamental rule that an employer cannot rely on a reason for dismissal which he did not know about at the time of dismissal.[185] Thus, contrary to the position at common law, if an act of gross misconduct comes to the employer's attention after the date of dismissal that ground cannot be argued before the tribunal; although it may be used to reduce compensation. However, this basic rule is subject to one exception applicable in a case where there is a right to an internal appeal. Any information which comes to light in the course of that appeal can be considered by the tribunal so long as the new evidence relates to the original ground of dismissal.[186] A failure to grant a right to such an appeal may of itself render a dismissal unfair.[187] However, a tribunal, when ascertaining the reason for dismissal, must ignore any pressure on the employer by way of calling, organising, procuring or financing a strike or other industrial action, or by threatening to do so.[188]

---

[180] But see *Harvard Security plc v. Younghusband* [1990] IRLR 17, EAT.
[181] *Clarke v. Trimoco Group Ltd* [1993] IRLR 148, EAT.
[182] *Nelson v. BBC* [1977] ICR 649, CA.
[183] *Bates Farms & Dairy Ltd v. Scott* [1976] IRLR 214, EAT.
[184] *Smith v. City of Glasgow District Council* [1987] ICR 796, HL. See also *Carlin v. St Cuthbert's Co-operative Association Ltd* [1974] IRLR 188, NIRC.
[185] *Devis (W.) & Sons Ltd v. Atkins* [1977] ICR 662, HL.
[186] *National Heart and Chest Hospitals v. Nambiar* [1981] ICR 441, EAT approved by the House of Lords in *West Midlands Co-operative Society Ltd v. Tipton* [1986] ICR 192, HL. Technically, of course, the employer is not changing the reason, he is merely adducing further evidence in support of it.
[187] *Tipton*, above.
[188] ERA, s. 107.

5.33 Fair grounds

The next stage is for the employer to show that the reason for the dismissal can be accommodated within the fair grounds of dismissal noted above. Occasionally, it may be difficult to categorise exactly the ground of dismissal. There are certainly times when a dismissal on the ground of capability can overlap with a misconduct dismissal. It would seem that where the lack of capability is attributable to the employee's failure to exercise the skills he possesses as opposed to an inherent deficiency in his work, then this would be a dismissal for misconduct.[189] In such a case there would be a need for the employer to issue warnings so that the tribunal could assess the reasonableness or otherwise of his decision to dismiss. If an employer is seeking to argue that a dismissal is fair on the ground of redundancy, the onus is upon him to show on a balance of probabilities that it was genuinely for this reason. The usual presumption which applies in redundancy law, *viz.* that a dismissal is by reason of redundancy until the contrary is proved, is not relevant in an unfair dismissal context. In the case of dismissal for breach of a statutory enactment it is necessary for the employer to show that the illegality actually exists. It is not enough for the employer simply to have a subjective belief that continued employment will break the law.[190] The final ground for dismissal — for some other substantial reason — is a deliberately wide category of dismissal which need not be construed *eiusdem generis* with the other reasons.[191] Thus the range of grounds for dismissal which fit this category is an open question so that this is one head where there are few limitations upon the exercise of managerial prerogative.[192]

THE ISSUE OF REASONABLENESS

5.34 Once the employer has proved that there is a fair reason for the dismissal, the tribunal must then consider whether in the circumstances he acted reasonably in treating it as a sufficient reason for dismissing the employee. In determining this question, there is no onus of proof upon either party, although the House of Lords has stated that the language of ERA, s. 98(4) requires the employer to show the reason for the dismissal so that the tribunal can consider whether the employer acted reasonably in treating that reason as a sufficient reason for dismissal.[193] In the end, legislation directs tribunals to reach their decisions on the basis of equity and the substantial merits of the case.[194] This is essentially a question of fact so that assuming that the correct test is applied the decision of the tribunal is really only challengeable on appeal where it can be shown that no reasonably instructed tribunal could have reached it.[195] There is a plethora of decisions bearing upon the issue of reasonableness. However, with a view to avoiding legalism and to encourage the parties to present their own cases tribunals have been advised to avoid a preoccupation with guideline authority and to frame their decisions in

---

[189] *Sutton & Gates (Luton) Ltd v. Boxall* [1979] ICR 67, EAT.
[190] *Bouchaala v. Trust House Forte Hotels Ltd* [1980] IRLR 382, EAT.
[191] *Components (R. S.) Ltd v. Irwin* [1973] IRLR 239, NIRC.
[192] See John Bowers and Andrew Clarke ''Unfair Dismissal and Management Prerogative; A Study of 'Other Substantial Reason' '' (1981) 10 ILJ 34.
[193] *Smith v. City of Glasgow District Council* [1987] ICR 796, HL.
[194] ERA, s. 98(4).
[195] *Spook Erection Ltd v. Thackray* [1984] IRLR 116, IH.

accordance with the statutory directions.[196] Indeed, it is advisable for tribunals to refer specifically to the language of ERA, s. 98(4), or, at the very least, to summarise its wording so as to make clear that they have applied the correct test.[197] This means that previous decisions do not have the same status as precedents as they would have in other legal fields. Nevertheless, they are important as indicating the general approach of the tribunals to the question of reasonableness.

5.35 The statutory directions are also important in two specific senses. First, tribunals are instructed to take account of the size and administrative resources of the employer's undertaking.[198] This means that the reasonableness test is variable and will not be applied so stringently in the case of a small employer as it would be for a large business. Second, tribunals are directed[199] to have regard to the ACAS Codes of Practice. In the context of unfair dismissal law, the ACAS Code on Disciplinary Practice and Procecdures in Employment[200] provides valuable guidance to tribunals in cases of dismissal for misconduct. The Code can be used both as a point of comparison when considering the reasonableness of an employer's own disciplinary procedures and sets out model arrangements in cases where there are no internal disciplinary rules.

5.36 Substantive and procedural issues

The issue of reasonableness has both a substantive and a procedural element, although, in the end, the decision has to be made on the basis of all the circumstances of the case. In terms of the substance of the decision, the tribunal must be satisfied that it was reasonable in the circumstances. In this regard it is not for the tribunal to substitute its own decision because it disagrees with the employer's particular conclusion in the circumstances of the case. The correct approach is to consider whether the decision of the employer is within a band of reasonable responses. The nature of this test is best explained in the judgment of Lord Denning MR in *British Leyland UK Ltd v. Swift*[201] where he declared as follows:

> "The correct test is: was it reasonable for the employer to dismiss him? If no reasonable employer would have dismissed him, then the dismissal was unfair. But if a reasonable employer might reasonably have dismissed him, then the dismissal was fair. It must be remembered that in all these cases there is a band of reasonableness, within which one employer might reasonably take one view; another quite reasonably take a different view ... if it was quite reasonable to dismiss him, then the dismissal must be upheld as fair; even though some other employers may not have dismissed him."

A tribunal should approach this issue in the following way:

---

[196] *Anandarajah v. Lord Chancellor's Department* [1984] IRLR 131, EAT. For recent developments on this issue see Chapter Eight, paras 8.21–8.26.

[197] *Conlin v. United Distillers* [1992] IRLR 503, EAT; [1994] IRLR 169, IH.

[198] ERA, s. 98(4).

[199] TULRCA, s. 207(1), (2).

[200] ACAS Code of Practice No. 1 effective from June 20, 1977. ACAS has tried to introduce a new and more extensive Code which was rejected by the Secretary of State. See (1987) D. of E. Gazette 150. However, there is now a useful ACAS handbook on Discipline and Dismissal.

[201] [1981] IRLR 91, CA applied in Scotland by the Inner House in *Gair v. Bevan Harris Ltd* 1983 SLT 487.

(1)   the starting point must always be the statutory language[202];

(2)   in applying this the tribunal must consider the reasonableness of the employer's conduct, not simply whether it considers the dismissal to be fair;

(3)   in judging reasonableness the tribunal must not substitute its decision as to what was the right course to adopt for that of the employer;

(4)   in many, though not all, cases there is a band of reasonable responses to the employee's conduct within which one employer might reasonably take one view, another quite reasonably take another;

(5)   the function of the industrial tribunal, as an industrial jury, is to determine whether in the particular circumstances of each case the decision to dismiss fell within the range of reasonable responses which a reasonable employer might have adopted.[203]

Thus in the end it is the function of the tribunal, as an industrial jury, to determine whether in the particular circumstances of each case the employer's decision fell within the band of reasonable responses which a reasonable employer might have adopted. If the decision falls within that band the dismissal is fair; if the dismissal falls outside the band it is unfair.[204]

5.37 A reasonable employer must not only have regard to the reason for the dismissal but also to the need for some sort of procedure relevant to the circumstances of the case. This is particularly important in misconduct cases where, as has already been noted, the ACAS Code of Practice must be a major focus of attention in order to establish the "procedural fairness" of the dismissal. Thus it might not be enough for an employer to have a fair substantive reason for dismissal: he must also ensure that a fair procedure is adopted. This would entail such elements as a proper investigation,[205] issuing warnings, and in serious cases meriting dismissal a right to a hearing and an appeal against the decision to dismiss. The importance of procedural fairness as an element in an unfair dismissal case has varied over the years. At least initially procedural fairness was a critical factor which could render an otherwise fair dismissal unfair simply through a want of procedure.[206] Later, procedural fairness was relegated to being one of a number of factors which established the reasonableness of the employer's decision. This approach became encapsulated in the *British Labour Pump*[207] test which allowed an employer to succeed in an unfair dismissal claim even where there had been a failure to follow the correct procedure if he could prove on a balance of probabilities that if he had applied the correct procedure there would have been no difference and the employee would still have been dismissed.

5.38 The decision of the House of Lords in *Polkey v. A. E. Dayton Services Ltd*[208] breathes fresh life into the procedural aspects of an unfair dismissal case. In

---

[202] ERA, s. 98(4).

[203] See generally the decision of the EAT in *Iceland Frozen Foods Ltd v. Jones* [1983] ICR 17, EAT particularly at pp. 24–25. Both *Swift* and *Jones* have been approved by the Second Division in *Scottish Midland Co-operative Society v. Cullion* [1991] IRLR 261, IH and in *Conlin v. United Distillers* [1994] IRLR 169.

[204] *Rentokil Ltd v. Mackin* [1989] IRLR 286, EAT.

[205] *British Home Stores Ltd v. Burchell* [1978] IRLR 379, EAT.

[206] See, for example, *Earl v. Slater & Wheeler (Airlyne) Ltd* [1972] IRLR 715, NIRC.

[207] *British Labour Pump Co. Ltd v. Byrne* [1979] ICR 347, EAT. Approved by the EAT in Scotland in *Gray Dunn & Co. Ltd v. Edwards* [1980] IRLR 23, EAT. See also the decision of the Court of Appeal in *Wass (W. & J.) Ltd v. Binns* [1982] ICR 486, CA.

[208] [1988] ICR 142, HL.

particular, it makes clear that the *British Labour Pump* test is unsound because it is inconsistent with the decision of the House of Lords in the *Devis* case[209] that the reason for the employer's decision to dismiss must be judged in light of his knowledge at the date of dismissal and because it concentrates unnecessarily upon the question of injustice to the employee and ignores the statutory direction to judge the employer's actions on the basis of the reasonableness test. It is now the case, therefore, that the question whether a particular dismissal is unfair must be judged in the light of what the employer actually did and not what he might have done. This should mean that in most cases a failure to apply a proper procedure will lead to a finding that the dismissal was unfair.[210]

5.39 Nonetheless, both Lord Mackay LC and Lord Bridge in *Polkey* recognised that there might be exceptional cases where a tribunal could hold that an employer had acted reasonably even where there had been a want of procedure. Lord Mackay argued that this arose where in the circumstances compliance with the code of practice would have been "utterly useless" and Lord Bridge observed that the usual procedural steps could be dispensed with when it would have been "futile" to comply with them. An important issue in the subsequent cases has been whether it is necessary for the employer to actually address his mind to the issue of procedural fairness and make a conscious decision based upon reasonable grounds to dispense with procedural requirements, or whether it is enough that a reasonable employer would have concluded in the circumstances that compliance with the procedural steps would have been utterly useless or futile.

The former approach has been favoured by the EAT in Scotland where it has been argued that the exception to *Polkey* will normally only be available where the employer himself has considered whether compliance with procedure would be useful and has reached the conclusion that it would not.[211] The EAT in England has adopted the alternative view and has concluded that the test is purely objective and requires the tribunal to ask whether a reasonable employer in the light of the facts known to him at the time would have dismissed the employee without complying with procedure.[212] The Court of Appeal in England has now supported the objective approach.[213] Balcombe LJ, for example, could find no warrant for the proposition that there had to be a deliberate decision by the employer that compliance with procedure would be useless. This means that it need not be fatal to an employer's case that he had not addressed his mind to the question of procedure. An employer who has failed to consider the issue can still succeed so long as it can be shown that a reasonable employer would have dispensed with

---

[209] *Devis (W.) & Sons Ltd v. Atkins* [1977] ICR 662, HL.

[210] See, for example, the speech of Lord Bridge of Harwich in *Polkey v. A. E. Dayton Services Ltd*, above, at p. 163 who argued that the language of ERA, s. 98(4) ensured that in the case of incapacity an employer would not normally act reasonably unless he gives the employee fair warning and an opportunity to mend his ways and show that he can do the job; in the case of misconduct a reasonable employer would be expected to investigate the complaint fully and fairly and to hear the employee in his defence or in mitigation and in a redundancy case an employer would not normally act reasonably unless he warns and consults employees and adopts a fair basis of selection. For a recent application of *Polkey* in a misconduct case see the decisions of the EAT in *Spink v. Express Foods Group Ltd* [1990] IRLR 320, EAT and *Louies v. Coventry Hood & Seating Co. Ltd* [1990] IRLR 324, EAT.

[211] *Robertson v. Magnet Ltd (Retail Division)* [1993] IRLR 512.

[212] *Duffy v. Yeomans & Partners Ltd* [1993] IRLR 368. See also *Heron v. Citylink-Nottingham* [1993] IRLR 372.

[213] *Duffy v. Yeomans & Partners Ltd* [1994] IRLR 642.

procedure in the circumstances of the case.[214] The objective approach has now been followed in Scotland.[215]

5.40 It is equally true that an employer who denies an employee a right to appeal against a decision to dismiss might also jeopardise his chances of proving that the dismissal was fair.[216] On the other hand, not every breach of an employee's contractual right of appeal renders a dismissal unfair. However, a dismissal is likely to be unfair, even where an employee has been granted an appeal, if the appellate procedure was defective because it could or should have found and demonstrated a flaw in the employer's disciplinary procedures and did not do so.[217] Equally, where an employee has a contractual right to an appeal it is reasonable to expect an employer to ensure that the composition of the members of the appeals panel conforms to that specified in the disciplinary procedure because a defect in the composition of such a body may well impede the employee in demonstrating that the real reason for his dismissal was not sufficient.[218] It is important for employers to comply fully with the appeals process stipulated in their disciplinary rules because a reasonable employer is expected to comply with the full requirements of the appeal procedure in the disciplinary code.[219]

5.41 It is clear that the tribunal must consider the reasonableness of the employer's decision in the circumstances of the case. One aspect of this is that the employer should take some account of the personal circumstances of the employee. Thus long-serving employees should obtain some recognition for that service when an employer is contemplating dismissal; although it is really the quality of that service which counts.[220] Length of service may be particularly important in redundancy cases and there can be no doubt that selection on the basis of last in first out is *prima facie* evidence of a reasonable choice by the employer. Another consideration, particularly in misconduct cases, is for the employer to act consistently so that employees in similar positions are treated in the same way and obtain the same sanctions for the same types of offence.[221] Employers should consider truly comparable cases of which they know or ought reasonably to have known.[222] However, although the issue of consistency must be important so also must be the question of flexibility of approach. Thus although it would seem sensible to treat like cases alike the Employment Appeal Tribunal has counselled both tribunals

---

[214] For analysis and criticism of this decision see Victor Craig, "British Labour Pump Revisited" (1994) Greens Emp. L.B. 10–6 and Douglas Brodie, "Procedural Fairness" 1995 SLT (News) 105.

[215] See, for example, *University of Glasgow v. Donaldson*, unreported, case no. 951/94, EAT and the discussion of the Second Division of the Inner House in *King v. Eaton Ltd* [1996] IRLR 199.

[216] *West Midlands Co-operative Society Ltd v. Tipton* [1986] ICR 192, HL. This is most likely to be the case where the employee has a contractual right to an appeal and is still challenging the sufficiency of the employer's reasons.

[217] *Post Office v. Marney* [1990] IRLR 170, EAT.

[218] *Westminster City Council v. Cabaj* [1996] IRLR 399, CA. Such a defect does not inevitably make the dismissal unfair; this is a matter for the tribunal.

[219] *Stoker v. Lancashire County Council* [1992] IRLR 75, CA.

[220] *AEI Cables Ltd v. McLay* 1980 SC 42.

[221] *Post Office v. Fennell* [1981] IRLR 221, CA. It is no defence for an employer to argue that the manager who dealt with previous cases was not the one who considered the circumstances of the complainant's dismissal. Consistency must be consistency as between all employees of the employer. See *Cain v. Leeds Western Health Authority* [1990] IRLR 168, EAT.

[222] *Procter v. British Gypsum Ltd* [1992] IRLR 7, EAT.

and employers to avoid applying a tariff approach to industrial misconduct cases.[223] Everything turns on the circumstances of the particular case and employers must have freedom to consider mitigating circumstances.[224] In many ways it is difficult to separate the issue of reasonableness from the employer's chosen ground for dismissal, so the fair reasons for dismissal must be discussed in more detail.

THE OPERATION OF THE FAIR REASONS

5.42 (a) Capability or qualifications

"Capability" is assessed by reference to skill, aptitude, health or any other physical or mental quality and "qualifications" as meaning any degree, diploma or other academic, technical or professional qualification relevant to the position which the employee held.[225] Clearly, dismissal for lack of capability is the more important reason. In some cases it may be difficult to establish that the employee is incompetent, and given that the qualifying period for a claim is currently two years it must be assumed that many employees who are considered incompetent by their employers will be dismissed without qualifying for any unfair dismissal rights. However, if an employee is being dismissed on the ground of incompetence it is usually the case that the employee cannot be dismissed for one single incompetent act; although there may be exceptions such as where the job involves such high standards that the employer cannot take the risk of repetition.[226]

5.43 To a large extent the requirement that the employee at least be given some warning that his job is at risk seeks to resolve the tension between the interest of the employer not to have his business affected adversely by an inefficient employee and the employee's right not to be treated unfairly. Ultimately, the tribunal must be satisfied that the employer honestly believed on reasonable grounds that the employee was incompetent and that there was a reasonable basis for that belief.[227] This test will require the employer to have conducted some sort of investigation into the employee's competence. There is also an obligation upon the employer to train the employee in the job and to ensure proper supervision. As far as the procedure for such dismissals is concerned, although the incompetent employee is not entitled to the same level of warnings as the employee who is guilty of misconduct, at the very least, he has the right to a fair warning from the employer.[228] This should inform the employee of the aspects of his work which he is not performing adequately and advise him of the likelihood of dismissal if there

---

[223] *Hadjioannou v. Coral Casinos Ltd* [1981] IRLR 352, EAT approved by the Court of Appeal in *Paul v. East Surrey District Health Authority* [1995] IRLR 305. This case stressed that the basic test is whether, in the particular case, dismissal was a reasonable response to the misconduct.

[224] *Proctor v. British Gypsum Ltd*, above.

[225] ERA, s. 98(3).

[226] *Alidair Ltd v. Taylor* [1978] IRLR 82, CA.

[227] *Taylor*, above.

[228] See, for example, the speech of Lord Bridge of Harwich in *Polkey v. A. E. Dayton Services Ltd* [1988] ICR 142, HL at p. 163. It should be remembered that where an employee's incapacity is attributable to his failure to exercise the skills that he possesses this would be a dismissal for misconduct where a warnings approach would be required. See generally *Sutton & Gates (Luton) Ltd v. Boxall* [1979] ICR 67, EAT.

is no improvement in his work after having been given a reasonable opportunity to improve his performance.[229]

5.44 *Ill health dismissals.* The most difficult type of capability case is that applying to the sick employee. As has already been discussed, the contract of employment of a sick employee absent from work for a substantial period might well terminate automatically through the doctrine of frustration. However, it is the clear thrust of the decisions on this subject that it is much the better route for the employer to consider all the options, and, where appropriate, to take the decision to dismiss. In reaching such a decision the critical issue is to balance the employer's need for the work to be done against the need of the employee to be given time to recover from his illness.[230] In the end, the tribunal must ask itself whether the employer should be expected to wait any longer and, if so, how much longer before dismissing the sick employee.[231] Although warnings are clearly not applicable here,[232] it is important for the employer to consult with the employee and to discuss the matter with him so that the true medical position can be established.[233] In deciding whether an employer has acted fairly in dismissing a sick employee the correct approach is for the tribunal to determine as a matter of fact and judgment what consultation, if any, was necessary or desirable in the known circumstances of the particular case; what consultation, if any, in fact took place; and whether or not that consultation process was adequate in all the circumstances.[234] Save in special circumstances, a failure to consult will show that the employer has acted unreasonably in the circumstances.[235]. But the issue of the degree and extent of consultation involves a question of fact for the tribunal so that there may be wholly exceptional circumstances where consultation with the employer can be avoided.[236]

5.45 In order to discover the true position it might also be important to discuss the employee's state of health with medical advisers and this may involve the employee undergoing an examination by a doctor nominated by the employer so long as there is contractual authority to this effect. But it has been stressed that the final decision to dismiss is not a medical one but one to be decided by the employer in the light of all the relevant facts.[237] Even where the employer forms the view that the sick employee is no longer capable of performing his work it does not necessarily follow that he should be dismissed. An employer should consider if there is other alternative work which the employee can do. The employer is certainly not obliged to create a special job for the sick employee.[238] However, an employer who does not consider this issue may be acting unreasonably; although it is certainly the case that he does not have to go out of his way to accommodate the sick employee.[239] Difficulties also arise in relation to the employee who is sick and absent from work on an intermittent basis. The Employment Appeal Tribunal has

---

[229] *Winterhalter Gastronom Ltd v. Webb* [1973] ICR 245, NIRC.
[230] *Taylorplan Catering (Scotland) Ltd v. McInally* [1980] IRLR 53, EAT.
[231] *Spencer v. Paragon Wallpapers Ltd* [1976] IRLR 373, EAT.
[232] *Spencer,* above.
[233] *East Lindsey District Council v. Daubney* [1977] IRLR 181, EAT.
[234] *Links (A.) & Co. Ltd v. Rose* [1991] IRLR 353, IH.
[235] *Leonard v. Fergus & Haynes Civil Engineering Ltd* [1979] IRLR 235, IH.
[236] *Eclipse Blinds Ltd v. Wright* [1992] IRLR 133, IH.
[237] *East Lindsey District Council v. Daubney* [1977] IRLR 181, EAT.
[238] *Merseyside & North Wales Electricity Board v. Taylor* [1975] IRLR 60, QBD.
[239] *Garricks (Caterers) Ltd v. Nolan* [1980] IRLR 259, EAT.

declared[240] that the correct approach in such a case is one based on sympathy, understanding and compassion and that a disciplinary approach is not appropriate. In the end there may come a time when the employee should be cautioned that his absences have reached the stage where it is impossible to continue with that employment.

5.46 (b) Misconduct

The sort of conduct which would justify dismissal has been described in *Thomson v. Alloa Motor Co. Ltd*[241] as being actions of such a nature, whether done in the course of employment or outwith it, that reflect in some way upon the employer/employee relationship. In terms of conduct within employment usually one act of misconduct will not justify dismissal. Only acts of gross misconduct such as thefts or assaults would merit dismissal for a single act. In this field, therefore, much will depend upon the previous disciplinary record of the employee and the employer's own disciplinary rules or, failing these, the ACAS Code. Thus the issue of warnings for previous acts of misconduct is likely to be an important focus for discussion in most conduct dismissals. Save for cases of gross misconduct, the sanction applied to a particular act or omission will depend upon the gravity of the offence and the employee's previous record. An employee who commits a fairly minor act may find himself dismissed because of the cumulative effect of his previous warnings. Obviously, therefore, it is important for employers with their own disciplinary rules to specify clearly the various acts of misconduct which employees can commit and to set out the penalties which can apply to them. The ACAS Code certainly envisages that for first offenders who commit a minor offence the penalty should be a formal oral warning; in more serious cases the sanction should be a written warning and only in cases of gross misconduct should the employee be dismissed. It also recognises that the disciplinary rules will vary depending on the circumstances of the case. Thus it is open to employers when devising their disciplinary rules to categorise some relatively trivial act which might usually only merit a warning as an act of gross misconduct justifying dismissal for certain classes of employees because of the impact of this type of misconduct upon their businesses. In the end, of course, the employer cannot circumvent the statutory test of reasonableness and it will be for the tribunal to decide whether or not the employer's decision to dismiss for this type of misconduct is reasonable in the circumstances.[242]

5.47 *Proof in misconduct dismissals.* One important question which arises in misconduct dismissals concerns the level of proof that the employer requires. It is clear that the employer does not have to prove the employee's guilt; it is enough if he has a genuine belief in the employee's guilt.[243] The *Burchell* case laid down a threefold approach to this question.[244] First, it is necessary for the employer to have a genuine belief in the employee's guilt; second, the employer must have reasonable grounds upon which to sustain that belief; and, third, there must have

---

[240] *Lynock v. Cereal Packaging Ltd* [1988] IRLR 510, EAT.
[241] [1983] IRLR 403, EAT.
[242] See the decision of the Inner House in *Ladbroke Racing Ltd v. Arnott* [1983] IRLR 154, IH.
[243] *British Home Stores Ltd v. Burchell* [1978] IRLR 379, EAT approved by the Court of Appeal in *Weddell (W.) & Co. Ltd v. Tepper* [1980] ICR 286, CA.
[244] This does not mean that an employer who fails one or more of the three elements, without more, is guilty of unfair dismissal: *Boys and Girls Welfare Society v. McDonald* [1996] IRLR 129, EAT. Tribunals must also avoid using *Burchell* in such a way as to place the onus of establishing reasonableness on the employer: *McDonald*.

been as much investigation into the matter as was reasonable in all the circumstances of the case.[245] The test was developed originally to deal with dishonesty cases, but its application has now been approved in other cases of breach of discipline.[246] The level of investigation required by the *Burchell* test will vary depending upon the nature of the case. At the one extreme will be the cases where the employee is virtually caught in the act and at the other end are cases where the issue is one of pure inference. As the scale moves towards a case based on inference so the amount of inquiry and investigation required of the employer will increase.[247] There is undoubtedly an obligation upon an employer to conduct a most stringent inquiry where his case depends entirely upon the uncorroborated evidence of an informant who refuses to be named.[248] Clearly, there is no requirement upon an employer to hold an investigation where the employee has already admitted the misconduct.[249] But even where the circumstances make the conduct of an investigation impossible, before deciding how to deal with an employee, a reasonable employer should discuss the issue with other interested parties such as important customers.[250] In deciding whether or not an employer has conducted a reasonable investigation, tribunals should avoid relying on material which came to light for the first time at the tribunal hearing. The correct approach is to judge the issue on the basis of the material which was before the employer when the decision to dismiss was taken.[251] Ultimately, the decision for the tribunal is whether on the facts that were known or ought to have been known to the employer, he genuinely believed on reasonable grounds that the employee was guilty.[252]

5.48 The full rigours of the *Burchell* test do not apply where the employer is convinced that one of two or three employees is responsible for an act of dishonesty but cannot identify the actual culprit. In such a case the employer would be entitled to dismiss all of the employees so long as three points are satisfied. First, the act must be one which if it had been committed by an identified individual would have justified dismissal; second, the tribunal must be satisfied that the act was committed by one or more of the group, all of whom can be shown to be individually capable of having committed the act complained of; and third, there must have been a proper investigation by the employer to identify the culprit.[253] Usually, the outcome will be the dismissal of all the members of the

---

[245] A tribunal must avoid substituting its own views when applying this test. See the decision of the Northern Ireland Court of Appeal in *Ulsterbus Ltd v. Henderson* [1989] IRLR 251, NICA.

[246] *Distillers Co. (Bottling Services) Ltd v. Gardner* [1982] IRLR 47, EAT.

[247] *ILEA v. Gravett* [1988] IRLR 497, EAT. In *Scottish Midland Co-operative Society v. Cullion* [1991] IRLR 261 the Second Division argued that the correct approach was to discover whether the employer believed that the employee was guilty of misconduct and was entitled so to believe, having regard to the investigation carried out.

[248] *Linfood Cash & Carry Ltd v. Thomson* [1989] IRLR 235, EAT.

[249] *RSPB v. Croucher* [1984] IRLR 425, EAT.

[250] *Securicor Guarding Ltd v. R.* [1994] IRLR 633, EAT. There may even be cases where some aspect of the background needs investigation so as to put the misconduct into proper context: *Chamberlain Vinyl Products Ltd v. Patel* [1996] ICR, 113, EAT.

[251] *Dick v. Glasgow University* [1993] IRLR 581, IH.

[252] *British Gas plc v. McCarrick* [1991] IRLR 305, CA.

[253] *Monie v. Coral Racing Ltd* [1980] IRLR 464, CA as developed by the EAT in *Whitbread & Co. plc v. Thomas* [1988] IRLR 43, EAT. See also *Parr v. Whitbread plc* [1990] IRLR 39, EAT, where the EAT again reiterated the need for a tribunal to be satisfied that the employer acted reasonably in identifying the group and that as between members of this group the employer could not reasonably identify the individual perpetrator.

group. However, it does not necessarily follow that a failure to dismiss one member of the group renders the dismissal of the remainder unfair. If the employer can show that there are solid and sensible grounds (which do not have to be related to the relevant offence) for differentiating between members of the group this will excuse the disparity of treatment.[254] These special rules are most likely to apply in dishonesty cases, although they may also operate in conduct cases generally and exceptionally in capability cases.[255]

5.49 The importance of procedural fairness in the wake of *Polkey v. A. E. Dayton Services Ltd*[256] has already been noted. In a misconduct case one would expect an employer to (1) investigate, (2) grant the employee a hearing and (3) permit an appeal where the employee is still challenging the grounds for dismissal. The right of the employee to be heard must be a critical step in a misconduct case. Its current importance can be gauged by *McLaren v. National Coal Board*[257] where it was held that an employee who had been dismissed for assault should have been given a hearing even although this would have been difficult to convene because of the miners' strike. In this case the court stressed that the standards of fairness are immutable.

5.50 As already indicated, procedural issues are central to unfair dismissal law. In the context of misconduct the *Polkey* case makes clear that normally a reasonable employer would be expected to investigate the complaint of misconduct fully and fairly and hear the employee's defence either in explanation or mitigation. These requirements have been fleshed out in the subsequent case law. In *Spink v. Express Foods Group Ltd*[258] the EAT made clear that fairness requires that the employee should know the case to be met, should hear or be told the important parts of the evidence in support of that case, should have an opportunity to criticise or dispute that evidence and to adduce his own evidence and argue his case. In *Clark v. Civil Aviation Authority*[259] these requirements were developed further and the EAT set out a checklist of good practice for hearings. It is clear that the employer cannot use the grievance procedure as a substitute for a disciplinary hearing.[260]

Usually in misconduct cases, the decision will turn on the evidence of witnesses. In such cases the employer must indicate the evidence against the employee either in statement form or by calling those witnesses at the hearing.[261] It is contrary to natural justice and *prima facie* unfair to refuse to let the employee see such statements. Where an employer relies almost entirely on them, it will be very rare for the procedure to be fair if the employee does not see the statements or is at least told very clearly what they say.[262] However, there may be exceptional cases where the employer need not disclose the witness statements to the employee. As the

---

[254] *Frames Snooker Centre v. Boyce* [1992] IRLR 472, EAT.
[255] *Thomas*, above.
[256] [1988] ICR 142, HL.
[257] [1988] IRLR 215, CA.
[258] [1990] IRLR 320, EAT.
[259] [1991] IRLR 412, EAT.
[260] *Clarke v. Trimoco Group Ltd* [1993] IRLR 148, EAT.
[261] *Clark v. Civil Aviation Authority* [1991] IRLR 412. For detailed guidance on the steps that a reasonable employer should take when dealing with a misconduct complaint based upon the allegations of an informant see *Linfood Cash & Carry Ltd v. Thomson* [1989] IRLR 235, EAT.
[262] *Louies v. Coventry Hood & Seating Co. Ltd* [1990] IRLR 324, EAT.

EAT indicated in *Fuller v. Lloyd's Bank plc*[263] for a dismissal to be unfair for a want of procedure either there must be a defect of such seriousness that the procedure itself is unfair or that the results of the defect taken overall are unfair.

Although an appeal against dismissal is important in its own right since it provides the employee with an opportunity of showing that the employer's reason for dismissal was not sufficient,[264] appeals might also be important as a means of correcting earlier procedural errors.[265] Whether the appeal can be used in this way will depend upon the degree of unfairness at the original hearing and the nature of the appeal.[266] Essentially, the appeal must be a full and proper one and amount to a re-hearing.[267] This means that the appeal must confer upon the employee all the rights which should have been accorded at the initial stage, notably proper notice of the complaint and a full opportunity of stating the employee's case.[268] But earlier defects cannot be cured in this way where the person conducting the appeal was so involved in the earlier stages that he can properly be regarded as a judge in his own cause.[269]

5.51 In conclusion a useful case which spells out the various steps which an employer should follow for misconduct dismissals is *Whitbread & Co. plc v. Mills*[270] in which it was suggested the question of reasonableness could be approached by asking the following subsidiary questions:
(1)   Has the employer complied with the pre-dismissal procedures which a reasonable employer would have applied in the circumstances?
(2)   Where there is a contractual appeal process, has the employer carried it out in its essentials?
(3)   Where conduct is the main reason, has the employer proved that at the time of dismissal he had a reasonable suspicion amounting to a belief in the guilt of the employee and, if necessary, complied with the *Burchell* principles?
(4)   During the disciplinary hearing and the appeals process, has the employer dealt fairly with the employee?

5.52 *Criminal offences.* The commission of a criminal offence, although a major act of misconduct, is merely one example of misconduct which may justify dismissal. Clearly, as far as criminal behaviour within employment is concerned, given that it is not necessary for an employer to prove guilt but merely to have a genuine belief as to the employee's misconduct which is based on reasonable grounds, an employer may be held to have been dismissed fairly even although the employee is subsequently acquitted at his trial or the procurator fiscal decides not

---

[263] [1991] IRLR 336.
[264] *West Midlands Co-operative Society Ltd v. Tipton* [1986] ICR 192, HL.
[265] A purpose approved by the Court of Appeal in *Sartor v. P. & O. European Ferries (Felixtowe) Ltd* [1992] IRLR 271. It might be argued that this subverts the real purpose of the appeal.
[266] *Whitbread & Co. plc v. Mills* [1988] IRLR 501.
[267] *Clark v. Civil Aviation Authority* [1991] IRLR 412, EAT.
[268] *Byrne v. BOC Ltd* [1992] IRLR 505, EAT.
[269] *Byrne,* above.
[270] [1988] IRLR 501, EAT.

to proceed with the criminal charge.[271] In the end, the issue for the tribunal is to discover whether the employer's behaviour complied with the statutory test of fairness.[272] On the other hand, where the criminal offence relates to conduct outside employment an employer would be well advised to dismiss only after the employee has been convicted. However, when there has been a plea of guilty or a finding of guilt it is reasonable for an employer to believe that the offence has been committed by the employee and to take steps to dismiss.[273] Even then the employer must also be sure that the nature of the offence makes the employee unsuitable to continue in his job.[274] The important point is for the employer to make a connection between the offence and the duties which the employee performs at work. In one sense this is a very simple task since it might be argued that any conviction has a bearing on the employer/employee relationship. However, it is necessary for the employer to show either that his business will be affected by continued employment because of the impact upon customers or the effect upon fellow employees or that the commission of the offence has seriously damaged the relationship of trust and confidence between the parties.[275] The more senior the employee the easier it will be for the employer to establish this latter point.[276] In appropriate cases, and where the size and administrative resources of the employer's undertaking permit, it may be necessary to consider whether the employee can be offered some other job, even though it is clear that he cannot continue in his original one. This possibility can be explored during the employee's notice period.[277]

5.53 (c) Redundancy

Where the employer establishes that his principal reason for dismissing an employee was one of redundancy that dismissal will be considered fair and the employer's primary obligation will be to pay the relevant statutory redundancy payment. However, such dismissals can be challenged in two ways. First, a redundancy dismissal can be regarded as unfair if it can be shown that the circumstances constituting the redundancy applied equally to one or more other employees in the same undertaking who held similar positions and who were not dismissed and the reason the applicant was selected for dismissal was his union membership or activities,[278] his non-union membership[279] or was an inadmissible

---

[271] See, for example, the decision of the Inner House in *Carr v. Alexander Russell Ltd* [1976] IRLR 220, OH where it was held that an employer could dismiss an employee before his trial where that employee had been caught red-handed by the police with the employer's property and later charged with theft. On the other hand the mere fact that an employee has been charged with theft would not of itself merit dismissal; in such a case an employer would be required to conduct some sort of investigation: *Scottish Special Housing Association v. Cooke* [1979] IRLR 264, EAT.

[272] *Harris (Ipswich) Ltd v. Harrison* [1978] IRLR 382, EAT.

[273] *P. v. Nottinghamshire County Council* [1992] IRLR 362, CA.

[274] See, for example, ACAS Code para. 15(c). Cf *Bradshaw v. Rugby Portland Cement Co. Ltd* [1972] IRLR 46, IT and *Nottinghamshire County Council v. Bowly* [1978] IRLR 252, EAT.

[275] *Norfolk County Council v. Bernard* [1979] IRLR 220, EAT; *Moore v. C. & A. Modes* [1981] IRLR 71, EAT.

[276] *Richardson v. Bradford City Metropolitan Council* [1975] IRLR 296, EAT.

[277] *P. v. Nottinghamshire County Council*, above.

[278] These activities must be carried out at an appropriate time. See TULRCA, s. 152(1), (2) and Chapter Ten. See also *O'Dea v. ISC Chemicals Ltd* [1995] IRLR 599, CA. The protection now extends to employee representatives and candidates for such posts: ERA, s. 105(6) and s. 103.

[279] TULRCA, s. 153.

reason.[280] This latter protection covers selection for redundancy where the reason relates to health and safety[281] or was for reasons of pregnancy or childbirth[282] or was because the employee has asserted a statutory right.[283] Formerly, employees were also protected when they were selected for redundancy in contravention of a customary arrangement or agreed procedure and there were no special reasons for departing from such an arrangement or agreement.[284] This protection was repealed by the Deregulation and Contracting Out Act 1994, s. 36(1) for dismissals taking effect after January 3, 1995.

5.54 A dismissal for redundancy can also be unfair on the basis that the employer has handled the redundancy in such a way that he cannot be held to have acted reasonably in all the circumstances. For example, an employer would be acting unreasonably when he dismisses an employee for redundancy and then offers to retain him at the expense of another employee because it is unfair to put the onus on the employee to decide whether he or another employee is to be selected for dismissal.[285] More particularly, a dismissal may be unreasonable and a breach of ERA, s. 98(4) either because there were no clearly adopted criteria to ascertain those selected for redundancy or that the criteria which were applied were inherently unreasonable. In England guidance has been provided in *Williams v. Compair Maxam Ltd*[286] where it was stated an employer should consider:
(1)   the need to give as much warning as possible about impending redundancies;
(2)   the need for consultation and discussion with trade unions so as criteria for selection can be agreed;
(3)   even where union agreement cannot be obtained the employer should devise criteria which are objectively justifiable;
(4)   those criteria should be applied fairly, taking account of any union representations;
(5)   the need to consider whether those selected could be offered alternative employment.

5.55 In the past, in Scotland there was some reluctance to accept the *Compair Maxam* principles. It was stated by the EAT in Scotland that the five principles were never intended to be considered in each and every redundancy case, nor that an employer had to comply with every one of the principles in order to avoid a finding of unfair dismissal.[287] The EAT in Scotland also argued that the *Compair Maxam* principles only had relevance to large organisations where a significant number of redundancies were contemplated and that they could not be applied to small employers, particularly if those employers did not recognise trade unions.[288] These comments should now be treated with considerable caution and are at odds

---

[280] ERA, s. 105(1).
[281] ERA, s. 100.
[282] ERA, s. 99.
[283] ERA, s. 104.
[284] EPCA, s. 59(1)(b).
[285] *Boulton & Paul Ltd v. Arnold* [1994] IRLR 532, EAT.
[286] [1982] ICR 156, EAT.
[287] *Simpson (A.) & Son (Motors) v. Reid* [1983] IRLR 401, EAT.
[288] *Meikle v. McPhail (Charleston Arms)* [1983] IRLR 351, EAT; *Gray v. Shetland Norse Preserving Co. Ltd* [1985] IRLR 53, EAT.

with the thrust of the most recent Scottish decisions.[289] They are also difficult to reconcile with the decision of the House of Lords in *Polkey v. A. E. Dayton Services Ltd*[290] and the repeal of the protection in the Employment Protection (Consolidation) Act 1978, s. 59 for dismissals in contravention of a customary arrangement or agreed procedure. As Lord Bridge made clear in *Polkey*, in the case of redundancy an employer will normally not act reasonably unless he warns and consults any employees affected or their representative, adopts a fair basis on which to select for redundancy and takes such steps as may be reasonable to avoid or minimise redundancy by redeployment within the organisation. The correct approach in cases where an employer fails to consult is to ask whether an employer acting reasonably would have failed to consult in the circumstances of the case: there is no requirement that there must be a deliberate decision by the actual employer that consultation would be useless.[291]

5.56 Nevertheless, it is also clear that there must be exceptional circumstances before the duty to consult will be excused. These are unlikely to arise when the employer believes that the applicant is the only person who can be made redundant since even in such a case there are other areas where consultation will be of benefit to the employee.[292] It is not a basis for avoiding consultation that on a previous occasion when redundancies were made some employees had indicated that they did not want to go through the process again and would prefer just to be told on the day.[293] Equally, it is no excuse to argue that the employer is a small undertaking. Size may affect the nature or formality of the consultation process, but it cannot excuse a total lack of consultation.[294] Consultation must be fair and genuine so that the employee understands fully the issues and is given an opportunity to express his views which are considered fully by the employer.[295] It may be necessary for the employer to consult with both the employee and his representative[296] and he must ensure that the consultation covers both the reason for the redundancy and the manner in which it is to be carried through.[297] Where selection for redundancy depends upon certain assessment criteria the employer must consult either with the affected employees or their representatives about the proposed selection method before the proposals have been finally formulated, give the consultees adequate information on which to respond, adequate time to do so and an indication that real consideration will be given to their response.[298]

---

[289] See, for example, the decision of the Second Division in *King v. Eaton Ltd* [1996] IRLR 199.

[290] [1988] ICR 142, HL. This decision overruled the ''no difference'' rule in redundancy cases as devised by the EAT in *British United Shoe Machinery Co. Ltd v. Clarke* [1978] ICR 70, EAT.

[291] *Duffy v. Yeomans & Partners Ltd* [1994] IRLR 642, CA approving the view of the EAT in this case reported at [1993] IRLR 368 and disapproving the view of the EAT in Scotland in *Robertson v. Magnet Ltd (Retail Division)* [1993] IRLR 512.

[292] *Heron v. Citylink-Nottingham* [1993] IRLR 372, EAT.

[293] *Ferguson v. Prestwick Circuits Ltd* [1992] IRLR 266, EAT.

[294] *De Grasse v. Stockwell Tools Ltd* [1992] IRLR 269, EAT.

[295] *Rowell v. Hubbard Group Services Ltd* [1995] IRLR 195, adopting the approach to consultation with representatives of recognised independent trade unions under TULRCA, s. 188 as stipulated by Glidewell LJ in *R. v. British Coal Corporation and Secretary of State for Trade and Industry, ex p Price* [1994] IRLR 72, HC. Approved in Scotland in *King v. Eaton Ltd* [1996] IRLR 199.

[296] *Rolls-Royce Motor Cars Ltd v. Price* [1993] IRLR 203, EAT. *Cf King*, above.

[297] *Hough v. Leyland Daf Ltd* [1991] ICR 697, EAT.

[298] *King v. Eaton Ltd*, above.

5.57 (d) Contravention of a statutory enactment

As has already been noted, for a dismissal to be accepted as fair under this head it is necessary for the employer to show that continued employment will contravene a statutory enactment and it has been held that this ground does not extend to encompass the idea of a genuine but erroneous belief on the part of the employer[299]; however, such a belief may allow the employer to plead there was some other substantial reason for the dismissal.[300] A reasonable employer who does have an employee whose continued employment will break the law should consider whether that employee can be employed in any other capacity, or whether making some modifications in the employee's contracual duties will ensure that any further employment is lawful, for example, redeployment of a driver who has lost his driving licence.

5.58 (e) Some other substantial reason

This category has been used to justify a variety of different reasons for dismissal. Employers have successfully argued for its application in such disparate cases as dismissal of an employee because of a personality clash with other workers[301]; dismissal on the instructions of a major customer who had been upset by the employee's conduct[302]; and dismissal because of the employee's sexual preference.[303] In all of these cases the crucial factor for the employers was to establish that the continued employment of the employees concerned would have had an adverse effect upon their businesses. In the case of dismissal because of a personality difference, for example, the employer would be expected to show that the breakdown was irredeemable and that he had no other option but to dismiss. It is clear that this head of dismissal requires the tribunal to assess the reason for dismissal by reference to an employee — and not the actual employee who was dismissed — but an employee who holds the position which that employee held.[304] A dismissal for a substantial reason cannot be for a whimsical or capricious reason which no person of ordinary sense would entertain. On the other hand, if the employer can show that he had a fair reason in his mind at the time when he decided on dismissal and that he genuinely believed it to be fair, this would bring the case within the category of some other substantial reason.[305]

5.59 *Business reorganisations.* The area of greatest controversy for some other substantial reason dismissals has been in relation to business reorganisations which fall short of redundancy. An employer may find that it is necessary to reorganise his business to make it more efficient or so as to react to a change in market conditions and this entails changing the employees' jobs or the duties that they perform. It has been accepted that an employer could be justified in dismissing an employee who refused to accept reasonable changes in his terms and conditions of employment on the basis of some other substantial reason.[306] Clearly, as far as the

---

[299] *Bouchaala v. Trust House Forte Hotels Ltd* [1980] IRLR 382, EAT.
[300] *Bouchaala,* above.
[301] *Treganowan v. Robert Knee & Co. Ltd* [1975] ICR 405.
[302] *Scott Packing & Warehousing Co. Ltd v. Paterson* [1978] IRLR 166, EAT.
[303] *Saunders v. Scottish National Camps Association Ltd* [1981] IRLR 277, IH.
[304] *Dobie v. Burns International Security Services (UK) Ltd* [1984] ICR 812, CA.
[305] See generally Lord McDonald in the EAT in *Harper v. National Coal Board* [1980] IRLR 260, EAT. See also the decision of the Court of Appeal in *Gilham v. Kent County Council (No. 2)* [1985] IRLR 18, CA which referred to some other substantial reason being designed to deter employers dismissing for some trivial or unworthy reason.
[306] *Components (R. S.) Ltd v. Irwin* [1973] IRLR 239, NIRC.

common law is concerned, an employer who unilaterally changes an employee's terms and conditions of employment is in danger of commiting a material breach of contract. However, as far as unfair dismissal law is concerned an employer's decision to change terms may well lead to a fair dismissal even although a serious breach of contract has been committed in the process. Thus it has been held that a breach of contract by the employer, such as a change in the place of work, which justifies the employee resigning and claiming constructive dismissal, can nonetheless be a dismissal for some other substantial reason.[307] In the end the task for the tribunal is to consider whether in all the circumstances the employer has acted reasonably and the fact that the reorganisation entails a breach of the employees' contracts or disregards collectively agreed terms would not preclude a tribunal from holding that the dismissal was fair because of the other circumstances.

5.60 Although all the circumstances must be taken into account one important issue in these types of case will always be to consider whether the change in terms is necessary for the needs of the business. In one of the early cases it was stated that a dismissal of an employee who refused to accept new terms could only be for some other substantial reason on the basis that if the reorganisation were not done the whole business would be brought to a standstill.[308] This undoubtedly set too high a standard and in *Hollister v. National Farmers' Union*[309] the Court of Appeal argued that the correct approach was to discover whether there was some sound, good business reason for the reorganisation. This particular test views the issue from the employer's perspective and widens the scope of management discretion. In other cases, an attempt has been made to take some account of the interests of the employee.[310] The modern approach is that it is necessary for a tribunal when considering the issue of reasonableness to make a finding as to the advantages to the employer of the reorganisation, and to assess whether it was reasonable for him to rely on those advantages despite the disadvantages which the employee will suffer when the changes are implemented. However, it has been stressed that the question of weighing the advantages to the employer against the disadvantages to the employee is merely one factor which the tribunal has to take into account.[311] In the final analysis the tribunal must approach this issue as it must in all other reasonableness questions on the basis of the band of reasonable responses test.[312] However, in assessing reasonableness the focus must not simply be on the terms of the employer's offer but on all the subsequent facts (including the employee's refusal to accept it) since ERA s. 98(4) directs the tribunal to assess the reasonableness or otherwise of the dismissal.[313]

---

[307] *Genower v. Ealing, Hammersmith & Hounslow Area Health Authority* [1980] IRLR 297, EAT.

[308] *Ellis v. Brighton Co-operative Society Ltd* [1976] IRLR 419, EAT.

[309] [1979] ICR 542, CA.

[310] Thus in *Evans v. Elemeta Holdings Ltd* [1982] ICR 323 the EAT argued that if it was reasonable for an employee to decline new contractual terms it would be unreasonable for an employer to dismiss for such a refusal but another EAT has criticised this approach as being inconsistent with *Hollister v. National Farmer's Union*, above: see *Chubb v. Fire Security Ltd v. Harper* [1983] IRLR 311, EAT.

[311] *Chubb*, above. *Catamaran Cruisers Ltd v. Williams* [1994] IRLR 386, EAT.

[312] *Richmond Precision Engineering Ltd v. Pearce* [1985] IRLR 179, EAT.

[313] *St John of God (Care Services) Ltd v. Brooks* [1992] IRLR 546, EAT. According to this case, one subsequent matter which is significant is the extent to which other employees who have been made the same offer have accepted it.

SPECIAL CASES

5.61 (a) Maternity

As well as protection against dismissal, pregnant employees also enjoy rights to maternity pay[314] and maternity leave,[315] a right to return to work after childbirth,[316] a right, in certain circumstances, to be suspended from work with pay on maternity grounds,[317] and a right to time off work for ante-natal care.[318] The current provisions on the dismissal of pregnant employees were enacted by the Trade Union Reform and Employment Rights Act 1993, s. 24(1) and were intended to comply with the Pregnant Workers Directive of the European Union.[319] They replaced the previous provisions on dismissal of pregnant employees in EPCA, s. 60 as of October 16, 1994. The provisions now contained in ERA, s. 99 enhance the protection against dismissal given to pregnant employees by extending the reasons which constitute dismissal on the ground of pregnancy or childbirth, by making such dismissals automatically unfair and by abolishing the qualifying period and upper age limit for competent claims. The protections also complement the other benefits given to pregnant employees, particularly the right to maternity leave which is a period of 14 weeks leave from work which is made available to all pregnant employees regardless of length of service.

5.62 An employee is to be treated as unfairly dismissed on the ground of pregnancy or childbirth if —
(a)   the reason for her dismissal is that she is pregnant or any other reason connected with her pregnancy;
(b)   her maternity leave period is ended by the dismissal and the reason for her dismissal is that she has given birth to a child or any other reason connected with her having given birth to a child;
(c)   the reason for her dismissal, where her contract of employment was terminated after the end of her maternity leave period, is that she took, or availed herself of the benefits of, maternity leave;
(d)   the reason for her dismissal is a relevant requirement or a relevant recommendation which triggers a pregnant employee's right to be suspended from work with pay;
(e)   her maternity leave period is ended by the dismissal, and the reason for her dismissal is that she is redundant and the employer has failed to comply with ERA, s. 77 as regards suitable available employment.[320]

An employee is also to be regarded as unfairly dismissed if (i) before the end of her maternity leave period, she gave to her employer a certificate from a registered medical practitioner stating that by reason of disease or bodily or mental disablement she would be incapable of work after the end of that period, (ii) her contract of employment was terminated within the four week period following the end of her maternity leave period in circumstances where she continued to be incapable of work and the certificate remained current, and (iii) the reason for the

---

[314] Social Security Contributions and Benefits Act 1992, Part XII.
[315] ERA, ss. 71–78.
[316] ERA, ss. 79–85.
[317] ERA, ss. 66–70.
[318] ERA, s. 55.
[319] Council Dir. 92/85.
[320] ERA, s. 99. Where there is more than one reason for dismissal, the employee is protected if the principal reason is one of those specified in (a)–(e).

dismissal is that she has given birth to a child or any other reason connected with her having given birth to a child.[320a]

It remains the case that s. 99 is part of social legislation aimed at putting women on an equal footing with men and requires employers to accept a degree of inconvenience as the price of such equal status.[321] Thus it is to be expected that the tribunals and courts will take the same broad interpretation of the current legislation as was the case with the original EPCA, s. 60. Moreover, since ground (a) uses the same language as its predecessor provision, cases decided under the previous law are still relevant. The phrase "any other reason connected with her pregnancy" must be construed widely and means simply that the reason must be associated with the pregnancy.[322] It includes cases where the employer's decision is based upon the side impact of the pregnancy such as the fact that she will require maternity leave[323] or that the employer will have to hire a temporary replacement to cover for her absence.[324]

Ground (b) protects employees from dismissal for having given birth or for any reason connected with that birth such as the need to breastfeed. During maternity leave all the employee's terms and conditions of employment are preserved except the right to remuneration. Ground (c), therefore, protects from dismissal an employee who claims any of the benefits of maternity leave such as accrued holiday rights. Ground (d) is linked to ERA, s. 66(2) and ensures that it is automatically unfair to dismiss an employee who is entitled to suspension from work with pay. Such suspension arises where continued employment breaches an HSC-approved Code of Practice or because the risk to the employee or her child cannot be avoided by altering her working conditions or hours of work or she is a nightworker and has a certificate from a registered medical practitioner or a registered midwife certifying that such work is a danger to her health and safety.[325] Ground (e) ensures that it is automatically unfair to dismiss an employee by reason of redundancy during her maternity leave period where there is a suitable available vacancy which has not been offered to her. Where no such vacancy exists the employee will have to rely on the usual provisions on unfair dismissal and redundancy. Pregnant employees are also protected from dismissal on the ground of disease or disablement so long as a medical certificate was submitted before the end of the period of maternity leave. There is no requirement that the disease or disablement be connected with the pregnancy.

5.63 In all of the above cases the burden is upon the applicant to establish the reason (or the principal reason) for the dismissal and that this reason is a prohibited one. But once this has been proved the dismissal is treated as being automatically unfair and there is no requirement that the tribunal should go on to consider the reasonableness or otherwise of that dismissal. As already indicated, there is no qualifying period for exercise of the right not to be dismissed on the ground of pregnancy or childbirth.

5.64 Additionally, a woman who has exercised her statutory right to return to work

---

[320a] ERA, s. 99(3).
[321] See the speech of Lord Griffiths in *Brown v. Stockton-on-Tees Borough Council* [1988] IRLR 263, at p. 265.
[322] *Clayton v. Vigers* [1990] IRLR 177, EAT.
[323] *Brown v. Stockton-on-Tees Borough Council* [1988] IRLR 263.
[324] *Clayton v. Vigers,* above.
[325] ERA, s. 66(1) as designated by the Suspension from Work (on Maternity Grounds) Order 1994 (SI 1994 No. 2930).

after childbirth and has complied with all the notice requirements[326] has the right to complain of unfair dismissal if the employer refuses to allow her to return.[327] An employee who is entitled to return to work and has exercised her right to do so but is not permitted to return to work shall be treated as if she had been employed until her notified date of return, as having been continuously employed until that day and as having been dismissed on the day she should have returned to work for the reason that she was not permitted to return.[328] The effect of a failure by the employee to comply with the 21-day-notice requirement about returning to work raises some uncertainty. In one EAT case it was held that this did not itself terminate the contract although it did mean that the employee had no statutory right to return to work. However, the EAT went on to hold that even though the employee loses her statutory right to return to work there is no forfeiture of the right not to be unfairly dismissed. Accordingly, there may be occasions where a dismissal is unfair even when there has been a failure on the part of the employee to comply with the requirement of notice.[329] But this should not be regarded as a rule of general application and it has recently been argued by another EAT that where an employee fails to exercise her right to return to work, there is no presumption that the contract continues in existence until terminated by the employer. Indeed, where the employer merely consents to the employee leaving work without compliance with the s. 96(1) requirements and remuneration ceases, the appropriate inference is that there has been an agreed termination.[330] There are special rules[331] for employees employed by employers with less than six employees who are prevented from returning to work because it is not reasonably practicable.

5.65 (b) Union membership dismissals and rights of non-union members

A dismissal is automatically unfair if the reason for it (or, if more than one, the principal reason) was that the employee

(i)   was, or proposed to become, a member of an independent trade union,[332] or

(ii)   had taken part, or proposed to take part, in the activities of an independent trade union at an appropriate time; or

(iii)   was not a member of any trade union, or of a particular trade union, or one of a number of particular trade unions, or had refused or proposed to refuse to become or remain a union member.[333]

Employees dismissed on any of these grounds also enjoy an additional benefit because there is no need for them to satisfy either the continuous employment requirements or be below the upper age limit in order to exercise these rights.[334]

5.66 The union membership and activities protections defined by heads (i) and (ii)

---

[326] ERA, ss. 79–82. The exercise of this right still depends on the employee having at least two years' continuous service by the eleventh week before the expected week of childbirth: ERA, s. 79(1) (b).

[327] See *Philip Hodges & Co. v. Kell* [1994] IRLR 568, EAT.

[328] ERA, s. 96(1).

[329] See generally *Hilton International Hotels (UK) Ltd v. Kaissi* [1994] IRLR 270, EAT.

[330] *Crouch v. Kidsons Impey* [1996] IRLR 79, EAT.

[331] ERA, s. 96(2)–(5).

[332] This phrase is defined by TULRCA, s. 5. See Chapter Ten, para. 10.15.

[333] TULRCA, s. 152(1).

[334] TULRCA, s. 154(1).

are identical to the statutory protections against action short of dismissal.[335] All of these protections are discussed at some length later.[336] For present purposes it is enough simply to discuss a few issues raised by head (ii). First, it is clear that an employee's right to be protected from dismissal for union activities only applies in relation to activities exercised by him after the commencement of his employment with the dismissing employer.[337] However, it will be a clear breach of TULRCA, s. 152(1)(b) for an employer to dismiss an employee because of union activities in a previous employment, when the only rational basis for doing so is the fear that those activities will be repeated in the present employment.[338] Second, these activities must be exercised at an appropriate time. This is defined to be a time outside working hours or within working hours but with the consent of the employer,[339] but participation in industrial action is not taking part in trade union activities.[340] Dismissal whilst taking part in industrial action is subject to special rules discussed shortly.

5.67 *The Closed Shop.* Although previous legislation provided for the fair dismissal of employees who were not union members all such provisions have now been repealed[341]; dismissal of an employee because of his non-membership of any or a particular trade union is now automatically unfair.[342] This protects the employee from dismissal in all circumstances for not being a member of any union, or of a particular trade union, or of one of a number of particular trade unions, or for refusing or proposing to refuse to become or remain a member. Moreover, there is also an equivalent protection for action short of dismissal against the non-union member.[343] These protections are limited in the sense that they only apply once employment has commenced. However, statute now regulates the pre-entry closed shop by making it unlawful to refuse a person employment because he is not a union member or because he is unwilling to accept a requirement to take steps to become a union member or to make payments to a third party (e.g. a charity) in the event of not being a union member.[344]

5.68 *Remedies for union membership dismissals.* There are also a number of other provisions which further enhance the rights relating to union membership, non-membership and activities. First, employees dismissed on these grounds have rights to a minimum basic award of not less than £2,770[345] regardless of length of service and, in addition to their basic award and compensatory award, enjoy a right to a special award where they have sought reinstatement or re-engagement and they have not got their jobs back. If reinstatement or re-engagement were sought but not ordered by the tribunal the special award is 104 weeks' pay or £13,775

---

[335] TULRCA, s. 146(1).

[336] See Chapter Nine, paras 9.53 ff.

[337] *City of Birmingham District Council v. Beyer* [1977] IRLR 211, EAT.

[338] *Fitzpatrick v. British Railways Board* [1991] IRLR 376, CA.

[339] TULRCA, s. 152(2).

[340] *Drew v. St Edmundsbury Borough Council* [1980] ICR 513, EAT.

[341] EA, 1988, s. 11; and see original provisions of EPCA, s. 58(3). The then state of the law was discussed by the European Court of Human Rights in *Young, James and Webster v. United Kingdom* [1981] IRLR 408, ECHR.

[342] TULRCA, s. 152(1) (c).

[343] TULRCA, s. 146(1).

[344] TULRCA, s. 137(1).

[345] TULRCA, s. 156(1). The Secretary of State can increase this sum by order. TULRCA, s. 159(1).

whichever is the greater up to a maximum of £27,500. Where the tribunal has made the relevant order but the employer has failed to comply with it the special award is 156 weeks' pay or £20,600 whichever is the greater, but, here, there is no maximum award.[346] The special award can be reduced in certain circumstances discussed later in this chapter. Union members and non-members also have a right to interim relief pending the hearing of their complaints of unfair dismissal.[347]

5.69 There are two final points which have to be made in relation to the dismissal of the non-union member. First, unlike any other type of unfair dismissal complaint, it is possible for a third party to be sisted as a respondent to the proceedings in addition to the employer. Where either the employer or the complainant claims that the employer was induced to dismiss the complainant by pressure which a trade union or other person exercised on the employer by calling, organising, procuring or financing a strike or other industrial action, or by threatening to do so, and that the pressure was exercised because the complainant was not a union member, the employer or the complainant may request the tribunal to direct that the person whom he claims exercised the pressure be sisted as a party to the proceedings.[348] If the employee succeeds in his complaint and an award of compensation is made that award can be made wholly or partly against the trade union or other person who has been sisted.[349] Secondly, the current law also protects the non-member who is dismissed because he objects to paying a sum of money equivalent to the union dues to some other organisation such as a charity. It provides that an employee who is dismissed because he failed to comply with a requirement that he makes payments, whether or not imposed by his contract of employment or in writing, to a third party if he refuses to become or ceases to remain a union member is to be treated as having been dismissed on the ground of non-union membership.[350] This provision ensures that his dismissal is automatically unfair and it fulfils the government's view that an employee should not be required to pay a financial price for his non-membership of a trade union.

5.70 (c) Industrial action dismissals

At common law, an employer is entitled to dismiss an employee who is taking part in industrial action because this is likely to constitute a material breach of contract. However, in unfair dismissal law special rules operate in cases of industrial action and lock-outs.[351] An employee has no right of complaint at all if at the time of dismissal he was taking part in unofficial industrial action. Otherwise the rules deny an industrial tribunal jurisdiction to hear complaints of unfair dismissal when the employee was taking part in official industrial action[352] or was locked out unless the employer has acted in a discriminatory or selective way either in terms

---

[346] See generally TULRCA, s. 158(1), (2). These sums can also be increased by order of the Secretary of State. The figures stated here are those specified in SI 1995 No. 1953.

[347] See para. 5.99.

[348] TULRCA, s. 160(1). Under the original provisions which were introduced by EA 1980 only the employer could sist. EA 1982, s. 7 extended this to cover the employee as well because the Government was concerned that employers were reluctant to exercise their sisting powers.

[349] TULRCA, s. 160(8).

[350] TULRCA, s. 152(3).

[351] TULRCA, s. 237 (unofficial industrial action), s, 238 (other industrial action).

[352] As to the distinction between official and unofficial action see para 5.75.

of dismissal or as regards re-engagement of those who have been dismissed.[353] There has been some disagreement as to the exact purpose of these special rules. On the one hand,[354] the rules were seen to be designed to protect the employer so that he could dismiss the entire labour force on strike and could take on another one without the stigma of any unfair dismissals. On the other hand, in more recent cases[355] it has been suggested that the purpose of this provision is to keep the law out of industrial disputes so that it can maintain an air of neutrality. But this position has become less tenable since the unfair dismissal rules applying to unofficial industrial action were introduced in 1990, and there is recent authority to the effect that tribunals should consider the merits of collective disputes, certainly as far as calculating compensation is concerned.[356] This latter reason is more in keeping with the notion of collective *laissez-faire* operative in other areas of collective labour law. Nevertheless, the enactment of rules applicable only where the industrial action is unofficial may require tribunals to resolve difficult questions as to the statutory distinction between unofficial industrial action and other industrial action.

5.71 *Official action.* The first question to be determined is whether at the date of dismissal either the employer was conducting a "lock-out" or the employee was taking part in "a strike or other industrial action". Although "lock-out" and "strike" are defined for determining whether there is continuity of employment[357] there is no definition of them for the purposes of s. 238; the general approach of the courts and tribunals has been to regard this lack of definition as deliberate and to ignore the definitions provided for continuity purposes. Thus as far as lock-outs are concerned the Court of Appeal has held that the fact that this amounts to a breach of contract will be a material consideration although not conclusive. In the end, it is the task of the tribunal to decide the question on the facts and merits of each case using its industrial relations expertise.[358] The reluctance to regard the issue as a legal question is also true for strikes.[359] As far as other industrial action is concerned there has also been an unwillingness to lay down any hard and fast rules: although it would appear that there is no need for such action to be in breach of contract. The important issue is to discover whether the action was intended to have a disruptive effect upon the employer's business.[360]

5.72 In the case of dismissal for taking part in strikes or other industrial action the next question is to discuss the legal approach to the issue of employee participation. This question is important for two reasons. First, under the current

---

[353] These rules do not apply to the dismissal of an employee if it is shown that the reason for the dismissal was on health and safety grounds or for reasons of pregnancy or childbirth: TULRCA, s. 238 (2A) as inserted by TURERA, s. 49(2), Sch. 8, para. 77.

[354] *Heath v. J. F. Longman (Meat Salesmen) Ltd* [1973] ICR 407, NIRC.

[355] *Gallagher v. Wragg* [1977] ICR 174, EAT; *Faust v. Power Packing Casemakers Ltd* [1983] ICR 665, CA.

[356] *TNT Express (UK) Ltd v. Downes* [1993] IRLR 432, EAT doubting *Courtaulds Northern Spinning Ltd v. Moosa* [1984] IRLR 43, EAT. But see *Crossville Wales Ltd v. Tracey (No. 2)* [1996] IRLR 91, CA.

[357] See Chapter Three.

[358] *Express & Star Ltd v. Bunday* [1988] ICR 379.

[359] See also *Bunday*, above.

[360] *Faust v. Power Packing Casemakers Ltd* [1983] ICR 665, CA.

provisions[361] it is necessary to discover whether or not the employee was taking part in the action on the date of his dismissal. Second, it is important to discover how other employees who were also taking part in the action were treated on that date. A tribunal will only have jurisdiction if there is discriminatory treatment as between the applicant and other employees who were taking part in the action at the date of his dismissal. This question is also one of fact since the meaning of taking part in a strike is just the kind of issue which the tribunal is best fitted to decide as an industrial jury.[362] The tribunal's finding should not be interfered with if there was evidence to support its conclusion and the words were given a meaning of which they were reasonably capable.[363] This may mean that on the same primary facts two tribunals could reach diametrically opposite, but equally correct, conclusions as to whether employees took part in industrial action[364] — surely an unsatisfactory state of affairs. All that can be said with any confidence is that an employer is entitled to judge the position on the basis of the employee's actions. Thus an employee who fails to carry out an instruction which the employer is entitled to give, can be treated as taking part in industrial action since his action was intended to coerce the employer into improving terms and conditions of employment.[365] Equally, an employer would be justified in believing that an employee who failed to turn up for work during a strike was taking part in that action.[366] This would arise even although the reason for the employee's non-appearance was because of a fear that he would be subjected to abuse by pickets if he should try to get to work,[367] or because he had fallen ill during the strike.[368] Indeed, it would seem that an absent employee who is not taking part in the action has a duty to maintain contact with his employer in order to ensure that the employer understands that his absence was not as a result of the strike.[369] A sick employee whose absence from work pre-dated the strike and who continues to inform the employer of his medical condition should not be treated as taking part in it even although he sympathises with its objectives.[370] Essentially, the correct approach is to discover whether or not there is evidence which enables the tribunal to find that the employee was not taking part in the industrial action. Even where employees are dismissed during a period of industrial action, it will still be necessary for the tribunal to decide the reasons for their dismissals. Such a

---

[361] TULRCA, s. 238 restricts the point of comparison to the date of the employee's dismissal. There was no such limitation under the original provisions (see EPCA, s. 62 before being amended by EA 1982, s. 9). This meant that an employer who allowed some strikers to return to work and then at some later date dismissed those who remained on strike could not rely on s. 62 to prevent a tribunal considering the fairness of those dismissals. See *Frank Jones (Tipton) Ltd v. Stock* [1978] ICR 347, HL. The current law reverses *Stock* and ensures that employees who do return to work on a date before the complainant's dismissal cannot be used as comparators.

[362] *Coates v. Modern Methods & Materials Ltd* [1982] ICR 763, CA.

[363] *Coates*, above.

[364] *Naylor v. Orton & Smith Ltd* [1983] IRLR 233, EAT.

[365] *Lewis and Britton v. E Mason & Sons* [1994] IRLR 4, EAT.

[366] *Coates*, above, where by a majority the Court of Appeal held that an employer was not required to discover the reasons for an employee's failure to work before deciding to dismiss him for not taking part in industrial action. It has been stated that the question as to whether an employee is taking part in industrial action is one of objective fact. See *Bolton Roadways Ltd v. Edwards* [1987] IRLR 392, EAT approved in *Manifold Industries v. Sims* [1991] IRLR 242, EAT. Cf *McKenzie v. Crosville Motors Ltd* [1990] ICR 172, EAT.

[367] *Coates*, above.

[368] *Williams v. Western Mail & Echo Ltd* [1980] ICR 366, EAT.

[369] *McKenzie*, above.

[370] *Hindle Gears Ltd v. McGinty* [1985] ICR 111, EAT.

requirement can cause difficulties where the industrial action is called at a time when the employer is seeking to reorganise the business.[371]

5.73 Because of the need to treat relevant employees equally it is necessary to consider which employees fall into this category. As far as lock-outs are concerned relevant employees are employees who were directly interested in the dispute in contemplation or furtherance of which the lock-out occurred.[372] It has been held that this issue involves a retrospective test.[373] This means that employees who have been able to return to work may still have a direct interest in the dispute and, therefore, be relevant employees so that unles they too are dismissed the tribunal would have jurisdiction to consider the fairness of any subsequent dismissals.[374] In the case of strikes or other industrial action, relevant employees are those employees at the establishment of the employer who were taking part in the action at the complainant's date of dismissal.[375] This test has two results — (1) it means that the employee can only compare himself with other employees who were taking part in the action at the date of his dismissal[376] — employees who returned to work at at earlier date cannot be used as comparators; and (2) it enables employers to treat employees differently who are employed at different establishments.[377] Clearly, therefore, where an employer does dismiss all his employees who are taking part in industrial action at a particular establishment so that there is no selectivity, a tribunal lacks jurisdiction to consider the fairness of those dismissals.

5.74 *Re-engagement after dismissal.* What is the position if the employer should decide to re-engage some of these employees who were dismissed? A tribunal has jurisdiction to consider an unfair dismissal complaint if within three months of the date of dismissal any employee in the same position as the complainant has been offered re-engagement and he has not.[378] This means that an employer who does re-engage selectively during this period may have to face unfair dismissal complaints from those who have not been re-hired. However, if the employer can sit out the three month period without taking back staff, any subsequent re-engagements outwith this period will not permit staff not offered re-engagement to complain to an industrial tribunal.

An offer of re-engagement means an offer, made by the original employer, a successor employer or an associated employer, to re-engage an employee, either in the job which he held immediately before the date of dismissal or in a different job which is reasonably suitable to him.[379] Given the width of this definition employers who do not wish to re-engage and who have several different locations must be careful in their recruitment arrangements during the three month period. For if they

---

[371] *Baxter v. Limb Group of Companies* [1994] IRLR 572, CA.

[372] TULRCA, s. 238(3)(a).

[373] *Campey (H.) & Sons Ltd v. Bellwood* [1987] ICR 311, EAT.

[374] For a recent illustration of the problems associated with dismissing employees during lock-outs see K. Miller and C. Woolfson, "Timex: Industrial Relations and the Use of the Law in the 1990s" (1994) 23 ILJ 209.

[375] TULRCA, s. 238(3)(b).

[376] In this context date of dismissal means time of dismissal. See *Hindle Gears Ltd v. McGinty* [1985] ICR 111, EAT.

[377] "Establishment" means that establishment of the employer at or from which the complainant works (TULRCA, s. 238(3)(b)).

[378] TULRCA, s. 238(2)(b).

[379] TULRCA, s. 238(4).

re-engage a dismissed employee at another establishment even by mistake the industrial tribunal will acquire jurisdiction to hear the employees' complaints. This is on the basis that the employer has at the very least constructive knowledge of the employee's re-engagement since he has the means to ascertain the true position.[380] A general advertising campaign for new staff does not constitute an offer of re-engagement but the position will be different if the employer offers work to applicants who respond to the advertisements and who are dismissed strikers.[381]

Employees who are offered their original jobs can be taken back on terms different from the original contract so long as the nature of their work and the capacity and place where they work are the same.[382] Further, it is also legitimate for an employer to offer re-engagement to dismissed strikers at different times so long as he ensures that by the expiry of the three month period all the strikers have received offers of re-engagement.[383]

5.75 *Unofficial action.* The above rules do not apply where the employee has taken part in an unofficial strike or other unofficial industrial action. Where an employee at the time of his dismissal was taking part in unofficial industrial action he loses all right to complain of unfair dismissal.[384] A strike or other industrial action is unofficial in relation to the employee unless —

(a)   the employee is a member of a trade union and the action is authorised or endorsed by that union,[385] or

(b)   the employee is not a member of the union but there are amongst those taking part in the industrial action members of the union by which the action has been authorised or endorsed. Thus only action which the union has repudiated is capable of being classified as unofficial. The mere fact that industrial action has been called by a shop steward does not make it unofficial. It will only become so once the union has repudiated the authorisation in the manner specified in the Trade Union and Labour Relations (Consolidation) Act 1992, s. 21.

A strike or other industrial action cannot be regarded as unofficial if none of those taking part in it are union members. However, in order to prevent union members from resigning *en masse* so as to avoid the action being treated as unofficial, an employee who was a member of the union when he began to take part in the action shall continue to be treated as a union member notwithstanding his resignation.[386] If a union decides to repudiate industrial action so that it must then be considered unofficial, the action cannot be treated as unofficial for unfair dismissal purposes until the end of the next working day after the day on which the repudiation takes place.[387] The effect of the above provisions is to enable an employer to dismiss selectively those of his employees who are taking part in unofficial industrial action without any of the employees so dismissed having

---

[380]   *Bigham and Keogh v. GKN Kwikform Ltd* [1992] IRLR 4, EAT. The position will be different where the employee submits a fraudulent application for work since such an application makes the contract of employment illegal and renders the offer of re-engagement void.

[381]   *Crosville Wales Ltd v. Tracey* [1993] IRLR 60, EAT.

[382]   *Williams v. National Theatre Board Ltd* [1982] IRLR 377, CA.

[383]   *Highland Fabricators Ltd v. McLaughlin* [1985] ICR 183, EAT.

[384]   TULRCA, s. 239(1). But this rule does not apply if the reason for the dismissal was health and safety or maternity: TULRCA, s. 237(1A) as inserted by TURERA, s. 49(2), Sch. 8, para. 76.

[385]   The question of authorisation or endorsement is dealt with by TULRCA, s. 20(2)–(4) and is considered in Chapter Eleven, paras 11.54–11.55.

[386]   TULRCA, s. 237(6).

[387]   TULRCA, s. 237(4).

recourse to an industrial tribunal. This state of affairs creates a major dilemma for a trade union. For if, on the one hand, it decides to endorse the industrial action it lays itself open to civil proceedings by the employer if the action should prove to be unlawful[388]; if, on the other hand, it repudiates the action the union takes the risk that some members (most probably the ringleaders of the action) will lose their jobs without any unfair dismissal rights.

5.76 (d) Dismissal on the transfer of an undertaking

Special rules regulate dismissals which take place because of the transfer of an undertaking or part of an undertaking.[389] As we have seen,[390] the Transfer of Undertakings (Protection of Employment) Regulations 1981, reg. 5(1) ensures that a relevant transfer does not terminate the contracts of employment of the employees employed in the undertaking who are being transferred and deems that after the transfer those contracts should be treated as having been made between the employees and the person acquiring the undertaking.[391] In addition, reg. 8(1) bestows unfair dismissal rights on employees who are dismissed either before or after a relevant transfer if the transfer or a reason connected with it is the reason or principal reason for their dismissals. The position is simple when the dismissals take place after the transfer since, in practical terms, only the transferee can be held responsible for such transfer-connected dismissals. However, the House of Lords has made clear in *Litster v. Forth Dry Dock & Engineering Co. Ltd*[392] that even when the employees are dismissed before the transfer their claims for unfair dismissal will still be against the transferee so long as their dismissals were for a reason connected with the transfer.[393] The EAT in Scotland has sought to argue that in such circumstances both the transferor and transferee should be held responsible for such dismissals.[394] However, the Second Division of the Court of Session has reversed this decision and has reiterated that the transferee alone is responsible under reg. 8(1) for transfer-connected dismissals even when they take place before the time of the transfer.[395]

However, difficult problems remain. First, as already noted, reg. 8(1) makes dismissals for a transfer-connected reason automatically unfair. An important issue is whether it is necessary for an employee who is dismissed for a reason connected with the transfer to serve the usual two years' qualifying period before the date of dismissal so as to claim. In *Milligan v. Securicor Cleaning Ltd*[396] the EAT has held that an employee who has been dismissed for a transfer-connected reason has a right of complaint of unfair dismissal irrespective of length of service on the basis that reg. 8(1) does not exempt any category of employee from protection against dismissal on the transfer of an undertaking. The decision has been subjected to

---

[388] The question of union repudiation is also discussed in Chapter Eleven.

[389] The Transfer of Undertakings (Protection of Employment) Regulations 1981 (SI 1981 No. 1794) as amended by TURERA, s. 33.

[390] Chapter Three.

[391] For the position of the employee who objects to being transferred, see reg. 5(4A) and (4B).

[392] 1989 SC (HL) 96.

[393] For the position where the dismissals are not connected with the transfer, see *Secretary of State for Employment v. Spence* [1985] ICR 646.

[394] *Allan v. Stirling District Council* [1994] IRLR 208. Cf *Berg and Busschers v. Besselsen* [1989] IRLR 447, ECJ. The EAT in England has refused to follow the reasoning in *Allan*. See *Ibex Trading Co. Ltd v. Walton* [1994] IRLR 564.

[395] *Stirling District Council v. Allan* [1995] IRLR 301.

[396] [1995] IRLR 288.

criticism[397] and has now been reversed by statutory instrument. The Collective Redundancies and Transfer of Undertakings (Protection of Employment) (Amendment) Regulations 1995[398] now ensure that the usual requirements about qualifying period and upper age limit apply to dismissals connected with the transfer of an undertaking. This change in the law took effect on October 26, 1995.

Another problem is to identify what constitutes a transfer-connected reason so as to make the transferee solely responsible. On this issue the authorities are difficult to reconcile. In *Harrison Bowden Ltd v. Bowden*[399] the ultimate purchaser of a business was held liable for the pre-transfer dismissal of the employee by the receiver even though at the time of dismissal no specific purchaser had come forward. On the other hand, in *Ibex Trading Co. Ltd v. Walton*[400] another EAT concluded that there was no dismissal for a transfer-connected reason when in similar circumstances an administrator dismissed staff before any prospective purchaser had been identified.[401] As already indicated, *Litster* makes the transferee liable for any pre-transfer dismissal which is connected with the transfer. But, strangely, transferees may be able to escape liability when instead of instructing the transferor to dismiss staff they indicate the employees who are to be retained with the consequence that the rest are dismissed by the transferor. In such circumstances, so long as it can be shown that the transferee had not put any pressure on the transferor to dismiss, the ensuing dismissals may not be unfair under reg. 8(1).[402] Where employees are dismissed by the transferor by the giving of notice which expires after the date of the transfer the reason for the dismissal is that of the transferor since the reason must be ascertained at the time when the notice was given. In such a case if the reason is a transfer-related one the dismissals may well be unfair and the transferee will be responsible for them even though the transferee might have been able to argue that the dismissals were for an economic, technical or organisational (ETO) reason.[403]

5.77 The protection granted by reg. 8(1) is qualified significantly by the statutory declaration that where an economic, technical or organisational reason entailing changes in the workforce of either the transferee or transferor employer is the reason or principal reason for the dismissal that dismissal will be for a substantial reason and whether it is fair or not will depend upon the application of the reasonableness principle.[404] It is clear that the economic, technical or organisational defence only applies when there are changes in the workforce, and changes in the identity of the individuals who make up the workforce do not constitute changes in the workforce itself so long as the overall numbers and functions of the

---

[397] See Victor Craig, "The Transfer of Undertakings Regulations and Unfair Dismissal Protection" (1995) Greens Emp. L.B. 7–9. See also *M.R.S. Environmental Services Ltd v. Marsh, The Times,* July 22, 1996, which overrules *Milligan* and makes it clear that any right conferred by reg. 8(1) is dependent upon the requirements of ERA, s. 94.

[398] SI 1995 No. 2587. Unsuccessfully challenged in *R. v. Secretary of State for Trade and Industry, ex parte Unison* [1996] IRLR 438, DC. See now 1981 Regulations, reg. 8(5).

[399] [1994] ICR 186, EAT.

[400] [1994] IRLR 564.

[401] The *Ibex* case may be contrary to the decision of ECJ in *P. Bork International A/S v. Foreningen af Arbejdsledere i Danmark* [1989] IRLR 41 and has not been followed by at least one industrial tribunal. These issues are discussed in more detail by Victor Craig, "TUPE and Receiverships" (1995) Emp.L.B. 6–11.

[402] *Longden v. Ferrari Ltd* [1994] IRLR 157, EAT. *Cf Wheeler v. Patel* [1987] ICR 631, EAT and *Gateway Hotels Ltd v. Stewart* [1988] IRLR 287, EAT.

[403] *BSG Property Services v. Tuck* [1996] IRLR 134, EAT.

[404] SI 1981 No. 1794, reg. 8(2).

employees looked at as a whole remain unchanged. Therefore reg. 8(2) cannot be applied where the employee resigned after the transfer because the transferee proposed to reduce his wages to that of their existing staff since the reason for the employer's decision was to produce standard rates of pay and was not intended to lead to a reduction in the number of employees.[405] On the other hand, there would be a change in the workforce when a transferee gives the employees who are kept on by him entirely different jobs to do since this entails changing the occupations of the workforce as a whole and amounts to much more than merely standardising their terms and conditions of employment.[406] Equally, the ETO defence is available to cover dismissals carried out by the transferee shortly after the transfer when he decides that the acquired business has too many employees to be viable.[407]

5.78 The statutory rules relating to dismissals and business transfers have been differently applied in the past. At one time in Scotland it was held that a dismissal that was for an economic, technical or organisational reason could not be for redundancy.[408] However, Scottish tribunals are now at liberty to follow the English decision in *Gorictree Ltd v. Jenkinson*[409] that such dismissals do not entail loss of redundancy rights.[410] Further, a later Scottish decision[411] on this issue has held that it would not be a dismissal for an economic, technical or organisational reason for the transferor to dismiss the workforce in order to comply with a condition of sale that the purchaser buy the business without staff. Hence such dismissals must now be automatically unfair.[412]

5.79 (e) Health and safety dismissals

The European Framework Directive on Health and Safety[413] requires employers to ensure that workers designated to carry out health and safety functions are not placed at any disadvantage because of their activities. In addition, the Directive requires that similar protections be granted to workers who take certain forms of action in the event of serious, imminent and unavoidable danger. The protections necessary for compliance with this Directive were first enacted by the Trade Union Reform and Employment Rights Act 1993, and are now contained in the

---

[405] *Berriman v. Delabole Slate Ltd* [1985] ICR 546, CA. Nor can reg. 8(2) be used to justify a consensual deterioration in terms: *Wilson v. St Helens Borough Council* [1996] IRLR 320, EAT.

[406] *Crawford v. Swinton Insurance Brokers Ltd* [1990] IRLR 42, EAT.

[407] *Trafford v. Sharpe and Fisher Building Supplies Ltd* [1994] IRLR 325, EAT. This decision runs counter to the opinion of the Advocate General under the equivalent provision of the Acquired Rights Directive that an ETO reason cannot be used to justify dismissing employees because the undertaking has been transferred. See *D'Urso & Ercole Marelli Elettromeccanica Generale SpA* [1992] IRLR 136, ECJ.

[408] *Canning v. Niaz* [1983] IRLR 431, EAT; *Meikle v. McPhail (Charleston Arms)* [1983] IRLR 351, EAT.

[409] [1985] ICR 51, EAT.

[410] See generally *Anderson v. Dalkeith Engineering Ltd* [1985] ICR 66, EAT.

[411] See *Gateway Hotels Ltd v. Stewart* [1988] IRLR 287, EAT which follows the decision of the English EAT in *Wheeler v. Patel* [1987] ICR 631, EAT. But see also the decision in *Anderson*, above, and the judgment of Lord Dunpark in *Forth Dry Dock and Engineering Co. Ltd v. Litster* [1988] IRLR 289, IH.

[412] But note *Longden v. Ferrari Ltd* [1994] IRLR 157, EAT.

[413] EC Directive on the Introduction of Measures to Encourage Improvements in the Health and Safety of Workers at Work 89/391/EEC.

Employment Rights Act 1996, as far as suffering a detriment[414] or being dismissed[415] on health and safety grounds. The dismissal protections are not dissimilar to those enacted for trade union membership dismissals and there is no need for an employee dismissed on health and safety grounds to satisfy any qualifying period.[416] In the case of dismissals, employees are protected where the reason or principal reason for their dismissals was that —

(a)   they were designated by the employer to carry out activities in connection with the prevention or reduction of risks to health and safety at work and they carried out or proposed to carry out those activities,[417]

(b)   they were safety representatives or members of safety committees and they performed, or proposed to perform, any relevant function,[418]

(c)   where there were no safety representatives nor a safety committee or where there were such representatives or such a committee but it was not reasonably practicable to raise the matter by those means, they brought to their employer's attention, by reasonable means, circumstances connected with their work which they reasonably believed were harmful or potentially harmful to health or safety,

(d)   they, in circumstances of danger which they reasonably believed were serious and imminent and which they could not reasonably be expected to avert, left, or proposed to leave, or (while the danger persisted) refused to return to their place of work or any dangerous part of such a place,

(e)   they, in circumstances which they reasonably believed[419] to be serious and imminent, took, or proposed to take, appropriate steps to protect themselves or other employees from the danger.[420]

The appropriateness of the steps taken under head (e) is to be judged by reference to all the circumstances including, in particular, the employee's knowledge and the facilities and advice available to him at the time.[421] A dismissal will not be unfair in the case of head (e) where the employer can show that it was so negligent for the employee to have taken the steps which were taken that a reasonable employer might have dismissed him for taking such steps.[422] Where the reason for the dismissal relates to either head (a) or head (b) the employee is entitled to a minimum basic award,[423] a special award[424] and is eligible for interim relief.[425] In the other cases the employee is entitled to the normal unfair dismissal remedies.

---

[414] ERA, s. 44.

[415] ERA, s. 100.

[416] ERA, s. 108.

[417] For the provisions on the appointment of employees to provide health and safety assistance, see the Management of Health and Safety at Work Regulations 1992 (SI 1992 No. 2051), reg. 6.

[418] For appointment of safety representatives and members of safety committees, see the Safety Representatives and Safety Committees Regulations 1977 (SI 1977 No. 500) as amended by SI 1992 No. 2051.

[419] Tribunals have been counselled not to place too onerous a duty of enquiring on the employee: *Kerr v. Nathan's Wastesavers Ltd*, unreported, case no. 91/95, EAT.

[420] ERA, s. 100(1).

[421] ERA, s. 100(2).

[422] ERA, s. 100(3).

[423] ERA, s. 120(1).

[424] ERA, s. 118(2), (3).

[425] ERA, ss. 128–132.

5.80 (f) Dismissal for asserting a statutory right

This particular protection also owes its origins to the Trade Union Reform and Employment Rights Act 1993, now the Employment Rights Act 1996, s. 104.[426] This provision makes it automatically unfair to dismiss an employee if the reason or the principal reason was that the employee —

(a)   brought proceedings against the employer to enforce a relevant statutory right;

(b)   alleged that the employer had infringed a right of his which is a relevant statutory right.[427]

The following statutory rights are covered, *viz.* any right conferred by ERA (including rights formerly in the Wages Act 1986) for which the remedy is by means of a complaint to an industrial tribunal, the right to minimum statutory periods of notice and rights in the Trade Union and Labour Relations (Consolidation) Act 1992 relating to deductions from pay, union activities and time off.[428] It is immaterial whether the employee has the right or not and whether it has been infringed or not so long as the claim to the right and that it has been infringed is made in good faith.[429] Employees are protected so long as they make reasonably clear to the employer what the right claimed to have been infringed was.[430] There is no need to serve the usual two year qualifying period in order to exercise this right.[431]

REMEDIES

5.81 Statute[432] creates a framework of remedies for employees whose complaints of unfair dismissal have been upheld by an industrial tribunal. The scheme of the legislation is to make re-employment — in the form of reinstatement or re-engagement — the primary remedy, although this has not been the case in practice,[433] with a right to compensation where an employee has not requested re-employment or it has not been ordered by the tribunal. Compensation is made up of two distinct elements — a basic award and a compensatory award. An employee who has sought re-employment and this has been ordered by the tribunal but has not been complied with by the employer also receives an additional award of compensation. Since 1982 an employee who has been dismissed for union membership, activities or non-membership also has a right to a special award.[434] A tribunal which finds a complaint to be well-founded must explain to the complainant the re-employment orders which can be made and ask him if he wishes to be reinstated or re-engaged. If re-employment is sought the tribunal must

---

[426] See TURERA, s. 29(1).

[427] ERA, s. 104(1).

[428] ERA, s. 104(4).

[429] ERA, s. 104(2).

[430] ERA, s. 104(3).

[431] ERA, s. 108. Such a relaxation has particular implications for claims under ERA, Part II, where there is also no qualifying period.

[432] ERA, ss. 111–132.

[433] In the UK reinstatement is awarded in less than 3% of unfair dismissal cases proceeding to a hearing. See Catherine Barnard, Jon Clark and Roy Lewis, *The Exercise of Individual Employment Rights in the Member States of the European Community* (D of E Research Series, No. 49) (1995), at p. 38.

[434] See para. 5.98.

then consider whether or not to make the relevant order and must give both the complainant and the employer the opportunity to be heard before exercising its discretion.[435] In Scotland the practice is to hear the evidence pertaining to remedies with the evidence on the merits and not to create a separate stage of procedure after the decision in favour of the complainant has been announced.

5.82 (a) Reinstatement and re-engagement

An order of reinstatement entails the tribunal ordering the employer to treat the complainant in all respects as if he had not been dismissed[436] and taking an employee back on less favourable terms does not constitute reinstatement.[437] The order must specify —

(a)   the amount payable by the employer in respect of any benefit which the complainant might reasonably be expected to have had but for the dismissal, including arrears of pay;

(b)   any rights and privileges, including seniority and pension rights, which must be restored;

(c)   the date for compliance with the order.[438]

5.83 A tribunal is directed to make an order of re-engagement on such terms as it may decide.[439] This is an order that the complainant be engaged by the employer, or by a successor of the employer or by an associated employer, in employment comparable to that from which he was dismissed or other suitable employment.[440] The order must specify the terms on which re-engagement is to take place including —

(a)   the identity of the employer;

(b)   the nature of the employment;

(c)   the remuneration;

(d)   the amount payable by the employer in respect of any benefit which the complainant might reasonably be expected to have had but for the dismissal, including arrears of pay;

(e)   any rights and privileges, including seniority and pension rights, which must be restored;

(f)   the date for compliance with the order.[441]

5.84 There is a clear procedure which must be followed in re-employment cases. First, the tribunal must consider whether to order reinstatement and only if this is not ordered should it then consider re-engagement and on what terms.[442] In doing so it must take into account the following considerations —

(a)   the wishes of the complainant;

(b)   whether it is practicable for the employer to comply;

(c)   where the complainant caused or contributed to the dismissal, whether it would be just to make the order.[443]

---

[435] *Pirelli General Cable Works Ltd v. Murray* [1979] IRLR 190, EAT.

[436] ERA, s. 114(1).

[437] *Artisan Press v. Srawley* [1986] IRLR 126, EAT.

[438] ERA, s. 114(2)(a)–(c).

[439] ERA, s. 115. However, this cannot be in a position which involves better terms: *Rank Xerox (UK) Ltd v. Stryczek* [1995] IRLR 568, EAT.

[440] ERA, s. 115(1).

[441] ERA, s. 115(2)(a)–(f).

[442] ERA, s. 116(1), (2).

[443] ERA, s. 116(1)(a)–(c), (3)(a)–(c).

Central to these provisions is the question of practicability. It is for the employer to show that re-employment is not practicable. It is worth noting that the employer can have two opportunities to show that it is not practicable to re-employ. First, when the tribunal is contemplating making the order; and, second, where the order has been made but not complied with and additional compensation becomes payable this can be avoided if the employer can satisfy the tribunal that it was not practicable to comply with the order.[444] Thus in Scotland a tribunal need not reach a final conclusion that re-employment is in fact practicable at the time when the order is made.[445] This approach has now been supported by the Court of Appeal in England in *Port of London Authority v. Payne*[446] where it was accepted that the legislation requires a two-stage approach to the issue of practicability. At the first stage, when the tribunal is contemplating making an order, its determination will be provisional and the final conclusion on practicability will only be made once the tribunal has discovered whether or not the employer can comply with the order within the period prescribed. At this second stage the burden of proof rests with the employer where the test is based upon the practicability of re-employment. This entails a lower standard than showing that re-employment was impossible.

5.85 *Practicability.* One issue which might be important as regards the issue of practicability is the extent to which personal relationships may have deteriorated between employer and employee particularly in small firms so as to make re-employment impracticable. In *Enessy Co. SA V. Minoprio*[447] it was declared that in the case of a small employer with few staff "where there must exist a close personal relationship, reinstatement can only be appropriate in exceptional circumstances and to enforce it upon a reluctant employer is not a course which an industrial tribunal should pursue unless persuaded by powerful evidence that it would succeed". It has been argued that these remarks were made in a case where the relationship was almost a domestic one and that tribunals should not shirk from their duty of inquiring into relationships, even in a small firm, to see whether the fears of continuing disharmony are exaggerated.[448] It is to be hoped that this latter view prevails since, as Smith and Wood point out, if the *Enessy* view were applied too widely it would resemble the old common law rules against enforcement of contracts of employment.[449] Reinstatement will not be practicable when it results either in redundancies or significant overstaffing.[450] The only further statutory guidance on the question of practicability is that where the employer has engaged a permanent replacement for a dismissed employee, the tribunal shall not take that fact into account in determining whether it is practicable to comply with a re-employment order, unless the employer shows —

(a)   that it was not practicable to have the work done without engaging a permanent replacement; or

(b)   that he engaged the replacement after the lapse of a reasonable period, without hearing from the complainant that he wished to be re-employed, and that when he engaged the replacement it was no longer reasonable for him to arrange for the work to be done except by a permanent replacement.[451]

---

[444]   ERA, s. 117(4). See also *Port of London Authority v. Payne* [1994] IRLR 9, CA.
[445]   *Timex Corporation v. Thomson* [1981] IRLR 522, EAT.
[446]   [1994] IRLR 9.
[447]   [1978] IRLR 489, EAT.
[448]   "Re-Employment and the Industrial Tribunals" (1982) JLSS 216.
[449]   *Industrial Law* (London, 5th edn) at p. 386.
[450]   *Cold Drawn Tubes Ltd v. Middleton* [1992] IRLR 160, EAT.
[451]   ERA, s. 116(6).

5.86 As has already been noted, a complainant who does obtain an order of re-employment is also entitled to be paid an amount to cover loss of benefits such as arrears of pay for the period from the date of termination to the date of his re-employment. In calculating the sum to be awarded, the tribunal must take into account, so as to reduce the employer's liability, any sums which the complainant has received by way of wages in lieu of notice or ex gratia payments paid by the employer, remuneration for employment with another employer and such other benefits as the tribunal thinks appropriate in the circumstances.[452] There is no statutory upper limit on the amount which an employee can be awarded to compensate for arrears of pay when the tribunal decides to make an order of re-employment.

5.87 If the employer does reinstate or re-engage the complainant but does not comply fully with the terms of the order, the tribunal will make an award of compensation of such amount as it thinks fit having regard to the loss sustained by the employee in consequence of the employer's failure to comply fully with the order.[453] This award cannot exceed the maximum compensatory award.[454] It is much more likely that the above provision will be activated because the employer has failed completely to comply with the order. In such a case the employee becomes entitled to compensation and will certainly receive a basic award and a compensatory award. The tribunal also has the authority to make an additional award. However, as we have seen, this can be resisted by the employer if he can satisfy the tribunal that it was not practicable for him to comply with the order. The additional award will be between 26 and 52 weeks' pay in a case of race or sex discrimination and between 13 and 26 weeks' pay in any other case.[455] This award is not intended to be a precisely calculated substitute for financial loss but rather a genuine *solatium*. It is capable of being reduced because of a failure to mitigate loss but only if this question is treated as a general factor and not something producing a quantifiable reduction in the sum which would otherwise be awarded.[456]

5.88 Since all these awards including the additional award are subject to a statutory maximum, an employer's failure to comply with the re-employment order could have had an unfortunate consequence for the complainant. For he may have received less by way of compensation for the employer's failure to comply with the order than he would have received for arrears of pay had the order been complied with! It was suggested[457] that the solution to this problem was for the tribunal to give the employee the option of receiving compensation for failure to obtain re-employment or to enforce the order for arrears of wages made as part of the original order of re-employment. However, the Court of Appeal in *O'Laoire v. Jackel International Ltd*[458] has made it clear that the employee does not have such an option because the statutory language is quite specific so that a complainant who has not been re-employed in pursuance of a tribunal order is only entitled to an award of compensation which is subject to a statutory maximum. This position

---

[452] ERA, s. 114(2), (4), s. 115(2)(d), (3).
[453] ERA, s. 117(1), (2).
[454] ERA, s. 124(1).
[455] ERA, s. 117(5), (6).
[456] See generally *Mabirizi v. National Hospital for Nervous Diseases* [1990] IRLR 133, EAT.
[457] *Conoco (UK) Ltd v. Neal* [1989] IRLR 51, EAT.
[458] [1990] IRLR 70, CA.

has been altered by new provisions which are contained in the Employment Rights Act 1996, s. 124. Subsection (3) now directs tribunals to exceed the maximum limit for the compensatory award (at time of writing, £11,300) to the extent necessary to enable the award fully to reflect the amount that the employee might reasonably have been expected to receive from the employer to cover benefits including arrears of pay during the period from the date of dismissal to the date when the order of re-employment should have been complied with. This power can only be exercised where an additional award falls to be made and the compensatory award should reflect the employee's true loss to the extent necessary when added to the additional award.[459]

5.89 (b) Compensation

A complainant's compensation is made up of two elements — a basic award and a compensatory award. The basic award is dependent upon the complainant's length of service and age whereeas the compensatory award is intended to compensate for loss consequent upon dismissal.

5.90 *(i) Basic award.* The basic award is calculated on the same basis as a redundancy payment. This means that the award is calculated by reference to the period, ending with the effective date of termination,[460] during which the employee has been continuously employed, by starting at the end of that period and reckoning backwards the number of years of employment and allowing —

(a)   one and a half weeks' pay for each year in which the employee was over the age of 41;

(b)   one week's pay for each year in which the employee was between 22 and 41; and

(c)   half a week's pay for each year of employment under 22.[461]

The maximum number of years which can be taken into account is twenty.[462] The amount of this award can be reduced in a number of circumstances. First, an employee who is aged over 64 has his basic award reduced by one twelfth for each whole month from the date of his last birthday (the specified anniversary) to his effective date of termination.[463] Thus an employee who is over 65 is ineligible to receive a basic award. The basic award is also reduced if the complainant has received a statutory redundancy payment,[464] or has received an ex gratia payment from his employer which is intended to satisy his legal rights.[465] It is also possible for the basic award to be reduced on grounds of justice and equity if the complainant has unreasonably refused an offer of reinstatement.[466] Finally, there is also provision to reduce the basic award where the complainant has contributed to his dismissal.[467] This would apply where the tribunal considers it just and equitable to reduce the award because of the conduct of the complainant before his dismissal. As has already been noted, this is most likely to arise where the employee commits an act of misconduct which only comes to light after the employer has taken the decision to dismiss on other grounds or where there is

---

[459] ERA, s. 124(4).
[460] See para. 5.27.
[461] ERA, s. 119(1), (2).
[462] ERA, s. 119(3).
[463] ERA, s. 119(4), (5). Formerly the ages were 64 for a man and 59 for a woman.
[464] ERA, s. 122(4).
[465] *Chelsea Football Club & Athletic v. Heath* [1981] ICR 323, EAT.
[466] ERA, s. 122(1).
[467] ERA, s. 122(2).

procedural unfairness.[468] Employees who have been dismissed for an automatically unfair reason related to trade union membership, non-membership or activities, certain health and safety grounds and for being employee representatives or candidates have the right to a minimum basic award before any reduction on any of the above grounds.[469]

5.91 *(ii) Compensatory award.* The compensatory award will be such amount as the tribunal considers just and equitable in all the circumstances having regard to the loss sustained by the complainant in consequence of the dismissal in so far as that loss is attributable to action taken by the employer.[470] The award is subject to a statutory maximum which is presently £11,300. Under this head of compensation the critical question is for the tribunal to ascertain the extent of the employee's loss. If there is no loss there can be no award. The award can also be reduced on account of the employee's conduct. Substantial reductions might be appropriate, for example, where the tribunal holds that the employee has been unfairly dismissed but considers that he would have been dismissed in any event. Such a state of affairs might arise in a case where the dismissal is unfair simply because of a want of procedure or a failure to consult.[471] In such cases, the compensation paid to the employee may be subject to three separate deductions. First, the basic award may be reduced on the basis that the conduct of the complainant before the dismissal was such that it was just and equitable to reduce the award.[472] Second, the compensatory award can be reduced on the basis of the loss which the complainant sustained and which was attributable to his dismissal.[473] The compensatory award can also be reduced by such proportion as the tribunal considers just and equitable where it finds that the complainant's dismissal was to any extent caused or contributed to by his action.[474]

It has been made clear that the deduction to the compensatory award made under ERA, s. 123(1) may have a significant bearing on what further deduction falls to be made under ERA, s. 123(6). The correct approach is for the tribunal to first assess the amount of the loss under s. 123(1), including the chance of employment continuing if the employee had not been unfairly dismissed. Thereafter, and in light of that finding, the tribunal should decide the extent to which the employee had caused or contributed to the dismissal and the amount by which it would be just and equitable to reduce the compensatory award under s. 123(6). Since the fact that a deduction has been made under s. 123(1) can affect what is just and equitable to be deducted under s. 123(6), it may turn out that the deduction to the compensatory award under s. 123(6) may not be of the same proportion as that made to the basic award by s. 122(2) even though the amount of this deduction

---

[468] *Devis (W.) & Sons Ltd v. Atkins* [1977] ICR 662, HL.

[469] ERA, s. 120(1) and see para. 5.68.

[470] ERA, s. 123(1). For a discussion as to whether or not the compensatory award can be deducted from any award of damages for common law breach of contract see the decision of the Court of Appeal in *O'Laoire v. Jackel International Ltd* [1991] IRLR 170. See Chapter Three, para. 3.62.

[471] *Polkey v. A. E. Dayton Services Ltd* [1988] ICR 142, HL; *Hough v. Leyland Daf Ltd* [1991] IRLR 194, EAT.

[472] ERA, s. 122(2).

[473] ERA, s. 123(1).

[474] ERA, s. 123(6).

also depends on justice and equity.[475] In making such deductions a tribunal must be satisfied that the unfairness is procedural. It has been held that a deducion under ERA, s. 123(1) is not appropriate where the unfairness suffered by the employee is substantive rather than procedural.[476] Another occasion where the tribunal would be justified in holding that the complainant has suffered no loss is where more serious misconduct comes to the employer's attention after the date of dismissal.[477]

5.92 In particular, the award can compensate for–
(a)   any expenses reasonably incurred by the complainant in consequence of the dismissal; and
(b)   loss of any benefit which he might reasonably be expected to have had but for the dismissal.[478]

However, where the complainant is being compensated for a loss of entitlement to a payment on redundancy, the compensatory award can only compensate him to the extent of the excess of this payment over his basic award.[479] A complainant has a duty to mitigate his loss and his compensatory award will be reduced if he has failed to do so.[480] Moreover, where an employee has received a payment on redundancy, whether statutory or otherwise, which exceeds the basic award, that excess must go to reduce the compensatory award.[481] As already noted, the compensatory award can also be reduced on a just and equitable basis where the tribunal finds that the dismissal was to any extent caused or contributed to by the action of the complainant.[482] Finally, a tribunal is directed to ignore any pressure exercised on the employer through a real or threatened strike or other industrial action when calculating the award.[483]

5.93 *Calculating the compensatory award.* A number of principles have been developed for ascertaining those losses which are capable of being compensated by this award. The major aim of the compensatory award is to compensate the complainant fully for the pecuniary losses which flowed from his unfair dismissal but not to award a bonus. He is not entitled to any compensation for injury to feelings.[484] The method of calculating the compensatory award was first discussed in *Norton Tool Co. Ltd v. Tewson*[485] — a decision under the unfair dismissal provisions of the Industrial Relations Act 1971 but which is still relevant. This decision sets out the basic heads of compensation which the compensatory award is capable of covering. A tribunal which is assessing the compensatory award must consider each of these heads in turn and must calculate the amount to be awarded under each. The tribunal has a duty to raise the various categories of loss even

---

[475] See, generally, the decision of the Court of Appeal in *Rao v. Civil Aviation Authority* [1994] IRLR 240 and see also the decision of an Extra Division of the Court of Session in *Campbell v. Dunoon & Cowal Housing Association Ltd* [1993] IRLR 496.
[476] *Steel Stockholders (Birmingham) Ltd v. Kirkwood* [1993] IRLR 515, EAT.
[477] *Devis (W.) & Sons Ltd v. Atkins* [1977] ICR 662, HL.
[478] ERA, s. 123(2).
[479] ERA, s. 123(3).
[480] ERA, s. 123(4).
[481] ERA, s. 123(7). Applied strictly by the EAT in *Rushton v. Harcros Timber & Building Supplies* [1993] IRLR 254, but see also *Roadchef Ltd v. Hastings* [1988] IRLR 142, EAT.
[482] ERA, s. 123(6).
[483] ERA, s. 123(5).
[484] *Norton Tool Co. Ltd v. Tewson* [1972] ICR 501, NIRC. Approved by the Court of Appeal in *Babcock FATA Ltd v. Addison* [1987] IRLR 173.
[485] [1972] ICR 501, NIRC.

where they are not raised by the complainant, although once a head of loss has been considered it is for the complainant actually to prove that he suffered a loss under it.[486]

5.94 *Heads of loss*

(1) *Immediate loss of wages.* This head compensates the complainant for his actual loss of earnings from the date of dismissal to the date of the hearing. This is done by calculating the complainant's net wage (i.e. his pay after deductions for tax and national insurance) and deducting from it any pay which he has received from other employment during the period from the date of the expiry of his notice until the hearing date.[487] If the complainant has obtained other employment which he then loses before the date of the hearing, then, that dismissal should be ignored when ascertaining the extent of his loss.[488] It is now clear that a tribunal is also required to deduct any money which the complainant has received as wages in lieu of notice.[489] The value of other benefits to the complainant such as the loss of a company car or cheap loan facilities can be included as a relevant loss.[490] Equally, the tribunal can also take account of any expenses which the employee incurred as a result of his dismissal.[491] This could include any expenses associated with moving house,[492] although it does not include any legal expenses incurred in complaining to the tribunal.

(2) *Future loss.* If the complainant is still out of work at the date of the hearing, the tribunal must consider awarding an element to cover his future loss of wages. This award must involve a degree of speculation for the tribunal since it is required to assess the likely period of continued unemployment for the complainant. Equally, even where the complainant has obtained fresh employment there will still be a future loss of earnings if he is paid at a lower rate by his new employer. In such a case the tribunal also has the difficult task of establishing how long it will be before the complainant achieves parity with his previous earnings. In considering these issues the tribunal is likely to base its decision upon its collective knowledge of industrial relations in the area.[493] The quantification of the likely period of continued unemployment will be based upon the evidence[494] and the tribunal's consideration of the complainant's personal characteristics, for example, that he was elderly or in poor health,[495] and a tribunal is entitled to take account of loss of earnings caused by an illness which was brought about by an unfair dismissal.[496] This calculation can include a sum to take account of loss of earnings after the employee has reached normal retiring age.[497] The tribunal may also include any anticipated salary increases so long as there is a high probability that the

---

[486] *Tidman v. Aveling Marshall Ltd* [1977] IRLR 218, EAT.
[487] *See Babcock FATA Ltd v. Addison* [1987] IRLR 173, CA. But different rules may apply where the employee has obtained a permanent job by the date of the hearing at a higher rate of pay. Here loss should be assessed from the date of dismissal to the date of the new employment: *Fentiman v. Fluid Engineering Products Ltd* [1991] IRLR 150, EAT.
[488] *Courtaulds Northern Spinning Ltd v. Moosa* [1984] IRLR 43, EAT.
[489] *Babcock FATA Ltd v. Addison*, above, disapproving *Finnie v. Top Hat Frozen Foods* [1985] IRLR 365, EAT.
[490] ERA, s. 123(2)(b).
[491] ERA, s. 118(2)(a).
[492] *Scottish Co-operative Wholesale Society v. Lloyd* [1973] IRLR 93, NIRC.
[493] *Bateman v. British Leyland (UK) Ltd* [1974] IRLR 101, NIRC.
[494] *Morganite Electrical Carbon Ltd v. Donne* [1987] IRLR 363, EAT.
[495] *Fougère v. Phoenix Motor Co. Ltd* [1976] IRLR 259, EAT.
[496] *Devine v. Designer Flowers Wholesale Florist Sundries Ltd* [1993] IRLR 517, EAT.
[497] *Barrel Plating & Phosphating Co. Ltd v. Danks* [1976] IRLR 262, EAT.

complainant would have received them.[498] However, where there is evidence that the complainant might have lost his job in the future because of redundancy the tribunal will be justified in taking this factor into account and, therefore, reduce the period of future loss accordingly.[499] The number of weeks which constitute the complainant's period of future loss will be used as a multiplier when calculating the amount of compensation to be awarded under this head. Thus the tribunal will also calculate the complainant's actual loss per week and then multiply this figure by the number of weeks of future loss in order to arrive at the appropriate sum. Clearly, the complainant's actual loss per week will depend upon whether or not he has obtained fresh employment and the rate of pay if new employment has been obtained. When calculating the complainant's net losses the tribunal is entitled to take account of loss of fringe benefits and may also include any additional expenses incurred in the new job.

(3) *Loss of pension rights.* A complainant is entitled to compensation for loss of pension rights. The sum awarded under this head is likely to be substantial particularly where the complainant contributed to an occupational pension scheme and remains unemployed or cannot take advantage of his existing pension rights in his new job.[500] The types of loss which a tribunal should take into account under this head were discussed in *Copson v. Eversure Accessories Ltd*[501] where it was stressed that a tribunal should take a broad common sense approach. Two forms of loss were identified — (a) loss of the present pension position; and (b) loss of future pension (i.e. the opportunity to improve the position until the time of retiral). Usually the tribunal will base its assessment of loss upon the sum of the contributions already made. This approach is particularly useful in cases of relatively short service or when calculating future loss. However, where the complainant is dismissed shortly before his retirement age, the better approach is to take an actuarial method and to assess the capital value of the pension and then discount it for accelerated payment. In 1980 the Government Actuary's Department (GAD) produced a paper which suggested ways of quantifying loss of pension rights.[502] A new set of guidelines entitled *Industrial Tribunals — Compensation for Loss of Pension Rights* was published by HMSO in 1990 and a second edition was published in 1991. These guidelines were prepared by three tribunal chairmen in consultation with GAD and are simple to operate. The new guidelines contain a simplified actuarial method for calculating deferred pension rights based on age and assume that the employee would not have left his employment for any reason other than death or disability. Given the amount of uncertainty associated with calculating loss of pension rights, industrial tribunals are likely to rely on these guidelines although it should not be forgotten that they have no statutory force and that tribunals are encouraged to take a broad common sense view.[503]

(4) *Loss arising from the manner of dismissal.* An employee has no right to any compensation for the distress caused by his dismissal. However, there may be rare occasions where an employee can claim compensation under this head when there is cogent evidence that the manner of the dismissal caused financial loss to him

[498] *York Trailer Co. Ltd v. Sparkes* [1972] IRLR 348, NIRC.
[499] *Young's of Gosport Ltd v. Kendell* [1977] IRLR 433, EAT.
[500] Since the Social Security Act 1986 it is now much easier to transfer occupational pensions.
[501] [1974] IRLR 247, NIRC.
[502] Discussed in (1980) 25 JLSS (Workshop).
[503] It has been held that tribunals do not have a duty to follow the guidelines so that there is no error of law when a tribunal does not give precise effect to them: *Bingham v. Hobourn Engineering Ltd* [1992] IRLR 298, EAT.

(e.g. by making it more difficult for him to find future employment).[504] Where a dismissal is unfair because of a failure to consult with an employee who has been made redundant, an important issue will be to assess compensation in light of the possibility that proper consultation could have led to an offer of alternative employment. In such a case tribunals should adopt a two-stage approach which requires them to ask whether an offer of employment would have been made if the proper procedure had been followed and what would that employment have been and what wage would have been paid in respect of it.[505] However, the tribunal has no obligation to consider the question of reduction of the compensatory award of its own volition where the employee has been dismissed in circumstances which entail an abrogation of the employee's responsibility to manage the business.[506]

(5) *Loss of statutory protection.* An employee who is dismissed and who obtains other employment will lose all those employment protection rights which depend upon continuity of employment and particularly his rights in redundancy. In *Norton Tool*[507] it was recognised that an employee could receive a sum to compensate for this. However, since the introduction of the basic award which is calculated on the same basis as a redundancy payment it was thought that this head would be largely ignored or lead to a nominal award. Nonetheless in *Daley v. A. E. Dorset (Almar Dolls) Ltd*[508] it was accepted that loss of a service-related notice entitlement is a head of damage which can be reflected in the compensatory award and awarded a sum equivalent to half the employee's statutory notice entitlement. The Scottish position is that loss of the statutory right to long notice may in principle be a head of loss provided it can be quantified, but it is so remote as to be significant only in an exceptional case.[509]

5.95 *Mitigation of loss and employee's contributory conduct.* As has already been noted the common law rules as regards mitigation of loss should apply in relation to the compensatory award.[510] The major issue as regards mitigation is to consider whether the employee has acted reasonably in the circumstances.[511] It is clear that this test does not require the employee to take any job that might be offered; although he should take employment that is reasonably and properly offered to him.[512] It is likely that an employee who fails to utilise the employer's grievance or appeals procedures after dismissal will not be taken to have failed to mitigate his loss.[513] Equally, an employee does not necessarily fail to mitigate his loss by setting up in business on his own account after dismissal rather than trying to get another job.[514] On the other hand, an employee is likely to find that a refusal by

---

[504] *Vaughan v. Weighpack Ltd* [1974] IRLR 105, NIRC.
[505] *Red Bank Manufacturing Co. Ltd v. Meadows* [1992] IRLR 209, EAT.
[506] *Boulton & Paul Ltd v. Arnold* [1994] IRLR 532, EAT (onus placed on employee to decide whether she or another employee should be dismissed).
[507] *Norton Tool Co. Ltd v. Tewson* [1972] ICR 501, NIRC.
[508] [1981] IRLR 385, EAT.
[509] *Gourley v. Kerr* February 18, 1982, EAT (unreported), discussed in *Stair Memorial Encyclopaedia of the Laws of Scotland*, Vol. 9, *Employment*, at para. 281.
[510] ERA, s. 123(4).
[511] *Bessenden Properties Ltd v. Corness* [1973] IRLR 365, NIRC.
[512] *Gallear v. J. F. Watson & Son Ltd* [1979] IRLR 306, EAT.
[513] *William Muir (Bond 9) Ltd v. Lamb* [1985] IRLR 95, EAT doubting *Hoover Ltd v. Forde* [1980] ICR 239, EAT. *Lamb* has been followed by the EAT in England in *Lock v. Connell Estate Agents* [1994] IRLR 444. It is now clear that as far as constructive dismissal cases are concerned there is no need to exercise grievance rights as far as mitigation is concerned: see *Seligman & Latz Ltd v. McHugh* [1979] IRLR 130, EAT.
[514] *Gardiner-Hill v. Roland Berger Technics Ltd* [1982] IRLR 498, EAT.

him to accept an offer of reinstatement from his employer amounts to a failure to mitigate so that he cannot claim for any loss.[515] The onus of proof as regard a failure to mitigate is likely to rest upon the employer.[516]

5.96 As has already been noted, the basic award can be reduced to any extent on a just and equitable basis because of the conduct of the complainant before his dismissal.[517] Equally, the compensatory award can also be reduced on a just and equitable basis where the tribunal finds that the dismissal was to any extent caused or contributed to by any action of the complainant.[518] In considering this question a tribunal is required to make three findings. First, that there was conduct on the part of the employee in connection with his dismissal which was culpable or blameworthy; second, that the matters to which the complaint relates were caused or contributed to, to some extent, by the culpable or blameworthy conduct; and, third, that it is just and equitable to reduce the assessment to a specified extent.[519] Culpable or blameworthy conduct includes not only breaches of contract and delicts but other conduct which is perverse or foolish or bloodyminded or simply unreasonable in the circumstances.[520] Tribunals have been advised to look at all the circumstances when conducting this exercise and to concentrate upon the realities rather than relying upon the technical reason for the dismissal.[521] This can entail the tribunal considering aspects of the complainant's conduct beyond those stated in the reasons for his dismissal.[522] In determining whether to reduce both the basic award and the compensatory award on the ground of conduct, tribunals must avoid considering what happened to other employees involved in the same act of misconduct and concentrate upon the causative or contributory conduct of the complainant.[523] Compensation can be reduced even where the employer has failed to show a reason for the dismissal.[524] Equally, there can be a reduction in compensation in a constructive dismissal case because constructive dismissal and contributory fault are separate and distinct processes.[525]

5.97 As already indicated,[526] a tribunal can reduce the compensatory award in a misconduct case where the dismissal has been held to be unfair because the employer failed to follow the correct procedure.[527] Equally, the compensatory award can be reduced because of other acts of misconduct which only came to light after the complainant's dismissal.[528] In both cases there is nothing to prevent the tribunal making a nil award. The question of contributory fault is more difficult to apply in a capability case. In *Kraft Foods Ltd v. Fox*[529] it was argued that

---

[515] *Sweetlove v. Redbridge and Waltham Forest Area Health Authority* [1979] IRLR 195, EAT.
[516] *Bessenden Properties Ltd v. Corness*, above. *Cf Scottish & Newcastle Breweries plc v. Halliday* [1986] IRLR 291, EAT where the onus was placed on the employee.
[517] ERA, s. 122(2).
[518] ERA, s. 123(6).
[519] *Nelson v. BBC (No. 2)* [1979] IRLR 346, CA.
[520] *Nelson*, above.
[521] *Maris v. Rotherham County Borough Council* [1974] IRLR 147, NIRC.
[522] *Jamieson v. Aberdeen County Council* [1975] IRLR 348, OH.
[523] *Parker Foundry Ltd v. Slack* [1992] IRLR 11, CA.
[524] *Polentarutti v. Autokraft Ltd* [1991] IRLR 457, EAT.
[525] *Polentarutti*, above.
[526] See para. 5.91.
[527] *Devis (W.) & Sons Ltd v. Atkins* [1977] ICR 662, HL; *Polkey v. A. E. Dayton Services Ltd* [1988] ICR 142, HL.
[528] *Devis*, above.
[529] [1977] IRLR 431, EAT.

contributory fault was best applied in misconduct cases or in capability cases where the employee is unwilling to increase his efforts; it had no place in cases of incapacity where the employee was doing his best but his best was not good enough because here the employee had no control over his actions. This proposition has been narrowed by the later case of *Moncur v. International Paint Co. Ltd*[530] where it was stated that it could not be an absolute rule that an act or failing which is attributable to a defect of character or personality of the claimant, and which is not within his control to alter, can never be material when considering contributory fault. The *Moncur* view has been preferred by the EAT in Scotland.[531] The compensatory award is most likely to be reduced in a capability case where the employee is lazy, negligent or unwilling to improve.[532] However, the possibility cannot be ignored that the award might also be reduced in cases where the employee's lack of skill is genuinely beyond his control.

5.98 (c) Trade union dismissals and certain health and safety dismissals, etc

It has already been noted that employees dismissed for union membership or activities or non-membership reasons have a right to a minimum basic award and a right to a special award where they have sought reinstatement or re-engagement and they have not been re-employed. Such benefits also accrue to employees designated to carry out health and safety activities and safety representatives and members of safety committees as well as elected employee representatives and candidates. Both the basic award and the special award are subject to reductions on account of the complainant's age.[533] The special award can also be reduced on a just and equitable basis because of the employee's conduct before his dismissal or, where dismissal was with notice, his conduct before that notice was given.[534] A reduction can also be made to this award on a just and equitable basis where the tribunal finds that the employee has unreasonably prevented an order of reinstatement or re-engagement being complied with or has unreasonably refused an offer of reinstatement made by his employer otherwise than in compliance with such an order.[535]

5.99 Interim relief. Employees who have been dismissed on grounds of union membership, non-membership or activities also enjoy the right to interim relief, as do employees designated to carry out safety activities, safety representatives and members of safety committees and employee representatives and candidates. This may involve the employee being re-employed by the employer until his unfair dismissal complaint is resolved. However, it is more likely that the tribunal will continue the employee's rights to wages and other benefits until this time. An application for interim relief must be presented to the tribunal within seven days of the employee's effective date of termination.[536] Where the dismissal is alleged to be for trade union membership or activities the application must be accompanied

---

[530] [1978] IRLR 223, EAT.
[531] See *Finnie v. Top Hat Frozen Foods* [1985] IRLR 365, EAT where it was held that the tribunal was entitled to take account of the employee's performance of his duties in assessing contributory fault.
[532] In such a case there is likely to be substantial reduction in the award: see *Sutton and Gates (Luton) Ltd v. Boxall* [1978] IRLR 486, EAT.
[533] For health and safety dismissals, etc, see ERA, s. 119(4) (basic award); ERA, s. 125(3) (special award) and for trade union dismissals, see TULRCA, s. 158(3).
[534] ERA, s. 125(4) (health and safety, etc); TULRCA, s. 158(4) (TU cases).
[535] ERA, s. 125(5) (health and safety, etc); TULRCA, s. 158(5) (TU cases).
[536] ERA, s. 128(2) (health and safety, etc); TULRCA, s. 161(2) (TU cases).

by a certificate, signed by an authorised official of the employee's union, stating that at the date of dismissal the complainant was, or had proposed to become, a member of the union and that there appear to be reasonable grounds for supporting that the reason or the principal reason was one alleged in the complaint.[537] An interim relief application is determined as soon as practicable, although the employer is entitled to at least seven days' notice of the application and the arrangements for the hearing.[538] The remedy will be awarded if it is likely that the tribunal which will later determine the complaint will find that the complainant was unfairly dismissed.[539] This has been interpreted as requiring the tribunal to consider whether the employee has a "pretty good" chance of succeeding — a higher standard than simply showing a reasonable prospect of success.[540]

5.100 If the tribunal upholds the application it must first ask the employer whether he is willing to reinstate or re-engage the complainant until the hearing and, if the employer is willing, it will make the appropriate order.[541] If the employer fails to attend the hearing or is unwilling to accept re-employment of the employee, the tribunal will make an order for the continuation of the employee's contract of employment.[542] This is an order continuing the employee's contract in force until the determination or settlement of his complaint but only for the purposes of pay or any other benefit derived from employment, seniority, pension rights and similar matters and as regards the computation of continuous employment.[543] The order must specify the amount which the employee is to receive at each normal pay period.[544] This will be the amount which he could reasonably have been expected to earn had he not been dismissed.[545] The employee can complain to the tribunal at any time (including at the hearing of his unfair dismissal complaint) that the employer has failed to comply with the relevant order. In the case where an order for reinstatement or re-engagement has not been complied with the tribunal has the power to order the continuation of the complainant's contract and may award such compensation as it considers just and equitable, taking account of the infringement and the loss to the employee.[546] Where the employer has failed to comply with a continuation order the tribunal will determine the amount of pay owed and in any other case will award such compensation as it considers just and equitable.[547]

5.101 (d) Recoupment of benefits

A person who has been dismissed from employment may well be entitled to state benefits such as unemployment benefit or income support. The question is whether a tribunal should take such benefits into account when determining the amount of compensation to be paid to a complainant. This issue is now regulated by the Employment Protection (Recoupment of Unemployment Benefit and Supplemen-

---

[537] TULRCA, s. 161(2).
[538] ERA, s. 128(3) and (4) (health and safety, etc); TULRCA, s. 162(1) and (2) (TU cases).
[539] ERA, s. 129(1) (health and safety, etc); TULRCA, s. 163(1) (TU cases).
[540] *Taplin v. C. Shippam Ltd* [1978] IRLR 450, EAT.
[541] ERA, s. 129(2) and (5) (health and safety, etc); TULRCA s. 163(2) and (4) (TU cases).
[542] ERA, s. 129(9) (health and safety, etc); TULRCA, s. 163(6) (TU cases).
[543] ERA, s. 130(1) (health and safety, etc); TULRCA, s. 164(1) (TU cases).
[544] ERA, s. 130(2) (health and safety, etc); TULRCA, s. 164(2) (TU cases).
[545] ERA, s. 130(7) (health and safety, etc); TULRCA, s. 164(7) (TU cases).
[546] ERA, s. 132(1) (health and safety, etc); TULRCA, s. 166(1) (TU cases).
[547] ERA, s. 132(3)–(6) (health and safety, etc); TULRCA, s. 166(3)–(5) (TU cases). Where this application is being dealt with at the same time as the unfair dismissal complaint, the tribunal must specify the amount of pay separately.

tary Benefit) Regulations 1977[548] which permit the recovery of sums from the prescribed element in unfair dismissal compensation. This element is the amount which the employee has received to cover loss of wages for the period up until the conclusion of the hearing.[549] When the tribunal makes a monetary award to which the Regulations apply it must set out (a) the monetary award; (b) the amount of the prescribed element, if any; (c) the dates of the period of the prescribed element; and (d) the amount, if any, by which the monetary award exceeds the prescribed element.[550] The effect of the Regulations is to assess the employer for the whole of the monetary award but to postpone payment of the prescribed element until a recoupment notice has been served on the employer by the Department of Employment.[551] Initially, therefore, the employee only receives the excess of the monetary award over the prescribed element. The effect of the recoupment notice is to require the employer to pay back to the Department the amount of the benefits paid during the period of the prescribed element.[552] Once this has been done the employer will be required to pay any remaining part of the required element to the successful complainant.

---

[548] SI 1977 No. 674, as amended by SI 1980 No. 1608. These regulations only apply to an award by a tribunal; they do not apply to a negotiated settlement. This fact may be an incentive to the parties to agree to some sort of negotiated settlement.

[549] Regulation 3, and paras 6–8 of Schedule.

[550] Regulation 5(3).

[551] Regulation 8.

[552] Regulation 9(2).

Chapter Six

REDUNDANCY PAYMENTS

INTRODUCTION

6.1 When an employee becomes redundant various legal questions can arise. For example, the selection for redundancy of part-time employees before full-time employees and contractual mobility clauses may raise issues of indirect sexual or marital status discrimination[1] and using absence as a selection criterion may raise the possibility of disability discrimination.[2] Alternatively, the selection for redundancy may raise issues of the fairness of the dismissal and it is the case that a perfectly genuine dismissal for redundancy may, for want of proper procedure, become an unfair dismissal.[3] Additionally prior to dismissing employees on the grounds of redundancy an employer may be obliged to inform and consult with employee representatives.[4] However, although reference will be made to Article 119 of the EC Treaty as necessary this Chapter is concerned with the simple question of whether an employee is entitled to receive a redundancy payment which is a payment, calculated in accordance with strict statutory rules, an employee[5] with at least two years'[6] continuous employment is entitled to receive from his employer[7] in the event is his dismissal on grounds of redundancy — in short, statutory compensation for loss of employment. The system of redundancy payments was first introduced by the Redundancy Payments Act 1965 and the current provisions are now contained in Part XI of the Employment Rights Act 1996.[8] The issues involved in whether an employee is entitled to receive a redundancy payment are as follows:

(1) Has the employee been dismissed?

(2) Is the dismissal due to redundancy?

(3) Has the employee's right to receive a redundancy payment been defeated by his refusal of alternative employment?

(4) Has the business in which the redundant employee worked been transferred to another employer?

---

[1] See Chapter Seven, para. 7.18.

[2] See Chapter Seven, para. 7.33.

[3] See Chapter Five, para. 5.53.

[4] See Chapter Nine, para. 9.26 ff.

[5] Defined to mean those employed under a contract of employment or apprenticeship (ERA, s. 235(1)); but note the special provisions made for others, e.g. office holders (ERA, ss. 171, 172, 173).

[6] The application of the 2 years' continuous employment rule may itself be indirect sexual discrimination: see para. 6.2.

[7] An employer's right to receive a rebate has been removed (WA, ss. 27–29; EA 1989, s. 17).

[8] For a detailed analysis of purpose of redundancy payments and the law regarding redundancy, see respectively, *The Effect of the Redundancy Payments Scheme* (HMSO, 1971) and C. Grunfeld, *The Law of Redundancy* (3rd edn 1989).

(5) Has the employee's right to a redundancy payment been affected by his misconduct or a strike or lock-out?

(6) Is the employee covered by an exclusion or exemption?

(7) What rules are there for claiming and calculating a redundancy payment?

(8) What payments may be received from the Redundancy Fund?

However, prior to dealing with these matters it is necessary to consider the effect of Article 119 on entitlement to a redundancy payment.

DISMISSAL

6.2 Article 119 and redundancy payments

Since the decision of the European Court of Justice in *Barber v Guardian Royal Exchange Assurance Group*[9] it has been clear that Article 119 encompasses statutory and ex gratia redundancy payments. Accordingly, as Article 119 is a directly applicable provision of the EC Treaty,[10] it renders unlawful and of no effect any domestic provision which results in direct and indirect discrimination. Thus the direct discrimination which resided in the rule whereby women aged 60 or over lost their entitlement to a redundancy payment while men did not do so until aged 65 could be overcome by relying on Article 119[11] and it has been held in relation to an unfair dismissal complaint that, having regard to the statistics available for the period prior to the female employees' dismissal and the reasons for it put forward by the Department of Employment, the requirement of two years' continuous employment discriminated indirectly against women.[12] It would seem to follow that the same requirement could be similarly challenged in respect of redundancy payments although, having regard to the different purposes of the legislation, arguments about justification may be different.[13]

6.3 General

Generally,[14] to become entitled to a redundancy payment an employee must have been dismissed. However, redundancy law[15] like unfair dismissal law[16] provides that an employee is to be treated as dismissed by his employer only if his contract of employment is terminated in certain ways. As the statutory declaration of the situations which amount to dismissal is discussed in detail in the context of unfair dismissal law,[17] it is sufficient here to set out the elements of the statutory declaration and consider any special rules which relate only to redundancy. Thus

---

[9]   [1990] IRLR 240, ECJ.

[10] *Defrenne v. Sabena* [1976] ICR 547, ECJ. And see Chapter Seven.

[11] See *Rankin v. British Coal* [1993] IRLR 69, EAT. The discriminatory rule in EPCA, s. 82(1) was amended by EA 1989, s. 16 but with effect from a date after Mrs Rankin had been dismissed for redundancy. See now ERA, s. 156(1).

[12] *R. v. Secretary of State for Employment, ex parte Seymour-Smith and Perez* [1995] IRLR 464, CA.

[13] The issues involved in relying on the decision in *ex parte Seymour-Smith and Perez* to claim a redundancy payment and the possibility of making claims in respect of redundancy dismissals which occurred some years ago are discussed in Emp.L.B. 10.

[14] The exceptions are where an employee has been put on short time or is laid off by his employer and where a dismissal is implied (see para. 6.4).

[15] ERA, s. 136(1).

[16] ERA, s. 95.

[17] See Chapter Five paras 5.14–5.25.

an employee is dismissed "if but only if"[18] (i) his contract is terminated by his employer with or without notice,[19] (ii) his fixed term contract expires without being renewed, or (iii) he terminates his contract with or without notice when his employer's conduct[20] entitles him (the employee) to terminate his contract without notice (i.e. rescind the contract) — commonly referred to as a constructive dismissal.

6.4 Special rules

(a) Employee leaving early. Although unfair dismissal and redundancy law both contain special rules which permit an employee who leaves by giving notice to terminate during a period of notice given by his employer to be regarded as dismissed,[21] the rules which operate in relation to redundancy are more strict than those for unfair dismissal. The object of the rules is to ensure that an employee under notice is not forced to choose between an offer of employment available during the period of the employer's notice and his redundancy payment. However, to preserve his right to a redundancy payment the employee's notice of earlier termination must be in writing[22] and it must be given during the "obligatory part" of the employer's notice.[23] The obligatory part of the employer's notice is the period of notice the employer is required by statute[24] to give. Thus if an employer's notice is longer than the period required by statute the employee must delay giving his notice of earlier termination until the obligatory part of the notice has commenced. Accordingly, if an employer gives four weeks' notice to an employee who by statute is entitled to only two weeks' notice, the employee to preserve his entitlement to a redundancy payment must not give written notice before the last two of the four weeks.[25] However, even if an employee gives written notice at the correct time his right to a redundancy payment depends on his employer's reaction. If his employer does not object to the employee's earlier termination, other conditions being met, the employee will be entitled to receive a payment. However, if the employer gives to the employee written notice requiring the employee to withdraw his notice but the employee persists in earlier termination, whether the employee retains an entitlement to a redundancy payment is determined by an industrial tribunal.[26]

(b) Implied termination. The statutory concept[27] of "dismissal" already mentioned is extended[28] so that where, in accordance with a rule of law, (a) any act on the part of, or (b) any event (including his death) affecting an employer operates to terminate the contract of employment, the act or event shall be treated as a termination by the employer. The result is that such implied or constructive

---

[18] It is therefore an exclusive definition which cannot be circumvented by contract — see ERA, s. 203.

[19] *Cf Brown v. Knowsley Borough Council* [1986] IRLR 102, EAT.

[20] However, a lock-out does not entitle termination without notice (ERA, s. 136(2)).

[21] The special rules are contained in ERA, ss. 95 (unfair dismissal) and 136 (redundancy) respectively.

[22] ERA, s. 136(3). Notice other than in writing results in loss of entitlement (*Brown v. Singer Manufacturing Co. Ltd* [1967] ITR 213).

[23] ERA, s. 136(3).

[24] ERA, s. 86.

[25] *Cf CPS Recruitment Ltd v. Bowen* [1982] IRLR 54 in which the EAT, perhaps to mollify the strictness of the rule, distinguished an employee's request for earlier termination (by the employer) from an employee's notice of earlier termination by himself.

[26] ERA, s. 142.

[27] ERA, s. 136(1).

[28] ERA, s. 139(4), (5).

terminations are deemed to be dismissals. Provision (b) above is to ensure that entitlement to a redundancy payment is not lost where the contract of employment is frustrated[29] by, for example, the death or long term illness or incapacity of an individual employer, a company's compulsory liquidation or the dissolution of a partnership.[30] However, obviously, there is no implied termination by an employer where it is the death, illness or incapacity of the employee which results in the termination of the contract[31] and where an event affects both the employer and employee there is an implied termination by the employer only where its effect on the employer terminates the contract. Thus when a statute transferred the policing functions at Heathrow Airport to the Metropolitan Police there was no implied termination of the employee's contract because it was brought about by his consenting to a transfer to the Metropolitan Police and not by the statutory transfer of functions.[32] On the other hand, with regard to provision (a) above, it is not clear what "acts on the part of an employer" (apart from those already declared to be a dismissal) operate to terminate the contract. It may have been intended to apply in a case where an employer, without expressly dismissing an employee, disposes of the business in which an employee is employed in the knowledge that the new owner will not offer him employment. However, strictly, because such an act would be a repudiation of the contract leaving the employee with no alternative but to rescind the contract, there would be a dismissal within the statutory definition.[33] Additionally, since the enactment of the Transfer of Undertakings (Protection of Employment) Regulations 1981[34] the sale of an undertaking (or part of one) operates to transfer to the new owner contracts of employment subsisting at the time of the transfer of the undertaking.[35]

(c) *Volunteers for redundancy.* Because entitlement to a redundancy payment is conditional on a dismissal, as previously explained, it follows that generally[36] a termination by agreement or by the employee leaving voluntarily will result in the loss of such entitlement. Because it is accepted as good industrial relations practice for employers to give advance warning of redundancies and, where possible, to reduce their workforce by inviting volunteers,[37] it is sometimes difficult to know whether a dismissal has occurred. However, the following principles have been established. After redundancies are announced without a date of dismissal being fixed or positively ascertainable, an employee who terminates his employment is not treated as dismissed.[38] It is necessary to distinguish an employee who consents

---

[29] See Chapter Four, para. 4.6 and Chapter Five para. 5.23.

[30] See Chapter Four para 4.7.

[31] *Cf Thomas v. John Drake & Co. Ltd* [1971] ITR 146 to the effect that the employer's intimation that he regarded the contract as frustrated was an act of the employer operating to terminate the contract.

[32] *British Airport Authority v. Fenerty* [1976] ICR 361, QB.

[33] ERA, s. 136(1)(c). However, when ERA, s. 139 was first enacted (see Redundancy Payment Act 1965, s. 22) the view may have been that certain repudiatory conduct itself terminated the contract.

[34] SI 1981 No. 1794.

[35] *Ibid.* reg. 5. Also see para. 6.12.

[36] ERA, s. 136(1)(b) may be seen as an exception because it provides for a dismissal where termination takes the form of the expiry of a fixed term contract without the contract being renewed.

[37] See *Handling Redundancy*, ACAS Advisory Booklet No. 12.

[38] *Morton Sundour Fabrics Ltd v. Shaw* [1976] ITR 84; *International Computers Ltd v. Kennedy* [1981] IRLR 28, EAT in which it was also held that an employer who indicated that those employees who leave at times convenient to the employer may be personally barred from subsequently pleading there was no dismissal.

to the termination of his contract from one who consents or volunteers to be dismissed. In the former case there is no dismissal,[39] whereas in the latter case there is a dismissal even if the employee went along with or encouraged it.[40] But, to be a dismissal, the eventual termination must be the act of the employer alone. Accordingly, because an employer's acceptance of an employee's application for early retirement results in the contract being terminated not by the employer alone but by the employer and employee together, it has been held there is no dismissal even although the employer had a discretion to accept or refuse the application.[41]

(d) Lay-off and short-time. An important exception to the rule that entitlement to a redundancy payment depends on the employee having been dismissed occurs where the employee has been laid-off or placed on short-time.[42] The purpose of the relevant provisions[43] is to prevent an employer avoiding liability for a redundancy payment by indefinite lay-off or short-time. Clearly, provided an employer had a contractual right to lay-off or impose short-time working, he may be able to meet the reduction in requirements for employees to do work without ever having to dismiss an employee.[44] An employee is laid-off for any week in which he is not entitled to any remuneration[45] under his contract by reason of no work being provided by his employer[46] and an employee is on short-time in any week for which he receives less than half a week's pay because of a diminution of his work.[47]

The effect of the provisions is that an employee who has been laid-off or on short-time (or a combination thereof) for at least four consecutive weeks or, in a period of 13 consecutive weeks, for three consecutive and three non-consecutive weeks is entitled to give his employer written notice[48] of his intention to claim a redundancy payment[49] and, if this is accompanied by his giving the notice required to terminate his contract,[50] the employee will become entitled to the appropriate redundancy payment unless (1) the employer gives to the employee "counter-notice" that he will contest his liability to make such a payment and (2) on the date of the employee's notice of intention to claim it was likely that within four weeks full employment lasting at least 13 weeks would be resumed.[51] While an offer of

---

[39] This is, of course, not the case where the termination agreement has been induced by force and fear; see for example *Hennessy v. Craigmyle & Co. Ltd* [1986] ICR 461, CA.

[40] *Burton, Allton and Johnson v. Peck* [1975] ICR 193, QBD; *Morley v. C. T. Morley Ltd* [1985] ICR 499, EAT.

[41] *Birch v. University of Liverpool* [1985] ICR 470, CA. The court was not prepared to separate the act of application from the act of acceptance and the contract was held to have been terminated by mutual consent. And see *Scott v. Coalite Fuels and Chemicals Ltd* [1988] IRLR 131, EAT.

[42] ERA, s. 135(1)(b).

[43] ERA, ss. 135(1)(b), 147–152.

[44] Of course, if he did not have such a contractual right by laying off or imposing short-time, the employer would risk the employee rescinding the contract and claiming a constructive dismissal within ERA, s. 136(1)(c). And see *McKenzie (D. & J.) Ltd v. Smith* 1976 SLT 216, OH.

[45] See *Powell Duffryn Wagon Co. Ltd v. House* [1974] ICR 123, NIRC.

[46] ERA, s. 147(1), which applies to piece-rate and time-rate workers. And see C. Grunfeld, *The Law of Redundancy* (2nd edn, 1980), p. 250.

[47] ERA, s. 147(2).

[48] The time at which the various notices have to be given is strictly regulated by ERA, ss. 148, 150(2), 152(1); and see *Allinson v. Drew Simmons Engineering Ltd* [1985] ICR 488, EAT.

[49] ERA, s. 148(1). However, these provisions do not apply where the lay-off or short-time is attributable to a strike or a lock-out (ERA, s. 154(b)).

[50] ERA, s. 150(3).

[51] ERA, s. 152(1), (2).

re-employment is not strictly a "counter-notice"[52] it has been held that the following was to be read as a week's notice of termination:

> "As I have now been laid off for four consecutive weeks with no work I have been advised (by ACAS) that after such a time you must either re-employ me full-time for a minimum of 13 weeks or make me redundant. If you do not wish to do any of the above, then I am left with no option but to resign and instigate industrial tribunal proceedings against you. I look forward to hearing from you within 7 days."[53]

Where liability to make a redundancy payment is contested by an employer giving counter-notice, the employee's entitlement to a payment is to be decided by an industrial tribunal.[54]

6.5 The relevant date

For various purposes[55] it is important to be able to ascertain the time of dismissal or as statute[56] describes it, the "relevant date".[57] The precise rules for determining the relevant date are complicated but they may be summarised thus.

(a) Termination with notice. The relevant date is the date the notice expires[58] unless the notice is given by the employer and it is shorter than that required by statute,[59] in which case it is postponed until the date on which the statutory minimum notice would have expired if given on the date the actual (shorter) notice was given.[60] However, although such a postponement applies "for the purposes" specified[61] it has been held they are not words of limitation and merely mean that it is the same relevant date that is used to decide whether the employee has the two years' continuous employment required to qualify for a redundancy.[62] Accordingly previous decisions[63] on the meaning of section 90(3) of the Employment Protection (Consolidation) Act 1978 will have to be reviewed.

(b) Termination without notice. The relevant date is the date of dismissal[64] unless the termination is by an employer who is not entitled — by reason of the employee's breach of contract — to terminate without giving notice, in which case it is postponed until the minimum statutory notice,[65] had it been given, would have expired.[66] Where termination is truly without notice (as opposed to with very short notice) the contract ends when the dismissal is communicated and does not

---

[52] *Fabar Construction Ltd v. Race* [1979] ICR 529, EAT.

[53] *Walmsley v. C. & R. Ferguson Ltd* [1989] IRLR 112, IH.

[54] ERA, s. 149.

[55] For (a) calculating continuous employment, (b) applying the time-limits for making a claim, and (c) applying the special rules regarding lay-off and short-time.

[56] ERA, s. 145.

[57] In the law of unfair dismissal, the equivalent concept is the "effective date of termination" as defined by ERA, s. 97(1). And see Chapter Five, para. 5.27.

[58] ERA, s. 145(2)(a). This also applies to notice of earlier termination given by the employee following notice by the employer (ERA, s. 145(3)).

[59] ERA, s. 86(1).

[60] ERA, s. 145(5), (6).

[61] ERA, s. 145(5). The specified purposes are for determining (1) a qualifying period, (2) a period of continuous employment and (3) a week's pay.

[62] *Secretary of State for Employment v. Staffordshire CC* [1989] IRLR 117, CA.

[63] *Slater v. John Swain & Co. Ltd* [1981] ICR 554, EAT; *Smith v. Clark's College Ltd* [1969] ITR 78.

[64] ERA, s. 145(2)(b).

[65] ERA, s. 86(1).

[66] ERA, s. 145(5).

continue until the employee has completed his journey home for which, by his contract, his employers are obliged to pay.[67] Furthermore, although employees and employers may waive their respective rights to minimum statutory notice[68] where such a waiver takes place, the relevant date is still postponed by statute[69] until the expiry of the notice required by the Employment Rights Act, section 86(1), because the fact that an employee has waived his right to notice or accepted a payment in lieu of notice under section 86(3) is relevant only to his rights in contract and not to his rights to a redundancy payment.[70] Where wages in lieu of notice are given the relevant date is the date of the dismissal but where the employee is merely excused from working out notice the relevant date is the date the notice expired.[71] Where termination occurs by the non-renewal of a fixed-term contract the relevant date is the date of the contract's expiry.[72]

(c) Special provisions. Special provisions determine the relevant date where there has been a trial period[73] and where the entitlement to a redundancy payment follows a period of lay-off or short-time.[74]

REDUNDANCY

6.6 The statutory definition of redundancy

Although the words "redundant" and "redundancy" are popularly used to denote "superfluous" or "outmoded", for the system of redundancy payments the concept of redundancy involves a two-part, technical legal definition.[75] Thus an employee is redundant if his dismissal is attributable[76] wholly or mainly to the fact that:

(a) his employer has ceased, or intends to cease, temporarily or permanently,[77] (generally or in the place the employee was employed) to carry on the business for the purposes of which the employee was employed,[78] or

(b) the requirements of that business for employees[79] to carry out work of a particular kind (generally or in the place the employee was employed) have ceased

---

[67] *Octavius Atkinson & Sons Ltd v. Morris* [1989] IRLR 158, CA.

[68] ERA, s. 86(3).

[69] ERA, s. 145(5).

[70] *Secretary of State for Employment v. Staffordshire CC*, above.

[71] Compare *Slater v. John Swain & Son Ltd*, above, *Belling & Lee Ltd v. Burford* [1982] ICR 454, EAT with *Adams v. GKN Sankey Ltd* [1980] IRLR 416, EAT, and *Chapman v. Letheby & Christopher Ltd* [1981] IRLR 440, EAT.

[72] ERA, s. 145(2)(c).

[73] See para. 6.8.

[74] ERA, s. 145(4) (trial periods); s. 153 (lay-off and short-time).

[75] The Transfer of Undertakings (Protection of Employment) Regulations 1981 have not altered the definition (*Chapman v. CPS Computer Group plc* [1987] IRLR 462, CA).

[76] As to the meaning of "attributable", see *Fleming v. Wandsworth London Borough Council, The Times* December 23, 1985, CA.

[77] ERA, s. 139(6). Thus closure of a business for a week has led to entitlement to a redundancy payment (*Whitworth v. Bilabbey Ltd* [1975] IRLR 206); cf *Higgs & Hill Ltd v. Singh* [1977] ICR 193, EAT. And where there is a right to lay-off short term closures may be dealt with by that method. See para. 6.4(d).

[78] ERA, s. 139(1)(a).

[79] Thus where one employee is replaced by another there is no redundancy because the requirements of the business for "employees" has not altered (*North Yorkshire CC v. Fay* [1985] IRLR 247, CA) and the opposite is the case where an employee is replaced by a self-employed person (*Gorictree Ltd v. Jenkinson* [1984] IRLR 391, EAT; and see *Willcox v. Hastings* [1987] IRLR 298, CA).

or diminished or are expected to case or diminish temporarily or permanently.[80] Thus it is not necessary that the employer ceased business permanently or that the requirements of the business diminish permanently; a temporary cessation or diminution is sufficient for the definition to be satisfied. While it has been held that the closure of a business for a week led to the employee being entitled to receive a redundancy payment[81] and it would not cover very short periods such as a day or two,[82] the important question is whether there is a cessation of business or a diminution of the requirements of the business rather than a closure, for example, for refurbishment.[83] However, because of (i) the difficulty in knowing whether a short term closure or diminution would be regarded as a temporary cessation of business or a temporary diminution in the requirements of the business and (ii) the presumption that a dismissal is due to redundancy,[84] employers make contractual provision for lay-off or short time working.

To satisfy either (a) or (b) it is permissible to have regard to the business(es) of an associated employer[85] and, similarly, the activities of local education authorities in respect of their schools may be treated as one business.[86] Although business is widely defined to include ''a trade, profession or any other activity'',[87] entitlement to a redundancy payment only occurs where the requirements of the business for the purposes of which the employee works has ceased or diminished. It is therefore necessary, occasionally, to be able to isolate the business for which the employee works from other business activities of the same employer. In *Babar Indian Restaurant v. Rawat*[88] two partners operated a restaurant, a frozen food shop and an off-sales shop. When the frozen food shop was closed down and an employee was transferred from there to the restaurant the dismissal of Rawat, a waiter in the restaurant, to accommodate the transfer of the employee from the frozen food was not due to redundancy in that the requirements of the restaurant business for whose purposes Rawat was employed had not ceased or diminished.[89] However, had the three businesses (the restaurant, the off-sales and the frozen food shop) been carried on by associated employers[90] the three businesses could have been treated as one[91] and the dismissal of Rawat would have been by reason of redundancy.

6.7 Place of employment

A key element in both parts of the definition of redundancy is ''the place where the employee (is) employed''[92] and it is critical to be able to determine this with some precision. This may require consideration of the written statement of employment particulars,[93] implied contractual terms, mobility clauses and issues of fact like where is an employee based. However, before considering these it is necessary to

---

[80] ERA, s. 139(1)(b).
[81] *Whitworth v. Bilabbey Ltd*, above.
[82] *Higgs & Hill v. Singh* [1976] IRLR 299, EAT.
[83] *Whitbread plc, trading as Berni Inns v. Flattery*, unreported, case no. 287/94, EAT.
[84] See para. 6.14.
[85] As to the meaning of ''associated employer'', see Chapter Three, para. 3.5(d).
[86] ERA, s. 139(1)–(3).
[87] ERA, s. 235(1).
[88] [1985] IRLR 57, EAT.
[89] In fact Rawat was unfairly dismissed because his employers did not prove the reason for his dismissal was redundancy.
[90] See Chapter Three, para. 3.5(d).
[91] ERA, s. 139(1), (2). And see para. 6.8.
[92] ERA, s. 139(1)(a), (b).
[93] See Chapter Two, para 2.1.

note that requiring an employee to be mobile or indeed perform duties at short notice may raise issues of indirect sexual or marital status discrimination.[94] The result is that the inclusion of a mobility clause in the contract of employment of a woman or a married person may be unlawful unless the employer is able to offer objective evidence that its justifiable and that is the case whether or not the term has in fact been invoked by the employer; according to the Court of Appeal judicial notice should be taken of the fact that a higher proportion of women than men are secondary earners so that a higher proportion of women would find it impossible in practice to comply with a direction of their employer to move their workplace to a destination which involved a change of home.[95] In *United Kingdom Atomic Energy Authority v Claydon*[96] it was held that to determine the place of an employee's employment it was necessary to consider, having regard to the express and implied terms, where he could by his contract of employment be required to work. The result was that an employee who worked at one location where the need for his work had ceased or diminished would not be entitled to a redundancy payment if he refused to transfer to another location at which there was work and to which he could be required to transfer in accordance with a mobility clause in his contract of employment. However, that "contractual" approach has been disapproved in *Bass Leisure Ltd v. Thomas*[97] because of the difficulties that would be met in industrial practice where it was stated that:

"The question of what is the place of employment concerns the extent or area of a single place, not the transfer from one place to another. The location and the extent of that 'place' must be ascertainable whether or not the employee is in fact to be required to move and therefore before any such requirement is made (if it is), and without knowledge of the terms of any such requirement, or of the employee's response, or of whether any conditions upon the making of it have been complied with."

Accordingly although an employee's contract provided that "the company reserves the right to transfer any employee whether temporarily or permanently to a suitable alternative place of work" and that "your geographic area may be altered provided it remains reasonably accessible from your normal residence" the place where she was employed was the Coventry depot so that her dismissal on the closure of that depot was due to redundancy even although there was work available at another depot 20 miles away.[98] However, it is necessary to distinguish contractual terms which permit the employer to require an employee to move to another place of employment from contractual terms which define the place of employment. Thus the place where an employee is required to work in accordance with express or implied terms of his contract may be "the Liverpool area"[99] or a complex of factories on a large site and not merely one of the factories[100] or any place within a daily reach of his home.[101] The approach which now seems to be required therefore is as follows:

---

94 See Chapter Seven.
95 *Meade-Hill and National Union of Civil and Public Servants v. British Council* [1995] IRLR 478, CA.
96 [1974] ICR 128, NIRC. And see *Rank Xerox Ltd v. Churchill* [1988] IRLR 280, EAT.
97 [1994] IRLR 101, EAT. And see *Curling v. Securicor Ltd* [1992] IRLR 549, EAT. *Cf Securicor Ltd v. Reid*, unreported, case no. 540/92, EAT.
98 *Bass Leisure Ltd v. Thomas*, above.
99 *O'Brien v. Associated Fire Alarms Ltd* [1968] 1 WLR 1916, CA.
100 *Briggs v. Imperial Chemical Industries Ltd* [1968] ITR 276, DC.
101 *Courtaulds Northern Spinning Ltd v. Sibson* [1988] IRLR 305, CA.

(1) Consider the express and implied terms in the contract of employment to determine where is the place that the employee is employed; if there is a diminution of work of a particular kind or if the employer proposes ceasing business at that place and the employee is dismissed, he will be entitled to a redundancy payment.

(2) If there is a mobility clause in the employee's contract the employer appears to have two options: (a) rely on the clause and require the employee to move to another location or (b) offer suitable alternative employment and invite the employee to accept.[102] Which option he adopts would seem to make little difference to liability for redundancy payments. In the former case, as *Bass Leisure Ltd* demonstrates, an employee's refusal to move as required does not prevent the dismissal being for redundancy,[103] while in the latter case, liability is conditional only on the suitability of the employment offered and the reasonableness of the employee's refusal. The significance of the mobility clause, therefore, is found more in the field of unfair dismissal and contract law disputes where the employer — not for reasons of redundancy but for structural or organisation reasons — requires employees to work in different areas.

Another question in considering the statutory concept of redundancy is whether there has been a reduction in the needs of the business for employees to carry out "work of a particular kind".[104] This question is answered by examining the particular kind of work the employee is by his contract bound to do.[105] However, as *Haden Ltd v. Cowen*[106] illustrates, this requires careful examination of the particular contract of employment. Although Cowen, a divisional contracts surveyor, was by his contract "required to undertake, at the direction of the company, any and all duties which reasonably fall within the scope" of his capabilities he was dismissed by reason of redundancy when the requirements of the business for a divisional contracts surveyor ceased because the effect of these words did not give his employer (Haden Ltd) the right to transfer him from his job as divisional contracts surveyor to any job as a surveyor; it merely required him to perform any duties reasonably within the scope of his capabilities as divisional contracts surveyor.[107] Similarly, although a job-title is to be construed with flexibility[108] it is wrong to rely solely on a general job-title without taking account of the surrounding circumstances.[109] However, where the kind of work the employee can be required to do is governed by an express term in the contract, it is wrong to imply a more restrictive term from the fact that the employee has for some considerable period of time carried out only a restricted range of duties.[110] The critical issue is whether the requirements of the business "for employees" has

---

[102] Would the fact that the employee could be compelled to move be relevant to (a) the suitability of the employment offered and (b) the reasonableness of the employee's refusal?

[103] *Cf Richardson v. Applied Imaging International Ltd*, unreported, case no. 311/93, EAT.

[104] ERA, s. 139(1)(b).

[105] *Nelson v. BBC* [1977] ICR 649, CA.

[106] [1982] IRLR 314, CA.

[107] *Cf Shook v. London Borough of Ealing* [1986] IRLR 46, EAT.

[108] *Glitz v. Watford Electric Co. Ltd* [1979] IRLR 89, EAT (job-title of "clerk/typist" held wide enough to require the employee to do photocopying).

[109] *Greater Glasgow Health Board v. Pate* [1983] SLT 90.

[110] *Nelson v. BBC*, above. Consider also the validity of an *ad hoc* agreement to permit the transfer of an employee to a job he was not bound by contract to perform. Would such an agreement "purport to limit the operation of a provision of the Act" (ERA, s. 203(1)) and therefore be void? See *Tocher v. General Motors Scotland Ltd* [1981] IRLR 55, EAT.

ceased or diminished and it is immaterial that the volume of work has not altered[111] or that an expected business expansion for which employees were specially recruited did not take place[112]; nor is it relevant to find out the reason for the reduction in requirements for employees.[113] Accordingly, an employee, dismissed when work previously performed by him is contracted out, is dismissed by reason of redundancy, as is an employee whose work is taken on by other employees or is performed by a machine or computer.[114] Determining whether there has been a reduction in requirements for employees to do work of a particular kind demands careful scrutiny of the functions required by the business and the skills and competence of employees and it is often a question of degree whether requirements for employees to do particular work have reduced. The following cases illustrate the approach that is necessary when considering whether requirements for employees to do work of a particular kind have ceased or diminished.

(a) *Vaux and Associated Breweries Ltd v. Ward.*[115] Mrs Ward was dismissed from her job as a waitress when her employers refurbished the pub in which she was employed changing its name from the Star and Garter Tavern to the Steamboat Inn. However, it was held her dismissal was not attributable to redundancy because although after the refurbishment her employers chose to replace her with attractive, younger waitresses—in keeping with the new atmosphere the employers wished to create—there was no reduction in their requirements for employees to do work of a particular kind, namely the job of a waitress.

(b) *Murphy v. Epsom College.*[116] Mr Murphy was one of two plumbers employed to maintain the heating system and do general plumbing work but after alterations to the system he indicated he would restrict the type of work he would do to it. This resulted in Mr Murphy being dismissed following the employer's decision to appoint a heating technician to maintain the improved system as well as to do general plumbing work. Murphy was dismissed for redundancy because his employers, having appointed a heating technician with different skills and qualifications who, as well as doing general plumbing, had to perform functions where were more extensive and responsible than those Mr Murphy was competent to perform, no longer required two plumbers; their requirements now were a plumber and a heating technician/plumber.

(c) *Johnson v. Nottinghamshire Combined Police Authority.*[117] Johnson was one of several clerical workers working a standard five-day, 38-hour week, employed by the police authority. To release more police officers from routine clerical work Johnson and her fellow workers were asked to change their work pattern so that they would work the same number of hours but at different times of the day and over a 6-day week. When they refused to comply with this pattern they were dismissed and claimed their dismissals were due to redundancy. However, their claims were rejected because the changes in the time of work did not alter the

---

[111] *North Yorkshire CC v. Fay* [1985] IRLR 247, CA; *Gorictree Ltd v. Jenkinson* [1984] IRLR 391, EAT; *Willcox v. Hastings* [1987] IRLR 298, CA. *Cf Lesney Products & Co. Ltd v. Nolan* [1977] IRLR 77, CA.

[112] *Cf O'Hare v. Rotaprint Ltd* [1980] ICR 94, EAT.

[113] *Association of University Teachers v. University of Newcastle* [1988] IRLR 10, EAT.

[114] *Cf Baxter v. Limb Group of Companies* [1994] IRLR 572, CA; *Frame It v. Brown*, unreported, case no. 177/93, EAT.

[115] [1969] VII KIR 308. And see *Loudon v. Crimpy Crisps Ltd* [1966] ITR 307 and *European Chefs (Catering) Ltd v. Currell* [1971] ITR 37, DC.

[116] [1985] ICR 80, CA, affirming [1983] ICR 715, EAT. And see *Robinson v. British Island Airways Ltd* [1978] ICR 304, EAT.

[117] [1974] ICR 170, CA.

essential nature of the work, it being noted that while the statutory definition of redundancy[118] expressly refers to the place of employment the same cannot be said for the time at which work is done.[119]

6.8 Bumping

"Bumping" describes what may frequently occur in a redundancy situation when, for example, a long serving employee capable of doing a variety of jobs in his employer's business is, on his redundancy, kept on in employment by being transferred into the job of another (usually more recently recruited) employee who, as a consequence, is dismissed. An early example is seen in *W. Gimber & Sons Ltd v. Spurrett*[120] in which Mr Spurrett was held entitled to a redundancy payment on being dismissed when another employee, whose sales territory had disappeared in a reorganisation, took over his job as warehouse manager. Lord Parker, CJ approved the following passage in the decision of the industrial tribunal—"if there is a reduction in the requirements for employees in one section of ... a business and an employee who becomes surplus or redundant is transferred to another section of that business, an employee who is displaced by the transfer of the first employee and is dismissed by reason of that displacement is dismissed by reason of redundancy." While the generality of such a statement has been subsequently questioned,[121] the effect is that an employee who is employed to do job "X" is entitled to a redundancy payment where the requirements for employees to do job "X" have not ceased or diminished provided they have ceased or diminished in relation to employees who do job "Y". The reason for this is that the definition of redundancy[122] does not expressly require that the redundant employee be one employed on the particular kind of work the requirements for which have ceased or diminished.[123] An important consequence of permitting an employer to argue that a "bumped" or displaced employee is dismissed by reason of redundancy is to enable him to overcome the first obstacle in defending an unfair dismissal complaint by proving the reason for dismissal was redundancy.[124]

ALTERNATIVE EMPLOYMENT

6.9 Offers of renewal and re-engagement

Even after an employee has been dismissed on grounds of redundancy his right to receive a redundancy payment may be defeated by his employer[125] offering to

---

[118] ERA, s. 139.

[119] However, changing the time of work may also involve a change in the particular kind of work: see *Archibald v. Rossleigh Commercial Ltd* [1975] IRLR 231, IT; *Macfisheries Ltd v. Findlay* [1985] ICR 160, EAT.

[120] [1967] ITR 308, QBD.

[121] *Gordon v. Adams (Dalkeith) Ltd* [1972] ITR 81, NIRC.

[122] ERA, s. 139(1)(b).

[123] Cf the comments in *Elliott Turbomachinery Ltd v. Bates* [1981] ICR 218, EAT. Also it would not seem difficult to imply a connection between the work for which there is a reduced requirement and the work performed by the dismissed employee; otherwise why does the statute create the idea of "work of a particular kind?"

[124] The alternative would have been for an employer to argue that dismissal was for some other substantial reason which, if successful, would result in a fair dismissal with no redundancy payment due. See Chapter Five, para. 5.58.

[125] Employer in this context includes an associated employer (ERA, s. 146(1)).

renew his contract or re-engage him. However, whether the right to receive a redundancy payment is defeated depends on the suitability of the employment offered and the reasonableness of the employee's refusal of re-employment; thus, generally, where an employer offers to continue the employment of an employee he will lose his right to a redundancy payment if the new employment is suitable and he unreasonably rejects the offer or, having accepted the offer on a trial basis, he unreasonably terminates the new employment. However, this is the result of a set of complicated statutory provisions which are strictly applied.[126] Although it is no longer[127] necessary for the employer's offer of renewal or extension[128] (of an existing contract) or re-engagement (under a new contract) to be in writing[129] it must be made (and communicated to the employee)[130] before[131] the ending of the original contract and must take place immediately on the ending of that contract or after an interval of not more than four weeks thereafter.[132] Where a change has occurred in the employee's terms of employment notice of such a change must be intimated *via* a revised or updated written statement issued in accordance with the relevant statutory provision.[133] However, it has to be emphasised that as there is no duty to issue a revised written statement before the new employment begins[134] it cannot be regarded as an alternative to the offer of renewal or re-engagement which must be made before the ending of the original contract, and although not required to be in formal, comprehensive terms it must be more than a vague indication that the contract may be extended for a few days.[135]

6.10 Same terms, different terms and trial periods

Where an employee accepts an offer of employment on the same terms for the purposes of redundancy payments law[136] he is not regarded as having been dismissed[137] and the law assumes that such an offer constitutes suitable employment so that an employee who declines such an offer is entitled to receive a redundancy payment only if his refusal is reasonable.[138] Where the offer is of employment on different terms[139] an employee's entitlement to a redundancy payment depends on whether the employment offered is suitable and, if the employee refuses the offer of suitable employment, whether his refusal is reasonable. If the employment offered is unsuitable the reaction of the employee to

---

[126] See, for example, *Davis (E. & J.) Transport Ltd v. Chattaway* [1972] ICR 267, NIRC.

[127] *Cf* Redundancy Payments Act 1965, s. 2(4) (repealed).

[128] ERA, s. 235(1).

[129] Accordingly an offer may be made collectively by the posting of a notice.

[130] Thus an employee who is off sick when the offer is made will not have received it unless it is sent directly to him (*Maxwell v. Walter Howard Designs Ltd* [1975] IRLR 77).

[131] See *Davis (E. & J.) Transport Ltd v. Chattaway*, above.

[132] ERA, s. 141(1).

[133] ERA, s. 1: see Chapter Two, para. 2.10.

[134] See Chapter Two, para. 2.10.

[135] Compare *Singer Co. (UK) Ltd v. Ferrier* [1980] IRLR 300, EAT with *Kitching v. Ward, Watson and Taylor* [1967] ITR 464, DC.

[136] In *Ebac Ltd v. Wymer* [1995] ICR 466 the EAT held that s. 138 had the effect of eliding the dismissal even for purposes of an unfair dismissal complaint but the decision (and reasoning) of another EAT in *Hempill v. W H Smith & Sons Ltd* [1986] ICR 365 that s. 138 relates only to redundancy payments seem preferable.

[137] ERA, s. 138(1).

[138] ERA, s. 141(2).

[139] Generally a difference in only one term will mean the offer is on different terms but trivial differences are disregarded (*Rose v. Henry Trickett & Sons Ltd* [1971] ITR 211, QBD).

the offer does not affect his right to receive a redundancy payment[140] but if the offer is of suitable employment an unreasonable refusal of the offer results in loss of redundancy payment.[141] Where before the original contract has ended the employee receives an offer of employment on different terms and renewal or re-engagement takes place immediately[142] on the ending of the original contract (or within four weeks thereof), the employee is not to be regarded as dismissed but a statutory trial period comes into play[143] and if either the employer or the employee terminates the new employment during the trial period then the employee is treated as having been dismissed at the date the original contract ended and for the reason(s) it ended.[144] However, this is subject to the qualification that where it is the employer who terminates during the trial period the reason for the termination must relate to the change to the new employment whereas where termination is by the employee a dismissal for the reason the original employment was terminated is reinstated whatever the reason for the employee terminating the new employment.[145] Thus where termination takes place during the trial period the original dismissal is reinstated but an employee who unreasonably terminates the new employment is not entitled to a redundancy payment if the new employment was suitable.[146]

Because of these provisions it is important to be able to determine when the trial period begins and ends and statute provides that it shall begin with the ending of the employment under the prior (original) contract and end with the expiration of a period of four weeks beginning with the date on which the employee starts work under the new contract.[147] If the trial period exceeds the statutory limits the employee whose employment is terminated will not be able to claim the reinstatement of the dismissal under the original contract and the phrase "period of four weeks" means four consecutive weeks calculated according to the calendar.[148] Thus, when an employee's employment terminated by reason of redundancy at midnight on December 21, 1986 and he was offered alternative employment commencing immediately, it was held the statutory trial period could not be extended to take into account the period of seven days the factory was closed for Christmas holidays; it was immaterial that the employee had not had a trial period of four weeks during which he was actually working.[149] While it is possible for a trial period to be extended by agreement between the employee and his employer,[150] the purpose of the extension must be to retrain the employee[151] and must be (1) in writing, (2) between the employer and the employee (or his representatives), (3) made before the employee starts work under the new contract and (4) specific about the date the trial period ends and the conditions which apply

---

[140] ERA, s. 141(4).
[141] ERA, s. 141(2).
[142] ERA, s. 146(2).
[143] ERA, s. 138(2).
[144] ERA, s. 138(4).
[145] *Ibid.*
[146] *Ibid.* Where an employer refuses to allow the employee to have a trial period, that can affect the reasonableness of his (the employee's) decision to reject the new employment: *Elliot v. Richard Stump Ltd* [1987] IRLR 215, EAT.
[147] ERA, s. 138(3).
[148] *Benton v. Sanderson Kayser Ltd* [1989] IRLR 19, CA.
[149] *Benton,* above.
[150] The agreement need not be a formal probative document but in addition to specifying the length of the extension it must cover matters like status, pay and job description (*McKindley v. William Hill (Scotland) Ltd* [1985] IRLR 492, EAT).
[151] ERA, s. 138(3).

thereafter.[152] Thus, extending a trial period to allow the employee an opportunity of deciding whether he could adapt to changed hours of work and night work is not permitted because it is not for retraining the employee.[153] It is necessary to appreciate the difference between a statutory trial period and the time an employee has to decide whether he will rescind his contract following a repudiation or conduct amounting to anticipatory breach by the employer. The relationship between the statutory trial period and, what might conveniently be termed, the common law trial period is illustrated by *Turvey v. C. W. Cheney & Son Ltd*[154] in which Turvey, without being dismissed, agreed to try alternative work he was not contractually bound to do. However, having worked at the new job for more than four weeks Turvey left because he did not find the job suitable and it was held that the statutory trial period was in addition to the common law trial period so that he had a reasonable time to decide whether to accept the new employment; only after the expiry of such a reasonable time would the statutory trial period begin to run.[155]

6.11 Is employment suitable; is refusal reasonable?

The answers given in response to these questions depend very much on the facts and circumstances of each case — they are questions of fact for determination by the industrial tribunal[156] and there is no rule that to be suitable the employment must be substantially equivalent to the employment which has come to an end.[157] Generally the onus of proof is on the employer to prove the employment offered is suitable and that the employee was unreasonable in refusing it.[158] To demonstrate how each case is dependent on its own facts and circumstances, compare the following decisions. In *Cahuac v. Allen Amery Ltd*[159] Mrs Cahuac was employed at the premises of her employers, Allen Amery Ltd, in Minerva Street, Hackney, London E2, when they moved to other premises in Goswell Road, London EC1 where she was offered employment but declined. The industrial tribunal held that the employment at Goswell Road was not suitable because it would involve a 40-minute bus journey, whereas Mrs Cahuac lived within a short walk of the Minerva Street premises; she looked after her widowed mother whom she could tend to during her lunch hour while employed at Minerva Street; the cost of travel to Goswell Road would reduce Mrs Cahuac's pay by 7% while the amount of travelling time would be greatly increased. In *Kerr v. National Coal Board*[160] on Mr Kerr's dismissal he was offered, but refused, employment at another colliery. His reasons for refusal were that the work was dangerous bearing in mind that he was deaf in one ear and for health reasons (he suffered from chronic *otitis medio*) he could not travel the 20 miles by bus to the new colliery. However, the Court of Session, emphasising the question of fact, upheld the decision of the industrial

---

[152] ERA, s. 138(6).
[153] *Meek v. J. Allen Rubber Co. Ltd* [1980] IRLR 21, EAT.
[154] [1979] ICR 341, EAT. *Turvey* was quoted with approval in *Kentish Bus and Coach Co. Ltd v. Quarry*, unreported, case no. 287/92, EAT.
[155] And see *Air Canada v. Lee* [1978] ICR 1202, EAT.
[156] *Kerr v. National Coal Board* [1970] ITR 48, IH; *Hitchock v. St Ann's Hosiery Co. Ltd* [1971] ITR 98, QBD.
[157] *Standard Telephones and Cables Ltd v. Yates* [1981] IRLR 21, EAT.
[158] *Jones v. Aston Cabinet Co. Ltd* [1973] ICR 292, NIRC.
[159] [1966] ITR 313.
[160] [1970] ITR 48, IH. Also see *Bruce v. National Coal Board* [1967] ITR 159, IT; *Taylor v. Kent County Council* [1969] ITR 294, QBD.

tribunal that he had been unreasonable in refusing the employment offered.[161] On the other hand, in *Cambridge & District Co-operative Society Ltd v. Ruse*[162] where an employee who had for more than 20 years worked as the manager of butcher shops belonging to the Co-operative Society was, on the closure of the shop of which he was the manager, offered employment as the manager of a butchery department in one of the Co-operative's supermarkets, his refusal of that was reasonable because he perceived he suffered a loss of status because he was to an extent under the jurisdiction of the store manager, did not have a key to the store and was no longer responsible for collecting and banking takings, the EAT adding that there is nothing in the legislation or the reported cases to restrict an employee's reasons for refusing a suitable job to factors not connected with the job itself so that it is possible for an employee reasonably to refuse an objectively suitable offer of alternative employment on the ground of his personal perception of the job offered.

BUSINESS TRANSFERS

6.12 Redundancy and the transfer of a business

Formerly a redundancy situation could arise when the business[163] in which an employee was employed was transferred to a new owner.[164] Where such a transfer took place and certain statutory conditions were satisfied[165] an offer of employment by the new owner was equated with an offer by the old owner so that an unreasonable refusal of suitable employment by the new owner resulted in the employee losing any entitlement to a redundancy payment.[166] Where the employee accepted an offer by the new owner the statutory trial period operated but if the employment was terminated (either by the employee or the new owner) the employee was deemed to have been dismissed by the old owner against whom a claim for a redundancy payment could be made.[167] However, these provisions had to be placed in the context of the Transfer of Undertakings (Protection of Employment) Regulations 1981[168] which provided for the statutory transfer of

---

[161] And see *Souter v. Henry Balfour & Co. Ltd* [1966] ITR 383; *Ryan v. Liverpool Warehousing Co. Ltd* [1966] ITR 69. From the Outer House decision in *British Steel Corporation v. Dingwall* 1976 SLT 230 it may be inferred that a substantial drop in wages would itself render the employment unsuitable.

[162] [1993] IRLR 156, EAT.

[163] " 'Business' includes a trade or profession and includes any activity carried on by a body of persons (whether corporate or unincorporated)": ERA, s. 235(1).

[164] The change in ownership could be by "sale or other disposition or by operation of law" (EPCA, s. 94(1)(a)) but did not include the transfer of shares in a limited company. In the latter situation there will be a transfer of shares but the business remains in the ownership of the limited company, no change of employer occurring.

[165] By the combined effect of EPCA, ss. 82(3) and 94(3) the new owner must make the offer (of renewal or re-engagement) before the employee's contract with the old owner ended and employment by the new owner had to take effect within four weeks of it so ending. But a failure to satisfy these conditions did not break continuity (*Secretary of State for Employment v. de Rosa* 1974 SLT 214, HL).

[166] EPCA, s. 94. *Cf* s. 150, Sch. 12, para. 13 (ownership passing to personal representatives).

[167] EPCA, ss. 84(6), 94(2). The substitution of a new owner did not itself affect the questions of whether the new employment was different or whether the employee had unreasonably refused the offer (s. 94(4)).

[168] SI 1981 No. 1794. The regulations were enacted to give effect to Directive 77/187, and in line with *Litster v. Forth Dry Dock and Engineering Co. Ltd* [1989] IRLR 161, HL it is necessary to construe the regulations to comply with the Directive.

contracts of employment which are in existence when an undertaking is transferred; the new owner (the transferee) of the undertaking was statutorily substituted for the old owner (the transferor) in the contract of employment and, clearly where such a substitution took place there was strictly no scope for the application of the statutory provisions[169] which equated an offer by the new owner with an offer by the old, the new owner being regarded as party to the contract of employment.[170] After the enactment of the Transfer of Undertakings etc. Regulations in 1981 it was unnecessary and illogical to provide that an offer of employment by the new owner (the transferee) should be equated with such an *offer* by the old owner (the transferor) when the contracts of employment of employees employed in the business were, in effect, the subject of a statutory novation. It was not until 1993, however, that that statutory provision[171] which equated an offer by the new owner with an offer by the old owner was recognised as being otiose and was repealed.[172]

STRIKES AND LOCK-OUTS

6.13 Special rules about misconduct, strikes and lock-outs

Although, generally, dismissal for misconduct does not entitle an employee to a redundancy payment[173] this is qualified where, after (a) the employer has given notice of termination by reason of redundancy or (b) a period of lay-off or short-time working[174] the employee has given notice of his intention to claim a redundancy payment, the employer terminates the contract because of the employee's conduct in circumstances such that he is entitled to terminate without notice.[175] In such a case the employee's right to receive all or part of a payment depends on whether that would be just and equitable.[176] Whether an employer is entitled to terminate without notice depends on whether the employee has repudiated the contract using the same approach as that to be adopted when dealing with an allegedly unfair constructive dismissal.[177] However, the special rule about dismissal for misconduct after notice of termination for redundancy or notice of intention to claim a payment is further modified where the conduct which entitles termination without notice is the employee's participation in a strike.[178] In such a case the employee does not lose all right to a redundancy payment; however, if he fails to make up for the days lost by his being on strike, entitlement to part or all of the payment depends on an industrial tribunal's discretion.[179] Although the special

---

[169] EPCA, s. 94.

[170] Transfer of Undertakings etc. Regulations, reg. 5.

[171] EPCA, s. 94.

[172] TURERA, s. 51, Sch. 10.

[173] And see the express provision to this effect in ERA, s. 140(1) where the misconduct justifies summary dismissal/rescission.

[174] See para. 6.4(d).

[175] ERA, s. 140(3)–(5).

[176] ERA, s. 140(3). And see *Lignacite Products Ltd v. Krollman* [1979] IRLR 22, EAT in which the EAT emphasised the discretion entrusted to the industrial tribunal and upheld a tribunal's aware of 60% of a payment to an employee convicted of theft from his employer during his period of notice. *Cf Jarmain v. E. Pollard & Co. Ltd* [1967] ITR 406.

[177] *Bonner v. H. Gilbert Ltd* [1989] IRLR 475, EAT.

[178] ERA, s. 140(2). ''Strike'' and ''lock-out'' are to receive the meanings given in ERA, s. 235(1).

[179] ERA, s. 143(5). Similarly an employee's termination without notice because of the employer's lock-out is not a (constructive) dismissal (s. 140(2)).

rules regarding strikes were extensively examined in *Simmons v. Hoover Ltd*[180] (whose conclusions may be summarised thus: an employee who is dismissed for striking after notice of redundancy will not automatically lose his right to a payment, whereas an employee who takes strike action first and is dismissed for redundancy during it is not entitled to a payment) the precise interaction between s. 140(1) (which excludes from the right to receive a redundancy payment an employee who the employer was entitled to dismiss by reason of the employee's conduct) and s. 140(2) (which disapplies that exclusion where the conduct takes the form of a strike — but not industrial action short of a strike — after notice of termination) is not clear. The need for employees to consider their position with care is illustrated by *Baxter v Limb Group of Companies*[181] in which equivalent provisions were considered. Dock workers who refused to comply with the employer's desire to change the terms of employment took industrial action by refusing to work overtime which led to their dismissal. Their employer responded by dismissing them and relying on employees supplied by another company in the group. The Court of Appeal rejected the industrial tribunal's decision that the redundancy and not the industrial action was the reason for the dismissal on the view that if an employer dismisses employees who refuse to call off industrial action and engages new employees who it is hoped will be more amenable, the reason for the dismissal is plainly the industrial action and it makes no difference to the reason for dismissal if the employer decides to obtain replacement workers not as direct labour but as contract labour from another company. Thus, workers who take industrial action when faced with a forced change of employment conditions or threatened but not notified redundancy dismissals are liable not merely to being dismissed without being able to claim unfair dismissal[182]; they also lose any entitlement to redundancy payments.[183]

PAYMENTS AND EXCLUSIONS

6.14 Claiming and calculating a redundancy payment

(a) The claim. To perfect his entitlement to a redundancy payment in accordance with domestic provisions an employee must within six months of the relevant date[184] either agree and receive a redundancy payment or make a written claim for one,[185] although late claims may be admitted by an industrial tribunal.[186] As indicated at the beginning of this Chapter, however,[187] a right to a redundancy payment may also be based on Art. 119 of the EC Treaty and the question which

---

[180] [1977] ICR 61 at 79, EAT.

[181] [1994] IRLR 572, CA.

[182] If the industrial action is unofficial no complaint is competent and where the action is official a complaint only lies where at least one participant has not been dismissed or offered re-engagement. See Chapter Five.

[183] Even if the dockers in *Baxter v. Limb Group of Companies* had taken the action after the employer had given notice of redundancy they would not have been able to obtain the benefits of ERA, s. 140(2) because that section applies only where the employee takes part in a strike which is defined (ERA, s. 235(1)) to exclude the action (overtime ban) undertaken by Baxter and others.

[184] See para. 6.5.

[185] ERA, s. 164(1).

[186] ERA, s. 164(3). *Cf Greenwich Health Authority v. Skinner* [1989] IRLR 238, EAT regarding EPCA, s. 112 (now ERA, s. 177) and contractual redundancy payments for which the time limit is the same as for ordinary contractual claims.

[187] See para. 6.2.

arises is when does a claim with such a basis have to be raised. Consider, for example, the case of a woman dismissed many years ago but denied a payment because she worked less than 16 (or 8) hours per week or a woman dismissed on the grounds of redundancy more than six months ago and denied a payment because she had not been continuously employed for at least two years.[188] Can either of them claim now under Art. 119? The answer would seem to depend on whether one subscribes to the dualist approach by which Art. 119 is regarded as creating a "free-standing" right, in addition to that created by domestic legislation, or the monist approach by which the jurisdiction of industrial tribunals is statutorily limited so that they may only give effect to Art. 119 by interpreting and applying the domestic jurisdictional rules. The former dualist approach is favoured by *Rankin v. British Coal*[189] which holds that while Art. 119 creates a free standing right for the sake of legal certainty it is necessary to import a time limit analogous to the time limit for enforcing the equivalent domestic right, while the monist approach is favoured by *Biggs v. Somerset County Council*[190] which regards all claims as originating from the domestic statute and governed by the jurisdictional and procedural rules therein so that the time limit for presenting a claim for a redundancy payment would begin to run from the time at which it became clear that such payments fell within Art. 119. Such an approach seems wholly artificial given the process of interplay between domestic courts and the European Court of Justice by which European Community law is developed. Nevertheless, such an approach has been endorsed by the Court of Appeal[191] so that any claim made after the period of six months beginning with the relevant date would be out of time.

In a redundancy payment claim the onus of proof may shift from one party to the other depending on the issue being contested. Thus it is for the employee to prove he has been dismissed,[192] whereas where alternative employment is offered the employer must prove compliance with the statutory conditions.[193] However, significantly, it is generally[194] presumed that employment has been continuous[195] and that dismissal is due to redundancy[196] so that where, for example, several factors together result in a dismissal, it is for the employer to prove that a reduction in the requirement of the business was not the main causative factor.[197] Ironically, since the introduction in 1972 of protection against unfair dismissal[198] employers

---

[188] See *R. v. Secretary of State for Employment, ex parte Seymour-Smith and Perez* [1995] IRLR 464, CA.

[189] [1993] IRLR 69, EAT. And see *Methilhill Bowling Club v. Hunter* [1995] IRLR 232, EAT.

[190] [1995] IRLR 452, EAT. And see *McManus v. Daylay Foods Ltd*, unreported, case no. 82/95, EAT.

[191] *Biggs v. Somerset County Council* [1996] IRLR 203, CA; *Barber v. Staffordshire County Council* [1996] IRLR 209, CA; and see *Fletcher v. Midland Bank plc, The Times*, July 2, 1996, EAT.

[192] The statutory concept of dismissal in s. 136 is exhaustive (*Dixon v. British Broadcasting Corporation* [1978] ICR 357, EAT).

[193] The employer cannot merely require the employee to prove his refusal was reasonable (*Cartin v. Botley Garages Ltd* [1973] ITR 150, NIRC).

[194] *Cf Secretary of State for Employment v. Cohen and Beaupress Ltd* [1987] IRLR 169, EAT (transfer of a business).

[195] ERA, s. 210(5).

[196] ERA, s. 163(2).

[197] *Hindle v. Percival Boats Ltd* [1969] ITR 86, CA, *per* Widgery LJ at p. 97. And see *Harrison v. Chamberlain Studios Ltd* [1966] ITR 162 (employer failed to rebut presumption that dismissal of Communist Party member who was alleged to be security risk was by reason of redundancy).

[198] See Chapter Five.

seek to prove that redundancy is the reason for dismissal — however, in such complaints no recourse to the statutory presumption that dismissal is due to redundancy is permitted.

(b) The payment. The amount of a redundancy payment is to be determined by reference to a statutory formula which takes account of the dismissed employee's continuous employment, age and "week's pay"[199] at date of dismissal. Only the most recent 20 years of continuous employment may be taken into account[200] with employment before the 18th birthday being discounted.[201] Broadly the payment is calculated as follows:

> for each year (of continuous employment)
> between 18 and 22 years of age — half a week's pay
> between 22 and 41 years of age — a week's pay
> between 41 years of age and the normal non-discriminatory retiring age or the employee's 65th birthday whichever occurs first — one and a half week's pay.[202]

Unless there operates a non-discriminatory earlier normal retiring age employees are excluded from entitlement to a redundancy payment on attaining 65 years of age[203] and for each month worked after the 64th birthday the redundancy payment is reduced by one twelfth.[204]

6.15 Exclusions, rebates and the Redundancy Fund

To be entitled to a redundancy payment an employee must have been employed for a period of two years at the relevant date, which will usually be the date when the employer's notice of termination expires.[205] However, such a qualification has, in the context of unfair dismissal law, been held to give rise to indirect sexual discrimination[206] and it would appear that similar arguments could be levelled against the qualification in respect of a claim for a redundancy payment.[207] If, in the period prior to dismissal, a female with less than two years' continuous employment could establish that there had been, and continued to be, a considerable and persistent difference between the number and percentages of men and women in the groups that did comply with the two year continuous employment qualification and that qualification could not be justified, an industrial tribunal would be required to award a redundancy payment irrespective of the qualifying condition contained in domestic rules.[208]

Those who have reached 65 years of age or an earlier non-discriminatory normal retiring age are excluded from receiving a redundancy payment[209] and various groups or classes of employee are excluded either expressly or because they do not

---

[199] ERA, s. 227 imposes a (reviewable) maximum amount of £210.00. And see Chapter Three, para. 3.12.

[200] ERA, s. 162(3).

[201] ERA, s. 211(2). *Cf* unfair dismissal.

[202] ERA, s. 162.

[203] ERA, s. 156(1).

[204] ERA, s. 162(1), (2).

[205] ERA, s. 155. "Relevant date" is defined by s. 145.

[206] See *R. v. Secretary of State for Employment, ex p Seymour-Smith and Perez* [1995] IRLR 464, CA.

[207] Strictly, of course, a redundancy payment is subject to challenge under Art. 119 which is, unlike the Equal Treatment Directive 76/207, a self-executing, directly applicable provision of the EC Treaty.

[208] For a discussion of the extent to which Art. 119 may be used to circumvent the indirectly discriminatory provisions of ERA, see Green's Emp.L.B. 10–9.

[209] ERA, s. 156(1).

have contracts of employment.[210] Thus an employee who ordinarily works outside Great Britain is not entitled to a redundancy payment unless on the relevant date[211] he is in Great Britain in accordance with his employer's instructions[212] and various employees are excluded from entitlement to a statutory redundancy payment because they are covered by a collective agreement which has been the subject of an exemption order by the Secretary of State.[213] Generally an agreement or contract to reduce an employee's entitlement to receive a redundancy payment is void[214] but this rule is subject to two important exceptions. First, an employee who enters into a contract for a fixed term[215] of two years[216] or more may lawfully (either by a written clause in the contract of employment or by entering a separate exclusion agreement in writing)[217] exclude his right to a redundancy payment which would be payable on the expiry of the fixed term contract without its renewal.[218] It must be emphasised, however, that such an exclusion clause only operates in the case of the expiry and non-renewal of the fixed term contract; it would have no effect if the employee were dismissed (for redundancy) during the term. Where the exclusion agreement is arrived at during the currency of a fixed-term contract of sufficient length it will not necessarily be incorporated into any extension of the original contract[219] and where there has been a succession of fixed term contracts it is the length of the final one which determines whether any exclusion of redundancy rights is valid.[220] However, a distinction exists between an extension of a fixed-term contract which is capable of carrying forward the exclusion clause and a new contract for less than two years which is not so capable. Thus where a fixed term contract for two years or more is extended for, say, six months the exclusion clause is carried forward so that on the expiry of the extension there will be no entitlement to a redundancy payment.[221] Entitlement to a rebate from the Redundancy Fund on paying a redundancy payment is now repealed[222] and the Redundancy Fund is merged with the National Insurance Fund.[223]

---

[210] E.g. police officers/cadets: *Robertson v. Bell* 1969 SLT 119, OH; *Wiltshire Police Authority v. Wynn* [1980] ICR 649, CA. And see Chapter Two.

[211] See para. 6.5.

[212] ERA, s. 196(6). And see *ibid.* ss. 161(1) (certain relatives), 199 (mariners and share-fishermen). And see Chapter Five, para. 5.7.

[213] ERA, s. 157. See e.g. Redundancy Payments Exemption Order 1980 (SI 1980 No. 1052).

[214] ERA, s. 203. And see *Tocher v. General Motors Scotland Ltd* [1981] IRLR 55, EAT.

[215] See Chapter Five, para. 5.16.

[216] *Cf* Unfair dismissal; see Chapter Five para. 5.10.

[217] ERA, s. 197(4).

[218] ERA, s. 197(3).

[219] ERA, s. 197(5).

[220] *BBC v. Ioannou* [1975] ICR 267, CA.

[221] *Mulrine v. University of Ulster* [1993] IRLR 545, NICA.

[222] WA 1986, s. 27; EA 1989, s. 17.

[223] EA 1990, s. 13.

Chapter Seven

DISCRIMINATION IN EMPLOYMENT

INTRODUCTION

7.1 That the contract of employment is based on consent, freely given, and that it involves the notion of *delectus personae*[1] emphasises that concluding a contract of employment will necessarily involve the consideration of many factors and criteria which are subjective in their conception and application. Consideration will be given to personal qualities ranging, on the employee's side, from education to appearance and, on the employer's side, from a good industrial relations record to the operation of a profit sharing scheme. In theory the terms of each contract of employment reflect a willingness of each party to accept those terms. Of course, there are limits imposed by law on that otherwise essential freedom to decide with whom one will contract and on what terms one will contract. For example, a contract of employment for an illegal purpose is not enforceable[2] and statute frequently attaches sanctions to the insertion of certain terms in contracts of employment either generally or in relation to particular classes of employee. Thus, contracts of employment cannot be lawfully terminated if less notice than that prescribed by statute is given,[3] nor can they exclude or limit the operation of many statutory employment rights.[4] Also, statute has forbidden certain types of work being done by women, young persons and children.[5] What these legal rules have in common is that they seek to prevent a contract of employment being concluded at all or on certain terms. Some could truly be described as "discrimination" laws because their direct result is that employees of one class are treated differently from employees of other classes. The different treatment is often, from the employee's point at any rate, less favourable.[6] Such well-meaning but unfavourable treatment has even been carried over into more recent legislation which itself was designed to ensure members of certain classes were no longer treated less

---

[1] Lord Fraser, *Master and Servant*, p. 66.
[2] Stair I, 10, 13(3); Bell, *Principles*. s. 35. And See *Salvesen v. Simon* [1994] IRLR 52, EAT; *Annandale Engineering v. Samson* [1994] IRLR 59, EAT. *Cf Leighton v. Michael and Another* [1996] IRLR 67 in which the EAT distinguished illegality for enforcing the contract from illegality for claiming sex discrimination.
[3] ERA, s. 86(3).
[4] ERA, s. 203; SDA 1975, s. 77 as amended by SDA 1986, s. 6 and TURERA, s. 32.
[5] See, for example, the Factories Act 1961, Part VI.
[6] See, for example the Factories Act 1961, s. 86 (now repealed by the Sex Discrimination Act 1986) whereby the working hours, and therefore the earning potential of female factory workers, were restricted.

favourably merely because of membership of a particular class.[7] Thus until the 1970s discrimination against employees of certain classes, notably women and members of different races and ethnic groups, was endorsed through the freedom to contract with whom and on what terms one liked and, in some instances, was required by ostensibly protective legislation.[8]

In the 1970s and 1980s, with the passage of the Equal Pay Act 1970, the Sex Discrimination Acts 1975 and 1986 and the Race Relations Act 1976, statute began to make inroads on the freedom of contract by proscribing criteria like sex, marital status, race, nationality and ethnic origin; and that trend has been continued most recently by the enactment of the Disability Discrimination Act 1995 which adds disability to the list of proscribed criteria. Deciding not to contract with, to terminate contractual relations with or to deal with a person to his detriment by reference to any of the above criteria were declared unlawful, giving the victim recourse to an industrial tribunal.[9] Further, many discriminatory legislative provisions have been repealed or amended by the Sex Discrimination Act 1986 and, with some exceptions, legislative provisions which require an act of discrimination to be committed are overridden by the Employment Act 1989.[10]

It is important to note, however, that discrimination is not unlawful unless and until the law declares it to be so. Thus, although it is unlawful to discriminate against a married person on the grounds of his or her marital status[11] it is not unlawful to discriminate against a single person on the grounds of his or her marital status although it is unlawful to treat a single woman differently from a single man on the grounds of marital status.[12] While the Sex Discrimination Act 1975 does not expressly proscribe discrimination on the grounds of pregnancy, it is clear from the decision of the House of Lords in *Webb v. EMO Air Cargo (UK) Ltd (No. 2)*[13] that in certain circumstances that Act has to be interpreted as protecting a woman unfavourably treated on the grounds of pregnancy. Thus a woman who, having been engaged to cover for another woman who was to take maternity leave, discovered that she herself was pregnant and would not be available during the period of the other woman's maternity leave was, on her dismissal, entitled to claim she had been the victim of sexual discrimination.[14] However, although the House of Lords limited its decision to a case in which a woman was engaged for an indefinite period and recognised that pregnancy was a circumstance that could not

---

[7] See SDA 1975, s. 51 prior to substitution by EA 1989, s. 3(3), and *Greater London Council v. Farrar* [1980] ICR 266, EAT (decided before the enactment of SDA 1986, s. 5), *Page v. Freight Hire (Tank Haulage) Ltd* [1981] ICR 299, EAT (decided before the enactment of EA 1989).

[8] There were some minor exceptions whereby statute had removed certain forms of discriminatory treatment of particular groups. Thus the Sex Disqualification (Removal) Act 1919 provides a person should not be disqualified by sex or marriage from exercising any public function or holding any civil or judicial office or from carrying on any profession. And see the now repealed Race Relations Acts 1965, 1968. For a survey of the legislative approach to sex discrimination, see W. B. Creighton, *Working Women and the Law* (1978).

[9] See paras. 7.23, 7.30. Victims of sexual or racial discrimination in fields other than employment have their disputes resolved by the courts (SDA 1975, s. 66; RRA, s. 57).

[10] EA 1989, ss. 1, 2.

[11] SDA 1975, s. 3.

[12] SDA 1975, s. 1(2).

[13] [1995] ICR 1021, HL, following a reference to the ECJ ([1994] IRLR 482). At the time of Mrs Webb's dismissal EPCA, s. 60 rendered unfair the dismissal of women on the grounds of pregnancy only if they had two years' continuous employment. ERA, s. 99 now renders unfair such dismissals without the need for any continuous employment. See Chapter Five.

[14] *Webb*, above.

be present in the case of a hypothetical man it also expressed the opinion that pregnancy would not be a relevant circumstance distinguishing her case from that of the hypothetical man where the woman was denied employment for a fixed period in the future during the whole of which her pregnancy would make her unavailable for work nor where after engagement for such a period the discovery of her pregnancy led to cancellation of her engagement. Even more confusingly the Court of Session, having considered the relevant European law,[15] has held that the dismissal of a woman whose pregnancy-related illnesses prevented her from working for the maximum period permitted by the employer's sickness policy rules was not unlawful sex discrimination.[16]

Similarly, it is not unlawful to treat a person less favourably on the grounds of his religion[17] or his political opinions or beliefs[18] or apply a policy of not recruiting homosexuals or others of whose sexual proclivities or private morality he disapprove[19]; and until the passage of the Employment Act 1990[20] the employer could lawfully refuse to engage a trade unionist or employ only members of a particular trade union.[21] Therefore, although certain types or groups of persons may derive some protection from general employment laws like unfair dismissal law or from statutes designed to give the type or group special legal entitlements,[22] employment law only proscribes generally discrimination on the grounds of sex, marital status, race, disability and union membership, non-membership or activities.[23]

SEX DISCRIMINATION

7.2 The law against sex and marital status discrimination is found principally[24] in the Equal Pay Act 1970,[25] the Sex Discrimination Acts 1975, 1986 and Article 119

---

[15] *Hertz v. Aldi Marked K/S* [1991] IRLR 31, ECJ.

[16] *Brown v. Rentokil Ltd* [1995] IRLR 211, IH. On appeal to the House of Lords the case has been referred to the European Court of Justice.

[17] But see *Mandla v. Dowell Lee* [1983] ICR 385, HL and other cases discussed at para. 7.25. In Northern Ireland discrimination on religious grounds is unlawful by virtue of the Fair Employment (Northern Ireland) Act 1976. And note the Local Government and Housing Act 1989, s. 7 which requires local authorities to appoint "on merit".

[18] *Cf* Fair Employment (Northern Ireland) Act 1976. However, in Scotland discrimination based on religious or political beliefs by a public body could probably be challenged by the flexible remedy of judicial review.

[19] And see *Saunders v. Scottish National Camps Association Ltd* [1981] IRLR 277, IH, *Boychuk v. H J Symons Holdings Ltd* [1977] IRLR 395, EAT. The policy of the Ministry of Defence to administratively discharge homosexuals is not irrational (*R. v. Ministry of Defence, ex parte Smith and Others* [1995] IRLR 585, CA).

[20] EA 1990, s. 1.

[21] Of course, dismissal or action short of it because of union membership, non-membership or activities was unlawful (TULRCA, ss. 152, 146); see Chapter Five, para. 5.65, Chapter Nine, para. 9.50.

[22] See, for example, the Rehabilitation of Offenders Act 1974.

[23] For coverage of discrimination based on trade union membership etc., see Chapter Nine, para. 9.50.

[24] The Sex Disqualification (Removal) Act 1919 removes sex disqualifications in public offices and professions.

[25] The scope of the Act was considerably increased by the Equal Pay (Amendment) Regulations 1983 (SI 1983 No. 1794).

of the European Community Treaty along with Council Directives 75/117, 76/207 and 92/85.[26]

EQUAL PAY

7.3 Domestic provisions

The Equal Pay Act 1970 which became effective at the same time as the Sex Discrimination Act 1975,[27] was amended by that Act and by the Equal Pay (Amendment) Regulations 1983.[28] The Equal Pay Act is designed to prevent discrimination in contractual terms and conditions of employment between men and women[29]; clearly it cannot directly[30] benefit women (men) whose terms of employment are worse than those of other women (men). The terms (whether they relate to pay or not) of every contract under which a woman is employed[31] are deemed to include an equality clause which has the effect of modifying any less favourable terms in, and inserting any terms which are absent from, the woman's contract when it is compared with the man's contract.[32] In *Hayward v. Cammell Laird Shipbuilders Ltd*[33] the House of Lords held that in the Act the word "term" should receive its natural meaning, namely, "a distinct provision or part of a contract which has sufficient content to permit a comparison from the point of view of the benefits it confers with a similar provision or part of another contract".[34] Thus it is correct to compare the term about basic pay in the woman's contract with the term about basic pay in the man's, whereas it is wrong to compare the entire remuneration packages in the two contracts.[35] However, unlike the Sex Discrimination Act 1975 and Article 119 of the EC Treaty, the Equal Pay Act does not embrace the distinction between direct and indirect discrimination so that if women are engaged on work rated equivalent[36] that is sufficient for them to become entitled to equal pay unless the employer can show the variation in pay is due to a genuine material factor.[37]

There are three situations in which a woman is entitled to receive pay and other

---

[26] See paras 7.11, 7.13 and Chapter Five para. 5.61.

[27] The two Acts became effective on December 29, 1975.

[28] SI 1983 No. 1794 made under the European Communities Act 1972.

[29] The EqPA is worded so that it benefits women but it is expressly provided that it applies equally to men and their treatment relative to women: s. 1(3). And see *Duke v. GEC Reliance* [1988] IRLR 118, HL in which Lord Templeman emphasises that the Act deals with contractual discrimination.

[30] Of course the indirect effect of one successful equal pay claim may be that pay differentials of other (female) workers are affected.

[31] "Employed" means employed under a contract of service or apprenticeship or a contract personally to execute any work or labour: s. 1(6).

[32] EqPA, s. 1(2).

[33] [1988] IRLR 257, HL.

[34] *Hayward*, above, *per* the Lord Chancellor Mackay at p. 259; and see *Barber v. Guardian Royal Exchange Assurance Group* [1990] IRLR 240, ECJ to the effect that genuine transparency of pay structures was assured only if the principle of equal pay applied to each of the elements of remuneration.

[35] The practical effect of their Lordships' decision may lead to "leap-frogging" i.e. mutual enhancement of benefits until equality is reached: but see *Leverton v. Clwyd C C* [1989] IRLR 28, HL discussed at para. 7.7.

[36] See para. 7.5.

[37] *Ratcliffe v. North Yorkshire County Council* [1995] IRLR 439, HL; *Cf Enderby v. Frenchay Health Authority* [1993] IRLR 591. And regarding "genuine material factor" see para. 7.7.

contractual benefits equal to those of a man — when she and the man are employed on (1) "like work",[38] (2) "work rated equivalent"[39] and (3) "work of equal value".[40] However, the woman and the man with whom she claims equal pay and benefits must be employed "in the same employment"[41] which restricts the effect of the legislation to men and women employed by the same employer (or any associated employer)[42] at the same establishment or at establishments in Great Britain at which common terms and conditions of employment are observed generally or for employees of the relevant class.[43] To determine whether such common terms exist it is incorrect to compare the terms of the complainant with those of the selected comparators of the opposite sex because the concept of common terms and conditions necessarily contemplates a wide range of employees whose individual terms will vary greatly as between each other.[44] However, the concept of "common terms and conditions" has been further refined by the Court of Appeal in the joined cases of *British Coal Corporation v. Smith* and *North Yorkshire County Council v. Ratcliffe*.[45] In the former, women canteen workers employed at over 200 establishments claimed equal pay with males who were employed as surface workers at different establishments. In the latter, dinner ladies in one administrative area compared themselves with men in another area and the Court of Appeal stated: (a) common terms means terms which are the same rather than terms which are broadly similar or of the same overall effect; (b) a woman can compare herself with a man at another establishment if the terms and conditions for the relevant class of men at that establishment are the same as those of that class at the woman's place of employment[46]; (c) it is not necessary that the terms of women employed at the two different establishments be the same although the terms which operate for women at the establishments is admissible and relevant evidence; and (d) the fact that one of the terms is the same (as between the men employed at the different establishments) is not enough to show there are "common terms and conditions". The result of the application of these propositions was that in the case against British Coal the women were unable to compare themselves with male surface workers at other establishments because the terms and conditions of such men employed at the women's establishment(s) and at other establishments differed in two important respects, namely, concessionary coal and incentive bonuses, while in the case against North Yorkshire County Council the

---

[38] EqPA, s. 1(2)(a).

[39] EqPA, s. 1(2)(b).

[40] EqPA, s. 1(2)(c) inserted by the Equal Pay (Amendment) Regulations 1983.

[41] EqPA, s. 1(2)(a), (b), (c).

[42] Employers are associated if one is a company of which the other (directly or indirectly) has control or if both are companies of which a third person (directly or indirectly) has control — EqPA, s. 1(6)(c). However this must be read to give effect to Art. 119 which applies to work in the same establishment or service and is not therefore limited to controlled or associated companies: *Scullard v. Knowles* [1996] IRLR 344, EAT.

[43] EqPA, s. 1(6). Note: (1) this is narrower than Art. 119 of the EC Treaty which is confined to men and women who work at the same establishment or service (*Macarthys Ltd v. Smith* [1980] ICR 672, ECJ and CA); (2) the issue of common terms of employment is relevant only where the applicant and the comparator(s) are employed at different establishments.

[44] *Leverton v. Clwyd C C*, above, in which it was held that a nursery nurse at one establishment was entitled to claim equal pay with male clerical workers at another, and see *Thomas v. NCB* [1987] ICR 757, EAT.

[45] [1994] IRLR 342, CA. Although the decision of the Court of Appeal was overturned by the House of Lords, the appeal did not concern the question of "common terms".

[46] Or, if no such men are employed at the woman's place of employment, the terms which such men would receive if they were employed there.

dinner ladies were able to compare themselves with men at other establishments because the males were employed on the same terms irrespective of the establishment at which they worked. Although the Court of Appeal also expressed the opinion that the male comparator chosen by the women must be representative of the class of male employees of which he is member, that issue, of course, is not concerned with whether there are common terms and conditions which affects the question of whether the woman's equal pay claim can be competently made but is a general consideration applying to all equal pay cases; should an applicant choose a comparator whom the tribunal judges to be unrepresentative the employer would be able to demonstrate any variation was genuinely due to a material factor other than the difference of sex. In any event the need to show there are common terms and conditions at different establishments may not limit the scope of Article 119 which applies to employment "in the same establishment or service, whether public or private".[47]

7.4 Like work

For a woman to be employed on like work her work and that of the man with whom she compares herself must be of the same, or of a broadly similar, nature and any differences between their jobs must not be of practical importance in relation to terms and conditions of employment.[48] Until the introduction of the equal value entitlement[49] the concept of like work was of great significance because in the absence of an employer introducing a job evaluation study, which rates the work of employees no matter what kind of work they do, the only method of obtaining equal pay was to prove the woman was doing like work with a man. Since the introduction of the equal value entitlement, absent a job evaluation study, equal pay no longer depends on the existence of like work.[50] Whether the man and woman are employed on like work is essentially a matter for the tribunal of first instance[51] which should not adopt "too pedantic" an approach.[52] A correct comparison involves a consideration of the whole of the respective jobs[53] and the duties actually performed as distinguished from those set out in the contract[54] and, although under the domestic law the like work entitlement applies only where the man and woman are employed contemporaneously, this limitation is overridden by European Community law.[55] Although additional responsibility and working shifts

---

[47] *Defence v. SABENA (No. 2)* [1978] 3 CMLR 312, ECJ; *Scullard v. Knowles*, above.

[48] EqPA, s. 1(4).

[49] See para. 7.6.

[50] However, if a woman and the man with whom she claims equality are employed on like work, no recourse may be had to the equal value entitlement (EqPA, s. 1(2)(c)). And see *Pickstone v. Freemans plc* [1988] IRLR 357, HL to effect that s. 1(2)(c) does not prevent an equal value claim because some (token) man is employed on like work; it only prevents an equal value claim where the woman and the comparator(s) is employed on like work.

[51] The EAT has indicated in *Capper Pass Ltd v. Lawton* [1976] IRLR 366, EAT and *Waddington v. Leicester Council for Voluntary Services* [1977] IRLR 32, EAT that s. 1(4) involves a two-stage inquiry. (1) Are jobs of a broadly similar nature? If yes, (2) Are differences of practical importance?

[52] *Capper Pass Ltd v. Lawton*, above.

[53] *Maidment v. Cooper & Co (Birmingham) Ltd* [1978] IRLR 462, EAT.

[54] *Shields v. Coomes Holdings Ltd* [1978] IRLR 263, CA; *Waddington v. Leicester Council for Voluntary Services*, above.

[55] See *Macarthys Ltd v. Smith* [1980] ICR 672, ECJ and CA and *Diocese of Hallam Trustee v. Connaughton, The Times*, June 11, 1996, EAT (comparison with male successor).

can prevent jobs being like work,[56] jobs do not cease to be like work merely because they are performed at different times.[57]

7.5 Work rated equivalent

A woman is employed on work rated equivalent to that of a man only where their respective jobs have been given an equal value on a study to evaluate the jobs to be done by all or any of the employees in an undertaking — a job evaluation study.[58] Until the introduction of the equal value entitlement only by being employed on work rated equivalent could a woman claim the same pay and other contractual benefits as a man who was not employed on like work. Although there is no duty on an employer to conduct a job evaluation study, where such a study has been conducted and results in different values for the woman's job and that of the man, a claim that the work of the woman is of equal value to that of the man is defeated.[59] However, to meet the requirements of the legislation[60] the job evaluation study must be analytical in nature,[61] although it may be sufficient to analyse only certain bench-mark jobs.[62] Thus an employer will not be able to rely on a job evaluation study to defend an equal pay claim unless the jobs of the woman and the man with whom she makes a comparison have been analysed in terms of the demands made on the jobholders under various headings like effort, skill and decision-making; allocating a value to the jobs of the applicant or comparator by"slotting" their jobs into a grading structure arrived at by analysing bench-mark jobs will not be regarded as a valid job evaluation study.[63] However, where a proper job evaluation study has been carried out the industrial tribunal is bound to act on the conclusions and content of the study[64] and although the House of Lords has held[65] a woman can rely on a job evaluation study to claim equal pay as soon as the study has resulted in the woman's job being given a value equal to that of a man even although the employers have not yet adopted the study or adjusted their pay structures, there is no completed job evaluation study unless and until the parties, normally the employer and the trade unions, have accepted its validity.[66]

---

[56] *Eaton Ltd v. Nuttall* [1977] IRLR 71, EAT (additional responsibility); *Thomas v. NCB* [1987] IRLR 451, EAT (shift-working).

[57] *NCB v. Sherwin* [1978] ICR 700, EAT; *Dugdale v. Kraft Foods Ltd* [1977] ICR 48, EAT in which the EAT approved of industrial tribunals awarding equal basic pay by discounting the extra premium the male night worker received as compensation for his inconvenient hours.

[58] EqPA, s. 1(5). It also provides for a woman to be regarded as employed on work rated equivalent but for the evaluation being made on a system setting different values for men and women.

[59] EqPA, s. 2A(2).

[60] EqPA, 1(5) requires the study to evaluate the demands made on the worker under various headings, for instance, effort, skill and decision.

[61] *Bromley v. H. & J. Quick Ltd* [1988] IRLR 249, CA in which support for such an interpretation of EqPA, s. 1(5) was derived from *Rummler v. Dato-Druck GmbH* [1987] IRLR 32, ECJ in which it was held that Dir. 75/117 (equal pay) requires that job evaluation schemes consider the nature of the work objectively.

[62] *Bromley v. H. & J. Quick Ltd,* above, *per* Woolf LJ at p. 256. However, where only bench-mark or representative jobs have been analysed under certain headings an employee will be able to contend that her job is materially different from the bench-mark job in which case the job evaluation study will not satisfy EqPA, s. 1(5).

[63] *Bromley v. H. & J. Quick Ltd,* above.

[64] *Greene v. Broxtowe DC* [1977] IRLR 34, EAT.

[65] *O'Brien v. Sim-Chem Ltd* [1980] IRLR 373, HL.

[66] *Arnold v. Beecham Group Ltd* [1982] IRLR 307, EAT. However, the EAT indicated that the parties could accept the validity of a study substantially before it is implemented.

7.6 Work of equal value

Until 1984 according to domestic law entitlement to equal pay depended on a woman being employed on "like work" or "work rated equivalent", the latter being dependent on the woman's employer conducting a job evaluation study. European Community law,[67] however, is less restrictive conferring equal pay rights where members of the opposite sex carry out the same work or work to which equal value is attributed[68] and in *EC Commission v, United Kingdom*[69] the European Court of Justice held that the United Kingdom, by making equal pay for different work (but to which equal value was attributed) depend on the employer agreeing to a job evaluation study, had failed to adopt such measures as European Community law required. To remedy the failure the Equal Pay Act 1970 was amended with effect from January 1, 1984, by the Equal Pay (Amendment) Regulations 1983,[70] so that along with equal pay claims based on "like work" and "work rated equivalent" a claim that the woman and a man are employed on "work of equal value" lies to an industrial tribunal.[71] However, the procedure to be followed by a tribunal on an "equal value" claim is different[72] from that when the claim is based on "like work" or "work rated equivalent". Thus on an equal value claim where a dispute arises about the value of any work the tribunal is prohibited from determining whether any work is of equal value unless (1) it is satisfied there are no reasonable grounds for deciding the work is of equal value or (2) it has received from a member of the panel of independent experts[73] a report on whether the work in question[74] is of equal value.[75] Although there may be other reasons for a tribunal concluding there are no reasonable grounds for deciding the work is of equal value,[76] it is statutorily declared that there shall be no such grounds where the jobs of the woman and her comparator(s) have been given different values on a job evaluation study[77] and that study was not itself discriminatory.[78] Nor may an equal value claim be brought if the woman and her chosen comparator(s) are employed on like work or work rated equivalent.[79]

---

[67] EC Treaty, Art. 119; Dir. 75/117.

[68] Dir. 75/117, Art. 1.

[69] [1982] IRLR 333, ECJ.

[70] SI 1983 No. 1794.

[71] Even though the equal pay claim might raise questions regarding the validity of the statutory authority on which the rates of pay are based, the correct procedure is still by way of a complaint to an industrial tribunal and not judicial review to challenge the statutory authority in the ordinary courts (*R. v. Secretary of State for Social Services, ex parte Clarke* [1988] IRLR 22, QBD).

[72] For details of the procedure to be followed, see the Industrial Tribunals (Constitution and Rules of Procedure) (Scotland) Regulations 1993 (SI 1993 No. 2688).

[73] The Advisory, Conciliation and Arbitration Service designates certain experts to be members of the panel (EqPA, s. 2A(4)).

[74] This will involve a comparison of the woman's work with that of her chosen comparator(s).

[75] EqPA, s. 2A.

[76] See, for example, *Kirby v. Cawoods (Fish Curers) Ltd* (IT Case No. 10673/84) in which the women's work was regarded as "repetitive" with "little skill content" and performed in "more ambiant (sic) temperature" while the man's job involved "his knowledge", "a range of work" and "responsibilities"; his work was so different that there were no reasonable grounds for concluding the work was of equal value.

[77] The study must analyse the work of the woman and her comparator(s) under various headings like skill, effort, decision. See para. 7.5.

[78] EqPA, s. 2A(2).

[79] This is the effect of the wording of s. 1(2)(c) as interpreted in *Pickstone v. Freemans plc* [1988] IRLR 357, HL. This interpretation prevents an employer using a token man — doing either like work or work rated equivalent to the women's—to defeat an equal value claim.

7.7 Genuine material factor

Where a woman is employed on work of equal value, entitlement to equal pay does not arise if the employer can prove that the variation between the woman's contractual benefits and those of the man with whom she compares herself is "genuinely due to a material factor which is not the difference of sex",[80] but where the claim is based on the woman doing like work or work rated equivalent, loss of entitlement to equal pay only occurs where the variation is genuinely due to a "material difference".[81] The reason for the apparently different criteria for losing entitlement to equal pay is largely due to the restrictive interpretation given to "material difference" by the Court of Appeal in *Clay Cross (Quarry Services) Ltd v. Fletcher*.[82] In order to ensure that such a restrictive interpretation did not affect equal value claims when that entitlement was introduced the new and wider concept of "material factor" was introduced. However, for all practical purposes the distinction between a material "factor" and a material "difference" has been removed by the decision of the House of Lords in the Scottish appeal of *Rainey v. Greater Glasgow Health Board*[83] which held that the meaning given to "material difference" by the Court of Appeal in *Clay Cross (Quarry Services) Ltd v. Fletcher*[84] was "unduly restricted"[85]; the proper meaning of those words — when account was taken of European Community law as contained in *Jenkins v. Kingsgate (Clothing Productions) Ltd*[86] and *Von Hartz v. Bilka-Kaufhaus*[87] — permitted taking account of personal and extraneous but objectively justified factors like economic or administrative matters. Thus the variation between the pay of Mrs Rainey a prostethist recruited directly into the National Health Service at Whitley Council pay rates and male prostethists who had previously been employed in the private sector and were recruited en bloc into the National Health Service at the rates of pay they had enjoyed in the private sector and subsequently increased by collective bargaining was genuinely due to a material difference other than the difference of sex because the employers could not have established the prostethist service within a reasonable time if the males who were previously employed in the private sector had not been offered the rate of pay they had been receiving there, and from the administrative view it would have been highly anomalous if those prosthetists like Mrs Rainey were, for the future as well as the present, to have a salary scale and negotiating machinery different from the rest of those employed in the National Health Service.

Although it is for the industrial tribunal to decide whether the reason for the variation between the contracts could be objectively justified, the following have been held sufficiently material to exclude the right to equal pay — regional

---

[80] EqPA, s. 1(3).
[81] *Ibid.*
[82] [1979] ICR 1. The Court of Appeal took the view that EqPA, s. 1(3) permitted consideration only of matters which were part of the "personal equation" (e.g. length of service, qualifications and preservation of special status "red-circling") and not extraneous factors (e.g. market forces or other economic or administrative reasons).
[83] [1987] IRLR 26, HL. If *Rainey* had been decided before the Equal Pay (Amendment) Regulations 1983 were enacted it might not have been necessary for the doubtful distinction between a material factor and a material difference to have been enacted at all.
[84] [1979] ICR 1.
[85] In *Albion Shipping Agency v. Arnold* [1981] IRLR 525, EAT the EAT restricted the rule in *Fletcher* to cases where employment was contemporaneous.
[86] [1981] IRLR 228, ECJ.
[87] [1986] IRLR 317, ECJ.

variations in pay and other conditions,[88] "red-circling",[89] longer service resulting in incremental differences,[90] different qualifications,[91] different pay rates for part-time and full-time workers[92] where the difference in rates are reasonably necessary to achieve some objective other than an objective related to the sex of the workers,[93] the fact that the jobs are done at different times[94] and the need to ensure the efficient carrying on of the employer's business.[95]

Similarly a premium, which amounted to 20% of the man's pay, paid to employees who worked rotating shifts was genuinely due to a material factor even where the employer was unable to demonstrate how much of the premium was due to unsocial working and how much due to the rotating nature of the man's shift because it was clear that the premium was paid to men and women working the rotating shifts.[96] However, this must now be seen in the context of the decision of the European Court of Justice in *Enderby v. Frenchay Health Authority*[97] that where the national tribunal is able to determine precisely what proportion of a difference is due to a reason it must accept that the difference is objectively justified to the extent of that proportion but if that is not the case the national court must assess whether the reason was sufficiently significant to provide objective justification for all or part of the difference. Although *Enderby* was concerned with a situation in which there was an appreciable difference in the pay of one group which was almost exclusively women and that of another group predominantly made up of men, the views of the European Court of Justice regarding proportion-ality and transparency would seem to apply to all cases so that an employer will not be deemed to have shown a difference is genuinely due to a material factor if the tribunal is unable to assess the extent to which a shift premium, for example, constitutes an objectively justified reason.[98]

It is not sufficient for an employer to show that the difference is not due to sex; the Equal Pay Act 1970[99] requires that the employer shows the difference is due to a material factor other than sex. To substitute saying that the cause of the variation

---

[88] *NAAFI v. Varley* [1976] IRLR 408, EAT. It may also be argued that the relevant employees are not in the same employment; see para. 7.3.

[89] This term is used to denote employees who are given exceptional terms of employment because, for example, they have agreed to transfer to a less well paid and lower status job on condition their terms of employment remain unchanged. See *Snoxell v. Vauxhall Motors Ltd* [1977] ICR 700, EAT and *Methven v. Cow Industrial Polymers* [1979] IRLR 276, EAT. Cf *NCB v. Sherwin* [1978] IRLR 122, EAT.

[90] *Shields v. Coomes Holdings Ltd* [1978] IRLR 263, CA. However, mere longer service will not necessarily be material: *Goutcher v. Monteith Building Services*, unreported, s/172/76, the first Scottish equal pay case.

[91] *Murray v. Lothian Regional Council*, unreported s/1783/76. Cf *Sampson v. Polikoff Universal Ltd*, unreported 9141/76.

[92] *Handley v. H. Mono Ltd* [1978] IRLR 534, EAT.

[93] *Jenkins v. Kingsgate (Clothing Productions) Ltd*, above.

[94] See *Thomas v. NCB* [1987] IRLR 451, EAT.

[95] *Rainey v. Greater Glasgow Health Board* [1987] IRLR 26, 1987 SC (HL) 1, HL.

[96] *Calder v. Rowntree Mackintosh Confectionery Ltd* [1993] IRLR 212, CA. And see *Baker v. Rochdale Health Authority*, unreported, case no. 295/91, EAT (premium paid to nurse with special expertise (catheterisation)).

[97] [1993] IRLR 591, ECJ.

[98] Cf *Calder v. Rowntree Mackintosh Confectionery Ltd*, above, where Kennedy LJ states that the transparency required by *Danfoss v. Dansk Abejdsgiverforening* [1989] IRLR 532, ECJ does not mean that the employer has to explain precisely how the premium is achieved.

[99] EqPA, s. 1(3).

was free from sex discrimination for saying that the variation was genuinely due to a material factor other than sex was to place an unwarranted gloss on the statutory words so that an employer who merely demonstrated that the difference was rooted in the process of collective bargaining failed to show it was due to a difference other than sex.[100] Similarly where the wages of school dinner ladies were reduced below those of male employees doing work rated equivalent in order for their employer to compete with a commercial organisation the variation was not due to a material difference other than sex.[101]

As a result of the decision of the House of Lords in *Hayward v. Cammell Laird Shipbuilders Ltd*[102] a woman who can mount a successful case based on "like work", "work rated equivalent" or "equal value" is entitled to equality with regard to each "term" of her contract. Thus she is entitled to, for example, the same basic pay as her male comparator but the fact that she has some other contractual benefit (for example entitlement to holiday pay or paid sick leave) which the man does not enjoy may be regarded as a material factor distinguishing her case from his.[103]

7.8 Bringing an equal pay claim

Since entitlement to equal pay is achieved through the statutory implication of an equality clause into the woman's contract, it follows that a failure to pay in accordance with an operative[104] equality clause is a breach of contract giving an action in the ordinary court. However, the court is empowered to (1) strike out any claim or counter claim based on an equality clause where it could be "more conveniently disposed of separately by an industrial tribunal" or (2) sist its own proceedings while directing the claim be referred directly to an industrial tribunal.[105] The normal route for an equal pay claim, therefore, is by way of a claim presented to an industrial tribunal which can award damages and arrears of remuneration in respect of the period of two years prior to the claim being made.[106] Although the claim will normally be brought by an employee or ex-employee, there is provision for the Secretary of State for Employment to bring a claim on

---

[100] *Barber v. NCR (Manufacturing) Ltd* [1993] IRLR 95, EAT. And see *Enderby v. Frenchay Health Authority*, above.

[101] *Ratcliffe v. North Yorkshire County Council* [1995] IRLR 439, HL. It may be worthy of note however that (a) all those employed as school dinner "ladies" (1300) except two were women and (b) the House of Lords merely held that the industrial tribunal, which was itself divided, on the evidence was entitled to conclude the employers had not shown a material difference other than sex.

[102] [1988] IRLR 257; and see *Barber v. Guardian Royal Exchange Assurance Group* [1990] IRLR 240, ECJ.

[103] *Leverton v. Clwyd CC* [1989] IRLR 28, HL. And see the view expressed by Lord Goff in *Hayward v. Cammell Laird Shipbuilders Ltd* [1988] IRLR 257, HL referring to *Reed Packaging Ltd v. Boozer* [1988] ICR 391, EAT that he might be prepared to accept the submission that the total value of all the contractual terms could be a material factor so as to prevent equality being obtained in one particular term.

[104] Clearly it will not be operative if the inequality is due to a material factor.

[105] EqPA, s. 2(3).

[106] EqPA, s. 2(1), (5). This limitation is probably not incompatible with Art. 119: see *Johnson v. Chief Adjudication Officer* [1995] IRLR 158, ECJ and *Preston v. Wolverhampton Healthcare NHS Trust*, unreported, case nos 5, 6/96, EAT.

behalf of women[107] and for an employer to obtain an order declaratory of his and the employee's rights.[108]

Rather oddly, although no period of continuous employment is required before an employee can claim equal pay, there are conflicting decisions of the Employment Appeal Tribunal as to whether the Equal Pay Act requires claims to be brought within a specific time. One decision is to the effect that while the Act[109] does require that a reference may be made to a tribunal only in respect of an employee employed within the period of six months preceding the reference, that time limit only operates where the reference is by a court of the Secretary of State[110] and does not operate where the claim is brought by an individual.[111] On the other hand, another decision applies the time limit to all types of claims and references.[112] Neither decision is of any significance, however, where the employee is still employed at the time of lodging the claim and an even more intractable problem arises with regard to claims for equal pay based on Article 119 of the EC Treaty. As will be indicated later, for the purposes of Article 119 "pay" is wide enough to include occupational pensions, statutory, contractual and *ex gratia* redundancy payments, and perhaps compensation for unfair dismissal, and since to an extent Article 119 permits retrospective claims, there is a need to clarify time limits for such claims but this will be dealt with later.[113]

Where the claim is based on "like work" or "work rated equivalent" the procedure before the tribunal is regulated by the tribunal's ordinary rules of procedure.[114] However, where the claim is based on the work being of "equal value" special rules of procedure operate[115] which permit the tribunal to determine the question of equal value itself or instruct an independent expert (from a panel of experts designated by ACAS)[116] to report on whether the work is of equal value unless (1) there are no reasonable grounds for determining the work is of equal value,[117] (2) the work of the woman and the man have been given different values on a valid[118] job evaluation study[119] or (3) at a preliminary stage the tribunal takes

---

[107] EqPA, s. 2(2).
[108] EqPA, s. 2(1A).
[109] EqPA, s. 2(4).
[110] As indicated, a court may refer under EqPA, s. 2(3) while the Secretary of State may refer under s. 2(2).
[111] *British Railways Board v. Paul* [1988] IRLR 20, EAT.
[112] *Etherson v. Strathclyde Regional Council* [1992] IRLR 392, EAT. *Etherson* has been approved and followed in *Fletcher v. Midland Bank plc, The Times*, July 2, 1996, EAT.
[113] See para. 7.11.
[114] Industrial Tribunals (Constitution and Rules of Procedure) (Scotland) Regulations 1993 (SI 1993 No. 2688), Sch. 1. Note that where the complaint involves the Equal Pay Act a tribunal must issue full reasons for its decision (*ibid.* Rule 10(4)(a)).
[115] SI 1993 No. 2688, Sch. 2.
[116] EqPA, s. 2A(1)(4) as amended by the Sex Discrimination and Equal Pay (Miscellaneous Amendments) Regulations 1996 (SI 1996 No. 438).
[117] 1993 Rules, Rule 8A(1). Although the rules of procedure do not require that such a conclusion (that there are no reasonable grounds for determining the work is of equal value) be based on evidence, the EAT has indicated that where evidence has been presented to the tribunal the correct approach is to take account of such evidence and look at the matter in the round; the tribunal should not limit itself to considering the originating application alone: *Dennehy v. Sealink UK Ltd* [1987] IRLR 120, EAT.
[118] To be valid the job evaluation study itself must not discriminate on grounds of sex: EqPA, ss. 1(5), 2A(3).
[119] 1993 Rules, Rule 8A(1); EqPA, ss. 2A(2).

the view that the employer has proved the variation between the contracts is genuinely due to a material factor.[120]

The independent expert. Where the tribunal refers the question of equal value to an independent expert the subsequent procedure can be fairly involved but can be summarised thus.[121] Reference to an expert results in the adjournment of the hearing.[122] The expert receives written information about the parties to the case, where the applicant works and the name of the comparator the value of whose work is involved.[123] The expert is required to take account of representations, summarise to the parties the information and representations received and report to the tribunal his conclusion (or failure to reach one) on the question of the value of the respective jobs.[124] Originally if, after 42 days, the tribunal formed the view that there was likely to be undue delay in receiving the expert's report, it could require him to provide an explanation for any delay or information on progress and, depending on the terms of the explanation or information, the tribunal could revoke the expert's instructions and require the procedure to be commenced *ab initio* perhaps with a new expert.[125] However, in order to forestall any avoidable delay it is now provided that within 14 days[126] of being instructed to prepare a report an expert must notify the Secretary of the Office of the Industrial Tribunal the date by which he expects to report to the tribunal (the projected date).[127] If an expert considers there will be a material delay he must notify the Secretary of the likely new projected date and the reasons for the delay including whether it has been contributed to by the actions of any party[128] and a tribunal may at any time require an expert to send it a progress report which may, depending on its terms, result in the revocation of the expert's instructions and the commencement of the procedure with another expert.[129] A report, once submitted, results in the hearing being resumed — with at least 14 days' notice to the parties beginning with their receipt of the report — and the report being admitted as evidence unless the

---

[120] EqPA, s. 1(3). Although s. 2A(1) and Rule 8A(1) seem to suggest that a tribunal may decline reference to an expert only where there are no reasonable grounds for determining the work to be of equal value the EAT in *Forex Neptune (Overseas) Ltd v. Miller* [1987] ICR 170, EAT, *McGregor v. GMBATU* [1987] ICR 505, EAT and *Reed Packing Ltd v. Boozer* [1988] IRLR 333 has taken the view that Rule 9(2E) (which empowers a tribunal to hear evidence and submissions on whether the inequality is due to a material factor before it requires an expert to report) also permits the tribunal, having heard the relevant evidence, to uphold the employer's defence and dismiss the claim without reference to an expert. And see *R. v. Secretary of State for Social Services, ex parte Clarke* [1988] IRLR 22, QBD to the effect that a defence under s. 1(3) cannot be taken as a preliminary point; it must be supported by evidence.

[121] The details of the procedure are contained in Rules 8A and 9 in Sch. 2 to the 1993 Rules.

[122] Rule 8A(4).

[123] Rule 8A(2).

[124] Rule 8A(3).

[125] Industrial Tribunals (Rules of Procedure) (Scotland) Regulations 1985 (SI 1985 No. 17), Rule 7A(5). These rules of procedure have been revoked and superseded by the Industrial Tribunals (Constitution and Rules of Procedure) (Scotland) Regulations 1993.

[126] If the expert cannot give the notification within 14 days he must "promptly" give notice of his reasons and the date by which he expects to be able to state the date by which he can give the projected date.

[127] Rule 8A(5), (6).

[128] Rule 8A(8).

[129] Rule 8A(9), (10).

tribunal sees fit to reject it[130] in which case a new report has to be instructed.[131] Assuming the report is not rejected by the tribunal at the resumed hearing parties are entitled to give evidence, call and cross-examine witnesses and address the tribunal.[132] The tribunal or a party to the proceedings may require the expert who prepared the report to attend for cross-examination by any party; any party may call only one expert witness — who may be cross-examined — to give expert evidence on the question which formed the subject of the independent expert's report.[133] There is no restriction on the number of non-expert witnesses who may be called although no evidence may be introduced if it relates to any matter of fact on which the independent expert based his report.[134] On completion of the resumed hearing the tribunal then decides[135] whether the respective jobs are of equal value or that the employer has proved there is a material factor between the woman's case and the man's. To assist the expert in preparing his report the tribunal is empowered, on the application of the expert, to require any person to provide for the expert's consideration information or documents which are relevant to the question of equal value.[136] It is an offence to unreasonably fail to comply with such a requirement[137] although there is a right to apply to the tribunal to have the requirement varied or set aside.[138]

7.9 Collective matters

Although in some cases an employer may agree to extend the decision of an industrial tribunal to employees doing the same job as a successful complainant, strictly, the decision of an industrial tribunal requires to be observed only with regard to the parties in each case.[139] However, although a complaint which is similar to complaints which have already been the subject of a tribunal decision may be regarded as vexatious and therefore struck out,[140] it has been held in Scotland that the principle of *res judicata* does not apply to a complaint brought under Article 119 where the previous unsuccessful claim was brought under domestic law.[141] Of course, many terms of individual contracts of employment

---

[130] Rule 8A(11), (12), (13). The tribunal may also require an expert to explain a report or to give further consideration to the question (Rule 8A(15)).

[131] Rule 8A(13), (18).

[132] Rule 9(2).

[133] Rule 9(2A), (2B).

[134] Rule 9(2C). But note the exception in Rule 9(2D) which deals with facts relating to the defence of a genuine material factor and where the failure of an expert to reach a conclusion is due to the refusal/omission of any person to provide the expert with such information as a tribunal may require.

[135] Note it is the decision of the tribunal and not the independent expert. His report is merely part of all the evidence before the tribunal. The tribunal must append to its decision the expert's report (Rule 10(4A)).

[136] Rule 4(2A). Certain persons including conciliation officers are exempt form this requirement to produce information/documents (Rule 4(2B)).

[137] ITA 1996, s. 7(4).

[138] Rule 4(5).

[139] Thus all females who do the same kind of work may require to apply; see, for example, the unreported cases 9142/76–9159/76 brought against Polikoff Universal Ltd and the background to *Thomas v. National Coal Board* [1987] IRLR 451, EAT in which claims by 1500 women were reduced to a sample of 14 on the instruction of the tribunal, but the decisions would not be binding on any other cases.

[140] *Ashmore v. British Coal Corporation* [1990] IRLR 283, CA.

[141] *Methilhill Bowling Club v. Hunter* [1995] IRLR 232, EAT. *Cf Biggs v. Somerset County Council* [1996] IRLR 203, CA; *Barber v. Staffordshire County Council* [1996] IRLR 209, CA. And see para. 7.11.

have their origins in a collective document which is, expressly or by implication, incorporated into the contracts of employment of individual employees. It follows, therefore, that if discriminatory terms and conditions can be eliminated at source, the terms of employment in the many individual contracts incorporating such collective documents will not themselves reflect the discrimination. It was to facilitate the elimination of discrimination at source that the Equal Pay Act in its original form provided[142] that collective agreements which had different provisions for men and women could be referred to the Central Arbitration Committee[143] for amendment.[144] However, the statutory procedure of referring discriminatory provision in collective agreements has been repealed by the Sex Discrimination Act 1986[145]. Discrimination in collective agreements and employers' rules is now dealt with under the Sex Discrimination Act 1975[146] which renders void any collective term or employer's rule which would be modified by, or supplemented by, the operation of an equality clause. The effect of this provision is that a term in a collective agreement — itself not legally enforceable *inter partes* — which provides for the inclusion of an unlawful[147] term in a contract of employment is void. However, this presupposes that terms are inserted into contracts of employment by the collective agreement whereas the orthodox British view is that the contract of employment, being the legal nexus between employee and employer, accepts or adopts terms of collective agreements.[148] Without incorporation by acceptance or adoption the term of the collective agreement exists in a legal vacuum and the precise effect of this statutory effort to deal with discrimination in collective agreements and employers' rules must await judicial elucidiation.[149]

7.10 Exclusion from the Equal Pay Act

Although the Act applies to employment for the purposes of a government department and statutory bodies and offices it does not extend to military service or any women's service administered by the Defence Council.[150] The Act applies whether or not the proper law of the contract under which the person is employed is the law of any part of the United Kingdom.[151] An equality clause does not affect terms of employment which result from complying with laws regulating the employment of women[152] or which afford special treatment to women in connec-

---

[142] Sections 3, 4, 5.

[143] See Chapter Eight, para. 8.35

[144] In *R. v. Central Arbitration Committee, ex parte Hy-Mac Ltd* [1979] IRLR 461, QBD it was held that a reference to the CAC could only occur in respect of provisions which were directly discriminatory, i.e. which applied to men only or women only.

[145] EqPA, s. 9.

[146] SDA 1975, s. 77 as amended by SDA 1986, s. 6.

[147] Unlawful in the sense of being contrary to an equality clause where there is no material factor to justify it.

[148] See Chapter Two.

[149] The amendments to SDA 1975, s. 77 were enacted to comply with the requirements of European Community law: see *EC Commission v. UK* [1984] IRLR 29, ECJ. Compliance with European Community law could have been achieved by remodelling EqPA, ss. 4, 5 and 6 to give the CAC wider powers to deal with discriminatory collective agreements etc.

[150] EqPA, s. 1(8), (9). But see s. 7 which seeks to ensure that pay allowances and leave of men and women in the forces are the same without giving them the right to complain to a tribunal or court.

[151] EqPA, s 1(11).

[152] Many such laws are now repealed; see Pt III of the Schedule to SDA 1986.

tion with pregnancy or childbirth,[153] and it has been held that where domestic law makes special provisions for employees absent because of pregnancy these provisions become a seperate code so that their position could not be compared with that of a man or a woman in work.[153a] Although an equality clause will apply to any terms relating to membership of an occupational pension scheme which deal with the equal access provisions of the Social Security Pensions Act 1975,[154] it will not apply to terms related to death or retirement[155] or any provision made in connection with retirement other than a term or provision which, in relation to retirement, gives access to promotion transfer or training or provides for a woman's dismissal[156] or demotion.[157]

7.11 The European Community provisions

The law on equal pay is complicated because Article 119 of EC Treaty is of direct application, that is it creates binding legal rights and duties within the Scottish legal system which override contradictory domestic legislation and can be relied on by individuals in private and public employment.[158] Article 119 requires each member state to maintain the application of the principle that "men and women should receive equal pay for equal work"[159] and is amplified by EC Council Directive 75/117[160] which provides that the "principle of equal pay" means, for the same work or for work to which equal value is attributed, the elimination of all discrimination on grounds of sex with regard to all aspects and conditions of remuneration and, where a job classification study is used, it must not discriminate on grounds of sex.

Although there is no statutory provision conferring on industrial tribunals

---

[153] EqPA, s. 6(1)(a), (b) as amended by SDA 1986, s. 9(1). And see *Coyne v. Exports Credits Guarantee Dept* [1981] IRLR 51, IT in which the employers unsuccessfully tried to use s. 6(1)(b) to justify less favourable treatment of a pregnant employee.

[153a] *Secretary of State for Employment v. Clark, The Times,* June 10, 1996, CA.

[154] Sections 53–59.

[155] "Retirement" includes voluntary retirement: EqPA, s. 6(2).

[156] "Dismissal" is to be construed in accordance with SDA 1975, s. 82(1A).

[157] EqPA, s. 6(1A)(a), (b) as amended by SDA 1986, s. 2(4). This amendment was introduced as a consequence of the decision of the ECJ in *Marshall v. Southampton and South West Hampshire Area Health Authority (Teaching)* [1986] IRLR 140 which dealt with the equivalent section of the Sex Discrimination Act 1975 (s. 6(4)) and its compliance with European Community law. By making similar amendments to both the EqPA and the SDA 1975, discrimination in relation to retirement is unlawful whether it results from a term in the contract which is the province of the EqPA or from a policy/practice of an employer which is the province of the SDA.

[158] *Defrenne v. SABENA* [1976] ICR 547, ECJ; *Jenkins v. Kingsgate (Clothing Production) Ltd* [1981] IRLR 228, ECJ. And see *Albion Shipping Agency v. Arnold* [1981] IRLR 525, EAT and *Garland v. British Rail Engineering* [1982] IRLR 257, HL. It may also be used as an aid to construing a domestic statute passed to bring domestic law into line with EC law — see *Pickstone v. Freemans plc* [1988] IRLR 357, HL and *Duke v. GEC Reliance* [1988] IRLR 118, HL. For further discussion of the direct applicability of EC provisions see D. J. Lasok and J. W. Bridge, *Law and Institutions of the European Communities* (1991).

[159] "Pay" is defined by Art. 119 to mean "the ordinary basic or minimum wage or salary and any other consideration, whether in cash or in kind, which the worker receives, directly or indirectly, in respect of his employment from his employer. Equal pay without discrimination based on sex means: (a) that pay for the same work at piece rates shall be calculated on the basis of the same unit of measurement; (b) that pay for work at time rates shall be the same for the same job."

[160] Directive 75/117 is merely interpretative; it does not create any rights additional to those contained in Art. 119 itself (*Jenkins v. Kingsgate (Clothing Productions) Ltd,* above).

jurisdiction to hear a claim based entirely on Article 119, it has been generally accepted in Scotland that Article 119 rights could be enforced by making a complaint to the industrial tribunal.[161] In England, the Employment Appeal Tribunal has disassociated itself from the Scottish decisions and has held that the jurisdiction of the industrial tribunal is restricted to proceeding under the domestic statute disapplied where necessary to give effect to Article 119 and such an approach has been endorsed by the Court of Appeal.[162] It may appear immaterial whether the industrial tribunal is entitled to hear a discrete claim based entirely on Article 119 (sometimes referred to as a "free-standing" claim and the product of a "dualist" approach by which it is meant that rights based on European law may receive effect by the application of that right simpliciter or through the modification or interpretation of a domestic statute) or whether it is required to proceed under a domestic provision (described in contrast as the "monist" approach by which it is meant that European law may receive effect only *via* the medium of the domestic law and tribunals)[163] but the distinction has practical importance, particularly regarding the time by which claims based on Article 119 have to be brought. Detailed analysis of the arguments is not appropriate here[164] but the effect of the "monist" approach is to require claims to be brought in accordance with the time limits set out in the relevant domestic statute unless not reasonably practicable, while the "dualist" approach considers a claim timeous if it is brought within a reasonable period which could begin when an employee is dismissed or when it became reasonably clear to him that a claim under the European provision could properly be made.[165]

7.12 Scope of Article 119

Given its direct applicability and that it is essentially a statement of the principle of equal pay for equal work rather than a series of detailed statutory rules, there is scope for conflict between the detailed rules of the Equal Pay Act 1970 and the general principle of Article 119. In one important respect Article 119 is more restricted than the 1970 Act because the former, even when read with Directive 75/117, is limited to inequality in pay[166] (whether payable under the contract or

---

[161] See, for example, *Secretary of State for Scotland and Greater Glasgow Health Board v. Wright* [1991] IRLR 187, EAT; *Rankin v. British Coal Corporation* [1993] IRLR 69, EAT; *Methilhill Bowling Club v. Hunter* [1995] IRLR 232, EAT. And see *R. v. Secretary of State for Employment, ex parte EOC* [1994] IRLR 176, HL.

[162] *Biggs v. Somerset County Council* [1995] IRLR 452, EAT; [1996] IRLR 203, CA; and see *Clark v. Secretary of State for Employment* [1995] IRLR 421, EAT and the decision of the EAT (Mr Justice Mummery) sitting in the Scottish case of *McManus v. Daylay Foods Ltd* (EAT, June 15, 1995, unreported). See too the decision of the Court of Appeal in *Barber v. Staffordshire County Council* [1996] IRLR 209, CA. Cf *Secretary of State for Employment v. Clark, The Times*, June 10, 1996, CA.

[163] See B. Napier's interesting article, "Time Limits and Procedural Questions after *Biggs*", Green's Emp.L.B. 8–2.

[164] Some of the issues are discussed in V. Craig, "The Implications of *Seymour-Smith*", Green's Emp. L.B. 10–9.

[165] It is respectfully submitted that the difficulty with the monist approach as applied in *Biggs* is that it makes no compensation for the uncertain and unsettled state of the law and presumes that because a discriminatory domestic law could have been challenged as being indirectly discriminatory it follows that it would have been reasonably practicable to make the claim within the domestic time limit.

[166] *Bilka-Kaufhaus GmbH v. Weber von Hartz* [1987] ICR 110, ECJ.

not[167]) whereas the latter deals with inequality in pay and other contractual terms. However, "pay" has been given a broad meaning both by domestic tribunals and the European Court of Justice. The latter has stated that the concept of pay within Article 119 comprises any other consideration whether in cash or in kind, whether immediate or future, provided that the worker receives it, albeit indirectly, in respect of his employment from his employer so that it includes redundancy payments whether contractual, statutory or *ex gratia* and benefits payable under pension schemes[168] as well as the right to join the scheme.[169] It has been held by the Employment Appeal Tribunal in England and Scotland that Article 119 is wide enough to include unfair dismissal compensation, although more recently the Court of Appeal has reserved its position on the question.[170] Whether a disparity is truly one of pay and therefore within Article 119 or a social security benefit and outside it requires an examination of each case individually having regard to the national legislation,[171] but a payment does not cease to be "pay" because it is paid by the Secretary of State where an employer is insolvent and unable to pay[172] or because a pension is payable not to the worker himself but to a survivor[173] and the European Court of Justice has recently decided that Article 119 does not require that while a woman is absent on maternity leave she is entitled to her full normal pay and benefits; however Article 119 does require that during her maternity leave she receives an amount of benefit which is not so low that it undermines the purpose of maternity leave and if the pay or benefit is calculated with regard to the pay she receives before her leave the pay or benefit must take account of rises awarded during the leave.[174]

Unlike the Sex Discrimination Act 1975, the Equal Pay Act 1970 does not make special provision for indirect discrimination and the House of Lords has resisted the opportunity of interpreting the Equal Pay Act so as to make provision for indirect pay discrimination and its associated component of "justification".[175] However, Article 119 is applied to the elimination of all discrimination on the

---

[167] *Barber v. Guardian Royal Exchange Assurance Group* [1990] IRLR 240, ECJ; and see *Hammersmith & Queen Charlotte's Special Health Authority v. Cato* [1987] IRLR 483, EAT and *McKechnie v. UBM Building Supplies (Southern) Ltd* [1991] IRLR 283, EAT.

[168] *Barber v. Guardian Royal Exchange Assurance Group*, above. And see *Commission of the EC v. Belgium* [1993] IRLR 404, ECJ ("pay" includes redundancy payments made under collective agreements entered into by State). *Cf Griffin v. London Pension Fund Authority* [1993] IRLR 248, EAT.

[169] *Vroege v. NCIV Instituut voor Volkschuisvesting BV en Stichting Pensioensfonds NCIV* [1994] IRLR 651, ECJ.

[170] Contrast the views of the EAT in *Mediguard Services Ltd v. Thame* [1994] IRLR 504 and *Methilhill Bowling Club v. Hunter* [1995] IRLR 232 with those of the Court of Appeal in *R. v. Seymour-Smith and Perez* [1995] IRLR 464.

[171] *Bilka-Kaufhaus GmbH v. Weber von Hartz*, above, *per* Adv. Gen. Darmon.

[172] *Clark v. Secretary of State for Employment* [1995] IRLR 421, EAT; *The Times*, June 10, 1996, CA.

[173] *Ten Oever v. Stichting Bedrijfspenioenfonds voor Het Glazenwassers en Schoonmakbedrijf* [1993] IRLR 601, ECJ. And see *Coloroll Pension Trustees Ltd v. Russell* [1994] IRLR 586, ECJ and *Fisscher v. Voorhuis Hengelo BV en Stichting Befrijfspenioenfonds voor de Detailhandel* [1994] IRLR 662, ECJ to the effect that Art. 119 may be relied on by employees and their dependants against trustees who administer schemes on behalf of employers.

[174] *Gillespie v. Northern Health and Social Services Board* [1996] IRLR 214, ECJ.

[175] *Ratcliffe v. North Yorkshire County Council* [1995] IRLR 439, HL, *per* Lord Slynn. The important result is that where a group of women is paid less than men it is not possible to argue in the context of the Equal Pay Act that the difference is "justifiable"; the difference must be due to a genuine material factor other than the difference of sex.

grounds of sex[176] and it is now well established that it may be used to challenge indirect discrimination in the form of different pay rates or other benefits, like pensions, for part-time and full-time workers on the grounds that invariably more women than men work part-time often for reasons associated with family responsibilities and child care. If the different rates of pay or pension affect a far greater number of women than men (or vice versa) they will infringe Article 119 unless the employer can show that the difference is based on objectively justified factors, like productivity or efficiency, unrelated to any discrimination based on sex.[177] Article 119 has been used to challenge a legislative exclusion of part-time workers from sick pay,[178] exclusion of part-time workers from severance pay[179] and paying a seniority element to full-time workers before part-time workers.[180] In the United Kingdom is has been held by the House of Lords[181] that the statutory rule that employees who worked fewer than 16 hours per week did not qualify for redundancy payments[182] was incompatible with Article 119 because the Secretary of State had not been able to justify it by adducing anything capable of being regarded as factual evidence demonstrating that it resulted in greater availability of part-time work with the result that amending legislation has been passed.[183] However, the exacting approach of the House of Lords may require to be modified in the light of more recent decisions of the European Court of Justice to the effect that a legislative measure is based on objective factors unrelated to discrimination where the measure reflects a legitimate social policy and the national legislature had concluded the legislation was necessary.[183a]

Where statistics disclose an appreciable difference in pay between two jobs of equal value, one carried out almost exclusively by women and the other predominantly by men, Article 119 requires the employer to show the difference is based on objectively justified factors unrelated to any sex discrimination which may include the state of the employment market, and the national court must determine the extent to which the shortage of candidates for a job and the need to attract them by higher salaries constitutes objectively justified ground.[184] However, it is not contrary to Article 119 to reward at premium or overtime rates only those hours which exceed, say, the normal working week even if that resulted in those who worked in excess of the hours provided for in their part-time contracts being paid at the ordinary rate because inequality has to be measured over the same number of hours worked.[185] The European Court of Justice noted that "a part-time worker whose contractual hours are 18 receives, if he works 19 hours, the same overall pay as a full-time worker who works 19 hours. Part-time workers also receive the same overall pay as full-time workers if they work more than the

---

[176] Dir. 75/129, Art. 1.

[177] *Jenkins v. Kingsgate (Clothing Productions) Ltd* [1981] ICR 592, ECJ; *Bilka-Kaufhaus GmbH*, above. Whether such an objective factor exists is for the national tribunal to determine (*R. v. Secretary of State for Employment, ex parte EOC* [1994] IRLR 176, HL).

[178] *Rinner-Kuhn v. FWW Spezialgebaudereinigung GmbH* [1989] IRLR 493, ECJ.

[179] *Kowalska v. Freie Hansestadt Hamburg* [1990] IRLR 447, ECJ.

[180] *Nimz v. Freie Hansestadt Hamburg* [1991] IRLR 222, ECJ.

[181] *R. v. Secretary of State for Employment, ex parte EOC* [1994] IRLR 176, HL.

[182] EPCA, ss. 81, 151, Sch. 13.

[183] See the Employment Protection (Part-time Employees) Regulations 1995 (SI 1995 No. 31). And see Chapter Three.

[183a] *Nolte v. Landesversicherungsanstalt Hannover* [1996] IRLR 225, ECJ; *Megher und Scheffel v. Innungskrankenkasse Voderpfalz* [1996] IRLR 236, ECJ.

[184] *Enderby v. Frenchay Health Authority and Secretary of State for Health* [1993] IRLR 591, ECJ.

[185] *Stadt Lengenrich v. Helmig* [1995] IRLR 216, ECJ.

normal working week ... because on doing so they become entitled to overtime supplements.'' Where an employer's payment scheme — which may include piece rates[186] — results in the pay of one group, predominantly female, being lower than the pay of another group, predominantly male, Article 119 requires that the scheme is transparent or that the employer proves no sex discrimination. Thus, where the piece work rates operated by the ceramic company Royal Copenhagen resulted in the average earnings of a group of female workers being less than the average earnings of a group of male workers whose work was of equal value, Article 119 was not automatically violated. However, if it was not possible to identify the factors which determined the rates or units of measurement used to calculate the variable pay element, thereby ensuring that the pay of the two groups was calculated on the same unit of measurement, the employer might have to show the difference in earnings was not due to sex discrimination.[187]

For Article 119 it is necessary to make a distinction between benefits payable under an occupational pension scheme and the right to participate in the scheme. Only since May 17, 1990 (the date on which the European Court of Justice handed down its judgment in the case of *Barber v. Guardian Royal Exchange Assurance Group)*[188] have workers been entitled to rely on Article 119 to receive equality in the benefits comprised in occupational pension schemes. Article 119 renders it unlawful to have different pensionable ages for men and women so that it is violated if a man made compulsorily redundant receives only a deferred pension when a woman in the same position would be entitled to receive an immediate pension[189] as it is by the repayment to a male employee of his compulsory contributions to a retirement benefit.[190] However, it is not unlawful to make a compulsory deduction from the salaries of males but not females to finance a widows' pensions scheme because the deduction is neither a benefit paid to the worker nor a contribution paid by an employer on behalf of a worker and there was no difference between the gross salaries of either men or women[191] or to reduce the amount of a woman's ''bridging'' pension to take account of the state pension to which she, but not a man, becomes entitled on reaching 60. Thus, where a female employee who retired early on ill health grounds received a bridging pension designed to place employees in a position they would have been in had they not been forced to discontinue their employment it was not contrary to Article 119 to reduce that pension by the amount of the state pension she received on reaching 60 even though in the case of men and women aged between 60 and 65 it results in female ex-employees receiving smaller bridging pensions than those paid to their male counterparts on the view that Article 119 presupposes that the men and women to whom it applies are in identical situations[192]; nor does Article 119 prevent an employer, when calculating the bridging pension, from taking into account a widow's pension or the full state pension which a married woman would have received if she had not opted in favour of paying reduced contributions because not to do so would result in an unfair advantage on married women who

---

[186] *Specialarbejderfobundet i Danmark v. Dansk Industri* [1995] IRLR 648, ECJ.
[187] *Dansk Industri*, above. Whether the onus of proof shifts to the employer is a matter for the national court and would be performed by the employer showing that the differences in pay were due to the different choices made by the workers regarding the rate at which they worked.
[188] [1990] IRLR 240, ECJ.
[189] *Barber v. Guardian Royal Exchange Assurance Group*, above.
[190] *Worringham v. Lloyds Bank Ltd* [1981] IRLR 178, ECJ.
[191] *Newstead v. Dept of Transport and H.M. Treasury* [1988] IRLR 66, ECJ.
[192] *Birds Eye Walls Ltd v. Roberts* [1994] IRLR 29, ECJ.

had in the one case opted to pay contributions at the lower rate — an option not available to men — and in the other had received the pension on the basis of their husband's contributions.[193] Article 119 does render unlawful the discriminatory effect of a pension scheme provision which reflects the different ages at which employees become entitled to a state pension.[194]

The apparent simplicity of the decision of the European Court of Justice in *Barber v. Guardian Royal Exchange Assurance Company*[195] required further elucidation by the European Court of Justice. In *Ten Oever v. Stichting Bedrijfspensioenfonds voor Het Glazenwassers en Schoonmakbedrijf*[196] Mr Ten Oever claimed entitlement to a widower's pension under his late wife's occupational pension scheme. However, because his wife had died in 1988 the question was whether his entitlement began (a) on the date of his wife's death, (b) on the date of the decision of the European Court in *Barber*, or (c) not at all because his wife had predeceased *Barber*? The answer, in effect, was (c) because equality in pension schemes can only be claimed for benefits payable in respect of periods of employment subsequent to the decision in *Barber*.[197]

Some employers responded to the decision in *Barber* by equalising pension ages but this in turn raised the issue of whether they should be levelled up or down. This has to be addressed by distinguishing three relevant periods. For the period prior to the judgment in *Barber* neither unequal ages nor benefits were in contravention of Article 119; for the period between *Barber* and the date an employer equalises pension ages the disadvantaged class of employees is entitled to be treated in the same way as the advantaged class[198]; for the period after the equalisation of pension ages Article 119 does not in any way prevent an employer reducing the benefits previously afforded to one sex only to achieve equality.[199] Also, the achievement of equality cannot be made gradual or progressive on a basis that still maintains discrimination, even if only temporary, so that where the retirement age of women is raised to that of men Article 119 does not allow transitional measures designed to limit the adverse consequences for women as regards benefits payable in respect of future periods of service.[200]

In *Vroege v. NCIV Instituut voor Volkshuisvesting BV en Stichting Pensioensfonds NCIV*[201] the European Court held not just that the exclusion of part-time employees from occupational pension schemes was contrary to Article 119 unless objectively justified by factors unrelated to sex but also that the temporal limitation of the *Barber* judgment applies only to the kinds of discrimination which employers and the trustees of occupational schemes could reasonably have considered to have been permissible owing to the transitional derogation permitted by the Community law in respect of unequal treatment with regard to the

---

[193] *Birds Eye Walls*, above.

[194] *Moroni v. Firma Collo GmbH* [1994] IRLR 130, ECJ.

[195] [1990] IRLR 240, ECJ.

[196] [1993] IRLR 601, ECJ. And see *Coloroll Pension Trustees Ltd v. Russell*, above.

[197] And see, regarding lump sum payments and transfer values, *Neath v. Hugh Steeper Ltd* [1994] IRLR 91, ECJ in which it was also held that the use of actuarial factors in calculating benefits was not contrary to Art. 119.

[198] Thus men will be entitled to have their benefits for this period calculated on the basis on which they are calculated for women.

[199] *Coloroll Pension Trustees Ltd v. Russell*, above. Thus women's pension age may be raised to that previously applied only to men.

[200] *Smith v. Avdel Systems Ltd* [1994] IRLR 602, ECJ.

[201] [1994] IRLR 651, ECJ.

determination of pension ages[202]; however, there was no reason why, with regard to the right to join a scheme, the professional groups concerned could, since the decision of the European Court in *Bilka-Kaufhaus v. Weber von Hartz*,[203] have been mistaken about the applicability of Article 119. Accordingly, the right to join an occupational pension scheme had been protected by Article 119 since it was held to be of direct effect in 1976, the year the Court decided *Defrenne v. SABENA*.[204] In a related case, *Fisscher v. Voorhuis Hengelo BV en Stichting Bedrijfspenioenfonds voor de Detailhandel*,[205] while the right of a part-time worker to claim retroactively to join the pension scheme was confirmed it was made clear that the worker who seeks to assert this right cannot do so without having to pay the relevant membership contributions and that the national rules relating to time limits for bringing actions under national law could be relied on against workers who seek to assert their right under Article 119 to join a pension scheme provided the national law is not less favourable than for similar actions of a domestic nature. The response of the United Kingdom government to *Vroege* and *Fisscher* has been to enact the Occupational Pension Schemes (Equal Access to Membership) Regulations 1995.[206] The regulations prohibit both direct and indirect discrimination in relation to pension scheme access; however, the regulations reflect both the Sex Discrimination Act and the Equal Pay Act in that claims must be lodged within six months of the employment terminating and tribunal awards in respect of backdated membership benefits is restricted to the period of two years prior to the date of claim which cannot begin before the date on which the regulations became effective. What the regulations do not deal with is the time limit for bringing actions to enforce Article 119 rights to membership for the period before May 31, 1995 and the Employment Appeal Tribunal has rejected such retroactive claims if they were made more than six months after employment ended but the decision is to be appealed.[207]

However, Article 119 does not require that employers organise their payment systems to take account of the particular difficulties faced by persons with family responsibilities.[208] Where a job evaluation system is used, neither Article 119 nor Directive 75/117 prohibits the use in such a system of the criterion of muscle demand or muscular effort or the heaviness of the work if the work requires the use of a certain degree of physical strength, provided the system as a whole, by taking account of other criteria, precludes any discrimination on grounds of sex and, because work which is objectively the same attracts the same rate of pay whether done by a man or a woman, the use of values reflecting the average performance of workers of one sex is contrary to Directive 75/117.[209]

---

[202] See Dir. 86/378, Art. 9(a) (equal treatment in occupational social security schemes) and Dir. 79/7, Art. 7(1)(a) (equal treatment in social security).

[203] [1986] IRLR 317, ECJ.

[204] [1976] ECR 455, ECJ.

[205] [1994] IRLR 662, ECJ.

[206] SI 1995 No. 1215, effective for all claims brought on or after May 31, 1995. Prior to this only discrimination in relation to age and length of service was prohibited by the Occupational Pension Schemes (Equal Access to Membership) Regulations 1976 (SI 1976 No. 142).

[207] *Preston v. Wolverhampton Healthcare NHS Trust*, unreported case nos 5 and 6/96, EAT, and the same view has been taken in *Fletcher v. Midland Bank plc, The Times*, July 2, 1996, EAT.

[208] *Bilka-Kaufhaus GmbH v. Weber von Hartz*, above.

[209] *Rummler v. Dato-Druck GmbH* [1987] IRLR 32, ECJ. However, the job evaluation/grading system must take into account criteria for which workers of each sex may show particular aptitude.

OTHER FORMS OF SEXUAL DISCRIMINATION

7.13 The European Community provisions

To supplement Article 119 which deals only with equality of remuneration[210] Directive 76/207 extends equality of treatment irrespective of sex, marital or family status to access to employment and training and working conditions, including conditions governing dismissal.[211] The Directive embraces discrimination on the grounds of gender re-assignment and involves a wider concept of employment than the Sex Discrimination Act.[211a] The Directive also prohibits discrimination on the grounds of pregnancy in certain circumstances. This is important in that, although domestic law has been amended[212] to give effect to Directive 92/85[213] so that it is no longer necessary for a woman dismissed on grounds of pregnancy or a reason connected therewith to found her claim on the Sex Discrimination Act 1975, it is necessary to note that the statutory provisions[214] which declare it unfair to dismiss a woman for pregnancy or a connected reason are subject to the compensation limits which apply in the law of unfair dismissal[215] whereas compensation for sex discrimination requires to be calculated without regard for any such arbitrary limit.[216] Additionally, Directive 76/207 is concerned with the elimination of unequal treatment generally (including selection, training and transfer) and not merely dismissal. In spite of the widening of the protection of pregnant women afforded by unfair dismissal law, basing a claim on the Sex Discrimination Act may be both more advantageous (in order to obtain more compensation) and necessary (where the claim deals with discrimination other than dismissal).

Accordingly, it is still necessary to know the extent to which Directive 76/207 embraces discrimination on the grounds of pregnancy and how the Directive has affected domestic law which had adopted the "comparative" approach[217] and required equating a woman's pregnancy with a similarly disabling medical condition of a man. In short, provided the employer did not treat the pregnant woman less favourably than a man in the nearest equivalent circumstances, the pregnant woman had no claim under the Sex Discrimination Act 1975. However, such an approach did not necessarily accord with Directive 76/207 as interpreted by the European Court of Justice in *Dekker v. Stichting Vormingscentrum*[218] to the effect that a refusal to engage an employee because she was pregnant could only be raised against a woman and thereby constituted direct discrimination based on sex, as was the refusal to take on a woman due to the financial consequences of

---

[210] *Bilka-Kaufhaus GmbH v. Weber von Hartz* [1987] ICR 110, ECJ.

[211] Directive 76/207, Art. 5(1).

[211a] See *P. v. S. and Cornwall County Council* [1996] IRLR 347, ECJ (gender re-assignment) and *Jepson v. The Labour Party* [1996] IRLR 116, IT (political candidacy).

[212] See in particular ERA, s. 99.

[213] Although the Directive addresses the matters of health and safety of pregnant workers, it also prohibits dismissal of pregnant employees in certain circumstances (Art. 10).

[214] ERA, s. 99.

[215] See ERA, ss. 118–124; and see Chapter Five.

[216] Sex Discrimination and Equal Pay (Remedies) Regulations 1993 (SI 1993 No. 2798).

[217] Such an approach is seen in the decision of the EAT in *Webb v. EMO Air Cargo (UK) Ltd* [1990] IRLR 124, EAT and endorsed by the Court of Appeal at [1992] IRLR 116, CA.

[218] [1991] IRLR 27, ECJ.

pregnancy.[219] The consistency of the domestic Sex Discrimination Act 1975 with the Directive was confronted in *Webb v. EMO Air Cargo (UK) Ltd*[220] in which Mrs Webb had been engaged by EMO to replace another employee who had become pregnant and was due to take maternity leave. However, shortly after being engaged Mrs Webb discovered that she herself had become pregnant and was expecting a baby at approximately the same time as the employee whom she was to replace and on learning of this EMO dismissed Mrs Webb. Mrs Webb claimed under the Sex Discrimination Act[221] but, although all the domestic courts dismissed her claim, the House of Lords referred to the European Court of Justice the question whether Mrs Webb's dismissal had been contrary to Directive 76/207. On receipt of the judgment of the European Court to the effect that the Directive[222] precludes dismissal of an employee who is engaged for an unlimited term, with a view, initially, to replacing another employee during the latter's maternity leave and who cannot do so because shortly after engagement she is herself found to be pregnant, the House of Lords, emphasising the difference between employment for a specific event or period and employment for an indefinite period, held in similarly prosaic terms that the Sex Discrimination Act 1975[223] was to be interpreted as meaning that in a case where a woman was engaged for an indefinite period the fact that the reason why she would be temporarily unavailable for work at a time when to her knowledge she would be particularly required was pregnancy, was a circumstance relevant to her case that could not be present in the case of hypothetical man[224]; the reason for her temporary unavailability — her pregnancy — was a relevant circumstance to be taken into account when applying s. 5(3) of the 1975 Act which requires that any comparison between the cases of a man and a woman must be such that the relevant circumstances are not materially different.[225] Mrs Webb had therefore been discriminated against on the grounds of sex.

In *Brown v. Rentokil Ltd*[226] the Court of Session has made a distinction between pregnancy dismissal and illness cases, although that decision might now require re-examination following the decision of the House of Lords in *Webb (No. 2)*. Mrs Brown was dismissed when she exceeded the number of weeks of continuous sickness absence permitted by her employer's rules. Her absence was due to a variety of pregnancy-related causes and undoubtedly, had it been a male employee with the same absence record, dismissal would also have occurred and the Inner House held, relying on the speech of Lord Keith in *Webb* prior to its being referred to the European Court of Justice, that it was not relevant that the precise reason for the illness was a condition capable of affecting only women and that under Directive 76/207 only dismissal due to the mere fact of pregnancy was unlawful;

---

[219] And see *Habermann-Beltermann v. Arbeiterwohlfahrt, Bezirksverband* [1994] IRLR 364, ECJ to the effect that the Directive prevents the avoidance of a non-fixed term contract by a domestic rule forbidding night work by pregnant woman because of the relatively short period of the prohibition.

[220] [1990] IRLR 124, EAT, [1992] IRLR 116, CA, [1994] IRLR 116, HL.

[221] At the time of her dismissal she was not protected against unfair dismissal law because she lacked the necessary 2 years' continuous employment.

[222] Articles 2(1) and 5(1).

[223] Sections 1(1)(a), 5(3).

[224] *Webb v. EMO Air Cargo (UK) Ltd (No. 2)* [1995] IRLR 645, HL.

[225] Unfortunately the House of Lords does not explain why pregnancy ceased to be a relevant circumstance in cases of contracts for fixed periods or specific events beyond stating that to fail to distinguish such cases would be unfair to employers and bring the sex discrimination law into disrepute.

[226] [1995] IRLR 211, IH.

even where an illness was directly related to pregnancy dismissal of the employee was not contrary to the Directive.[227]

Article 5(1) of Directive 76/207 is directly applicable in that it can be relied upon by an individual in a domestic court or tribunal against a member state or an agency which is an "emanation of the state".[228] The theory is that a member state cannot plead its own failure to implement a European Community directive in an issue between an individual and the member state or an agent or organ of the state. Thus where domestic legislation permitted employers to discriminate between men and women with regard to the ages at which they could be required to retire,[229] an employee could rely on Directive 76/207 to base her case against her public authority employer which was treated as an "emanation of the state".[230] According to the European Court of Justice, a body (whatever its legal form) which has been made responsible, pursuant to a measure adopted by the state, for providing a public service under the control of the state and has for that purpose special powers beyond those which resulted from the normal rules applicable between individuals, is a body against which a directive, which is capable of having direct effect, may be relied on.[231] Similarly, although domestic law formerly provided for compensation for indirect discrimination only where it was intentional,[232] it has been held that an employee of an emanation of the state may rely on Directive 76/207 for compensation even where the discrimination has been unintentional.[233] However, where the employer was not an emanation of the state an employee had no recourse to the Directive because the domestic provision[234] was sufficiently clear to prevent it being construed to give effect to the Directive.[235]

In Article 5 "working conditions" include the need to satisfy rules regarding eligibility for a benefit or payment[236] while in Article 3 "access to ... jobs or posts" includes the qualifying conditions for Family Credit even although it is within the national social security system[237]; and "dismissal" is to receive a wide meaning and includes a requirement to retire[238] and the automatic termination of employment on becoming entitled to a company pension.[239] However, although it

---

[227] The Inner House refused to distinguish the case of Mrs Brown, in which the incapacity occurred during pregnancy, from that in *Handels-og Kontorfunktionaernes Forbund I Danmark v. Dansk Arbejdsgiverforening* [1991] IRLR 31, ECJ in which the incapacity had its origins in pregnancy but occurred after the woman had returned to work. On appeal to the House of Lords the questions raised in *Brown* have been referred to the European Court of Justice.

[228] *Marshall v. Southampton and South West Hampshire Area Health Authority (Teaching)* [1986] IRLR 140, ECJ; *Becker v. Finanzamt Munster-Innenstadt* [1982] ECR 53, ECJ.

[229] See the SDA 1975, s. 6(4) before its amendment by the SDA 1986, s. 2.

[230] *Marshall v. Southampton and South West Hampshire Area Health Authority*, above. Cf *Duke v. GEC Reliance* [1988] IRLR 118, HL.

[231] *Foster v. British Gas Corporation* [1990] IRLR 353, ECJ; and see *NUT v. Governing Body of St Mary's School* [1995] ICR 317, EAT; *Griffin v. S.W. Water Services* [1995] IRLR 15, Ch D; *Kelman v. Care Contract Services Ltd* [1995] ICR 260, EAT.

[232] SDA 1975, s. 66(3). Cf *Hussain v. J H Walker Ltd, The Times*, November 13, 1995.

[233] *Tickle v. Governors of Riverview CF School and Surrey County Council*, unreported, case no. 32420/92, COIT. But see now Sex Discrimination and Equal Pay (Miscellaneous Amendments) Regulations 1996 (SI 1996 No. 438).

[234] SDA 1975, s. 66(3). And see note 233 above.

[235] *MacMillian v. Edinburgh Voluntary Organisations Council* [1995] IRLR 536, EAT.

[236] *Burton v. British Railways Board* [1982] ICR 329, ECJ.

[237] *Meyers v. The Adjudication Officer* [1995] IRLR 498, ECJ.

[238] *Marshall v. Southampton and South West Area Health Authority (Teaching)* [1986] IRLR 140, ECJ.

[239] *Beets-Proper v. F. Van Lanschot Bankiers* [1986] ICR 706, ECJ.

has been held that where eligibility to participate in an early retirement scheme merely reflects the different national retirement/pensionable ages for men and women there is no violation of Directive 76/207,[240] it has been questioned[241] whether this is reconcilable with the decision in *Barber v. Guardian Royal Exchange Assurance Group*.[242] Nor is the Directive infringed if in a mass redundancy scheme men and women of the same age can participate even although their normal retirement ages are different.[243]

Member states are required to provide individuals with opportunities to pursue their claims about equal treatment by judicial process[244] and while full implementation of the Directive requires that the sanction guarantees real and effective judicial protection,[245] it does not require payment of exemplary damages.[246] Directive 76/207[247] could allow a member state to restrict general policing duties to armed male officers but it[248] does not permit special treatment of women except against risks, like pregnancy or maternity, which affect women as such[249]; and although the Directive[250] is without prejudice to measures to promote equal opportunity for men and women, in particular by removing existing inequalities which affect women's opportunities, it does not permit a member state to enact laws which guarantee women absolute and unconditional priority over men in appointment or promotion.[251]

7.14 Domestic provisions

To complement the Equal Pay Act 1970 which deals only with discriminatory contractual provisions, the Sex Discrimination Act 1975 was enacted to deal with non-contractual discrimination on the grounds of sex and marital status. In relation to employment the Sex Discrimination Act[252] deals with sexual discrimination by, first, defining discrimination,[253] then indicating when it is unlawful to discriminate in the employment context,[254] and finally listing the circumstances in which discrimination by an employer is lawful either because sex is a "genuine

---

[240] *Burton*, above. This is the result of reading Art. 1(2) of Dir. 76/207 in light of Art. 7 of Dir. 79/7 which deals with elimination of discrimination in social security matters.

[241] *McKechnie v. UBM Building Supplies (Southern) Ltd* [1991] IRLR 283, EAT.

[242] [1990] IRLR 240, ECJ. And see *Moroni v. Firma Collo GmbH* [1994] IRLR 131, ECJ.

[243] *Roberts v. Tate & Lyle Industries Ltd* [1986] ICR 371, ECJ.

[244] Dir. 76/207, Art. 6. And see *Johnston v. Chief Constable RUC* [1987] ICR 83, ECJ in which it was held Art. 53(2) of the Sex Discrimination (Northern Ireland) Order 1976 by which the Secretary of State could, by certifying national security was involved, prevent an industrial tribunal from hearing a case, contravened the right to judicial process conferred by Art. 6 which could be relied on by an individual against a public authority. The equivalent provision for other parts of the UK is the Sex Discrimination Act 1975, s. 52.

[245] *Marshall v. Southampton and South West Area Health Authority (No. 2)* [1993] IRLR 445, ECJ.

[246] *Ministry of Defence v. Meredith* [1995] IRLR 539, EAT.

[247] Article 2(2).

[248] Article 2(3).

[249] *Johnston v. Chief Constable RUC*, above.

[250] Article 2(4).

[251] *Kalanke v. Freie und Hansestadt Bremen* [1995] IRLR 660, ECJ. A distinction must be made between equality of opportunity and the result which such equality of opportunity is eventually designed to achieve. But see the Commission's proposal to amend the Directive (COM (96) 93 final, OJ 22/6/96).

[252] The SDA 1975 was amended by the SDA 1986 in various respects and references are to the SDA 1975 as amended.

[253] SDA 1975, ss. 1–3.

[254] SDA 1975, ss. 6, 9, 37–42.

occupational qualification''[255] or the type of employment is excluded in some respects from the provisions of the Act.[256] The Act also creates the Equal Opportunities Commission (EOC) and invests it with powers of investigation and enforcement.[257] Many of the issues involved in sex discrimination also arise in racial discrimination which is covered later in this chapter.

7.15 Definition of discrimination

The Act applies to both direct and indirect discrimination on the grounds of sex and marital status[258] and while it is couched in terms of benefiting women the Act applies equally to men.[259] It also protects a person who has been the victim of discrimination which takes the form of less favourable treatment because, for example, he has brought proceedings under the Act (or the Equal Pay Act)[260] and where the word ''discriminate'' is used it embraces discrimination as defined by sections 1, 2, 3 and 4.[261]

7.16 Victimisation

Victimisation occurs where a person (the discriminator) discriminates against another person (the victimised person) if he treats that person less favourably than he treats or would treat other persons because[262] the victimised person has (a) brought proceedings[263] against the discriminator or any other person, (b) has given evidence or information in connection with these proceedings, (c) done anything under or by reference to sex discrimination law[264] in relation to the discriminator or any other person, or (d) alleged that the discriminator or any other person has committed an act which would amount to a contravention of sex discrimination law.[265] Thus no protection is given against an employee who is victimised for having brought proceedings by virtue of European law in the form of Article 119 or Directive 76/207 and a complaint of victimisation only lies against an employer where either the employer himself or an employee acting in the course of his employment is alleged to have committed an unlawful act of discrimination. Accordingly, where a policewoman who had made a complaint of sexual assault against a male colleague (against whom no action was taken) found that her name had been removed from a list of personnel to be used in special operations, her complaint of victimisation failed because the colleague had not been acting in the course of his employment; for a successful complaint of victimisation under

---

[255] SDA 1975, s. 7.

[256] SDA 1975, ss. 17–21, 47, 48, 51, 52.

[257] SDA 1975, ss. 53–61, 67–75.

[258] SDA 1975, ss. 1, 2, 3.

[259] SDA 1975, s. 2.

[260] SDA 1975, s. 4.

[261] *Cornelius v. University College of Swansea* [1987] IRLR 141, CA.

[262] It is not necessary that the only reason for victimising the person is that he/she had previously brought proceedings etc. but it must be sufficiently prominent to be the cause of the less favourable treatment (*Swiggs v. Nagarajan* [1994] IRLR 61, EAT).

[263] The proceedings must have been brought under the Equal Pay Act, the Sex Discrimination Act or Schedule 5 to the Social Security Act 1989 and do not include bringing an internal complaint (*British Telecommunications plc v. Grant*, unreported, case no. 816/92, EAT) but being victimised for having brought an internal complaint would be covered by (d) below (*Waters v. Commissioner of Police of the Metropolis* [1995] ICR 510, EAT).

[264] The relevant law is the Equal Pay Act, the Sex Discrimination Act or Schedule 5 to the Social Security Act 1989.

[265] SDA 1975, s. 4(1). The relevant law is the Equal Pay Act, the Sex Discrimination Act or Schedule 5 to the Social Security Act 1989.

section 4(1)(d) against an employer it is necessary that the discriminator himself (the employer) or an employee acting in the course of his employment commits an unlawful act of discrimination.[266]

7.17 Direct discrimination

Clearly direct discrimination occurs where an employer treats or would treat[267] a woman less favourably on the ground of her sex.[268] Thus it includes the straightforward refusal to appoint a woman,[269] permitting women to leave their work stations earlier than men,[270] reserving unpleasant, dirty work for men,[271] dismissal and compulsory retirement,[272] and sexual harassment.[273] However, it also includes unfavourable treatment which derives from the application of a gender-based criterion like state pension age which is different for men and women.[274] Also, following the decision of the House of Lords in *Webb v. EMO Air Cargo (UK) Ltd (No. 2)*,[275] unfavourable treatment of a woman on the grounds of her pregnancy must be regarded as sex discrimination in certain circumstances. However, whether an employer treats an employee less favourably by insisting on particular dress rules has until recently been confused. Thus, in *Schmidt v. Austicks Bookshop Ltd*[276] the complaint of a woman who was not permitted to wear trousers was rejected because "the realistic and better way of [dealing with dress rules] is to say that there were in force rules restricting wearing apparel and governing appearance which applied to men and women, although obviously women and men being different, the rules in the two cases were not the same." However, in *Smith v. Safeway plc*[277] the lay members of the Employment Appeal Tribunal distinguished *Schmidt* because it did not address the question of appearance (hair length) which extended beyond working hours so that rules which prevented male but not female delicatessen assistants from having pony-tails did result in men being treated less favourably. The grounds of that distinction are dubious and the Court of Appeal, in allowing the employer's appeal, has dispelled some of the confusion by holding that there is an important distinction between discrimination between the sexes and discrimination against one sex, and that an appearance code which applies a standard of what is conventional applies an even-handed approach

---

[266] *Waters v. Commissioner of Police of the Metropolis*, above. As to "the course of employment" in this context, see *Tower Boot Co. Ltd v. Jones* [1995] IRLR 529, EAT.

[267] It is not necessary that less favourable treatment actually occurs.

[268] SDA 1975, s. 1(1)(a).

[269] *Roadburg v. Lothian Regional Council* [1976] IRLR 283, IT; *Grieg v. Community Industry* [1979] IRLR 158, EAT.

[270] *Automotive Products Ltd v. Peake* [1977] IRLR 365, CA.

[271] *Ministry of Defence v. Jeremiah* [1979] IRLR 436, CA.

[272] *Coleman v. Skyrail Oceanic Ltd* [1981] IRLR 398, CA (dismissal of woman after marriage to man who worked for rival on assumption that husband was the "breadwinner"); *Marshall v. Southampton and South West Hampshire Area Health Authority (Teaching)* [1986] IRLR 140, ECJ (requiring woman to retire earlier than men).

[273] *Porcelli v. Strathclyde Regional Council* [1986] ICR 564, IH.

[274] *James v. Eastleigh Borough Council* [1990] IRLR 288, HL.

[275] [1995] IRLR 645, HL, discussed at para. 7.13.

[276] [1977] IRLR 360, EAT. *Schmidt* was followed and applied in *Burnett v. West Birmingham Health Authority* [1994] IRLR 7, EAT.

[277] [1995] IRLR 132, EAT.

between men and women.[278] Direct discrimination against a married person occurs when a married person is treated less favourably than an unmarried person of the same sex.[279] In all cases of direct discrimination the reason of the alleged discriminator is irrelevant.[280]

7.18 Indirect discrimination

Indirect discrimination occurs when a gender-neutral requirement or condition, which cannot be objectively justified, is applied to both sexes but the proportion of one sex which can comply with it is considerably smaller than the proportion[281] of the other sex which can comply and by not being able to comply the person suffers a detriment.[282] Following the decision in the racial discrimination case of *Meer v. London Borough of Tower Hamlets*[283] that the words "requirement" and "condition" denote something mandatory or in the form of an "absolute bar" and not merely one of several (weighted) criteria to be considered, the Equal Opportunities Commission proposed that indirect discrimination be extended to include a policy or practice but the legislation remains unamended. Indirect discrimination may be described as "covert" discrimination because on the surface, by applying the same criterion to both sexes, there would appear to be equal treatment. However, when the impact or effect of the criterion is considered it clearly disadvantages one sex more than the other.[284] Insisting that employees work a certain pattern or number of hours per week is a requirement or condition. Thus not permitting part-time work or job-sharing can be expressed as imposing a requirement or condition[285] that employees have to work a minimum of hours per week which, arguably, is a requirement that fewer women, because of family responsibilities, can comply with[286] as is selecting for redundancy part-timers before full-timers[287] and requiring applicants to be between certain ages.[288] A requirement to be mobile

---

[278] *Smith v. Safeway plc* [1996] IRLR 456, CA: the industrial tribunal must consider, in the context of the code as a whole, whether the restriction results in men (or women) being treated less favourably. And see *McConomy v. Croft Inns Ltd* [1992] IRLR 561, NICA (acceptance that men wearing earrings is now common).

[279] *Bick v. Royal West of England Residential School for the Deaf* [1976] IRLR 326, IT (dismissal as from date of marriage).

[280] *James v. Eastleigh Borough Council*, above.

[281] See *Greater Manchester Police Authority v. Lea* [1990] IRLR 372, EAT.

[282] SDA 1975, s. 1(1)(b). And see *James v. Eastleigh Borough Council* [1990] IRLR 288, HL.

[283] [1988] IRLR 399, CA; and see para. 7.26.

[284] For an early appreciation of the importance of controlling indirect discrimination, see *Griggs v. Duke Power Co.* 401 US 424 (1971).

[285] The decision in *Clymo v. Wandsworth London Borough Council* [1989] IRLR 241, EAT — that a contractual term that a job is full-time does not involve applying a requirement or condition but is part of the nature of the job — has been disapproved in *Briggs v. North Eastern Education and Library Board* [1990] IRLR 181, NICA. And see *Meade-Hill v. British Council* [1995] IRLR 478, CA.

[286] *Home Office v. Holmes* [1984] IRLR 299, EAT.

[287] *Clarke and Powell v. Eley (IMI) Kynoch* [1982] IRLR 482, EAT; *Kidd v. DRG (UK) Ltd* [1985] IRLR 190, EAT; and see *Brook v. London Borough of Haringey* [1992] IRLR 478, EAT regarding application of LIFO for redundancy selection.

[288] *Price v. Civil Service Commission* [1977] IRLR 291, EAT. Other instances of a requirement or condition with disproportionate effect have included a seniority test for allocation of more attractive work (*Steel v. Post Office* [1977] IRLR 288, EAT), a height and strength test for admission to certain types of work (*Thorn v. Meggitt Engineering Ltd* [1976] IRLR 241), operating a promotion procedure which was subjective and unadvertised (*Watches of Switzerland Ltd v. Savell* [1983] IRLR 141, EAT) and requiring previous experience in particular job (*Conway v. Queen's University of Belfast* [1981] IRLR 137, NICA).

may also be a requirement or condition. Thus in *Meade-Hill v. British Council*[289] a female employee who, on promotion, accepted a contractual term to the effect that she would "serve in such parts of the United Kingdom ... as the company may in its discretion require" successfully claimed that the term amounted to indirect discrimination, the Court of Appeal holding that the inclusion of a contractual term which imposes an obligation on a party to the contract amounts to the application of a requirement or condition against that party even although the employer has not yet sought to enforce it. Reflecting the similar approach of European equal pay jurisprudence,[290] insisting on previous experience of work in a section or for a particular employer may be a requirement which, if not justifiable, will give rise to a claim of indirect discrimination.[291]

Disproportionate effect

To determine whether a smaller proportion of one sex "can comply" with the requirement or condition the test to be used is a practical and not a theoretical one. Thus, in *Price v. Civil Service Commission*[292] the fact that there were approximately the same numbers of men and women between the stipulated ages of $17\frac{1}{2}$ and 28 years, fewer women than men could in practice comply because women between those ages were, to a considerably greater extent than men, due to family responsibilities unable to take up employment.[293] While the effect or impact of a requirement or condition is to be judged at the time it is applied to the employee,[294] it appears that where the requirement or condition involves the introduction of a new contractual term the impact is to be judged at the time the term is incorporated rather than the time at which the employer may require the employee to comply with it[295] and an inability to comply with a requirement or condition must be judged at the time of the alleged act of discrimination.[296] Although the applicant must show disproportionate effect by adducing appropriate evidence, tribunals need not proceed by any particular process of reasoning or by reference to specified statistical evidence, so that a tribunal may properly be able to conclude that the proportion of women who could comply with a particular requirement was considerably smaller than the proportion of men who could comply with it if that fact was first established with reference to a particular section of the population of men and women which could be safely accepted as typical.[297] However, where a

---

[289] [1995] IRLR 478, CA; but note the case concerns the relationship between s. 1(1)(b)(iii) and s. 77 of the SDA 1975 and the dissent of Stuart-Smith LJ.

[290] *Nimz v. Freie und Hansestadt Hamburg* [1991] IRLR 222, ECJ.

[291] *Meikle v. Nottinghamshire County Council*, unreported, case no. 35780/90, COIT; and see *McCausland v. Dungannon District Council* [1993] IRLR 583, NICA.

[292] [1977] IRLR 291, EAT.

[293] *Cf Wright v. Civil Service Commission*, unreported, 9324/79B in which W failed to show that an age-bar of 32 years for internal promotion had a disproportionate effect on women because there were more men than women in the "pool" of employees to which the age-bar was applied.

[294] *R. v. Secretary of State for Employment, ex parte Seymour-Smith* [1995] IRLR 464, CA.

[295] *Meade-Hill v. British Council* [1995] IRLR 478, CA; but note that the case concerns the relationship between s. 1(1)(b)(iii) and s. 77 of SDA 1975 and the dissent of Stuart-Smith LJ.

[296] *Clarke and Powell v. Eley (IMI) Kynoch* [1982] IRLR 482; the fact that C could have worked full-time was immaterial because there were no full-time jobs available when she was selected for redundancy. And see *Turner v. Labour Party Superannuation Society* [1987] IRLR 101, CA that a woman may be able to comply by change of status before the date by which compliance is judged.

[297] *University of Manchester v. Jones* [1993] IRLR 218, CA.

university advertised the post of careers officer stating that the person appointed will be a graduate, preferably aged 27–35 years with a record of relevant experience, when dealing with a complaint from a 44-year-old woman the industrial tribunal was wrong to take as the relevant "pool" not the body of graduates as a whole but the body of graduates who were mature students; according to the Court of Appeal the relevant total was the number of men and women referred to in section 1(1) of the 1975 Act and that meant all men and all women graduates with the relevant experience. However, the section refers not to the number of men and women who could comply with the requirement but to the proportion of men and women who could comply and this shows that those who could comply with the requirement were to be considered as a proportion of another number and that that number is the relevant total of men and women to whom the requirement is applied.[298] Such an approach is consistent with the Equal Treatment Directive[299] as interpreted by the Court of Appeal in *R. v. Secretary of State for Employment, ex parte Seymour-Smith and Perez*[300] although for the Directive it may be appropriate to have regard to the percentage (or proportion) of the sex which cannot comply with the relevant requirement as an alternative to the percentage (or proportion) which can comply; and provided the difference between the proportions of men and women is more than *de minimis* the weight to be attached to "considerably" (smaller) must not be exaggerated.[301] The importance of the "pool" with respect to which disproportionate effect is to be judged is also illustrated by *Pearse v. City of Bradford Metropolitan Council*[302] in which the applicant's statistical evidence related only to the academic staff of a college and not to those with appropriate qualifications which was the appropriate pool in the circumstances.

Justification

However, even if the employee can show she has suffered a detriment because of the inability to comply with a requirement or condition which is of disproportionate effect, there is no discrimination if the employer can show that the requirement or condition is justifiable irrespective of the sex of the person to whom it is applied.[303] It has been stated that what is justification is a question of fact for the industrial tribunal[304] and means what is acceptable to right-thinking people[305] but the better view which requires the employer to demonstrate some objective reason for the application of the requirement or condition[306] has now been authoritatively confirmed. Thus in *R. v. Secretary of State for Employment, ex*

---

[298] *Jones*, above.

[299] Dir. 76/207.

[300] [1995] IRLR 464, CA.

[301] *Ibid. Cf McCausland v. Dungannon District Council* [1993] IRLR 583, NICA.

[302] [1988] IRLR 379, EAT. See also *R. v. Secretary of State for Education, ex parte Schaffter* [1987] IRLR 53, QBD.

[303] SDA 1975, s. 1(1)(b)(ii).

[304] *Greater Glasgow Health Board v. Carey* [1987] IRLR 484, EAT; and see the speech of Lord Fraser of Tulleybelton in *Mandla v. Dowell Lee* [1983] IRLR 385, HL.

[305] *Ojutiku v. Manpower Services Commission* [1982] IRLR 418, CA.

[306] See *Hampson v. Department of Education and Science* [1989] IRLR 69, CA and *Pearse v. City of Bradford Metropolitan Council*, above, in which the remarks of Lord Keith in *Rainey v. Greater Glasgow Health Board* [1987] IRLR 26 were suggested to require a more stringent test than that contained in *Ojutiku*. And note the application of the test in *Briggs v. North Eastern Education and Library Board* [1990] IRLR 181, NICA.

parte Equal Opportunities Commission[307] and *R. v. Secretary of State for Employment, ex parte Seymour-Smith and Perez*,[308] although dealing with whether the social policy of a member state — as reflected in the qualifying thresholds of employment statutes — could be justified in the context of Article 119 and Directive 76/207, both the House of Lords and the Court of Appeal have indicated that objective justification must be assessed according to whether there is factual evidence to the effect that the means (the requirement or condition) adopted by the employer correspond to a real need on the part of the undertaking and are appropriate and necessary to achieve the undertaking's objectives, and such an approach should be adopted when considering justification in the context of the Sex Discrimination Act.

Marital status

Indirect discrimination against a married person[309] occurs where an employer[310] applies without justification[311] a requirement or condition to both married and unmarried people but which is such that a considerably smaller proportion of married people than unmarried people of the same sex can comply with it and a married person suffers a detriment thereby, for example, by not being appointed to a job or being dismissed.[312] Instances of requirements with which fewer married people can comply include not employing people who have children[313] and selecting for redundancy part-time workers before full-time workers on the basis that fewer married women can comply with the need to work full-time to avoid primary selection for redundancy because fewer married women than unmarried women were free of family and domestic responsibilities.[314]

7.19 Discrimination in employment

Discrimination by employers is dealt with by Part II of the Sex Discrimination Act 1975[315] (complemented by the EOC's Code of Practice)[316] which renders unlawful

---

[307] [1994] IRLR 176, HL.

[308] [1995] IRLR 464, CA. *Cf Megher und Scheffel v. Innungskrankenkasse Vorderpfalz* [1996] IRLR 236, ECJ and *Nolte v. Landesversicherungsanstalt Hannover* [1996] IRLR 225, ECJ regarding the test of justification of social policy of a member state. And see para. 7.12.

[309] Note EC Dir. 76/207 (Equal Treatment) is wider than domestic law by prohibiting not just discrimination against a married person on the grounds of marital status but also discrimination against married *and* single persons on the grounds of "marital or family status". And see *R. v. Secretary of State for Education, ex parte Schaffter*, above.

[310] The rules preventing discrimination against married persons only apply to acts of discrimination in the context of employment (SDA 1975, s. 3).

[311] See notes 304–306.

[312] SDA 1975, s. 3(1)(b).

[313] *Hurley v. Mustoe* [1981] IRLR 208, EAT; *Thorndyke v. Bell Fruit (North Central) Ltd* [1979] IRLR 1, IT, which proceed on the view that a smaller proportion of married women can comply with the "no children" requirement than unmarried women.

[314] *Kidd v. DRG (UK) Ltd* [1985] IRLR 190.

[315] Part II also deals with discrimination by other bodies in the employment field-partnerships (s. 11), trade unions (s. 12), qualifying bodies (s. 13), vocational and training bodies (ss. 14, 16) and employment agencies (s. 15). In relation to s. 13 see *Jepson v. The Labour Party* [1996] IRLR 116, IT (all-women ahort lists).

[316] Code of Practice for Elimination of Discrimination on grounds of Sex and Marriage and the Promotion of Equality of Opportunity in Employment (1985).

discrimination[317] at an establishment in Great Britain by an employer[318] (a) in the arrangements he makes for determining who should be offered employment,[319] (b) in the terms on which employment is offered[320] unless it is a contractual term for the payment of money,[321] (c) by refusing to offer employment,[322] (d) in the way he affords access to promotion, training, benefits, facilities or services,[323] and (e) by dismissing or subjecting to any other detriment.[324] Although the *de minimis* rule may present some differences of treatment being regarded as a detriment[325] it can be the same detriment as that which founds a claim of indirect discrimination[326] and it need not sound in financial terms[327] but it must involve a disadvantage.[328]

7.20 Genuine occupational qualifications

Even where a person has been the subject of unlawful discrimination it is possible for the employer to obtain a complete defence by proving that being a man or a woman is a "genuine occupational qualification" (GOQ) for the job or part of it.[329] However, such a defence is not available where the discrimination is in the terms on which employment is offered or by dismissal or subjection to a detriment[330] nor, generally,[331] where the employer already has sufficient men or women to perform the duties for which sex is a genuine occupational qualification.[332] An employer's contention that being a man or a woman is a genuine occupational qualification is likely to be carefully examined.[333] Being a man (or a woman) is a genuine

---

[317] Note that in Part II "discriminate" means (1) to discriminate (directly or indirectly) on grounds of sex (s. 1) and marital status (s. 3), and (2) to discriminate by victimisation (s. 4) (*Cornelius v. University College of Swansea* [1987] IRLR 141, CA).

[318] An employer is liable for acts of employees committed in the course of their employment (SDA 1975, s. 41). And see *Bracebridge Engineering Ltd v. Darby* [1990] IRLR 3, EAT and *Yaseen v. Strathclyde Regional Council* 1991 GWD 20–1200. Discrimination against contract workers is dealt with by s. 9; and see *BP Chemicals Ltd v. Gillick and Roevin Management Services Ltd* [1995] IRLR 128, EAT.

[319] SDA 1975, s. 6(1)(a). And see *Roadburg v. Lothian Regional Council* [1976] IRLR 283, IT; "arrangements" would include how a vacancy is publicised, how interviews are conducted, how application forms are constructed and the use of selection tests.

[320] SDA 1975, s. 6(1)(b).

[321] SDA 1975, ss. 6(5), 8(3),(4).

[322] SDA 1975, s. 6(1)(c).

[323] SDA 1975, s. 6(2)(a),(b). But contractual money benefits are covered by the Equal Pay Act and generally services which are also offered to the public are excluded (SDA 1975, s. 6(6), (7)). And note s. 50 which brings in indirectly provided benefits etc.

[324] The definition of dismissal is extended to include expiry of a fixed term contract and constructive dismissal (SDA 1986, s. 2(3)).

[325] *Schmidt v. Austicks Bookshops Ltd* [1977] IRLR 360, EAT; *Ministry of Defence v. Jeremiah* [1980] ICR 13, CA.

[326] *Home Office v. Holmes* [1984] IRLR 299, EAT.

[327] *Ministry of Defence v. Jeremiah* [1980] ICR 13, CA. Subjection to a detriment would include being selected for redundancy, a reduction in working hours, unpleasant working conditions, having to pay a baby-sitter and being the victim of sexual harassment. But requiring women but not men to wear overalls might not be a detriment (*Schmidt v. Austicks Bookshops Ltd*, above).

[328] *Porcelli v. Strathclyde Regional Council* [1986] ICR 564, IH.

[329] SDA 1975, s. 7(1)(3).

[330] SDA 1975, s. 6(1)(b), (2)(b).

[331] The exceptions are those genuine occupational qualifications which relate to (a) the job being done in a private home and (b) jobs for a married couple.

[332] SDA 1975, s. 7(4).

[333] See, for example, *Roadburg v. Lothian Regional Council* [1976] IRLR 283, IT and *Sisley v. Britannia Security Systems Ltd* [1983] IRLR 404, EAT.

occupational qualification for a job only where (a) the essential nature of the job calls for a man for reasons of physiology (excluding physical strength or stamina)[334] or in dramatic performances or entertainment, for reasons of authenticity, so that the essential nature of the job would be materially different if carried out by a woman,[335] (b) for decency or privacy the job needs to be held by a man because (i) it is likely to involve physical contact with men in circumstances where they might reasonably object to its being carried out by a woman[336] or (ii) the holder of the job is likely to do his work in circumstances where men might reasonably object to the presence of a woman because they are in a state of undress or using sanitary facilities,[337] (c) the job is likely to involve working or living in a private home and needs to be done by a man because objection might reasonably be taken to allowing a woman to have the degree of social or physical contact with, or knowledge of intimate details of, the person living in the private home,[338] (d) the nature or location of the establishment makes it impracticable for the job-holder to live other than on the premises and (i) the only available premises are not equipped with separate sleeping accommodation and sanitary facilities and (ii) it is not reasonable to expect the employer to provide separate accommodation or facilities for women,[339] (e) where the work requires the job-holder to be a man because (i) it is a hospital, prison or place for providing persons with special care, supervision and attention and (ii) those persons are all men, and (iii) it is reasonable that the job should not be held by a woman,[340] (f) the job-holder provides individuals with personal services promoting their welfare education or the like and they can be more effectively provided by a man,[341] (g) the job is likely to involve working in a country whose laws or customs are such that a woman could not operate effectively[342] and (h) that the job is one of two to be held by a married couple.[343]

7.21 Special cases, exceptions and exclusions

Limited discrimination is permitted with regard to: (a) *police* — discrimination is permitted only with regard to (i) height, uniform or equipment and allowances in lieu, (ii) special treatment of women with regard to pregnancy or childbirth and (iii) pensions, special constables and cadets;[344] (b) *prison officers* — discrimination with regard to height is permitted and the governor of a prison need not be the same sex as the prisoners;[345] (c) *ministers of religion* — discrimination is permitted in so far as doctrine requires it.[346]

---

[334] While physical strength and stamina are excluded here it must be remembered that requiring all employees for a particular job to possess a certain degree of strength or stamina may be a requirement which, although of disproportionate effect on women, may be justifiable, in which case there would be no discrimination at all. See *Thorn v. Meggitt Engineering Ltd* [1976] IRLR 241, IT.

[335] SDA 1975, s. 7(2)(a).

[336] See *Wylie v. Dee & Co. Menswear Ltd* [1978] IRLR 103, IT, *Sisley*, above and *Etam plc v. Rowan* [1989] IRLR 150, EAT.

[337] SDA 1975, s. 7(2)(b). It is not necessary that the job *requires* that people be in a state of undress: *Sisley*, above.

[338] SDA 1975, s. 7(2)(ba), added by the SDA 1986, s. 1.

[339] SDA 1975, s. 7(2)(c).

[340] SDA 1975, s. 7(2)(d).

[341] SDA 1975, s. 7(2)(e). And see *London Borough of Lambeth v. CRE* [1990] IRLR 231, CA.

[342] SDA 1975, s. 7(2)(g).

[343] SDA 1975, s. 7(2)(h).

[344] SDA 1975, s. 17.

[345] SDA 1975, s. 18.

[346] SDA 1975, s. 19.

Part V contains several general exceptions to the operation of the Act of which the following have relevance for employment.

(a) Training. Although there is a freedom to discriminate with regard to training for certain work (where very few people of one sex, during the 12 month period preceding the act complained of having been engaged in that kind of work) for the purpose of (i) affording women only or men only training to fit them for that work, (ii) encouraging women only or men only to do that work or (iii) affording training for work for persons who have been excluded from full-time employment by family or domestic responsibilities, this freedom does not extend to protecting any discrimination by an employer which is unlawful by section 6 of the 1975 Act.[347] However, a similar exception is made specifically for employers who seek to afford training for employees[348] of one sex only to encourage or facilitate workers of that sex to take up work which has generally not been performed by members of that sex.[349]

(b) Statutory authority. Previously a discriminatory act was not unlawful if it was done to comply with a requirement of legislation passed before the 1975 Act itself.[350] Thus an employer who refused to permit a woman of child-bearing age to be concerned with the transport of dimethylformamide because of his duties under the Health and Safety at Work etc. Act 1974 was not required to prove that removing a woman from the job (tanker driver) was the only method of complying with his duties under the prior Act.[351] The position is now different as a result of the Employment Act 1989[352] which only permits discrimination if it is necessary to comply with (1) an existing statutory provision[353] concerning the protection of women or (2) a relevant statutory provision (within Part I of the Health and Safety at Work etc. Act 1974) for the purpose of protecting a particular woman or a class including that woman. However, a statutory provision may only operate to defend an act of discrimination if it is for the purpose of protecting women as regards (a) pregnancy or maternity or (b) other circumstances giving rise to risks specifically affecting women.[354] However, these provisions of the Employment Act 1989 are properly appreciated only when it is noted that the same Act (1) declares that legislation passed before the Sex Discrimination Act 1975 is of no effect if it requires an act of unlawful discrimination,[355] (2) empowers the amendment or repeal of such legislation by order,[356] (3) lists statutory provisions which, because

---

[347] SDA 1975, s. 47 as amended by SDA 1986, s. 4. The principal effect of the amendments is to extend the limited exceptions in s. 47 to any person who provides training as opposed to designated training bodies.

[348] Note SDA 1975, s. 48(1)(a) applies only in respect of "employees'. It would not therefore permit recruiting people of one sex only. However, s. 48(1)(b), which is an alternative to s. 48(1)(a), is cast in wider terms of encouraging "women" to do certain work. And see *Kalanke v. Freie and Hanstadt Bremen* [1995] IRLR 660, ECJ.

[349] SDA 1975, s. 48(1). Similar provision is made for trade unions and other organisations by s. 48(2), (3) and s. 49 permits such bodies to discriminate to ensure that on elected bodies there is a minimum number of persons of one sex.

[350] SDA 1975, s. 51 which also applies to an Act re-enacted after the passage of the SDA 1975.

[351] *Page v. Freight Hire (Tank Haulage) Ltd* [1981] IRLR 13, EAT. And see *Greater London Council v. Farrar* [1980] ICR 266, EAT (lawful refusal to employ female wrestler in order to comply with licence issued for premises under London Government Act 1963).

[352] EA 1989, s. 3(3) substitutes the original provision of SDA 1975, s. 51.

[353] This includes Acts passed before November 16, 1989 and instruments made under them no matter when made (*ibid*).

[354] SDA 1975, s. 51 as substituted by EA 1989, s. 3(3).

[355] EA 1989, s. 1.

[356] EA 1989, s. 2 and see s. 6.

they concern the protection of women, continue to excuse acts of discrimination,[357] and (4) amends and repeals many statutory provisions which have operated to discriminate.[358]

(c) *National security.* A discriminatory act is not unlawful if it is done for the purpose of safeguarding national security[359] and, although a Crown certificate that an act was done for such a purpose is conclusive,[360] an individual cannot be deprived of enforcing by judicial process the rights conferred by EC Directive 76/207.[361] The Directive itself allows for exceptions on the grounds of public safety[362] but whether the exception can be relied upon is to be determined by the domestic tribunal taking into account whether the discriminatory action is appropriate and necessary to achieve public safety. Thus where the policy of not permitting female officers to carry firearms led to the non-renewal of the contract of a female police officer, whether the discrimination fell within the public safety exception was a matter to be determined by the domestic tribunal whose jurisdiction could not be excluded by ministerial certificate.[363]

(d) *Other exclusions.* Part II of the Act relates to discrimination in the field of employment which is defined to mean "employment under a contract of service or apprenticeship or a contract personally to execute any work or labour, and related expressions shall be construed accordingly".[364] While this includes any contracts which involve personal performance of work or labour,[365] it will not include a contract with an individual for the distribution of newspapers unless its dominant purpose is that the party contracting to provide the services under the contract performs personally the work or labour which forms the subject matter of the contract.[366] However, it is also unlawful to discriminate against existing and prospective contract workers *viz.* those who are employed by a third party who has a contract with the discriminator.[367] Although service for the Crown is treated as if it were under a contact of employment,[368] military service is partly excluded from the Act's operation[369] in that it will not be unlawful sex discrimination if an act was

---

[357] EA 1989, s. 4; Sch. 1; and see s. 5 (exemptions regarding certain educational appointments).

[358] EA 1989, s. 29; Schs. 6, 7.

[359] SDA 1975, s. 52.

[360] SDA 1975, s. 52(2).

[361] *Johnston v. Chief Constable of the RUC* [1986] IRLR 263, ECJ. The decision in *Johnston* deals with the equivalent (but wider) provision in the Sex Discrimination (Northern Ireland) Order 1976 (Art. 53) which includes acts to protect public safety.

[362] Article 2(2).

[363] *Johnston,* above.

[364] SDA 1975, s. 82(1).

[365] *Hugh-Jones v. St Johns College* [1979] ICR 848, EAT; *Quinnen v. Hovells* [1984] ICR 525, EAT; *BP Chemicals Ltd v. Gillick and Roevin Management Services Ltd* [1995] IRLR 128, EAT.

[366] *Mirror Group Newspapers Ltd v. Gunning* [1986] ICR 145, CA: although in practice there was an element of personal supervision, the dominant purpose of the contract was for the efficient distribution of newspapers. Another approach might be to require the contract contains an element of *delctus personae.* And see *Tanna v. Post Office* [1981] ICR 374, EAT.

[367] SDA 1975, s. 9. In *Rice v. Fon-A-Car* [1980] ICR 133, EAT, s. 9 was limited to where the contract worker is employed by a person/company who contracts with the principal to supply workers. And regarding prospective workers see *BP Chemicals Ltd v. Gillick and Roevin Management Services Ltd* [1995] IRLR 128, EAT.

[368] SDA 1975, s. 85(1).

[369] SDA 1975, s 85(4), (5).

done to ensure "combat effectiveness"[370] and, although it is not unlawful for the Crown to discriminate in appointing to an office or post,[371] the Crown is prohibited from doing any act which would be unlawful if the Crown were the employer.[372]

Discrimination in employment is only unlawful if it occurs at an establishment in Great Britain.[373] Employment is at an establishment in Great Britain unless the employee does his work "wholly or mainly outside Great Britain"[374] and employment on a British registered ship or an aircraft or hovercraft registered in the United Kingdom is at an establishment in Great Britain unless the employee works wholly outside Great Britain.[375] Until the passage of the Sex Discrimination Act 1986 discrimination in relation to death or retirement was excluded from the operation of the Sex Discrimination Act 1975.[376] However, as a result of the decision of *Marshall v. Southampton and South West Hampshire Area Health Authority*[377] in which the policy of requiring women but not men to retire at age 60 was held to contravene the Equal Treatment Directive 76/207, the 1975 Act was amended[378] so that discriminatory retirement provisions are now unlawful if they involve promotion, transfer, training, dismissal, demotion or subjecting to a detriment. Thus if an employer operates an age-bar for access to promotion, transfer or training expressed in relation to proximity to retirement the age-bar must be the same for men and women and, although the amended exclusion in relation to retirement does not include voluntary retirement,[379] permitting women to opt for voluntary retirement earlier than men could be contrary to the Equal Treatment Directive 76/207.[380]

7.22 Sexual harassment, advertisements, other discrimination and vicarious liability

"Sexual harassment" is shorthand for activity which is easily recognisable as subjecting a person to "any other detriment"[381] and, although there has been some debate about whether sexual harassment is properly within the province of sexual

---

[370] SDA 1975, s. 85(4) as amended by the Sex Discrimination Act 1975 (Application to Armed Forces Etc) Regulations 1994 (SI 1994 No. 3276).

[371] SDA 1975, s. 86(2).

[372] SDA 1975, s. 86(2). But note in *Knight v. Attorney-General* [1979] ICR 194 the EAT ruled that s. 86(2) does not give an industrial tribunal jurisdiction.

[373] SDA 1975, s. 6. Note the same limitation is not contained in s. 9 (contract workers) or any other provisions in Part II of the Act.

[374] SDA 1975, s. 10(1). The area of the Act's application may be extended by Order in Council (s. 10(5)). The SDA 1975 and the EpPA have been extended to the continental shelf by the Sex Discrimination and Equal Pay (Offshore Employment) Order 1987 (SI 1987 No. 930). In 1987 only 1% of the continental shelf workforce was female.

[375] SDA 1975, s. 10(2). In *Haughton v. Olau Line (UK) Ltd* [1986] ICR 357 the Court of Appeal stated that s. 10 excludes claims by those whose work was wholly or mainly outside Great Britain unless done on a British registered ship, aircraft etc. and was not done *wholly* outside Great Britain; it therefore excluded a claim by an employee who worked mainly outside Great Britain on a German registered ship.

[376] SDA 1975, s. 6(4).

[377] [1986] IRLR 140, ECJ.

[378] SDA 1986, s. 2.

[379] *Cf* SDA 1975, s. 82(1).

[380] *Burton v. British Railways Board* [1982] ICR 329, ECJ; *Roberts v. Tate & Lyle Industries Ltd* [1986] ICR 371, ECJ. And see para. 7.11.

[381] *Wileman v. Minilec Engineering Ltd* [1988] IRLR 144, EAT. It is also a breach of contract for an employer to fail to investigate allegations of sexual harassment: *Bracebridge Engineering Co. v. Darby* [1990] IRLR 3, EAT.

discrimination,[382] in *Porcelli v. Strathclyde Regional Council*[383] the First Division held that sexual harassment is a particularly degrading and unacceptable form of sex discrimination which it must have been the intention of Parliament to restrain.[384] However, as in any complaint of sexual discrimination the burden of proof is on the complainant, the industrial tribunal has to be satisfied that the harassment took the form of less favourable treatment on the grounds of the victim's sex.[385] Whether there has been less favourable treatment is a question for the industrial tribunal as the "industrial jury" guided by *Porcelli* and the European Commission's Recommendation on the Protection of the Dignity of Men and Women at Work[386] which states that "sexual harassment means unwanted conduct of a sexual nature or other conduct based on sex affecting the dignity of men and women at work ... and can include physical, verbal or non-verbal conduct".[387] Thus an "industrial jury" has lawfully rejected a woman's complaint of subjection to a detriment by (a) continuing to permit the display of nude women in her workplace when they knew that the display was offensive to her and (b) failing to deal with her complaints because it was satisfied that the employers "would have treated a man just as badly whether he was complaining about the display of nude women or nude men".[388] On the other hand a tribunal was entitled to conclude that greeting a female employee with "Hiya, big tits" was less favourable treatment on the grounds of sex because such a remark could not have been made to a man in relation, say, to a balding head or a beard.[389] Where a complaint of discrimination in the form of harassment is successful evidence as to the victim's sexual attitudes will be admissible in calculating compensation for injured feelings.[390]

It is also unlawful for any person (a) to operate a "discriminatory practice,"[391] (b) to publish or cause to be published an advertisement which indicates an intention to discriminate unlawfully unless the intended act would not in fact be unlawful,[392] (c) to instruct a person over whom he has authority, or who usually carries out his wishes, to do an act of unlawful discrimination or to procure that

---

[382] See, for example, Pannick, "Sexual Harassment and the Sex Discrimination Act", 1982 *Public Law* 42.

[383] [1986] ICR 564, IH.

[384] In response to the argument, accepted by the industrial tribunal, that a man would have been treated in the same way Lord Brand opined that the sexual harassment involved (comparing Mrs Porcelli to pictures of nude females, offering her a screw nail while asking if she would like a screw and whether she could use a piece of laboratory equipment shaped like a penis) was a "form of unfavourable treatment to which a man would not have been vulnerable" while Lord Grieve described it as "a sexual sword used against the victim because she was a woman."

[385] *Balgobin v. Tower Hamlets London Borough Council* [1987] ICR 829, EAT.

[386] OJ 1992 L 49/1.

[387] *Wadman v. Carpenter Farrer Partnership* [1993] IRLR 374, EAT. And see *Insitu Cleaning Co. Ltd v. Heads* [1995] IRLR 4, EAT to effect that as the Recommendation refers to "unwanted" conduct one incident, if serious enough, could itself amount to sexual harassment.

[388] *Stewart v. Cleveland Guest (Engineering) Ltd* [1994] IRLR 440, EAT.

[389] *Insitu Cleaning*, above.

[390] Thus in *Snowball v. Gardner Merchant Ltd* [1987] ICR 719, EAT evidence that the complainant had, allegedly, referred to her bed as a "play-pen" was admitted because of its bearing on the extent to which her feelings had been injured.

[391] SDA 1975, s. 37. A discriminatory practice is the application of a requirement or condition which results in an act of discrimination within Part II (Employment) or which would be likely to result in such an act if the persons to whom it is applied were not all of one sex (*ibid*).

[392] SDA 1975, s. 38(1), (2).

person to do such an act,[393] and (d) to pressure another person to do an act of unlawful discrimination.[394] Although legal action in respect of such forms of unlawful discrimination can be brought only by the Equal Opportunities Commission[395] and, although it has been held[396] that publishing an unlawful advertisement may also be the subject of a complaint by an individual who can show that the discriminatory advertisement falls into the category of "arrangements for the purpose of determining who should be offered employment" the decision has been criticised.[397] "Advertisement" is widely defined to include public and internal or in-house advertisements.[398] However, the publisher (for example, a newspaper) of an unlawful advertisement can escape liability if he can prove he reasonably relied on a statement that the actual act of discrimination itself would not be unlawful.[399]

Although section 41(1) of the 1975 Act provides that anything done by a person in the course of his employment shall be treated as done by his employer as well as by him, this must be seen in the context of section 6 which regulates discrimination in the employment field and provides that "[i]t is unlawful for a person, in relation to employment *by him* ... to discriminate against a woman ... ". The result is that, generally, the employee who commits an act of unlawful discrimination whether in the course of his employment or not will escape liability under Part II of the Act.[400] However, Part IV of the Act, which relates to other unlawful acts, is not confined to the employment field with the result that proceedings (by the Equal Opportunities Commission) may be taken against an individual employee. On the other hand, it is clear from section 41(1) that an act of unlawful discrimination committed by an employee in the course of his employment is treated as the act of his employer whether or not it was done with the employer's knowledge or approval, although the employer has a defence of showing that he took such steps as were reasonably practicable to prevent the employee from doing acts of such description.[401] Once it is accepted that the unlawful act was committed in the course of employment the burden of proof shifts to the employer to prove that they had taken such steps as were reasonable.[402] However, to determine whether an act is done in the course of employment the Employment Appeal Tribunal has indicated that the test to be applied is whether the unauthorised wrongful act of the employee is so connected with that which he was employed to do as to be a mode

---

[393] SDA 1975, s. 39. This would include instructing a personnel manager not to select males/females for a particular post unless the discrimination itself was lawful because, for example, the post was covered by a GOQ. And see the unreported industrial tribunal decisions in *EOC v. Jack Adams* (refusal to interview males referred by Jobcentre), *EOC v. Foulds and Riding (Synthetics)* (request that Careers Office send only female applicants for vacancies as "sorters") and *EOC v. British Car Auctions* (request that Jobcentre refers only females for a vacancy).

[394] SDA 1975, s. 40. The pressure has to take the form of offering a benefit of subjecting to a detriment but neither needs to be made directly to the person pressured.

[395] SDA 1975, ss. 37(3), 72(1).

[396] SDA 1975, s. 6(1)(a). And see *Brindley v. Tayside Health Board* [1976] IRLR 364, IT.

[397] *Cardiff Women's Aid v. Hartup* [1994] IRLR 390, EAT.

[398] SDA 1975, s. 82(1). Newspapers, radio, television, notices, signs, catalogues, pictures, models and films are all included.

[399] SDA 1975, s. 38(4). A false or misleading statement to the publisher is an offence (*ibid* s. 38(5)).

[400] *Cf Enterprise Glass Co. v. Miles* [1990] ICR 787, EAT in which the EAT made no comment on the tribunal's award of compensation against the employee.

[401] SDA 1975, s. 41(3).

[402] *Enterprise Glass Co.* above.

of doing it, with the result that an employer escaped liability where one employee was subjected to (racial) insults and assaults from fellow employees.[403] However, the case was remitted to the tribunal to consider whether the employer, having become aware of the abuse, might have been personally as opposed to vicariously liable under s. 6(2)(b) for having subjected the employee to the detriment of exposing him to further abuse.

7.23 Enforcement

A person who believes he has been the victim of unlawful discrimination may present a complaint to an industrial tribunal within three months of the date of the act which forms the subject of complaint.[404] While the Equal Opportunities Commission may present a preliminary[405] complaint to an industrial tribunal,[406] generally[407] no proceedings shall be brought for unlawful discrimination except those provided by the Act itself and, although a minister of the Crown has the power to bar the hearing of a case on the grounds of national security,[408] the exercise of such a power is inconsistent with EC Directive 76/207.[409] If the industrial tribunal finds the complaint well-founded[410] it must make such of the following as it considers just and equitable: (a) an order declaring the rights of the complainant and respondent, (b) an order requiring the respondent to pay compensation,[411] and (c) a recommendation that the respondent take, within a specified time, action to obviate or reduce the effect of the discrimination on the complainant[412] but a tribunal has no power to require a respondent to pay a specific

---

[403] *Tower Boot Co. Ltd v. Jones* [1995] IRLR 529, EAT. *Cf Bracebridge Engineering Ltd v. Darby* [1990] IRLR 3 EAT.

[404] SDA 1975, ss. 63, 76(1). A complaint may be admitted outside the period if it is just and equitable and there are provisions for deeming the date of an act or omission to be extended until the end of a period (s. 76(5)). The interpretation of "employment" so as to exclude ex-employees adopted in the race discrimination case of *Post Office v. Adekeye (No. 2)* [1995] IRLR 297 is probably inconsistent with the Equal Treatment Directive: *Jepson v. The Labour Party* [1996] IRLR 116, IT.

[405] It is preliminary in the sense that it will facilitate the EOC itself taking action under s. 71 or s. 72 (application to sheriff court for interdict).

[406] SDA 1975, s. 73.

[407] There is a limited exception in respect of the Court of Session to review, reduce or suspend any order or determination (*ibid* s. 62(3). as substituted by the Race Relations Act 1976, Sch. 4, para. 2).

[408] SDA 1975, s. 52.

[409] *Johnston v. Chief Constable of the RUC* [1986] IRLR 263, ECJ. And see *von Colson and Kamann v. Land Nordrhein-Westfahlen* [1986] CMLR 430, ECJ to effect that while Dir. 76/207 leaves the matter of penalty to the Member States, it has to be of such a nature so as to have actual disuasive effect. And see note 411.

[410] A complaint may, of course, be settled by conciliation at any stage prior to the industrial tribunal determining the matter (SDA 1975, ss. 64, 77).

[411] SDA 1975, s. 65. The statutory maximum has been removed by the repeal of SDA 1975, s. 62(2) (Sex Discrimination and Equal Pay (Remedies) Regulations 1993 (SI 1993 No. 2798)). In England it is possible for exemplary damages to be awarded (*City of Bradford Metropolitan Council v. Arora* [1991] IRLR 16 CA) but they are not available for breach of the Equal Treatment Directive at the instance of an employee of an emanation of the state (*Ministry of Defence v. Meredith* [1995] IRLR 539, EAT).

[412] SDA 1975, s. 65(1)(a), (b), (c). But a tribunal does not have power to order that a victim be promoted/appointed at next suitable vacancy: *British Gas plc v. Sharma* [1991] IRLR 101, EAT.

wage to the complainant in respect of a future time.[413] However, in relation to an act of indirect discrimination originally no award of damages could be made if the respondent proved that the requirement or condition in question was not applied with the intention of treating the claimant unfavourably on the ground of his sex[414] and this was a major defect in the legislation. Thus, in *MacMillan v. Edinburgh Voluntary Organisations Council*[415] although an industrial upheld a woman's case that she had been the victim of indirect discrimination by refusing to increase her hours to full-time — a requirement which the employers had not been able to justify — which resulted in her dismissal, it was unable to award any compensation because the employers proved the requirement had not been applied with the intention of treating her unfavourably; the Employment Appeal Tribunal rejected the argument that the domestic statutory provisions could be interpreted in such a way as to give effect to the Equal Treatment Directive[416] which requires that victims of sexual discrimination be provided with an effective and adequate judicial remedy because the domestic provisions were clear and unambiguous. Of course, had the employer been an emanation of the state the employee would have been able to rely on the Directive irrespective of domestic law.[417] However, whether an employer could prove that the requirement was not applied with the intention of treating the employee unfavourably depended on the intention with which the requirement was applied rather than the more generalised question relating to the introduction of the requirement so that an industrial tribunal could infer that a requirement, which was applied with the knowledge of its unfavourable consequences for a woman, was applied with the intention to produce those consequences.[418] The position has been altered with regard to acts of discrimination committed on or after March 25, 1996, so that if the employer proves the requirement or condition was not applied with the intention of treating the employee unfavourably, a tribunal may now award compensation if it is just and equitable to do so.[418a]

7.24 The Equal Opportunities Commission

The Equal Opportunities Commission (EOC) was established by the Sex Discrimination Act 1975 and is charged with (a) working towards the elimination of discrimination, (b) promoting equality of opportunity between men and women generally, and (c) reviewing and suggesting amendment of the Sex Discrimination Act itself and the Equal Pay Act 1970 and other statutory provisions in so far as they require men and women to be treated differently.[419]

---

[413] *Irvine v. Prestcold Ltd* [1981] IRLR 281, CA. The loss of wages is to be dealt with under s. 65(1)(b) while s. 65(1)(c) deals with, for example, ensuring the complainant has equal opportunity of participating in training etc.

[414] SDA 1975, ss. 65(1)(b), 66(3).

[415] [1995] IRLR 536, EAT.

[416] Dir. 76/207.

[417] *Tickle v. Governors of Riverview CF School and Surrey County Council*, unreported, case no. 32420/92, COIT.

[418] *London Underground Ltd v. Edwards* [1995] IRLR 355, EAT. And see in the context of racial discrimination *Hussain v. J. H. Walker Ltd, The Times* November 13, 1995.

[418a] Sex Discrimination and Equal Pay (Miscellaneous Amendments) Regulations 1996 (SI 1996 No. 438).

[419] SDA 1975, ss. 63(1), 55. Detailed provision for the financing, staffing and proceedings of the Commission is set out in Sch. 3.

Formal investigations

The EOC is empowered, on prescribed terms of reference, to conduct formal investigations for the purpose of carrying out any of its duties.[420] The investigation may be general or in respect of named persons. However, an investigation in respect of named persons must be preceded by a belief, which has to be based on sufficient evidence, that these persons are committing acts which are unlawful by virtue of the Sex Discrimination Act 1975 or the Equal Pay Act 1970.[421] Subject to certain limits,[422] for the purpose of a formal investigation the Commission may serve a notice requiring the production of written information and attendance of any person to give oral information and produce documents in his possession or control.[423] To enforce a notice the EOC may apply to the sheriff court[424] and it is an offence to wilfully alter, suppress, conceal or destroy a document or knowingly or recklessly to make a false statement.[425] Either during or after a formal investigation the EOC may make recommendations for changes in the policies or procedures of an employer to promote equality of opportunity or for changes in the law.[426] Any information given to the EOC for a formal investigation shall not be divulged[427] unless disclosure is (a) compelled by a court, (b) with the informant's consent, (c) in a summary which does not identify the informant or other person, (d) in a report published or available for inspection or (e) to other members of the EOC or its staff or for certain litigation to which the EOC is a party.[428]

Non-discrimination notices

Where the EOC in the course of a formal investigation, believes that certain unlawful acts[429] are being or have been committed it may, after giving the addressee at least 28 days in which to make representations, issue to the person (the addressee) believed to be committing the unlawful act a "non-discrimination notice" which requires the person not to commit any such acts, inform the EOC that any necessary changes in his practices or arrangements have been taken and take appropriate steps for informing others concerned (for example employees, employment agencies) or such changes.[430] If the notice relates to employment there

---

[420] SDA 1975, s. 58. And see the Sex Discrimination (Formal Investigations) Regulations 1975 (SI 1975 No. 1993).

[421] *In re Prestige Group plc* [1984] ICR 473, HL.

[422] These are that, unless the formal investigation follows the issue of a non-discrimination notice, (a) the notice was authorised by the Secretary of State, (b) the investigation is confined to the acts specified in s. 59(2)(b) and (c) no order regarding information or documents may be made if a similar order could not be made by the Court of Session in civil proceedings (SDA 1975, s. 59(2)).

[423] SDA 1975, s. 59(1)–(3).

[424] SDA 1975, s. 59(4), (5).

[425] SDA 1975, s. 59(6), (7).

[426] SDA 1975, s. 60(1). Unless the Secretary of State requires otherwise, the Commission's report on a formal investigation is required to be published or available for inspection (s. 60(2)–(7)).

[427] It is a criminal offence for the Commission, any Commissioner or any employee of the Commission to divulge any such information (SDA 1975, s. 61(2)).

[428] SDA 1975, s. 61(1).

[429] These are set out in s. 67(1) to be (1) an unlawful discriminatory act, (2) a contravention of ss. 37, 38, 39 or 40, and (3) breach of a term included by virtue of an equality clause.

[430] SDA 1975, s. 67(1)–(5). Where the Secretary of State can exercise the powers conferred by s. 25(2), (3) the Commission must give notice of unlawful acts to the Secretary of State.

is a right of appeal within six weeks to an industrial tribunal[431] (if the notice relates to matters which are outside the jurisdiction of the industrial tribunals the right of appeal is to the sheriff court).[432] The tribunal has a wide discretion[433] to quash a notice or direct that it be replaced by an amended notice.[434] A non-discrimination notice becomes final when an appeal is dismissed, withdrawn or abandoned or when the time for appealing expires.[435]

Orders, codes and assistance

Additional powers are conferred on the Commission to permit it to deal with persistent discrimination. Thus in the period of five years after the service of a non-discrimination notice or a finding by a tribunal or court that a person has done an unlawful discriminatory act or has breached an equality clause, the EOC may apply to the sheriff court for an order restraining such a person from doing such an unlawful act.[436] The EOC may issue codes of practice for elimination of discrimination and promotion of equality of opportunity in the field of employment;[437] such codes are admissible in evidence in proceedings before any industrial tribunal.[438] An individual may apply to the EOC for assistance for bringing proceedings under the Sex Discrimination Act 1975 and it has a wide discretion for granting assistance, which can range from giving advice to arranging legal representation.[439]

RACIAL DISCRIMINATION

7.25 Introduction and definitions

The Race Relations Act 1976 and its complementary Code of Practice[440] regulate racial discrimination in the employment field. The Act follows the same scheme as that adopted by the Sex Discrimination Act 1975 in that it embraces the concepts of direct and indirect discrimination,[441] and discrimination by way of victimisation before setting out in Part II the circumstances in which discrimination is unlawful in the context of employment (subject to the exceptions set out in Part VI), while Parts VII and VIII deal with the constitution and powers of the Commission for Racial Equality (CRE) and the provisions for enforcement respectively.

However, before dealing with these matters it is necessary to note that

---

[431] SDA 1975, s. 68(1). And see the Industrial Tribunals (Non-Discrimination Notices Appeals) (Scotland) Regulations 1977 (SI 1977 No. 1095).

[432] SDA 1975, s. 68(1)(b).

[433] *Commission for Facial Equality v. Amari Plastics Ltd* [1982] ICR 304, CA.

[434] SDA 1975, s. 68(2), (3).

[435] SDA 1975, s. 82(4); an appeal is treated as dismissed even if the tribunal directs it to be amended under s. 68(3).

[436] SDA 1975, s. 71.

[437] SDA 1975, s. 56A inserted by RRA 1976, Sch. 4. And see Code of Practice for Elimination of Discrimination etc. (1985) approved by Secretary of State.

[438] SDA 1975, s. 56A.

[439] SDA 1975, s. 75.

[440] Code of Practice for the Elimination of Racial Discrimination and the Promotion of Equality of Opportunity in Employment, prepared by the Commission for Racial Equality and approved by the Secretary of State under the Race Relations Act 1976 (hereinafter RRA), s. 47.

[441] Cross reference should be made to paras 7.15–7.18.

segregation on racial grounds is itself deemed to be less favourable treatment[442] and to mention two pivotal definitions specific to the Race Relations Act —

(a) "Racial grounds" means any of the following grounds — colour, race, nationality and citizenship or ethnic or national origins.

(b) "Racial group" means a group of persons defined by reference to colour, race, nationality or citizenship[443] or ethnic or national origins[444] and references to a previous racial group refer to any racial group into which a person falls.[445] Whether a group of persons constitutes an ethnic group was considered in *Mandla v. Dowell Lee*[446] with the word "ethnic" being construed relatively widely in a "broad, cultural/historic sense". Before a group can be regarded as an ethnic group it must regard itself, and be regarded by others, as a distinct community by virtue of certain characteristics. The essential characteristics of an ethnic group are: (1) a long shared history, or which the group is conscious as distinguishing it from other groups, and the memory of which it keeps alive; (2) a cultural tradition of its own, including family and social customs and manners often but not necessarily associated with religious observance.[447] Thus it has been accepted that Sikhs are one of a group defined by reference to ethnic origins and applying a "no turban" or a "no hats" rule has been held to set up a case based on indirect discrimination.[448] Similarly, Jews form an ethnic group;[449] and, while a notice stating "Sorry no travellers" indirectly discriminated against gypsies who were regarded as forming an ethnic group because they were a minority with a long shared history, a common geographical origin, distinctive customs or language derived from Romany and a common culture,[450] neither an ability to speak a particular language (Welsh) nor an accent defined membership of a particular ethnic group.[451] However, there may be such a close association between a racial or ethnic group and a religion that to impose on a group of workers a requirement with which members of a religion are unable to comply also results in a higher proportion of

---

[442] RRA, s. 1(2). Thus equal but separate toilet facilities would be discriminatory. *Cf Pel Ltd v. Modgill* [1980] IRLR 142, EAT where one racial group congregated in one section of the business of their own volition.

[443] On the question of nationality and citizenship see *Orphanos v. Queen Mary College* [1985] IRLR 349, HL.

[444] In *Tejani v. Superintendent Registrar for District of Peterborough* [1986] IRLR 502, CA, there was no discrimination of grounds of "national origins" where less favourable treatment was because the complainant was born abroad without any reference to any particular place or country of origin; but see the speech of Lord Fraser of Tullybelton in *Orphanos*, above.

[445] RRA, ss. 3(1), 78(1). A racial group can itself be comprised of two or more distinct racial groups (s. 3(2)) or more than one ethnic group (*London Borough of Lambeth v. CRE* [1990] IRLR 231, CA).

[446] [1983] ICR 385, HL.

[447] *Mandla*, above, *per* Lord Fraser of Tullybelton at p. 390. Other relevant but not essential characteristics are: (a) a common geographical origin, or descent from a small number of common ancestors; (b) a common language, not necessarily peculiar to the group; (c) a common literature peculiar to the group; (d) a common religion different from that of neighbouring groups or from the general community surrounding it; and (e) being a minority or being an oppressed or a dominant group within a larger community.

[448] *Mandla*, above; *Gurmit Singh Kambo v. Vaulkhard, The Times* December 7, 1984, CA.

[449] *Seide v. Gillette Industries Ltd* [1980] IRLR 427, EAT.

[450] *Commission for Racial Equality v. Dutton* [1989] IRLR 8, CA. *Cf Dawkins v. Department of Environment* [1993] IRLR 284, CA (Rastafarians); *Commission for Racial Equality v. Precision Manufacturing*, unreported, case no. 4106/91, COIT (Muslims).

[451] *Gwynedd County Council v. Jones, The Times* July 28, 1986, EAT; *Vizzini v. BBC, The Herald* October 24, 1995, IT.

one racial group in the workforce being unable to comply and this could give rise to a claim of indirect racial discrimination.[452]

7.26 Direct and indirect discrimination and victimisation

Direct discrimination occurs where one person is treated (or would be treated) less favourably than other persons on racial grounds.[453] However, it does not follow from the fact that one racial group has been treated differently that the different treatment is on racial grounds. Thus, in *Barclays Bank plc v. Kapur (No. 2)*[454] employees of East African Asian origin had not been discriminated against on racial grounds when, on taking up employment in the United Kingdom, the bank refused to credit their previous employment with banks in Africa as pensionable service but did credit the previous service of employees of European origin because the bank's reason for not crediting the East African Asians with previous service was because they had already been compensated for the loss of those pension rights while white employees engaged at the same time had not been paid compensation. Also, as with the Sex Discrimination Act 1975, when judging whether there has been less favourable treatment it is necessary that the comparison of a person of one particular racial group with a person not of that group must be such that the relevant circumstances in the one case are the same or not materially different in the other.[455] It is probably not necessary that the complainant/victim is a member of a racial group before a complaint of direct discrimination will lie. Thus, employees dismissed for refusing to carry out instructions not to admit or serve coloured customers were held to be treated less favourably on racial grounds.[456] However, although it may be an offence under the Public Order Act 1986,[457] the use of racially insulting words to describe an employee does not amount to less favourable treatment unless the person who used the words intended the employee to overhear them or knew the insulting words would be passed on to the employee.[458] An employer's motive or intentions are irrelevant so that treating a black employee less favourably by changing his employment, not because the employer is prejudiced against the employee but because he is being discriminated against by his fellow employees contrary to the employer's wishes, is nevertheless unlawful.[459]

Cases of indirect racial discrimination are dealt with in broadly the same way as cases of indirect sexual and marital status discrimination although, of course, the latter are not concerned with the notion of the "racial group". Thus indirect racial discrimination is concerned with overtly neutral employment rules or practices having an adverse effect on members of one or more particular racial groups, and occurs where one person applies to another a requirement or condition which he applies (or would apply) to persons not of the same racial group as that other

---

[452] See, for example, *Commission for Racial Equality v. Precision Manufacturing*, unreported, case no. 4106/91, COIT; and see para. 7.26.

[453] RRA, s. 1(1)(a).

[454] [1995] IRLR 87, CA.

[455] RRA 1976, s. 3(4). See *Dhatt v. McDonald's Hamburgers Ltd* [1991] ICR 226, CA.

[456] *Zarczynska v. Levy* [1978] IRLR 532, EAT; *Showboat Entertainment Centre Ltd v. Ownes* [1984] IRLR 7, EAT. Similarly a white woman refused a job because her husband was West Indian has had her complaint heard (*Wilson v. T B Steelwork Co. Ltd* 1978, unreported, case no. 706/441, COIT).

[457] Section 18 prohibits the use of insulting or abusive words likely to stir up racial hatred.

[458] *De Souza v. Automobile Association* [1986] IRLR 103, CA.

[459] *R. v. Commission for Racial Equality, ex parte Westminster City Council* [1984] IRLR 230, QBD. And see *Din v. Carrington Viyella Ltd* [1982] IRLR 281, EAT.

person but (1) which is such that the proportion of persons of the same racial group as that other who can comply[460] with it is considerably smaller than the proportion of persons not of that racial group who can comply with it, (2) which he cannot show to be justifiable irrespective of the colour, race, nationality, or ethnic or national origins of the person to whom it is applied and (3) which is to the detriment of that other person because he cannot comply with it.[461]

Indirect discrimination and religion. As indicated earlier there may be such a close association between a religion and a racial group or groups as to give rise to a claim of indirect racial discrimination. For example, where an employer imposed a requirement that all workers be at work during the period of the Muslim religious festival of *Id al-Fitr* on a workforce which consisted of employees from the Indian sub-continent and from Europe it was held that the proportion of Asian workers who could comply with the requirement to work over the period of *Id al-Fitr* was considerably smaller than the proportion of European workers who could comply.[462] In some cases the requirement may relate to dress,[463] hair[464] or safety equipment.[465] Of course, as with any claim of indirect discrimination, the imposition of a requirement with which a smaller proportion of a religious/racial group can comply may be justified.[466]

Justifiable. "Justifiable" means capable of being justified and is a question of fact.[467] Although it has been doubted whether the meaning of "justifiable" adopted by the Court of Appeal in *Ojutiku v. Manpower Services Commission*[468] is consistent with the meaning of justifiable in the context of sex discrimination, the House of Lords has approved[469] the Court of Appeal's analysis[470] of the judgments in *Ojutiku* that although its previous decision in that case is binding with regard to the meaning of "justifiable" that word merely connotes a value judgment, and in accordance with the judgment of Stephenson LJ in *Ojutiku* it requires an objective balance between the discriminatory effect of the requirement and the reasonable needs of the person applying it; thus there is no significant difference between that test and the one adopted by the House of Lords in *Rainey v. Greater Glasgow*

---

[460] As in the Sex Discrimination Act the words "can comply" are to mean "can in practice comply"; *Mandla v. Dowell Lee* [1983] ICR 385, HL; *Raval v. DHSS* [1985] ICR 685, EAT.

[461] RRA, s. 1(1)(b).

[462] *Azam v. J. H. Walker Ltd*, unreported, case no. 41161/92, COIT. And see *Hussain v. J. H. Walker Ltd, The Times* November 13, 1995, EAT as to whether the imposition of such a requirement may be intentional so as to give rise to compensation. *Cf Esson v. London Transport Executive* [1975] IRLR 48, IT (Seventh-day Adventist).

[463] See, for example, *Kingston and Richmond Area Health Authority v. Kaur* [1981] ICR 631, EAT and *Malik v. British Home Stores*, unreported, case no. 987/92, COIT, both cases concerning the employer's requirement that female staff wore skirts — a requirement with which fewer Pakistani women, who were required by their predominantly Muslim religion to dress modestly, could comply.

[464] *Singh v. Rowntree Mackintosh Ltd* [1979] IRLR 199, EAT; *Panesar v. Nestlé Co. Ltd* [1980] IRLR 60, EAT.

[465] *Dhanjal v. British Steel General Steels*, unreported, case no. 2692/119, COIT.

[466] See *Panesar*, above and *Dhanjal v. British Steel General Steels*, unreported, case no. 2692/119, COIT.

[467] *Per* Lord Fraser of Tullybelton in *Orphanos v. Queen Mary College* [1985] IRLR 349 at p. 353.

[468] [1982] IRLR 418, CA.

[469] *Hampson v. Department of Education and Science* [1990] IRLR 302, HL *per* Lord Lowry at p. 307.

[470] [1989] IRLR 69, CA.

Health Board[471] that to justify a material difference (in the context of equal pay) the employer has to show a real need on the part of the undertaking, objectively justified. The following requirements or conditions have been held to be justifiable in particular circumstances: (a) forbidding beards on grounds of hygiene,[472] (b) requiring that a female nurse conform with the uniform prescribed by regulations by not wearing trousers,[473] (c) requiring employees to wear protective headgear,[474] (d) requiring previous managerial experience,[475] and (e) requiring highly qualified and skilled employees to produce written reports in English promptly.[476] On the other hand the following have been held not to be justifiable: (a) a requirement that labourers complete application forms in English in their own handwriting,[477] (b) a requirement that pupils attending a Christian school did not wear a turban,[478] and (c) a requirement that students who had not been ordinarily resident in the European Community for three years pay higher fees.[479]

Requirement or condition. However, a requirement or condition has to be justifiable without regard to the racial group to which the complainant belongs.[480] Although it must make it more difficult to establish a case of indirect discrimination, it has been confirmed[481] that the decision in *Perrera v. Civil Service Commission (No. 2)*[482] to the effect that a requirement or condition means an absolute bar or a "must" has to be followed unless it can be distinguished. Accordingly a claim of indirect discrimination could not succeed where a selection criterion — the need to have previous experience of Tower Hamlets — was merely one factor taken into account in not considering a job application.[483]

Racial group. In view of the significance of the "racial group" when issues of proportionality are being considered it is important for industrial tribunals to identify clearly the racial group in respect of which the proportional inability to comply (with a requirement or condition) was to be assessed and a failure to do so is illustrated by the decision in *Tower Hamlets London Borough Council v. Qayyum*[484] in which the Employment Appeal Tribunal suggested that a complaint of indirect racial discrimination be tackled by (1) identifying the colour, race, nationality or ethnic origin of the complainant, (2) ascertaining whether there is a racial group of similar colour or nationality or ethnic origin as the complainant, (3)

---

[471] [1987] IRLR 27, HL.
[472] *Singh v. Rowntree Mackintosh Ltd*, above; *Panesar*, above.
[473] *Kingston and Richmond Area Health Authority v. Kaur* [1981] IRLR 337, EAT.
[474] *Singh v. British Rail Engineering Ltd* [1986] ICR 22, EAT. But see now the Employment Act 1989, s. 12 to the effect that a requirement that a Sikh on a construction site wear a safety helmet instead of a turban is a requirement which cannot be shown to be justifiable.
[475] *Ojutiku*, above.
[476] *Chiu v. British Aerospace plc* [1982] IRLR 56, EAT.
[477] *Isa & Rashid v. B.L. Cars* [1981] COIT 1103/125. And see the Code of Practice on racial discrimination, para. 1.13.
[478] *Mandla v. Dowell Lee* [1983] ICR 385, HL. Lord Fraser observed, however, "it might be possible for the school to show that a rule insisting on a fixed diet, which included some dish (for example pork) which some racial groups could not conscientiously eat was justifiable if the school proved the cost of providing special meals for the particular group would be prohibitive.
[479] *Orphanos v. Queen Mary College* [1985] IRLR 349, HL; but note no reference was made to s. 41(2) to effect that nothing in Parts II to IV or RRA makes unlawful discrimination on basis of length of residence in UK if done to comply with a requirement of the Crown.
[480] *Orphanos*, above.
[481] *Meer v. London Borough of Tower Hamlets* [1988] IRLR 399, CA.
[482] [1983] IRLR 166, CA.
[483] *Meer*, above; *Meikle v. Nottingham City Council*, unreported, case no. 249/92, EAT.
[484] [1987] ICR 729, EAT.

considering whether there has been imposed a requirement or condition irrespective of race, nationality or ethnic origin, and finally (4) deciding whether the proportion of the racial group (to which the complainant belongs and to which the requirement or condition applies) is considerably smaller than the relevant comparable proportion of the indigenous population.[485]

Victimisation. Like the Sex Discrimination Act 1975[486] the Race Relations Act 1976 contains a provision[487] whose purpose is to ensure that victims of racial discrimination shall not be deterred from raising proceedings under the Race Relations Act. Thus it is provided[488] that a person (the discriminator) discriminates — though not on racial grounds[489] — against another if he treats that other person (the victim) less favourably than he treats or would treat other persons and does so because the victim has or will do any of the following: (a) brought proceedings under the Race Relations Act,[490] (b) given evidence or information in connection with proceedings[491] under the Act, (c) otherwise done anything under or by reference to the Act,[492] or (d) alleged in good faith that someone has contravened the Act.[493] The correct approach is to compare the treatment accorded to the victim with the treatment the discriminator has applied or would apply to persons who have not done an act in paragraphs (a) to (d) above.[494] However, more importantly, the less favourable treatment must be by reason of the fact that the victim had done an act set out in one of the paragraphs (a) to (d) and the complaint will fail if the less favourable treatment would have occurred irrespective of the victim doing such an act. Thus in *Aziz v. Trinity Street Taxis Ltd*[495] the complainant, an Asian taxi operator, failed to establish discrimination by victimisation when he was expelled from an association of taxi operators after making secret tape recordings of conversations held with other members even although the existence of the tape recordings was disclosed in industrial tribunal proceedings because "the evidence [did] not establish that the fact that the recordings were made by [Aziz] by

---

[485] In practice this may often be the comparison but the position is probably correctly stated by Lord Fraser of Tullybelton in *Orphanos v. Queen Mary College*, above, p. 353 (in a case dealing with nationality), " ... consider ... the group consisting of Cypriot [the complainant's] nationality and compare it with the group consisting of persons not of Cypriot ... nationality, i.e. consisting of all persons (except Cypriots) of every nationality from Chinese to Peruvian inclusive."

[486] SDA 1975, s. 4.

[487] RRA, s. 2.

[488] *Ibid.*

[489] Discrimination on racial grounds is covered by RRA s. 1. In view of the decisions in *Zarczynska v. Levy* [1978] IRLR 532, EAT, and *Showboat Entertainment Centre Ltd v. Owens* [1984] IRLR 7, EAT could it be argued that certain discrimination by way of victimisation could also be covered by s. 1?

[490] The proceedings do not have to be brought against the discriminator.

[491] The proceedings need be neither against the discriminator nor brought by the victim.

[492] Although "under" relates to a specific statutory provision under which an act was done, "by reference to" has a much wider meaning; thus an act can be done by reference to the Race Relations Act if it is done by reference to it "in the broad sense, even though the doer does not focus his mind specifically on any provision of the Act", *per* Slade LJ, *Aziz v. Trinity Street Taxis Ltd* [1988] ICR 534 at p. 542, CA.

[493] RRA, s. 2.

[494] *Aziz*, above, overruling, on this point, *Kirby v. Manpower Services Commission* [1980] ICR 420, EAT.

[495] [1988] ICR 534, CA.

reference to the race relations legislation in any way influenced [the alleged discriminator] in expelling [Aziz] from membership''.[496]

7.27 Racial discrimination and employment

Part II of the Race Relations Act 1976 deals with discrimination in the employment field. It is unlawful for a person in relation to employment[497] by him[498] at an establishment in Great Britain[499] to discriminate[500] against another (a) in the arrangements made for offering employment,[501] (b) in the terms on which employment is offered or afforded,[502] (c) by refusing to employ a person,[503] (d) in access to promotion, transfer, training, benefits, facilities or services,[504] and (e) by dismissing or subjecting a person to some other detriment[505] and in this context "detriment" is not limited to circumstances akin to dismissal or disciplinary action but includes any situation in which a reasonable worker would or might feel disadvantaged in the circumstances and conditions in which he had therefore to work.[506] It does not have to be a different detriment from that shown in making a case of indirect discrimination[507] and is wide enough to embrace racial harassment.[508] Discrimination in relation to partnerships,[509] trade unions,[510] qualifying and vocational training bodies,[511] employment agencies[512] and public training agencies[513] is also unlawful.

---

[496] *Aziz*, above, *per* Slade L.J. at p. 548.

[497] "Employment", which by s. 16 includes the police, is defined by s. 78(1) and may include the self-employed (*Hill Samuel Investment Services Group Ltd v. Nwauzu*, unreported, case nos 582/93, 87/94, EAT) but not an ex-employee (*Post Office v. Adekeye (No. 2)*. [1995] IRLR 297, EAT).

[498] Generally, the employee who commits the act of discrimination will not be liable: see para. 7.22.

[499] For the meaning of "employment at an establishment in Great Britain" see s. 8; and note s. 9 which disapplies ss. 4 and 7 in respect of persons employed on a ship who were engaged outside Great Britain. In *Deria v. General Council of British Shipping* [1986] IRLR 108, CA, it was held that whether there is employment in Great Britain depends on what the parties intended at the date of the act complained of. And note that nothing in s. 4 applies to persons not ordinarily resident in Great Britain in connection with employment to provide training in skills which are to be exercised wholly outside Great Britain (s. 6).

[500] "Discriminate" means on racial grounds or by way of victimisation (*Cornelius v. University College of Swansea* [1987] IRLR 141, CA).

[501] RRA, s. 4(1)(a). This includes advertisements, application forms and other literature, interviews, instructions to personnel officers etc. And see Code of Practice paras. 1.5–1.14.

[502] RRA, s. 4(1)(b), (2)(a).

[503] RRA, s. 4(1)(c). *Johnson v. Timber Tailors (Midlands) Ltd* [1978] IRLR 146, IT.

[504] RRA, s. 4(2)(b). But note the partial exemption where the employer provides the services etc. to the public (s. 4(4)).

[505] RRA s. 4(2)(c).

[506] *De Souza v. Automobile Association* [1986] IRLR 103, CA. Thus referring to an employee as "the wog" would constitute subjecting her to a detriment if it was intended that she should hear the remark and she could reasonably feel disadvantaged thereby.

[507] *Home Office v. Holmes* [1984] IRLR 299, EAT.

[508] *Barclays Bank plc v. Kapur* [1989] IRLR 387, CA.

[509] RRA, s. 10.

[510] RRA, s. 11.

[511] RRA, s. 12, 13.

[512] RRA, s. 14. And see *Harrods Ltd v. Remick, The Times*, May 28, 1996, EAT (contract workers).

[513] RRA, s. 15.

7.28 Genuine occupational qualifications

However, none of the discrimination in paragraphs (a)–(e) above is unlawful if the employment is for the purposes of a private household.[514] Also akin to the Sex Discrimination Act 1975,[515] the Race Relations Act provides that discrimination within (a), (c) and (d) above is not unlawful where being a member of a particular racial group is a genuine occupational qualification (GOQ) for the job.[516] A GOQ may be used to defend an act of discrimination (a) where the job involves participation in a dramatic performance or other entertainment in a capacity for which a person of a particular racial group is required for reasons of authenticity,[517] (b) the job involves participation as an artist's or photographic model in the production of a work of art, visual image, or sequence of visual images for which a person of a particular racial group is required for reasons of authenticity,[518] (c) the job involves working in a place where food or drink is provided to, and consumed by, members of the public in a particular setting for which a person of a particular racial group is required for reasons of authenticity,[519] or (d) the holder of the job provides persons of a particular racial group with personal services promoting their welfare and those services can most effectively be provided by a person of that racial group.[520]

However, although the "provision of welfare" and "effective provision of services" are issues of fact for the industrial tribunal,[521] as a matter of principle the provisions relating to GOQs generally should be narrowly or strictly construed and the particular GOQ relating to the provision of personal services envisages circumstances where there is direct contact — mainly face to face, or where there could be susceptibility to personal, physical contact — and where language or a knowledge and understanding of cultural and religious background are of material importance.[522] Also, the particular racial group in respect of whom the personal services are to be provided by the job holder has to be clearly identified.[523]

7.29 Exceptions

In addition to the exceptions already mentioned, certain general exceptions operate in relation to employment. Thus although, generally, conferring preferential treatment on a racially disadvantages group — positive discrimination — is unlawful, an employer may encourage, by affording them access to facilities for

---

[514] RRA, s. 4(3). Note this exemption does not apply to discrimination by victimisation (s. 2) nor to discrimination against contract workers (s. 7) and the circumstances may allow an ordinary claim of unfair dismissal under ERA.

[515] SDA 1975, s. 7. And see para. 7.20.

[516] RRA, s. 5(1): but note, similar to s. 7(3), (4) of the Sex Discrimination Act 1975, s. 5(3), (4) permits the operation of a GOQ even where only part of the duties involve a GOQ but not where such duties could be done by existing employees of the relevant racial group. Thus, provided a duty is not so trivial as to be disregarded, it is not for the tribunal to evaluate the importance of the duty: *Tottenham Green Under Fives' Centre v. Marshall (No. 2)* [1991] IRLR 162, EAT.

[517] RRA, s. 5(2)(a).

[518] RRA, s. 5(2)(b).

[519] RRA, s. 5(2)(c).

[520] RRA, s. 5(2)(d).

[521] *Tottenham Green Under Fives' Centre v. Marshall* [1989] IRLR 147, EAT.

[522] *London Borough of Lambeth v. Commission for Racial Equality* [1989] IRLR 379, EAT, affirmed [1990] IRLR 231, CA; accordingly s. 5(2)(d) did not justify the Borough of Lambeth limiting two managerial jobs in their Housing Benefit department to black Afro-Caribbean or black Asian candidates because over half the tenants dealt with fell into those groups.

[523] *Tottenham Green Under Fives' Centre v. Marshall*, above.

training or otherwise, employees[524] of a particular racial group to do work which during the previous year has generally not been done by employees of that racial group.[525] However, that provision is permissive and does not require an employer to provide special facilities for an employee to allow him to qualify for a promoted post so that it is not unlawful for an employer to refuse to provide a Thai croupier with English lessons to assist him in obtaining a level of proficiency in English required to become casino manager.[526] Additionally, the exceptions in respect of (1) affording special treatment to meet the needs of a particular racial group[527] and (2) facilities for persons not ordinarily resident in Great Britain,[528] may be relevant to employers. For example, offering a training course only to employees who are members of a particular racial group which has a special need for such training would be covered by the exception (1) above.[529] Nothing in the Race Relations Act 1976 may compromise national security[530] or acts done (1) in pursuance of an enactment (or instrument made thereunder by a Minister) or Order in Council, or (2) to comply with any condition or requirement imposed by a Minister by virtue of any enactment.[531] However, the phrase ''in pursuance of'' is to be narrowly construed to avoid defeating the object of the Race Relations Act.[532] Thus refusing to employ a person who is required to, but does not, have a work permit may be defended by relying on the fact that the requirement that the person has a work permit is done in pursuance of an enactment.[533] However, while it was discriminatory to ask an Indian who, by the Immigration Act 1971, was entitled to work here without the need for a work permit for proof of his right to work in the United Kingdom when such a request was not made of EC nationals, the employee had not been treated less favourably because Parliament, by giving the right of freedom to work in the United Kingdom to British and EC citizens, had made a distinction between them and nationals of other states; the proper comparison required by section 3(4) of the Race Relations Act 1976 was between the applicant and others who were neither British nor EC citizens and, as all such others required either a

---

[524] Thus discriminatory recruitment is not permitted; see *Riyat v. London Borough of Brent*, unreported, case no. 1405/59, COIT.

[525] RRA, s. 38(1), (2). And see the complementary provisions of s. 38(3) which qualifies s. 11 (trade unions, professional organisations and employers' associations) and s. 37 (positive discrimination permitted by official training agencies).

[526] *Mecca Leisure Group Ltd v. Chatprachong, The Times*, March 5, 1993, EAT.

[527] RRA, s. 35.

[528] RRA, s. 36; and see s. 6.

[529] Note that by s. 40 the benefit of these exceptions can be obtained not just where an employer provides the training course etc. but also where he arranges for another person to do so.

[530] RRA, s. 42.

[531] RRA, s. 41(1); and see s. 41(2), discussed in *Savjani v. Inland Revenue Commissioners* [1981] QB 458, CA regarding discriminatory treatment on basis of nationality or residence in accordance with ministerial decisions. *Cf Orphanos v. Queen Mary College* [1985] IRLR 349, HL.

[532] *Hampson v. Department of Education and Science* [1990] IRLR 302 HL, disapproving, in part, *General Medical Council v. Goba* [1988] IRLR 425, EAT. According to Lord Lowry at p. 307 the fallacy of a wide construction ''can be recognised when one reflects that almost every discretionary decision such as that which is involved in the appointment, promotion and dismissal of individuals in, say, local government, the police, the National Health Service and the public sector of the teaching professions, is taken against a statutory background which imposes a duty on someone.''

[533] As to work permits see the Statement of Immigration Rules for Control of Entry (HC Papers 1972–73, nos 80, 81, as amended by Statement of Changes in Immigration Rules 1989 H.C. 388). Work permits are not required by nationals of EC member states.

work permit or indefinite leave to enter the United Kingdom, they were all treated alike by the employer's request for proof of entitlement to work here.[534]

7.30 Enforcement

Individuals who believe they have been the victims of unlawful racial discrimination enforce their rights by presenting a complaint to an industrial tribunal within three months[535] of the alleged discriminatory act taking place. Where a copy of such a complaint is sent to a conciliation officer he must endeavour to promote a settlement and as an alternative, but without prejudice to an eventual complaint to an industrial tribunal, an individual may request the services of a conciliation officer.[536] In the event of an industrial tribunal upholding a complaint it may make such of the following as it considers just and equitable — (a) a declaratory order, (b) an order requiring the respondent to pay to the complainant a sum of compensation, and (c) a recommendation that the respondent take action to reduce the effect on the complainant of any act of discrimination to which the complaint relates.[537] With the exception of an application for judicial review, no proceedings other than those provided by the Act may be brought in respect of an act of unlawful discrimination[538] but the amount of compensation that may be awarded by an industrial tribunal is no longer subject to a statutory maximum[539] and while no compensation may be awarded in respect of unintentional indirect discrimination,[540] compensation may include a sum in respect of injury to feelings whether or not compensation is payable for other heads of loss.[541]

7.31 The Commission for Racial Equality

The Commission for Racial Equality (CRE) was established by the Race Relations Act 1976[542] with powers and responsibilities similar to those of the EOC.[543] The duties of the CRE as (a) elimination of racial discrimination by way of victimisation, (b) promotion of equality of opportunity and good relations between persons of different racial groups,[544] and (c) to review the working of the Race Relations Act and prepare proposals for amending it[545] and, to perform these, it has the following powers — (a) the preparation and issue of codes of practice in the

---

[534] *Dhatt v. McDonald's Hamburgers Ltd* [1991] ICR 226, CA.

[535] RRA, ss. 54, 68. But note the distinction between a ''deliberate omission'' (s. 68(7)(c)) and an ''act extending over a period'' (s. 68(7)(b)) for calculating the time limit: *Barclays Bank plc v. Kapur* [1991] IRLR 136, HL. And see *Adekeye v. Post Office* [1993] ICR 464, EAT.

[536] RRA, s. 55.

[537] RRA, s. 56(1). But see *British Gas plc v. Sharma* [1991] IRLR 101, EAT.

[538] RRA, s. 53(1), (2).

[539] Race Relations (Remedies) Act 1994; Race Relations (Interest on Awards) Regulations 1994 (SI 1994 No. 1748).

[540] RRA, ss. 56(1)(b), 57(3). But see *Hussain v. J. H. Walker Ltd, The Times* November 13, 1995, EAT. *Cf* the position regarding indirect sexual discrimination: see para. 7.23.

[541] RRA, ss. 56(1)(b), 57(4). *Cf Coleman v. Skyrail Oceanic Ltd* [1981] IRLR 398, CA. And see the indications on *quantum* in *Noone v. North West Thames Regional Health Authority* [1988] IRLR 195, CA.

[542] RRA, s. 43; Sch. 1.

[543] See para. 7.24.

[544] And note the duty to make reports on recommendations in the context of a formal investigation (s. 51); as to the timing and publication of reports see *Commission for Racial Equality v. Amari* [1982] IRLR 252, CA.

[545] RRA, s. 43(1).

field of employment;[546] (b) conducting formal investigations in connection with carrying out its statutory duties but before doing so the terms of reference of the investigation must be set in accordance with the appropriate statutory provisions;[547] where the CRE proposes to conduct a formal investigation into a named person it should have formed the belief, and state so in the terms of reference, that the persons named in the terms of reference might have done or might be doing unlawful acts of a kind specified in the reference;[548] and (c) issuing and enforcing non-discrimination notices, which are recorded in a public register,[549] in respect of certain discriminatory acts.[550] A person on whom a non-discrimination notice has been served may appeal against it within six weeks[551] and a notice may not be formally served without the addressee being given the opportunity of making representations of which the CRE must take account.[552] Where the CRE fears that discrimination may be persisted in it may apply to the sheriff court for an interdict to restrain further acts of unlawful discrimination[553] and proceedings in respect of certain types of unlawful discrimination are reserved to the CRE.[554] In cases where a complaint may be brought by an individual the CRE may grant assistance including (a) giving advice, (b) procuring a settlement, (c) arranging for legal advice, and (d) providing other appropriate assistance.[555]

ONUS OF PROOF

7.32 Onus of proof

In common with other legal disputes, a person who claims that another person has discriminated against him has to prove that to be the case. However, where the reason for treating a person in a particular way plays such an important part it is difficult to obtain direct evidence of discrimination; circumstantial evidence from which certain inferences may be drawn will frequently be all that is available but there has to be some evidence from which an inference can be drawn.[556] The onus of proof can be further complicated by the fact that at different stages of a complaint of discrimination the issue requiring proof will be put forward either by the complainant or the respondent. For example, once a complainant has proved

---

[546] RRA, s. 47. A draft is submitted to the Secretary of State for approval and laying before Parliament. A code is admissible evidence in industrial tribunal proceedings (s. 47(10)).

[547] RRA, ss. 48, 49.

[548] *R. v. Commission for Racial Equality v. ex parte Hillingdon London Borough Council* [1982] 3 WLR 159, HL. In *In re Prestige Group plc* [1984] 1 WLR 335, HL, it was stated the CRE must have some grounds for suspecting unlawful discrimination albeit they were no more than tenuous because at that stage they had not yet been tested.

[549] RRA, s. 61.

[550] RRA, ss. 58, 60, 62.

[551] RRA, s. 59.

[552] RRA, s. 58(5); but the process of making and considering such representations is not in the nature of a judicial hearing (*R. v. Commission for Racial Equality, ex parte Cottrell & Rothon* [1980] 1 WLR 1580, QBD).

[553] RRA, s. 62. And note the ability of the Commission to make a preliminary complaint to an industrial tribunal under s. 64(1).

[554] RRA, s. 63. The reserved provisions relate to s. 30 (instructions to discriminate), s. 31 (pressure to discriminate) and s. 29 (discriminatory advertisements). Regarding advertisements, see the equivalent provisions in the Sex Discrimination Act 1975 discussed at para. 7.22.

[555] RRA, s. 66.

[556] *Chapman v. Simon* [1994] IRLR 124, CA.

that she has been subjected to less favourable treatment on the grounds of her sex, the employer may wish to argue that the discrimination can be defended by showing there is a genuine occupational qualification for the relevant job or that an appropriate exclusion or exception is applicable. In those instances it is for the employer/respondent to prove the existence of the defence he puts forward. Similarly, where the complainant makes out a case of indirect discrimination it would be for the respondent to show the requirement or condition is justifiable. Acknowledging the difficulty of proving discrimination, courts and tribunals have frequently attempted to assist a complainant by holding that the onus of proof shifts from the complainant to the respondent and a failure by the latter to prove he did not discriminate results in a finding for the complainant.[557] However, that approach has been criticised because although an industrial tribunal can infer discrimination in the absence of a satisfactory explanation[558] it is wrong to understand *Khanna v. Ministry of Defence*[559] and *Chattopadhyay v. Headmaster of Holloway School*[560] as implying that the burden of proof is formally cast on the respondent; the burden of proof of discrimination is on the applicant, and to prove it on the balance of probabilities.[561]

A complainant's task of proving discrimination may be eased by an industrial tribunal ordering recovery or inspection of documents as might be granted by a sheriff.[562] Production of a document will be ordered if it is regarded by the tribunal chairman as relevant to the proceedings and in cases where confidential information may be involved, whether disclosure will be ordered depends on whether the tribunal chairman considers it necessary to fairly dispose of the proceedings.[563] Thus an employer has been ordered to produce a schedule showing, over the two-year period prior to the complainant's application, the number of white and non-white persons who had applied for particular posts categorised as to whether or not they had been appointed because the statistical information contained therein was relevant to the complaint.[564] However, it has been suggested that production of documents will not be ordered if such an order would be oppressive.[565]

Additionally, a person who believes he has been the victim of discrimination

---

[557] See *Moberly v. Commonwealth Hall* [1977] IRLR 176, EAT; *Wallace v. South Eastern Education and Library Board* [1980] IRLR 193, NICA; *Dornan v. Belfast City Council* [1990] IRLR 179, NICA; *Baker v. Cornwall CC* [1990] IRLR 194, CA.

[558] *Noone v. North West Thames Regional Health Authority* [1988] IRLR 195, CA.

[559] [1981] IRLR 331, EAT.

[560] [1981] IRLR 487, EAT.

[561] *London Borough of Barking v. Camara* [1988] IRLR 373, CA. This, of course, applies to proving whether discrimination has taken place but it would not affect issues in respect of which the onus is clearly placed on the employer/respondent, e.g. s. 1(1)(b)(ii) (whether a condition is justifiable). And see the analysis of the question of the burden of proof in *British Gas plc v. Sharma* [1991] IRLR 101, EAT.

[562] Industrial Tribunals (Constitution and Rules of Procedure) (Scotland) Regulations 1993 (SI 1993 No. 2688), Sch. 1, rule 4(1)(b).

[563] *Science Research Council v. Nasse* [1979] ICR 921, HL.

[564] *West Midlands Passenger Transport Executive v. Singh* [1988] IRLR 186, CA disapproving *Jalota v. I.M.I. (Kynoch) Ltd* [1979] IRLR 313, EAT. But an employer will not be ordered to prepare a document which in effect creates evidence (*Carrington v. Helix Lighting Ltd* [1990] IRLR 6, EAT).

[565] *West Midlands Passenger Transport Executive*, above, *per* Balcombe LJ at p. 189. Ordering the production of documents may be oppressive because the material might not be readily to hand and expensive to provide or because its effect will unreasonably extend the length and cost of the hearing.

may send to the alleged discriminator a statutory questionnaire.[566] The questions and any replies are admissible as evidence in tribunal or court proceedings and although the recipient is not under any legal duty to respond to the questions a tribunal or court may infer from a failure to reply or making an evasive reply the recipient committed an unlawful act.[567] Although legal aid is not available for applicants to industrial tribunals,[568] the EOC and the CRE may grant assistance in respect of complaints based on the Sex Discrimination Act 1975, the Equal Pay Act 1970 and the Race Relations Act where (1) the case raises a question of principle, (2) it is unreasonable to expect an applicant to deal with a case unaided, or (3) for any other special consideration[569]; codes of practice giving practical guidance on the avoidance and elimination of sexual and racial discrimination and the promotion of equal opportunity have been issued by the EOC and the CRE and, while a failure to observe a code does not render a person liable to proceedings, the provisions of the codes are admissible in proceedings before an industrial tribunal.[570]

AIDS, SEXUAL ORIENTATION, DISABILITY AND SPENT CONVICTIONS

7.33 As indicated earlier,[571] certain vulnerable classes of applicant and employees may derive protection from general legal principles, others from special rules.

AIDS. People who have Acquired Immune Deficiency Syndrome (AIDS) which is generally understood to be caused by the Human Immunodeficiency Virus (HIV) may be the subject of discrimination in relation to employment through fear — seldom real, often imagined — and prejudice.[572] Although no rule of law specifically protects against such discrimination[573] it is arguable that applying a policy of not employing people who suffer from AIDS or HIV could support a case of indirect sexual or racial discrimination. Thus it could be argued, at least in terms of present statistics, that such a policy disproportionately disadvantages men and would require to be justified for it to be lawful[574] Alternatively, to refuse to employ a person from an African country where the incidence of AIDS is very high could be unlawful direct racial discrimination,[575] whereas to apply a policy of not recruiting applicants who had spent many years in such countries could be seen to be indirect discrimination against their nationals and require to be justified. The

---

[566] The form of the questionnaire and of the recipient's reply have been prescribed by the Secretary of State under SDA 1975, s. 74. The Order also sets out the time limits and manner of service of the questions and replies. And see RRA, s. 65.

[567] SDA 1975, s. 74(2); RRA, s. 65(2); *Brighton Borough Council v. Richards*, unreported, case no. 431/92, EAT. And see *Carrington v. Helix Lighting Ltd*, above regarding use of second (supplementary) questionnaire.

[568] Industrial tribunals are not mentioned in the Legal Aid (Scotland) Act 1986 but the EAT is.

[569] SDA 1975, s. 75. And see RRA, s. 66 regarding equivalent powers of the CRE.

[570] SDA 1975, s. 56A; RRA, s. 47.

[571] See para. 7.1.

[572] For a detailed analysis of this area of the law see B.W. Napier, ''AIDS Sufferers at Work and the Law'' in M. Davidson, J. Earnshaw (eds), *Vulnerable Workers: Psychosocial and Legal Issues*.

[573] See ''Guide to AIDS in the Workplace'' published jointly by Department of Employment and Health and Safety Executive (1988).

[574] SDA 1975, s. 1(1)(b).

[575] RRA 1976 s. 1(1)(b).

Council of Ministers of the European Community has concluded that employees (of the EC) who are HIV positive but do not show any symptoms are to be treated as normal employees and fit for work[576] but this does not apply to an applicant who, after examination, showed symptoms of AIDS and other infections.[577] It is likely that those who are HIV positive or suffer from AIDS will derive some protection from the Disability Discrimination Act 1995.

Sexual orientation. Provided no sexual discrimination is committed it is not unlawful to refuse to employ a person because of his/her lifestyle or private morality although it has been held that a law which prohibits (male) homosexual activity constitutes an interference with a person's right to respect for his private life as guaranteed by Article 8 of the European Convention on Human Rights[578] but it is not unlawful for the Ministry of Defence to adopt a policy of administratively discharging homosexuals or lesbians[579] because that policy was not irrational at the time of discharge (1994) having been supported by both Houses of Parliament and the Ministry's professional advisers; nor was it contrary to the Equal Treatment Directive (76/207) or the European Commission's Code of Practice on the Dignity of Men and Women because that is directed to unacceptable behaviour in the workplace and not employment policy. On the other hand the European Court of Justice has held that the Directive does protect against unfavourable treatment where the discrimination arises from gender re-assignment in which case comparison is required with persons of the sex to which the victim belonged before the re-assignment.[579a]

Disability. Rather ironically, although disabled people have for some time been the subject of special statutory protection,[580] the lofty principles of the legislation were placed in proper perspective by statistics which demonstrated only token observance and by the fact that a disabled person who was refused employment in breach of these special provisions had no legal procedure or remedy which he himself could initiate, the previous policy being that prosecution of recalcitrant employers is less productive than education, advice and encouragement.[581] After considerable vacillation on the part of the government, legislation designed to remedy the plight of disabled people who were discriminated against in employment has eventually been enacted in the form of the Disability Discrimination Act 1995, although its employment provisions will not be in force until December 2, 1996. To an extent the Act follows the patterns of the Sex Discrimination Act and the Race Relations Act by first of all defining "disability", declaring when it is unlawful in the context of employment and creating a National Disability Council. However, in many respects it differs from the approach of these Acts in that (1) it protects only the disabled person and creates no legal rights for those who are not

---

[576] Conclusion of Council of Ministers (OJ 1989 C28/2).

[577] *A. v. Commission of European Communities, The Times* June 30, 1994, ECJ.

[578] *Norris v. Ireland, The Times*, October 10, 1988, ECHR.

[579] *R. v. Ministry of Defence, ex parte Smith* [1996] IRLR 100, CA.

[579a] *P. v. S. and Cornwall County Council* [1996] IRLR 347, ECJ. *Cf Smith v. Gardner Merchant* [1996] IRLR 342, EAT decided before *P. v. S. and Cornwall County Council.*

[580] Disabled Persons (Employment) Acts 1944, 1958; and see the Chronically Sick and Disabled Persons Act 1970 and the Disabled Persons Act 1981 (access to and accommodation at work) and the Companies Act 1985, s. 235 (company policy on disabled employees).

[581] See Code of Good Practice on the Employment of Disabled People (MSC, 1985); Employment and Training for People with Disabilities: Consultative Document (Department of Employment, 1990).

disabled,[582] (2) permits certain forms of direct discrimination to be "justified", and (3) confers on the National Disability Council only limited powers. However, perhaps the most striking feature of the legislation is the extent to which it requires implementation by delegated legislation, codes of practice and Ministerial "guidance".[583]

Definition

A disabled person is a person who has (or has had)[584] a physical or mental impairment which has a substantial and long-term adverse effect on his ability to carry out normal day-to-day activities.[585] While the Secretary of State may issue guidance (including the giving of examples) about matters to be taken into account for determining whether an impairment has a substantial adverse effect on day-to-day activities and has long-term effect, it is provided that the effect of an impairment is to be regarded as long term if it has lasted, or is likely to last, 12 months or the rest of the person's life and where an impairment ceases to have a substantial long-term adverse effect on day-to-day activities it is to be regarded as continuing to have that effect if that effect is likely to recur.[586]

A mental impairment includes an impairment resulting from or consisting of a mental illness only if the illness is a clinically well-recognised illness[587] while a severe disfigurement may be regarded as having an adverse effect on the ability of the person to carry out normal day-to-day activities.[588] Where as a result of a person having a progressive degenerative condition (such as cancer, multiple sclerosis, muscular dystrophy or infection by the human immunodeficiency virus) he has an impairment which has or had an effect on his normal day-to-day activities but if that effect is or was not a substantial adverse effect, it is to be taken to have a substantial adverse long-term effect if the condition is likely to have such an effect.[589]

However, an impairment only affects a person's ability to carry out normal day-to-day activities if it affects one of the following: (a) mobility, (b) manual dexterity, (c) physical co-ordination, (d) continence, (e) ability to lift, carry or otherwise move everyday objects, (f) speech, hearing or eyesight, (g) memory or ability to concentrate, learn or understand, or (h) perception of the risk of physical danger although this may be modified by delegated legislation.[590] The provision of a prosthesis or other aid (except spectacles or contact lenses) is to be ignored when assessing the effect on day-to-day activities.[591] Although the 1995 Act repeals the main provisions of the Disabled Persons (Employment) Act 1944 and the Disabled Persons (Employment) Act 1958, a person who was registered under the former

---

[582] Thus it does not prohibit discrimination on the grounds of disability but only such discrimination *against* a disabled person; the nearest equivalent is s. 3 of the SDA 1975.
[583] See in particular Code of Practice (ISBN 0-11-270954-0) and Guidance in relation to definition of disability (ISBN 0-11-270955-9).
[584] Section 2 of the DDA 1995 makes special provision for those who have had a disability by providing that the question whether a person had a disability before the Act came into force is to be decided as if the Act was in force at the relevant time; and see Sch. 2.
[585] DDA 1995, s. 1.
[586] DDA 1995, Sch. 1, para. 2.
[587] DDA 1995, Sch. 1, para. 1.
[588] DDA 1995, Sch. 1, para. 3.
[589] DDA 1995, Sch. 1, para. 8.
[590] DDA 1995, Sch. 1, para. 4.
[591] DDA 1995, Sch. 1, para. 6.

Act on January 12, 1995 and is so registered when the relevant provision[592] of the 1995 Act becomes effective (December 2, 1996) is deemed to be a disabled person for a period of three years thereafter.[593]

Employment

Echoing the provisions of the Sex Discrimination Act 1975 it is declared to be unlawful for an employer[594] to discriminate against a disabled person at the selection stage, during employment and by dismissal[595] but the Disability Discrimination Act does not embrace the notions of direct and indirect discrimination providing instead that discrimination in employment occurs where an employer, for a reason which relates to a person's disability, treats him less favourably than others to whom the reason does not apply or where an employer fails to comply with a duty to make adjustments (to the arrangements for determining who should be offered employment or the terms of employment or to the physical features of the employment premises) and he cannot show such treatment or failure to make adjustments was justified.[596] However, the duty to make such adjustments only arises where the existing arrangements or features of premises place a disabled person at a substantial disadvantage in comparison with those who are not disabled and the duty is to take such steps as are reasonable to prevent the arrangements or features having that effect.[597] The duty to adjust premises is on the employer who is the occupier of the premises but special provisions are made where the employer occupies the premises as a tenant.[598] Where a disabled person believes he is the victim of unlawful discrimination in the field of employment his remedy is by way of complaint to an industrial tribunal which can make a declaration of rights, award compensation and recommend that action be taken for the purpose of reducing or obviating the adverse effect on the complainant.[599] Where an advertisement, which may be understood as indicating that success might be determined by reference to an applicant's disability or an employer's reluctance to make adjustments, is placed by an employer a tribunal may assume the reason for not offering the job to the complainant was related to his disability.[600]

The National Disability Council and the Secretary of State

In spite of strong pressure to set up a body with the investigative and enforcement powers of the EOC and the CRE, the Disability Discrimination Act has created in the National Disability Council a body which is essentially advisory.[601] Thus it has

---

[592] DDA 1995, Sch. 1, para. 7.

[593] *Ibid.*

[594] DDA 1995, s. 7 excludes employers who have fewer than 20 employees and while that figure may be reduced by delegated legislation, it cannot be increased.

[595] DDA 1995, s. 4. Contract workers are also protected: s. 12.

[596] DDA 1995, s. 5(1), (2). And regulations may make provision as to when treatment or failure to adjust is justified (s. 5(6)).

[597] DDA 1995, s. 6(1). Section 6(3) gives certain examples of the steps an employer may reasonably be required to take including altering working hours, acquiring or modifying equipment and providing a reader or interpreter. But note the exclusion of money or benefits payable under an occupation pension scheme or arrangement for the benefit of employees (s. 6(7)). And see s. 17 regarding the duty of trustees and membership of the scheme.

[598] DDA 1995, s. 16.

[599] DDA 1995, s. 8.

[600] DDA 1995, s. 11.

[601] DDA 1995, s. 50; the advice can also include recommendations and while s. 50(3) allows the Secretary of State to confer additional functions on the NDC these may not include investigative powers: s. 50(4).

no powers — only duties to (a) advise the Secretary of State on (i) matters relevant to the elimination of discrimination against disabled persons or related to the operation of the Act and (ii) measures likely to reduce such discrimination, and (b) when requested to do so by the Secretary of State, to prepare and review codes of practice.

However, the Secretary of State may issue codes of practice containing such practical guidance as he considers appropriate with a view to (a) the elimination of discrimination in the employment field or (b) encouraging good practice in relation tot he employment of disabled persons[602] and, rather oddly it might seem, the Secretary of State is not required to consult the National Disability Council before issuing such a code of practice.[603] The Secretary of State also has the power to assist persons in bringing a complaint by formulating statutory questionnaires which are admissible in industrial tribunal proceedings and in respect of which the tribunal may draw certain inferences.[604]

Spent convictions. Although ex-offenders receive special treatment by the Rehabilitation of Officers Act 1974 in that neither a ''spent'' conviction (including a failure to disclose) nor any of its ancillary circumstances is a ''proper ground'' for dismissal or exclusion from office or a profession or for prejudicing a person in employment[605] the legislation creates no special remedies for people whose rights are infringed. Thus although the dismissal of an employee because of a ''spent'' conviction cannot be used to found a fair dismissal[606] such protection comes from the ordinary law of unfair dismissal and would be of no avail to an employee who lacked the requisite period of continuous employment. Similarly it is not clear what remedy would be available to an applicant who was refused employment because he had a spent conviction no matter how ''improper'' such exclusion might be. This area of the law is currently under review and is discussed in relation to England in the White Paper ''On the Record''[607] and in relation to Scotland in the consulation document ''On the Record in Scotland''.

---

[602] DDA 1995, s. 53. And see note 583.

[603] DDA 1995, s. 54. And see s. 60 which allows the Secretary of State to appoint such persons as he thinks fit to advise and assist him with matters relating to the employment of disabled persons.

[604] DDA 1995, s. 56.

[605] Rehabilitation of Offenders Act 1974, s. 4; but see the Rehabilitation of Offenders Act 1974 (Exceptions) Order 1975, SI 1975 No. 1023.

[606] *Hendry v. Scottish Liberal Club* [1977] IRLR 5, IT and see *Torr v. British Railways Board* [1977] IRLR 184, EAT.

[607] Cm 3308.

Chapter Eight

MACHINERY FOR EMPLOYMENT DISPUTES

INTRODUCTION

8.1 This chapter will concentrate upon those agencies and institutions charged with the resolution of disputes which arise in an employment law context. There are some agencies such as the Advisory, Conciliation and Arbitration Service (ACAS) and the industrial tribunals which have been created specifically to deal with certain forms of employment law disputes in ways directed by the statutory provisions which created them. Their actual functions will be discussed in more detail later in this chapter. Equally, the Central Arbitration Committee (CAC) is the only statutory agency in labour law which has been created in order to exercise arbitration functions. Despite the creation of the above agencies which are unique to employment law, one cannot under-estimate the importance of the civil courts which also exercise a wide jurisdiction in this field. The jurisdiction of the courts is important in two senses. First, they continue to exercise a significant first instance jurisdiction in such common law matters as breach of contract[1] and delictual liability (this latter area is particularly important as regards the law of industrial conflict). Further, the whole question of judicial review is becoming an increasingly important issue for employment law.[2] The other sense in which the courts are important arises through the jurisdiction of the Inner House of the Court of Session in Scotland and the Court of Appeal in England and Wales to hear appeals from the Employment Appeal Tribunal which itself is charged with hearing appeals from the industrial tribunals and the certification officer.

INDUSTRIAL TRIBUNALS

8.2 Composition and jurisdiction

Industrial tribunals were first created by the Industrial Training Act 1964 to hear appeals from employers against their assessment for industrial training levy. The

---

[1]   Industrial tribunals now enjoy a concurrent jurisdiction with the courts for certain types of breach of contract action. Most crucially, tribunals only have jurisdiction for breach of contract complaints where the claim arises or is outstanding on the termination of employment. There is also a limit on the amount available in respect of any complaint which is £25,000. See the Industrial Tribunals Extension of Jurisdiction (Scotland) Order 1994 (SI 1994 No. 1624), effective as of July 12, 1994.

[2]   For the current law on judicial review in employment cases, see the decision of the First Division of the Court of Session in *West v. Secretary of State for Scotland* [1992] IRLR 399.

accompanying regulations[3] which established these tribunals recognised the need for a separate system of industrial tribunals for Scotland with their own personnel and administrative arrangements. This separate jurisdiction has been maintained ever since. However, the work of the industrial tribunals has changed substantially since the 1964 Act and they have acquired a wide and extensive jurisdiction to adjudicate upon a large number of employment law questions. As was noted in Chapter Five, one reason why industrial tribunals were selected as the appropriate adjudicative bodies to hear labour law complaints was because they appeared to possess the virtues of relative accessibility, informality, speed and lack of expense. To this end legal aid is not available before industrial tribunals, although an applicant may be able to use the Legal Advice and Assistance Scheme for advice on the presentation of his case and have a case supported by the Equal Opportunities Commission or the Commission for Racial Equality. One issue that will be considered in this chapter is the extent to which these virtues have been eroded over the years through the increasing volume and complexity of cases[4] and the growth of legalism which reduces the opportunities for unrepresented litigants to present effectively their own cases. Tribunals should also enjoy the confidence of both sides of industry since they are tripartite bodies consisting of a legally qualified chairman and two "wingpersons" or "lay members" (one selected from employer bodies and the other from organisations representing employees) and are independent of the Department of Education and Employment and the Department of Trade and Industry.

8.3 Membership

As has already been noted, an industrial tribunal usually consists of a chairman and two lay members. There are three panels of members for industrial tribunals in Scotland. The first panel consists of advocates or solicitors of not less than seven years' standing who are appointed by the Lord President of the Court of Session and who chair the hearings. The members of the other two panels are lay members and are appointed by the Secretary of State after consultation with such organis- ations or associations of organisations representative of employees and of employers as he sees fit.[5] There is also a President of the Industrial Tribunals (Scotland) who is also appointed by the Lord President and is an advocate or solicitor of not less than seven years' standing[6] and two regional chairmen who are appointed by the President from the panel of chairmen and who are responsible for the administration of justice by tribunals in their area.[7] The President exercises

---

[3] See the Industrial Tribunals (Scotland) Regulations 1965, SI 1965 No. 1117 as amended by SI 1967 No. 302, SI 1972 No. 638 and SI 1977 No. 1474. But see now the Industrial Tribunals (Constitution and Rules of Procedure) (Scotland) Regulations 1993 (SI 1993 No. 2688) and the Industrial Tribunals Act 1996, s. 1.

[4] This is an issue which is of concern to the Government. See the Green Paper *Resolving Employment Rights Disputes: Options for Change* (Cm 2707, December 1994) and Resolving Employment Rights Disputes: Draft Legislation for Consultation (July 1996).

[5] Industrial Tribunals (Constitution and Rules of Procedure) (Scotland) Regulations 1993 (SI 1993 No. 2688), reg. 5(1). The most obvious bodies who are consulted are, on the employer's side, the CBI, and for employed persons the TUC and STUC. Other employer associations such as the Convention of Scottish Local Authorities are also consulted. Until 1981 only the TUC and STUC were consulted as bodies of employed persons. In April 1981 the Secretary of State announced that consultations would take place with non-TUC bodies such as the Management, Professional and Staff Liasion Group. See generally Linda Dickens *et al.*, *Dismissed: A Study of Unfair Dismissal and the Industrial Tribunal System* (Oxford, 1985).

[6] 1993 Regs., reg. 3(1).

[7] 1993 Regs., reg. 6(1)

overall supervision of tribunals in Scotland though regional chairmen have responsibility over the times and places where industrial tribunals in their area sit.[8] For each hearing the President or the regional chairman must select a chairman, who is a member of the panel of chairmen,[9] and two other members, one from each of the two panels of lay members.[10] The lay members are appointed because of their knowledge and experience of industrial relations matters and they can make use of their industrial experience in order to help the tribunal reach its decision. However, the lay members cannot rely on their industrial experience to such an extent that it leads to a decision which is contrary to the plain meaning of a statutory provision.[11] All three members have the same voting rights and participate equally in the activities of the tribunal, although it is the chairman who conducts the hearing and writes and signs the decision. Decisions may be by majority. There is provision for a tribunal to hear a case in the absence of one of the lay members, with the consent of the parties.[12] In Scotland there is a President, 2 regional chairmen, 7 full-time chairmen, approximately 26 part-time chairmen and 250 lay members.[13]

8.4 Administration

The industrial tribunals in Scotland are administered by the Secretary of Tribunals and an assistant secretary. It is the Secretary who exercises many of the procedural duties associated with industrial tribunals and he is responsible for the day-to-day administration of the Scottish system. The Secretary operates from the Central Office of the Industrial Tribunals (Scotland) in Glasgow which is the administrative headquarters of the Scottish tribunals and is the place where originating applications to the tribunal should be made. There are also offices in Edinburgh, Aberdeen and Dundee where a tribunal will hear cases from those areas. When a tribunal is hearing a case there will be a clerk appointed by the Secretary of Tribunals to deal with the administrative details.

8.5 Jurisdiction

It is not intended to provide an exhaustive list of the types of complaint which are competent before industrial tribunals. For more detailed information on the rules for qualification and entitlement to each of the rights referred to below, the reader is referred to the appropriate chapter which deals with the substantive law pertaining to the relevant statutory rights. However, the following should provide some indication of the width and variety of case which a tribunal is entitled to hear. The jurisdiction of industrial tribunals includes:

(a) claims for equal terms and conditions of employment under the Equal Pay Act 1970;[14]

(b) appeals against improvement notices and prohibition notices issued under the Health and Safety at Work etc. Act 1974[15] and complaints relating to time off

---

[8]   1993 Regs., reg. 4(1) and (2).
[9]   1993 Regs., reg 7(1). The President or regional chairman can select themselves to chair a tribunal hearing.
[10] 1993 Regs., reg. 7(2).
[11] *British Coal Corporation v. Cheesbrough* [1988] IRLR 351, CA.
[12] 1993 Regs., reg. 7(3).
[13] *Industrial Tribunals in Scotland: Fact Sheet* May 1995.
[14] For the procedure for such claims see the 1993 Regs., Sch. 2 (The Industrial Tribunals Complementary Rules of Procedure (Scotland)).
[15] For the procedure for such appeals see the 1993 Regs., Sch. 4 (The Industrial Tribunals (Improvement and Prohibition Notices Appeals) Rules of Procedure (Scotland)).

work for safety representatives under the Safety Representatives and Safety Committee Regulations 1977;[16]

(c) complaints under Part II of the Sex Discrimination Act 1975 and appeals against non-discrimination notices;[17]

(d) complaints under Part II of the Race Relations Act 1976 and appeals against non-discrimination notices[18];

(e) complaints of unfair dismissal under the Employment Rights Act 1996, Part X;

(f) complaints about entitlement to redundancy payments and the amount of such payments under the Employment Rights Act 1996, Part XI;

(g) complaints of infringement of maternity rights under the Employment Rights Act 1996, Part VIII (right to maternity leave, right to return to work after childbirth) and ss. 66–68 (right not to be suspended from work on pregnancy grounds);

(h) miscellaneous employment protection rights under the Employment Rights Act 1996 (e.g. written particulars of terms and conditions of employment, guarantee payments, action short of dismissal on health and safety grounds, time off for public duties, time off for ante-natal care, and written statement of reasons for dismissal);

(i) complaints that an employer has not informed and consulted with a trade union or employee representatives under the Transfer of Undertakings (Protection of Employment) Regulations 1981;[19]

(j) complaints alleging unauthorised deductions from wages under the Employment Rights Act 1996, Part II;

(k) complaints that an employer has failed to consult with a trade union or employee representatives regarding redundancies under the Trade Union and Labour Relations (Consolidation) Act 1992;

(l) complaints alleging denial of access to employment, action short of dismissal on union membership grounds under the Trade Union and Labour Relations (Consolidation) Act 1992;

(m) complaints alleging denial of time off for trade union duties and activities under the Trade Union and Labour Relations (Consolidation) Act 1992;

(n) complaints alleging exclusion or expulsion from a trade union or unjustifiable union discipline contrary to the Trade Union and Labour Relations (Consolidation) Act 1992;

(o) claims for damages for breach of contract (Industrial Tribunals Extension of Jurisdiction (Scotland) Order 1994).

However, there can be no doubt that in terms of volume of cases the industrial tribunal's jurisdiction over unfair dismissal complaints constitutes its most important function,[20] though in the past few years complaints under the Wages Act

---

[16] SI 1977 No. 500.

[17] For the procedure for such appeals, see the 1993 Regs., Sch. 5 (The Industrial Tribunals (Non-Discrimination Notices Appeals) Rules of Procedure (Scotland)).

[18] *Ibid.*

[19] SI 1981 No. 1794.

[20] Figures supplied by the Department of Employment show that for the period April 1993–March 1994 unfair dismissal applications represented 61.4% of all applications registered. The equivalent percentage for 1992–93 was 63%. See Employment Gazette, October 1994. In Scotland, in the period from April 1994–March 1995, unfair dismissal applications were approximately 53% of all cases. In 1993–94 this was nearly 65%. See *Industrial Tribunals in Scotland: Fact Sheet*, May 1995.

1986 have been another significant feature of tribunal jurisdiction constituting about 20% of the caseload in Scotland in 1994–95.[21]

8.6 Procedure

The procedure applicable before the industrial tribunals in Scotland is regulated by the Industrial Tribunals (Constitution and Rules of Procedure) (Scotland) Regulations 1993, Schedule 1.[22] Proceedings are commenced before the tribunal by presenting to the Secretary of Tribunals an originating application in writing.[23] This application must set out the name and address of the applicant, the name and address of the person(s) against whom relief is sought and the grounds of complaint.[24] There is an appropriate form which the applicant can complete, entitled Form IT1. However, so long as the applicant provides all the necessary information in writing, any form of application will suffice.[25] Once the application has been received it is the duty of the Secretary to send a copy of it to the respondent, give every party written notice of the case number of the application and of the address to which notices and other communications to the Secretary shall be sent and send a written notice to the respondent which includes information about the means and time for entering an appearance, the consequences of failure to do so, and the right to receive a copy of the decision.[26] The Secretary must enter particulars of the originating application either within 28 days of receiving it or, if that is not practicable, as soon as reasonably practicable thereafter.[27] Where the Secretary is of the opinion that the originating application does not disclose a proper ground of complaint, he can give notice to that effect stating the reasons for his opinion and informing the applicant that his application will not be registered unless he states in writing that he wishes to proceed with it.[28] The respondent also receives a notice of appearance (Form IT3) which must be returned to the Secretary within 14 days.[29] A respondent who fails to return a completed notice within this time may lose his entitlement to take any further part in the tribunal proceedings.[30] A completed notice of appearance will contain the full name and address of the respondent, states whether or not he intends to resist the application and, if he intends to resist it, sufficient particulars to show the grounds of his defence.[31]

8.7 Conciliation

An important feature of most types of industrial tribunal application is the authority exercised by ACAS to conciliate a settlement of the dispute. These

---

[21]   See *Industrial Tribunals in Scotland: Fact Sheet*, May 1995.

[22]   SI 1993 No. 2688. There are also special rules in Sch. 2 which deal with the procedural aspects of a complaint of equal pay for work of equal value. These are discussed in Chapter Seven.

[23]   1993 Regs., Sch. 1, rule (1)(1). Where the applicant gives an address outside the UK he must specify an address within the UK to which he requires notices and documents relating to the proceedings to be sent: rule 1(1)(a).

[24]   1993 Regs., rule 1(1)(a)–(c).

[25]   *Coates v. C. J. Crispin Ltd.* [1973] ICR 413, NIRC.

[26]   1993 Regs., rule 2(1).

[27]   1993 Regs., rule 2(2). The Secretary must also indicate in cases where conciliation is competent that the services of a conciliation officer are available to the parties: rule 2(3).

[28]   1993 Regs., rule 1(2).

[29]   1993 Regs., rule 3(1).

[30]   1993 Regs., rule 3(2).

[31]   1993 Regs., rule 3(1)

conciliation powers are most important in unfair dismissal applications, in equal pay cases and in complaints alleging unlawful sex or race discrimination complaints about unauthorised deductions from wages and in claims for breach of contract.[32] Usually ACAS can expect to conciliate a settlement in around 37 per cent of applications where it has the authority to conciliate.[33] In Scotland the Secretary of Tribunals will send copies of all the relevant documents to ACAS and will notify the parties that the services of a conciliation officer are available to them.[34] A conciliation officer must endeavour to promote a settlement of the complaint if either party requests him to do so, or if he believes that there is a reasonable prospect of conciliation succeeding.[35] In an unfair dismissal complaint, the officer is first required to promote reinstatement or re-engagement of the applicant on equitable terms, and only if this fails or is not requests should he attempt to promote agreement as to the amount of compensation.[36] If the conciliation officer succeeds in achieving a settlement between the parties that settlement will be recorded on ACAS Form COT3 which is signed by the parties. A copy of the form will be sent to the Secretary of Tribunals, so that the complaint can then be dismissed by the chairman. An applicant who does sign Form COT3 cannot proceed with a complaint to an industrial tribunal based on the same facts[37] unless his agreement to settle the complaint can be vitiated in some way.[38]

8.8 Preliminary matters

There is a number of preliminary matters which can arise before a complaint actually gets to a full hearing. A tribunal has the power on the application of either party, or of its own motion, to require the other party to furnish in writing further particulars of his case.[39] Clearly a person who will be appearing before a tribunal should ensure that he has all the necessary documents for the hearing and can rely on all his witnesses agreeing to give evidence on his behalf. However, there may be occasions when necessary documents are in the possession of the other party, who should provide them when so requested. If he should fail to do so an application can be made to the tribunal for recovery and inspection of documents (including the right to take copies).[40] Equally, a party who is experiencing trouble ensuring that witnesses attend the hearing can apply to the tribunal for a witness order requiring the attendance of any person, including a party, as a witness and, where necessary, requiring that person to produce any document relating to the case.[41] A person who without reasonable excuse fails to comply with an order for recovery and inspection or a witness order can be prosecuted and on summary conviction can be fined up to level 3 on the standard scale.[42] In addition, a tribunal has the power, either on the application of either party or of its own motion, to

---

[32] See, generally, ITA 1996, s. 18.
[33] See ACAS Annual Report for 1994 at 51.
[34] 1993 Regs., Sch. 1, rule 20(7) and rule 2(3).
[35] See, for example, ITA 1996, s. 18(2).
[36] ITA 1996, s. 18(4).
[37] *Moore v. Duport Furniture Products Ltd.* [1982] ICR 84, HL.
[38] See *Hennessy v. Craigmyle & Co.* [1986] ICR 461, CA.
[39] 1993 Regs., Sch. 1, rule 4(1)(a).
[40] 1993 Regs., rule 4(1)(b). For the procedure which operates in sex and race discrimination cases where documents are claimed to be confidential, see the decision of the House of Lords in *Science Research Council v. Nasse* [1979] ICR 921.
[41] 1993 Regs., rule 4(2). The party must state his reasons for the witness order: *Dada v. Metal Box Co. Ltd* [1974] ICR 559, NIRC.
[42] ITA 1996, s. 7(4).

require the other party to furnish to the tribunal a written answer to any question if it considers that such an answer would clarify an issue likely to arise during the proceedings and that the provision of the answer before the hearing would be likely to assist the progress of the proceedings.[43] Finally, there may be occasions where it is necessary for the tribunal to convene a preliminary hearing in order to consider a question of jurisdiction. In the past, tribunals in Scotland have been exercising such a power informally. However, rule 6(1) now gives the tribunal the power, either on the application of either party or of its own motion, to determine any issue relating to the entitlement of any party to bring or contest the proceedings. Such a preliminary hearing can be conducted by a chairman sitting alone.[44] Such a power is important, for example, in an unfair dismissal case where the respondent argues that the complainant is not an employee or that he lacks the necessary period of continuous employment in order to make a competent complaint. This issue will have to be decided in the complainant's favour before the case can proceed to a full hearing.

8.9 Pre-hearing reviews

There is one further issue which can arise before a case goes to a full hearing. This concerns the possibility that there will be a preliminary hearing in order to ascertain the prospects of success for either party. At one time the procedure regulations provided for a system of pre-hearing assessment whereby a full tribunal could be required, by either party or on its own motion, at any time before the hearing to consider the contents of the complaint or the defences and any other written or oral representations.[45] This procedure was first introduced in 1980 in order to weed out hopeless or ill-founded cases. The system was not a success[46] and by the government's own admission the pre-hearing assessment system had not achieved its objective.[47] Accordingly, a consultation paper on tribunal procedure was published in May 1988 which recommended that at the pre-hearing stage either party could be required to pay a deposit of up to £150 as a condition of proceeding further. Section 20 of the Employment Act 1989 gave statutory effect to this recommendation and gave the Secretary of State increased powers to make regulations to provide for a system of pre-hearing review to be carried out by such person as may be determined by the regulations, or by the tribunal itself.

8.10 The necessary legislative sanction for such an arrangement was provided for the first time by the 1993 Regulations which replace the old system of pre-hearing assessment with pre-hearing review. Regulation 7(1) enables a tribunal at any time before the hearing of an originating application, on the application of either party or of its own motion, to conduct a pre-hearing review so as to consider:
    (a) the contents of the originating application and notice of appearance;
    (b) any representations in writing;
    (c) any oral argument advanced by either party.[48]
If upon a pre-hearing review the tribunal considers that the contentions put forward

---

[43] 1993 Regs., reg. 4(3).
[44] 1993 Regs., rule 13(8).
[45] Industrial Tribunals (Rules of Procedure) (Scotland) Regulations 1985, Sch. 1, rule 6(1) (repealed).
[46] For example, in Scotland for the period from April 1, 1990 to March 31, 1991 there were only eight pre-hearing assessments. See *Industrial Tribunals in Scotland: Fact Sheet*, May 1991.
[47] See the White Paper *Building Businesses . . . Not Barriers* (1986, Cmnd 9794).
[48] A pre-hearing review can be conducted by the chairman alone: 1993 Regs., rule 13(8).

by one of the parties have no reasonable prospect of success, it can make an order against that party requiring him to pay a deposit of an amount not exceeding £150 as a condition of being permitted to continue to take part in the proceedings.[49] However, no order can be made unless the tribunal has taken reasonable steps to ascertain the ability of the party to comply with the order.[50] Such information must also be used to determine the amount of the deposit.[51] Any such order must be recorded in summary form by the chairman and the party against whom the order has been made must be warned that if he persists in participating in the proceedings, he may have an award of expenses made against him and could lose his deposit.[52] If the party fails to pay the deposit within 21 days the tribunal must strike out the originating application or notice of appearance (or the part to which the order relates).[53] If the case proceeds to a full hearing the deposit will be refunded in full except where the tribunal finds against the party as regards the matter for which the deposit was paid and an award of expenses is made against that party.[54] A member of the tribunal which conducted the pre-hearing review cannot be a member of the tribunal at the full hearing.[55] It would seem that the system of pre-hearing review is being used in Scotland almost as infrequently as was the case with pre-hearing assessment.[56]

8.11 The hearing

If a case is to go to full hearing a notice of hearing must be sent to the parties by the Secretary of Tribunals at least 14 days before the date fixed.[57] It is the practice of the tribunals in Scotland to consider both the merits of the case and the question of remedies at the hearing, so that the parties should be in a position to lead evidence on both of these points.[58] Tribunal hearings must take place in public except where a Minister of the Crown has directed a tribunal to sit in private on grounds of national security[59] or, in certain specific circumstances, where the tribunal itself decides.[60] A party at a hearing is entitled to give evidence, to call and question witnesses, and to address the tribunal.[61] Industrial tribunals are encouraged, so far as it seems to them appropriate, to seek to avoid formality in their proceedings and they are not bound by an enactment or rule of law relating to the admissibility of evidence in proceedings before the courts.[62] A tribunal also has the statutory duty of making such enquiries of persons appearing before it and witnesses as it considers appropriate and it must conduct the hearing in such a manner as it considers most appropriate for the clarification of the issues before it and generally

---

[49] 1993 Regs., rule 7(4).
[50] 1993 Regs., rule 7(5).
[51] 1993 Regs., rule 7(5).
[52] 1993 Regs., rule 7(6).
[53] 1993 Regs., rule 7(7). There is power to extend the period for a further period not exceeding 14 days: rule 7(7)(b).
[54] 1993 Regs., rule 7(8).
[55] 1993 Regs., rule 7(9).
[56] The number of pre-hearing reviews held in Scotland between April 1994 and March 1995 was 24. Of this number 19 were at the instance of the respondent and 5 were at the instance of a tribunal chairman. Deposits were ordered in 10 cases with the value of the deposits ranging between £10 and £150. See *Industrial Tribunals in Scotland: Fact Sheet*, May 1995.
[57] *Ibid.* rule 5(2).
[58] For the position in England, see *Iggesund Converters Ltd. v. Lewis* [1984] ICR 544, EAT.
[59] 1993 Regs., rule 8(2).
[60] 1993 Regs., rule 8(3).
[61] 1993 Regs., rule 9(2).
[62] 1993 Regs., rule 9(1).

to the just handling of the proceedings. These strictures are intended to facilitate the informal and inquisitorial nature of proceedings before industrial tribunals. Despite this, recent studies have suggested that parties who present their own cases still encounter difficulties in case preparation and presentation.[63] In Scotland there are no opening statements at the hearing and witnesses are excluded until they give their evidence on oath or by affirmation.[64] If the applicant fails to appear or be represented at the hearing the tribunal may dismiss his application. Alternatively, and in any other case where a party fails to appear, the tribunal can dispose of the case in the absence of that party or adjourn the hearing to a later date.[65]

8.12 The decision, interest and expenses

As has already been noted, decisions of industrial tribunals can be unanimous or by majority with the chairman only having a second or casting vote in cases where for some reason the tribunal has been reduced to two members.[66] The decision may be given orally at the end of the hearing or reserved, but in either case must be recorded in writing and signed by the chairman.[67] The tribunal must give reasons for its decision in a document signed by the chairman and the document must also specify whether the tribunal's reasons are given in summary or extended form.[68] Formerly, decisions of industrial tribunals could be given in summary form except in equal pay, sex and race discrimination cases and certain trade union cases where the tribunal's reasons had to be recorded in full.[69] However, in Scotland it was very common for full reasons to be issued as a matter of course.[70] Under the current rules the decision of the tribunal must be given in summary form except where

(a) the proceedings involve a complaint of equal pay or sex or race discrimination,

(b) there is an oral request by one of the parties at the hearing,

(c) there is a written request by one of the parties after the hearing,[71]

(d) the tribunal considers that reasons given in summary form would not sufficiently explain the grounds of decision, in which case the reasons must be given in extended form.[72] On the other hand, tribunals must now provide more detailed information in any case where an award of compensation is made. Where compensation is awarded or the tribunal makes any other determination which requires one party to pay a sum of money (excluding expenses) to the other, the decision must contain a statement of the amount of compensation awarded, or of the sum required to be paid, followed either by a table showing how the amount or sum has been calculated or by a description of the manner in which it has been

---

[63] See, generally, Linda Dickens et al., Dismissed: A study of Unfair Dismissal and the Industrial Tribunal System (Oxford, 1985). This is an issue to which we shall return later in the chapter.

[64] 1993 Regs., Sch. 1, rule 9(4).

[65] 1993 Regs., rule 9(3).

[66] 1993 Regs., rule 10(1).

[67] 1993 Regs., rule 10(2).

[68] 1993 Regs., rule 10(3). The reasons must be sufficient to show the parties why they have won or lost: Speciality Care plc v. Pachela [1996] IRLR 248, EAT.

[69] Industrial Tribunals (Rules of Procedure) (Scotland) Regulations 1985, SI 1985 No. 17, Sch. 1, rule 9(5)(a).

[70] Anon, "Industrial Tribunals — New Rules on Procedure" (1994) Emp.L.B. 10–2, 4.

[71] A written request for extended reasons can be made either before the decision with summary reasons is sent to the parties or within 21 days of the date the decision is sent: 1993 Regs., rule 10(4)(c)(i) and (ii).

[72] 1993 Regs., Sch. 1, rule 10(4).

calculated.[73] It is now possible for interest at the rate of 15% to be levied on late payments of compensation awarded by industrial tribunals.[74]

It has always been rare for expenses to be awarded to the successful party after an industrial tribunal hearing.[75] Formerly, the basic test for the award of expenses was whether a party had acted frivolously, vexatiously or otherwise unreasonably. Now the test has been extended so that expenses can be awarded where, in the opinion of the tribunal, a party has in bringing or conducting the proceedings acted frivolously, vexatiously, abusively, disruptively, or otherwise unreasonably.[76] The current rules grant the tribunal the power to limit the amount of expenses awarded. Thus, unless the parties otherwise agree, the amount awarded can be restricted by the tribunal to a sum not exceeding £500.[77] In any other case the expenses must be taxed in accordance with the sheriff court table of fees.[78] Expenses can also be awarded in two further circumstances. First where the tribunal has postponed or adjourned the hearing on the application of a party and the other party has incurred any expenses;[79] and, second where, in an unfair dismissal complaint, an adjournment or postponement has been caused by the respondent's failure to adduce evidence on job availability and the applicant has expressed a wish to be reinstated or re-engaged which has been communicated to the respondent at least seven days before the hearing, or the proceedings arose out of the respondent's failure to permit a return to work after pregnancy or confinement.[80] There are also special rules as regards expenses where a party has been ordered to pay a deposit as a condition of continued participation in the proceedings and that party loses at the full hearing but no award of expenses is made. In such circumstances the tribunal must consider whether to award expenses against that party on the ground that he conducted the proceedings unreasonably in persisting in having his case determined by the tribunal. However, a tribunal cannot award expenses on this ground unless it has considered the reasons which led to the tribunal ordering the payment of a deposit after pre-hearing review and is of the opinion that the reasons which caused the tribunal to find against the party in its decision were substantially the same as the reasons for requiring the deposit.[81] Where expenses are awarded against a party who has been ordered to pay a deposit that deposit must be used in part or full settlement of the award of expenses.[82]

8.13 Review and appeal

Except in the case of a minor clerical error, the decision of an industrial tribunal can only be altered by review or by means of an appeal to the Employment Appeal

---

[73] 1993 Regs., rule 10(3).
[74] See Industrial Tribunals (Interest) Order 1990 (SI 1990 No. 479) which provides for interest to be applied after 42 days from the date that the decision is sent to the parties.
[75] In 1988–89 expenses were awarded by the tribunals in Britain in only 207 cases and in 1989–90 this figure was 185. See ''Industrial Tribunals — An Update'' (1991) Department of Employment Gazette 303.
[76] 1993 Regs., rule 12(1).
[77] 1993 Regs., rule 12(3)(a) and (b).
[78] 1993 Regs., rules 12(3)(c) and (6).
[79] 1993 Regs., rule 12(4).
[80] 1993 Regs., rule 12(5).
[81] 1993 Regs., rule 12(7).
[82] 1993 Regs., rule 12(8).

Tribunal. A tribunal has the power to review its own decision[83] on the following grounds:

(a) the decision was wrongly made because of an error by the tribunal staff;

(b) a party did not receive notice of the proceedings leading to the decision;

(c) the decision was made in the absence of one of the parties;

(d) new evidence has become available since the decision provided that its existence could not have been reasonably known of or foreseen;

(e) the interests of justice require such a review.[84]

An application for review may be made at the hearing or at any time until 14 days after the date when the decision is sent to the parties[85] and the original tribunal can only review a decision of its own motion if, within the same 14-day period, it has sent notice to each of the parties in summary form of the ground and reasons for the review and given them the opportunity to show cause why there should be no review.[86] If, in the opinion of the President, a regional chairman or the chairman of the tribunal, the application has no reasonable prospect of success it will be refused.[87] Otherwise a full tribunal will be convened which may confirm, vary or revoke the earlier decision.[88] The purpose of review is to enable the tribunal to reconsider its decision in the light of some procedural error or the discovery of new evidence; it is not intended as a means of providing a dissatisfied party with a second opportunity to succeed before the tribunal.[89]

8.14 Miscellaneous powers and restricted reporting orders

Subject to the Procedure Regulations, a tribunal has the power to regulate its own procedure.[90] In particular, it can:

(a) dismiss the proceedings where the applicant gives notice of withdrawal;

(b) decide the outcome on the basis of the agreed decision of the parties;

(c) consider written representations submitted less than seven days before the hearing;

(d) order to strike out or amend any originating application or notice of appearance on the grounds that it is scandalous, frivolous or vexatious;

(e) order to strike out any originating application or notice of appearance on the grounds that the manner in which the proceedings have been conducted has been scandalous, frivolous or vexatious;

(f) on the application of the respondent, or of its own motion, order an originating application to be struck out for excessive delay in proceeding with it.[91]

There are also special rules in cases involving allegations of sexual misconduct. In such cases both the tribunal and the Secretary have the power to ensure that the Register, decision, document or record of the proceedings do not contain any identifying matter which is likely to lead members of the public to identify any person affected by or alleging the commission of a sexual offence.[92] In addition, in

---

[83] Such a power can be exercised either on the application of a party or a tribunal's own motion: 1993 Regs., rule 11(1).

[84] 1993 Regs., Sch. 1, rule 11(1)(a)–(e).

[85] 1993 Regs., rule 11(4).

[86] 1993 Regs., rule 11(3).

[87] 1993 Regs., rule 11(5).

[88] 1993 Regs., rules 11(6) and 11(7).

[89] *Flint v. Eastern Electricity Board* [1975] ICR 395, QBD.

[90] 1993 Regs., rule 13(1).

[91] 1993 Regs., rule 13(2)(a)–(f).

[92] 1993 Regs., rule 13(6).

any case which involves allegations of sexual misconduct, the tribunal has the power at any time before the promulgation of its decision, either on the application of a party or of its own motion, to make a restricted reporting order.[93] No such order can be made unless each party is given the opportunity to advance oral argument at a hearing.[94] The effect of the order is to specify the persons who may not be identified and it remains in force (unless the tribunal revokes it) until the date when the decision is sent to the parties.[95] The Assistant Secretary has the duty to publicise such an order on the tribunal notice board beside the list of proceedings and on the door of the room to be used for the hearing.[96]

8.15 Likely reforms

As already indicated, the case load of industrial tribunals has increased considerably over the last few years. In Scotland, for example, in 1987/88 there were 3,684 applications to the industrial tribunals. This figure had nearly doubled to 7,216 for the year 1994/95.[97] As a result there have been attempts to simplify and streamline industrial tribunal procedure. The 1993 Regulations, for example, sought to improve the speed and accessibility of the tribunal system and were intended to modernise the law so as to make the Regulations easier to follow. In particular, they encourage tribunals to adopt a more investigatory approach and to make greater efforts to weed out hopeless cases. But concern continues to be expressed that increased case load has made it much more difficult for tribunals to provide accessible, cheap, informal and relatively speedy justice.

This is a concern which is shared by the Government and which is most clearly expressed in the Green Paper, *Resolving Employment Rights Disputes: Options for Reform*.[98] This policy document recognises that the increased workload of industrial tribunals has put at risk their original objectives. Accordingly, there are a series of proposals aimed at reducing delays and making industrial tribunals more efficient. The proposals seek to pursue three key themes: encouraging settlements in-house, strengthening the role of conciliation and encouraging voluntary arbitration, and improving tribunal procedure.

As regards the first theme, the Green Paper contemplated introducing statutory requirements that employees pursue grievances with their employer before a tribunal complaint can be made and that tribunals should take account of whether applicants have sought to resolve their dispute with the employer before applying to the tribunal. There were also suggestions that the exemption arrangements for dismissal procedures agreements in ERA, s. 110 should be promoted and that the scope for compromise agreements should be strengthened. On the second theme, the Green Paper recommended greater liaison between ACAS and the industrial tribunals. It also considered extending conciliation to redundancy cases and amending the law to make independent voluntary arbitration a binding alternative to a tribunal hearing. On the third issue, the most significant ideas were the extension of the right of tribunal chairmen to sit alone for all except discrimination

---

[93] 1993 Regs., rule 14(1).

[94] 1993 Regs., rule 14(2).

[95] 1993 Regs., rule 14(3) and (5).

[96] 1993 Regs., rule 14(3)(c).

[97] See *Industrial Tribunals in Scotland: Fact Sheet*, May 1995. The figures are for the year from 1 April to 31 March. The Department of Employment's own figures also show a steady increase in workload. In 1992–93, 53,445 cases were dealt with by industrial tribunals. In 1993–94 this had risen to 69,612 representing a percentage increase of 30%. See Employment Gazette, October 1994.

[98] Cm 2707, December 1994.

and unfair dismissal cases, granting tribunals greater powers to dismiss hopeless cases and giving them the express power to time-limit proceedings, encouraging chairmen to be more interrogative and enabling tribunals to award expenses where an applicant has unreasonably refused a respondent's offer of compensation which is larger than the tribunal award. The government has indicated its intention to introduce legislation which will implement many of the proposals in the Green Paper. Although the proposal that employees would be required to exhaust in-house procedures as a condition for applying to an industrial tribunal has been dropped and the proposal that tribunal chairmen be given extensive powers to sit alone has been modified severely, the bulk of the Green Paper proposals are likely to become law. In particular, future legislation will authorise ACAS to fund and provide a scheme for arbitiation in unfair dismissal cases, extend the scope of compromise agreements, provide for conciliation in redundancy cases, permit the appointment of legal officers for tribunals and enable them to take account of the availability of in-house appeals procedures when awarding compensation for unfair dismissal.[98a] It is likely that industrial tribunals will be renamed employment tribunals.

EMPLOYMENT APPEAL TRIBUNAL

8.16 General

The Employment Appeal Tribunal was first established in 1975[99] and continues to operate under the powers conferred upon it by the Industrial Tribunals Act 1996.[100] It is a superior court of record[101] and is a tripartite body like the industrial tribunals. It consists of a number of judges of the High Court or Court of Appeal who are nominated by the Lord Chancellor, at least one judge of the Court of Session nominated by the Lord President, and a number of other members (the appointed members) who are appointed by the Queen on the joint recommendation of the Lord Chancellor and Secretary of State.[102] The appointed members are persons who appear to the Lord Chancellor and Secretary of State to have special knowledge or experience of industrial relations, either as representatives of employers or as representatives of workers.[103] A hearing of the Employment Appeal Tribunal will be made up of a judicial member who acts as chairman and usually two, although possibly four, appointed members taken in the same proportion from each side of industry.[104] Decisions can be by majority. The Employment Appeal Tribunal has a central office in London and a Scottish office in Edinburgh although it can sit anywhere in Great Britain.[105] The members of the Employment Appeal Tribunal can also sit anywhere in Great Britain and it is not unusual for the President of the Employment Appeal Tribunal, an English judge, to sit in Edinburgh. A party may appear before the Employment Appeal Tribunal in person or be represented by counsel or by a solicitor or by a representative of a

---

[98a] Department of Trade and Industry, Resolving Employment Rights Disputes: Draft legislation for Consultation (July 1996).

[99] ERA, s. 147.

[100] ITA 1996, Part II.

[101] ITA 1996, s. 20(3).

[102] ITA 1996, s. 22(1).

[103] ITA 1996, s. 22(2).

[104] ITA 1996, s. 28(2). For examples of a tribunal of five, see *Webb v. Emo Air Cargo (UK) Ltd* [1990] IRLR 124 and *Enderby v. Frenchay Health Authority* [1991] IRLR 44.

[105] ITA 1996, s. 20(2).

trade union or employers' association or by any other person.[106] Expenses can only be awarded if, in the opinion of the Employment Appeal Tribunal, the proceedings were unnecessary, improper or vexatious, or there was unreasonable delay or other unreasonable conduct in bringing or conducting them.[107]

8.17 The principal task of the Employment Appeal Tribunal is to hear appeals on points of law from decisions of the industrial tribunals.[108] It also hears appeals on questions of law from decisions of the certification officer under the Trade Union and Labour Relations (Consolidation) Act 1992, Part I, Chapter VI (political funds)[109] and Part I, Chapter VII (union mergers)[110] and appeals on questions of law and fact from his decisions under the Trade Union and Labour Relations (Consolidation) Act 1992, s. 3 (listing of trade unions) and ss. 6 and 7 (certificates of independence).[111] The Employment Appeal Tribunal also exercises a limited originating jurisdiction to determine applications for compensation as regards the right not to be unjustifiably disciplined by a trade union[112] and the right not to be excluded or expelled from a trade union.[113] The Employment Appeal Tribunal also has the power to make a restriction of proceedings order prohibiting a person who has instituted vexations proceedings before an industrial tribunal or the Employment Appeal Tribunal instituting further proceedings before these tribunals without the leave of the Employment Appeal Tribunal.[114] There is a further right of appeal on a point of law with leave of the Employment Appeal Tribunal or Court of Session, to the Inner House of the Court of Session.[115]

8.18 Errors of law

In *Watling v. William Bird & Son (Contractors) Ltd*[116] Phillips J declared that proving an error of law on the part of the tribunal entailed the appellant establishing one or more of the following:

(a) that the tribunal misdirected itself in law, misunderstood the law or misapplied the law; or

(b) that it misunderstood the facts or misapplied the facts; or

---

[106] ITA 1996, s. 29(1).

[107] ITA 1996, s. 34(1).

[108] ITA 1996, s. 21(1). It might appear surprising that there should be two laypersons sitting on a tribunal which is hearing appeals on points of law. However, the former President of the EAT, Sir John Wood, has argued that the appointed members are essential. He argued that it is the mix of experience in industrial problems, coupled with their knowledge of industrial practice and the ways in which the law is being seen to be worked that is all important. He also saw their role as vital in cases of considerable factual complexity. See "The Employment Appeal Tribunal as it Enters the 1990s" (1990) 19 ILJ 133.

[109] TULRCA, s. 95.

[110] TULRCA, s. 104.

[111] TULRCA, s. 9.

[112] TULRCA, ss. 66 and 67(2).

[113] TULRCA, ss. 174(5) and 176(2).

[114] ITA 1996, s. 33. Such a power can only be exercised on an application by the Lord Advocate or Attorney General: s. 33(1).

[115] ITA 1996, s. 37(1), (2). In England and Wales there is a right of appeal to the Court of Appeal. The EAT in Scotland has made it clear that it is bound to follow decisions of the Court of Appeal in England in appeals from the EAT there unless the case before the EAT in Scotland relates purely to a particular aspect of Scots Law: *Brown v. Rentokil Ltd* [1992] IRLR 302, EAT.

[116] (1976) 11 ITR 70.

(c) that the decision was either perverse of that there was no evidence to justify the conclusion which was reached.

In a similar vein, Lord President Emslie declared in *Melon v. Hector Powe Ltd*[117] as follows:

"The law is clear that where it cannot be shown that the tribunal of original jurisdiction has either misdirected itself in law, entertained the wrong issue, or proceeded upon a misapprehension or misconstruction of the evidence, or taken into account matters which were irrelevant to its decision, or has reached a decision so extravagant that no reasonable tribunal properly directing itself on the law could have arrived at, then its decision is not open to successful attack. It is of no consequence that the appellate tribunal or court would itself have reached a different conclusion on the evidence."

8.19 Misdirection

Clearly, the simplest error to detect is that disclosed by head (a). This head would cover such obvious errors as a wrong construction of a statutory provision or a misapplication of its terms. The other two types of error are more difficult to classify; particularly since there has been a tendency over the last 10 years for the Employment Appeal Tribunal and the appeal courts to narrow the grounds of appeal. Indeed, since the decision of the Court of Appeal in *Sheridan v. British Telecommunications plc*[118] it is doubtful whether head (b) can still be classified as a separate ground. Here it was argued that head (b) was not a separate category and thus not a sufficient ground for appeal unless the misunderstanding or misapplication amounted to an error of law on the basis that there was no evidence to support it. This view appears to merge the second and third heads of appeal. Certainly, this was the position adopted by McCowan LJ in *Sheridan* who, when discussing the three heads, declared:

"I have no difficulty in understanding and accepting the first and third, but I am bound to say for my part I have difficulty in accepting the second as a separate category. Either the second means nothing more than the third, or it means something less. If the latter, I would respectfully doubt if it can be right since this would suggest that the EAT is entitled to allow an appeal if it takes a different view of the facts from that of the Industrial Tribunal."[119]

In similar vein, the Inner House of the Court of Session has made it clear that the weight to be attached to any evidence is a matter for the industrial tribunal and not an issue for an appellate tribunal.[120] Equally, any inference which is to be drawn from the facts is a matter to be determined exclusively by the tribunal which hears and decides those facts. The only exception would be where the tribunal draws inferences in circumstances where there are no facts from which any particular inference can properly be drawn.[121]

---

[117] [1980] IRLR 80, IH at p. 82, approved by Lord Fraser of Tullybelton on appeal to the House of Lords at [1980] IRLR 477.
[118] [1990] IRLR 27, CA.
[119] *Sheridan*, above, at p. 29.
[120] *Eclipse Blinds Ltd v. Wright* [1992] IRLR 133, IH.
[121] *Eclipse Blinds*, above.

8.20 Perversity

As far as head (c) is concerned, the traditional test for perversity is to show that no reasonable tribunal properly directing itself could, upon the facts before it, have come to the conclusion which it did.[122] It is vital that when the Employment Appeal Tribunal applies this test it ensures that it does not substitute its own views for those of the industrial tribunal. This significant factor has caused the appellate courts to take a narrow view of what amounts to a perverse decision. In *Retarded Children's Aid Society Ltd v. Day*[123] the Court of Appeal approved the statement of the Employment Appeal Tribunal that it would be a very rare case indeed for the Employment Appeal Tribunal to conclude that a tribunal had arrived at a result not tenable by any reasonable tribunal properly directed in law. Moreover, Russell LJ in the same case counselled the Employment Appeal Tribunal to avoid "searching around with a fine tooth-comb" for a point of law so as it could take a different view from that of the industrial tribunal.

This reluctance to interfere with the decisions of industrial tribunals has been a major aspect of statutory employment law. In *Spook Erection Ltd v. Thackray*,[124] for example, the Second Division reminded the Employment Appeal Tribunal that the adequacy of an employer's procedures in an unfair dismissal case is essentially a question of fact for the tribunal to decide and re-emphasised that the Employment Appeal Tribunal could only overrule the tribunal when it had moved outside the range of reasonable decisions open to a reasonable tribunal. May LJ in the Court of Appeal in *Hereford and Worcester County Council v. Neale*[125] argued that there was an instinctive element to the question of perversity when he stated that an appellate body should only reverse a tribunal's decision if it could be said "My goodness, that was certainly wrong"! However, there are clear dangers in adopting this type of approach since the appellate tribunal may very easily persuade itself that, as it certainly would not have reached the same conclusion, the industrial tribunal that did so must be "certainly wrong".[126] An appellate tribunal which is tempted to take this line commits a grievous error of law since it is likely to involve it in substituting its own views for those of the first instance tribunal. A decision of an industrial tribunal can only be characterised as perverse where it is not a permissible option. The Court of Appeal has held in *Piggott Brothers & Co Ltd v. Jackson*[127] that in order to hold that a decision is not a permissible option the Employment Appeal Tribunal will almost always have to identify a finding of fact which was unsupported by any evidence, or a clear misdirection in law by the tribunal. But this approach does not necessarily ensure that perversity is an independent ground of appeal and it has been argued that its application has caused

---

[122] See, for example, *Global Plant Ltd v. Secretary of State for Social Security* [1972] 1 QB 139 and for its application in the context of industrial tribunals see *Palmer v. Vauxhall Motors Ltd* [1977] ICR 24 where the EAT also applied the dicta of Lord Radcliffe in *Edwards v. Bairstow* [1956] AC 14 at p. 36.

[123] [1978] ICR 437. For a recent Scottish case where the EAT was held to have substituted its views for those of the tribunal see *Scottish Midland Co-operative Society v. Cullion* [1991] IRLR 261, IH.

[124] [1984] IRLR 116, IH where the Second Division applied the statement of Lord President Emslie in *Melon v. Hector Powe Ltd* [1980] IRLR 80, IH.

[125] [1986] IRLR 168, CA.

[126] See the decision of the Court of Appeal in *Piggott Brothers & Co. Ltd v. Jackson* [1991] IRLR 309, CA.

[127] [1991] IRLR 309, CA.

difficulties for the industrial members of the Employment Appeal Tribunal.[128] As a result, the Employment Appeal Tribunal has sought to claim that perversity is a free-standing basis in law on which it can interfere with the decision of an industrial tribunal.[129] In this same case the EAT went very close to returning to the *Neale* formulation of perversity when it argued that it involved a decision which was so clearly wrong that it just cannot stand.[130]

THE COURTS AND THE TRIBUNALS

8.21 Legalism

It has already been suggested in this chapter that industrial tribunals have been criticised for operating in an unnecessarily legalistic manner. Although it is arguable that the Scottish industrial tribunals have avoided some of the worst aspects of legalism in comparison with their counterparts in England and Wales, it is still the case that the industrial tribunal system has been criticised for not delivering the levels of accessibility, informality, speed and lack of expense as had been hoped. The question of legalism has been raised at two levels. First, there is the question of the complex nature of the employment laws which tribunals are required to interpret and apply. Second, it has been argued that the physical arrangements for hearings, the tribunal procedure itself and the requirement that tribunals rely upon the adversarial system all contribute towards an atmosphere which inhibits parties (and applicants, in particular) from arguing their own cases.[131] ACAS has also been concerned about the growth of legal representation before industrial tribunals. The Annual Report for 1989, for example, declared "1989 saw mounting concern about the nature of proceedings in some industrial tribunal jurisdictions and the expenses often incurred by the parties in bringing and defending cases. In part this derived from the apparently irreversible increase in the use of legal representation in many jurisdictions, which was a feature of the decade as a whole; and which undoubtedly led to an increase in the time taken to clear applications".[132] Since this time there is evidence to support the view that

---

[128] See the decision of the EAT in *East Berkshire Health Authority v. Matadeen* [1992] IRLR 336, EAT.

[129] *Matadeen*, above.

[130] *Matadeen*, above. The EAT also supported a number of other formulations of perversity in *Matadeen* such as a conclusion which offends reason or is one to which no industrial tribunal could come or that it is a decision which was so outrageous in its defiance of logic or of accepted standards of industrial relations that no sensible person who had applied his mind to the question and with the necessary experience could have arrived at. It is noticeable that Wood J was keen to involve the lay members in this formulation. Indeed, Wood J sought to argue that the "not a permissible option" test should be applied where the members of the EAT were satisfied of this on the basis of their own experience and sound industrial practice.

[131] These points are discussed in much more detail in Linda Dickens *et al., Dismissed: A Study of Unfair Dismissal and the Industrial Tribunal System* (Oxford, 1985); the Justice *Report on Industrial Tribunals* (1987), and Hazel Genn and Yvette Genn, *The Effectiveness of Representation at Tribunals: A Report to the Lord Chancellor* (1989).

[132] ACAS Annual Report for 1989 at p. 17. In Scotland in 1990/91, 35.0% of applicants were legally represented at industrial tribunal hearings and 56.1% of respondents had legal representation. See *Industrial Tribunals in Scotland: Fact Sheet*, May 1991.

levels of legal representation before industrial tribunals have dropped.[133] However, it is important to bear in mind that during the same period there has been a very large increase in total caseload. This has meant that the absolute numbers of both applicants and respondents with legal representation at tribunal hearings have increased even though they have fallen as a proportion of total caseload.[134] Equally, there remains a disparity in levels of legal representation as between applicants and respondents:[135] though this is offset to some extent by applicants' use of trade union representation.[136]

8.22 Issues of fact

Judges and policy-makers have been aware of these criticisms of the industrial tribunals. Attempts have been made to speed up the procedure before tribunals. For example, as has already been noted, the procedure regulations were redrafted in 1993 to permit tribunals to extend the use of summary cases in tribunal decisions and the strengthening of the system of pre-hearing scrutiny must be viewed, in part, as an attempt to reduce the burden of cases on tribunals.[137] Equally, the recent consolidation Acts have sought to make the law more accessible. As far as the judges are concerned they have responded principally to the first charge that tribunals administer an area of law which is now too complex. Their response has taken a number of different forms. First, there has been a tendency to categorise most issues as questions of fact, thus limiting the opportunities for appeal to the Employment Appeal Tribunal. This is an issue which permeates most of the statutory employment protection laws but is most noticeable as regards such questions as to whether or not an applicant is an employee,[138] whether or not an employer has acted reasonably when dismissing an employee,[139] and the meaning of justifiable in cases of indirect discrimination.[140] This determination to leave most issues to be determined by the tribunal as a finding of fact is no better illustrated than by the case law as to whether employees were dismissed while taking part in industrial action.[141] Much of the uncertainty in this area has been

---

[133] In Scotland, for example, in 1990–91, 35% of applicants had legal representation at industrial tribunals and 56.1% of respondents used lawyers. See *Industrial Tribunals in Scotland: Fact Sheet*, May 1991. In 1994–95 the figures were that 24.4% of applicants and 47.3% of respondents had legal representation. See *Industrial Tribunals in Scotland: Fact Sheet*, May 1995. A similar trend is identified in the 1994 Green Paper.

[134] See the 1994 Green Paper, at para. 6.4.

[135] As the 1994 Green Paper identifies, this disparity has widened as a result of the increasing caseload of tribunals. The absolute increase in legal representation over the period 1987–88 to 1992–93 was 13.5% for applicants and 36% for respondents: see Green Paper at para. 6.4.

[136] In Scotland in 1994–95, 14.1% of applicants were represented by trade union officials: see *Industrial Tribunals in Scotland: Fact Sheet*, May 1995.

[137] There is also a procedure in England and Wales whereby appeals to the EAT can be listed for a preliminary hearing in order to assess whether or not the appeal discloses a genuine point of law. See Practice Direction (EAT Procedure), rule 14 [1996] ICR 422. The procedure does not apply in Scotland.

[138] *O'Kelly v. Trusthouse Forte plc* [1983] ICR 728, CA; *Nethermere (St Neots) Ltd v. Taverna* [1984] ICR 612, CA. See also *Lee v. Chung* [1990] IRLR 236, PC where the Judicial Committee of the Privy Council approved the statement of the law in *O'Kelly* and declared that where the relationship is to be determined by an investigation and evaluation of the factual circumstances in which the work is performed, the question should be regarded by an appellate court as one of fact to be determined by the trial court.

[139] *Spook Erection v. Thackray* [1984] IRLR 116, IH.

[140] See, for example, *Greater Glasgow Health Board v. Carey* [1987] IRLR 484, EAT.

[141] See, for example, *Coates v. Modern Methods & Materials Ltd* [1982] ICR 763, CA; *Naylor v. Orton & Smith Ltd* [1983] IRLR 233, EAT.

fuelled by the reluctance of the EAT and the appellate courts to classify disputes over the meaning of many of the key statutory words and phrases as disclosing questions of law.

8.23 Errors of law

This tendency to classify issues as raising pure questions of fact has been taking place in tandem with another theme prevalent in appellate decisions of the last ten years, *viz*, the narrowing of the definition of an error of law. As we noted in the last section, doubts have been cast on the width of application of Phillips J's definition of an error of law in *Watling*. In many cases a potential appellant's only means of appeal is to argue that the decision is perverse. However, as was noted in *Retarded Children's Aid Society v. Day*,[142] it will be rare for the Employment Appeal Tribunal to hold that an industrial tribunal has reached a decision which is so perverse that no reasonable tribunal, properly instructed as to the relevant law, could have come to it.

8.24 Guidelines

Finally on this issue, the view that industrial tribunals should be left to reach their own decisions as industrial juries has also led in recent years to a discouragement of guideline authorities. There was a time, particularly in the early years of the Employment Appeal Tribunal, when it was prepared to give guidance to the tribunals as to how they should interpret some of the key provisions of statutory employment law. This was intended " ... to introduce into the decisions of something over 60 industrial tribunals up and down the country, dealing day after day with questions of this kind something in the nature of a uniform approach".[143] This tactic ensured that the tribunals were briefed properly on the legal issues and also brought some certainty to the law. On the other hand, it had the effect of developing a large body of case law in an area where lay people were encouraged to participate and, so it was argued, of encouraging the likelihood of appeals. The guideline approach to employment issues was criticised by the Court of Appeal in *Bailey v. BP Oil (Kent Refinery) Ltd*[144] where Lawton LJ reminded tribunals that each case must depend upon its own facts and argued that it was wrong for either the Court of Appeal or Employment Appeal Tribunal to set out guidelines, to make rules or to establish presumptions. The attack on guideline authority was supported by Waite J when he was President of the Employment Appeal Tribunal. He was concerned to prevent the growth of legalism before industrial tribunals and to create an environment where lay people could conduct their cases with the same confidence as professional representatives. In the view of Waite J, a preoccupation with guideline authority put this objective in jeopardy. He considered that "[i]t should seldom be necessary (and may sometimes even be unwise) for an industrial tribunal to frame its decisions by reference to any direction other than the express terms of the statute".[145]

8.25 Guidelines in Scotland

If anything, the Employment Appeal Tribunal in Scotland and the Court of Session have had even less respect for guideline authority. The traditions of the Scottish

---

[142] [1978] ICR 437, CA.

[143] Phillips J, "Some Notes on the Employment Appeal Tribunal" (1978) 7 ILJ 137.

[144] [1980] ICR 642, CA.

[145] *Anandarajah v. Lord Chancellor's Department* [1984] IRLR 131, EAT. See also "Lawyers and Laymen as Judges in Industry" (1986) 15 ILJ 32.

legal system with its reliance on principle rather than precedent have had an impact on the conduct of employment law cases before the industrial tribunals. Thus the question of guideline authority has been less of an issue in Scotland since there has not been the same tendency to cite a plethora of previous decisions to the tribunals. Equally, the Employment Appeal Tribunal in Scotland and the Court of Session have considered that tribunals need little guidance beyond the statutory language for the meaning of the key concepts such as fairness or reasonableness. Thus, perhaps the most well-known of the remaining guideline cases, *Williams v. Compair Maxam Ltd*,[146] which deals with the reasonableness of the employer's procedures on redundancy, has not received wholehearted backing in Scotland.[147] More recently, however, the EAT in Scotland, with Lord Coulsfield as the judicial member, has sought to ensure that tribunals articulate reasons for their decisions which are consistent with the appropriate legal tests[148] and that in the area of unfair dismissal law, for example, the House of Lords' requirements for procedural fairness as set out in *Polkey v. A. E. Dayton Services Ltd*[149] are adhered to fully.[150]

8.26 Re-emergence of guidelines?

Nonetheless, it may be that under the previous president of the Employment Appeal Tribunal, Wood J, the value of guideline authority has been reappraised. In a recent article,[151] Wood J argued that there was some virtue for the industrial tribunals to have access to what he referred to as "guidance cases". These were cases where the Employment Appeal Tribunal was not necessarily indicating how the law could properly be applied, but rather indicating industrial practice. In this regard, Wood J placed particular importance on the role of the lay members as people with experience of industrial relations and argued that their views " . . . are given with one voice, it is the expression of opinion from *both* sides of industry and to seek to eliminate these cases is, to my mind, to waste the reservoir of experience which is contained within the Employment Appeal Tribunal".[152] This has even been extended to attempting to devise a test for perversity which draws upon the industrial experience of the lay members.[153] More significantly, Wood J presided in a number of cases where the Employment Appeal Tribunal had sought to provide guidance on good practice for employers as regards dismissal procedures. In *Linfood Cash & Carry Ltd v. Thomson*,[154] for example, the Employment Appeal Tribunal provided a ten-point guide on the steps that an employer might take when dealing with allegations about an employee's conduct! He also wrote decisions of the Employment Appeal Tribunal which provide detailed guidance as to good practice for hearings in the case of dismissal for misconduct.[155]

---

[146] [1982] ICR 156, EAT.
[147] See, for example, *Buchanan v. Tilcon Ltd* [1983] IRLR 417, IH; *A Simpson & Son (Motors) v. Reid* [1983] IRLR 401, EAT; *Meikle v. McPhail (Charleston Arms)* [1983] IRLR 351, EAT.
[148] See, for example, *United Distillers v. Conlin* [1992] IRLR 503, EAT.
[149] [1987] IRLR 503, HL.
[150] See, for example, *Robertson v. Magnet Ltd (Retail Division)* [1993] IRLR 512, EAT.
[151] "The Employment Appeal Tribunal as it Enters the 1990s" (1990) 19 ILJ 133.
[152] *Ibid.* at p. 139.
[153] *East Berkshire Health Authority v. Matadeen* [1992] IRLR 336, EAT.
[154] [1989] IRLR 235. See also *Whitbread & Co. plc v. Mills* [1988] IRLR 501, EAT.
[155] See, for example, *Clark v. Civil Aviation Authority* [1991] IRLR 412, EAT.

ACAS

8.27 Although ACAS came into operation in 1974 its constitution and powers are regulated by statute.[156] ACAS has the general duty of promoting the improvement of industrial relations and, in particular, by exercising its functions in relation to trade disputes.[157] It is directed by a council which consists of a full-time chairman and eleven other members appointed by the Secretary of State. The ACAS Council conforms to the traditional tripartite arrangements for British industrial relations bodies since of the eleven other members four have been selected from organisations representing employers, and four from trade unions. The other members are independent people such as academics. ACAS cannot be subject to directions from any minister as to the way it exercises its functions and has the authority to appoint its own staff subject to the consent of the Secretary of State as to numbers.[158] It has a head office in London and a regional office for Scotland in Glasgow. There is also a Welsh regional office in Cardiff and seven regional areas in England. ACAS is required to make an annual report on its activities and those of the CAC to the Secretary of State, which will be laid before Parliament and published.[159]

8.28 Conciliation — general

ACAS exercises conciliation functions in relation to collective labour disputes and also provides conciliation facilities for a wide range of industrial tribunal complaints. As regards collective conciliation, where a trade dispute exists or is apprehended ACAS may, at the request of one of the parties to the dispute or of its own volition, offer its assistance to the parties with a view to bringing about a settlement.[160] This assistance will be by conciliation or by other means, and may include the appointment of a person from outside the service to settle the dispute.[161] ACAS is also directed when exercising its collective conciliation functions to have regard to the desirability of encouraging the parties to use any appropriate agreed procedures for negotiation or settlement of disputes.[162] It is clear that use of these facilities is voluntary. This means that ACAS does not normally intervene in a collective dispute until any agreed procedures for direct negotiations have been exhausted. In recent years resort to ACAS conciliation services has often been written into procedures by the voluntary agreement of the parties as an optional or mandatory final stage for the settlement of disputes.[163]

8.29 Conciliation and industrial tribunals

ACAS also has a duty to conciliate in complaints presented to industrial tribunals alleging unfair dismissal, breaches of statutory employment protection rights (but not redundancy payments),[163a] breaches of the equal pay and sex and race discrimination legislation, breaches of the Wages Act 1986, failures to consult trade unions and employee representatives on proposed redundancies, complaints

---

[156] TULRCA, ss. 209–214 and ss. 247–258.
[157] TULRCA, s. 209.
[158] TULRCA, ss. 247(5) and 251(1) and (2).
[159] TULRCA, ss. 253 and 265.
[160] TULRCA, s. 210. ACAS still maintains a wide authority to offer conciliation facilities in trade disputes since the narrowing of the definition of a trade dispute in TULRCA, s. 244(1) for industrial action immunity does not apply to ACAS. See TULRCA, s. 218(1).
[161] TULRCA, s. 210(2).
[162] TULRCA, s. 210(3).
[163] ACAS Annual Report for 1994 at p. 27.
[163a] But see the draft Employment Rights (Dispute Resolution) Bill.

of unreasonable exclusion and expulsion from a trade union, unjustifiable union disciplinary action and refusal of employment on grounds related to trade union membership, and claims for breach of contract.[164] In Scotland the Secretary of Tribunals sends copies of all the relevant documents to the Scottish regional office of ACAS and informs the parties of the availability of ACAS's conciliation services. A conciliation officer can endeavour to promote a settlement of a complaint without it being determined by the tribunal if, either, he is requested to do so by both the complainant and the respondent or, in the absence of such request, where the officer considers that he has a reasonable prospect of success.[165] ACAS also has the authority to conciliate in cases which have not been presented to industrial tribunals so long as the case entails a matter which could form the basis of a tribunal complaint and provided that either of the parties to the dispute has requested the services of the conciliation officer.[166] Individual conciliation not only ensures financial savings to the parties and a benefit to the public purse since tribunal time is saved, but also there is a benefit through the early resolution to the dispute without resort to a tribunal.[167] The success of the conciliation process requires that the parties and ACAS recognise the confidential nature of their discussions. Accordingly, anything communicated to a conciliation officer in connection with his conciliation functions shall not be admissible in evidence before a tribunal, except with the consent of that person.[168]

8.30 Arbitration

ACAS does not actually conduct any arbitrations. Instead, it has the authority, where a trade dispute exists or is apprehended, at the request of one or more of the parties and with the consent of all of them, to refer all or any matters to which the dispute relates for settlement by arbitration either by persons appointed by ACAS but who are neither officers nor employees of the service or by the CAC.[169] In deciding whether to refer a matter to arbitration ACAS must consider the likelihood of the dispute being settled by conciliation, and where there are appropriate agreed procedures for negotiation must not refer a matter to arbitration until these procedures have been exhausted unless there is a special reason which justifies arbitration.[170] ACAS's ability to refer a matter to arbitration depends upon the agreement of all the parties and is therefore a voluntary process so that the arbitration award is not legally binding on the parties. Nonetheless, it is the policy of ACAS, when arbitration is being sought, to ask the parties to give an unqualified undertaking that the arbiter's award will be accepted as settling the disputed issue.[171] Resort to arbitration and mediation has continued to decline in the 1990's with only 156 requests to ACAS for arbitration in 1994. Nonetheless arbitration and mediation continue to make a valuable contribution to dispute resolution across a very wide range of industries and services.[172] One particular development in the field of arbitration has been the growth of "pendulum" or "straight choice"

---

[164] See generally ITA 1996, s. 18 and TULRCA, s. 290.
[165] ITA 1996, s. 18(2).
[166] ITA 1996, s. 18(3).
[167] ACAS Annual Report for 1994 at p. 54.
[168] ITA 1996, s. 18(7).
[169] TULRCA, s. 212(1).
[170] TULRCA, s. 212(2) and (3).
[171] See generally ACAS Annual Report for 1989, ch. 3.
[172] ACAS Annual Report for 1994 at p. 47.

arbitration.[173] This system reduces the flexibility of the arbitration process by requiring the arbiter to choose one or other of the two competing propositions advanced by the parties. ACAS believes that pendulum arbitration is much better suited to non-pay issues. However, where the dispute is over pay its advantages are less clear because of its inhibiting effect upon employer/union negotiations.

8.31 Advice

ACAS has very broad powers to provide advice to employers, employers' associations, workers and trade unions, on request or of its own volition, on any matter concerned with or affecting industrial relations.[174] Such advice may include the following:

    (a) the organisation of workers or employers for collective bargaining purposes;

    (b) trade union recognition;

    (c) negotiation machinery and joint consultation;

    (d) disputes machinery and grievance procedures;

    (e) questions relating to communications between employers and workers;

    (f) facilities for trade union officials;

    (g) procedures relating to the termination of employment;

    (h) disciplinary matters;

    (i) manpower planning;

    (j) recruitment, retention, promotion and vocational training;

    (k) payment systems.

ACAS can also publish general advice on any matter concerned with industrial relations. It has used this power extensively to produce advisory booklets, handbooks and occasional papers. However, in its Annual Report for 1994, ACAS noted a significant decline in the number of advisory booklets and handbooks issued since it started to charge for this service.[175] ACAS believes that its general duty to promote the improvement of industrial relations lies at the heart of its advisory work. It has also used this function to organise workshops for small firms where good practice in employment policies and procedures is stressed.[176]

8.32 Inquiry

ACAS may, if it thinks fit, inquire into any question relating to industrial relations generally or to industrial relations in any particular industry, undertaking or part of an undertaking.[177] The findings of any such inquiry may be published.

8.33 Codes of Practice

ACAS is authorised to issue Codes of Practice containing practical guidance for the purpose of promoting the improvement of industrial relations.[178] When ACAS proposes to issue a Code it must first prepare and publish a draft of that Code and must consider any representations about the draft and may modify it accordingly.[179] Thereafter the draft will be transmitted to the Secretary of State who may

---

[173] For an analysis of the growth of pendulum arbitration in Britain, see Roy Lewis, ''Strike-free Deals and Pendulum Arbitration'' (1990) 28 BJIR 32.

[174] TULRCA, s. 213(1).

[175] See Annual Report for 1994 at pp. 59–60.

[176] *Ibid.* at p. 60.

[177] TULRCA, s. 214(1) and (2).

[178] TULRCA, s. 199(1).

[179] TULRCA, s. 200(1).

either approve of it, in which case it will be laid before both Houses of Parliament, or if he does not approve of the draft, publish details of his reason for withholding approval.[180] So long as no resolution is passed by either House negativing the draft, ACAS will issue the Code in the form of the draft and the Code will come into effect on such day as the Secretary of State by order appoints.[181] A failure on the part of any person to observe any provision of a Code of Practice does not of itself render that person liable to any proceedings; but in any proceedings before an industrial tribunal or the CAC any ACAS Code is admissible in evidence, and if any provision of the Code appears to the tribunal or the CAC to be relevant it will be taken into account.[182] Currently, ACAS has issued three Codes of Practice — on Disciplinary Practices and Procedures (1977), Disclosure of Information to Trade Unions for Collective Bargaining Purposes (1977), and on Time Off for Trade Union Duties and Activities (reissued in revised form in May 1991). In 1987 ACAS sought to revise and expand its Code of Practice on Disciplinary Procedures. However, the Secretary of State did not approve of it and so the original Code which came into force on June 20, 1977 continues to operate.[183]

8.34 As already indicated, ACAS now has the power to charge a fee for exercising its functions.[184] Such a fee can be charged when ACAS thinks it appropriate to do so.[185] However, the Secretary of State can also direct ACAS to charge fees for any function specified in the direction but only after consultation with it.[186]

CAC

8.35 The Central Arbitration Committee was formerly the Industrial Arbitration Board and before that the Industrial Court. It consists of a chairman appointed by the Secretary of State after consultation with ACAS and other members who are appointed by the Secretary of State from persons nominated by ACAS because of their experience of industrial relations.[187] The CAC's functions are performed on behalf of the Crown, but it is not subject to directions of any kind from any minister as to the manner in which it exercises those functions.[188] The CAC was intended to be an arbitration body which exercised a wide authority over a number of different statutory matters. However, the legislation of the 1980s has denuded the committee of many of its functions. Currently, it possesses the power to arbitrate in two circumstances. First, it can arbitrate where a trade dispute exists or is apprehended on a matter which has been referred to it by ACAS at the request and with the consent of all the parties.[189] Second, it can adjudicate on complaints by independent trade unions alleging failures by employers to disclose information for collective bargaining purposes.[190]

[180] TULRCA, s. 200(2) and (3).
[181] TULRCA, s. 200(4) and (5).
[182] TULRCA, s. 207(1) and (2).
[183] It should also be remembered that the Secretary of State has the power to issue Codes of Practice for certain matters: see TULRCA, s. 203. He has issued Codes on Picketing and on Trade Union Ballots on Industrial Action (revised 1991 and 1995).
[184] See, generally, TULRCA, s. 251A as inserted by TURERA, s. 44.
[185] TULRCA, s. 251A(1).
[186] TULRCA, s. 251A(2).
[187] TULRCA, s. 206(1) and (2). The CAC must include some members whose experience is as employers' representatives and others who have represented workers.
[188] TULRCA, s. 259(2).
[189] TULRCA, s. 212(1).
[190] TULRCA, s. 183.

Chapter Nine

THE LAW OF COLLECTIVE BARGAINING

INTRODUCTION

9.1 The unique feature of the system of industrial relations operative in Britain is the limited extent to which the law directly regulates collective bargaining between employers and trade unions. In the past the attitude of the State has been to create an environment where the law provides as much support as it can towards the promotion and furtherance of collective bargaining but interferes as little as possible in the actual process. Thus, unlike the United States and Canada, for example, there has never been a legal duty upon trade unions and employers to bargain collectively in this country. The approach of the law has been to eschew any involvement in the collective bargaining process. This approach has been described by Kahn-Freund as a system of "collective laissez-faire".[1]

9.2 Voluntarism

In 1968 the Donovan Commission Report considered that the distinctive feature of British industrial relations was the extent to which the state remained aloof from the process of collective bargaining in private industry.[2] However, the report identified serious problems with British collective bargaining arising from the conflict between the formal system of industry-wide bargaining and the informal system of plant-level bargaining. Yet Donovan recognised that collective bargaining had to be supported and promoted by the state since it constituted the most fair and effective means of settling terms and conditions of employment. Consequently, the commission's recommendations for reform were not based on the belief that the traditional system should be abandoned but rather on a need to ensure its voluntary reform and extension. One important recommendation consistent with this objective was that there should be a statutory agency, the Industrial Relations Commission, charged with encouraging employers and trade unions to improve their bargaining arrangements themselves without reference to external interference. Equally, further statutory supports to collective bargaining were recommended such as the authority to be given to the Industrial Relations Commission to deal with recognition disputes, the relaxation of the rules permitting the abolition of Wages Councils where it could be established that voluntary collective bargaining could operate effectively, and the extension of the authority of the industrial court (now the Central Arbitration Committee) to hear

---

[1] Otto Kahn-Freund, "Labour Law" in M. Ginsberg (ed.), *Law and Opinion in England in the Twentieth Century* at p. 224.
[2] Report of the Royal Commission on Trade Unions and Employers Associations (the Donovan Report) Cmnd 3623, at para. 39.

complaints over the refusal by an employer to observe relevant terms and conditions.[3]

9.3 Statutory intervention

The approach of the Donovan Commission, therefore, reflected the view that the voluntarist nature of British collective bargaining should not only continue but be encouraged. The Industrial Relations Act 1971, however, rejected this philosophy in favour of one which supported the improvement of collective bargaining by creating a legal framework to ensure that the parties acted in a reasonable and responsible way towards each other.[4] This legal framework was swiftly repealed by legislation passed by the incoming Labour government in 1974,[5] following which there was developed and enacted a series of statutory supports to collective bargaining along lines similar to those recommended by the Donovan Commission. Some of these were enacted as part of the government's stated preference for collective bargaining as the exclusive means for setting terms and conditions of employment at the workplace.[6] Others were enacted as part of the obligations placed upon the United Kingdom as a member of the European Economic Community.[7]

The most important statutory supports which were enacted during this period were as follows:

(a) the power of the Advisory Conciliation and Arbitration Service (ACAS) to have a request for recognition referred to it by an independent trade union and to investigate and report[8];

(b) the right of recognised independent trade unions to seek disclosure of information for the purpose of collective bargaining;[9]

(c) the duty imposed upon employers to consult with representatives of recognised independent trade unions as regards redundancies.[10]

9.4 As well as this, new and increased powers were enacted which complemented and built upon a number of existing legislative provisions encouraging the extension of collective bargaining. Legislation was introduced, for example, to extend the work of Wages Councils.[11] This not only extended the scope of Wages Councils to make orders applying to other terms and conditions apart from wages and holidays but also made provision for the creation of Statutory Joint Industrial Councils which were supposed to act as halfway houses between the regulated forum of the Wages Council and free collective bargaining.[12] Legislation enhanced the jurisdiction of the Central Arbitration Committee (CAC) by not only continu-

---

[3] See generally the Donovan Report, Chapter V.

[4] Although the Industrial Relations Act created a procedure for union recognition (IRA, ss. 45–55), it also presumed that collective agreements were legally binding (IRA, ss. 34–35). See Thomson and Engleman, *The Industrial Relations Act: A Review and Analysis* at pp. 126–7.

[5] TULRA, ss. 1 and 25.

[6] Encapsulated in statutory form by the direction to ACAS in EPA 1975, s. 1(2) to encourage the extension of collective bargaining.

[7] As we shall see, some of the present statutory supports to collective bargaining only exist because of the UK's duty to implement EC Directives.

[8] EPA 1975, ss. 11–16.

[9] EPA 1975, ss. 17–21.

[10] EPA 1975, ss. 99–107 (now TULRCA, ss. 181–185) originally based on EC Council Directive No. 75/129 (now TULRCA, ss. 188–198).

[11] See EPA 1975, ss. 89–96 and later, Wages Councils Act 1979.

[12] Wages Councils Act 1979, s. 10.

ing its existing power to hear complaints by unions that employers were observing terms and conditions of employment which were less favourable than recognised terms, but also by giving it the right to hear a wider type of complaint.[13] This operated so that in the absence of recognised terms a union could also complain that the employer was observing terms less favourable than the general level of terms and conditions in the particular trade, industry or section.[14] The CAC also had jurisdiction under the Fair Wages Resolution 1946 to arbitrate on claims that a government contractor was failing to observe terms and conditions recognised in the industry or area. It is clear from the above that the government believed that this indirect approach was the best way of extending collective bargaining.

9.5 Moreover, a number of statutory rights were also created or developed which, although applying to individual employees, only acquired true significance through the organisational strength of trade unions at the collective level.[15] Their purpose, therefore, was to protect and encourage union organisation at the workplace. The most important of the statutory rights which were created at this time and which applied to the individual employee but which really only have significance where a trade union was recognised by an employer for collective bargaining purposes, were as follows:

(a) the right not to be dismissed or to have action short of dismissal taken on the grounds of trade union membership or activities;[16]

(b) the right given to an employee who is a union official to time off with pay in order to carry out trade union duties;[17] and

(c) the right given to an employee to unpaid time off to take part in trade union activities.[18]

The legislation of this time also sought to improve and strengthen union security arrangements. The most important example of this aspect of the law concerned the provisions in the Employment Protection (Consolidation) Act 1978 on the closed shop. These authorised the creation of union membership agreements and made dismissal for non-union membership unfair only in the special circumstances of the religious objector.[19]

PRESENT LEGAL FRAMEWORK

9.6 The policy of the Conservative government which has been in power since 1979 has been to challenge the post-war consensus that collective bargaining requires the support of the State as the best way of establishing terms and conditions of employment. Instead, there has been a preference for a "lightly regulated, decentralised and flexible approach to employment and social affairs".[20] This has necessitated encouragement for a movement away from the system of national collective bargaining towards a much more localised and individual

---

[13] EPA 1975, Sch. 11, para. 1 repealing the Terms and Conditions of Employment Act 1959, s. 8. See B. Bercusson, "The New Fair Wages Policy: Schedule 11 to the Employment Protection Act" (1976) 5 ILJ 129.

[14] EPA 1975, Sch. 11, para. 2(b).

[15] Lord Wedderburn, *Worker and the Law* (3rd edn), pp. 309–310.

[16] EPCA, ss. 58 and 23–26 (now TULRCA, s. 146 and s. 151).

[17] EPCA, s. 27 (now TULRCA, s. 168).

[18] EPCA, s. 28 (now TULRCA, s. 170).

[19] TULRA, s. 30(1) and EPCA, s. 58 (now TULRCA, s. 152).

[20] See the White Paper, *People, Jobs and Opportunities* (Cm. 1810, 1992).

system. The Conservative government's approach has been to seek to reward skills and performance through a legal framework which encourages individuals to take responsibility for negotiating their own terms and conditions of employment.[21] Such an approach reflects the government's concerns about the burdens on businesses and the need for employers to devise affordable pay systems.[22] Equally, the present framework represents a movement towards a much more market-oriented system where neither the State nor even trade unions have much of a role in pay determination and fulfils the government's economic policy of deregulation of the labour market.[23] This policy has necessitated the repeal or erosion of most of the statutory supports which were in place in 1979. The power that ACAS formerly enjoyed to recommend that a union be recognised by an employer for collective bargaining purposes was repealed in 1980.[24] (There was no doubt that some of the early court decisions created difficulties for ACAS in the exercise of its functions over union recognition[25]; indeed, the chairman of ACAS was moved to argue in a letter to the then Secretary of State for Employment in 1979 that the procedures could no longer operate satisfactorily[26].) This repeal has meant that at the present moment there is no legal provision creating a regime for the compulsory recognition of trade unions in Great Britain. As was noted in Chapter Eight, while ACAS still retains some authority over union recognition questions through its statutory power to provide conciliation or other assistance to parties involved in a trade dispute,[27] few of the measures enacted by previous governments and aimed at the encouragement of collective bargaining remain on the statute book.

9.7 The role of the law

As already indicated, other priorities have underpinned much of the government's legislation of the 1980s and 1990s.[28] Some of the changes such as those prohibiting union membership or union recognition requirements in contracts[29] can be viewed as examples of a policy of legal restriction of trade unions. Other changes such as the abolition of Wages Councils in 1993[30] illustrate the government's preference for the operation of the market as a means of setting terms and conditions of employment for many employees. Even in those activities where collective bargaining continues, the government appears to have a preference for local bargaining over national collective agreements in order to avoid inflationary wage deals. Moreover, a major emphasis of the legislation since 1980 has been the need to protect the rights of the individual. Thus the Employment Acts 1980, 1982 and 1988 ensured the removal of all the previous statutory supports for the post-entry

[21] *Ibid.*
[22] See *Lifting the Burden* (Cmnd 9571, 1985) and *Building Businesses not Barriers* (Cmnd 9794, 1986).
[23] These issues are discussed in much more detail by Kenneth Miller and Mairi Steele in ''Employment Legislation: Thatcher and After'' (1993) 24 Industrial Relations Journal 224.
[24] EA 1980, s. 19.
[25] *Powley v. ACAS* [1978] ICR 123, ChD; *Grunwick Processing Laboratories Ltd v. ACAS* [1978] ICR 231, HL; *UKAPE v. ACAS* [1979] ICR 303, CA. See generally R. Simpson, ''Judicial Control of ACAS'' (1979) 8 ILJ 69.
[26] See ACAS Annual Report for 1979, Appendix C.
[27] See originally EPA 1975, s. 2 and now TULRCA, s. 210.
[28] For a more detailed analysis of these priorities, see Simon Auenbach, *Legislating for Conflict* (Oxford, 1990) and Lord Wedderburn, ''Freedom of Association and Philosophies of Labour Law'' (1989) 18 ILJ 1.
[29] EA 1982, ss. 12–14 (now TULRCA, ss. 144, 186 and 222).
[30] See TURERA, s. 35. Repeal took effect on August 30, 1993.

closed shop; whereas the Employment Act 1990 tackled the pre-entry closed shop by creating for the first time a right not to be denied access to employment on the ground of non-membership of a trade union. The effect of the changes introduced by the Employment Act 1988, in particular, ensure that now under British law the right to join and the right not to join a trade union must be considered as equal and correlative rights. These changes also have a de-stabilising effect upon existing collective bargaining arrangements. However, the clearest indication as to where the present government's priorities lie is evidenced by two significant changes to the law brought about by the Trade Union Reform and Employment Rights Act 1993. The first is the repeal of the statutory direction to ACAS to encourage the extension of collective bargaining and the development and reform of collective bargaining machinery.[31] The second is the limitation of the protection for action short of dismissal on grounds of trade union membership and activities where the employer seeks to change the basis of the relationship between employer and employee.[32] This change facilitates the offer of personal contracts to employees and if such offers are made by employers enhances their ability to reduce the role of trade unions to mere representation in grievance and disciplinary matters.[33] Such changes support the Government's preference for a much more individualistic system of wage determination and encourage union derecognition.

9.8 The influence of Europe

It is noteworthy that the few statutory supports to collective bargaining owe their origins to European law. Indeed, there has been one legislative measure this decade which goes against this trend. This concerns the provisions of the Transfer of Undertakings (Protection of Employment) Regulations 1981[34] which (a) continue a union's recognition rights after the relevant transfer of a business so long as that business retains its separate identity and (b) grant information and consultation rights in respect of the transfer to representatives of recognised independent trade unions.[35] However, these regulations were only introduced in compliance with the United Kingdom's obligations under EC law when default proceedings were threatened against this country for a failure to implement the requisite directive.[36] These regulations together with the consultation provisions in the Trade Union and Labour Relations (Consolidation) Act 1992, ss. 188–198 are the two most important supports to collective bargaining which remain. Both provisions are necessary so as to comply with European law. It is fast becoming the case, therefore, that the statutory supports which remain are those which the British government must provide under its obligations as a member of the European Union. This raises an interesting paradox for at the same time as the government has repealed many of the other statutory supports it not only has had to continue but also to strengthen the two statutory supports which are required by

---

[31] See TULRCA, s. 209 as amended by TURERA, s. 43.
[32] See TULRCA, s. 148(3)–(5) as inserted by TURERA, s. 13.
[33] As it happens, this legislative change has proved to be unnecessary. See the decision of the House of Lords in *Associated Newspapers Ltd v. Wilson*; *Associated British Ports v. Palmer* [1995] ICR 406, HL and Chapter Ten.
[34] SI 1981 No. 1794.
[35] Discussed in more detail at para. 9.35.
[36] See Bob Hepple, "The Transfer of Undertakings (Protection of Employment) Regulations" (1982) 11 ILJ 29.

European law.[37] Thus the Trade Union Reform and Employment Rights Act 1993 extended the rights of representatives of recognised independent trade unions to be consulted over redundancies and on the transfer of an undertaking, and enhanced an employee's rights to compensation for a breach.[38] However, even after the amendments of 1993, the rights to consultation only accrued to representatives of trade unions which were recognised for collective bargaining purposes. This was despite the fact that the corresponding European directives grant a right of consultation for both redundancy dismissals and the transfer of an undertaking to "worker representatives".[39] The European Court of Justice has held that the United Kingdom remains in breach of both directives by not providing for a compulsory system for the designation of representatives to whom information can be supplied.[40] The government has now introduced legislation which amends the pre-existing law to ensure that consultation can either take place with representatives of recognised independent trade unions or elected representatives of the affected employees.[41]

9.9 Individual rights

On the whole the individual rights of trade unionists have not been affected greatly by the Conservative government's labour legislation apart from the changes in relation to the dismissal of employees taking part in industrial action introduced by the Employment Acts 1982 and 1990[42] and the provisions enacted by the Trade Union Reform and Employment Rights Act 1993 concerning action short of dismissal and personal contracts.[43] Indeed, in one sense members' rights have been increased as a result of the provisions which create larger awards of compensation not only to cover the dismissal of the non-unionist but the trade union member and activist as well,[44] and the right not to be denied access to employment because of trade union membership.[45] In both of these cases it must also be recognised, however, that these enhanced rights were only introduced as part of a package of measures aimed primarily at protecting the non-member. Finally, in keeping with the government's encouragement for collective bargaining conducted at local level the Employment Act 1989 introduced restrictions on a union official's rights to paid time off work.[46]

It is now time to look at the present legislative provisions concerning collective bargaining in more detail.

---

[37] This was done largely because in October 1992 the EC Commission had commenced infraction proceedings in the ECJ against the UK for breach of both the collective redundancies directive and the acquired rights directive.

[38] See TURERA, s. 34 (redundancy) and s. 33 (transfer of an undertaking). These amendments were basically introduced so as to remedy most of the breaches identified in the EC Commission's action against the UK.

[39] See Council Dirs. 75/117 and 92/56 (collective redundancies) and Council Dir. 77/187 (acquired rights).

[40] *Commission of the European Communities v. United Kingdom* (Case C-383/92) [1994] IRLR 412 (redundancies) and *Commission of the European Communities v. United Kingdom* (Case C-382/92) [1994] IRLR 392 (transfer of undertaking).

[41] See the Collective Redundancies and Transfer of Undertakings (Protection of Employment) (Amendment) Regulations 1995 (SI 1995 No. 2587) and paras 9.35–9.40 and 9.48.

[42] See now TULRCA, ss. 237–239.

[43] See now TULRCA, s. 148(3)–(5).

[44] See now TULRCA, ss. 156–158.

[45] See now TULRCA, s. 137.

[46] See TULRCA, s. 168.

COLLECTIVE BARGAINING

9.10 Meaning and status of a collective agreement

The purpose of collective bargaining is to provide a mechanism whereby terms and conditions of employment for a given group of employees are reached by means of negotiation and agreement between an employer or association of employers and a trade union or confederation of unions. As was noted in Chapter Two, there is no system in British law which permits these collectively agreed terms automatically to form part of an employee's terms and conditions of employment. This must be brought about by some arrangement which permits the incorporation of collectively agreed provisions into the individual contracts of employment of the employees concerned. This system makes no distinction between the terms of employment of the union member compared with those of the non-unionist. A collective agreement is also likely to have another function and that is to act as an "industrial peace treaty"[47] setting the method and procedure by which disputes between management and labour can be resolved. It is unlikely that this aspect of the collective agreement will be incorporated into the employees' contracts. The importance of the collective agreement as a means of ensuring order has been judicially noted in Scotland although Lord McDonald may have overstated the position when he declared in one case[48] "[w]here employers negotiate a detailed agreement with a recognised union they are entitled to assume that all employees who are members of the union know of and are bound by its provisions. There could be no stability in industrial relations if this were not so".

9.11 National and plant level agreements

The two most significant features of British collective bargaining are the different levels at which negotiations are conducted and the lack of precision as regards the contents of collective agreements. Bargaining may be conducted at national level involving associations of employers. The purpose of these agreements is to set minimum terms and conditions which apply to all employees within a given description in the industry. It is likely that these agreements will be augmented by bargaining at local or plant level. The purpose of these local negotiations is to deal with the problems of applying the national agreement to the special circumstances of the area. Equally, bargaining may be conducted exclusively at the local plant or factory.[49] In the last few years there has definitely been a movement supported by the government towards a more localised system of bargaining: indeed, in the public sector there has been an attempt to target higher wage increases to employees in particular geographical areas or types of work and to encourage local employers to take a greater role in negotiating rates of pay and conditions of employment. As far as the language of British collective agreements is concerned, it is often vague, and although there is evidence that agreements are becoming more formalised[50] there can be no doubt that they still lack the detail and sophistication of, for example, those in the United States.

---

[47] See, generally, Kahn-Freund's *Labour and the Law*, Ch. 6.
[48] *Gray Dunn & Co. Ltd v. Edwards* [1980] IRLR 23 at p. 24, EAT.
[49] These issues are discussed in more detail in the Donovan Commission Report, Ch. III.
[50] See Brown (ed.), *The Changing Contours of British Industrial Relations: A Survey of Manufacturing Industry.*

9.12 Legal enforceability of the collective agreement

Statute declares that any collective agreement shall be conclusively presumed not to have been intended by the parties to be legally enforceable and this presumption can be overcome only by ensuring that the agreement is in writing and that it contains a provision, however expressed, which declares that the parties intend the agreement to have legal effect.[51] This is consistent with the decision of Geoffrey Lane J in *Ford Motor Co. Ltd v. AEF*[52] to the effect that under English common law a collective agreement was not a legally enforceable contract. Looking at the wording of such agreements, their nature and the climate of opinion at the time,[53] the judge concluded that the parties did not intend that collective agreements should be enforceable. Instead, they were intended to be binding in honour only.

9.13 The position in Scots law

There is some limited support for this decision in *International Tailors' Machinists' and Pressers' Union v. Goldberg*[54] where it was held that an employer was not bound by a written undertaking that he had given to a trade union that he would not hire non-union labour on the basis that this undertaking was a mere voluntary and gratuitous act. However, one academic writer[55] has argued that under Scots law an intention to create legal relations is always presumed to exist is commercial or industrial cases.[56] Accordingly, a collective agreement as a form of industrial agreement should be assumed to create a legally binding relationship at the time when the agreement is made. Therefore, if the Scottish courts were to reach the same conclusion as the *Ford* case at common law, it would have to be on different grounds, for example, the need for certainty as to the terms of a valid contract.[57]

9.14 The statutory presumption

The existence of s. 179 of the Trade Union and Labour Relations (Consolidation) Act 1992 renders these arguments otiose. Unless a contrary intention is expressed in writing s. 179 ensures that a collective agreement is conclusively presumed not to be a legally binding contract. There are no decisions of the Scottish courts on the language of s. 179. However, two English decisions shed light upon its effect. In the first,[58] it was held that the effect of the presumption in s. 179 was to ensure that a collective agreement was not a contract at all in the eyes of the law. Indeed, it was merely an arrangement between the parties, the enforcement of which was to be achieved, if at all, by other means. Accordingly, it is wrong to view a collective agreement as a form of contract which statute has made unenforceable in the courts. It has no contractual status whatsoever.

9.15 Rebutting the presumption

Moreover, if the parties wish the agreement to be legally enforceable the written term which is intended to rebut the presumption must clearly express this desire.

---

[51] TULRCA, s. 179(1) and (2).
[52] [1969] 2 QB 303.
[53] Geoffrey Lane J referred in particular to several articles by Otto Kahn-Freund and to the Report of the Donovan Commission.
[54] (1903) 19 Sh Ct Rep 312.
[55] James Casey, "Collective Agreements: Some Scottish Footnotes", 1973 JR 22.
[56] See Stair 1.10.6; 1.10.13.
[57] And see Chapter Two, paras 2.9, 2.14.
[58] *Monterosso Shipping Co. Ltd v. International Transport Workers Federation* [1982] IRLR 468, CA.

This was held in the second case, *National Coal Board v. National Union of Mineworkers*,[59] where there was a clause in the agreement between the coal board and the union which declared that "the parties hereto be bound thereby accordingly". The union argued that the use of the word "bound" displayed an intention that the agreement should be legally binding. However, Scott J concluded that the statutory presumption had not been displaced. It was his view that a statement in a collective agreement that the parties are to be bound by that agreement cannot be equated with a statement that the parties intend the agreement to be legally enforceable. At the very least, for the presumption to be rebutted the collective agreement must contain a statement showing that the parties have directed their minds to the question of legal enforceability and have decided in favour of such enforceability.

UNION RECOGNITION

9.16 It has been noted that the original statutory provisions[60] permitted ACAS to inquire and report on a request for union recognition by an independent trade union. In exercising these powers ACAS had to have regard to the desirability of settling the issues by conciliation. ACAS was also obliged in the course of its inquiries to ascertain the opinions of the workers affected by the issue by any means it thought fit, and this would often involve the use of a questionnaire. At the end of its inquiries ACAS was required to make a report which set out its findings and, where necessary, make a recommendation for recognition by the employer. This recommendation was not legally binding. If the employer chose to ignore it all that ACAS could do was to attempt to settle the matter by conciliation. The ultimate sanction was for the union to complain to the CAC that the employer was not complying with ACAS's recommendation, and to have incorporated into the contracts of the relevant employees particular terms and conditions of employment except a term requiring the employer to recognise the applicant union.[61]

9.17 The repeal of the statutory procedure

There were some who argued that the provisions on union recognition did not go far enough.[62] However, the courts, at least initially, adopted the view that the procedure involved an interference with individual liberty.[63] In *Grunwick Processing Laboratories Ltd v. ACAS*[64] Lord Salmon, for example, considered that it was the court's duty to ensure that the rights of the individual were not lost except in strict accordance with the statutory procedure. As already pointed out, this statutory procedure was discontinued in 1980.[65] Thus apart from the provisions of

---

[59]   [1986] IRLR 439, Ch D.
[60]   EPA 1975, ss. 11–16.
[61]   See, for example, *Phoenix Timber (Grangemouth) Ltd v. TGWU* (CAC Award No. 272).
[62]   During the 1977/78 Session of Parliament two Private Member's Bills were introduced which would have increased the powers of ACAS, particularly as regards obtaining access to the names of employees whose opinions the Service had to ascertain. These Bills are discussed by B. James and R. C. Simpson in "Grunwick v. ACAS" (1978) 41 MLR 372.
[63]   See Browne-Wilkinson J in *Powley v. ACAS* [1978] ICR at p. 135; Lord Denning MR in *Grunwick Processing Laboratories Ltd v. ACAS* [1978] ICR 231 at p. 237, HL and in *UKAPE v. ACAS* [1979] ICR 303 at pp. 316–317, CA. Later House of Lords' decisions took a less damaging tack. See *UKAPE v. ACAS* [1980] ICR 201, HL.
[64]   [1978] ICR 231 at p. 268, HL.
[65]   EPA 1975, ss. 11–16 repealed by EA 1980, s. 18.

certain statutes applying in the public sector which impose a duty of consultation with "appropriate"[66] organisations or organisations appearing to represent "substantial proportions"[67] of employees, there is no legal obligation upon an employer to recognise a trade union. To a large extent, therefore, unions must rely on self-help in order to obtain recognition rights. However, the extent to which a union can apply self-help measures is limited since it is unlawful for a union to pressure an employer to impose a union-only or union-recognition requirement in contracts,[68] or for the union to take industrial action to enforce union membership.[69]

9.18 Recognition for collective bargaining

Despite the lack of an enforceable union recognition procedure the remaining statutory supports to collective bargaining are highly dependent on there being a trade union which is recognised for collective bargaining purposes. Thus the concept of union recognition is still a central aspect of the law. It is defined to mean the recognition of the union by the employer, or two or more associated employers, to any extent for the purpose of collective bargaining.[70] Collective bargaining is defined as negotiations relating to or connected with one or more of the following matters:

(a) terms and conditions of employment;

(b) engagement or non-engagement, or termination or suspension of employment or the duties of employment;

(c) allocation of work;

(d) matters of discipline;

(e) membership or non-membership of a union;

(f) facilities for union officials;

(g) machinery for negotiation or consultation.[71]

9.19 The act of recognition

There is no doubt that before a union can be considered to be recognised by an employer in terms of the above definition there must be consent[72] or a meeting of the minds of the parties.[73] This requires the employer to acknowledge the role of the union and for the union to assent to such acknowledgement. This is best achieved through some form of express agreement to this effect. More difficult is the case where a decision about recognition has to be resolved by reference to the actings of the parties. In such a case, as Lord McDonald declared in *Transport and General Workers' Union v. Dyer*,[74] the actings "... must be clear and unequivocal, usually though not necessarily, involving a course of conduct over a period of time". This approach which sets a heavy burden of proof on the party claiming

---

[66] *R. v. Post Office, ex parte ASTMS* [1981] ICR 76, CA.

[67] *R. v. British Coal Corporation, ex parte Union of Democratic Mineworkers* [1988] ICR 36, QBD. See also *Cannon v. Secretary of State for Scotland* 1964 SLT 91, OH.

[68] EA 1982, s. 14. See Chapter Eleven, para. 11.51.

[69] EA 1988, s. 10. See Chapter Eleven, para. 11.52.

[70] TULRCA, s. 178(3).

[71] TULRCA, s. 178(1) and (2).

[72] *TGWU v. Dyer* [1977] IRLR 93, EAT.

[73] *National Union of Tailors and Garment Workers v. Charles Ingram & Co. Ltd* [1977] ICR 530.

[74] [1977] ICR 93, EAT.

recognition[75] has been applied in subsequent cases. The thrust of these decisions is summed up in the statement of Lord Denning MR in *National Union of Gold, Silver & Allied Trades v. Albury Brothers Ltd*[76] that "a recognition issue is a most important matter for industry: and therefore an employer is not to be held to have recognised a trade union unless the evidence is clear". Usually the employer's conduct should establish not only a willingness on his part to discuss but also to negotiate about one or more matters listed above. It would not be sufficient proof of recognition for the union merely to show that the employer is a member of an association with whom it negotiates.[77] On the other hand, this factor could be an element in establishing recognition if there are other facts in the case which also point in this direction.[78]

9.20 Under the statutory definition it is competent for a union to be recognised "to any extent" for the purpose of collective bargaining. This phrase does not refer to the strength of conviction of the recognition but to the subject matters to which it relates.[79] Thus there is nothing to prevent a union acquiring partial recognition and exercise as a result rights which are conditional on being recognised for collective bargaining. However, the case law does make a distinction between negotiating rights which is the essence of recognition and mere rights to represent members. A union would not be considered recognised for collective bargaining purposes where its role is restricted simply to representing its members in individual grievances before the employer.[80] The distinction also applies as regards a collective agreement which grants full negotiating rights over some matters but as regards other matters only offers rights of representation. In such circumstances a union cannot complain about a failure on the part of the employer to disclose information about a method of evaluating work if this is an aspect of terms and conditions where only representation rights have been accorded.[81]

STATUTORY SUPPORTS FOR COLLECTIVE BARGAINING

9.21 Disclosure of information

An employer must disclose to the representatives of an independent trade union on request all the information relating to his undertaking as is in his possession for the purposes of all stages of collective bargaining.[82] This duty only arises where the union is recognised for collective bargaining purposes. Information need not be disclosed by an employer, therefore, where the union only possesses representation rights in relation to the type of information which the union is seeking.[83] Equally, there is no duty to disclose where, for example, the information is required to assist the union in its campaign against privatisation since this does not fall within the

---

[75] As Kilner Brown J stated in *Joshua Wilson & Brothers Ltd v. Union of Shop, Distributive & Allied Workers* [1978] ICR 614, EAT the side of the scales labelled recognition must "go down with a bump".

[76] [1979] ICR 84 at p. 89, CA.

[77] *Albury Brothers*, above.

[78] *Joshua Wilson*, above.

[79] *Per* Lord McDonald in *TGWU v. Dyer* [1977] IRLR 93 at p. 94, EAT.

[80] *USDAW v. Sketchley Ltd* [1981] ICR 644, EAT.

[81] *R. v. Central Arbitration Committee, ex parte BTP Tioxide Ltd* [1981] ICR 843, QBD.

[82] TULRCA, s. 181.

[83] *BTP Tioxide Ltd*, above.

statutory concept of collective bargaining.[84] Two further conditions must be satisfied before the duty applies. The request must be for information without which the trade union representatives would be to a material extent impeded in carrying out collective bargaining and it must be in accordance with good industrial relations practice for the information to be disclosed.[85] Beyond this there is no further definition in the statute as to the types of information for which there is a duty to disclose. However, the ACAS Code of Practice on Disclosure of Information to Trade Unions for Collective Bargaining Purposes[86] does provide examples of the types of information which might be relevant to collective bargaining. These are under the headings of pay and benefits; conditions of service; manpower; performance and financial matters. This list is by no means exhaustive, and the Code stresses that it would be far better if the parties could reach agreement over the matters relevant for disclosure.

9.22 *Exempted information.* On the other hand the employer is exempt from disclosing certain types of information.[87] An employer need not disclose:

(a) any information the disclosure of which would be against the interests of national security;

(b) any information the disclosure of which would involve contravening a prohibition imposed by or under an enactment;

(c) any information which has been disclosed to the employer in confidence,[88] or which the employer has otherwise obtained in consequence of the confidence reposed in him by another person;

(d) any information relating specifically to an individual, unless he has consented to its disclosure;

(e) any information the disclosure of which would cause substantial injury to the employer's undertaking for reasons other than its effect on collective bargaining;

(f) any information obtained by the employer for the purpose of bringing, prosecuting or defending any legal proceedings.

9.23 *Commercial information.* One specific head which leaves scope for widely divergent views is that which exempts disclosure where "substantial injury" is likely to be caused to the employer's undertaking. Although this phrase is not defined, the Code does give some guidance as to the types of information where disclosure might cause substantial injury. The examples provided include cost information on individual products; detailed analysis of proposed investment; marketing or pricing policies and price quotas or the make-up of tender prices. Moreover, the Code advises that substantial injury is likely to arise where disclosure would result in certain customers being lost to competitors, or suppliers refusing to supply necessary materials, or an impairment in the ability of the employer to raise funds.[89] Also an employer is not required to produce or allow for inspection any document other than the one prepared for the purpose of conveying the information[90] and there is no requirement on an employer to compile or

---

[84] TULRCA, s. 178 and see *Civil Service Union v. Central Arbitration Committee* [1980] IRLR 274, QB.
[85] TULRCA, s. 181(2)(a) and (b).
[86] ACAS Code No. 2, effective August 22, 1977.
[87] TULRCA, s. 182(1).
[88] Discussed by Forbes J in *CSU v. CAC* [1980] IRLR 274, QB.
[89] Para. 15.
[90] TULRCA, s. 182(2)(a).

assemble information which would entail an amount of work or expenditure out of reasonable proportion to the value of the information in the conduct of collective bargaining.[91]

9.24 *Enforcement*. Enforcement of these provisions is by means of an application by the union to the Central Arbitration Committee.[92] However, where there is a reasonable likelihood that the complaint can be settled by conciliation the CAC has the authority to refer the matter to ACAS. In such a case it is the duty of ACAS to attempt to promote a settlement.[93] Where conciliation fails or no reference has been made, the CAC will proceed to determine the complaint. The principal remedy where the whole or part of the complaint is well-founded is for the CAC to make a declaration.[94] In such a case the CAC is required to specify the information which should have been disclosed, the date when the employer refused to disclose it, and the period of time within which the employer ought to disclose that information.[95] Where the employer refuses to comply with the terms of the declaration the union is entitled to make another complaint to the CAC[96] which entitles the union to submit a claim for improved terms and conditions for the class of employees specified in the complaint. If this further complaint is upheld the CAC is empowered to make an award requiring the employer to observe the terms and conditions which the union has specified in its claim or such other terms as it thinks appropriate.[97] The sanction under this procedure, therefore, is not to force disclosure, but to impose upon the employer an obligation to improve the employees' terms and conditions of employment. These terms become part of the contracts of employment of each of the employees concerned and can be enforced where necessary by an action for breach of contract in the civil courts, or, possibly by a complaint to an industrial tribunal where the matter is still outstanding on the termination of the contract.

9.25 The right to consultation

Statute places upon an employer a duty to consult with employee representatives in three specific circumstances. An employer must consult on health and safety matters so as to ensure that he and his employees can co-operate effectively in promoting and developing measures to ensure health and safety and to check the effectiveness of these measures.[98] There is also a duty to consult as regards proposals for redundancies and as regards the transfer of the employer's undertaking. These last two obligations have been introduced in compliance with the United Kingdom's membership of the European Union.

9.26 *Consultation on redundancy*. The statutory procedure[99] for handling redundancies (which is intended to comply with the United Kingdom's obligations

---

91 TULRCA, s. 182(2)(b).
92 TULRCA, s. 183. See H. Gospel and P. Willman, "Disclosure of Information: the CAC Approach" (1981) 10 ILJ 10.
93 TULRCA, s. 183(2).
94 TULRCA, s. 183(3).
95 TULRCA, s. 183(5).
96 TULRCA, s. 184.
97 TULRCA, s. 185(3).
98 Health and Safety at Work etc. Act 1974, s. 2(6). Further discussion of this subject is outwith the scope of this work. But see V. Craig and K. Miller, *The Law of Health and Safety at Work in Scotland* (1995) paras 5.18–5.32.
99 TULRCA, ss. 188–198 as amended by TURERA, s. 34.

under the EC Directive on Collective Redundancies)[100] also imposes a duty to consult. This procedure was the subject of considerable amendment by the Trade Union Reform and Employment Rights Act 1993 so as to ensure proper compliance with the 1975 directive and compliance with the 1992 directive. As will be indicated, it is debatable whether these changes satisfy fully the requirements of the two directives. Until recently, such a duty only arose where the employer proposed to dismiss as redundant an employee of a description in respect of which an independent trade union possessed recognition rights.[101] Formerly, redundancy had the same meaning as it did in Part VI of the Employment Protection (Consolidation) Act 1978 as regards an employee's entitlement to a redundancy payment.[102] However, since 1993 the duty to consult is triggered whenever an employer proposes to dismiss an employee for a reason not related to the individual concerned.[103] Moreover, there is a presumption that where an employee is or is proposed to be dismissed that dismissal is dismissal for redundancy unless the contrary can be proved.[104] It is central that the employer propose to dismiss the employee as redundant as so defined. Where the employer seeks to deal with the problem by some other method which does not involve any dismissals (such as redeployment or the non-filling of vacancies) the statutory procedure does not operate. As already indicated, consultation under TULRCA, s. 188 need only begin once an employer proposes to dismiss an employee as redundant. This requirement is in contrast to the terms of the collective redundancies directive which requires the employer to begin consultation as soon as he is contemplating collective redundancies. It would seem that consultation as required by the directive is likely to start at an early stage when the employer is first envisaging the possibility that employees may have to be made redundant. On the other hand, consultation under s. 188 need only begin when the employer has decided that it his intention, however reluctant, to make employees redundant. This means that consultation under s. 188 does not have the same meaning as that required by the directive and so this is a possible further ground where the United Kingdom could be in default.[105] On the other hand, as was argued in *Griffin v. South West Water Services Ltd*,[106] the important issue is that consultation can only begin once an employer has formulated a proposal. If this view is correct, then, British law is not out of step with European requirements.

9.27 *Consultation with representatives.* The duty is to consult with representatives of independent trade unions, *viz.* officials or other persons authorised to carry on collective bargaining with the employer.[107] The employer must ensure, therefore, that any consultations only take place with those union officials who have

---

[100] Council Dir. 75/129 as amended by Council Dir. 92/56.

[101] TULRCA, s. 188(1). But see now the Collective Redundancies and Transfer of Undertakings (Amendment) Regulations 1995 (SI 1995 No. 2587) discussed at para. 9.35. The Regulations were challenged unsuccessfully in *R. v Secretary of State for Trade and Industry, ex parte UNISON* [1996] IRLR 438, DC.

[102] Discussed in more detail in Chapter Six, paras. 6.5–6.7.

[103] TULRCA, s. 195(1) as substituted by TURERA, s. 34(1) and (5).

[104] TULRCA, s. 195(2) as substituted by TURERA, s. 34(1) and (5).

[105] The issue is discussed by Glidewell LJ in *R. v. British Coal Corporation and Secretary of State for Trade and Industry, ex parte Vardy* [1993] IRLR 104, QBD.

[106] [1995] IRLR 15, ChD.

[107] TULRCA, s. 196.

responsibility for conducting collective bargaining with him.[108] However, once this provision has been satisfied the duty to consult will apply to all of those employees whom the employer is proposing to dismiss. The only condition for consultation is that the employees concerned be of a description for which an independent trade union has acquired recognition rights. Once this has been established the duty to consult will operate regardless of whether or not the employees concerned are union members.[109]

9.28 *Commencing consultation.* The employer is required to begin consultation at the earliest opportunity[110] regardless of the number of employees to be dismissed. Where, however, the employer is proposing to dismiss 100 or more employees at one establishment within a period of 90 days or less, consultation must begin at least 90 days before the first of these dismissals takes effect.[111] Equally, where the proposal was to dismiss 10[112] or more employees at one establishment within a period of 30 days or less, consultation had to begin at least 30 days before the first of these dismissals took effect.[113] Consultation must begin as soon as the employer proposes to make redundancies. This means, for example, that an employer would be breaking the consultation requirements where he began to consult with the union at the same time as individual notices of dismissal had been sent out to the affected employees.[114] This would be the case even although the first dismissal would not take effect until after the periods for consultation mentioned in the statute had expired.[115] Equally, an employer would be in breach of his statutory obligations where the employees' dismissal notices and a memorandum to the union setting out details of the redundancies were sent out simultaneously.[116] In *Transport and General Workers' Union v. Ledbury Preserves (1928)*[117] the Employment Appeal Tribunal made it clear that consultation had to be meaningful, so that the employer should start consultation before issuing redundancy notices and should give the union representatives time to consider the proposals. This point has been developed further in a case involving consultation under the Coal Industry Nationalisation Act 1946.[118] Here it was made clear that the process of consultation is not one which obliges the employer to adopt any or all of the views expressed by the union representatives. Nevertheless, the consultation must be fair. This entails giving the representatives a fair and proper opportunity to understand fully the matters about which they are being consulted and to express their views on the subject. The employer has an obligation thereafter to consider those views

---

[108] *Amalgamaged Union of Engineering Workers v. Sefton Engineering Co. Ltd* [1976] IRLR 319, EAT.
[109] *Governing Body of the Northern Ireland Hotel and Catering College v. National Association of Teachers in Further and Higher Education* [1995] IRLR 83, NICA.
[110] TULRCA, s. 188(2) Now "in good time." See para. 9.36.
[111] TULRCA, s. 188(2)(a).
[112] The obligation to consult now only arises where 20 or more employees are to be dismissed. See the Collective Redundancies and Transfer of Undertakings (Protection of Employment) (Amendment) Regulations 1995 (SI 1995 No. 2587) and para. 9.36.
[113] TULRCA, s. 188(2)(b).
[114] See, for example, *Sovereign Distribution Services Ltd v. TGWU* [1990] ICR 31, EAT.
[115] *National Union of Teachers v. Avon County Council* [1978] ICR 626, EAT; *E. Green & Son (Castings) Ltd v. ASTMS* [1984] ICR 352, EAT.
[116] *General & Municipal Workers' Union v. British Uralite Ltd* [1979] IRLR 409, IT.
[117] [1985] IRLR 412, EAT (notification of planned redundancies intimated half n hour before issue of dismissal notices).
[118] *R. v. British Coal and the Secretary of State for Trade and Industry, ex parte Price* [1994] IRLR 72, DC.

properly and genuinely.[119] On the other hand, the fact that the procedure only operates once the employer proposes to dismiss means that there must be something concrete to put before the union. As Lord McDonald stated in *Association of Patternmakers & Allied Craftsmen v. Kirvin Ltd*,[120] s. 99 of the Employment Protection Act (now TULRCA, s. 188) "... connotes a state of mind directed to a planned or proposed course of events. The employer must have formed some view as to how many are to be dismissed, when this is to take place and how it is to be arranged".

9.29 *Multi-location businesses.* The reference to the dismissals being at one "establishment" has also created difficulties for there is no definition of this word for the purposes of consultation. This issue has obvious implications for the timing of any consultations for an employer running a multi-location business like retailing. In *Barratt Developments (Bradford) Ltd v. Union of Construction, Allied Trades and Technicians*[121] the company had employees engaged in house-building at 14 different sites, each with a temporary shed housing the foreman and a telephone link to the head office. Due to a reduction in demand, it was decided that redundancies were necessary. As a result, 24 employees working at eight of the company's sites were given one week's notice of dismissal and at the same time the union was notified about the impending dismissals. The union argued that these eight sites amounted to one establishment and that, since more than 10 employees were being dismissed at one time, the amount of prior notification that had been given was inadequate. It was held that the question of what was an establishment was essentially one of fact and that the industrial tribunal in this case had been right to conclude that it would be contrary to common and business sense to regard each of these sites as a separate establishment. Accordingly, the company had provided insufficient time for consultation. It was significant that in this case all the important decision-making functions were exercised at head office. In another case, where the facts disclose that far greater autonomy resides with the management at each location, the decision might be different.

9.30 *The extent of the duty.* The extent of the consultation duty is to be found in the statutory requirement that an employer disclose in writing to union representatives the following:

    (a) the reasons for the proposals;

    (b) the numbers and descriptions of employees whom it is proposed to dismiss as redundant;

    (c) the total number of employees of the appropriate description employed by the employer at the establishment in question;

    (d) the proposed method of selection;

    (e) the proposed method of carrying out the dismissals;

---

[119] This obligation is enhanced by the additional requirements inserted by TURERA, s. 34. These now require that consultation be "with a view to reaching an agreement". See further at para. 9.30.

[120] [1978] IRLR 318 at p. 310. See also *Hough v. Leyland DAF Ltd* [1991] IRLR 194, EAT where the EAT held that an employer should be taken as "proposing" to discuss redundancy with employees so as to be under an immediate duty to consult when a specific proposal had been formulated.

[121] [1978] ICR 319, EAT. Under the Collective Redundancies Directive "establishment" means the unit to which the redundant workers have been assigned. See *Rockfon A/S v. Special Arbejderfor Bundet i Danmark* [1996] IRLR 168, ECJ.

(f) the proposed method of calculating the amount of the redundancy payment where that amount is not to be based upon the statutory formula.[122]
The above information should be delivered to the trade union representatives, or sent by post to an address notified by them to the employer, or sent by post to the union at the address of its head or main office.[123] Any consultation must include consultation about ways of (a) avoiding the dismissals, (b) reducing the numbers to be dismissed, and (c) mitigating the consequences of the dismissals, and must be undertaken with a view to reaching agreement with the union representatives.[124] These requirements were first introduced in 1993 and undoubtedly extend the scope of consultation. Moreover, the requirement that the consultation be with a view to reaching agreement may create difficult questions of judgment for industrial tribunals but it does provide statutory support for the notion that consultation should be meaningful and real.

9.31 *Qualification of the duty.* The duty to consult is qualified by the Trade Union and Labour Relations (Consolidation) Act 1992, s. 188(7) which provides that where there are special circumstances which render it not reasonably practicable for the employer to comply with any of the above requirements, he must take all such steps towards compliance as are reasonably practicable in the circumstances. This is also a matter for the tribunal to decide. The Court of Appeal considered the meaning of "special circumstance" in *Clarks of Hove Ltd v. Bakers' Union*[125] where the employers had been in financial difficulties for some time. After their last hopes of financial aid had disappeared they dismissed 368 of their employees for redundancy and ceased trading on the same day. The Bakers' Union — the recognised trade union — complained to an industrial tribunal that the employers had failed to consult at least 90 days before the first dismissals were to take effect. The employers argued that there were special circumstances excusing their lack of consultation. The Court of Appeal held that insolvency was not necessarily a special circumstance. Everything would depend on the cause of that insolvency. A sudden disaster, either physical or financial, which suddenly struck a company making it necessary for the business to close could be capable of being a special circumstance. On the other hand, if the insolvency came about after a gradual run-down of the company such a circumstance would not be special.

9.32 *Special circumstances.* In general terms, therefore, to be a special event the occurrence must be something out of the ordinary or uncommon. A similar approach has been applied in Scotland in the *Kirvin* case[126] where Lord McDonald declared that insolvency would not be a special case where it was foreseeable. However, he did take the view that it would be a special circumstance for an employer to delay consultation until it became clear that the last potential purchaser of the business as a going concern had disappeared and that a receiver would have to be appointed. It has also been held to be a special circumstance where a prospective employer withdrew from negotiations and a receiver was appointed immediately by the bank.[127] On the other hand, this defence cannot operate where the employer's excuse for a failure to consult was his genuine belief

---

[122] TULRCA, s. 188(4) as amended by TURERA, s. 34.
[123] TULRCA, s. 188(5).
[124] TULRCA, s. 188(6) as inserted by TURERA, s. 34.
[125] [1978] ICR 1076, CA.
[126] [1978] IRLR 318, EAT.
[127] *USDAW v. Leancut Bacon Ltd* [1981] IRLR 295, EAT.

that there was no recognised trade union.[128] It is not a special circumstances defence for an employer to argue that the failure to consult was because the decision leading to the proposed dismissals was taken by a controlling organisation who had failed to provide the requisite information about those dismissals to the employer.[129] This provision, which was also introduced in 1993, is intended to meet an objective of the 1992 directive which seeks to prevent employers avoiding their consultation responsibilities by arguing that the decision to dismiss was taken by a controlling interest in another member state.

9.33 *Failure to consult.* The sanction for breach of these provisions is for an industrial tribunal to declare that a complaint by a recognised trade union is well-founded and to make a protective award.[130] The purpose of this award is to require the employer to continue to pay the wages of the employees who are the subject of the complaint for a protected period. Individual employees have no right to complain under this procedure, although any award will apply to union members and non-unionists alike. The duration of the protective award will be for such period as the tribunal considers just and equitable in all the circumstances, having regard to the seriousness of the employer's default,[131] and begins with the date on which the first of the dismissals took effect, or the date of the award whichever is earlier.[132] However, the duration of any award is subject to certain maximum periods. In the case of 100 or more dismissals conducted within 90 days or less, the maximum award remains at 90 days. Formerly, the protected period in the case of 10 or more dismissals was 30 days, and 28 days in all other cases.[133] Now, where 20 or more employees are being dismissed the protective award will be for a maximum of 30 days. Any employee covered by the award is entitled to one week's wages for each week of the protective award. It is now no longer competent to deduct from the protective award the amount of any contractual payment (such as pay in lieu of notice) which is made to the employee during the protected period.[134] Employees who fail to receive their protective awards have the right to complain to an industrial tribunal.[135] If the tribunal finds that the complaint is well-founded it will order the employer to pay the sum of money which is due.[136]

9.34 *The protective award.* There has been some judicial disagreement within the Employment Appeal Tribunal as regards the purpose of the protective award. In *Talke Fashions Ltd v. Amalgamated Society of Textile Workers and Kindred Trades*,[137] Kilner Brown J considered that the purpose of the award was not to punish employers for their failure to consult. Instead, it was intended merely to compensate the employees for any losses they had incurred as a result of the employer's default. This appears to be the dominant view in England, although in

[128] *Joshua Wilson & Brothers Ltd v. USDAW* [1978] ICR 614, EAT.
[129] TULRCA, s. 188(7): proviso inserted by TURERA, s. 34.
[130] TULRCA, s. 189(1) and (2).
[131] TULRCA, s. 189(4)(b).
[132] TULRCA, s. 189(4)(a).
[133] TULRCA, s. 189(4). These requirements were amended for dismissals taking place after March 1, 1996. Now the duty to consult only arises where 20 or more employees are being dismissed as redundant. See the Collective Redundancies and Transfer of Undertakings (Protection of Employment) (Amendment) Regulations 1995 (SI 1995 No. 2587).
[134] TULRCA, s. 190(3) repealed by TURERA, s. 34 as from August 30, 1993.
[135] TULRCA, s. 192(1).
[136] TULRCA, s. 192(3).
[137] [1977] ICR 833, EAT.

recent times protective awards have become more punitive.[138] In Scotland, on the other hand, Lord McDonald has declared in *Kirvin*[139] that since a tribunal was required to take account of the seriousness of the employer's default in assessing the period of the award, this introduced a punitive element into the jurisdiction of industrial tribunals in this area.

9.35 Reforms

The Collective Redundancies and Transfer of Undertakings (Protection of Employment) (Amendment) Regulations 1995[140]

As has already been noted, the provisions on consultation on redundancy have been amended by the Trade Union Reform and Employment Rights Act 1993 so as to ensure compliance with European standards. This legislation was timely since the European Court of Justice has held subsequently that the British legislation breached European requirements in four respects *viz.* failing to designate worker representatives where this does not happen voluntarily in practice; limiting the scope of the legislation as regards the definition of redundancy dismissals; failing to ensure that consultation is done with a view to reaching agreement and failing to provide an effective remedy for a failure to consult.[141] The last three breaches have been tackled by the 1993 Act. However, the Act did nothing to change the law as far as the introduction of a system for the compulsory designation of worker representatives is concerned. The process of consultation continued to rest solely upon whether or not an employer had voluntarily recognised an independent trade union for the purpose of collective bargaining.

Research evidence has suggested that the trend in the last 10 years has been for there to be a movement away from collective bargaining so that union recognition is now less prevalent[142] and so there were fewer occasions when the consultation provisions applied. Public sector unions who lack recognition rights have supported actions by employees who have sought to rely on the Collective Redundancies Directive as a means of forcing an employer to consult with them when there is no recognised independent trade union. In *Griffin v. South West Water Services Ltd*[143] the Divisional Court held that such an action was incompetent because the terms of the directive were not sufficiently unconditional and clear and precise to permit direct effect.

9.36 The Collective Redundancies and Transfer of Undertakings (Protection of Employment) (Amendment) Regulations 1995[144] are intended to rectify the defective implementation of the Directive by granting rights of consultation to employee representatives as well as continuing the present arrangements where there is a recognised independent trade union. In addition, the Regulations are intended to achieve certain deregulatory purposes. Thus, the Regulations remove

---

[138] See Smith and Wood, *Industrial Law* (5th edn), at pp. 58–59.
[139] [1978] IRLR 318.
[140] SI 1995 No. 2587. The Regulations came into force on Ocober 26, 1995, but they did not take effect until March 1, 1996.
[141] See *Commission of the European Communities v. United Kingdom* (Case C-383/92) [1994] IRLR 412, ECJ.
[142] See, for example, Neil Millward *et al.*, *Workplace Industrial Relations in Transition: the ED/ ESRC/PSI/ACAS Surveys* (1992).
[143] [1995] IRLR 15, ChD.
[144] SI 1995 No. 2587.

the duty to consult where the employer is proposing to dismiss as redundant less than 20 employees at one establishment within a period of 90 days or less. This may be the most significant change to the law which the Regulations will make, since it will exclude entirely a large number of smaller organisations from the duty to consult. The Regulations also ensure that consultation must be in good time which implies a lesser standard than the original provisions which required consultation at the earliest opportunity. The net effect of these two changes is that where an employer proposes to dismiss 100 or more employees at one establishment the consultation should begin in good time and at least 90 days before the first of these dismissals takes effect and in all other cases the period of consultation will be 30 days.

9.37 The Regulations create a new breed of representative — the employee representative who has the right to be consulted on redundancy. Under the new s. 196(1) of the Trade Union and Labour Relations (Consolidation) Act 1992 employee representatives are (1) employees elected by their fellow employees for the specific purpose of being consulted by the employer about proposed redundancies, or (2) employees who have been elected for another purpose (either before or after the dismissals have been proposed) but it is appropriate (having regard to the purposes for which they were elected) to consult them about the proposed dismissals. It is necessary in both cases for the representatives to be employed by the employer at the time when they are elected.

The Regulations do not specify any requirements as to how many employee representatives should be elected, the process by which they are chosen or the geographical base in which they operate. This is a matter for the employer. However, the Guidance issued by the Department of Trade and Industry advises employers to consider such matters as whether:

(a) the arrangements adequately cover all the categories of employees who might be made redundant and provide a reasonable balance between the interests of different groups;

(b) the employees have sufficient time to nominate and consider candidates;

(c) the employees can freely choose who to vote for;

(d) there is any normal company custom and practice for similar elections and, if so, whether there are good reasons for departing from it.

9.38 Employers now have the choice as to who is to be consulted. They must consult with "appropriate representatives" who are (1) employee representatives; (2) union representatives where the employees are of a description where a trade union has been recognised by the employer; or (3) where there are both elected representatives and representatives of a recognised trade union the employer must consult either the employee representatives or the union representatives as the employer chooses. Any such representatives must be given access to the employees whom it is proposed to dismiss as redundant and the employer must provide them with appropriate accommodation and other facilities.

If the employer chooses to consult through employee representatives who are to be elected specifically for this purpose, he must take steps to ensure that such representatives are elected in proper time to allow for effective consultation. This means that where an employer invites the dismissed employees to elect employee representatives, that invitation must be issued long enough before the 90-day or 30-day periods to allow them to elect representatives by that time and he must comply with the basic consultation requirements as soon as is reasonably practicable after the representatives have been elected.

9.39 A complaint about a breach of the consultation provisions can now be made by the following:

(1) where the failure to consult relates to employee representatives, by any of the representatives to whom the failure related;

(2) where the failure relates to union representatives, by the trade union;

(3) in any other case, by any of the employees who have been or may be dismissed as redundant.

This means that, where there are no union representatives and there have been no elections for employee representatives, it will be competent for any of the affected employees to complain over a failure to consult. The maximum period of the protective award is now 90 days where there are 100 or more dismissals or 30 days in any other case.

9.40 *Protections for employee representatives.* Employee representatives are granted three specific rights by the 1995 Regulations. First, both employee representatives and candidates for election as employee representatives have the right not to be subjected to any detriment by any act, or any deliberate failure to act[145] where they perform, or propose to perform, any functions or activities as such an employee representative or candidate. Second, it is automatically unfair to dismiss both employee representatives and candidates where they perform, or propose to perform any functions or activities as such an employee representative or candidate. Such employees do not have to serve the normal two year qualifying age for unfair dismissal and can be above normal retiring age. Such employees also have rights to a minimum basic award, a special award and interim relief. Third, employee representatives and candidates have the right to reasonable time off with pay during normal working hours in order to perform their functions. They have the right to complain to an industrial tribunal if the employer does not allow them reasonable time off or does not pay for such time off.

9.41 Notification to the Secretary of State

There is also an obligation placed upon an employer to notify the Secretary of State for Trade and Industry over mass redundancies. Where he proposes to dismiss as redundant 100 or more employees at one establishment within a period of 90 days or less at least 90 days prior written notice of these dismissals should be given. In the case where 20 or more employees are being dismissed from one establishment within 30 days or less at least 30 days notice is required.[146] Representatives of any recognised union are entitled to a copy of the notice. The only sanction now available for a failure to notify the Secretary of State is a fine on level 5 of the standard scale after summary conviction.[147]

9.42 Consultation on the transfer of an undertaking

The Transfer of Undertakings (Protection of Employment) Regulations 1981[148] constitute the United Kingdom's response to the Directive[149] of the European

---

[145] *Cf* the protection against action short of dismissal on union membership grounds in the Trade Union and Labour Relations (Consolidation) Act 1992, s. 146(1) as interpreted by the House of Lords in *Associated Newspapers Ltd v. Wilson; Associated British Ports Ltd v. Palmer* [1995] IRLR 406, HL.

[146] TULRCA, s. 193(1) and (2) as amended by the 1995 Regulations.

[147] TULRCA, s. 194(1).

[148] SI 1981 No. 1794.

[149] See Council Dir. 77/187.

Union safeguarding employees' rights in the event of a transfer of an undertaking. Unlike the case of consultation on redundancies the government chose to comply with its EC obligations on this occasion by means of regulations made under the European Communities Act 1972. The regulations fulfil two purposes. First, they ensure that when the transfer of a business takes place the contracts of employment of the employees concerned will be transferred automatically from the one employer to the other.[150] Second, they require that when an employer proposes to transfer his business or part of it to another employer, both employers inform and in certain circumstances consult with representatives of the relevant trade unions about the proposed transfer. Moreover, as we have seen, union recognition rights can also be transferred and it is also declared that any collective agreement operating before the transfer will continue to apply after the transfer becomes effective.[151] However, as regards the continued operation of the collective agreement, the transferee is only required to honour its terms as regards those employees who were employed in the undertaking at the date of the transfer. The transferee is not obliged to honour its terms as regards those employees recruited after that date.[152] As regards recognition rights, reg. 9(2) declares that where before a transfer an independent trade union was recognised in respect of employees who are being transferred, then, after the transfer, the union is to be deemed to have been recognised by the transferee. However, reg. 9(2) goes on to make clear that any agreement for recognition can be rescinded accordingly. This provision has little practical effect. Moreover, under reg. 9(1) the obligation to recognise only operates where the undertaking transferred maintains an identity distinct from the remainder of the transferee's business.

9.43 *The nature of the duty.* The 1981 Regulations impose a specific duty to inform and a separate duty to consult. The duties only arise where there is a relevant transfer[153] and formerly where there was a recognised trade union.[154] Further, the obligations only operate where there is an employee who will be affected by the transfer. This covers any employee of the transferor or the transferee (whether or not employed in the undertaking or the part of the undertaking to be transferred) who may be affected by the transfer or may be affected by measures taken in connection with it.[155] In the case of the duty to inform, the transferor employer must inform representatives of his own workforce about his intention to transfer them. The duty on the transferee employer is to inform the representatives of those of his own employees who will be affected by the transfer. The information must be provided long enough before a relevant transfer to enable consultations to take place. This is all that the regulations say about the timing of the information. However, in the only case to shed light on this question[156] Millet J argued that the crucial issue was for the information to be provided as soon as measures are envisaged. This is the primary obligation under the regulation. The information

---

[150] Regulation 5 discussed in more detail in Chapter Three.

[151] Regulation 6.

[152] See the decision of the European Court of Justice in *Landsorganisationen i Danmark v. Ny Molle KRO* [1989] IRLR 37, ECJ.

[153] See Reg. 3.

[154] But see now the Collective Redundancies and Transfer of Undertakings (Protection of Employment) (Amendment) Regulations 1995 (SI 1995 No. 2587) which extends rights of information and consultation to employee representatives; and para. 9.48.

[155] Regulation 10(1).

[156] *Institution of Professional Civil Servants v. Secretary of State for Defence* [1987] IRLR 373, ChD.

should be provided, therefore, as long as possible before the transfer is to take place. But where no measures are envisaged before the transfer, there is no requirement that information be provided before that transfer.

9.44 *The duty to inform.* The representatives should be informed about:

(a) the fact that the relevant transfer is to take place, when it is to take place and the reasons for it;

(b) the legal, economic and social implications of the transfer;

(c) the measures, if any, which it is envisaged will be taken in relation to those employees in connection with the transfer; and

(d) where the employer is the transferor, the measures which the transferee envisages he will take in connection with the transfer in relation to the employees being transferred.[157]

The necessary information for this last head must be given by the transferee to the transferor at such a time as will enable the latter to perform his duty. The information which union representatives are to receive should be delivered to them, or sent by post to an address notified by them to the employer, or sent by post to the union's head office.[158]

9.45 *When does it operate?* The nature of this duty to inform is vague. However, some light has been shed on its restrictive nature by the judgment of Millet J in *Institution of Professional Civil Servants v. Secretary of Defence.*[159] There the judge confirmed that the obligation to provide information about measures which are envisaged under heads (c) and (d) only arises where some definite plan or proposal has been formulated which it is intended to implement. Where no measures are envisaged there is no need to inform. This may mean that these obligations will not assist employees to obtain information on such matters as manpower, redundancy and changes in working practices to which they might claim that they are entitled under head (d). For, although Millet J accepted that the word measure has a wide import and involved any action, step or arrangement about these matters, he also argued that the use of the word ''will'' excluded mere hopes or possibilities. Consequently, an employer would have to formulate some definite plan or proposal which he is intending to implement before a duty to inform under head (d) would arise.

9.46 *The duty to consult.* The regulations also impose a duty of consultation. This duty arises where the employer envisages that he will be taking measures in relation to employees who are affected by the transfer.[160] If the employer is required to consult, any such consultation must be conducted with a view to seeking the representatives' agreement to the measures to be taken.[161] The employer is required in the course of these consultations to consider any representations made by representatives, to reply to them, and, if he rejects any of their representations, to state his reasons.[162] Consultation with representatives is only compulsory where an employer envisages that he will be taking measures in

---

[157] Regulation 10(2). If no measures are envisaged under heads (c) and (d) the union representatives should be informed of that fact.

[158] Regulation 10(4).

[159] [1987] IRLR 373, ChD.

[160] Regulation 10(5).

[161] Regulation 10(5) as amended by TURERA, s. 33.

[162] Regulation 10(6).

connection with the transfer. This is the only topic for which consultation is mandatory. There is no obligation on an employer under the regulations to consult on any of the other topics for which information has been provided. This would be a voluntary matter for the employer alone to decide.[163] Where there are special circumstances rendering it not reasonably practicable for the employer to perform his information and consultation duties, he is required to take all such steps towards performing any duty as are reasonably practicable in the circumstances.[164] Since this is a similar defence to that applicable in redundancy consultation, it can be presumed that that case law will also apply to a transfer of an undertaking.

9.47 *Failure to inform or consult.* A complaint that there has been a breach of these provisions must be presented to an industrial tribunal by the appropriate union before the end of the period of three months beginning with the date on which the relevant transfer is completed;[165] though this provision does not prevent a union from complaining of a failure to inform and consult before the completion of the relevant transfer.[166] Where the complaint is well-founded the tribunal will make a declaration to that effect and will award appropriate compensation to the employees concerned.[167] A tribunal is no longer required to take account of any protective award which may already have been made or to deduct any contractual payment when assessing compensation.[168] An employee who has not been paid in pursuance of this order can complain to the tribunal, and if the complaint is well-founded the employer will be ordered to pay the sum due.[169] However, the maximum compensation which can be awarded under this procedure is limited to four weeks' pay.[170]

9.48 Employee representatives

Like the redundancy consultation requirements, the information and consultation provisions in the 1981 Regulations were also considered by the European Court of Justice in default proceedings brought by the Commission.[171] In the context of information and consultation the most significant holding was that the United Kingdom had breached the Acquired Rights Directive by not introducing a system for the compulsory designation of worker representatives where that did not occur voluntarily in practice.[172]

The Collective Redundancies and Transfer of Undertakings (Protection of Employment) (Amendment) Regulations 1995[173] are intended to remedy this defect by extending the information and consultation requirements on a transfer to cover employee representatives. Such representatives can be elected for the specific purpose of consultation on a transfer or for some other purpose where it is

---

[163] See the decision of Millett J in *IPCS* case, above, at p. 376.
[164] Regulation 10(7).
[165] Regulation 11(8)(a).
[166] *South Durham Health Authority v. UNISON* [1995] IRLR 407, EAT.
[167] Regulation 11(4).
[168] Regulation 11(7) repealed by TURERA, s. 33.
[169] Regulation 11(5).
[170] Regulation 11(11).
[171] See *Commission of the European Communities v. United Kingdom* (Case C-382/92) [1994] IRLR 392, ECJ.
[172] The other breaches as regards information and consultation requirements were the failure to require consultation to be undertaken with a view to reaching agreement and the lack of an effective sanction for breach. Both of these matters were dealt with in TURERA, s. 33.
[173] SI 1995 No. 2587.

appropriate to inform and consult with them on transfer matters. As with redundancy consultation employers can now choose to consult with employee representatives, or, where there is a recognised independent trade union, union representatives. Where there are both employee representatives and a recognised independent trade union, the employer may choose which one of them to consult. Such representatives must also be allowed access to the affected employees and be afforded appropriate accommodation and other facilities. Complaints to industrial tribunals alleging a breach of the information and consultation requirements can be made by employee representatives, union representatives or by any employee affected by the transfer as the case may be. The new arrangements apply to transfers which took place on or after March 1, 1996.

UNION ORGANISATION — THE RIGHT TO ASSOCIATE

9.49 In Britain the right of workers to join and to take part in the affairs of trade unions is protected by means of three specific rights: (i) a right not to be refused employment because of trade union membership,[174] (ii) a right not to have action short of dismissal taken against them because of trade union membership or activities[175] and (iii) a right not to be dismissed on the grounds of union membership or activities.[176] Each of these three rights also applies to a person who is not a member of a trade union. The protection against refusal of employment on union membership grounds marks a new departure for British law because for the very first time applicants for employment enjoy protection against discrimination because of their membership or non-membership of a trade union.

9.50 Refusal of employment

The Trade Union and Labour Relations (Consolidation) Act 1992 renders it unlawful to refuse a person employment because he is, or is not, a member of a trade union; or because he is unwilling to accept a requirement;

(i) to take steps to become or cease to be, or to remain or not to become, a member of a trade union, or

(ii) to make payments or suffer deductions in the event of his not being a member of a trade union.[177]

Although this provision is aimed principally at the practices of the pre-entry closed shop it applies also to the applicant for employment who is denied a job because he is a union member. However, the protection given to union members seeking employment differs in two material respects from the right not to suffer action short of dismissal or the right not to be unfairly dismissed. First, it does not protect the applicant from discrimination as far as his trade union activities are concerned — arguably a major omission as regards active trade union members. The effect of such an omission could have been ameliorated by a broad interpretation of union membership. In *Discount Tobacco and Confectionery Ltd v. Armitage*[178] the EAT argued that there was no genuine distinction between membership of a union and making use of its essential services. This approach has been followed in the context of refusal of employment where the Employment Appeal Tribunal has

---

[174] TULRCA, s. 137.
[175] TULRCA, ss. 146–151.
[176] TULRCA, s. 152.
[177] TULRCA, s. 137(1).
[178] [1990] IRLR 15, EAT.

argued that there must be some overlap between the concepts of union membership and union activities and concluded that union membership also protected the incidents of union membership.[179] Such an approach is now less tenable since the decision of the House of Lords in *Associated Newspapers Ltd v. Wilson* and *Associated British Ports v. Palmer*.[180] Second, the right applies to membership of any trade union and is not restricted to those unions which hold a certificate of independence from the certification officer.[181]

9.51 *Deemed refusals of employment.* A person is taken to have been refused employment if he seeks a job with a person and that person does any of the following:

(a) refuses or deliberately omits to entertain and process his application or enquiry;

(b) causes him to withdraw or cease to pursue his application or enquiry;

(c) refuses or deliberately omits to offer him employment;

(d) makes him an offer of employment (which he does not accept) the terms of which are such as no reasonable employer who wished to fill the post would offer; or

(e) makes him an offer of such employment but withdraws it or causes him not to accept it.[182]

Further, it is conclusively presumed that a person has been refused employment for being a member or not being a member of a trade union when an advertisement is published which indicates or might reasonably be understood as indicating (a) that employment to which the advertisement relates is open only to a person who is, or is not a union member, or (b) that there will be requirements about taking steps to join or resign from a trade union or about making payments or suffering deductions in the event of not being a union member and a person who does not satisfy any of the above conditions seeks employment to which the advertisement relates and is refused that employment.[183] Finally, where there is an arrangement or practice under which employment is offered only to persons put forward or approved by a union — a "hiring hall" arrangement — and the union puts forward or approves only persons who are union members, a person who is not a union member and who is refused employment because of that arrangement or practice is to be taken as having been refused employment because he is not a union member.[184] All of the above provisions apply equally to an employment agency acting on behalf of the employer as it does to the employer himself, and it is unlawful for such an agency to refuse a person any of its services because he is or is not a union member, or because he is unwilling to accept a requirement to become or cease to be, or to remain or not to become, a union member.[185] While "employment agency" is defined in very broad terms[186] as meaning a person, who, for profit or not, provides services for the purpose of finding employment for

---

[179] *Harrison v. Kent County Council* [1995] ICR 434, EAT.
[180] [1995] ICR 406, HL discussed in more detail at para. 9.53. But see *Speciality Care plc v. Pachela* [1996] IRLR 248, EAT decided after *Wilson*.
[181] For the meaning of "independence" see Chapter Ten, para. 10.15.
[182] TULRCA, s. 137(5).
[183] TULRCA, s. 137(3).
[184] TULRCA, s. 137(4).
[185] TULRCA, s. 138(1).
[186] TULRCA, s. 143(1).

workers or supplying employers with workers,[187] a trade union is not to be regarded as an employment agency by reason of services provided only to members.[188]

9.52 *Remedies.* Applicants for employment who believe that they have been discriminated against on any of the above grounds have the right to complain to an industrial tribunal.[189] If the tribunal finds the complaint to be well-founded it can award compensation and can recommend that the respondent take within a specified period such action as appears practicable in order to obviate or reduce the adverse effect of his conduct upon the complainant[190]; the maximum amount of compensation that a complainant can receive is the maximum compensatory award in an unfair dismissal complaint.[191] The complainant or respondent may sist a third party to the proceedings where the respondent claims that he was induced to act as he did because of pressure which a trade union or other person exercised on him by calling, organising, procuring or financing a strike or other industrial action, or by threatening to do so; if the tribunal awards compensation it can order that the award be paid jointly or wholly by the third party.[192]

9.53 Action short of dismissal

The right against action short of dismissal on grounds of union membership or activities operates in two circumstances. First, where the employer takes action short of dismissal for the purpose of preventing or deterring the employee from being or seeking to become a member of an independent trade union, or penalises him for doing so. This right is also breached where the employer's action prevents or deters the employee from taking part in the activities of an independent trade union at any appropriate time, or penalises him for doing so.[193] Here also, the employer's action must be taken with the purpose of preventing or deterring the employee from taking part in union activities. Such purpose must be established and connotes an object which the employer desires or seeks to achieve. This is different from the case where the employer takes action for another purpose but its impact is to deter the employee from continuing his union activities.[194] As far as the non-member is concerned, it is also unlawful for an employer to take action to compel an employee to be or become a member of any trade union or of a particular trade union or of one of a number of particular trade unions.[195]

In all cases it is for the employer to show the purpose for which the action was taken against the employee.[196] But in determining that purpose no account is to be taken of any pressure which was exercised on the employer by calling, organising, procuring, or financing a strike or other industrial action, or by threatening to do so.[197] Difficulties have arisen in establishing the relevant purpose in cases where the employer seeks to alter the basis for determining terms and conditions of

---

[187] For the width of operation of the similar definition in race and sex legislation see *Commission for Racial Equality v. Imperial Society of Teachers of Dancing* [1983] IRLR 315, EAT.
[188] TULRCA, s. 143(2)(b).
[189] TULRCA, s. 143(4).
[190] TULRCA, s. 140(1).
[191] TULRCA, s. 140(4).
[192] TULRCA, s. 142(1)–(3).
[193] TULRCA, s. 146(1)(a) and (b).
[194] *Gallacher v. Department of Transport* [1994] IRLR 231, CA.
[195] TULRCA, s. 146(1)(c).
[196] TULRCA, s. 148(1).
[197] TULRCA, s. 148(2).

employment by offering personal contracts with incentives for those who accept and which involve individual negotiation rather than collective bargaining.[198] Such a policy is likely to have a disproportionate adverse impact on union members. This point is now addressed specifically in the 1992 Act. Where there is evidence that the employer's purpose was to further a change in his relationship with all or any class[199] of his employees, and there is also evidence that his purpose was to prevent, deter or penalise union membership, the tribunal is directed to regard the former purpose as the purpose for which the employer took the action, unless it considers that the action was such that no reasonable employer would take it in the circumstances.[200]

It is now clear that employees have no protection under these provisions where the penalty comes about through an omission to provide a benefit.[201] Thus, for example, withholding a pay increase from employees who are union members does not give them a cause of complaint as action short of dismissal. Moreover, it must be shown that the employer's action was taken against the employee as an individual.[202] This means that it is not action short of dismissal where the employer's action is aimed at the union but that action also has a consequential effect upon employees who are union members. Thus, for example, employees cannot complain of action short of dismissal where the employer's action takes the form of the derecognition of a trade union of which they are a member.[203] However, a complaint will be competent where the employee can show that the action of the employer had a direct effect upon him because it breached his rights as an individual employee.[204] But this protection is limited and will not apply where the action of the employer takes the form of the withholding of a benefit since this involves an omission which is not covered by the legislation.[205] Action in the form of disciplinary action[206] or the transfer of an employee to a less desirable job[207] is undoubtedly action short of dismissal for this purpose. However, it has been doubted whether a threat by an employer to dismiss in the future can amount to action short of dismissal.[208]

9.54 Dismissal

As was noted in Chapter Five, the right not to be unfairly dismissed applies where the reason (or, if more than one reason, the principal reason) was that the employee

---

[198] See the decision of the House of Lords in *Associated Newspapers Ltd v. Wilson* and *Associated British Ports v. Palmer* [1995] ICR 406, HL.

[199] "Class" means those employees employed at a particular place of work, and those employees of a particular grade, category or description either generally or at a particular place of work: TULRCA, s. 148(5) as inserted by TURERA, s. 13.

[200] TULRCA, s. 148(3) as inserted by TURERA, s. 13. In any event, this arrangement does not amount to action short of dismissal since it involves an omission to provide a benefit; see *Associated Newspapers Ltd v. Wilson* and *Associated British Ports v. Palmer*, above.

[201] *Associated Newspapers Ltd v. Wilson* and *Associated British Ports v. Palmer*, above. See, in particular, the speech of Lord Bridge of Harwich (Lord Slynn of Hadley and Lord Lloyd of Berwick dissenting).

[202] TULRCA, s. 146(1).

[203] See the decision of Dillon LJ in *Associated Newspapers Ltd v. Wilson* [1994] ICR 97 at p. 104 and the speech of Lord Slynn of Hadley in the House of Lords in the same case.

[204] *National Coal Board v. Ridgway* [1987] ICR 641, CA.

[205] *Associated Newspapers Ltd v. Wilson* and *Associated British Ports v. Palmer*, above overruling *Ridgway*, above, on this point.

[206] *British Airways Engine Overhaul v. Francis* [1981] IRLR 9, EAT.

[207] *Robb v. Leon Motor Services Ltd* [1978] ICR 506, EAT.

[208] *Brassington v. Cauldon Wholesale Ltd* [1978] ICR 405, EAT.

was, or proposed to become, a member of an independent trade union or had taken part, or proposed to take part, in the activities of an independent trade union at an appropriate time.[209] Equally, it is an automatically unfair dismissal to dismiss an employee because he is not a member of any trade union, or of a particular trade union, or has refused or proposed to refuse to become or remain a member.[210] The protection against dismissal for union activities is undoubtedly the more significant right for the union member. The Employment Appeal Tribunal in *Discount Tobacco & Confectionery Ltd v. Armitage*[211] has sought to define broadly the union membership protection so as to cover any incident of trade union membership such as making use of the essential services of a union officer to negotiate on the member's behalf. This decision hinges upon the view that the right not to be unfairly dismissed on the ground of union membership also applies so as to protect the consequences of that membership as well. However, in *Associated Newspapers Ltd v. Wilson* and *Associated British Ports v. Palmer*[212] the House of Lords has taken a much narrower view of the meaning of union membership. While not challenging the correctness of the *Armitage* decision on its facts, the House of Lords refused to accept that union membership should be equated with using the essential services of the union. Lord Bridge of Harwich even rejected the contention that the use of collective bargaining was an essential service of the union and Lord Lloyd of Berwick could see little justification for regarding trade union membership and the use of trade union services as the same thing. The *Wilson* and *Palmer* decision undoubtedly limits the effectiveness of the protections against dismissal and action short of dismissal on union membership grounds.[213] But it may have a greater impact in refusal of employment cases where there is no additional protection against discrimination for trade union activities.

9.55 Job applicants and new members

The protections against dismissal and action short of dismissal only apply after employment has commenced. However, even after a trade union activist has obtained employment he is only protected from discriminatory action in respect of trade union activities which took place after his employment had begun and the statutory protections do not cover trade union activities outside of and before the particular employment had begun.[214] However, this position is now subject to a major caveat which was discussed by the Court of Appeal in *Fitzpatrick v. British Railways Board*[215] where it was argued that it would be wrong to conclude that what happened in previous employment could never form the basis for a relevant complaint. What happened in a previous job may form the reason for a dismissal in subsequent employment and therefore cannot be ignored. In such a case the tribunal must ask itself if the fear of trade union activities in the future played any part in the employer's decision to dismiss. If the only rational explanation is that the employer feared repetition of those activities then the tribunal would be entitled to find the dismissal unfair because it is clear that the employer expected the employee to take part in such activities in his current employment. A tribunal

---

[209] TULRCA, s. 152(1)(a) and (b).
[210] TULRCA, s. 152(1)(c). This protection is discussed in much more detail in Chapter Five, paras 5.57–5.59.
[211] [1990] IRLR 15, EAT.
[212] [1995] ICR 406, HL.
[213] For a recent consideration of its impact see the decision of the EAT in *Speciality Care plc v. Pachela*, [1996] IRLR 248, EAT a case which adheres to the principle set out in *Armitage*.
[214] *City of Birmingham District Council v. Beyer* [1977] IRLR 211, EAT.
[215] [1991] IRLR 373, CA.

must also establish the belief held by the employer in cases where employees are selected for redundancy and they allege that this is because of their trade union activities. Here it is necessary for the tribunal to discover whether those past activities were the activities of an independent trade union and whether the employer believed that the employees would engage in disruptive activities in the future which were related to those in the past. If this is the case the dismissals are automatically unfair and constitute a breach of the Trade Union and Labour Relations (Consolidation) Act 1992, ss. 153 and 152(1)(b).[216] However, there is no need for an employer to be motivated by malice or a deliberate desire to be rid of a trade union activist for the above provisions to be broken.[217] The statutory protections may be of limited effect as regards employees who have recently joined a union during a campaign to obtain recognition rights. In *Carrington v. Therm-a-stor Ltd*[218] the Court of Appeal held that four employees who had been dismissed after their union had made a request to be recognised by their employer had not been dismissed for an automatically unfair reason because the reason for their dismissal was the union's request for recognition and not because they *personally* had joined or proposed to take part in the union's activities.

9.56 Activities of a trade union

An employee is protected from dismissal and action short of dismissal for taking part in the activities of an independent trade union. There is no definition of the word "activities" and it has been held that this lack of definition was deliberate since the word connotes a wide variety of possibilities varying with the circumstances of each case.[219] "Activities" should be reasonably, and not too restrictively, interpreted[220] but includes forming a union branch,[221] calling a meeting to consider the recognition of an employee as a shop steward[222] and complaining to the union about the provision of safety cover.[223] Moreover, it is not restricted to activities involving the status of an employee as a trade unionist. It might even apply where a meeting of women union members is called in order to pass a resolution complaining about the union's inability to obtain equal pay with the men.[224] On the other hand, the mere fact that an employee who makes representations to an employer is a trade unionist does not necessarily make those representations the activities of a trade union. In *Chant v. Aquaboats Ltd*[225] a union member who was not an accredited shop steward was held not to be taking part in union activities when he organised a petition complaining about the safety standards which was signed by a majority of employees who were not union members. Equally, where the employee carries out wholly unreasonable, extraneous or malicious acts in support of union activities, none of the statutory protections will apply.[226] This might also be the case where the employee indulges in union activities simply in order to ventilate a private grievance.[227] It is

---

[216] *Port of London Authority v. Payne* [1992] IRLR 447, EAT.
[217] *Dundon v. GPT Ltd* [1995] IRLR 403, EAT.
[218] [1983] ICR 208, CA.
[219] *Chant v. Aquaboats Ltd* [1978] ICR 643, EAT.
[220] *Dixon v. West Ella Developments Ltd* [1978] ICR 856, EAT.
[221] *Lyon v. St James Press Ltd* [1976] ICR 413, EAT.
[222] *Marley Tile Co. Ltd v. Shaw* [1980] ICR 72, CA.
[223] *Dixon v. West Ella Developments*, above.
[224] *British Airways Engine Overhaul Ltd v. Francis* [1981] IRLR 9, EAT.
[225] [1978] ICR 643, EAT.
[226] *Lyon v. St James Press*, above.
[227] *Per* Goff LJ in *Marley Tile Co.*, above, at p. 79.

undoubtedly the case that going on strike or taking part in industrial action short of a strike are not protected activities for the purposes of either dismissal or action short of dismissal.[228]

9.57 "Appropriate time"

This right to take part in union activities is circumscribed by the requirement that the activities take place at an appropriate time. This is defined as a time either outside working hours, or, alternatively, within working hours where, in accordance with arrangements agreed with or consent given by his employer, the employee is permitted to take part in those activities.[229] The best course would be to ensure that there is some express agreement defining the terms of this right. However, the requirement that union activities should take place outside working hours unless the employer has consented has not been interpreted as involving a complete embargo on the use of the employer's premises. It would be legitimate for employees to use the employer's premises for union business at times when no work is being done, such as during meal breaks or tea breaks, so long as their contracts entitle them to be on those premises at that time.[230] The exercise of this right might even involve the employer tolerating minor infringements of his strict legal rights so long as no harm is caused and the employees who are taking part in those activities on his premises are doing so at a time when they are not actually working.[231]

9.58 Implied consent

As has been noted, the greater right to participate in union affairs during working hours can only be exercised with the employer's consent or agreement. Although such consent need not be stated expressly and can be implied, clear evidence of its existence must be established. Mere silence on the part of the employer is unlikely to suffice. In *Marley Tile Co. Ltd v. Shaw*[232] the Court of Appeal held that the silence of the employer when an employee denied the status of shop steward announced his intention to hold a meeting during working hours did not imply consent. Equally, a statement in an employee's written particulars providing a right to take part in union activities at an appropriate time does not constitute the necessary agreement or consent nor does it provide any guidance as to what is meant by appropriate time.[233]

9.59 Remedies for action short of dismissal

An employee who alleges that action short of dismissal has been taken against him because of his union membership or trade union activities or because of non-union membership has the right to complain to an industrial tribunal.[234] If the complaint is upheld, the tribunal has the authority to make a declaration and to award

---

[228] *Drew v. St Edmondsbury Borough Council* [1980] ICR 513, EAT. The effect of TULRCA, ss. 237 and 238 upon a dismissed striker's right to complain of unfair dismissal is discussed in Chapter Five, paras. 5.70–5.75.

[229] TULRCA, s. 146(2) and s. 152(2).

[230] *Post Office v. Crouch* [1974] ICR 378, HL. A decision reached under the equivalent provisions of IRA.

[231] *Per* Lord Reid in *Crouch*, above at pp. 398–400.

[232] [1980] ICR 72.

[233] *Robb v. Leon Motor Services Ltd* [1978] ICR 506, EAT.

[234] TULRCA, s. 151(2).

compensation to the employee.[235] The amount of compensation awarded is such as the tribunal considers just and equitable in all the circumstances having regard to the infringement of the complainant's rights and to any loss sustained by him which is attributable to the employer's action.[236] The loss includes (a) any expenses reasonably incurred by the employee in consequence of the employer's action and (b) loss of any benefit which the employee might reasonably be expected to have but for that action.[237] In assessing compensation the tribunal must ignore any pressure exercised on the employer by a real or threatened strike or other industrial action.[238] The award can be reduced where the tribunal finds that the employee caused or contributed to the action taken by the employer.[239] It has been held[240] that the purpose of the award is to compensate an employee for the infringement of his rights; it is not intended to act as a fine against the employer. The amount should be calculated by reference to any monetary loss suffered by the employee plus an additional sum to compensate for non-pecuniary loss. It might be appropriate when assessing compensation to take account of the fact that an employee's sincere desire to enjoy the benefits of trade union membership have been frustrated as a result of the employer's actions.

9.60 Remedies for dismissal

An employee who has been dismissed because of his trade union membership and activities has the same rights of complaint to an industrial tribunal as an employee who has been dismissed for non-union membership. As was noted in Chapter Five these include the right to interim relief and the right to receive enhanced levels of compensation if dismissal for an automatically unfair reason is established.

9.61 Deducting union subscriptions

The Employment Act 1988 sought to ensure that employees who had terminated their membership of trade unions could prevent any union subscriptions being deducted from their wages by their employer from the date of termination of their union membership.[241] The Trade Union Reform and Employment Rights Act 1993 has replaced this provision with a much wider protection as regards union subscriptions which are deducted by the employer from a worker's wages.[242] It requires employers, where check-off arrangements exist for the deduction of union subscriptions, to ensure (a) that no deduction is made unless it is an authorised deduction and (b) that the amount of the deduction does not exceed the permitted amount.[243] A subscription deduction will only be authorised where there is a document containing the worker's authorisation for the deduction which he has signed and dated and which is in force on the day of the deduction.[244] Authorisations only remain in force for a period of three years from the date the worker signs and dates the document of authorisation.[245] After the end of this period the relevant authorisation will lapse and the employer will have to obtain a fresh authorisation

---

[235] TULRCA, s. 149(1).
[236] TULRCA, s. 149(2).
[237] TULRCA, s. 149(3).
[238] TULRCA, s. 149(5).
[239] TULRCA, s. 149(6).
[240] *Brassington v. Cauldon Wholesale Ltd* [1978] ICR 405, EAT.
[241] See the original provisions of TULRCA, s. 68.
[242] "Worker" and "wages" have the same meaning as in ERA, Part II and s. 230(3).
[243] TULRCA, s. 68(1) as inserted by TURERA, s. 15.
[244] TULRCA, s. 68(2).
[245] TULRCA, s. 68(3).

if subscription deductions are to be continued. As well as authorisations lapsing automatically after the expiry of three years an employee can also withdraw his consent at any time by giving written notice to the employer. In this case subscription deductions must cease as soon as is reasonably practicable to enable the employer to secure that no further deductions are made.[246]

As already noted, subscription deductions are limited to the permitted amount. This is the amount which falls to be made from wages in accordance with subscription deduction arrangements.[247] If the amount of the deduction is to be increased the employer must give the appropriate notice to the worker at least one month before the increased amount is deducted.[248] This notice must be in writing and must state (a) the amount of the increase and the increased amount of the subscription deductions, and (b) that the worker may at any time withdraw his authorisation for the deduction by giving written notice to the employer.[249]

Where the employer makes a deduction from wages without the necessary authorisation or deducts more than the permitted amount, the worker may present a complaint to an industrial tribunal.[250] Such a complaint must be presented within three months of the last deduction complained of, unless it was not reasonably practicable to present the complaint within that period.[251] If the tribunal finds the complaint to be well-founded it will make a declaration to that effect and will order the employer to pay to the worker the whole of the deduction (in the case of an unauthorised deduction) or the amount by which the deduction exceeded the permitted amount (in the case of any deduction above the permitted amount) less any part that has already been paid to the worker by the employer.[252]

TIME OFF

9.62 Trade union duties

The original statutory provisions[253] created a right to time off with pay during working hours for employees who were officials[254] of recognised independent trade unions in two circumstances. First, they were entitled to time off to enable them to carry out those duties as officials which were concerned with industrial relations between their employer and any associated employer and their employees.[255] They were also entitled to time off in order to undergo training in aspects of industrial relations which were relevant to their duties and which had been approved by the TUC or by their own union.[256] The case law on the right to time off adopted a liberal interpretation of this provision. In *Sood v. GEC Elliott*

---

[246] TULRCA, s. 68(4).
[247] TULRCA, s. 68(5)(a).
[248] TULRCA, s. 68(5)(b).
[249] TULRCA, s. 68(7).
[250] TULRCA, s. 68A(1) as inserted by TURERA, s. 15.
[251] TULRCA, s. 68A(1).
[252] TULRCA, s. 68A(2).
[253] EPCA, s. 27 before amendment by EA 1989.
[254] An official is defined by TULRCA, s. 119 as a person who is an officer of the union or a branch or section or a person elected or appointed in accordance with the union's rules to be a representative of its members or some of them.
[255] EPCA, s. 27(1)(a). See now TULRCA, s. 168(1)(a).
[256] EPCA, s. 27(1)(b). See now TULRCA, s. 168(1)(b). *Cf* the provisions for time off for training for safety representatives in the Safety Representatives and Safety Committees Regulations 1977 (SI 1977 No. 500) where there is no need for TUC or union approval. See *White v. Pressed Steel Fisher* [1980] IRLR 176, EAT.

Process Automation Ltd,[257] for example, although it was held that there was no statutory right to time off simply to attend meetings of union officials where information would be exchanged, it was accepted that the right to time off should not be restricted exclusively to those purposes falling within the statutory definition of recognition. Moreover, it need not even have been restricted to the industrial relations structure of the employer. The Court of Appeal confirmed this approach in *Beal v. Beecham Group Ltd*[258] where that court held that work preparatory to collective bargaining could give rise to a right to time off with pay. It was reiterated that the right of a union official to time off was not restricted by the extent of his union's recognition rights and the court accepted that it could encompass attendance at meetings with other officials of the union employed by the same or an associated employer called to plan union negotiating strategy prior to collective bargaining taking place.

9.63 *Development of the right to time off.* In another Court of Appeal decision, *Thomas Scott & Sons (Bakers) Ltd v. Allen*,[259] the right to paid time off was extended even further. In this case it was held that attending a meeting with union officials was within the industrial relations duties of a shop steward even although the meeting related to a matter over which the union had no authority to bargain collectively with that employer. This was on the basis that it was a shop steward's duty to give senior officials the benefit of his experience at meetings. The only limitation on the right to paid time off was that the official's duties had to have a connection with industrial relations between an employer and his employees. However, it was possible that an official might have a right to paid time off in order to attend a meeting called to plan a union's campaign against the repeal of an Act of Parliament so long as it could be established that the repeal of that Act would have some impact on the continued operation of the employer's arrangements for collective bargaining.[260]

9.64 *Time off for training.* The right to time for training was also liberally interpreted, particularly in England. In *Young v. Carr Fasteners Ltd*,[261] for example, it was held that an employee had the right to time off to attend a training course on pensions even although the employer's own pension scheme did not call for any union involvement because advising about pensions was as much about industrial relations as negotiating and advising about wage levels. A different approach to this question has been adopted in Scotland[262] where it was held that an employee had to show that the subject of the course was directly related to his duties as a union official. Moreover, before paid time off could be granted it had to be the purpose of the course to teach material which would be of assistance in negotiation with the employer. This decision is more in keeping with the current statutory regime for time off.

---

[257] [1979] IRLR 416, EAT. See also *RHP Bearings Ltd v. Brookes* [1979] IRLR 452, EAT.

[258] [1982] ICR 460, CA.

[259] [1983] IRLR 329, CA.

[260] See the decision of the Court of Appeal in *Adlington v. British Bakers (Northern) Ltd* [1989] IRLR 218 reversing the decision of the EAT reported at [1988] ICR 488. See also *Luce v. London Borough of Bexley* [1990] IRLR 422 where the EAT argued that whether a trade union organised lobby of parliament is a trade union activity depends upon whether it is in some way linked to the employment relationship between the employee, the employer and the trade union.

[261] [1979] IRLR 420, EAT.

[262] *Menzies v. Smith & McLaurin Ltd* [1980] IRLR 180, EAT.

9.65 *Restricting the right to time off.* The scope for time off under both of the above heads has been considerably narrowed[263] by restricting an official's right to time off for union duties to time off in relation to matters over which the union has obtained recognition rights with his particular employer. Now an employer must permit an employee of his who is an official of a recognised independent trade union to take paid time off during his working hours so as to carry out any duties of his, as such an official, concerned with:

(a) negotiations with the employer related to or connected with matters of collective bargaining[264] for which the union is recognised by the employer; or

(b) the performance of functions for the employees related to or connected with matters falling within collective bargaining which the employer has agreed may be performed by the union.[265]

The right to time off for training in aspects of industrial relations is similarly circumscribed so that it must now be relevant to the carrying out of collective bargaining duties.[266] Such training must also be approved by the TUC or by an independent trade union of which the employee is an official.[267] These changes mean that there is a restriction in the number of duties which qualify for time off. In addition, those duties must be related to or connected with collective bargaining and the union must be recognised in relation to those matters.[268] So employees will only be entitled to time off to attend a co-ordinating committee of their union where that committee acts as a forum for discussing the union's approach to collective bargaining and so long as there is sufficient nexus between any subsequent collective bargaining and those discussions.[269] Thus, under the present law there can be no repetition of decisions such as that in the *Allen* case where entitlement to time off for duties unconnected with collective bargaining was upheld. On the other hand, there are aspects of the decisions in both *Sood* and *Beal* which would be decided in the same way under the current definition since they related to time off in connection with negotiations with the employer over collective bargaining matters. This exclusion of industrial relations duties and the restriction of the right to matters involving the employee's own employer are consistent with the government's objective of weakening national collective bargaining and encouraging bargaining at local level so as to create greater flexibility in the setting of wage rages.

9.66 *The extent of the right to time-off.* Employees are entitled to take time off during working hours.[270] Those are the hours which the employee would normally have been at work.[271] In addition, the amount of time off which an employee is to be permitted to take and the purposes for which, and the occasions on which and any conditions subject to which, time off may be taken are those that are reasonable in all the circumstances having regard to any Code of Practice issued by ACAS.[272] The remedy is by complaint to an industrial tribunal that the employer

---

[263] First introduced by EA 1989, s. 14.
[264] These matters are listed in TULRCA, s. 178(2).
[265] TULRCA, s. 168(1)(a) and (b).
[266] TULRCA, s. 168(2)(a).
[267] TULRCA, s. 168(2)(b).
[268] *London Ambulance Service v. Charlton* [1992] IRLR 510, EAT.
[269] *Charlton*, above.
[270] TULRCA, s. 168(1).
[271] *Hairsine v. Kingston-Upon-Hull City Council* [1992] IRLR 211, EAT.
[272] TULRCA, s. 168(3).

has failed to permit the applicant to take time off.[273] The ACAS Code of Practice on Time Off for Trade Union Duties and Activities[274] provides guidance on these issues. In particular, para. 12 of the Revised Code contains a detailed list of the matters for which time off should be granted (assuming that the union has collective bargaining rights). These cover:

(a) terms and conditions of employment, or the physical conditions in which employees are required to work (e.g. pay, hours of work, holiday pay and entitlement, sick pay arrangements, pensions, vocational training, equal opportunities, notice periods, the working environment, utilisation of machinery and other equipment);

(b) engagement or non-engagement, or termination or suspension of employment or the duties of employment, of one or more workers (e.g. recruitment and selection policies, human resource planning, redundancy and dismissal arrangements);

(c) allocation of work, or the duties of employment as between workers and groups of workers (e.g. job grading, job evaluation, job descriptions, flexible working practices);

(d) matters of discipline (e.g. disciplinary procedures, representing members at internal interviews, appearing for members before agreed outside appeal bodies or industrial tribunals);

(e) trade union membership or non-membership (e.g. representational agreements, induction arrangements);

(f) facilities for officials of trade unions (e.g. accommodation, equipment, names of new workers to the union);

(g) machinery for negotiation and consultation and other procedures (e.g. collective bargaining, grievance procedures, joint consultation, communicating with members or officials).

The Code also recommends that union officials have the right to reasonable time off in order to prepare for negotiations and meetings, inform members of their progress and to explain the results to members.

9.67 *Reasonable time-off.* As has already been noted, the amount of time off is that which is reasonable in all the circumstances. There is no definition of reasonableness in the Act, though the ACAS Code of Practice, section 4 does give guidance on the general considerations which unions and employers should have in mind in relation to time off. The issue has also been judicially considered but without any definite guidelines being laid down because it is for the tribunal to decide the question of reasonableness on the facts. This point is illustrated in the *Allen* case[275] where the Court of Appeal refused to disturb the finding of the tribunal that it was not unreasonable in the circumstances for the employer to refuse paid time off to all eleven shop stewards who had requested time off in order to attend their meeting. Although this approach is consistent with that applied in other areas of employment law, it does have a number of questions unanswered.

For instance, it is not clear whether it would be legitimate for an employer who believes that a request for time off for union duties is unreasonable, to grant such time off on an unpaid basis. May LJ was clearly of the view in *Allen* that an

---

[273] TULRCA, s. 168(4). It is necessary for the employer to know of the request before he can fail to permit him time off: *Ryford Ltd v. Drinkwater* [1996] IRLR 16, EAT.

[274] ACAS Code No. 3. The original Code was brought into force on April 1, 1978. The present revised code took effect on May 13, 1991.

[275] [1983] IRLR 329. See also Code of Practice, section 4.

employer would be entitled to offer time off without pay in such circumstances. However, in *Beecham Group Ltd v. Beal (No. 2)*[276] it was held that if it was established that the time off was for industrial relations duties, the employer could not impose a condition that it be unpaid. It would be legitimate, however, for an employer, when assessing the reasonableness of a particular request, to take account of the amount of paid and unpaid time off which that employee has already received.[277] The amount of pay that an employee receives for time off is that amount which he would have received had he worked his normal hours, although an employee paid by piece rates will receive an amount calculated by reference to his average hourly earnings for that work.[278] There is no justification for paying the equivalent number of hours for the time it took to perform the duties if these hours were not within the normal working hours.[279]

9.68 Trade union activities

As far as trade union activities are concerned, an employee who is a member of a recognised independent trade union is entitled to take time off without pay to take part in the activities of that union, together with any activities in relation to which the employee is acting as the representative of the union.[280] Like time off for trade union duties, the amount, purposes, occasions and conditions under which time off can be taken for those activities are those that are reasonable in all the circumstances.[281] It would be lawful for an employer to refuse time off for union activities to an employee who has already taken a considerable amount of time off for other purposes.[282] The ACAS Code of Practice is once again useful for guidance on this issue. The Code (para. 21) advises, for example, that employees should be permitted reasonable time off in order to attend workplace meetings to discuss and vote on the outcome of negotiations, meeting full-time officials, voting in properly conducted ballots on industrial action or in union elections. There is no right to time off, however, in order to participate in industrial action whether or not that action is in contemplation or furtherance of a trade dispute.[283]

9.69 Remedies

An employee who is denied the right to time off for trade union duties, relevant training or activities has the right to complain to an industrial tribunal within three months of the date when the failure occurred unless it was not reasonably practicable.[284] There is also a right of complaint where the employer has granted time off for trade union duties but has failed to pay the wages that fell due. Where a complaint against a refusal to allow time off is made the tribunal has the authority to make a declaration to that effect and may also award such compensation as it considers just and equitable having regard to the employer's default and any loss sustained by the employee attributable to that refusal.[285] By analogy with the right to compensation for action short of dismissal for trade union membership

---

[276] [1983] IRLR 317, EAT.
[277] *Wignall v. British Gas Corporation* [1984] ICR 716, EAT.
[278] TULRCA, s. 169(1)–(3).
[279] *Hairsine v. Kingston-Upon-Hull City Council* [1992] IRLR 211, EAT.
[280] TULRCA, s. 170(1).
[281] TULRCA, s. 170(3).
[282] *Wignall v. British Gas Corporation* [1984] ICR 716, EAT.
[283] TULRCA, s. 170(2).
[284] TULRCA, s. 171. ACAS can also exercise conciliation functions over such complaints: TULRCA, s. 290.
[285] TULRCA, s. 172(1) and (2).

or activities, the purpose of any award of compensation should not be to punish the employer for his default.[286] Where the complaint relates to a failure by the employer to pay the employee for the time off for trade union duties, the tribunal is entitled to order the payment of the amount which it considers that the employee is due.[287]

---

[286] See *Brassington v. Cauldon Wholesale Ltd* [1978] ICR 405, EAT.
[287] TULRCA, s. 172(3).

Chapter Ten

THE LEGAL REGULATION OF TRADE UNIONS

INTRODUCTION

10.1 The internal affairs of trade unions are regulated both by common law principles and by statute. As far as Scots common law is concerned a trade union is a voluntary unincorporated association with no separate legal identity from that of its members. The nearest analogous organisations are the non-established churches or social clubs. In the same way as the constitution of a club regulates the rights of the members so, in the case of a union, the rule book constitutes the contract of membership. It is the rule book which sets out a person's rights to join, to be disciplined and even to take part in the affairs of the union. As we shall see, the practice of the Scottish courts has been to examine these rules closely in order to establish the contractual rights of the member.[1] One important theme which will be explored in this chapter is the extent to which the courts no longer regard this voluntary association/social club model as suitable when reviewing the conduct of trade unions. There can be no doubt that in modern times trade unions exercise important functions in society far beyond those of the social club. In the past the practice of the closed shop was the most obvious manifestation of the economic power of trade unions. However, the very process of collective bargaining also had important implications for the union member, the employer and for society as a whole, particularly when resort is made to industrial action. It will be important to discover to what extent the law has taken account of these factors in its present attitude towards trade union government.

10.2 Trade unions originally operated in a hostile legal environment where the law provided little or no legal protection for their activities or against abuse of their funds.[2] However, with the enactment of the Trade Union Act 1871, a new legal regime was created whereby trade unions were permitted to regulate their own internal affairs without the threat that their activities would be tainted with illegality.[3] This legislation set the tone for the approach of the State towards internal union affairs. Thus until recently, and with the exception of the period of the Industrial Relations Act 1971, recently, the role of legislation had been to provide a legal framework where trade unions could organise their own affairs

---

[1] See, for example, *Martin v. Scottish Transport and General Workers Union* 1951 SC 129; 1952 SC (HL) 1.

[2] *Procurator Fiscal v. Wool-Combers in Aberdeen* (1762) M 1961 and *Barr v. Carr* (1766) M 9564. See also *Hornby v. Close* (1867) LR 2 QB 153; *Farrer v. Close* (1869) LR 4 QB 602.

[3] See, in particular, TUA 1871, s. 3 which declared that the purposes of a trade union were not to be considered unlawful simply because they were in restraint of trade, and s. 4 which sought to exclude the courts from entertaining certain types of legal action against trade unions.

without external interference. As Kahn-Freund has observed,[4] "in this country, it has, on the whole, been common ground that in the dilemma between imposing standards of democracy and protecting union autonomy the law must come down on the side of union autonomy". This policy has now been rejected in favour of one which seeks to ensure that trade unions behave in a manner which conforms with certain democratic standards as laid down in statute. Thus the Trade Union Act 1984 and the Employment Act 1988, for example, ensured that union executive ballots and political fund ballots had to be conducted by secret postal ballot and were subject to independent scrutiny.[5] Equally, the legislation has introduced a series of provisions to ensure probity and transparency in union affairs.[6] In addition, the legislation enacted since 1980 has displayed a belief in the primacy of the rights of the individual union member above and beyond the collective interests of his trade union. As we shall see, for example, statute prevents a union from disciplining a union member who has refused to obey a lawfully executed strike call,[7] and there is now a right not to be excluded or expelled from a trade union except in very limited circumstances.[8]

DEFINITION OF A TRADE UNION

10.3 The original definition of a trade union as enacted by the Trade Union Act 1871 was undoubtedly wider than the one operative in modern times since it also applied to employers' associations and even to trade associations unconnected with industrial relations.[9] The present statutory definition of a trade union concentrates upon both the nature of the organisation and upon its objects by providing that a trade union is "an organisation (whether temporary or permanent) which consists wholly or mainly of workers of one or more descriptions and whose principal purposes include the regulation of relations between workers of that description or those descriptions and employers or employers' associations".[10] An organisation which is made up wholly or mainly of constituent associations or affiliates or representatives of such constituents of affiliates can also be a trade union in law so long as either the organisation itself or its constituents or affiliates consist wholly or mainly of workers and also seek to regulate worker/employer relations.[11]

10.4 The members

The members of a trade union must be wholly or mainly workers. A worker is defined as a person who works or normally works or seeks to work under a contract of employment or any other contract whereby he undertakes to do or perform personally any work or services for another party to the contract who is

---

[4] *Kahn-Freud's Labour and the Law* (3rd edn, Davies & Freedland) at p. 274.
[5] See now TULRCA, Chapter IV (elections) and TULRCA, ss. 73–81 (political funds).
[6] See, for example, TULRCA, ss. 15 and 16 (protections against unlawful use of union funds), originally enacted by EA 1988, ss. 8 and 9.
[7] EA 1988, s. 3, now TULRCA, s. 64.
[8] TULRCA, s. 174 originally enacted by TURERA, s. 14.
[9] See *G & J Rae v. Plate Glass Merchants' Association* 1919 SC 426; *Edinburgh Master Plumbers' Association v. Munro* 1928 SC 565; *Edinburgh and District Aerated Water Manufacturers' Defence Association v. Jenkinson & Co.* (1903) 5 F 1159.
[10] TULRCA, s. 1(a).
[11] It is unclear whether the TUC or STUC satisfies the definition of a trade union. See Kidner *Trade Union Law* (2nd edn) at p. 3.

not his professional client.[12] The legislation declares specifically that individuals in employment under or for the purposes of a government department (otherwise than as a member of the naval, military or air forces of the Crown) are workers.[13] The term worker is clearly wider in scope than that of employee. However, certain groups of workers cannot be members of trade unions. Members of the police service[14] and, as already noted, those in the armed forces are specifically excluded from the statutory definition.[15] On the other hand, both Crown employees[16] and health service practitioners[17] are expressly declared to be workers.

10.5 The organisation's objects

The fact that a trade union must be an organisation whether temporary or permanent has been described as being "pregnant with elasticity".[18] At the very minimum the union must possess some of the attributes of an organisation. In *Frost v. Clarke & Smith Manufacturing Co. Ltd.*[19] a claim that an employees' works committee could be a trade union was rejected because it possessed none of the organisational qualities expected of such a body. It had no name, no constitution and no rules; it held no meetings, kept no minutes, and did not have any officers, property or funds. A union must also have the regulation of worker/ employer relations as one of its principal objects. This entails establishing that the organisation has some ambition to regulate the relations between an employer and workers by means of collective bargaining. It is not enough for the organisation simply to be involved in organising industrial action.[20] At the very least the organisation must have attempted to obtain recognition rights from an employer.[21] There is nothing to prevent an organisation which seeks to promote the professional interests of its members from satisfying the statutory definition. So long as it is also involved in some way in worker/employer relations it will be a trade union in law. In deciding this question the court is entitled to look beyond the organisation's rules and to consider how it operates in practice.[22]

10.6 Legal status

There is no doubt that in the past the exact legal status of a trade union was uncertain. As we have seen, Scots common law considered that a trade union had no legal existence separate from the membership. Consequently, it could not sue in its own name — although it could take advantage of the procedures which permitted an unincorporated body to sue by the addition of certain of its members clothed with such responsibility.[23] However, with the enactment of the 1871 Act which *inter alia* granted a trade union the right voluntarily to register with the Chief Registrar of Friendly Societies, the English courts construed this provision

---

[12] TULRCA, s. 296(1)(a) and (b); and see *Carter v. Law Society* [1973] ICR 113 NIRC.
[13] TULRCA, s. 296(1)(c).
[14] TULRCA, s. 280(1).
[15] TULRCA, s. 274(1).
[16] TULRCA, s. 273.
[17] TULRCA, s. 279.
[18] *Per* Megarry L. in *Midland Cold Storage v. Steer* [1972] Ch. 630.
[19] [1973] IRLR 216, NIRC.
[20] *Midland Cold Storage v. Turner* [1972] ICR 230, NIRC.
[21] *Turner*, above.
[22] *British Association of Advisers and Lecturers in Physical Education v. National Union of Teachers* [1986] IRLR 497, CA.
[23] See the decision of Lord McLaren in *Renton Football Club v. McDowall* (1891) 18 R 670; *Wilson v. Scottish Typographical Society* 1912 SC 534.

as bestowing upon it a near corporate status.[24] The exact position in Scotland was unclear. Lord President (Inglis) declared in *Aitken v. Associated Carpenters and Joiners of Scotland*[25] that the 1871 Act made "no change ... into the constitution of these societies. They remain voluntary associations of which the law can take no special cognisance as collective bodies". This approach was followed in a later sheriff court decision.[26] On the other hand, in *Johnstone v. Associated Iron-moulders of Scotland*[27] Lord Skerrington, following the decision of the House of Lords in *Amalgamated Society of Railway Servants v. Osborne*,[28] concluded that a trade union was an example of "a statutory quasi-corporation". Moreover, in later Scottish cases registered trade unions were sued in their descriptive names alone without the addition of any of their responsible members or trustees.

10.7 The present provisions on union status reassert the position at common law by declaring that a trade union "is not a body corporate".[29] However, the Act does provide trade unions with certain corporate characteristics. Trade unions are capable of making contracts, suing or being sued in their own names and of being the subjects of criminal prosecution.[30] It is also the case that any judgment, order or award made against a union by a court can be enforced against it to the same extent and in the same manner as if the union were a body corporate.[31] The purpose of providing these corporate characteristics is not to create a near corporation but rather to overcome the specific difficulties which can arise particularly under English law when an unincorporated body is raising or defending a court action. However, its effect is wider than this because it was held in *Electrical, Electronic, Telecommunications and Plumbing Union v. Times Newspapers Ltd*[32] that the lack of corporate status meant that a union could not sue in damages for defamation. Any such action had to be based upon the possession of a personality and reputation and the clear and unambiguous statutory direction that a trade union should not be treated as a body corporate denied it that necessary personality.[33]

10.8 Restraint of trade

There can be no doubt that one major obstacle to the development and growth of trade unions was the common law doctrine of restraint of trade. The law considered that the objects of trade unions were unlawful because they restrained a person's freedom to earn a living in whatever occupation and upon whatever salary or wage that person could obtain. In particular, where a trade union sought to achieve its objectives by the threat or use of industrial action[34] or by the

---

[24] *Taff Vale Railway Co. v. Amalgamated Society of Railway Servants* [1901] AC 426, HL; *Amalgamated Society of Railway Servants v. Osborne* [1910] AC 87, HL; *National Union of General and Municipal Workers v. Gillian* [1946] KB 81, CA; *Bonsor v. Musicians' Union* [1956] AC 104, HL. *Cf* Lord Macdermott in *Bonsor*, at pp. 143–144.

[25] (1885) 12 R 1206 at p. 1211.

[26] *International Tailors' Machinists' and Pressers' Union v. Goldberg* (1903) 19 Sh Ct Rep 312.

[27] 1911 2 SLT 478.

[28] [1910] AC 87.

[29] TULRCA, s. 10(1).

[30] TULRCA, s. 10(1)(a)–(c).

[31] TULRCA, s. 12(2).

[32] [1980] QB 585.

[33] It has been doubted whether this decision represents the law of Scotland: though, since it is based on a UK statute the same result is likely to be reached in both jurisdictions. See K. Norrie, *Defamation and Related Actions in Scots Law* (1995) at pp. 67–68.

[34] *McKernan v. United Operative Masons' Association* (1874) 1 R 453.

negotiation of closed shop agreements[35] it was held at common law to be an illegal organisation. The position under Scots common law was summarised by Lord President (Dunedin) in *Wilkie v. King*[36] who declared that "trades unions were judged by the decisions of the court to be illegal organisations in restraint of trade, and, as such illegal associations, were denied the assistance of the courts in recovering under any contracts made by them". Thus from a Scottish perspective it was not so much the fact that a trade union possessed an unincorporated status as common law which constituted an obstacle to the courts entertaining its legal actions, since, in any case, the Scottish courts had already devised ways of permitting an unincorporated body to sue and be sued at common law, but, rather, it was the restraint of trade doctrine which denied a union the necessary authority to pursue or defend a court action.

10.9 Statutory intervention

Statute remedied this situation by declaring that the purposes of a trade union should not be considered unlawful by reason merely that they were in restraint of trade.[37] The exact scope of this provision became the subject of doubt as a result of the opinion of Sachs LJ in *Edwards v. Society of Graphical and Allied Trades*.[38] There he declared that it only protected the purposes of trade unions and did not, therefore, prevent the courts from holding that a specific union rule was void and in restraint of trade when it was not "proper" for the attainment of those purposes. Consequently, statute now declares that not only shall the purposes of a trade union not be unlawful so as to make any member of a trade union liable to criminal proceedings or to make any agreement or trust void or voidable by reason only that they are in restraint of trade,[39] but also that no union rule shall be unlawful or unenforceable for the same reason.[40] However, it is possible that even this extended provision may not insulate the rules of a trade union from judicial scrutiny. In *Greig v. Insole*[41] Slade J suggested that a distinction might be made between rules which are in restraint of trade and rules which restrain a person's right to work. He considered that, as regards this latter category of rule, the courts may not be prevented from interfering where an association exercises a virtual monopoly right to control entry to a particular trade or profession.

10.10 Ownership of property

The property of a trade union vests in its trustees.[42] Such vesting of property is in trust for the union itself. On this basis, the union must be the sole beneficiary. However, as a result of its unincorporated status the members are entitled to represent their union "collectively and severally".[43] The rights and obligations of the member, therefore, depend not on the notion of property but upon the contract of membership which all union members possess.[44] In the case of a union's branch funds, however, much will depend upon the terms of the union rule book when

---

[35] *Bernard's Executrix v. National Union of Mineworkers* 1971 SC 32.

[36] 1911 SC 1310 at p. 1314.

[37] TUA 1871, s. 3.

[38] [1971] Ch 354, CA.

[39] TULRCA, s. 11(1)(a) and (b).

[40] TULRCA, s. 11(2).

[41] [1978] 1 WLR 302.

[42] TULRCA, s. 12(1).

[43] *Per* Lord Lindley in *Yorkshire Miners' Association v. Howden* [1905] AC 256 at p. 280.

[44] *Cf* the rights of members in other forms of unincorporated association under Scots law. See, in particular, *Murray v. Johnstone* (1896) 23 R 981.

ascertaining who enjoys the beneficial rights to that property. In *News Group Newspapers Ltd v. SOGAT 82*[45] the Court of Appeal held that the branch property was being held in trust for the members of the branch and not the union, because the clear purport of the rules was to vest that property in trustees who held it on behalf of the branch members for the time being. However, it is unlawful for a union's property to be used in order to reimburse an individual who has been fined or is likely to be fined for the commission of an offence or for contempt of court[46] and for a union to offer indemnity to an individual as regards a fine for any such offence or for contempt of court.[47] Where the property of a union is used in this way, then an amount equal to the payment is recoverable by the union from the member and he is liable to account to the union for the value of the property applied.[48] If a union should fail to bring or continue the necessary proceedings in order to recover unlawful payments made to individuals from union funds any union member who claims that the failure is unreasonable may seek the authorisation of the court to pursue such an action at the union's expense.[49]

10.11 The trustee's responsibilities

Union trustees are bound by the normal law of trusts and owe fiduciary duties as regards their stewardship of the union property. Thus trustees can be removed from office by the court at common law if they act in such a way as to show that they are not fit and proper persons to administer the union's assets.[50] Under Scottish common law this could entail the appointment of a judicial factor by the court to take over the management of the union's assets.[51] In any case, statute now gives the courts important new powers to intervene at the suit of a member when trustees are alleged to have used a union's property unlawfully, or are proposing to carry out their functions so as to cause or permit any unlawful application of the union's property or where the trustees have complied, or are proposing to comply, with an unlawful direction which has been given to them under the union's rules.[52] If the court is satisfied that the member's application is well-founded it can make such order as it considers appropriate and has the power to make interim orders.[53] In particular, the courts may:

    (a) require the trustees to take all such steps as the order may require for the protection or recovery of the union's property;

    (b) appoint a judicial factor on the property of the union; and

    (c) remove one or more of the trustees from office.[54]

EMPLOYERS' ASSOCIATIONS

10.12 Unlike the earlier legislation, modern law recognises employers' associations as separate and distinct organisations.[55] It is clear that such an association can

---

[45] [1986] ICR 716, CA.
[46] TULRCA, s. 15(1)(a) and (b).
[47] TULRCA, s. 15(1)(c).
[48] TULRCA, s. 15(2).
[49] TULRCA, s. 15(3).
[50] See the decision of Mervyn Davies J in *Clarke v. Heathfield, The Times* December 1, 1984. Approved on appeal at [1985] ICR 203, CA.
[51] *Munro v. Edinburgh and District Trades Council Social Club* [1989] GWD 6–240, OH.
[52] TULRCA, s. 16(1)(a) and (b).
[53] TULRCA, s. 16(3) and (5).
[54] TULRCA, s. 16(3).
[55] TULRCA, ss. 122–136.

either be a body corporate or an unincorporated association.[56] An unincorporated employers' association is provided with the same corporate benefits in respect of title to sue etc. as is granted to a trade union.[57] However, it is clear that, unlike the trade union, an unincorporated employers' association is a quasi corporation.[58] An employers' association can remain unincorporated even although it has more than twenty members and would otherwise require to be incorporated under s. 716 of the Companies Act 1985.[59] An unincorporated employers' association enjoys the same exemption from the restraint of trade doctrine as does a trade union.[60] However, its corporate counterpart has its rules and purposes protected only in so far as they relate to the regulation of relations between employers and workers or trade unions.[61]

THE ROLE OF THE CERTIFICATION OFFICER

10.13 The Certification Officer exercises an extensive independent statutory jurisdiction over trade union affairs.[62] The Office was first created by the Employment Protection Act in 1975. However, as well as being given the authority to award certificates of independence to trade unions the Certification Officer also had transferred to him certain functions which were exercised formerly by the Chief Registrar of Friendly Societies. There is authority for an Assistant Certification Officer for Scotland to be appointed.[63] This officer has the responsibility for maintaining the lists of trade unions and employers' associations whose principal offices are in Scotland. The original duties of the Certificating Officer have been extended considerably by the legislation enacted since 1980. He has been responsible for the administration of the scheme whereby independent trade unions have been entitled to claim payment towards expenditure incurred in the conduct of secret postal ballots for certain prescribed purposes[64] and his jurisdiction has been extended to hear complaints over the conduct of union executive elections[65] and the conduct of political fund ballots.[66] He also exercises important new powers as regards the investigation of a union's financial affairs.[67]

10.14 List of trade unions and employers' associations

The Certification Officer, or his assistant in Scotland, is required to keep a list of organisations which satisfy the statutory definition of a trade union[68] and also a list of employers' associations.[69] Therefore, the only requirements for inclusion on the

56   TULRCA, s. 127(1).
57   TULRCA, s. 127(2).
58   *Electrical, Electronic, Telecommunications and Plumbing Union v. Times Newspapers Ltd* [1980] QB 585.
59   TULRCA, s. 127(3).
60   TULRCA, s. 128(1).
61   TULRCA, s. 128(1) and (2).
62   TULRCA, s. 254. Although ACAS provides the Certification Officer with the necessary staff, accommodation and finance, he is independent of both ACAS and the Secretary of State in the exercise of his functions.
63   TULRCA, s. 254(3).
64   TULRCA, s. 116, repealed as from April 1, 1996.
65   TULRCA, s. 55.
66   TULRCA, s. 80.
67   TULRCA, s. 37B as inserted by TURERA, s. 10.
68   TULRCA, ss. 2 and 3.
69   TULRCA, s. 123.

list of trade unions are that the organisation be made up wholly or mainly of workers and that it has the regulation of worker/employer relations as one of its principal purposes. There is a right of appeal to the Employment Appeal Tribunal against a refusal to list or against a withdrawal from the list.[70] The listing of a trade union is a simple process, and by itself it has very little significance. Indeed, there are certain obligations which are imposed upon a trade union even where it remains unlisted. Thus, any organisation which meets the statutory definition of a trade union, whether listed or not, is required to maintain proper accounting records, to have those accounts audited and to submit annual returns to the Certification Officer. The main benefit of listing is that it is a prerequisite for any union which intends to seek a certificate of independence from the Certification Officer. The only other important benefit is that a listed trade union is guaranteed tax relief for expenditure on provident funds.[71]

10.15 Independence

In deciding whether to issue a certificate of independence the Certification Officer is guided by the statutory definition of an independent trade union.[72] This declares that an independent trade union means a trade union which is not under the domination or control of an employer or a group of employers or of one or more employers' associations; and is not liable to interference by an employer or any such group or association (arising out of the provision of financial or material support or by any other means whatsoever) tending towards such control. Any union seeking a certificate must satisfy the Certification Officer that it meets both parts of the test. As regards the first requirement that the union should not be dominated or controlled by the employer, it has been suggested that this might require both a subjective and an objective approach.[73] However, it has been the second limb of the definition which has been the major barrier to the acquisition of a certificate of independence. Most unions who have been denied a certificate have failed because they could not prove that they were not liable to interference tending towards employer control.

10.16 Interference by an employer

The approach of the Certification Officer towards this second limb has been to ask how vulnerable the organisation is to employer interference. This test has been criticised as being more suited to discovering whether the union was subject to employer domination or control.[74] Nevertheless, the Court of Appeal has made it clear that the appropriate test under limb two is vulnerability to employer interference.[75] This requires the Certification Officer to look beyond the issue of the quality of relations between union and employer and to consider such factors as the extent to which the union has to rely on employer financed or employer provided facilities for its existence. A union is vulnerable to employer interference when its existence depends upon employer approval since the threat of disapproval by the employer must necessarily affect its conduct of industrial negotiations.[76]

---

[70] TULRCA, s. 9(1).
[71] Income and Corporation Taxes Act 1988, s. 467.
[72] TULRCA, s. 5.
[73] *Association of HSD (Hatfield) Employees v. Certification Officer* [1979] ICR 21, EAT.
[74] *Squibb UK Staff Association v. Certification Officer* [1977] IRLR, EAT.
[75] *Squibb UK Staff Association v. Certification Officer* [1979] ICR 235, CA.
[76] *Government Communications Staff Federation v. Certification Officer* [1993] IRLR 260, EAT.

The duty of the Certification Officer is to assess the independence of a trade union on the basis of these statutory criteria. The effectiveness of the union in collective bargaining is irrelevant except in so far as it impinges upon independence. Equally, the Certification Officer has no authority to consider the impact that certification will have on existing collective bargaining arrangements.[77]

10.17 The relevant criteria

The Certification Officer has drawn up a series of criteria which he takes account of when deciding whether or not to issue a certificate. These criteria have been approved.[78] They are:

(1) *History* If there is evidence in the recent past that the union has received employer support and encouragement, this is a powerful argument against certification.

(2) *Membership Base* A union which recruits from the employees of a single employer is much more vulnerable to employer interference than a broadly based union.

(3) *Organisation and Structure* Looking at the union rules and its practices as well, the union should be organised in such a way as to enable the members to play a full part in the union's decision-making process free from employer interference or involvement.

(4) *Finance* A union with weak finances and inadequate reserves is more likely to be susceptible to employer interference than one with a strong financial base.

(5) *Employer-Provided Facilities* The greater a union's reliance on such facilities, the more vulnerable it must be to employer interference.

(6) *Collective Bargaining Record* A weak record does not of itself indicate employer dependence. On the other hand, proof of a strong record and the display of a robust attitude in negotiation will be significant and, indeed, may even outweigh other factors unfavourable to the union's case.

There is no need for a union to satisfy each of these criteria separately. The final decision will be based on "the whole nature and circumstances" of the application.[79]

10.18 The importance of independence

In contrast to the issue of listing, there are considerable and numerous advantages which accrue to a trade union which has been awarded a certificate of independence. Privileges accrue to both the union and to its members. For example, union members have protection so far as their trade union membership and activities are concerned,[80] have the right to time off for trade union activities[81] and can be appointed as safety representatives.[82] Amongst the advantages which accrue to an independent trade union are the rights to information for collective bargaining,[83] to

---

[77] This is a matter which has caused some TUC-affiliated trade unions to criticise the role of the Certification Officer. See his Annual Report for 1977 at p. 12. The Certification Officer has the power to withdraw a certificate from a union which is no longer independent. See TULRCA, s. 7(1).

[78] *Blue Circle Staff Association v. Certification Officer* [1977] ICR 224, EAT.

[79] Annual Report of the Certification Officer for 1979 at pp. 10–11.

[80] TULRCA, s. 146 (action short of dismissal), TULRCA, s. 152 (dismissal).

[81] TULRCA, s. 168.

[82] Health and Safety at Work etc. Act 1974, s. 2(4).

[83] TULRCA, s. 181.

consult with a trade union over redundancies,[84] to obtain funds from the Certification Officer for the cost of postal ballots,[85] and to use the employer's facilities for secret ballots.[86]

10.19 Mergers

The Trade Union and Labour Relations (Consolidation) Act 1992, s. 97 recognises two forms of merger: a transfer of engagements and an amalgamation. In the former case only members of the union seeking to transfer are balloted. If the ballot result is for transfer, the membership of the transferor organisation joins the transferee union with the result that the transferor union ceases to exist in law. In the case of an amalgamation, two or more unions will come together in order to form one new union with new rules. All the unions involved must return a membership vote in favour of merger before such an amalgamation can take place. The Certification Officer's authority over union mergers has been delegated to the Assistant Certification Officer for Scotland in the case of transfers where the transferee union is based in Scotland and in the case of amalgamations where the new union will have its principal office north of the border. Important new requirements as regards the conduct of such ballots were added by the Trade Union Reform and Employment Rights Act 1993.

10.20 Procedure

Before any transfer or amalgamation can take place, a number of steps laid down in the Act must be carried out. The completion of these steps is necessary before the Certification Officer can authorise the merger. As a first step, the Certification Officer must be given the opportunity to approve the instrument setting out the terms of the merger.[87] There is also a requirement that a notice which explains the merger proposals be drawn up and distributed to the members who will be voting on it.[88] The notice must be in writing and must either set out in full the instrument of amalgamation or transfer, or give a sufficient account to enable those receiving the notice to form a reasonable judgment of the main effects of the merger.[89] Any such notice must be approved by the Certification Officer.[90] The notice must not contain any statement making a recommendation or expressing an opinion about the merger.[91] There will then be a ballot which takes the form of a resolution upon which the members vote.

10.21 The ballot

The fundamental aspect of the procedure is the ballot. There are four basic requirements for the conduct of this ballot. First, all members of the union must be accorded an equal entitlement to vote on the resolution.[92] This means that the union cannot restrict the vote to certain groups even if the union rule book provides

---

84 TULRCA, s. 188.
85 TULRCA, s. 115 (repealed as of April 1, 1996)
86 EA 1980, s. 2. TULRCA, s. 116 (repealed as of April 1, 1996).
87 TULRCA. s. 98(1).
88 TULRCA, s. 99(1).
89 TULRCA, s. 99(2).
90 TULRCA, s. 99(1).
91 TULRCA, s. 99(3A) as inserted by TURERA, s. 5.
92 TULRCA, s. 100B as inserted by TURERA, s. 4.

this authority.[93] But problems do arise as to the meaning of the word "member" since there is no definition of the word in the Act. The phrase "members of the trade union" is expressive of a constitutional relationship between individuals and the organisation to which they belong. However, the nature of this relationship can differ as between different classes of member and it will be necessary to examine the rule book closely to ascertain whether certain classes of member do genuinely have an entitlement to participate fully in the union's affairs.[94] Second, every member of the union must be allowed to vote without interference or constraint and must, so far as reasonably practicable, be able to do so without incurring any direct costs.[95] The phrase "without interference or constraint" has been interpreted by the Certification Officer as being concerned with intimidation, physical interference and the like.[96] The third requirement is that, so far as reasonably practicable, every person who is entitled to vote should have a voting paper sent to him at his home address[97] and be given a convenient opportunity to vote by post.[98] Finally, the ballot must be conducted so as to secure that, so far as reasonably practicable, those voting do so in secret and that the votes are fairly and accurately counted.[99] Thus all union merger ballots can only be conducted by means of a secret postal ballot. In addition, there are a series of requirements aimed at ensuring the fairness and accuracy of the ballot result. Thus there must be an independent scrutineer appointed who is responsible for supervising the ballot[100] and for reporting to the union[101] on its outcome and the extent to which the ballot complies with the statutory requirements,[102] and the storage, distribution and counting of the voting papers must be conducted by an independent person.[103] A simple majority of those voting is sufficient to pass a merger resolution unless the rules of the trade union expressly require it to be approved by a greater majority or by a specified proportion of the members of the union.[104]

10.22 Registration of the transfer

If the resolution is approved in the ballot, it is for the union or unions concerned to request the Certification Officer to register the instrument.[105] An application for registration cannot be sent to the Certification Officer until the union has ensured that the report of the independent scrutineer has been sent to all its members.[106] There are two important points about registration. First, the Certification Officer would be entitled to refuse to register the instrument if its terms are inconsistent

---

[93] *McLaren and Ognall and Association of Cinematograph, Television and Allied Technicians,* CO Annual Report, 1979, p. 18; *Young and National Union of Agricultural and Allied Workers,* CO Annual Report, 1982, p. 21.

[94] *National Union of Mineworkers (Yorkshire Area) v. Millward* [1995] IRLR 411, EAT.

[95] TULRCA, s. 100C(3).

[96] *Clare and Eagle Star Staff Association,* Annual Report, 1981, p. 19; *Ammonds and Society of Lithographic Artists, Designers, Engineers and Process Workers,* Annual Report, 1982, p. 20.

[97] Or such other address as he has requested the union in writing to treat as his postal address.

[98] TULRCA, s. 100C(4).

[99] TULRCA, s. 100E(6).

[100] See, generally, TULRCA, s. 100A.

[101] A copy of the report must also be sent to all members of the union: TULRCA, s. 100E(6).

[102] See, generally, TULRCA, s. 100E.

[103] See, generally, TULRCA, s. 100D.

[104] TULRCA, s. 100(2).

[105] TULRCA, s. 101(1).

[106] TULRCA, s. 101(3) as inserted by TURERA, s. 49(2), Sch. 8, para. 55.

with the rules of a participating union.[107] Second, registration can only be effected after a period of six weeks has elapsed in order to enable complaints from members about the conduct of the merger process to be received.[108] Any complaint made to the Certification Officer during this time will prevent the instrument from being registered until that complaint is finally determined.[109] A member can complain either on the basis that one of the statutory requirements has not been complied with or because the union has breached its own rules.[110] Once the instrument it recorded, however, the merger will become effective and there will be an automatic transfer of union property without any express conveyance.[111]

10.23 Union accounts

Both listed and unlisted trade unions[112] and employers' associations are required to keep proper accounting records and to establish and maintain a satisfactory system of control of those records.[113] The records must be such as to give a true and fair view of the state of the affairs of the union and to explain its transactions.[114] Union branches are also required to comply with these provisions.[115] Formerly, a member did not have any statutory right to inspect the union's accounts, although such a right may well have been provided under the rule book.[116] However, now a union is required to keep its accounting records available for inspection and to ensure that union members have the right to inspect those records on request.[117] A member who is exercising his right to inspect has the statutory right to be accompanied by an accountant.[118] A union must also ensure that a properly qualified auditor has been appointed to make a report on these accounts.[119] The auditor's report which is included in the annual return made to the Certification Officer must state whether the accounts present a true and fair view of the union's financial position.[120]

10.24 Annual returns

All trade unions and employers' associations are required to submit annual returns to the Certification Officer for each calendar year.[121] Any such return must contain a revenue account, a balance sheet, and any other accounts required by the Certification Officer.[122] A copy of the union's current rules should also be included

---

[107] *R v. Certification Officer, ex parte AUEW (Engineering Section)* [1983] ICR 125, CA.

[108] TULRCA, s. 101(2) and s. 103.

[109] TULRCA, s. 103(2). There is a right of appeal on a point of law to the EAT. TULRCA, s. 104.

[110] TULRCA, s. 101(3) as substituted by TURERA, s. 49(2), Sch 8, para. 56

[111] TULRCA, s. 105(1).

[112] The only excluded organisations are federated trade unions which consist wholly or mainly of constituent or affiliated organisations — TULRCA, s. 118(4)(b).

[113] TULRCA, s. 28(1) (trade unions), TULRCA, s. 131(1) (employers' associations).

[114] TULRCA, s. 28(2).

[115] TULRCA, s. 44(2).

[116] For the extent of this right, see *Dodd v. Amalgamated Marine Workers' Union* [1924] 1 Ch 116, CA; *Taylor v. National Union of Mineworkers (Derbyshire Area)* [1985] IRLR 65, Ch D.

[117] TULRCA, ss. 29 and 30.

[118] TULRCA, s. 30(2) and (3).

[119] TULRCA, s. 33(1). It is necessary for a union's rules to make provision for the appointment and removal of an auditor — TULRCA, s. 35(1).

[120] TULRCA, s. 36(2).

[121] TULRCA, s. 32(1) (trade unions); TULRCA, s. 131(1) (employers' associations).

[122] TULRCA, s. 32(3)(a).

in the return together with a copy of the auditor's report.[123] In addition, trade unions must now ensure that their annual returns contain the following additional information, viz. (a) the salary and other benefits paid to each member of the executive, the president and the general secretary,[124] and (b) a statement of the number of names on the register of members' names and addresses as at the end of the period to which the return relates and the number of those names which were not accompanied by an address.[125] It is the duty of the Certification Officer to keep these annual returns available for public inspection at all reasonable hours.[126] Both trade unions and employers' associations are under an obligation to provide any person who so requests with a copy of the rule book and the most recent annual return.[127]

10.25 Statement to members

Unions are now also required to take all reasonable steps to secure that, not later than eight weeks after the day on which the annual return is sent to the Certification Officer, members receive a detailed statement of the union's financial affairs.[128] This statement must specify:

(a) the union's total income and expenditure for the period;

(b) how much of the income consisted of membership payments;

(c) total income and expenditure for the period of any political fund; and

(d) the salary and benefits of executive members, the president and the general secretary.[129]

Additionally, the statement should set out in full the auditor's report together with his name and address and may include any other matter which the union believes will enable members to make informed judgments about the financial activities of the union.[130] The statement must also include a three paragraph statement setting out the options open to any member who believes that there may be some irregularity in the union's financial affairs.[131] A copy of the whole statement must be sent to the Certification Officer.[132]

10.26 Investigation of financial affairs

The Certification Officer also has additional new powers to require the production of union documents[133] and to investigate the financial affairs of a trade union.[134] Any such investigation will be conducted by one or more members of the Certification Officer's staff or other persons appointed as inspectors.[135] An investigation can only be conducted where there is evidence that:

(a) the union's financial affairs are being or have been conducted for a fraudulent or unlawful purpose;

---

123 TULRCA, s. 32(3)(b) and (c).
124 TULRCA, s. 32(3)(aa) as inserted by TURERA, s. 8.
125 TULRCA, s. 32(3)(d) as inserted by TURERA, s. 8.
126 TULRCA, s. 32(6).
127 TULRCA, ss. 27, 32(5) and 131(1).
128 TULRCA, s. 32A(1) as inserted by TURERA, s. 9.
129 TULRCA, s. 32A(3).
130 TULRCA, s. 32A(5).
131 TULRCA, s. 32A(6).
132 TULRCA, s. 32A(7).
133 TULRCA, s. 37A as inserted by TURERA, s. 10.
134 TULRCA, s. 37B as inserted by TURERA, s. 10.
135 TULRCA, s. 37B(1).

(b) the union's financial managers have been guilty of fraud, misfeasance or other misconduct;

(c) the union has failed to comply with any duty imposed by the 1992 Act in relation to its financial affairs; or

(d) the union has breached one of its financial rules.[136]

The inspectors must report their findings to the Certification Officer who is required to publish a final report.[137] This report must be supplied free of charge to the union, its auditors and any member who has complained of financial irregularities.[138] A copy of the report of the inspectors is admissible as evidence in any subsequent legal proceedings.[139]

It is an offence for any person to contravene any duty or requirement as regards the production of union documents or the conduct of any investigation by inspectors.[140] Any such offence is punishable by a fine not exceeding level 5 on the standard scale[141] and there are higher penalties for more serious offences.[142] Trade unions must ensure that those convicted of any of the above offences are prevented from being members of the executive or the president or general secretary for a period of five or 10 years from the date of conviction depending upon the severity of the offence.[143] A member who claims that the union has failed to comply with the above requirement can apply to the Certification Officer or to the court for a declaratory order.[144]

SECESSION AND DISSOLUTION

10.27 There is an implied term in every union rule book permitting a member to resign from the union on giving reasonable notice and after complying with any reasonable conditions.[145] Thus a union has no legal remedy if a large number of members decide to resign from the union at the same time. However, the position is undoubtedly different when those disaffected members seek to leave the union as one distinct unit, for example, where a branch or section of the union decides to secede. In such a case, secession is only competent where there is a specific union rule providing for such an event. If a union does not possess such a rule it would be necessary for one to be created before the severance of any branch of the union would be legitimate.[146] Moreover, even where secession is permitted under the rules, those leaving the union have no right to any of its property, unless there is a specific union rule granting them rights over the union's property as well.[147] Usually, the union's property will remain vested in its original trustees. The need for express rule book authority also applies where it is the union which seeks to dissolve one of its branches. It has been held that such dissolution would only be

---

[136] TULRCA, s. 37B(2).
[137] TULRCA, s. 37C. There is also provision for interim reports: TULRCA, s. 37C(1).
[138] TULRCA, s. 37C(6).
[139] TULRCA, s. 37C(8).
[140] TULRCA, s. 45(5) as inserted by TURERA, s. 11(1).
[141] TULRCA, s. 45A(1)(a) as inserted by TURERA, s. 11(2).
[142] TULRCA, s. 45A(1)(b).
[143] TULRCA, s. 45B(1) and (2) as inserted by TURERA, s. 12.
[144] TULRCA, s. 45C as inserted by TURERA, s. 12.
[145] TULRCA, s. 69.
[146] *John v. Rees* [1970] Ch. 345.
[147] *Burnley, Nelson, Rossendale and District Textile Workers Union v. Amalgamated Textile Workers Union* [1986] IRLR 298, QB.

legitimate where there is an express provision in the rule book clothing the union with such power.[148] Equally, it would not be competent for the union to rely on the general power given to the executive council by the rules to manage the affairs of the union as authority for dissolution of a branch.

10.28 There is no statutory provision which requires a union to possess a rule authorising its dissolution where necessary.[149] However, such a rule would be advisable because under the common law an unincorporated association has no right to dissolve itself without the consent of every member.[150] If a union does not possess a dissolution rule it is always free to adopt one so long as it complies with all the democratic requirements necessary before any additional rules can be created. Where no such rule exists a simple resolution authorising winding-up passed at a delegate meeting of the union will not be sufficient.[151] There must be an express rule setting out the dissolution procedure and that procedure must be followed to the letter. A union should also possess a rule which explains in detail how its assets are to be distributed on dissolution. Otherwise the general law should be applied. This should ensure that the union's net assets are distributed amongst the members. However, the exact method of calculation for distribution of those assets is as yet unclear.[152]

MEMBER'S RIGHTS AT COMMON LAW

10.29 There is no doubt that in law the union rule book constitutes a contract of membership between the member and his union.[153] However, there is also both statutory[154] and judicial[155] authority for the view that the contract is between the members *inter se*. Any action raised by a member alleging unfair treatment by his union must be based upon breach of this contract. It will be the provisions of the rule book, as a contract, which will be relied upon by the courts to resolve any disputes about the extent of members' rights on the basis that those rules constitute "an exhaustive code".[156] The Scottish courts have always relied upon the notion of contract as the mechanism for reviewing the internal affairs of all unincorporated voluntary associations and not just trade unions.[157] This sets the position in Scotland apart from that under English law where at least initially a member's rights were thought to be based on property[158] and where, in more

---

[148] *Maddock v. EETPU* 1972 SLT (Sh Ct) 54.
[149] It is possible that a union could be wound up as an unregistered company under Part XXI of the Companies Act 1985.
[150] *Free Church of Scotland v. Overtoun* (1904) 7 F (HL) 1.
[151] *Gardner v. McLintock* (1904) 11 SLT 654, OH.
[152] Compare *Re Printers and Transferers Amalgamated Trades Protection Society* [1899] 2 Ch 184 with *Re Sick and Funeral Society of St John's Sunday School* [1973] Ch 51.
[153] See, for example, the judgment of Lord Blades in *Martin v. Scottish TGWU* 1951 SC 129, particularly at p. 136.
[154] See TULRCA, s. 20(7) which defines a union's rules as meaning "the written rules of the union ... forming part of the contract between a member and the other members".
[155] See. in particular, the speech of Lord MacDermott in *Bonsor v. Musicians' Union* [1956] AC 104, HL.
[156] *Martin v. Scottish TGWU*, above.
[157] See *Robinson v. Scottish Amateur Athletic Association* (1900) 7 SLT 356, OH; *Anderson v. Manson* 1909 SC 838.
[158] *Rigby v. Connol* (1880) 14 Ch D 482.

modern times, alternative bases for review of trade union affairs have been canvassed.[159]

10.30 If the union rule book is the source for the terms of the contract of membership, this must also mean that the law would expect that any disciplinary action would comply with rule book requirements. As has been stated, there is ample authority in Scotland that all voluntary associations must comply with their constitutions when disciplining members. However, another ground of action has also been recognised and this arises where the member complains that there has been a denial of natural justice.[160] Thus, even where the association complies with its constitution, its decision may still be impugned by reference to natural justice rules because the member had no notification of the charge against him and had not been given any opportunity to be heard in his defence.[161] As we shall see, these two grounds of review still constitute the bedrock upon which a member's rights to complain about a union's decision to discipline or expel him have been built.

10.31 Patrimonial loss

Before examining the application of this area of the law to trade unions in more detail, one final point has to be made. This concerns the additional requirement that not only does a member suing an unincorporated body have to show some breach of the rules but must also establish patrimonial loss. This entails establishing that the pursuer has been deprived of something more substantial than merely the enjoyment of membership,[162] although loss of status or reputation might be enough.[163] There is no doubt that in the early cases, and, particularly those decided during the time of the Trade Union Act 1871, the need to establish patrimonial loss was a major obstacle in the path of a member suing his union.[164] Nowadays it is no longer an issue. An averment of breach of the contract of membership by a trade union member seems to constitute sufficient patrimonial interest to permit the action to proceed.[165]

10.32 Admission

The fact that there is no contract in existence between the applicant and the union has made it far more difficult for the courts to discover a theoretical tool with which to review a union's decision to exclude a person from membership. There is no doubt that, at least initially, the courts adopted a fairly benign attitude to union exclusion cases. Indeed, in the only major case on the subject in Scotland —

---

[159] Lord Denning, for example, sought to argue that union rules were akin to bye-laws. See his judgments in both *Bonsor v. Musicians' Union*, above and *Cheall v. Association of Professional, Executive, Clerical and Computer Staff* [1982] ICR 543, CA. This theory has been rejected by the House of Lords in both *Faramus v. Film Artistes' Association* [1964] AC 925 and in *Cheall* [1983] ICR 398, HL. The idea that a member may have a cause of action based on status was firmly rejected by Lord President Cooper as being ''completely false'' in *Martin v. Scottish TGWU*, above at p. 143.

[160] See Lord Justice-Clerk Aitchison in *M'Donald v. Burns* 1940 SC 376.

[161] *Walker v. Amalgamated Union of Engineers and Foundry Workers* 1969 SLT 150.

[162] *Ellis v. Neilston Bowling Club* 1987 GWD 3–81.

[163] Per Lord Prosser in *Gunstone v. Scottish Women's Amateur Athletic Association* 1987 SLT 611, OH.

[164] *Aitken v. Associated Carpenters and Joiners of Scotland* (1885) 12 R 1206; *Drennan v. Associated Ironmoulders of Scotland* 1921 SC 151.

[165] See, for example, *McGregor v. National and Local Government Officers' Association* 1979 SC 401.

Martin v. Scottish Transport and General Workers' Union[166] — the House of Lords restricted themselves exclusively to an examination of the union's rules in order to discover whether the decision to exclude complied with them. In this case the pursuer had become a member of the union in 1940 and was placed in a category which restricted membership to the duration of the war. In 1948 the union resolved to terminate his membership. Martin sought a declarator that he was still a union member and reduction of that resolution. Lord Normand accepted that it was for the union to decide its own rules over admission. It was held, therefore, that since there was no authority in the rule book to admit a person into temporary membership, the pursuer's purported membership was *ultra vires*. Thus, although Martin had enjoyed *de facto* rights of membership, he had never in law been a member. This broad approach was followed in the later House of Lords decision in *Faramus v. Film Artistes' Association*[167] where the judges were not prepared to question the application of a union rule which had the effect of barring the plaintiff from membership because of criminal convictions, even although these related to offences committed almost twenty years before during the German occupation of Jersey. This conclusion was reached despite their Lordships' recognition that since Faramus' employment was the subject of a closed shop agreement, loss of union membership would also entail loss of employment.

10.33 Although the *Martin* case still remains the last word on the law of Scotland as regards union admission decisions, there have been cases decided by the English courts which have developed some legal basis with which to review union admission decisions. This has come about through the development of the concept of a right to work. The original architect of this theory was Lord Denning who believed that powerful organisations such as trade unions should be prevented from denying individuals the right to exercise their skills in their chosen area of employment. In the area of union admission policies the right to work theory has been used to declare invalid union refusals to admit[168] or readmit[169] applicants where the union acted arbitrarily or capriciously in processing those applications. Its most effective application arose in cases where there was a closed shop.[170]

10.34 Hepple has argued that the concept of a right to work is merely "a reformulation in positive terms of the old doctrine or restraint of trade"[171] applied to protect the individual. Nevertheless, other judges have recognised its existence. Sachs LJ, for example, has referred to a right of equal opportunity to obtain work under English law.[172] Another judge[173] has acknowledged that the notion of a right to work is a category of public policy wider than restraint of trade. It entitles the courts to review the application of job controls by trade unions and other professional bodies in order to ensure fair treatment for applicants.[174] Megarry V-C

---

[166] 1952 SC (HL) 1.
[167] [1964] AC 925, HL.
[168] *Nagle v. Feilden* [1966] 2 QB 633, CA. See also *Lee v. Showmen's Guild* [1952] 2 QB 329, CA.
[169] *Edwards v. SOGAT* [1971] Ch 354, CA.
[170] *Edwards*, above; *Goring v. British Actors' Equity Association* [1987] IRLR 122, Ch D.
[171] "A Right to Work?" (1981) 10 ILJ 65 at pp. 79–80.
[172] *Edwards v. SOGAT* [1971] 1 Ch 354 at p. 383.
[173] Slade J in *Greig v. Insole* [1978] 1 WLR 302.
[174] See also Browne Wilkinson V-C in *Goring v. British Actors' Equity Association* [1987] IRLR 122.

in *McInnes v. Onslow Fane*[175] has argued that it should be more properly referred to as a liberty to work. This case is important because it provides a clear indication about the direction taken by English law on this subject. Here Megarry V-C argued that unions must act fairly in exercising their authority to exclude or expel. In most admission cases, this simply means that a union should ensure that its decision is reached honestly without bias or caprice. However, in other cases where a person has a legitimate expectation that he will be admitted into membership because the union is merely acting as a confirming body or the person has been a member previously, higher standards of fairness are required. The nature and extent of this higher duty was not explained by Megarry V-C. However, Elias has argued that such a higher duty not only permits the courts to review the substantive unfairness of a union admission rule but also ensures that the courts' right of review is no longer confined exclusively to closed shop cases.[176] Although there is no express authority on this point in Scotland,[177] it is submitted that the courts in Scotland would apply a similar concept, at least in the sense of providing an applicant facing union job controls with a right to fair and equal treatment.

10.35 Discipline and expulsion

As has already been noted, Scots law has always recognised two bases for reviewing the activities of an unincorporated association. The first has involved discovering whether the organisation has acted in breach of its rules and the second has concerned the application of the rules of natural justice. It is also legitimate for a judge to intervene where there is evidence of malice or bad faith so that the decision can be challenged on the basis that it is not one which could have been reached *bona fide*.[178] As far as trade unions are concerned, this latter ground for review has been refined so that it now involves a consideration of whether or not the decision was one which a reasonable trade union could have reached.[179]

10.36 As far as breach of the rules is concerned, it is clear that if a union is intending to discipline or expel a member it must ensure that it has both the necessary authority in its rule book[179a] and that it complies with those rules. The court will always demand that a union comply with rule book requirements on the basis of the contract of membership. Thus if a union conducts its disciplinary procedures in breach of its rules or imposes a penalty which is not authorised by the rule book, the member will be entitled to sue the union for breach of contract. A union must ensure, for example, that the person or body conducting the disciplinary proceedings has the necessary authority under the rules;[180] and that any disciplinary penalty imposed against a member is implemented at a time

---

[175] [1978] 3 All ER 211.

[176] "Admission to Trade Unions" (1979) 8 ILJ 111.

[177] The *Lee* decision was applied in Scotland by Lord Allanbridge in *Partington v. NALGO* 1981 SC 299 but only as regards the question of expulsion.

[178] *Dawkins v. Antrobus* (1881) 17 Ch D 615, CA.

[179] *Lee v. Showmen's Guild* [1952] 2 QB 329, CA applied in Scotland by Lord Allanbridge in *Partington v. NALGO* 1981 SC 299.

[179a] Though there may be circumstances where the court is prepared to imply a disciplinary rule: *McVitae v. UNISON* [1996] IRLR 34, HCt.

[180] See, for example, *Bonsor v. Musicians' Union* [1956] AC 104, HL where it was held that an expulsion by a branch secretary was unlawful because he had no such authority under the rules.

specified in the rule book.[181] The Scottish courts have been just as determined as their English counterparts to ensure that the requirements of the rule book are enforced to the letter. In *McGregor v. National and Local Government Officers' Association*,[182] for example, Lord Dunpark held that a union which had rescinded a decision to expel a member could not reinstate that decision simply by means of a resolution of the annual conference. If disciplinary action was to be reactivated, this entailed starting these proceedings afresh so that the member enjoyed all the procedural safeguards as provided by the rules and could exercise his full rights of appeal as prescribed by the rule book.

10.37 Expulsion and the Bridlington Rules

The same strict approach has also been applied by the courts as regards union expulsion decisions which comply with a disputes decision of the TUC under its Bridlington Rules. The thrust of these rules is to avoid inter-union disputes over organisation and negotiation rights. It is not lawful, for example, for a union to expel a member in conformity with an award of a disputes committee where it has no specific provision authorising such expulsion under its own rules.[183] Moreover, the Bridlington Principles themselves have been subjected to very close scrutiny by the courts.[184] However, where it appears that neither the Bridlington Rules nor the expelling union's own rules have been misapplied, the courts cannot intervene simply because the decision to expel is unreasonable.[185] It is clear, therefore, that in this area where a union makes rules which it considers to be in the best interests of its members and applies those rules to the letter, it would normally be beyond judicial challenge.[186] The STUC also applies the Bridlington Rules. However, where a trade union has been suspended from membership of the TUC for breach of Bridlington the STUC has no right automatically to invoke the same penalty in Scotland simply because it has a reciprocal agreement with the TUC. Such suspension requires the express authority of a specific STUC rule.[187]

10.38 The content of union rules

Union rule books normally provide for two types of offence — a specific offence where an express rule of the union has been broken and a blanket offence for conduct which the union believes is detrimental or prejudicial to its interests. In both cases the courts have applied a strict construction of the rules. Where the allegation is that a member has broken a specific disciplinary rule, it must be established that the actual conduct satisfies the terms of that offence. For example, a union would not be justified in disciplining a member who left a mandatory

---

[181] In *Blackall v. National Union of Foundryworkers* (1923) 39 TLR 431, KBD it was held that B's expulsion was unlawful because he was expelled two days earlier than the rule about expulsion for arrears would allow.

[182] 1979 SC 401.

[183] *Spring v. National Amalgamated Stevedores and Dockers Society* [1956] 2 All ER 221.

[184] See *Rothwell v. APEX* [1975] IRLR 375, Ch D where it was held that a transfer of engagements does not constitute organisation activities under Bridlington. See also the majority decision of the Court of Appeal in *Cheall v. APEX* [1982] ICR 543.

[185] *Cheall v. APEX* [1983] ICR 398, HL.

[186] See the speech of Lord Diplock in *Cheall*, above, at p. 405.

[187] See *Electrical, Electronic, Telecommunications and Plumbing Union v. STUC, Glasgow Herald*, August 10, 1988, where Lord Davidson accepted an undertaking from the STUC that it would lift its suspension of the EETPU because it was admitted that the STUC did not possess the power to suspend affiliated unions under its constitution.

meeting early when the rule book merely required attendance at such meetings.[188] Equally, where such a rule is ambiguous or unclear the court will apply the meaning which is more favourable to the member concerned.[189] Where a member is charged with a blanket offence, the function of the court is to discover whether the facts as proved are reasonably capable of establishing that offence. In *Silvester v. National Union of Printing, Bookbinding and Paper Workers*[190] for example, it was held that a member who had refused to work overtime contrary to the instructions of his union branch had not acted in a manner detrimental to the interests of his union because there was no union rule which made the working of overtime compulsory.

10.39 The blanket offence cases raise the question about how far the courts are prepared to go in examining the facts and the interpretation which the union has placed upon them. There is an obvious tension in the area of union discipline between the interest of the union to determine its own affairs and the right of the individual member not to be unreasonably treated. In the early days this tension was reflected in the court's insistence that it would only intervene where there was no evidence of rule book irregularities nor any denial of natural justice if it could be proved that the actual decision was reached in bad faith.[191] This test was very similar to that applied in the case of a social club. The modern test for trade unions, however, is to consider whether the facts are reasonably capable of supporting the decision reached. There is no doubt that an important factor in the development of this test has been the recognition that union disciplinary decisions can affect a person's livelihood.[192] The test grants to the court a discretion to consider factual questions as well as legal ones. Its scope is best illustrated by the decision of the Court of Appeal in *Lee v. Showmen's Guild*.[193] In that case Lee had been expelled from the Guild for "unlawful competition" by taking a site at a fair which had already been allocated to another member. In considering the extent to which the courts could review the disciplinary decision of a trade union, Lord Denning argued that union disciplinary committees performed two functions. First, they construed the rules and, second, they applied those rules to the facts. The second issue may appear to be solely a question of fact. However, Lord Denning argued that the two issues were so inextricably mixed together that they could not be separated. This decision undoubtedly enlarged the scope for judicial intervention. In the end, the Court of Appeal held unanimously that the facts in this case did not establish the offence and concluded that the union had come to a decision which no reasonable union could have reached.

10.40 Discipline and industrial action

It has been in the area of union disciplinary proceedings against the member who fails to take part in industrial action that this test has been most important. Its widest application was that of Templeman J in *Esterman v. NALGO*[194] who suggested that a member being disciplined for not taking part in industrial action

---

[188] *MacLelland v. NUJ* [1975] ICR 116, Ch.

[189] *Amalgamated Society of Carpenters v. Braithwaite* [1922] 2 AC 440, HL.

[190] (1966) I KIR 679. See also *Kelly v. NATSOPA* (1915) 31 TLR 632, CA.

[191] *Maclean v. Workers' Union* [1929] 1 Ch 602; *Wolstenholme v. AMU* [1920] 2 Ch 388.

[192] See Somervell LJ in *Lee v. Showmens' Guild* [1952] 2 QB 329, CA and Lord Allanbridge in *Partington v. NALGO* 1981 SC 299.

[193] [1952] 2 QB 329, CA.

[194] [1974] ICR 625, Ch D.

had the right to doubt whether the union had the authority to issue such instructions in the first place. Templeman J paid lip service to the now traditional test as to whether this was a decision which no reasonable union could have reached. However, as Davidson has argued, the *Esterman* case inverts the test because it concentrates upon whether it was reasonable for the member being subjected to the disciplinary process to refuse to engage in industrial action.[195]

10.41 The Scottish courts have also recognised that where a member is being disciplined for non-participation in industrial action the facts must be reasonably capable of supporting the disciplinary decision reached. However, the *Esterman* decision has been specifically distinguished in Scotland on the basis that it goes beyond the *ratio* of the *Lee* case.[196] In *Partington v. NALGO*[197] Lord Allanbridge declared invalid a decision to expel the pursuer for returning to work during a strike. He argued that the correct test was whether the facts were reasonably capable of establishing a breach of the union's rules. In deciding whether the facts did prove the offence, Lord Allanbridge declared that the union had to look outside its own rules and also consider the terms of the pursuer's contract. The fact that Partington's contract had a term which had been reached after agreement between NALGO and the employer that he would be required to provide safety cover during industrial action rendered the expulsion unlawful. A reasonable union in this case would not only have taken account of its rules but also the terms of the agreement which recognised the employer's right to require members to return to work in order to provide safety cover.

10.42 Natural justice and discipline

It has been held in Scotland that a union disciplinary committee acts in a quasi-judicial manner.[198] It is upon this footing that a union must comply with the rules of natural justice, although such an issue is no longer significant since the modern law applies the rules to administrative proceedings as well.[199] Under Scots law the rules of natural justice constitute implied terms of the contract of membership and it would therefore be unlawful for any trade union to attempt to exclude their operation.[200] Natural justice demands that at the very least a member should have proper notice of the charge against him and a fair opportunity to be heard in his defence.[201] The union disciplinary committee should also act in an unbiased way. Each of these issues will be considered in turn.

10.43 Fair notice involves giving the member sufficient notice of the charge against him so as to enable him to prepare his defence and sufficient time within which to do so. This notice should specify the offence(s) the member is alleged to have committed, the rule(s) which have been violated and any relevant penalties.[202] A union cannot give the member notice of one charge and then find him guilty of

---

[195] *The Judiciary and the Development of Employment Law* at p. 100.
[196] See Lord Allanbridge in *Partington v. NALGO* 1981 SC 299.
[197] 1981 SC 299.
[198] *Milton v. Nicolson* 1965 SLT 319.
[199] *Ridge v. Baldwin* [1964] AC 40, HL; *Breen v. Amalgamated Engineering Union* [1971] 2 QB 175, CA.
[200] *McDonald v. Burns* 1940 SC 376.
[201] *Walker v. Amalgamated Union of Engineers and Foundry Workers* 1969 SLT 150; *Lawlor v. Union of Post Office Workers* [1965] Ch 712.
[202] *Walker v. Amalgamated Union of Engineers and Foundry Workers* 1969 SLT 150.

an offence under another rule for which he has received no notice.[203] Equally, where a union is relying upon the report of an investigation conducted by a union official, it cannot take disciplinary action on the basis of that report until the member has been informed about the report's contents. This is to ensure that the member has a fair opportunity to correct or contradict any adverse comments made in it.[204] It would also be a breach of the rules for a disciplinary committee to consider a record of previous complaints outwith the presence of the member concerned.[205]

10.44 A member must be given the opportunity to be heard in his defence. This is to enable him to rebut the charge, or, if that is not possible, at least to explain the circumstances under which the breach of the rules was committed.[206] A failure to provide such a hearing even in an ''open and shut'' case will render the decision of the disciplinary committee *ultra vires* and invalid.[207] The member's right to a hearing is not an absolute one — it only operates to the extent of providing a fair opportunity to be heard. Thus, if the member does not avail himself of this opportunity the union would be entitle to proceed with the case in his absence as long as it could be established that he had proper notice of the charges.[208] The test applied in Scotland to assess the fairness of those proceedings is ''whether the proceedings were truly and essentially consistent with fair justice between man and man or whether on the other hand they were such as to permit of any possibility of injustice''.[209] It is not competent for some defect in the procedure before the disciplinary committee to be corrected by means of an appeal to a higher union tribunal.[210] It is undoubtedly the case in Scotland that a member has the right to request that he be represented by counsel and that the union must grant this request where the nature of the charge is likely to affect reputation or live-lihood.[211]

10.45 It is a fundamental requirement of the rules of natural justice that nobody should be judge in their own cause. A strict application of this rule creates difficulties in trade union cases because there is a sense in which the association is both prosecutor and judge. Moreover, it is invariably lay people who are involved in a trade union's disciplinary procedures. Accordingly, the task of the members of a union's disciplinary committee is to have ''a will to reach an honest conclusion after hearing what was urged on either side and a resolve not to make up their minds beforehand''.[212] This involves not only ensuring that there is no actual bias

---

[203] *Annamunthodo v. Oilfield Workers' Trade Union* [1961] AC 945, PC.

[204] *Walker*, above.

[205] *Tait v. Central Radio Taxis (Tollcross) Ltd* 1989 SLT 217.

[206] *Burn v. National Amalgamated Labourers' Union* [1920] 2 Ch 364.

[207] *Burn*, above. See also Megarry J in *John v. Rees* [1970] Ch 345 at p. 402 who declared that ''the path of the law is strewn with examples of open and shut cases which, somehow, were not''.

[208] *Annamunthodo v. Oilfield Workers' Trade Union* [1961] AC 945, PC.

[209] *Per* Lord Stott in *Walker v. Amalgamated Union of Engineers and Foundry Workers* 1969 SLT 150 at pp. 151–152 applying the dicta of Lord President Clyde in *Black v. John Williams & Co. (Wishaw) Ltd* 1923 SC 510.

[210] *Jamieson v. Central Federation of Homing Pigeon Societies* unreported January 11, 1983, Lord Dunpark following *Leary v. National Union of Vehicle Builders* [1970] 2 All ER 713.

[211] *Walker*, above, distinguishing the decision of Maugham J in *Maclean v. Workers' Union* [1929] 1 Ch 602 and applying the dictum of Lord Denning MR in *Pett v. Greyhound Racing Association* [1969] 1 QB 125, CA.

[212] *Per* Viscount Simon in *White v. Kuzych* [1951] AC 585 at p. 596, PC.

but that there can be no appearance of bias. If, for example, a member is expelled by a union committee which has as its non-voting chairman the person who pressed for charges in the first place, justice is not seen to be done since there must be an impression that the dice are loaded against the member.[213]

10.46 Exhaustion of internal remedies

Any union rule which seeks to prevent a member complaining to the courts against expulsion from that union is a nullity in law.[214] However, there was a time when the member had to exhaust all stages of his union's disciplinary procedure before he could approach the courts.[215] Nowadays, the courts will not demand that internal remedies are exhausted. This is on the basis of one of two propositions. In the first case, if the union rule book should declare expressly that a member must first exhaust all internal remedies, the courts will not be bound by this rule since their jurisdiction cannot be ousted. In this case, the member may have to show cause why the court should interfere with the contractual position. On the other hand, if the rule book merely provides for a right of appeal, the court can more readily grant relief without recourse to any domestic remedies.[216] This basic approach was followed by Lord Allanbridge in the *Partington* case[217] who entertained the member's action before he had appealed to the union's national council because it was considered that the interpretation of the rule book fell exclusively within the province of the courts and because the judge was concerned about the injustice which might result if court action were delayed.

10.47 The question of injustice is one which has also surfaced in other cases where a member is being disciplined for not taking part in industrial action. In *Porter v. NUJ*,[218] for example, the House of Lords was even prepared to grant the member interim relief before the disciplinary proceedings had commenced. Such relief may now be exceptional because it has been held by the Court of Appeal in *Longley v. NUJ*[219] that an injunction should only be granted to prevent a hearing from taking place where there was evidence that the disciplinary tribunal had acted improperly in the past or was likely to do so. Parliament has also been concerned to ensure that members should not be prevented from complaining to the courts by union rules or be delayed by union rules which provide for inordinately long and drawn out internal procedures. Thus, the Trade Union and Labour Relations (Consolidation) Act 1992, s. 63(1) declares that, where under the union's rules a matter must be submitted for determination or conciliation and those rules provide that this is to be a person's only remedy, such rules are to have no effect. In addition, the Act ensures that where court proceeding relate to a matter which a member began to pursue against his union under its rules more than six months before applying to the court, the court should not dismiss, sist or adjourn those proceedings on the ground that further procedures for resolving the grievance are available under the union's rules.[220] There is provision for an extension of this period where the reason

---

[213] *Roebuck v. National Union of Mineworkers (Yorkshire Area) (No. 2)* [1978] ICR 676, Ch.
[214] *Lee v. Showmens' Guild* [1952] 2 QB 329, CA.
[215] *White v. Kuzych* [1951] AC 585, PC.
[216] Goff J in *Leigh v. NUR* [1970] Ch 326 at p. 334.
[217] 1981 SC 299.
[218] [1980] IRLR 404, HL.
[219] [1987] IRLR 109, CA.
[220] TULRCA, s. 63(2).

for the delay in resolving the grievance is attributable to the unreasonable conduct of the member who initiated the court case.[221]

STATUTORY CONTROL OF ADMISSION, DISCIPLINE AND EXPULSION

10.48 Both the Sex Discrimination Act 1975 and the Race Relations Act 1976 contain provisions which outlaw discrimination on grounds of sex or marital status or on racial grounds by trade unions and employers' associations. The Acts protect not only applicants for membership[222] but those in membership as well.[223] Until recently, the only other major statutory control on a union's treatment of its members was the statutory protection against unreasonable exclusion or expulsion from a trade union which only applied where, in accordance with a union membership agreement (UMA), a person was required to belong to a specified trade union or one of a number of specified trade unions.[224] In the Green Paper, *Industrial Relations in the 1990s*,[225] the Government expressed concern about the restrictive nature of the TUC's "Bridlington Principles". As already noted, these seek to prevent unions poaching the members of other unions and create a disputes procedure to resolve inter-union disputes over organisation rights. The Green Paper viewed the Principles as denying individuals freedom to obtain membership of the union of their choice and recommended that, subject to qualification requirements, workers should be entitled to join their chosen union. The crux of this recommendation was that where a union represents workers of a similar skill or occupation, individuals possessing that skill or occupation should be legally entitled to become a member of that union. The Trade Union Reform and Employment Rights Act 1993, s. 14 implemented this recommendation and repealed the previous provisions on unreasonable exclusion or expulsion from a trade union.[226] Instead, there was enacted a general right not to be excluded or expelled from a trade union except in accordance with certain specific statutory requirements.[227]

Now the exclusion or expulsion of a person from a trade union is permitted if (and only if) any of the four following requirements applies:

(a) the person does not satisfy, or no longer satisfies, an enforceable membership requirement contained in the union's rules;

(b) the person does not qualify, or no longer qualifies, for membership because the union only operates in particular part(s) of Great Britain;

(c) in the case of a union which organises members employed by one particular employer or a number of particular associated employers, the person is not, or is no longer, employed by that employer(s); or

(d) the exclusion or expulsion is entirely attributable to the person's conduct.[228]

As far as the first head is concerned, a membership requirement will only be

---

[221] TULRCA, s. 63(4).

[222] SDA, s. 12(2); RRA, s. 11(2).

[223] SDA, s. 12(3); RRA, s. 11(3).

[224] Originally EA 1980, s. 4.

[225] Cm 1602, 1991.

[226] See now TULRCA, ss. 174–177.

[227] TULRCA, s. 174(1) as inserted by TURERA, s. 14.

[228] TULRCA, s. 174(2)(a)–(d). "Exclusion" means a refusal to admit into membership, not to a suspension of the privileges of membership: *NACODS v. Gluchowski* [1996] IRLR 252, EAT.

enforceable if it restricts membership solely because of one or more of the following criteria:

(a) employment in a specified trade, industry or profession,

(b) occupational description (including grade, level or category of employment),

(c) possession of specified trade, industrial or professional qualifications or work experience.[229]

As regards the last head, conduct cannot include any of the grounds of conduct which constitute unjustifiable union discipline under the Trade Union and Labour Relations (Consolidation) Act 1992, s. 65 nor conduct which consists of being, or ceasing to be, a member of another trade union, or employed by a particular employer at a particular place, or a member of a political party.[230]

The enforcement provisions for the above right are broadly similar to those which applied under the previous right not to be unreasonably excluded or expelled. A person who has been excluded or expelled from a trade union for a non-permitted reason is entitled to complain to an industrial tribunal at any time before the end of six months from the date of the exclusion or expulsion.[231] In the first instance, the tribunal has the power to make a declaration where the complaint is well-founded.[232] Thereafter, there is a right to seek compensation.[233] This application will be heard by the industrial tribunal if the union has complied with the declaration; otherwise the application will be to the EAT.[234] The amount of compensation will be that which is just and equitable in all the circumstances.[235] However, the award can be reduced by such amount as the tribunal considers just and equitable where the applicant has caused or contributed to his exclusion or expulsion.[236] The maximum that can be awarded by both the industrial tribunal and the EAT cannot exceed the maximum basic and compensatory awards for unfair dismissal (currently £17,600): though in the case of an application before the EAT there is a minimum award of £5,000.[237]

10.49 Unjustifiable discipline

Since 1988, union members have enjoyed a comprehensive and extensive right not to be unjustifiably disciplined by their union.[238] The provisions were based upon the 1987 Green Paper, *Trade Unions and Their Members*,[239] which had expressed the government's clear view in the context of industrial action that every union member should have the right to decide whether to break his contract of employment and run the risk of dismissal without compensation. Accordingly, it was recommended that no union member should be penalised by his union for exercising his right to cross a picket line and go to work. The original provisions, although seeking to outlaw union disciplinary action against the non-striking member, applied in a great many other circumstances. They were extended even

---

[229] TULRCA, s. 174(3).
[230] TULRCA, s. 174(4)(a) and (b).
[231] TULRCA, ss. 174(5) and s. 175(a). The tribunal has the power to extend this period where it was not reasonably practicable to submit it in time: TULRCA, s. 175(b).
[232] TULRCA, s. 176(1).
[233] TULRCA, s. 176(2).
[234] TULRCA, s. 176(2).
[235] TULRCA, s. 176(4).
[236] TULRCA, s. 176(5).
[237] TULRCA, s. 176(6).
[238] See originally EA 1988, s. 3.
[239] Cm 97.

further by the Trade Union Reform and Employment Rights Act 1993, s. 16. Under the Trade Union and Labour Relations (Consolidation) Act 1992, s. 64(1), an individual who is or has been a member of a trade union has the right not to be unjustifiably disciplined by the union. It is unjustifiable union discipline to discipline a union member for any of the following:

(a) failing to participate in or support a strike or other industrial action (whether by members of his own union), or indicating opposition to, or a lack of support for, any such strike or other industrial action;

(b) failing to contravene, for a purpose connected with such a strike or other industrial action, a requirement imposed on him by his contract of employment or any other agreement between the member and any person for whom he works or normally works[240];

(c) asserting (whether by bringing proceedings or otherwise) that the union, any official or representative of it or a trustee has contravened, or is proposing to contravene, any requirement imposed by the union' rules or by any other agreement or by any enactment or rule of law[241];

(d) encouraging or assisting a person to perform an obligation imposed upon him by his contract of employment or to make or attempt to vindicate an assertion made under para. (c);

(e) contravening a requirement imposed by, or in consequence of, a determination which infringes the individual's or another individual's right not to be unjustifiably disciplined[242];

(f) consulting or seeking advice or assistance from the Commissioner for the Rights of Trade Union Members or the Certification Officer on any matter whatsoever[243];

(g) consulting or seeking advice or assistance from any other person with respect to a matter which forms or might form the subject matter of an assertion that the union or one of its officials, representatives or trustees has contravened a requirement[244];

(h) proposing to engage in or doing anything preparatory or incidental to conduct set out above.[245]

The 1993 Act has extended the conduct for which a person cannot be disciplined by a trade union, largely so as to support the protection against an unauthorised deduction of union subscriptions and the right not to be excluded or expelled from a trade union which were also enacted in 1993. This was achieved by adding five new circumstances where disciplinary action cannot be taken against a member. These are as follows:

(a) failing to agree, or withdrawing agreement, to deductions from wages in accordance with check-off arrangements of union subscriptions;

(b) resigning or proposing to resign from the union or from another union, becoming or proposing to become a member of another union, refusing to become a member of another union, or being a member of another union;

---

[240] See also TULRCA, s. 65(7). The test for what amounts to industrial action under s. 65 is a mixed question of fact and law: *Knowles v. FBU, The Times*, August 15, 1996, CA.

[241] This would cover, for example, an allegation that there has been a failure to ballot or to hold an election in conformity with statutory requirements. It is a defence to show that the assertion was false and that it was made in the belief that it was false or in bad faith and that these were the reasons for the disciplinary action: TULRCA, s. 65(5).

[242] TULRCA, s. 65(2)(a)–(e).

[243] TULRCA, s. 65(3).

[244] TULRCA, s. 65(3).

[245] TULRCA, s. 65(4).

(c) working with, or proposing to work with, individuals who are not members of the union or who are or are not members of another union; or

(d) working for, or proposing to work for, an employer who employs or who has employed individuals who are not members of the union or who are or are not members of another union; or

(e) requiring the union to do an act which the union is required to do under the 1992 Act on the requisition of a member.[246]

10.50 An individual is disciplined by a trade union if a determination[247] is made, or purportedly made, under the rules of the union or by a union official or a number of persons including an official that:

(a) he should be expelled from the union or any of its branches or sections;[248]

(b) he should pay a sum to the union, to a branch or section or to any person (e.g. a donation to a charity);

(c) sums paid by the member by way of subscription should be treated as unpaid or paid for a different purpose;

(d) he should be deprived to any extent of, or access to, any of the benefits, services or facilities which would otherwise be provided or made available to him by virtue of his membership (e.g. preferential insurance rates for members);[249]

(e) advising or encouraging another trade union or branch or section of that other union not to accept the individual as a member;

(f) he should be subjected to some other detriment.[250]

10.51 Complaint of unjustifiable discipline

An individual who claims that he has been unjustifiably disciplined by a union has the right to complain to an industrial tribunal within three months of the date of the union's determination.[251] Any attempt by a union to preclude such a complaint is void.[252] If the complaint is well-founded, the tribunal will make a declaration to that effect.[253] Thereafter, the individual is entitled to compensation. Where the union has revoked the disciplinary action, the application for compensation will also be to an industrial tribunal. Otherwise the individual's right is to complain to the Employment Appeal Tribunal.[254] In both cases the amount awarded will be that

---

[246] TULRCA, s. 65(2)(f)–(j) as inserted by TURERA, ss. 16(1), 51, Sch. 10.

[247] This entails a decision of the union which disposes of that issue and not one which contains with it a condition subsequent: *Transport and General Workers' Union v. Webber* [1990] IRLR 462, EAT. It does not apply to action taken by the union before the provisions took effect: *Medhurst v. NALGO* [1990] IRLR 459, EAT; [1992] IRLR 229, CA.

[248] This provision will only be breached once the expulsion has taken place. See *Webber*, above.

[249] The suspension of a member is a breach of s. 64(2)(d) since it involves depriving that person of access to benefits, services or facilities. See *NALGO v. Killorn* [1990] IRLR 464, EAT.

[250] TULRCA, s. 64(2)(a)–(f). Naming a person as a strike-breaker in a union circular involves a detriment. See *Killorn*, above. "Detriment" has been construed broadly in anti-discrimination legislation to mean being placed at a disadvantage. See the decision of the Court of Appeal in *Ministry of Defence v. Jeremiah* [1979] IRLR 436, CA.

[251] TULRCA, s. 66(1) and (2). There are grounds specified in TULRCA, s. 66(2)(b)(i) and (ii) for extending this period.

[252] TULRCA, s. 288(1).

[253] TULRCA, s. 66(3).

[254] TULRCA, s. 67(1) and (2). For the industrial tribunal to have jurisdiction the union must have revoked the determination or reversed anything done for the purpose of giving effect to it: TULRCA, s. 67(2)(a) and (b). This latter step requires the union to put the member back into the same position he was in before he was unjustifiably disciplined: *NALGO v. Courteney-Dunn* [1992] IRLR 114, EAT.

which is just and equitable in all the circumstances.[255] The maximum compensation available under this provision is thirty times the maximum week's pay for a basic award for unfair dismissal plus the maximum compensatory award.[256] However, in the case of an application to the Employment Appeal Tribunal there is a minimum award of compensation which is an amount equal to the minimum basic award for trade union membership or non-union membership dismissals.[257] Any applicant under this provision has a duty to mitigate his loss and may also have his compensation reduced because he has caused or contributed to the disciplinary action.[258]

UNION DEMOCRACY AT COMMON LAW

10.52 The rights of union members to participate in the affairs of their unions depend just as much upon a strict construction of the rule book as do their rights over discipline or expulsion. It is the rule book which sets out the constitution of the union in the eyes of the law. The extent to which the Scottish courts rely on the rule book as the means of establishing a member's democratic rights is best illustrated by the statement of Lord President Cooper in *Martin v. Scottish TGWU*[259] who argued that the rules of a trade union are as fundamental and exhaustive a statement as the memorandum and articles of association of a limited company. Any deviation from the requirements of the rule book would show that the union has acted beyond its constitution and make it amenable to the *ultra vires* doctrine. In order to pursue such an action in court, the member need only show that he has been denied his constitutional right to participate fully in the democratic affairs of his union.[260] However, where a member applies for an interdict to prevent further *ultra vires* conduct by the union, that person must remain in membership of the union throughout the whole course of the action.[261] The Scottish decisions in this field have been fixed firmly upon the *ultra vires* doctrine. This may be the reason why our courts have not found it necessary to consider the application of the rule in *Foss v. Harbottle*[262] to trade unions. This is a doctrine which restricts the circumstances in which an individual member can sue for alleged irregularities in procedure on the basis that the proper plaintiff should be the association itself. The English courts have applied it in the trade union field[263] and it was recently considered in one of the English decisions arising out of the miners' strike of 1984–85.[264] However, its application to trade unions has never been judicially considered in Scotland.

---

[255] TULRCA, s. 67(5).
[256] TULRCA, s. 67(8). This award cannot be exceeded because of injury to feelings. See *Bradley v. NALGO* [1991] IRLR 159, EAT.
[257] TULRCA, s. 67(8).
[258] TULRCA, s. 67(6) and (7).
[259] 1951 SC 129 at p. 142.
[260] See the decision of Lord Cameron at first instance in *Paterson v. NALGO* 1977 SC 345.
[261] *Donaghy v. Rollo* 1964 SC 278.
[262] (1843) 2 Hare 461.
[263] *Cotter v. National Union of Seamen* [1929] 2 Ch 58, CA; *Edwards v. Halliwell* [1950] 2 All ER 1064, CA; *Hodgson v. NALGO* [1972] 1 WLR 130.
[264] *Taylor v. NUM (Derbyshire Area)* [1985] IRLR 99, Ch D.

10.53 The member and the rule book

There is English authority to the effect that, in this area, union rule books should not be interpreted literally or like a statute. Some account should be taken of the authors of union rules and their likely readership.[265] No such statement has been made by any Scottish judge. The Scottish approach has been to subject union rules to a close and detailed analysis. This is best illustrated by the decision of the First Division in *Paterson v. NALGO*[266] where it was held that the respective powers of the union's conference as compared to the National Executive Council (NEC) were contained in the rule book as a constitutional document. Moreover, it was declared that the conference cannot rely on its power to direct the general policy of the union as authority for making decisions which clearly fall within the competence of the NEC under the rules. It is also wrong to view a union's conference as analogous to the general meeting of an unincorporated society since in this latter case every single member has the right to attend, whereas in the case of the union conference attendance is restricted to delegates.[267] One area where the need to follow rule book requirements closely is paramount concerns union authorisation for industrial action. If the union's rules demand a ballot, for example, any failure to ballot or a defect in balloting procedures will render subsequent industrial action unlawful. Consequently, the votes in support of industrial action must at least reach the necessary majority specified in the rules,[268] and the ballot must not be held at a time which is too remote from the date of the proposed action.[269] Any authorisation of union expenditure in support of such action is also unlawful at common law, and any union officer who so authorised that expenditure could be held personally liable for breach of fiduciary duty.[270]

10.54 A full compliance with the requirements of the union's rules is particularly important where the union is seeking to change those rules. A change in the rules of a union cannot be implied from conduct alone.[271] Equally, where a particular rule change requires a successful ballot of the members, the union cannot avoid this procedure simply by calling a rules revision conference to repeal the balloting requirement and then change the rule at a later union conference. It has been held that a rule requiring a ballot of the members prior to any such change is an entrenched provision, so that no lawful change in the rule can be accomplished without the necessary ballot.[272] A union cannot cancel a ballot for the election of an officer unless there is express powers under the rule to do so or it can be shown that the whole election process is a nullity. It will be difficult to establish such a nullity if the independent scrutineer who has to be appointed under statute[273] in order to supervise such a ballot submits a favourable report.[274] Moreover, where the union rule book requires that the conduct of a ballot be delegated to an independent returning officer and there are allegations that the ballot was defective no action

---

[265] The cases are analysed and discussed by Warner J in *Jacques v. AUEW (Engineering Section)* [1986] ICR 683, Ch D.

[266] 1977 SC 345.

[267] See Lord Johnston in *Paterson*, above, at p. 359.

[268] *Taylor v. NUM (Derbyshire Area)* [1984] IRLR 440.

[269] *Taylor v. NUM (Yorkshire Area)* [1984] IRLR 445.

[270] *Taylor v. NUM (Derbyshire Area)* [1985] IRLR 99. See also TULRCA, ss. 15–16.

[271] *Wilson v. Scottish Typographical Society* 1912 SC 535.

[272] *Jacques v. AUEW (Engineering Section)* [1986] ICR 683, Ch D.

[273] See TULRCA, ss. 49 and 52.

[274] *Douglas v. Graphical Paper and Media Union* [1995] IRLR 426, HCt.

will be competent against the union so long as it can be shown that the union properly delegated its functions in accordance with the rules.[275]

10.55 The rule book and officials

A union must also ensure that it complies with the rule book in its treatment of union officers or officials. Thus, if a union wishes to suspend a person from office it must make sure that it has that specific authority in its rules.[276] The courts apply a very strict construction of the rules affecting union officers. For example, it does not follow that a union would be acting lawfully at common law when it insists that candidates for the office of president be members of a particular political party, even although there is a union rule requiring the holder of that office to be a member of that party. In such a case, the question of a person's election to that office is too remote at the time of nomination to insist that a candidate hold a particular allegiance.[277] The courts also adopt the same strict approach if a person is being dismissed from office. For example, the union can only implement those disciplinary sanctions which the rules authorise. A union officer appointed for a fixed term under a contract of employment who is also a member and who is challenging a union decision to dismiss him has two options under Scots common law. He can sue for damages for breach of his contract of employment, or he can seek reduction of the decision to dismiss on the basis that it is *ultra vires*.[278] If he chooses the former route he must be able to prove the existence of the contract.[279] As regards the authority to dismiss, it has been held in *Milton v. Nicolson*[280] that a union's general powers under the rule book to conduct the business of the union are sufficient authority for the dismissal of a union official. There is no doubt that any dismissal of a union officer from that office must also comply with the rules of natural justice.[281] The rules may even apply where a union official has a legitimate expectation that his election to a particular post will be confirmed by the executive and this does not happen.[282] Certainly, they would operate where there are allegations of improper behaviour against that candidate.[283] However, natural justice rules would not necessarily apply to a union delegate attending a Labour Party Conference whose nomination is withdrawn by his union because it is doubtful whether the withdrawal of such a nomination is a disciplinary measure relating to an office in the union.[284] Nor do the rules of natural justice apply where, for genuine financial reasons, a union decides to reorganise its staff structure so that a member is unable to take up a post as a divisional officer which had previously been offered to him.[285]

---

[275] *Veness v. National Union of Public Employees* [1991] IRLR 76, HCt.
[276] *Burn v. Amalgamated Labourers' Union* [1920] 2 Ch 364.
[277] *Leigh v. NUR* [1970] Ch 326.
[278] See Lord President Cooper in *Nisbet v. Percy* 1951 SC 350 particularly at p. 355. An employed official who has sufficient service could also seek a remedy for unfair dismissal under ERA, Part X.
[279] *Nisbet*, above.
[280] 1965 SLT 319.
[281] *Stevenson v. United Road Transport Union* [1977] ICR 893, CA.
[282] *Breen v. Amalgamated Engineering Union* [1971] 2 QB 175, CA.
[283] See judgment of Megaw LJ in *Breen*, above at p. 200.
[284] *Hudson v. GMB* [1990] 1990 IRLR 67, Ch D.
[285] *Meacham v. Amalgamated Engineering and Electrical Union* [1994] IRLR 218.

UNION DEMOCRACY UNDER STATUTE

10.56 There can be no doubt that one major thrust of the Conservative government's trade union legislation has been to attempt to make trade unions more responsible and more responsive to the wishes of their members. As the Green Paper which preceded the Trade Union Act 1984 declared " ... union leaders are seen to be out of touch with their rank and file and often appear to be neither representative of the majority of their members nor directly responsible to them".[286] In particular, the government has sought to ensure the primacy of the secret postal ballot over other forms of union democracy because of its belief that this form of balloting constitutes the most accurate means of ascertaining the views of the members.[287] At first postal balloting was encouraged indirectly through the scheme authorised by the Employment Act 1980 which enabled the Certification Officer to refund certain costs incurred by independent trade unions in the conduct of postal ballots.[288] The Trade Union Act 1984 took this a stage further by introducing a rebuttable statutory presumption that union executive election ballots and political fund ballots would be conducted by post. The Employment Act 1988 completed this process by stipulating that the secret postal ballot is the only lawful means of electing a union's executive or voting on a political fund.[289] Moreover, the impact of the legislation has been to create one uniform system for the election of all members of a union's principal executive committee (PEC) and president and general secretary.

10.57 Reimbursing ballot costs

The Trade Union and Labour Relations (Consolidation) Act 1992, empowered the Secretary of State to create a scheme allowing independent trade unions to claim reimbursement of expenses for certain ballots from the Certification Officer. The actual scheme which was created by regulations[290] was more tightly drawn than the enabling legislation since it only applied to secret postal ballots and also restricted the ballot purposes for which funds were available. The scheme provided funds for ballots for the following purposes:

    (a) calling or ending a strike or other industrial action;

    (b) carrying out elections to a union's PEC as required by the 1992 Act;

    (c) carrying out elections required by the union's rules for the posts of president, chairman, secretary, or treasurer of the union or any other elected post which a person holds as employee of the union;

    (d) amending the union's rules[291];

    (e) obtaining a decision about an amalgamation or transfer of engagements under the Trade Union (Amalgamations etc.) Act 1964;

    (f) deciding whether a union with a political fund wishes to retain that fund;

---

[286] *Democracy in Trade Unions* (1983), Cmnd 9571 at p. 3.

[287] See *Trade Unions and their Members* (1987), Cm 95 at p. 25.

[288] See now TULRCA, s. 115 repealed as of April 1, 1996.

[289] See now TULRCA, s. 51(4).

[290] Funds for Trade Union Ballots Regulations 1984 (SI 1984 No. 1654) as amended by the Funds for Trade Union Ballots (Amendment) Regulations 1988 (SI 1988 No. 1123) and the Funds for Trade Union Ballots (Amendment No. 2) Regulations 1988 (SI 1988 No. 2116).

[291] The ballot does not have to lead automatically to a rule change so as to qualify for funding: see *R. v. Certification Officer, ex parte Royal College of Nursing* [1991] IRLR 258, QBD.

(g) accepting or rejecting a proposal by an employer relating to remuneration, hours of work, level of performance, holidays or pensions.[292]

Funds could not be obtained for ballots to elect worker representatives, although this purpose was an appropriate ballot purpose as far as the enabling legislation is concerned.

10.58 Conditions for reimbursement

There are also a number of conditions about the conduct of the ballot which had to be satisfied before the Certification Officer could authorise payment.[293] The first condition was that the method of voting must be by the marking of a voting paper. Every voter had to be allowed to vote without interference or constraint on the part of the union or any of its members, officials or employees. It was a fundamental requirement of the scheme that, so far as reasonably practicable, a voter should have been sent a ballot paper by post to his home address and be given a convenient opportunity to return the paper by post.[294] The member had to be able to vote without incurring any direct cost.[295] The result of the ballot had to be determined solely by counting the individual votes cast fairly and accurately.[296] It was clear that, in determining the outcome of the ballot, the Certification Officer had to take account of the rules of the applicant union.[297] The Certification Officer was empowered to repay two types of expense — stationery and printing expenditure and postal costs.[298] Since the TUC's change of policy in 1986 concerning the use of the scheme by affiliated trade unions, substantial sums of money had been paid out. Thus, it is not surprising that the government's decision to revoke the scheme was greeted with dismay by many unions. The scheme itself has been repealed entirely since April 1, 1996.[299] There have also been transitional provisions in operation since March 31, 1993 which have reduced progressively the amount that a union can reclaim for expenditure incurred in a ballot.[300]

10.59 Electing the union's executive and president and general secretary

In the past, trade unions were left to arrange their own methods of electing members to their executives. So long as the union complied with its rules, the law did not interfere with union election arrangements. The Conservative governments of the 1980s, however, expressed considerable disquiet that unions were not properly consulting their members in such elections. Eventually, when the government became convinced that the unions were not prepared to instigate voluntary reforms, legislation was enacted to ensure all unions conducted certain elections in a particular way, despite anything to the contrary in their rules.[301]

---

[292] Regulation 5(a)–(b).
[293] See, generally, reg. 11. Under the 1988 Amendment (No. 2) Regulations it was also necessary for the union to ensure that the ballot had been independently scrutinised where appropriate.
[294] Regulation 11(c).
[295] Regulation 11(b)(ii).
[296] Regulation 11(e).
[297] See the decision of the House of Lords in *R. v. Certification Officer, ex parte Electrical Power Engineers' Association* [1990] IRLR 398 overruling the decision of the Court of Appeal reported at [1990] IRLR 98.
[298] Regulations 14 and 15.
[299] The right in TULRCA, s. 116 to use an employer's premises for secret ballots has also been repealed since this date.
[300] See Funds for Trade Union Ballots Regulations (Revocation) Regulations 1993 (SI 1993 No. 233) and, in particular, reg. 4.
[301] Originally enacted TUA, s. 3. See now TULRCA, s. 46.

Initially the statutory requirements about union executive elections applied only to those members of a union's executive who had a deliberative or casting vote. And it was possible for a union to hold a workplace or semi-postal ballot where the union was satisfied that there were no reasonable grounds for believing that such ballots could not satisfy the requirements of secrecy, freedom from interference or constraint, fairness and accuracy in the counting of votes required for postal ballots.[302] Now unions must secure that every person who holds the office of president or general secretary or who is a member of the executive or who holds any position by virtue of which a person is a member of the executive, is elected in accordance with the requirements of the Trade Union and Labour Relations Act 1992, Chapter IV.[303] No person can continue to hold any of the above positions for more than five years without being re-elected.[304] A member of the executive includes any person who, under the rules or practice of the union, may attend and speak at some or all of the meetings.[305] But the Act exempts from the election requirements persons who are entitled to attend the executive merely to provide the committee with factual information or with technical or professional advice.[306] Equally, union presidents and general secretaries whose positions are purely ceremonial are exempted so long as they are neither voting members of the executive nor union employees, hold office for less than thirteen months and have not held that position within the previous twelve months.[307] There are also special exemptions for newly formed trade unions[308] and for executive members and presidents and general secretaries who are approaching retirement.[309]

10.60 The conduct of the ballot

Since 1988 a union must elect and re-elect, at least every five years, all members of the executive and the president and general secretary, by the sole method of a secret postal ballot.[310] The basic requirement is for the method of voting to involve the marking of a voting paper by the person voting.[311] So far as reasonably practicable, a union must send a voting paper to a member's home address or any other address which he has requested in writing to be treated as his postal address and give that member a convenient opportunity to vote by post.[312] Each voting paper must state the name of the independent scrutineer and clearly specify the address to which and the date by which it is to be returned, and be consecutively numbered.[313] Every person who is entitled to vote at the election must have an equal entitlement to vote.[314] Members must be allowed to vote without interference from, or constraint imposed by, the union or any of its members, officials or employees and, so far as reasonably practicable, be enabled to do so without incurring any direct cost.[315] The ballot must be conducted so as to secure, so far as

---

[302] TUA, ss. 1–2(7).
[303] TULRCA, s. 46(1)(a) and (2).
[304] TULRCA, s. 46(1)(b).
[305] TULRCA, s. 46(3).
[306] TULRCA, s. 46(3).
[307] TULRCA, s. 46(4).
[308] TULRCA, s. 57. For the position of special register bodies see TULRCA, s. 117(5).
[309] TULRCA, s. 58.
[310] See now TULRCA, ss. 46–61.
[311] TULRCA, s. 46.
[312] TULRCA, s. 51(4).
[313] TULRCA, s. 51(2).
[314] TULRCA, s. 50(1).
[315] TULRCA, s. 51(3).

reasonably practicable, those voting do so in secret and the outcome must be determined by counting the number of votes cast directly for each candidate, and all those votes must be fairly and accurately counted.[316] There are occasions when a union can lawfully exclude certain classes of members under its rules from voting, so long as every member in that class is excluded.[317] Equally, union rules may restrict entitlement to vote to members who fall within a class determined by reference to trade or occupation, geographical area, separate section or any combination of the above.[318]

10.61 Independent scrutiny

These provisions are now reinforced by the system of independent scrutiny of elections for a union's executive and for the offices of president and general secretary. It is for the union to appoint its own independent scrutineer for each ballot, although there are regulations which specify the categories of person or organisation who can act as scrutineers.[319] The scrutineer must supervise the production and distribution of all voting papers, be the person to whom these papers are returned and retain custody of them for at least one year after the announcement of the election result.[320] He is also required to take such steps as appear to him appropriate for making his report, and to make his report to the union as soon as reasonably practicable after the last date for return of voting papers.[321] The report must state the number of voting papers distributed, the number of papers returned to him, the number of valid votes cast for each candidate, the number of spoiled papers and the name of the independent person required to store, distribute and count the votes cast.[322] The report must also state whether the scrutineer is satisfied that there are no reasonable grounds for believing that the ballot contravened any statutory balloting requirement, that the security arrangements for the production, storage, distribution, return or other handling of the voting papers and for the counting of them were, so far as reasonably practicable, sufficient to minimise the risk of any unfairness or malpractice and that he was able to carry out his functions without interference.[323] A union must ensure that, before a scrutineer has begun to carry out his functions, every member is notified of his name.[324] Unions are also required to appoint an independent person to store, distribute and count the votes cast in the election.[325] This person can either be the independent scrutineer or some other person who will carry out his functions competently and whose independence in relation to the union or the election cannot reasonably be called into question.[326] The person

---

[316] TULRCA, s. 51(5) and (6). It may be legitimate to have regard to the rules of the union on this question. See the decision of the House of Lords in *R. v. Certification Officer, ex parte EPEA* [1990] IRLR 398.

[317] TULRCA, s. 50(2).

[318] TULRCA, s. 50(3).

[319] Trade Union Ballots and Elections (Independent Scrutineer Qualifications) Order 1993 (SI No. 1909). This authorises solicitors and accountants and organisations such as Electoral Reform Ballot Services Ltd to act as independent scrutineers.

[320] TULRCA, s.49(3)(a) and (d).

[321] TULRCA, s. 49(3)(b) and (c).

[322] TULRCA, s. 52(1).

[323] TULRCA, s. 52(2).

[324] TULRCA, s. 49(5).

[325] TULRCA, s. 51A(1) as inserted by TURERA, s. 2(1).

[326] TULRCA, s. 51A(2).

appointed must carry out his functions so as to minimise the risk of any statutory contravention or the occurrence of any unfairness or malpractice.[327]

10.62 Candidature

No member of a trade union can be unreasonably excluded from standing as a candidate at an election.[328] It is arguable that this right is infringed when a union prevents members of a particular political party standing for office. The test for unreasonable exclusion is to consider the practical application of the union's arrangements. A procedure which does not specifically exclude a union member from standing would be unreasonable if it effectively precludes any real possibility that the ordinary member will put himself forward.[329] On the other hand, a member is not unreasonably excluded from standing as a candidate if he is excluded because he belongs to a class of which all the members are excluded by the rules of the union.[330] The Act clearly prohibits a union from requiring, whether directly or indirectly, that a candidate be a member of a political party.[331] There are also detailed rules which enable candidates to prepare an election address in their own words and to have that address sent out with the voting papers without incurring any cost.[332]

10.63 Register of members' names and addresses

In order to facilitate the requirement that executive ballots be open to all members, a statutory duty is imposed on trade unions to compile and thereafter to maintain, by means of a computer or otherwise, a register of the names and proper addresses of members.[333] This register must, so far as reasonably practicable, be kept up to date and be accurate, and any member has the right free of charge at any reasonable time, to check whether or not he is included on that register and, if he so requests, to receive a copy of his entry either for no fee or on the payment of a reasonable fee.[334]

10.64 These statutory obligations are enforced through rights provided to every member of the union. A member can complain either to the Court of Session (High Court of Justice for England and Wales) or to the Certification Officer.[335] The power of the Certification Officer is restricted to the making of a declaration which specifies the breaches which the union has committed.[336] As well as having the power to make a declaration, the courts possess the more potent remedy of an enforcement order[337] and can also make interim orders.[338] The Certification Officer must give written reasons for his decision and can make written observations on any matter connected with the proceedings.[339] The order can be made at the same time as the declaration or after it since there is nothing to prevent a member

---

[327] TULRCA, s. 51A(3).
[328] TULRCA, s. 47(1).
[329] *Paul v. NALGO* [1987] IRLR 43.
[330] TULRCA, s.47(3).
[331] TULRCA, s. 47(2).
[332] TULRCA, s. 48.
[333] TULRCA, s. 24.
[334] TULRCA, s. 24(3).
[335] TULRCA, s. 54(1).
[336] TULRCA, s. 55(1) and (3).
[337] TULRCA, s. 56(4).
[338] TULRCA, s. 56(7).
[339] TULRCA, s. 55(5).

applying to the courts for a remedy in respect of a matter which has already been dealt with by the Certification Officer.[340] The order may require the union to ensure the holding of an election, to take the necessary steps to remedy its breach of the Act and to abstain from specified acts so that a repetition of the breach does not take place.[341] If the enforcement order is not observed, any member (and not just the one who made the original application) can apply to the Court of Session to enforce obedience.[342] This enables contempt of court proceedings to be taken against the union.

THE COMMISSIONER FOR THE RIGHTS OF TRADE UNION MEMBERS

10.65 The Secretary of State has authority to appoint a Commissioner for the Rights of Trade Union Members.[343] The Commissioner has the power to provide assistance to a union member who is contemplating or is already taking certain proceedings against his union or one of its officers. The assumption underpinning this provision is that union members acting on their own behalf experience considerable disadvantages in pursuing cases against their unions in the courts and tribunals. Accordingly, the Commissioner is directed to assist a union member in a number of ways. The assistance may include making arrangements for or bearing the costs of:

(a) the giving of legal advice or assistance by a solicitor or advocate;

(b) the representation of the applicant, or the provision to him of such assistance as is usually given by a solicitor or advocate in steps preliminary or incidental to the proceedings, or in arriving at, or giving effect to, a compromise to avoid or bring an end to the proceedings.[344]

In exercising this discretion, the Commissioner is not obliged to provide assistance in every case. The matters which she may consider in deciding whether, and to what extent, to grant assistance include whether the case raises a question of principle, whether given the complexity of the case it is reasonable to expect the member to pursue the case unaided and whether the case involves a matter of substantial public interest.[345] There are also special rules where a member seeks assistance from the Commissioner in a case where the Certification Officer has already made a declaration concerning a breach of the balloting requirements for executive elections, or for industrial action ballots or in the case of a failure to maintain a register of members for political funds and the member intends to enforce the declaration before the courts.[346] In such case the Commissioner must grant assistance if the applicant has a reasonable prospect of securing the making of the enforcement order.

10.66 Where assistance may be given

The Commissioner has the power to provide assistance to union members in actions brought under the Trade Union and Labour Relations (Consolidation) Act 1992 as well as common law actions against their unions. As far as statutory

---

[340] See *Lenahan v. UCATT* [1991] IRLR 78, Ch D.
[341] TULRCA, s. 56(4)(a)–(c).
[342] TULRCA, s. 56(6).
[343] TULRCA, s. 266(1)(a) and (2).
[344] TULRCA, s. 111(2).
[345] TULRCA, s. 110(2).
[346] TULRCA, s. 110(3).

actions are concerned, the Commissioner can assist in the following circumstances:

(a) where a union has failed to take proceedings to prevent the use of funds to indemnify unlawful conduct;

(b) where union trustees have caused or permitted any unlawful use of union property;

(c) where a union has failed to maintain a register of members or secure confidentiality;

(d) where a union has failed to comply with a request for access to a union's accounts;

(e) where a union has allowed positions to be held by officers who have committed certain offences under the 1992 Act;

(f) where a union has breached the statutory requirements for union elections;

(g) where a union has authorised industrial action without the support of a ballot;

(h) where a union has unlawfully applied its funds for political purposes;

(i) where the union has breached the statutory requirements for political fund ballots.[347]

The government has continued to be concerned about union malpractices and announced in 1989 that it was contemplating extending the powers of the Commissioner to cover proceedings against a trade union alleging a breach of its rule book requirements where the complaint was viewed as a matter of substantial public interest.[348] These proposals were given statutory effect by the Employment Act 1990 and now the Trade Union and Labour Relations (Consolidation) Act 1992, s.109(2) authorises the Commissioner to provide assistance to a member who, in proceedings in the Court of Session, alleges that the union has breached or is threatening to breach its rules. The Commissioner can grant assistance in the following cases:

(a) appointment or election to, or the removal of a person from, any office;

(b) disciplinary proceedings by the union (including expulsion);

(c) the authorising or endorsing of industrial action;

(d) the balloting of members;

(e) the application of the union's funds or property;

(f) the imposition, collection or distribution of any levy for the purposes of industrial action;

(g) the constitution or proceedings of any committee, conference or other body.[349]

The Commissioner cannot grant assistance for any of the above matters unless it appears to her that the breach of the rules affects, or may affect, union members other than the applicant, or that similar breaches of the rules have been or may be committed in relation to other members of the union.[350]

TRADE UNIONS AND POLITICS

10.67 The starting point for any discussion on this point must be the decision of the House of Lords in *Amalgamated Society of Railway Servants v. Osborne*[351] in

---

[347] See, generally, TULRCA, s. 109(1)(a)–(h) as amended by TURERA, s. 49(3), Sch. 8, para. 58(a).

[348] *Removing Barriers to Employment* (1989), Cm 655, Ch. 4.

[349] TULRCA, s. 109(2)(a)–(g).

[350] TULRCA, s. 110(4).

[351] [1910] AC 87, HL.

1910. There it was held that the Trade Union Act 1871 did not confer any power authorising a trade union to maintain a political fund. This decision was quickly followed in Scotland in *Johnstone v. Associated Ironmoulders of Scotland*[352] where Lord Skerrington held that a union rule which allowed the association to take such steps as necessary for labour representation was *ultra vires*. In *Wilson v. Scottish Typographical Society*[353] the effect of the *Osborne* judgment was extended by the Second Division to cover unions which had not registered under the Trade Union Act 1871. It was clear, therefore, that if trade unions were to be able to finance and to participate in political activities, statutory intervention was required. This came in the form of the Trade Union Act 1913 whose basic framework continues largely to form the basis for the modern legal approach to expenditure by trade unions on political purposes.[354]

10.68 The Trade Union and Labour Relations (Consolidation) Act 1992

The 1992 Act fulfils three functions. First, it provides a mechanism by which the members of a trade union can be balloted in order to approve the creation and maintenance of a political fund. Second, it creates a system whereby those union members who do not wish to contribute to the fund can be exempt from paying the political levy, and, third, it ensures that an exempt member who does not contribute cannot be put at any disadvantage as a union member save in relation to the fund's administration.[355] Under the 1913 Act, once a union had balloted to create a political fund it never had to ballot again to obtain authorisation for the continuance of that fund. However, since the Trade Union Act 1984 unions have to ballot at least every 10 years in order to maintain their political funds. The 1984 Act also extended the definition of political objects because of government concern that unions were using their general funds to finance campaigns which were really political in nature. In addition, since 1988 union members can complain to the Certification Officer about a breach of the balloting arrangements for political funds.[356]

10.69 Political objects

If a union wishes to spend money on a political object, it must possess a political fund which has been approved in a ballot of the members. the following forms of expenditure are defined as constituting political objects:

(a) contributions to the funds of, or on the payment of any expenses incurred directly or indirectly by, a political party;

(b) the provision of any service or property for use by or on behalf of any political party;

(c) payments in connection with the registration of electors, the candidature of any person, the selection of any candidate or the holding of any ballot by the union in connection with any election to a political office;

(d) payments to maintain any holder of a political office;

(e) payments towards the holding of any conference or meeting by, or on behalf of, a political party or of any other meeting the main purpose of which is the transaction of business in connection with a political party;

---

[352] 1911, 2 SLT 478. See also *McArdle v. United Society of Boilermakers* 1915, 1 SLT 437.
[353] 1912 SC 534.
[354] See, generally, K. D. Ewing *Trade Unions, the Labour Party and the Law*.
[355] See, generally, TULRCA, s. 82(1). Contribution to the political fund cannot be a condition for admission to the union: TULRCA, s. 82(1)(d).
[356] Originally enacted by EA 1988, s. 16.

(f) payments on the production, publication or distribution of any literature, document, film, sound recording or advertisement, the main purpose of which is to persuade people to vote for a political party or candidate or to persuade them not to vote for a political party or candidate.[357]

10.70 Political fund ballots

As already noted, there must be a ballot to approve the creation of a political fund and a review ballot every 10 years to maintain it. These ballots must be in accordance with union rules approved by the Certification Officer.[358] Entitlement to vote in the ballot must be accorded equally to all members of the union.[359] Any person voting must be entitled to do so without interference or constraint and so far as reasonably practicable must be able to do so without incurring any direct cost.[360] So far as reasonably practicable the ballot must be conducted by post and members must be given a convenient opportunity to vote by post.[361] The ballot must be conducted so as to secure that, so far as reasonably practicable, those voting do so in secret by means of the marking of a voting paper by the person voting,[362] and the votes cast must be fairly and accurately counted.[363] Moreover, the voting paper must clearly specify the address to which, and the date by which, it is to be returned and the union must ensure that the voting papers are consecutively numbered.[364]

Both the Court of Session and the Certification Officer have jurisdiction to hear complaints about irregularities in the conduct of political fund ballots.[365] Political fund ballots must be subjected to independent scrutiny and the independent scrutineer must submit a report of the ballot. In addition, the storage, distribution and counting of the votes must be undertaken by independent persons.[366]

10.71 There are also a series of requirements as regards the management of the political fund. It is made clear that no property can be added to the fund other than from contributions by members, donations from other persons (other than the union itself) and income which accrues to the fund in the course of administering its assets.[367] The Act also forbids the union using assets from its general fund in order to discharge liabilities incurred by the political fund.[368] Where there ceases to be any political resolution in force the union must take all necessary steps to ensure that political contributions are discontinued as soon as reasonably practicable.[369] Any union member can request repayment of any political contributions he has made after the political fund resolution has ceased to have effect.[370] Further, all expenditure on political objects must cease within six months of the date of the

---

[357] TULRCA, s. 72(1)(a)–(f). The meaning of para. (f) is discussed by Browne-Wilkinson V-C in *Paul and Fraser v. NALGO* [1987] IRLR 413, Ch D.
[358] TULRCA, s. 74(1).
[359] TULRCA, s. 76.
[360] TULRCA, s. 77(3).
[361] TULRCA, s. 77(4).
[362] TULRCA, s. 77(1).
[363] TULRCA, s. 77(5).
[364] TULRCA, s. 77(2).
[365] TULRCA, ss. 79–81.
[366] TULRCA, s. 77A as inserted by TURERA, s. 3, Sch. 1, para. 3.
[367] TULRCA, s. 83(1).
[368] TULRCA, s. 83(3).
[369] TULRCA, s. 90(1).
[370] TULRCA, s. 90(3).

adverse ballot result.[371] A union which ballots against the continuation of the political fund may, if it wishes, transfer the assets in that fund into its general fund so that they can be spent on non-political objects, or, alternatively, it may simply retain its political fund and freeze the assets contained therein.[372] In this latter case, the union would have to obtain a positive vote in a subsequent ballot in order to revive the union's right to spend money on political objects.[373]

10.72 Despite criticisms of the system whereby union members who do not wish to contribute to the political fund are required to seek exemption from the payment of the political levy,[374] the present law retains the system of contracting-out.[375] Once a union has adopted a resolution for a political fund, notice must be given to the members of their right to contract-out of the political levy and they must be informed that an exemption notice is available from the union head office, its branches or from the Certification Officer.[376] A member of a trade union may give notice in the form prescribed by the 1992 Act or on any other form to like effect, that he objects to contributing to the political fund.[377] So long as such exemption notice is returned to the union within one month of notice of the ballot result the member's exemption will operate from the date on which the notice was given; otherwise, the exemption will become effective from the first of January following.[378] An exempted member cannot be excluded from any of the benefits of the union, nor can he be placed in any respect either directly or indirectly under any disability or at any disadvantage compared with other members of the union (except in relation to the control and management of the political fund) simply because he is exempt.[379] The right to exclude an exempt member from control and management of the political fund does not permit a union denying that person the right to stand for union office.[380] The Certification Officer has the authority to hear complaints about irregularities in the management of a union's political fund or alleging discriminatory treatment against an exempt member.[381] There is a right of appeal on a question of law to the EAT.[382]

10.73 One area of controversy under this provision concerns a union's treatment of its exempt members. In particular, disquiet was expressed at the practice whereby unions charged exempt members the full subscription (including the political fund element) and then repaid them the political levy portion. Occasionally, this was done at the beginning of the year, but more often the political levy was paid in arrears. The lawfulness of these practices was considered by the EAT in *Reeves v.*

---

[371] TULRCA, s. 89(2).

[372] TULRCA, s. 89(4) and s. 71.

[373] TULRCA, s. 89(5).

[374] An unsuccessful attempt was made by some Tory backbenchers to add a clause to the then Trade Union Bill 1984 which would have provided for contracting-in. See HC, *Official Report*, Parl. Debs, Vol. 57, No. 133, Cols. 721–761. The clause was defeated by 472 votes to 57.

[375] However, the TUC has issued a Statement of Guidance on Political Funds to affiliated unions. See Report of TUC General Council to 1984 Congress at pp. 84–85.

[376] TULRCA, s. 84(2).

[377] TULRCA, s. 84(1).

[378] TULRCA, s. 84(4).

[379] TULRCA, s. 82(1)(c). For the meaning of disability or disadvantage see, for example, *Cleminson v. POEU* [1980] IRLR 1, CO.

[380] *Birch v. NUR* [1950] Ch 602.

[381] TULRCA, ss. 82(2)–(4).

[382] TULRCA, s. 95.

TGWU[383] where the member was required to pay the full subscription and then was refunded the political levy as an exempt member. Some refunds were given in arrears of payment and some were paid in advance. It was argued that both types of refund were unlawful since they placed him at a disability or disadvantage. The Certification Officer held that those refunds paid in advance were lawful but that those paid in arrears were in breach of the 1913 Act. The EAT, on appeal, concluded that it was not only legitimate for a union to repay an exempted member's political levy in advance, it was also lawful for refunds to be paid in arrears so long as they were made as soon as reasonably possible after the collection of subscriptions by the employer. This point is now dealt with in the Trade Union and Labour Relations (Consolidation) Act 1992, s. 86(1) which declares that where an exempt member has certified in writing to the employer that he has contracted-out, that employer must ensure that no amount representing a contribution from the political fund is deducted from his wages.[384] It is therefore a breach of this provision for an employer to refuse to deduct this smaller subscription from the wages of an exempted member. This ensures that an employer will have to provide different levels of deduction for union subscriptions, depending on whether or not the member pays the political levy, when carrying out check-off arrangements. An exempt member who alleges that his employer has failed or has refused to deduct a rate of subscription which does not include the political fund element has a right of complaint to the sheriff court.[385] The court has the power to award a declarator and can make an order requiring the employer to take such steps as the order may specify in order to ensure that the employer's failure is not repeated.[386]

---

[383] [1980] IRLR 307.

[384] For the impact of such a certificate on the amount of any deduction authorised by ERA, Part II, see TULRCA, s. 88.

[385] TULRCA, s. 87(1).

[386] TULRCA, s. 87(2) and (3).

Chapter Eleven

THE LAW OF INDUSTRIAL CONFLICT

INTRODUCTION

11.1 There can be no doubt that without the intervention of parliament through the provision of immunities against legal action, the organisation of industrial action in Scotland would be fraught with legal difficulties. Except in the unusual case where union members have given proper notice of termination to their employer, the act of calling employees out on strike ensures that not only are the members in breach of their contracts of employment when they participate in the action but the union and its responsible officers, at the very least, are also liable in delict for inducing breaches of those contracts. Thus, some statutory protection for industrial action is necessary if that action is to be organised without the fear of proceedings in the civil courts. As we saw in Chapter Ten, it might have been difficult for any legal action to be sustained against the trade union concerned because of its unincorporated status at common law. However, in 1901 the House of Lords held in *Taff Vale Railway Co. v. Amalgamated Society of Railway Servants*[1] that a trade union registered under the Trade Union Act 1871 possessed a quasi-corporate status and accordingly it became competent to bring a court action against a union which authorised industrial action.

11.2 Statutory immunities

It was as a direct result of this decision that Parliament enacted the Trade Disputes Act 1906. This statute is important not only because it gave trade unions complete immunity in law for actions in delict but also because it developed the concept of the ''golden formula'' which protected union officers and the like *inter alia* for inducing breaches of their members' contracts of employment when the industrial action was ''in contemplation or furtherance of a trade dispute''. Thus, in deciding how to protect those who authorise industrial action in Britain the law has sought to provide protection through a system of immunities for those who organise that action rather than create a positive right to strike as in many Continental legal systems. This notion of a ''golden formula'' defence remains the bedrock for the operation of the immunities.[2] However, the particular delicts which can apply to industrial action have been developed considerably by the courts since 1906. Moreover, the present law no longer grants trade unions complete protection against legal actions in delict.[3] This means that their legal position is now the same as that of any other person who is responsible for calling industrial action. It is also

---

[1]   [1901] AC 426, HL.
[2]   TULRCA, s. 219.
[3]   Originally EA 1982, s. 15 repealing TULRA, s. 14.

worth pointing out that statutory developments have also redefined the meaning of a trade dispute[4] in British Law and have outlawed virtually all secondary action.[5]

11.3 English decisions

There are three further introductory points that have to be made before examining the present state of the law in more detail. The first is that much of the development of the law in this field has been carried out by the English courts. In Scotland the common law delicts remain imprecise and underdeveloped in comparison with their English counterparts. This can make it difficult on occasions to state definitively the Scots law on the relevant delicts. Consequently, unless there is appropriate Scottish authority reference will be made to the important English decisions. Second, given the fact that the immunities are intended to give protection against the operation of certain common law delicts, any redefinition or extension of these delicts is likely to have an effect upon the scope of the immunities. It is certainly the case that Parliament has had to extend the immunities on a number of occasions in order to take account of common law developments.[6] As we shall see, it is even arguable that certain forms of primary action might be unlawful because they entail delictual liability in circumstances where there is no corresponding statutory immunity. Lastly, it must be noted that the statutory immunities protect only those who organise or authorise the action. The law provides no protection for those employees who participate in the industrial action — even where the action is in contemplation or furtherance of a trade dispute. If their participation in the action involves a breach of their contracts of employment, the employer is entitled to sue for damages,[7] or, more likely, to treat those breaches as material and summarily dismiss the employees concerned. As far as unfair dismissal law is concerned, in the case of official action, so long as all the strikers are dismissed and none taken back within three months of dismissal an industrial tribunal would have no jurisdiction to hear complaints of unfair dismissal from those who were dismissed unless the industrial action is unofficial; in the case of unofficial action participants may be dismissed selectively.[8]

11.4 In *Merkur Island Shipping Corporation v. Laughton*[9] Lord Diplock declared that this area of the law should be approached in three stages. First, does the common law provide the pursuer with a cause of action against the defender? Second, if the pursuer satisfies this requirement, has the pursuer's cause of action been removed as a result of immunities in the Trade Union and Labour Relations Act 1974, s. 13? Third, if one of these immunities does apply, has the pursuer's cause of action been restored by any of the statutory developments which have restricted the scope of protected industrial action? This is the approach to this subject which will be adopted in this chapter.

---

4   TULRCA, s. 244.
5   TULRCA, s. 224.
6   See, for example, the enactment of the Trade Disputes Act 1965 to provide statutory relief for the delict of intimidation which had been applied to trade unions by the House of Lords in *Rookes v. Barnard* [1964] AC 1129 and the extension of immunity to cover inducement of breach of all contracts by the Trade Union and Labour Relations (Amendment) Act 1976 in accordance with the recommendations of the Royal Commission on Trade Unions and Employers' Associations 1965–68 (Donovan Commission) Cmnd 3623 who had argued that the earlier legal decisions had created a "legal maze". See paras 892–893 of the Report.
7   *NCB v. Galley* [1958] 1 All ER 91, CA.
8   TULRCA, ss. 237 and 238.
9   [1983] ICR 490, HL.

THE COMMON LAW

11.5 (a) Conspiracy

The essence of conspiracy is a combination of two or more persons to commit an unlawful act or to commit a lawful act by unlawful means. A conspiracy cannot be committed by one person alone. It is clear that there are two forms of conspiracy which can give rise to liability in delict. The first arises where two or more persons combine in order to injure the pursuer through the use of means which are unlawful in themselves and which do not depend on the combination for their illegality. The second exists when two or more persons combine in order to injure the pursuer using lawful means, but where their predominant purpose is not to advance their own legitimate interests. In both cases it is now clear that there must be an intention to injure the pursuer[10] who must also establish that he has suffered some patrimonial loss.[11] The critical question as regards the first form of the delict concerns the meaning of unlawful means. There can be no doubt that any conspiracy to commit a delict[12] or to commit a crime[13] would be unlawful. There has been some doubt expressed as to whether combining in order to break a contract can constitute an unlawful conspiracy[14] although the preponderance of opinion is now in favour of liability.[15] At one time it was thought that this form of delictual liability was established as soon as the unlawful means were proved. However, it now seems as a result of the decision of the House of Lords in *Lonrho Ltd v. Shell Petroleum Ltd (No. 2)*[16] that it is also necessary to show some intention to injure the pursuer. But this does not entail establishing a predominant purpose: all that is required is that there be proof of an intention to harm the pursuer.[17]

11.6 *Simple conspiracy.* The second form of conspiracy — simple conspiracy to injure without lawful means — became important as far as industrial conflict law is concerned through the trilogy of cases decided by the House of Lords in the late Victorian era.[18] The effect of one of these decisions, *Quinn v. Leathem*,[19] ensured that an otherwise lawful act could become unlawful if it was done by two or more persons and with the intent to injure a third party.[20] Clearly, such a principle would have a significant impact on the legality of industrial action since the very basis of

---

[10] *Lonrho Ltd v. Shell Petroleum Co. Ltd. (No. 2)* [1982] AC 173, HL.

[11] See the decision of the House of Lords in *Crofter Hand Woven Harris Tweed Co. Ltd v. Veitch* 1942 SC (HL) 1.

[12] *Crofter*, above; *Sorrell v. Smith* [1925] AC 700.

[13] However, a conspiracy to breach a penal statute may not constitute unlawful means. See the decision of the House of Lords in *Lonrho*, above.

[14] See the speech of Lord Devlin in *Rookes v. Barnard* [1964] AC 1129 at p. 1210.

[15] See "Trade Unions and Trade Disputes", *Stair Memorial Encyclopaedia of the Laws of Scotland*, Vol. 23, (1991) para. 850.

[16] [1982] AC 173. This decision has been construed by the Court of Appeal as requiring proof of a predominant purpose to injure for both types of conspiracy. See the decision of the Court of Appeal in *Metall und Rohstoff AG v. Donaldson Lufkin & Jenvette Inc* [1990] 1QB 391, CA. The House of Lords had now overruled *Metall und Rohstoff* in part by declaring that there is no need to establish a predominant purpose in the case of a conspiracy using unlawful means. An intention to injure will suffice. See *Lonrho plc v. Fayed* [1991] 3 All ER 303, HL.

[17] See J. M. Thomson, "An Island Legacy — the Delict of Conspiracy" in D. L. Carey Miller and D. W. Meyers, *Comparative and Historical Essays in Scots Law* (Edinburgh, 1992).

[18] *Mogul SS Co v. McGregor Gow & Co.* [1892] AC 25; *Allen v. Flood* [1898] AC 1; *Quinn v. Leathem* [1901] AC 495.

[19] [1901] AC 495.

[20] *Sorrell v. Smith* [1925] AC 700.

such action involves employees combining together to cause economic harm to their employer's business. However, later cases have reduced the impact of this delict by taking a broad interpretation of the predominant object behind the action and by accepting a defence of justification. Thus if the union can show that its predominant purpose is to pursue genuine trade union objectives the pursuer will have no cause of action even though his business is being injured as a result. In *Crofter Hand Woven Harris Tweed Co. v. Veitch*,[21] for example, island mill-owners combined with the union to keep out the pursuer because his yarn was produced on the mainland. As part of this campaign, the union instructed its members, without breaking their contracts, to boycott the pursuer's yarn so as not only to protect the local industry but also to ensure that the local mill-owners improved the wages of the employees and permitted the extension of union membership. The House of Lords held that, since the interests of the union and the employer were similar because both wanted to protect the local tweed industry which relied upon home produced wool, there was no unlawful conspiracy by the union and its members.[22] On the other hand, where the predominant object is to pursue a grudge against a former union member by seeking to have him dismissed, a conspiracy to injure will be established since this is not a legitimate union objective.[23]

11.7 (b) Inducement of breach of contract

This form of illegality was established as far as English law is concerned in *Lumley v. Gye*[24] where an opera singer was induced to break her contract of employment by singing at another theatre. This decision has been followed in Scotland in *Rose Street Foundry and Engineering Co. Ltd v. Lewis & Sons*.[25] It is clear that the delict does not just apply to an inducement to break a contract of employment but extends to inducing a breach of any type of contract.[26] The delict is committed where one person intentionally and without lawful justification procures or induces a breach of a contract between two other persons causing damage to one of them.[27] This delict takes three forms.

(a) *Direct inducement* where the defender (U) directly approaches one of the contracting parties (B) and persuades him to break his contract with a third party (A). See Figure 1.

In this case A will have a cause of action against U for inducement for breach of contract.

(b) *Direct procurement* where one of the contracting parties is forced to break the contract as a result of an unlawful act committed against him by the defender such as false imprisonment, trespass or theft.

(c) *Indirect procurement or inducement* this arises where the defender (U) is able to induce a breach of the pursuer's (A) contract with B (the other contracting

---

[21] 1942 SC (HL) 1. See also *Scala Ballroom (Wolverhampton) Ltd v. Ratcliffe* [1958] 3 All ER 220, CA where it was held that a boycott of a dance hall by members of the Musician's Union in protest at a colour bar did not constitute an unlawful conspiracy because the union was pursuing its legitimate interests.

[22] See also *Reynolds v. Shipping Federation* [1942] Ch 28 where the union's action to enforce a closed shop was held not to be an unlawful conspiracy because it was intended to advance the business interests of employers and employed alike.

[23] *Hunter v. Thornton* [1957] 1 All ER 234.

[24] [1853] 2 E & B 216.

[25] 1917 SC 341.

[26] See the judgment of Lord President Cooper in *BMTA v. Gray* 1951 SC 586 at p. 599.

[27] *Per* Lord Russell in *Gray*, above, at p. 603.

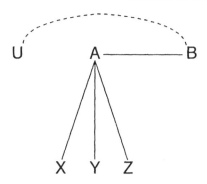

Figure 1

party) by inducing the employees (K, L & M) of B to break their contracts of employment bringing about a consequent breach of the contract between A and B.[28] See Figure 2.

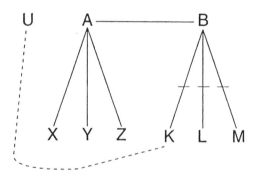

Figure 2

Once again A will be able to sue U for inducement of breach of contract.

It is the first and third versions of the delict which are most important as far as industrial action is concerned. The essential difference between these two forms of wrong is causation. If the person immediately responsible for bringing the pressure of inducement to bear is the defender or someone for whose acts he was legally responsible, the inducement is direct. If it is a third party, responding to the defender's inducement or persuasion but exercising his own choice in the matter and not being a person for whom the defender is legally responsible, the inducement is indirect.[29]

---

[28] See the judgment of Evershed MR in *D. C. Thomson & Co. Ltd v. Deakin* [1952] Ch 646 at p. 678. This is the most likely form of the delict for trade dispute purposes. However, it can be committed by the commission of any unlawful act by a third party which causes one of the contracting parties to break the contract. This point is developed further later in this chapter.

[29] See the judgment of Hoffman LJ in *Middlebrook Mushrooms Ltd v. Transport and General Workers' Union* [1993] IRLR 232, CA.

11.8 The elements of the delict

There are a number of elements to this delict. These were best outlined by Jenkins LJ in *D. C. Thomson & Co. Ltd v. Deakin*[30] which is still relied upon today as the basis for the delict, albeit that some of the strict requirements mentioned by Jenkins LJ have been diluted. First, the inducer must have knowledge of the contract and intend to bring about its breach. As far as knowledge is concerned, at one time it was thought that this required the defender to possess a knowledge of the precise terms of the contract.[31] Now, however, general knowledge about the existence of the contract is enough.[32] Indeed, it is possible for the courts to deem that the inducer had knowledge of the existence of contracts from the circumstances of the case.[33] Moreover, it would not be a defence for the inducer to argue that he genuinely believed that there was no such contractual term between the parties which could be broken.[34]

11.9 *Intention.* In one of the few authoritative statements on this branch of the law in Scotland, Lord Russell declared in *British Motor Trade Association v. Gray*[35] that the defender's actings must be intentional. However, the present English position is that the tort is no longer one of intention since liability can be established where the inducer acts recklessly or turns a blind eye to the likelihood of breach.[36] The present state of the law in Scotland is unclear although there is a recent Outer House decision in a landlord and tenant case to the effect that the delict is still one of intention and that "turning a blind eye" is not sufficient unless such action is tantamount to enable the court to conclude that the actings were in effect intentional.[37] If one can induce a breach without intending to damage the actual pursuer, this has obvious implications for the range of people who have title to sue for inducement of breach of contract in a trade dispute. This issue was discussed in the County Court in England in *Falconer v. ASLEF and NUR*[38] where a passenger on British Rail sued the two unions for damages for inducement of breach of contract. He had bought his ticket in advance but was unable to travel on the appointed day because of industrial action. The unions' defence that F was not the object of the action and that any damage to passengers was merely consequential was rejected by the judge as being both naïve and divorced from reality. In his view the action could succeed because the intention of the unions was to direct the strike against passengers in order to put pressure on the employers. In any case, the unions also acted recklessly because they knew and appreciated the effects of their action upon F and his contract but nevertheless pursued it.

11.10 On the other hand, in *Barretts & Baird (Wholesale) Ltd v. IPCS*[39] Henry J introduced an element of predominant purpose in order to establish liability. He argued that where the industrial action was called in order to improve the

---

[30] [1952] Ch 646, at pp. 696–697.
[31] See *D. C. Thomson*, above.
[32] *J. T. Stratford & Son Ltd v. Lindley* [1965] AC 269, HL applied in Scotland by Lord Milligan in *Square Grip Reinforcement Co. Ltd v. Macdonald* 1968 SLT 65, OH.
[33] *Merkur Island Shipping Corporation v. Laughton* [1983] ICR 490, HL.
[34] *Metropolitan Borough of Solihull v. NUT* [1985] IRLR 211, Ch.
[35] 1951 SC 586 at p. 603.
[36] *Emerald Construction Co. Ltd v. Lowthian* [1966] 1 WLR 691, CA.
[37] *Rossleigh Ltd v. Leader Cars Ltd* 1987 SLT 355, OH. See particularly the decision of Lord Mayfield at p. 360.
[38] [1986] IRLR 331.
[39] [1987] IRLR 3.

members' terms and conditions of employment, the union would not be held liable for inducing consequent breaches of commercial contracts if these were merely "unavoidable by-products". There is no direct authority on this point in Scotland, although statements by Lord Milligan in *Square Grip Reinforcement Co. Ltd v. Macdonald*[40] could be construed as supporting the *Falconer* decision because he argued that although actual knowledge of the terms of the contract on the part of the defender could not be proved, liability could be established when the defender should have realised that his action would injure the pursuer and cause a breach of contract. However, despite the fact that Henry J's view does have the advantage in a labour law context of limiting the legal consequences of industrial action, it has to be acknowledged that in other areas of the law there is no need to prove a predominant intention to injure the plaintiff for the purposes of the tort.[41] In Scotland, of course, the issue may yet be resolved purely on the basis that the defender did not intend to damage the pursuer.[42]

11.11 *Inducement or advice?* Second, it must be shown that the defender definitely and unequivocally persuaded, induced or procured the breach of an existing contract.[43] This requirement is particularly important as far as direct inducement is concerned. The issue here is to discover the forms of direct approach to one of the contracting parties which can constitute the necessary persuasion for the purposes of the delict; for example, would it be unlawful persuasion for a union officer merely to inform a supplier that a customer was in dispute with his employees? In *D. C. Thomson & Co Ltd v. Deakin*[44] this question appeared to be answered in the negative because the court suggested that merely to advise one of the contracting parties about the current state of facts would not constitute the necessary persuasion for the delict. However, in the only major case on this topic in Scotland a contrary view was expressed. In *Square Grip Reinforcement Co. Ltd v. Macdonald*[45] Lord Milligan, adopting a similar approach to that of Lord Pearce in *J. T. Stratford & Son Ltd v. Lindley*,[46] took the view that informing customers that the union had a recognition dispute with the other contracting party amounted to inducement of breach of contract because the union was "desperately anxious" to achieve a successful conclusion to the dispute. It would be important in deciding whether the approach amounted to inducement to consider the relative positions of the parties involved in order to assess the impact of the information upon the contract-breaker.[47] It is clear that for there to be direct inducement that inducement must be directed at one of the parties to the contract so as to force them to break it. There is no direct inducement when potential customers of one of the parties to the contract are approached not to buy the product which is the subject of the contract. Here, any influence which they can exert is dependent upon their anticipated action in not buying the product, but since they have no contractual relationship with the seller they are free to make up their own minds whether or not to buy it. Hence it is

---

[40] 1968 SLT 65 at p. 72.
[41] See the decision of the Court of Appeal in *Lonrho plc v. Fayed* [1989] 3 WLR 631, CA.
[42] *Rossleigh Ltd v. Leader Cars Ltd* 1987 SLT 355, OH.
[43] *BMTA v. Gray* 1951 SC 586 at p. 603. In England, the Court of Appeal has held in *Union Traffic Ltd v. TGWU* [1989] IRLR 127 that interlocutory relief could be provided in order to prevent a party inducing a breach of a future contract.
[44] [1952] Ch 646.
[45] 1968 SLT 65 at pp. 72–73.
[46] [1965] AC 269 at p. 333.
[47] *Square Grip Reinforcement Co. Ltd v. Macdonald* 1968 SLT 65, OH.

far from definite what effect the approach would have on the customers of the seller.[48]

11.12 *Indirect inducement.* As far as indirect inducement is concerned, it is also necessary to show in a trade dispute context that the employees concerned did actually break their contracts of employment and that the breach of the contract between A and B came about as a necessary consequence of the employees' breaches of their contracts of employment. The necessary consequence point has not proved a major obstacle in the cases.[49] It simply entails the pursuer showing as a matter of practical possibility that the other contracting party did not perform his contract.[50] Much more important is the requirement that the breach of the contract between A and B be procured by unlawful means. If there is not unlawful means, there can be no delictual liability for indirect inducement of breach of contract.[51] In the context of industrial action, unlawful means will usually be established by the employees of B being called upon by their union to take strike action or boycott goods destined for delivery to or collection from A; although, as we shall see, the unlawful means can exist in other ways such as inducement of breach of statutory duty.[52] Whatever action the employees of B actually take must entail a breach of their contracts of employment. This means that the necessary illegality would be lacking where B, having been informed of the union's dispute with A, withdraws his instructions to his employees to deliver goods to A so that the employees are never put in a position to break their contracts.[53]

11.13 *Justification.* In the *BMTA* case[54] Lord Russell declared that it was also necessary to show that the defender had acted without lawful justification. Although this is a widely recognised defence, it has been applied very restrictively in trade dispute cases. It would not be a defence in a case involving industrial action to show that that action was called without any malice or ill-will towards the pursuer.[55] The only occasion where a defence of justification has been accepted in an employment case is *Brimelow v. Casson*[56] where it was acknowledged that the defendants were justified in inducing theatre proprietors to refuse the use of their theatres to the plaintiff when it was clear that the wages he was offering his chorus girls was so low that there was a danger that some of them would seek to supplement their income through immoral behaviour. As we shall see shortly, this specific delict has been extended considerably, certainly as far as English law is

---

[48] *Middlebrook Mushrooms Ltd v. Transport and General Workers' Union* [1993] IRLR 232, CA.

[49] See, for example, the decision of the House of Lords in *J. T. Stratford & Son Ltd v. Lindley* [1965] AC 269 reversing the decision of the Court of Appeal on this point (reported at [1965] AC 276). See also *Merkur Island Shipping Corporation v. Laughton* [1983] ICR 490, HL.

[50] *Per* Jenkins LJ in *D. C. Thomson & Co. Ltd v. Deakin* [1952] Ch 646 at p. 697.

[51] See the judgment of Lord Denning MR in *Torquay Hotel Co. Ltd v. Cousins* [1969] 2 Ch 106, CA at pp. 138–139 reversing his earlier statement in *Daily Mirror Newspapers Ltd v. Gardner* [1968] 2 QB 768, CA.

[52] But there are no unlawful means where the action takes the form of a leaflet campaign to persuade potential customers not to buy a particular product: *Middlebrook Mushrooms Ltd v. TGWU* [1993] IRLR 232, CA.

[53] *D. C. Thomson*, above.

[54] *BMTA v. Gray* 1951 SC 586 at p. 603.

[55] *South Wales Miners' Federation v. Glamorgan Coal Co.* [1905] AC 239. *Cf Findlay v. Blaylock* 1937 SC 21.

[56] [1924] 1 Ch 302.

concerned, so that there is now a broad innominate tort of interference with contractual relations.

11.14 (c) Intimidation

The basis of intimidation involves the pursuer suffering damage as a result of action by a third party which that party is forced to take because of unlawful threats made to the third party by the defender. This form of liability was developed by the House of Lords in the context of industrial action in *Rookes v. Barnard*.[57] Previously it was thought that intimidation only applied to threats which were in themselves unlawful, usually threats of physical violence, although it might have extended to cover any crime or delict.[58] The *Rookes* case makes it clear that the concept of intimidation is wide enough to cover threats to break a contract. In that case the plaintiff was held to have a cause of action against a number of his fellow employees for intimidation when their employer terminated his contract of employment by proper notice. The basis for this was that his dismissal came about as a direct result of threats to take industrial action by the other employees in breach of their contracts of employment. Clearly, this form of liability has significant implications for those organising industrial action[59] since the critical element is that the defender must make an unlawful threat — something that may arise frequently in the preliminary stages before any industrial action is actually taken. If this is the case, then it is of no moment whether the damage caused to the pursuer by the person who has been threatened is committed lawfully through, for example, the termination of a contract by proper notice. There is no express authority on this form of liability in Scotland although there are some older Scottish cases where a threat to break a contract has been held to constitute an actionable wrong.[60] However, it must be accepted that a wrong of the type envisaged by the judges in the *Rookes* case would fall within the general principle of *culpa* in the Scots law of reparation. Thus we can assume that a wrong of the same kind as intimidation would be recognised by the Scottish courts.[61]

11.15 (d) Interference with contractual relations or with trade or business

As we saw earlier in this chapter there is no doubt that it is an actionable to induce a breach of contract. However, in the last twenty years or so liability has been extended to encompass another form of wrong *viz*. interference with the performance of a contract. This arises where the defender interferes with the performance of a contract without actually causing either of the contracting parties to break it. Although there are statements in the *Thomson* case[62] which could be construed as being wide enough to encompass this type of liability, its origins can be traced to the decision of the Court of Appeal in *Torquay Hotel Co. Ltd v. Cousins*.[63] In that case the contract which was the target of the union's action had a *force majeure* clause. This allowed the contract to be terminated without breach in the event of

---

[57] [1964] AC 1129.
[58] See K. W. Wedderburn "Intimidation and the Right to Strike" (1964) 27 MLR 257.
[59] One other feature of the *Rookes* case was the fact that the House of Lords also held that the union officer who had informed the employer about the likelihood of strike action could be held responsible for a conspiracy to intimidate for which there was then no trade disputes protection. See Wedderburn, *ibid.* at pp. 272–275.
[60] See, for example, *Hewit v. Edinburgh and District Operative Lathsplitters and Lathdrivers' Association* (1906) 14 SLT 489, OH.
[61] See J. T. Cameron, "Intimidation and the Right to Strike", 1964 SLT (News) 81.
[62] [1952] 1 Ch 646. See, in particular, the judgment of Jenkins LJ at pp. 690–694.
[63] [1969] 2 Ch 106, CA.

industrial action. When industrial action was called at the hotel the company which supplied the hotel with heating oil activated the *force majeure* clause. Thus we had the situation where it was obvious that the *force majeure* clause was implemented because of the industrial action. However, technically, there was no breach of contract. The majority of the court considered that the clause only provided an immunity as between the contracting parties and therefore concluding that Cousins was still responsible for inducement of breach of contract. However, Lord Denning MR considered that there was also a tort of interference with contractual relations which arose where a third person prevents or hinders one of the contracting parties from performing his contract so long as that interference is deliberate.

11.16 *Interference without breach.* This view has been supported by Lord Diplock in *Merkur Island Shipping Corporation v. Laughton.*[64] He argued that the analysis of the law in the *Thomson* case was restricted to inducement of breach of contract simply because this was the legal issue which the facts in that case disclosed. In Lord Diplock's opinion, although he used the expression ''breach'' in that case, Jenkins LJ did not intend to restrict the tort of actionable interference with contractual rights to situations where a breach of contract was actually induced. Thus, as far as English law is concerned, an interference with the performance of a contract will give rise to liability in tort even although no breach of contract has been induced. It most likely arises where the action of the defender prevents or hinders the performance of the pursuer's contract without a breach.[65] It is important to discover whether this wrong applies in both the direct and indirect forms of the tort. In *Cousins*, Lord Denning certainly envisaged that both forms of interference would give rise to liability. As far as indirect interference is concerned, there can be no doubt that there must be unlawful means — usually through the employees of one of the contracting parties being induced to break their contracts of employment. However, in the case of direct interference, it would seem that mere interference alone without the commission of some other unlawful act by the inducer would not be tortious.[66] There is no clear authority on the existence of this form of liability in Scots law. However, Lord Cameron in *St Stephen Shipping Co. Ltd v. Guinane*[67] did accept without argument that it would be unlawful in Scotland to interfere with the performance of an existing contract. The exact limits of this form of liability still await clearer articulation and analysis.

11.17 In the *Thomson* case,[68] Evershed MR argued that at the time of the enactment of the Trade Disputes Act in 1906 it was unlikely that the law recognised that a person would be liable for merely interfering in some way with the trade or business of some other person. However, English law now undoubtedly recognises this type of liability so long as, and this is crucial, the defender uses unlawful means.[69] Interference with trade or business was certainly relied upon by Lord Denning in *Daily Mirror Newspapers Ltd v. Gardner*[70] and in the

---

[64] [1983] ICR 490.
[65] *Merkur*, above, *per* Lord Diplock at p. 506.
[66] See the judgment of Lord Denning MR in *Acrow (Automation) Ltd v. Rex Chainbelt Inc* [1971] 3 All ER 1175, CA.
[67] 1984 SLT 25, OH.
[68] [1952] Ch 646 at p. 688.
[69] *Torquay Hotel Co. Ltd v. Cousins* [1969] 2 Ch 106, CA.
[70] [1968] 2 QB 768, CA at p. 783.

Cousins case[71] and it was referred to by Lord Reid in both *Stratford v. Lindley*[72] and *Rookes*.[73] There is, therefore, ample authority in English law to support its existence. Indeed, in English law, it is likely that the concept of wrongful interference with trade or business constitutes a broad category of tortious liability encompassing the other specific delicts to which we have already referred.[74] In the *Merkur* case[75] Lord Diplock certainly recognised the existence of a common law tort of interfering with the trade or business of another person by doing unlawful acts. There is no express authority on this point in Scotland. However, if the Scottish courts were to follow the English position the delict would be committed where damage is caused intentionally to the pursuer's business by the use of unlawful means. It is undoubtedly the case that the wrong is only actionable when there is proof of unlawful means — there would be no wrong where the interference is brought about by means which are themselves lawful. The exact scope of the unlawful means is not yet clear, although it is not restricted to procuring another person to break a subsisting contract nor to interfering with the performance of that contract. As a final point, there is authority in a trade disputes case that it is a strong requirement of the delict that the defender's predominant purpose must be injury to the pursuer and not his own self-interest.[76] However, in *Lonrho plc v. Fayed*[77] the Court of Appeal held that it was not necessary to establish a predominant intention to injure for the purposes of the tort; it is enough if the unlawful act is in some sense directed against the plaintiff or is intended to harm him.

11.18 *What constitutes unlawful means?* It has already been noted that, although the existence of unlawful means is critical to the delict of interference with business, the exact limits of those means for the purposes of liability have not been fully defined. Commission of another delict or of a crime would constitute the necessary unlawful act. Equally, as we shall see, inducement of breach of a statutory duty can constitute unlawful means — although not the breach of a penal statute.[78] The area of doubt is whether a breach of contract would be enough.[79] This is a point which is discussed by Henry J in *Barretts & Baird (Wholesale) Ltd v. IPCS*.[80] In this case, it was held that the plaintiffs had an arguable case against a number of fatstock officers employed by the Meat and Livestock Commission for interference with their business by unlawful means when the officers took part in a one day strike causing disruption to their business through the non-availability of EC subsidies. The critical aspect of this case was Henry J's holding that the

---

71   [1969] 2 Ch 106 at p. 139.
72   [1965] AC 269, HL.
73   [1964] AC 1129.
74   See Patrick Elias and Keith Ewing, "Economic Torts and Labour Law: Old Principles and New Liabilities" (1982) 41 Cam LJ 321.
75   [1983] ICR 490, HL. See also *Barretts & Baird (Wholesale) Ltd v. IPCS* [1987] IRLR 3; *Associated British Ports v. TGWU* [1989] IRLR 305, CA; [198] IRLR 399, HL; *Lonrho plc v. Fayed* [1989] 2 WLR 631, CA.
76   *Per* Henry J in *Barretts & Baird (Wholesale) Ltd v. IPCS* [1987] IRLR 3 at p. 10 misapplying the speech of Lord Diplock in *Lonrho Ltd v. Shell Petroleum Co. Ltd (No. 2)* [1982] AC 173.
77   [1989] 2 WLR 631. See, in particular, the judgment of Dillon LJ at p. 637.
78   *Lonrho Ltd v. Shell Petroleum Co. Ltd (No. 2)* [1982] AC 173.
79   In *Rookes v. Barnard* [1964] AC 1129 the House of Lords had held that a breach of contract was unlawful means for the purposes of intimidation, but left open the question of whether it would be so for the purpose of other delicts. See, for example, Lord Devlin at p. 1210.
80   [1987] IRLR 3, QBD.

unlawful means existed in the form of the officers' breaches of their own employment contracts when they took part in the action. He came to this conclusion because of the repeal of the Trade Union and Labour Relations Act 1974 s. 13(3)(b) by the Employment Act 1980, s. 17(8). This provision had declared that "a breach of contract in contemplation or furtherance of a trade dispute shall not be regarded as the doing of an unlawful act for the purpose of establishing liability in [delict]". Its repeal forced Henry J to accept that a simple breach of contract would be enough to constitute the necessary unlawful means for liability for wrongful interference with another's business.[81]

11.19 (e) Other actionable wrongs

In this developing area of the law there have been a number of other potential forms of liability which have been discussed in the cases. The importance of most of these is that given their novelty, no immunity is provided in the Trade Union and Labour Relations (Consolidation) Act 1992 against their application to trade unions in a trades dispute case. One possible wrong which has been discussed is inducement of breach of statutory duty. In *Meade v. Haringey LBC*[82] industrial action was called involving school janitors and cleaners. When the council closed the schools a number of parents sought an injunction against the council for failing to comply with its statutory duties under the Education Acts. In the Court of Appeal both Lord Denning MR and Eveleigh LJ considered that it was not only competent to sue the council for breach of statutory duty but also that a cause of action lay against the union for inducing such a breach.

11.20 *Inducing breach of statutory duty.* An important element in this delict is to discover whether the statute does actually impose a mandatory duty upon the person induced which the pursuer alleges has been broken as a result of the defender's inducements. This will entail a careful examination of the terms of the relevant statute.[83] The dangers of this type of liability for primary industrial action and the extent to which the appropriate statute will have to be scrutinised are illustrated in *Associated British Ports v. TGWU*.[84] There the union sought to call a strike of dockers as part of its campaign for similar terms and conditions to be applied to the dockers which they had previously enjoyed under the National Dock Labour Scheme. The Court of Appeal held that the scheme imposed a statutory duty upon registered dockers to work for such periods as were reasonable so that the union was inducing a breach of this statutory duty by calling the dockers out on strike. While this decision was reversed by the House of Lords,[85] it was simply on the ground that the Court of Appeal was wrong in its interpretation of the scheme. In the view of the House of Lords, it did not place a clear statutory duty on the dockers to perform work. Their Lordships did not question the existence of such a wrong and so the dicta of the Court of Appeal are still relevant. The other important aspect of this form of liability is that there is no doubt that in certain

---

[81] As had already been noted, the action against the employees for interference failed because the plaintiffs could not show that the action was taken with the predominant purpose of injuring them. This holding must now be open to doubt as a result of the Court of Appeal's decision in *Lonrho plc v. Fayed* [1989] 3 WLR 631.

[82] [1979] ICR 494, CA. See also the judgment of Lord Denning MR in *Associated Newspapers Group Ltd v. Wade* [1979] ICR 644, CA where he also argued that an interference with press freedom would also involve liability.

[83] *Per* Henry J in *Barretts & Baird (Wholesale) Ltd v. IPCS* [1987] IRLR 3.

[84] [1989] IRLR 305, CA.

[85] [1989] IRLR 399, HL.

circumstances inducing a breach of statutory duty can constitute the necessary unlawful means for the purpose of wrongful interference with the pursuer's trade or business.[86] However, the critical point is to show that the statutory contravention is independently actionable so that the pursuer has a right to sue *per se*.[87] Once again liability will turn upon the exact terms of the statute concerned.[88]

11.21 *Economic duress*. A final potential form of liability which could apply to trade unions is economic duress. This arises where one party to a contract is forced to enter into that contract or to agree to one of its terms because of unlawful coercion by the other party. In such a case the innocent party can argue that the contract is voidable and seek restitution of any money paid under it. The House of Lords has held in *Universe Tankships Inc of Monrovia v. ITWF*[89] that this form of liability is applicable in trade dispute cases. In this case it was held that the plaintiffs could seek restitution of $6,480 which they had been forced to pay into the union's welfare fund as a result of industrial pressure caused when the union authorised the blacking of one of their ships. In *Dimskal Shipping Co. SA v. ITWF*[90] the House of Lords confirmed that under English law the blacking of a ship or the threat to black it constituted economic duress. Accordingly, the plaintiffs were entitled to avoid contracts and recover money paid to the union as a result of a threat to black a ship. There is no direct authority on this type of liability in Scotland. However, it is doubtful whether such a cause of action would apply given the underdeveloped state of the law relating to force and fear and duress.[91]

THE IMMUNITIES

11.22 Introduction

Once a pursuer has established that he has a cause of action at common law, it is then necessary to discover whether that right to sue had been removed by any of the statutory immunities. Before any immunity operates, it must be shown that the industrial action was called "in contemplation or furtherance of a trade dispute" and is therefore protected by the golden formula. However, immunity is not provided against all the forms of delictual liability that are likely to arise in the course of a trade dispute.

11.23 The scope of s. 219

The Trade Union and Labour Relations (Consolidation) Act 1992, s. 219(2) declares that an agreement or combination to do or procure the doing of an act in contemplation or furtherance of a trade dispute shall not be actionable in delict if the act is one which, if done without any such agreement or combination, would not be actionable in delict. This immunity applies in the case of simple conspiracy to injure — that is the case where two or more persons combine in order to injure the pursuer by lawful means, but have an unlawful predominant purpose.

---

[86] *Barrets & Baird*, above.
[87] *Lonrho Ltd v. Shell Petroleum Ltd (No. 2)* [1982] AC 173.
[88] See, generally, the litigation arising out of the dockers' strike of 1989. See *Associated British Ports v. TGWU* [1989] IRLR 291, HCt; [1989] IRLR 305, CA; [1989] IRLR 399, HL.
[89] [1982] ICR 262.
[90] [1992] IRLR 78, HL.
[91] The present state of Scots law in this area is discussed by Andrew Thompson, "Economic Duress", 1985 SLT (News) 85 and Ewan McKendrick, "Economic Duress — A Reply", 1985 SLT (News) 277.

However, there is no protection in the case where the combination seeks to achieve its objective by means which would be unlawful if perpetrated by one person alone. The Trade Union and Labour Relations (Consolidation) Act 1992, s. 219(1)(a) declares that an act done by a person in contemplation or furtherance of a trade dispute is not actionable in delict on the ground only that it induces another person to break a contract or interferes or induces another person to interfere with its performance. When initially passed in 1974 this provision only applied to inducement or interference with a contract of employment. Immunity was extended to cover all types of contract in 1976.[92] This immunity has remained unchanged since that date and in the case of primary action it is unaffected by any of the statutory changes enacted in the 1980s and 1990s. Immunity is also provided against the delict of intimidation. The 1992 Act declares that an act done in contemplation or furtherance of a trade dispute will not be actionable in delict on the ground only that it consists in the defender threatening that a contract (whether one to which he is party or not) will be broken or its performance interfered with, or that he will induce another person to break another contract or to interfere with its performance.[93] This protection was first introduced by the Trade Disputes Act 1965 in order to negate the decision of the House of Lords in *Rookes v. Barnard*[94] and in 1976 it was extended to cover intimidation of any type of contract.[95]

11.24 There are a number of other wrongs which can be committed in the course of industrial action for which statute provides no protection. For example, there is no protection for assault or trespass although arguably until 1982 there existed immunity for the consequences of a trespass since statute[96] protected any interference with trade, business or employment of some other person, or with the right of some other person to dispose of his capital or his labour as he wills.[97] More importantly, as has already been noted, there is no immunity against the new actionable wrongs. Thus there is no protection against economic duress or inducement of breach of statutory duty.

11.25 The position is rather more complicated in the case of an interference with business by unlawful means. The repeal of the Trade Union and Labour Relations Act 1974, s. 13(2) by the Employment Act 1982, s. 21(3) might have been relevant since, as we have seen, it sought to protect an interference with a person's trade, business or employment. However, it was made clear by Lord Reid in *Rookes v. Barnard*[98] that this provision only provided protection if it was ever decided that a person could be liable for simple interference with business and nothing more. As we know, such interference is only actionable where unlawful means are used. It seemed, therefore, that s. 13(2) protected nothing.[99] However, in *Hadmor*

---

[92] TULR(A)A 1976, based on the proposals of the Donovan Commission (1968, Cmnd 3623) which had recommended that in order to bring clarity to this area of the law the immunities should be extended to cover inducement of breach of contract. See paras 891–894.

[93] TULRCA, s. 219(1)(b).

[94] [1964] AC 1129.

[95] Brought about by TULR(A)A 1976, s. 3(2).

[96] TULRA 1974, s. 13(2) which was repealed by EA 1982, s. 21(3).

[97] See the interpretation placed upon this provision by the First Division as regards the legality of factory occupations in *Plessey Co. plc v. Wilson* 1983 SLT 139.

[98] [1964] AC 1129 at p. 1177.

[99] As Lord Wedderburn put it, TULRA, s. 13(2) was of "limited value since it has been made clear that such interference is not a tort anyway, so there is nothing to protect". See K. W. Wedderburn, "The Trade Union and Labour Relations Act" (1974) 37 MLR 525 at p. 539.

Productions Ltd v. Hamilton[100] Lord Diplock suggested that s. 13(2) was intended to cover interference by unlawful means. No authority was cited in support of this proposition and certainly one writer has argued that it was *per incuriam*.[101] The better view is that Lord Reid's assessment in *Rookes* is correct. Since the repeal of s. 13(2) there is now no specific statutory protection against interfering with business by unlawful means. However, there may be some indirect protection against liability. This would arise where the means adopted to bring about the interference are themselves declared not actionable by s. 219. Thus, if the interference involved employees being induced to break their contracts of employment the necessary unlawful means would not exist since this form of inducement cannot form the basis of an action under the Trade Union and Labour Relations (Consolidation) Act 1992, s. 219(1)(a).[102]

11.26 Golden formula

The parties to a dispute. Once it has been established that the delict which the defender is alleged to have committed is one covered by s. 219 the next task is to consider whether it was done in contemplation or furtherance of a trade dispute. This entails discovering whether or not there is a trade dispute and then considering whether or not the industrial action is in contemplation or furtherance of that dispute. The first question raises two issues. First we must consider who can be the parties to a trade dispute and then examine the definition of a trade dispute provided by the statute. A trade dispute means a dispute between workers and their own employer.[103] To qualify as a worker a person must be employed by the employer in dispute, or, in the case of a person who has ceased to be employed by that employer, either have had his employment terminated in connection with the dispute, or, prove that the termination of his employment was one of the circumstances giving rise to the dispute.[104] It would seem that the present definition would exclude inter-union disputes or demarcation disputes since these are unlikely to involve the workers' employer. It also ensures that workers cannot use this provision as a means of taking solidarity action in support of other trade unionists, since they are not employed by the employer in dispute. The only way by which these other workers would be protected would be by establishing that they had a separate dispute with their own employer. The present definition would also exclude a dispute with another employer in the same group of companies as the workers' employer. In such a case the workers would have no trade dispute with their own employer because of the judges' reluctance to lift the "corporate veil".[105]

---

[100] [1982] IRLR 102 at p. 109. Lord Diplock's interpretation of s. 13(2) was followed by the First Division in *Plessey Co. plc v. Wilson* 1983 SLT 139.

[101] See K. D. Ewing, "Industrial Action: Another Step in the 'Right' Direction" (1982) 11 ILJ 209 at p. 214.

[102] See the speech of Lord Diplock in *Hadmor Productions Ltd v. Hamilton* [1982] IRLR 102, HL at p. 109.

[103] TULRCA, s. 244(1). Formerly under the original provisions of TULRA 1974, s. 29(1) a trade dispute could be between workers and workers or workers and employers. The present more restrictive definition was introduced by EA 1982, s. 18. It should be noted that a dispute between a trade union and an employer does satisfy the present statutory definition of a dispute between workers and their employer, since a union has the authority to negotiate terms and conditions on behalf of its members. See the decision of Millett J in *Associated British Ports v. TGWU* [1989] IRLR 291.

[104] TULRCA, s. 244(5).

[105] *Dimbleby & Sons Ltd v. NUJ* [1984] ICR 386, HL.

11.27 *The subject matter of a trade dispute.* A trade dispute must relate wholly or mainly to one of the following —

(a) terms and conditions of employment, or the physical conditions in which any workers are required to work;

(b) engagement or non-engagement, or termination or suspension of employment or the duties of employment, of one or more workers;

(c) allocation of work or the duties of employment as between workers or groups of workers;

(d) matters of discipline;

(e) a worker's membership or non-membership of a trade union;

(f) facilities for officials of trade unions; and

(g) machinery for negotiation or consultation, and other procedures, relating to any of the above matters, including the recognition by employers or employers' associations of the right of a trade union to represent workers in such negotiation or consultation or in the carrying out of such procedures.[106]

11.28 The above definition covers a large number of issues. As far as terms and conditions of employment are concerned, it is clear that this phrase has a wide meaning and covers not only the express and implied terms of the contract but also customary arrangements applied in practice by the parties.[107] The only limitation seems to be that it is restricted to those terms which regulate the relationship between the employee and his employer.[108] As regards head (c) concerning allocation of work, given that a trade dispute is now restricted to disputes between workers and their employer, disputes over allocation of work are only covered where the work is being reallocated between workers employed by the same employer. It does not apply where the employer chooses to reallocate the work to an outside agency.[109]

11.29 Some matters lie outside the definition. Strikes which are primarily political are not covered;[110] nor is industrial action aimed at showing employee disapproval of the employer's policy of selling his products to a particular country.[111] The most important point about this definition is that the dispute must "relate wholly or mainly" to one or more of the matters listed above. This phrase was inserted by the Employment Act 1982, s. 18 to replace the original requirement that the dispute by "connected with" one or more of the above-noted matters. This previous phrase undoubtedly covered a wider category of dispute and had been interpreted broadly by the courts. The only requirement was that the dispute had to have some genuine connection with one of the matters listed in (a)–(g). It was

---

[106] TULRCA, s. 244(1)(a)–(g).

[107] *BBC v. Hearn* [1977] ICR 685, CA approved by the House of Lords in *Hadmor Productions Ltd v. Hamilton* [1982] IRLR 102.

[108] *Per* Lord Diplock in *Universe Tankships Inc of Monrovia v. ITWF* [1982] ICR 262. Both Lord Scarman and Lord Brandon dissented from this view and placed a wider interpretation on this phrase.

[109] *Dimbleby & Son Ltd v. NUJ* [1984] ICR 386, HL.

[110] See, for example, *Express Newspapers Ltd v. Keys* [1980] IRLR 247, CA. The general strike of 1926 was held to be illegal by Astbury J in *National Sailors' and Firemen's Union v. Reed* [1926] Ch 536.

[111] *BBC v. Hearn* [1977] ICR 685. In this case the Court of Appeal held that H had no immunity when he authorised industrial action to protest against the BBC's decision to televise the FA Cup Final to South Africa. However, Lord Denning MR conceded that, had the union sought to include as a term and condition of employment of its members, a right not to be involved in broadcasts to South Africa, this might make the dispute a trade dispute.

therefore irrelevant that the dispute was primarily concerned with some extraneous subject-matter like a political issue provided that the dispute was also concerned with one of the matters listed.[112]

11.30 The current definition is much more restrictive. The meaning of the present phrase has been considered by the Court of Appeal in *Mercury Communications Ltd v. Scott-Garner*[113] where it was concluded that although the union had called industrial action because of the fear of redundancies amongst its members given the liberalisation and ultimate privatisation of British Telecom, the main reason for the action was the union's opposition to the government's privatisation programme. This case makes it clear that judges may be required to make a critical choice as to what is the predominant purpose or main matter behind the action. In doing so they must consider the reason for the dispute very carefully[114] and this may entail considering the contents of statements made by union officers both before and during the action. As the *Mercury* case illustrates, under the present definition there can be no such thing as a mixed industrial/political strike. One or other of these two possibilities must be selected as the main reason for the action. This state of affairs means that public sector unions, in particular, have to be very careful about how they manage their disputes with employers. This point is illustrated by the case arising out of the proposed repeal of the National Dock Labour Scheme.[115] Millett J had to decide whether the union's strike call was in protest at the government's proposal to abolish the scheme or against the port employers for replacement terms and conditions of employment after the scheme was abolished. The judge considered that initially these two issues were intermingled. However, the union had clearly been able to separate them. Thereafter, the union only threatened strike action in relation to its dispute with the employers over the terms and conditions of employment applying to the dockers after the scheme was repealed. Accordingly Millett J concluded that the dispute was a trade dispute because it wholly related to the matters specified in the statutory definition. More recently, in *London Borough of Wandsworth v. NAS/UWT*[116] the Court of Appeal held that a boycott by schoolteachers of tests and assessments associated with the national curriculum was mainly about terms and conditions of employment and therefore constituted a trade dispute. Here the court was satisfied that the action had been taken in order to complain about the perceived excessive workload that the national curriculum had created for teachers rather than to protest against its educational merit.

11.31 There are two further points about the statutory definition of a trade dispute. First it is possible to have a trade dispute even though it relates to matters occurring outside the United Kingdom. For this to happen, however, it must be

---

[112] *NWL Ltd v. Woods and Nelson* [1979] ICR 744, HL. See also the decision of the House of Lords in *Hadmor Productions Ltd v. Hamilton* [1982] IRLR 102 where it was held that a trade dispute did exist when ACTT sought to prevent "facility companies" being permitted to broadcast on the ITV network. The House of Lords accepted that although the dispute was mainly about the union's objection to such companies being granted network time, the dispute also concerned fears about redundancies amongst ACTT members and on this basis was a trade dispute. See also *General Aviation Services (UK) Ltd v. TGWU* [1975] ICR 276, CA.

[113] [1984] ICR 74, CA. *Cf Hadmor*, above.

[114] *Per* Dillon LJ in *Mercury*, above at p. 123.

[115] See, for example, the tactics of the TGWU prior to the calling of a dockers' strike after the abolition of the National Dock Labour Scheme. See *Associated British Ports v. TGWU* [1989] IRLR 399, HL.

[116] [1993] IRLR 344, CA.

shown that the person(s) whose actions in the United Kingdom are said to be in contemplation or furtherance of a trade dispute relating to matters outside the UK are likely to be affected in respect of one of the matters specified by the outcome of the dispute.[117] Second, a trade dispute can still exist in law even where the employer accedes to the union's demands because an act, threat or demand done or made by one person or organisation against another which, if resisted, would have led to a trade dispute, shall, notwithstanding that the other submits to the act or threat or accedes to the demand, be treated as being done or made in contemplation or furtherance of a trade dispute.[118]

11.32 *"Contemplation"*. Once it has been established that there is a trade dispute the next step is to show that the action taken was called in contemplation or furtherance of that dispute. As far as "in contemplation" is concerned it is clear that this phrase refers to something which is impending or likely to occur. There must be some objective event or situation which is before the defender's mind. A person would not be acting in contemplation of a trade dispute where he has a resolve in regard to something which is as yet wholly within his mind and is of an entirely subjective character.[119] The dispute must be real and imminent. Accordingly, preparing for something which is merely a possibility and not certain to arise cannot be considered to be in contemplation.[120]

11.33 *"Furtherance"*. The essence of "in furtherance" is that the dispute should be in existence and that the act is done in the course of it and for the purpose of promoting the interests of one of the parties to it.[121] The meaning of this phrase has been the subject of considerable judicial disagreement in the past. In the 1970s the Court of Appeal sought to define this phrase narrowly as a means of restricting the categories of lawful industrial action. Three strands of approach could be identified in the cases. First, the motive test which required unions to organise industrial action for a legitimate trade object and not for some extraneous motive;[122] second, the remoteness test which restricted lawful industrial action to action which directly furthered the dispute;[123] and the objective test which required that the action be "reasonably capable" of furthering the dispute.[124] These qualifications on the statutory language were swept away by the House of Lords. In *NWL Ltd v. Woods and Nelson*[125] the House of Lords declared that the motive test was wrong and inconsistent with the intention of parliament. Then in *Express Newspapers Ltd v. McShane*[126] the objective test was rejected by the House of Lords in favour of a subjective approach which concentrated upon the state of mind of the defender and simply required him to show that he had an honest belief

---

[117] TULRCA, s. 244(3).

[118] TULRCA, s. 244(4).

[119] See, generally, Lord Shaw of Dunfermline in *Conway v. Wade* [1909] AC 506 at p. 522.

[120] *Bents Brewery Co. Ltd v. Hogan* [1945] 2 All ER 570.

[121] *Per* Lord Loreburn in *Conway v. Wade* [1909] AC 506 at p. 512, and Lord Shaw of Dunfermline, at p. 522.

[122] *Star Sea Transport Corporation v. Slater* [1979] 1 Lloyd's Rep 26, CA.

[123] *Beaverbrook Newspapers v. Keys* [1978] ICR 582; *Associated Newspapers Group Ltd v. Wade* [1979] ICR 664, CA.

[124] *Express Newspapers Ltd v. McShane* [1979] ICR 210, CA. Lord Denning MR would have applied an even narrower objective test than that of the majority of the court. In his view before action could be held to further a dispute it had to provide "practical" assistance. See his judgment at p. 218.

[125] [1979] ICR 744, HL.

[126] [1980] ICR 42, HL.

that the action would further the dispute.[127] This approach was later confirmed by the House of Lords in *Duport Steels Ltd v. Sirs*[128] where it was reiterated that the important task for the judges was to give effect to the statutory language. The net effect of these three decisions was to re-establish that "furtherance" requires nothing more than an honest purpose to assist one party to the dispute.[129] Before it can be shown that a union is not furthering a dispute it must be established that the union called the action without any intention of pursuing trade dispute objectives.[130] The test is not restricted by any limitations based upon causation or the non-wisdom of the action taken.

RESTRICTIONS ON THE STATUTORY IMMUNITIES

11.34 Even where a union has established that the action is in contemplation or furtherance of a trade dispute and that it involves the commission of one or more of the protected delicts that action could still give rise to a civil claim because of a failure to comply with certain requirements laid down in the present legislation. Four limitations on the immunities will be discussed *viz.* secondary action, action not authorised by a secret ballot, action without notice to the employer, and action to enforce union membership or recognition requirements.

11.35 (a) Secondary industrial action

Prior to its repeal by the Employment Act 1990, s. 4, s. 17 of the Employment Act 1980 limited the legality of industrial action taken against a person other than the employer in dispute. It outlawed all forms of industrial action taken beyond a first customer or supplier of the employer in dispute and severely restricted legitimate secondary action. In particular, section 17 created three situations or gateways in which secondary action could be protected. The first was secondary industrial action taken at a first customer or supplier of the employer in dispute; the second was secondary action involving an associated employer and the third concerned the delictual secondary effects of lawful primary picketing.

11.36 *The present law.* Now only the third gateway remains. This gateway, as reconstituted by the Employment Act 1990 and as presently contained in the Trade Union and Labour Relations (Consolidation) Act 1992, s. 224, is now the sole type of legitimate secondary action and fulfils the recommendations contained in the Green Paper, *Removing Barriers to Employment*.[131] It ensures that lawful secondary action will be restricted to acts which affect an employer who is not a party to the dispute only where they are induced in the course of lawful primary picketing. There is secondary action in relation to a trade dispute, when, and only when, a person:

(a) induces another to break a contract of employment or interferes or induces another to interfere with its performance, or

(b) threatens that a contract of employment under which he or another is

---

[127] This was the majority view. Lord Wilberforce, although concurring in the result, applied an objective test that the action should be reasonably capable of achieving its objective. See his speech at pp. 54–56. Lord Salmon also added the rider that the honest belief should be on reasonable grounds: see *ibid.* p. 60.

[128] [1980] ICR 161, HL.

[129] See R. C. Simpson, "Gilt Back on the Formula" (1980) 43 MLR 319.

[130] *Associated British Ports v. TGWU* [1989] IRLR 291, ChD.

[131] March 1989, Cm. 665.

employed will be broken or its performance interfered with, or that he will induce another to break a contract of employment or to interfere with its performance, and the employer under the contract of employment is not the employer party to the dispute.[132]

These requirements for protected secondary action are only satisfied if the action is done in the course of such attendance as a picket as is declared lawful by the Trade Union and Labour Relations (Consolidation) Act 1992, s. 220. This will require the picket to be peaceful and for the action to be conducted either by a worker employed (or, in the case of a worker not in employment, last employed) by the employer party to the dispute or by a trade union official whose attendance is lawful because he is accompanying a member of that union whom he represents.[133]

11.37 The effect of these measures is to compartmentalise industrial action by restricting it exclusively to the employer in dispute. Now only the consequential secondary effects of such primary action may attract immunity. This state of affairs is enhanced by the Trade Union and Labour Relations (Consolidation) Act 1992, s. 224(4) which prevents unions extending a primary dispute to involve another employer in order to circumvent these extended restrictions on secondary action. This provision declares than an employer must not be treated as party to a dispute between another employer and workers of that employer; and where more than one employer is in dispute with his workers, the dispute between each employer and his workers must be treated as a separate dispute. On the other hand, the law prevents an employer who is one of a number who are involved in a trade dispute from arguing that protected primary action should lose its immunity because it could also involve secondary action of a type which does not enjoy any statutory immunity. Thus it is declared that an act in contemplation or furtherance of a trade dispute which is primary action in relation to that dispute may not be relied on as secondary action in relation to another dispute.[134]

11.38 (b) Industrial action ballots

The Trade Union and Labour Relations (Consolidation) Act 1992, as amended by the Trade Union Reform and Employment Rights Act 1993, creates detailed rules for the conduct of ballots for trade unions who wish to authorise strikes or other forms of industrial action. These provisions develop the requirements for ballots first introduced by the Trade Union Act 1984 which required trade unions to conduct secret ballots before calling industrial action. The current provisions ensure that only a secret postal ballot is acceptable as a legitimate means for ascertaining the views of the members and that any such ballot is subject to independent supervision. The present law also requires trade unions to fulfil certain notice requirements as regards the ballot arrangements and outcome.

Entitlement to vote in the ballot must be accorded equally to all the members of the trade union who it is reasonable at the time of the ballot for the union to believe will be induced to take part in the industrial action, and to no others.[135] This provision does not of itself necessitate a union arranging separate ballots where the members who will be asked to take part in the action are employed by different

---

[132] TULRCA, s. 224(2).
[133] TULRCA, s. 224(3).
[134] TULRCA, s. 224(5).
[135] TULRCA, s. 227(1).

employers.[136] A union breaches the above requirement if any person who was a member of the trade union at the time of the ballot was denied settlement to vote but was induced to take part in the action.[137] It would seem that this provision does not require absolute compliance and a ballot will not be invalidated simply because the union has inadvertently failed to give a member an entitlement to vote. A breach should involve something more than trifling errors in the way the ballot has been conducted.[138]

11.39 *Support of a ballot.* An act done by a trade union to induce a person to take part, or to continue to take part, in industrial action is not protected unless the industrial action has the support of a ballot and the trade union has served notice on the employer of its intention to hold a ballot and has given him a sample of the voting paper.[139] Industrial action is to be regarded as having the support of a ballot if the union has held a ballot which involves the appointment of an independent scrutineer, satisfies the statutory requirements for the conduct of the ballot and results in the majority of those voting in the ballot answering "Yes" to the appropriate question.[140] In addition, the union must ensure that there is a report on the ballot from the independent scrutineer and that any subsequent industrial action is called by a specified person.[141] These rules constitute a detailed and elaborate procedure which unions must satisfy if they are to call industrial action which remains within the immunities.

A critical decision which provides valuable guidance on the meaning of the phrase "support of a ballot" is the decision of the Court of Appeal in *London Underground Ltd v. RMT*.[142] Here the court distinguished between industrial action which meant collective action and the position of the members who are asked to take part in that action. It was the view of the court that individual members could not take collective action but as individuals could merely take part in it. This means that in the context of ballots it is the industrial action which must have the support of the ballot, not the participation of those who have been induced to take part in it.[143] Accordingly, a union will still have immunity when it calls upon new members to take industrial action even though they have not been balloted because they joined the union after the ballot on the action had taken place. This is because the industrial action, as collective action, already has the support of a majority of those voting in the ballot who declared themselves prepared to take part in the action.

---

[136] *University of Central England v. NALGO* [1993] IRLR 81. But see TULRCA, s. 228 for the provisions on separate workplace ballots discussed at para. 11.44.

[137] TULRCA, s. 227(2). The position is different for persons induced to take part in the action who were not members of the union at the time of the ballot and who joined subsequently. See the decision of the Court of Appeal in *London Underground Ltd v. RMT* [1995] IRLR 636.

[138] *British Railways Board v. NUR* [1989] IRLR 349, CA. At first instance Vinelott J argued that a ballot would only be invalidated under s. 227(2) where the denial of entitlement was of such magnitude that it might affect the result: see [1989] IRLR 345. This may be going too far.

[139] TULRCA, s. 226(1) as amended by TURERA, s. 18(1).

[140] TULRCA, s. 226(2)(a) as amended by TURERA, s. 49(2); Sch. 8, para. 73(b). Where the ballot poses two separate questions, one relating to strike action and the other to industrial action short of a strike, each question falls to be regarded as a separate matter which has to be voted upon individually and the majority in respect of each question considered separately. See *West Midlands Travel Ltd v. TGWU* [1994] IRLR 578, CA.

[141] TULRCA, s. 226(2)(b) and (c) as amended by TURERA, s. 49(2); Sch. 8, para. 73(b).

[142] [1995] IRLR 636.

[143] *Cf* Lord Donaldson MR in *Post Office v. UCW* [1990] IRLR 143, CA.

11.40 *The result of not balloting or a defective ballot.* Under the original provisions on industrial action ballots, enacted by the Trade Union Act 1984, the remedy for a failure to ballot properly was for immunity to be withdrawn. This meant that the employer or any other person affected by that action could apply to the courts for relief. The present law ensures that the immunities provided by the Trade Union and Labour Relations (Consolidation) Act 1992, s. 219 will not apply where an act is done by a trade union to induce a person to take part, or to continue to take part, in industrial action unless that action is supported by a ballot. Thus, the sanction for a failure to ballot is that any statutory immunities are removed and the union becomes liable for all the common law wrongs which are committed in the course of that action. This would apply even though the industrial action falls within the golden formula or is legitimate secondary action. It is not a defence for the union to argue that it could not comply with the statutory balloting requirements because such ballots were not authorised by its rules.[144]

11.41 *Balloting arrangements.* The method of voting in the ballot must be by the marking of a voting paper by the person voting.[145] The voting paper must state the name of the independent scrutineer, must clearly specify the address and date for return, and be consecutively numbered.[146] The members must be asked at least one of two questions — whether they would be prepared to take part (or continue to take part) in a strike; whether they would be prepared to take part (or continue to take part) in other industrial action short of a strike, and such questions must be framed in such a way that the person answering it is merely required to answer "Yes" or "No".[147] If a union wishes to ballot for approval for both strike action and action short of a strike it must ensure that the ballot paper gives the members the opportunity to vote separately on each of these questions. A single "rolled-up" question does not satisfy the balloting requirements.[148] In addition, action must be in support of an issue which constitutes a trade dispute. Immunity is lost if the union poses a question, either wholly or in part, which asks whether the member would be prepared to take part in action involving issues which are not trade dispute matters.[149] The voting paper must also contain a statement in these exact words *viz.* "if you take part in a strike or other industrial action, you may be in breach of your contract of employment". This statement cannot be commented upon or qualified by anything else on the voting paper.[150]

The voting paper must also specify who it is that has the authority to call the industrial action in the even of a majority "Yes" vote.[151] It has been argued that these quite specific requirements for the content of the voting paper constitute an attempt by the State to influence unduly the outcome.[152] Yet it does seem that strike

---

[144] *Shipping Co. Uniform Inc. v. ITWF* [1985] IRLR 71, QB.

[145] TULRCA, s. 229(1).

[146] TULRCA, s. 229(1A) as inserted by TURERA, s. 20(2).

[147] TULRCA, s. 229(2).

[148] *Post Office v. UCW* [1990] IRLR 143, CA.

[149] *London Underground Ltd v. NUR* [1989] IRLR 341.

[150] See, generally, TULRCA, s. 229(4). Apart from the contents of the voting paper, a union can make its support for industrial action known to the members. As the Courts of Appeal made clear in *London Borough of Newham v. NALGO* [1993] IRLR 83, a union is perfectly entitled to be partisan so long as it complies with the legislation.

[151] TULRCA, s. 229(3). The person specified on the voting paper must be within the range of persons for whose acts the union is taken to be responsible. See TULRCA, s. 229(3) and TURERA, s. 20(2).

[152] Ewan McKendrick, "The Rights of Trade Union Members: Part I of the Employment Act 1988" (1988) 17 ILJ 141.

ballots have become a permanent feature of negotiating processes and that in the majority of cases the ballot result supports industrial action.[153]

11.42 The primary obligation on trade unions is to ensure that every person who is entitled to vote in an industrial action ballot is allowed to do so without interference from, or constraint imposed by, the union or any of its members, officials or employees and that, so far as reasonably practicable, those voting do so without incurring any direct cost.[154] Such ballots can only be conducted by post so that unions must ensure that, so far as reasonably practicable, every person voting in the ballot has a voting paper sent to him by post at his home address or any other address which he has requested in writing to be treated as his postal address, and that he is given a convenient opportunity to vote by post.[155] The ballot must be conducted so as to secure that, so far as reasonably practicable, those voting do so in secret and that the votes cast are fairly and accurately counted.[156]

11.43 *Scrutiny of ballots.* Previously, trade unions were encouraged to ensure that industrial action ballots were subject to independent scrutiny.[157] Now, however, there is a statutory requirement that trade unions appoint an independent scrutineer for industrial action ballots[158] unless the number of members entitled to vote in the ballot does not exceed 50.[159] His key function is to submit a report to the union about the conduct of the ballot.[160] The union must ensure that the scrutineer duly carries out his functions and that there is no interference with the carrying out of those functions from the union or any of its members, officials or employees.[161] It is also obligatory for the union to comply with the scrutineer's reasonable requests.[162]

The report or the independent scrutineer must state whether he is satisfied about three things. First, that there were no reasonable grounds for believing that there was a contravention of any statutory provision in relation to the ballot. Second, that the arrangements made with respect to the production, storage, distribution, return or other handling of the voting papers, and the arrangements for the counting of the votes, included all such security arrangements as were reasonably practicable so as to minimise the risk of any unfairness or malpractice. Third, that he was able to carry out his functions without any interference from the trade union or any of its members, officials or employees.[163] Any person entitled to vote in the ballot and any employer is entitled to receive, on request, a copy of the scrutineer's report from the trade union.[164]

---

[153] ACAS Annual Report for 1994 at p. 36.
[154] TULRCA, s. 230(1).
[155] TULRCA, s. 230(2) as substituted by TURERA, s. 17. there are special rules for merchant seamen: see TULRCA, s. 230(2A)–(2C).
[156] TULRCA, s. 230(4).
[157] See, in particular, the Code of Practice on Trade Union Ballots on Industrial Action (revised as of May 20, 1991). For the current Code see para. 11.49.
[158] TULRCA, s. 226B as inserted by TURERA, s. 20(1). For provisions on the qualification of scrutineers, see TULRCA, s. 226B(2) and the Trade Union Ballots and Elections (Independent Scrutineer Qualifications) Order 1993 (SI 1993 No. 1909).
[159] For limitation, see TULRCA, s. 226C inserted by TURERA, s. 20(4).
[160] TULRCA, s. 226B(1). He must report to the union as soon as reasonably practicable after the date of the ballot and no later than four weeks from that date: TULRCA, s. 226B(1)(b).
[161] TULRCA, s. 226B(2)(b).
[162] TULRCA, s. 226B(4).
[163] See, generally, TULRCA, s. 231B(1) as inserted by TURERA, s. 20(3).
[164] TULRCA, s. 231B(2).

11.44 *Separate workplace ballots.* There is a requirement that where the members who will be asked to take part in the industrial action have different places of work, separate ballots must be held for each place of work.[165] However, this requirement can be displaced in two circumstances. First, if at the time of the ballot it is reasonable for the union to believe, and it does believe, that all the members entitled to vote have the same place of work.[166] The second circumstance arises where the members have different places of work. Here, the requirement in favour of separate workplace ballots can be avoided where, at the time of the ballot, it is reasonable for the union to believe, and it does believe, that the members entitled to vote in the ballot share some factor in common relating to terms and conditions of employment or to occupational description, provided that all the employees employed by the same employer who have that factor in common are entitled to vote.[167] Thus, a union would be justified in holding an aggregated ballot covering different places of work so long as all of its members who shared the same pay arrangements, for example, or the same job description, were balloted. Such a ballot is appropriate even where the employees with the common factor are not employed by the same employer.[168] "Place of work", in relation to any person who is employed, means the premises occupied by his employer at or from which that person works or, where he does not work at or from any such premises or works at or from more than one set of premises, the premises occupied by his employer with which his employment has the closest connection.[169] So workplaces are defined by reference to the particular premises of the employer where the employee works or has the closest connection.

11.45 *Notice requirement for ballots.* There are now detailed provisions requiring unions to give notice to employers of their intention to ballot for industrial action, to provide a sample voting paper and to inform employers of the result. A failure to comply with any of these requirements means that the union loses its immunity for the industrial action as against the employer. First, unions must give notice to employers of their intention to hold industrial action ballots. Unions must take such steps as are reasonably necessary to ensure that not later than the seventh day before the opening of the ballot, notice of its intention to hold a ballot is received by every person who it is reasonable for the union to believe is the employer of members who will be entitled to vote in the ballot.[170] The notice to employers must be in writing and must (1) state that the union intends to hold a ballot, (2) specify the date which the union reasonably believes will be the opening of the ballot, and (3) describe (so that he can readily ascertain them) the employees of the employer who it is reasonable for the union to believe will be entitled to vote in the ballot.[171] This final condition will require the union to actually specify by name the individual members who are to be balloted unless less specific information nonetheless enables the employer readily to ascertain which of his employees are

---

[165] TULRCA, s. 228(1).
[166] TULRCA, s. 228(2).
[167] TULRCA, s. 228(3).
[168] *University of Central England v. NALGO* [1993] IRLR 81.
[169] TULRCA, s. 228(4) as added by TURERA, s. 49(1); Sch. 7, para. 24.
[170] TULRCA, s. 226A(1)(a) as inserted by TURERA, s. 18(2). The opening day of the ballot is the first day when a voting paper is sent to any person entitled to vote in the ballot: TULRCA, s. 226A(4).
[171] TULRCA, s. 226A(2).

to be balloted.[172] Employers must also receive, not later than the third day before the opening of the ballot, the sample voting paper.[173]

Union members who vote in an industrial action ballot have the right to be informed about the number of votes cast, the number of "Yes" votes, the number of "No" votes and the number of spoiled voting papers.[174] Since 1993, unions are also required to inform employers of the ballot result. As soon as reasonably practicable after holding the ballot, a union must take such steps as are reasonably necessary to ensure that every relevant employer receives the same information as the members.[175]

11.46 *Calling of industrial action.* Industrial action is to be regarded as not having the support of a ballot unless it is called by a specified person.[176] Such person must be specified on the voting paper or be of a description which is so specified.[177] If action is called by a person who is not so specified, that action will not be regarded as having the support of a ballot even where there has been compliance with all the other statutory balloting requirements. However, the otherwise harsh effect of such a result has been mitigated by the decision of the Court of Appeal in *Tanks & Drums Ltd v. TGWU*[178] where it was held that industrial action still had the support of a ballot even though the senior official specified on the voting paper authorised another official to implement it if negotiations with the employer proved to be unsuccessful. Here the Court of Appeal recognised the importance in industrial relations of leaving some judgment to those on the ground.

Equally, industrial action cannot be regarded as having the support of a ballot unless certain conditions are satisfied. These are that (1) there must have been no call by the trade union to take part or continue to take part in industrial action to which the ballot relates, or any authorisation or endorsement by the union of that action, before the date of the ballot; (2) there must be a call for industrial action by a specified person which takes place before the ballot ceases to be effective. The first condition does not require the union to adopt a neutral stance. Nor does it prevent a union from widening industrial action and instructing a further ballot to this effect even though some members are already taking industrial action on the basis of an earlier ballot.[179]

11.47 *Period of effectiveness of the ballot.* The mandate provided by a majority "Yes" vote only operates for four weeks. As the Trade Union and Labour Relations (Consolidation) Act 1992, s. 234(1) makes clear, a ballot ceases to be effective at the end of the period of four weeks beginning with the date of the ballot. This period ends at the stroke of midnight of the last day of the fourth week.[180] To retain immunity, industrial action must be called and have started within this time and courts may be asked difficult questions as to whether particular union instructions constitute calls for industrial action within the relevant period.[181]

---

[172] *Blackpool and the Fylde College v. NATFHE* [1994] ICR 648, CA.
[173] TULRCA, s. 226A(1)(b).
[174] TULRCA, s. 231.
[175] TULRCA, s. 231A as inserted by TURERA, s. 19.
[176] TULRCA, s. 233(1).
[177] TULRCA, s. 233(2).
[178] [1991] IRLR 372.
[179] *London Borough of Newham v. NALGO* [1993] IRLR 83, CA.
[180] *RJB Mining (UK) Ltd v. NUM* [1995] IRLR 556, CA.
[181] See *Secretary of State for Scotland v. Scottish Prison Officers' Association* [1991] IRLR 371.

Such a tight schedule may also cause problems for unions who are using the strength of a "Yes" vote as a bargaining lever in negotiations with an employer. Yet, if a union does get its calculations wrong and makes a call for industrial action to start outwith the four week period, it will lose its immunity.[182] The only exception is where industrial action has already been called under the authority of a ballot and that action is suspended temporarily in order to allow for the re-start of negotiations with the employer.[183]

Equally, there may be problems for unions who are prevented from calling industrial action during the four weeks because of court proceedings.[184] Some amelioration from this difficulty is provided by the Trade Union and Labour Relations (Consolidation) Act 1992, s. 234(2) which declares that, where for the whole or part of the period the calling of industrial action is prohibited because of a court order which subsequently lapses, the union may apply to the court for an order that the period of the prohibition should not count towards the period of four weeks.[185] Such an application must be made forthwith to the same court and no application can be made after the end of the period of eight weeks beginning with the date of the ballot.[186] An order need not be made if it appears to the court that the results of the ballot no longer represents the views of the union members concerned or that an event is likely to occur as a result of which the members would now vote against industrial action if another ballot were to be held.[187]

11.48 *Rights of members.* As already indicated, the remedy for a failure to comply with any of the above provisions is a loss of immunity. Such actions will invariably be raised by an employer who is a party to the dispute. However, union members also have rights as regards breaches of the balloting requirements. The Trade Union and Labour Relations (Consolidation) Act 1992, s. 62(1) enables a member to apply to the court for an order where he claims that union members, including himself, are likely to be or have been induced by the union to take part or to continue to take part in industrial action which does not have the support of a ballot.[188] If the court is satisfied that the claim is well-founded it must make an order[189] which requires the union to take steps for ensuring that there is no, or no further, inducement of members to take part in the action and that no member continues to engage in industrial action in breach of the order.[190] Although, in practical terms, the effect may be the same, in the case of an application by a member the law creates a specific procedure with a particular remedy and does not rely on loss of immunity, as is the sanction for actions brought by employers.

11.49 *Ballots and the Code of Practice.* The above procedures are fairly complex and elaborate and it is very possible that a union could be subject to court action

---

[182] See the facts in *RJB Mining*, above.

[183] *Monsanto plc v. TGWU* [1986] IRLR 406, CA. But unions may have to be careful about the length of any such interruption: see *Post Office v. UCW* [1990] IRLR 143, CA.

[184] See, for example, the litigation over the decision of the TGWU to call industrial action as a result of the repeal of the National Dock Labour Scheme: see *Associated British Ports v. TGWU* [1989] IRLR 291, HCt; [1989] IRLR 305, CA; [1989] IRLR 399, HL.

[185] There is no appeal against the decision of the court on this matter: see TULRCA, s. 234(5).

[186] TULRCA, s. 234(3).

[187] TULRCA, s. 234(4).

[188] Such an application can be supported by the Commissioner for the Rights of Trade Union Members: see TULRCA, s. 109.

[189] This can be an interim order. See TULRCA, s. 62(4).

[190] TULRCA, s. 63(3).

because of an inadvertent failure to comply precisely with the requirement of the law. To this extent the Trade Union and Labour Relations (Consolidation) Act 1992, s. 203 authorises the Secretary of State to issue Codes of Practice which provide practical guidance and promote desirable practices on, *inter alia*, ballots. There is a Code of Practice on Industrial Action Ballots and Notice to Employers[191] which seeks to set out these complicated requirements in a form which is accessible to the non-lawyer. However, it has been argued that the present Code goes beyond this aim by laying down additional requirements for ballots which are not in the 1992 Act and, in some places, by misrepresenting the law.[192]

11.50 (c) Notice to employer of intention to call industrial action

As has already been noted, an employer has a right to be informed of the ballot result. However, the present legislation also creates further requirements for unions to notify employers about the nature and timing of industrial action. The Trade Union and Labour Relations (Consolidation) Act 1992, s. 234A[193] ensures that industrial action called by a trade union will not be protected as respects employers unless the union has taken or takes such steps as are reasonably necessary to ensure that the employer receives, within the appropriate period, a relevant notice of industrial action. A relevant notice must be in writing and it must (1) describe (so that he can readily ascertain them[194]) the employees of the employer who the union intends to induce to take part in the industrial action, (2) state whether the industrial action is intended to be continuous or discontinuous, and (3) state that it is given for statutory purposes.[195] Where the action is to be continuous, the notice must specify the intended date for the start of the action; where it is to be discontinuous, the intended dates of the action must be specified.[196]

The appropriate period for the notice is the period beginning with the day when the union informed the employer of the ballot result and ending with the seventh day before the day when the industrial action will commence.[197] This means that, at the very least, unions must give seven days' notice to employers of their intention to call industrial action. If a union starts industrial action without providing this notice or without complying with the appropriate period requirements, it will lose its immunity against civil action by the employer. However, immunity will also be lost if any of the relevant employees who are to be induced to take part in the industrial action take part in the action before the date specified in the notice.[198] Equally, in the case of discontinuous industrial action, that action will not be protected if there is industrial action on a date not specified in the notice.[199]

Unions also have duties where the action is suspended, for example, so as to enable negotiations with employers to recommence, and it is later renewed. In such circumstances, the union must notify employers where it had originally authorised

---

[191] Present version took effect on November 17, 1995.
[192] See Bob Simpson, "Code of Practice on Industrial Action Ballots and Notice to Employers" (1995) 24 ILJ 337.
[193] As inserted by the TURERA, s. 21.
[194] This may entail notification of the names of individual members: see the decision of the Court of Appeal in *Blackpool and the Fylde College v. NATFHE* [1994] ICR 648.
[195] TULRCA, s. 234A(3).
[196] TULRCA, s. 234A(2)(b)(i) and (ii). Industrial action is discontinuous where the union intends it to take place only on some days on which there is an opportunity to take the action, and continuous industrial action arises if a union intends it to be not so restricted: TULRCA, s. 234A(6).
[197] TULRCA, s. 234A(4).
[198] TULRCA, s. 234A(5)(a).
[199] TULRCA, s. 234A(5)(b).

or endorsed industrial action which then ceases to be so authorised or endorsed for reasons other than compliance with a court order, and at a later date then seeks to renew its authorisation or endorsement. Here the action cannot be restarted until the union has given the employer a further notice, of at least seven days, of such an intention.[200]

11.51 (d) Pressure to impose union membership or recognition requirements

It has been one of the major objectives of the legislation of the 1980s and 1990s to provide protections against practices associated with the closed shop.[201] This aim is also supported through provisions in the Trade Union and Labour Relations (Consolidation) Act 1992, which outlaw terms in contracts seeking to enforce union only or recognition only requirements and which remove immunity for industrial action called in support of such industrial practices. Any term in a contract for the supply of goods or services is void if that term seeks to impose union membership requirements.[202] It is also unlawful to refuse to deal with a supplier or prospective supplier of goods or services on union membership grounds.[203] Moreover, it is a breach of statutory duty if on the ground of union membership a person excludes the name of a particular person from a list of approved contractors; or excludes a person from the right to tender for the supply of goods or services; or otherwise determines not to enter into a contract for the supply of goods or services.[204] Further, any term which purports to require a party to a contract for the supply of goods or services to grant recognition rights to a trade union or to negotiate or consult with any union official is void.[205] It is also a breach of statutory duty to refuse to deal with a supplier or prospective supplier of goods or services on the grounds that that person does not, or is not likely to, recognise a trade union or negotiate or consult with a union official.[206] These provisions are intended to outlaw discrimination against employers who employ non-union labour. However, the law goes further by removing the immunities from trade unions who call industrial action in support of union-only practices. Thus industrial action will not be protected if the reason, or one of the reasons, for which it is done is the fact or belief that a particular employer is employing, has employed or might employ a person who is not a member of a union, or is failing, has failed or might fail to discriminate against such a person.[207] This is an extensive provision which appears to remove immunity from all industrial action associated with non-union membership.[208] Equally, industrial action will not be protected if it constitutes an inducement or attempted inducement of a person to incorporate in a contract for goods or services a term or condition requiring union membership or to refuse to deal with a supplier on union membership grounds.[209] Thus a person who has been denied the right to tender for a contract because he

---

[200] See, generally, TULRCA, s. 234A(7).

[201] See, for example, TULRCA, s. 137 (access to employment), TULRCA, s. 146 (action short of dismissal) and TULRCA, s. 152 (dismissal).

[202] TULRCA, s. 144.

[203] TULRCA, s. 145(1).

[204] TULRCA, s. 145(3).

[205] TULRCA, s. 186.

[206] TULRCA, s. 187(1).

[207] TULRCA, s. 222(1).

[208] It might also be taken as limiting the trade dispute protection provided in TULRCA, s. 244 since s. 244(1)(e) includes as a trade dispute a worker's membership or non-membership of a trade union.

[209] TULRCA, s. 222(3).

refuses to provide union-only labour may not only have a cause of action against the person who prevented him from tendering but also against the trade union which induced that person to exclude him.

11.52 There are also a series of parallel provisions which seek to remove immunity from industrial action aimed at union recognition requirements. Industrial action is not protected if it constitutes an inducement or attempted inducement of a person to incorporate in a contract for the supply of goods or services a term or condition requiring union recognition or to refuse to deal with a supplier or prospective supplier on union-recognition grounds.[210] Further, a union has no immunity where it seeks to interfere with the supply (whether under a contract or not) of goods or services by inducing or threatening to induce employees to break or interfere with their contracts of employment if the supplier is not the employer under the contract of employment and the reason, or one of the reasons, for the interference is the fact or belief that the supplier does not or might not recognise a trade union or negotiate or consult with its officials.[211] In a similar vein, industrial action is not protected if the reason, or one of the reasons, for calling it is the fact or belief that an employer has dismissed one or more employees who have taken part in unofficial industrial action.[212] In sum, these provisions concentrate upon the subject matter of a dispute and withdraw immunity even where there is a primary dispute which has the support of a ballot.

UNION LIABILITY

11.53 The Employment Act 1982

As we saw at the start of this chapter, the Trade Disputes Act 1906 granted trade unions complete immunity from actions in delict. This arrangement was continued by the Trade Union and Labour Relations Act 1974.[213] However, this provision was repealed in 1982[214] so that trade unions were put in the same position as their officials and only had protection from legal action if they could establish immunity under the Trade Union and Labour Relations Act 1974, s. 13. The result is that presently unions are liable for unlawful industrial action if, but only if, that action was authorised or endorsed by union officials or committees.[215] Initially this requirement was satisfied where the action was authorised or endorsed by any of the following:

(a) by the principal executive committee (PEC);

(b) by any other person empowered by the union's rules to authorise or endorse acts of the kind in question;

(c) by the president or general secretary;

(d) by any other official who is an employed official;

(e) by any committee of the union to whom an employed official regularly reports.[216]

---

[210] TULRCA, s. 225(1).
[211] TULRCA, s. 225(2).
[212] TULRCA, s. 223.
[213] Section 14.
[214] EA 1982, s. 15.
[215] TULRCA, s. 20(1) and (2).
[216] EA 1982, s. 15(3).

11.54 The present law

However, these rules on the liability of trade unions for industrial action were amended by the Employment Act 1990[217] so as to widen the categories of people who could authorise or endorse industrial action on behalf of a trade union and stiffen the rules on repudiation.[218] The present law is that an act will be taken to have been authorised or endorsed by a trade union if it was done, or was authorised or endorsed —

(a) by any person empowered by the rules to do, authorise or endorse acts of the kind in question; or

(b) by the PEC or the president or general secretary; or

(c) by any other committee of the union or any other official of the union (whether employed by it or not).[219]

The principal effect of this change has been to make unions responsible for the acts of shop stewards or committees of shop stewards who call or take part in industrial action even although the union rule book does not authorise or may even specifically deny shop stewards the right to call industrial action on behalf of their union. This also means that unions are required to ballot members to obtain their support for industrial action called by a shop steward unless the repudiation rules discussed in the next paragraph are activated. The idea of union responsibility is developed further by providing that, as far as para. (c) is concerned, any group of persons constituted in accordance with the rules of the union is a committee of the union; and that an act shall be taken to have been done, authorised or endorsed by, or by any member of, any group of persons of which he is a member, the purposes of which include organising or co-ordinating industrial action.[220] These vicarious liability rules apply notwithstanding anything in the rules of the union, or in any contract or rule of law.[221]

11.55 *Repudiation.* An act shall not be taken to have been authorised or endorsed by the union by virtue of para. (c) if it was repudiated by the PEC or the president or general secretary as soon as reasonably practicable after coming to the knowledge of any of them.[222] For such repudiation to be effective, a number of detailed and complex requirements have to be fulfilled. Written notice of the repudiation must be given to the committee or official in question without delay.[223] Further, the union must do its best to give individual written notice of the fact and date of repudiation without delay to every member of the union who the union has reason to believe is taking part, or might otherwise take part, in the repudiated action and to the employer of every such member.[224] The notice which the members receive must contain the following statement —

"Your union has repudiated the call (or calls) for industrial action to which the notice relates and will give no support to unofficial industrial action taken in

---

[217] EA 1990, s. 6.
[218] It fulfils the proposals contained in the Green Paper, *Unofficial Action and the Law* (Cm. 821, October 1989).
[219] TULRCA, s. 20(2).
[220] TULRCA, s. 20(3).
[221] TULRCA, s. 20(4).
[222] TULRCA, s. 21(1).
[223] TULRCA, s. 21(2)(a).
[224] TULRCA, s. 21(2)(b)(i) and (ii).

response to it (or them). If you are dismissed while taking unofficial industrial action, you will have no right to complain of unfair dismissal''[225]

If the union should fail to comply with any of these notice requirements, the repudiation must be treated as ineffective.[226] A party to a commercial contract which has or may be interfered with and who has not received written notice of the repudiation, may request the PEC president or general secretary to confirm the repudiation within three months and a failure to confirm forthwith in writing will render that repudiation ineffective.[227] Finally, enhanced powers are given to a court which is granting an interdict against a trade union to require the union to take such steps as the court considers appropriate for ensuring —

(a) that there is no, or no further, inducement of persons to take part or to continue to take part in industrial action; and

(b) that no person engages in any conduct after the granting of the interdict by virtue of having been induced before it was granted to take part or to continue to take part in industrial action.[228]

11.56 Delicts outwith s. 219

These statutory rules setting out the liability of a trade union only apply where the acts in question entail the commission of a delict listed in the Trade Union and Labour Relations (Consolidation) Act 1992, s. 219. If another type of wrong is committed such as trespass or nuisance[229] or the proceedings against the union are for contempt of court[230] a union's liability will depend upon the common law. The exact nature of a union's vicarious liability at common law was discussed in *Heatons Transport (St Helens) Ltd v. TGWU*[231] where the House of Lords had to consider the scope of the authority of a shop steward where the union's rules were unclear. In this case it was held that union officers not only bind their union when they act in conformity with their express authority but that they also possess some sort of implied authority which also makes the union responsible for their acts. The exact extent of this implied authority is unclear although when considering its scope, reference can be made to the union rule book, its customs and practices and even to a shop steward's handbook.[232]

11.57 Damages

The effect of these provisions is to make trade unions the subjects of court proceedings. In the past when trade unions enjoyed blanket immunity, actions raised by employers against union officials tended to be for interdicts only. Interdicts can now be awarded against the union as well. However, given the fact that unions do have assets, there is an increased likelihood that employers will sue trade unions in damages where unlawful industrial action has caused them loss. However, the Trade Union and Labour Relations (Consolidation) Act 1992 places

---

[225] TULRCA, s. 21(3). See Chapter Five, para. 5.75 for the unfair dismissal rules for unofficial industrial action.
[226] TULRCA, s. 21(4).
[227] TULRCA, s. 21(6).
[228] TULRCA, s. 20(6). For the problems associated with these repudiation requirements, see K. Miller and C. Woolfson, ''Timex: Industrial Relations and the Use of the Law in the 1990s'' (1994) 23 ILJ 209.
[229] *Thomas v. NUM (South Wales Area)* [1985] ICR 886; *News Group Newspapers Ltd v. SOGAT 82 (No. 2)* [1987] ICR 181.
[230] *Express Star Ltd v. NGA (1982)* [1986] IRLR 222, CA.
[231] [1973] AC 15.
[232] *Heatons*, above. *Cf General Aviation Services (UK) Ltd v. TGWU* [1976] IRLR 224, HL.

limits on the amount of damages which can be awarded against trade unions in actions in delict. The present limits are as follows:

    (a £10,000, if the union has less than 5,000 members;

    (b) £50,000, if it has 5,000 or more members but less than 25,000 members;

    (c) £125,000 if it has 25,000 or more members but less than 100,000 members;

    (d) £250,000, if it has 100,000 or more members.[233]

Clearly, these limits only apply where the pursuer can establish that his losses are at least as much as the appropriate maximum statutory award. On the other hand, if the employer was awarded damages against the union and the industrial action continued, he would be at liberty to sue the union anew for further damages. It is also worth pointing out that the limits are only applicable to an action by an individual pursuer. If there are a number of pursuers, each can sue and be awarded the appropriate maximum sum assuming that the necessary level of loss can be established. Finally, it must be stressed these limits only apply in relation to damages actions in delict.[234] They have no relevance in the case of a fine against a union for contempt of court.[235]

11.58 *Protected property.* Certain categories of union property are protected in terms of damages awards. Where a pursuer is seeking to recover damages or expenses against a trade union, its trustees acting in their official capacity, or, its members or officials on behalf of themselves and all the other members, no part of that amount can be recovered against the union's protected property.[236] This encompasses any property:

    (a) belonging to trustees otherwise in their capacity as such;

    (b) belonging to any member of the union otherwise than jointly or in common with the other members;

    (c) belonging to any official of the union who is neither a member nor a trustee;

    (d) comprised in a political fund; or

    (e) comprised in a provident benefits fund.[237]

11.59 Award of interdicts

It was mentioned in the previous section that although it was always possible to sue a union official in damages for authorising unlawful industrial action, the usual remedy was that of interdict to stop the action taking place or to prevent it

---

[233] TULRCA, s. 22(2). The Secretary of State may by order vary these limits — TULRCA, s. 22(3).

[234] Moreover, certain actions in delict and quasi-delict are also exempted from the above limits. Thus, actions for personal injury for negligence, nuisance or breach of duty; or actions for breach of duty in connection with the ownership, occupation, possession, control or use of property (whether heritable or moveable) and proceedings under the Consumer Protection Act 1987, Pt I are not subject to the appropriate limits: see TULRCA, s. 22(1).

[235] See, for example, the fines imposed against the NGA in connection with the Stockport Messenger dispute, discussed in John Gennard, "The Implications of the Stockport Messenger Group Dispute," (1984) 15(3) IRJ 7.

[236] TULRCA, s. 23(1).

[237] TULRCA, s. 23(2). "Provident benefits" includes any payment, expressly authorised by the rules of the union, which is made to a member during sickness or incapacity from personal injury or while out of work, or to an aged member by way of superannuation, or to a member who has met with an accident or has lost his tools by fire or theft, and includes funeral expenses paid on the death of a member or his wife, or a payment as provision for the children of a deceased member — TULRCA, s. 23(3).

continuing. Although, as we have seen, damages actions are now competent against trade unions, it is still the case that, even where the union is the defender, the initial proceedings will be for interdict. The normal remedy is that of interim interdict.[238] This is on the premiss that at some later date there will be a full trial of the action where a permanent interdict will be awarded and possibly damages as well. In most cases, however, the pursuer is happy to obtain a remedy which effectively ends the action and will not insist that the case proceed to proof.[239] This means that interim interdict can be considered as the primary remedy in industrial conflict case.[240]

11.60 *Interim interdicts.* In order to prevent interdicts being awarded without the union being given the opportunity to state a defence, it is declared that where there is an application for an interdict in the absence of the union and the union has claimed, or in the opinion of the court would be likely to claim, that it acted in contemplation or furtherance of a trade dispute, the court shall not grant the interdict unless satisfied that all steps which in the circumstances were reasonable have been taken with a view to securing that notice of the application and an opportunity of being heard with respect to the application have been given to the union.[241] There is evidence from both sides of the border that judges have sometimes ignored these directions.[242] This is the extent of the statutory directions for the award of interdicts in Scotland.

11.61 *Statutory immunity in England and Wales.* There is, however, an additional provision applicable only south of the border. This declares that, for the avoidance of doubt, where an interlocutory injunction is sought against a union and the union claims that it acted in contemplation or furtherance of a trade dispute, the court shall, when exercising its discretion, have regard to the likelihood of the union establishing a statutory defence.[243] This provision was enacted in the wake of the decision of the House of Lords in *American Cyanamid Co. v. Ethicon Ltd*[244] which had held that in interlocutory proceedings the important issue was whether there was a serious issue to be tried and, if so, then to consider where the balance of convenience lay. This latter point entails discovering whether the plaintiff would

---

[238] See, for example, *Scottish and Universal Newspapers Ltd v. Smith* 1982 SLT 160.

[239] See the speech of Lord Diplock in *NWL Ltd v. Woods and Nelson* [1979] ICR 876, HL at p. 880 who declared that because of the "practical realities" trade disputes actions rarely came to full trial. In *Dimbleby & Sons Ltd v. NUJ* [1984] ICR 386, HL, at pp. 405–406, Lord Diplock argued that because of the Employment Acts 1980 and 1982 these practical realities were no longer apposite so that employees were much more likely to sue trade unions in damages.

[240] Although an employer may also seek interim suspension of a union's instruction to cease work. See the decision of Lord Cullen in *Maersk Co. Ltd v. NUS* 1988 SLT 828, OH.

[241] TULRCA, s. 221(1).

[242] See, for example, K. D. Ewing's letter to the Editor of the Scots Law Times published at 1981 SLT (News) 99, complaining about the decision of the vacation judge in *Scottish and Universal Newspapers Ltd v. Smith* 1982 SLT 160 to grant interim interdict without appearance by the respondent. See also Sandra Fredman, "The Right to Strike: Policy and Principle" (1987) 103 LQR 176 who points out that in *Barretts & Baird (Wholesale) Ltd v. IPCS* [1987] IRLR 3, an *ex parte* injunction was initially granted over the telephone. See also the litigation ensuing out of the Timex dispute in Dundee, discussed by K. Miller and C. Woolfson in "Timex: Industrial Relations and the Use of the Law in the 1990s" (1994) 23 ILJ 209.

[243] TULRCA, s. 221(2).

[244] [1975] AC 396. Formerly under English law it was necessary for the plaintiff to establish that he had a *prima facie* case, i.e. one to which there was *prima facie* no defence.

suffer more damage by the non-award of the injunction than the defendant would if it was awarded. Although this was not a labour law case, the decision did have important consequences for interlocutory relief in trades disputes. For, if a plaintiff can be awarded an injunction simply by establishing that there is a serious issue to be tried, there is an obvious danger than an injunction will be awarded to an employer in an industrial dispute case without any consideration as to whether or not the union can establish a statutory defence. The award of the injunction is all the more likely when one considers that, given the nature of industrial action, the employer will invariably be able to show that the balance of convenience lies with him because of the economic losses which he is or is likely to suffer. Since the award of the injunction is almost certain to end the dispute, the *American Cyanamid* approach would have meant that the case would have gone against the union without any real consideration of the substantive legal questions.[245]

11.62 *The position in Scotland.* It has been claimed that the reason why such a provision was not applied in Scotland was because parliament thought that such a provision was unnecessary because it would merely have given effect to the existing Scots law.[246] This claim is borne out by the decision of Lord Avonside in *Square Grip Reinforcement Co. Ltd v. Macdonald*,[247] where a clear distinction was made between the merits of the case and the balance of convenience question. This case represents the traditional approach of the Scottish judges and entails a consideration of two questions. First, whether a *prima facie* or substantial case has been established; and second, an analysis of where the balance of convenience lies. It has been argued that this approach gives substantial weight to the legal rights of the parties.[248] In the last few years, however, an alternative "palm tree"[249] approach has been applied in the Scottish cases. In this approach the question of the defender's legal rights is not considered as a separate issue but is subsumed within the question of the balance of convenience. Its application has been supported by Lord Fraser of Tullybelton in *NWL Ltd v. Woods and Nelson*[250] who declared that "[w]hether the likelihood of success should be regarded as one of the elements of the balance of convenience, or as a separate matter, seems to me to be an academic question of no real importance, but my inclination is in favour of the former alternative".

11.63 Nevertheless, there is a problem with this alternative approach in that the likelihood of establishing a trade dispute defence simply becomes one issue amongst others in establishing where the balance of convenience lies. A great deal is left to the discretion of the judge in establishing what weight to give to the likelihood factor. This is illustrated in *Scottish and Universal Newspapers Ltd v. Smith*,[251] where Lord Cowie accepted that the defenders had a fair chance of

---

[245] These points are discussed in the speeches of Lords Diplock and Scarman in *NWL Ltd v. Woods and Nelson* [1979] ICR 867, HL.

[246] *Per* Lord Fraser of Tullybelton in *NWL Ltd*, above at p. 884.

[247] 1966 SLT 232. The *Square Grip* case does illustrate one of the major problems for trade unions even with the traditional balance of convenience test, i.e. establishing that they would suffer financial loss if the interdict were awarded. As Lord Avonside put it, in this case "[d]amage to the petitioners might be disastrous and irreparable. Damage to the respondents would be minimal": see his judgment at p. 234.

[248] K. D. Ewing, "Interim Interdicts in Labour Law: A Case for Reform" (1981) JLSS 422.

[249] A soubriquet applies to this approach by Ewing, above.

[250] [1979] ICR 867 at p. 884.

[251] 1982 SLT 160.

establishing that there was a trade dispute and that they were acting in furtherance of it. However, he was of the opinion that this was only one of the elements which had to be taken into account when deciding where the balance of convenience lay. Other matters such as the economic consequences of the action for the pursuers had to be considered. In the end, Lord Cowie concluded that interim interdict should be issued because the balance of convenience lay heavily in favour of the pursuers since the industrial action was having "disastrous effects" on the viability of their business.[252]

11.64 This case illustrates the dangers of the alternative approach in a trade dispute case. It concentrates upon the economic losses sustained by the employer to the detriment of the statutory provisions providing immunity from legal action which parliament has created. The most extreme example of this inversion of priorities is *Phestos Shipping Co. Ltd v. Kurmiawan*[253] where the Second Division introduced an additional element to the balance of convenience question by arguing that the workers' grievances could be resolved better by legal action for breach of contract rather than by a strike when deciding whether or not the industrial action could continue. In this case Lord Justice-Clerk Wheatley considered that it was unnecessary for him to form a view as to whether or not the Lord Ordinary was correct on the substantive law. In his opinion, the balance of convenience was so overwhelmingly in favour of the pursuers, given the amount of losses that they were sustaining, that consideration of the legal issues was irrelevant. As one commentator has argued, this decision turns the traditional test on its head because it permits legal questions to be ignored if the balance of convenience question is heavily in favour of one side.[254] This modern "palm tree" approach pays insufficient regard to the statutory immunity issue and is, on this basis, contrary to the intention of parliament.

11.65 *Breach of interdict.* It is worth noting that Scots law demands that the pursuer must specify the reasons for his request for interdict in his written pleadings.[255] It is at the discretion of the court whether or not to grant the interdict and whether or not to award it in the exact terms sought. In addition, where an interdict is awarded it should be no wider than is necessary to curb the alleged illegal actings.[256] In the context of industrial action this means that the terms of the interdict must be clear and specific and no wider than is necessary to prevent any unlawful conduct, so that lawful conduct remains unaffected by it.[257] If the defenders should fail to comply with the terms of the interdict after it has been served on them, the pursuer can commence proceedings for breach.[258] Such proceedings require the concurrence of the Lord Advocate.[259] The usual remedies are fines or even imprisonment. Although there is no express authority on the

---

[252] This decision was upheld by an Extra Division reported at 1982 SLT 162. See also *Star Offshore Services plc v. NUS* 1988 SLT 836, OH (Lord Allanbridge).

[253] 1983 SLT 388.

[254] Douglas Brodie (1984) 13 ILJ 170.

[255] See Lord M'Laren in *Fleming v. Liddesdale District Committee* (1897) 24 R 281.

[256] *Murdoch v. Murdoch* 1973 SLT (Notes) 13.

[257] See the decision of the First Division in *Timex Electronics Corporation v. AEEU* 1994 SLT 438.

[258] The difficulties that this procedure can present in cases such as factory occupations where there are a large number of defenders are illustrated in *Plessey Co. plc v. Wilson* 1983 SLT 139 discussed by K. Miller at (1982) 11 ILJ 115.

[259] For the appropriate procedure for this type of case, see W. W. McBryde and N. J. Downie, *Petition Procedure in the Court of Session* (1988) at pp. 145–147.

point, in Scotland, sequestration of the assets of a trade union which has failed to obey an interdict does appear to be a competent remedy since it has been used for breach of interdict in family law cases.[260] In England, sequestration proceedings have become a regular feature of modern trade dispute cases. It would seem that, in deciding whether the union can be held vicariously liable for the contempts of its officers or members, it is the common law rules which must be applied.[261] Before a union will be entitled to return of its assets after they have been sequestrated, it must be shown to have purged its contempt. Usually this will entail some apology to the court, although it may be enough for the union by its actions to recognise the authority of the court.[262]

11.66 *Rights of members of the public.* Since the Trade Union Reform and Employment Rights Act 1993, individuals who are affected by unlawful industrial action have the right to seek an order against the union in court. Individuals have the right to apply to the Court of Session for an order where they claim that any trade union or other person has done, or is likely to do, an unlawful act to induce any person to take part in industrial action, and an effect or a likely effect of that action is or will be to (1) prevent or delay the supply of goods or services, or (2) reduce the quality of goods or services supplied.[263] Industrial action is unlawful if it is actionable in delict, or, where it is called by the union, if it could form the basis of an application by a union member that the action has not been supported by a ballot.[264] It is immaterial whether or not the individual is entitled to be supplied with the goods or services in question.[265] There appears to be no need to show that material loss or damage, or even inconvenience, has been, or would be, suffered by the individual as a result of the industrial action. The provision undoubtedly constitutes a significant extension of the range of individuals who have the authority by court order to restrain unlawful industrial action. It also renders it unnecessary for it to be established that the union had any intention to harm the actual individual or that in some sense the action was directed against him, as is usually required by the economic delicts.[266]

If a court is satisfied that a claim is well-founded, it must make such an order as it considers appropriate for requiring the union to take steps for ensuring (1) that no, or no further, act is done to induce any persons to take part or to continue to take part in the industrial action, and (2) that no person engages in industrial action after the making of the order.[267] The court has the power to award such an interim order as it considers appropriate.[268] If the proceedings are interim, it is likely that the balance of convenience will be important as it is in other cases where interdict is sought to restrain alleged unlawful industrial action.

---

[260] *Ross v. Ross* (1885) 12 R 1351; *Edgar v. Fisher's Trs* (1893) 21 R 59.

[261] *Express Star Ltd v. NGA (1982)* [1986] IRLR 222, CA.

[262] *Richard Read Transport Ltd v. NUM (South Wales Area)* [1985] IRLR 67. For a discussion of contempt under English law see Lord Wedderburn *The Worker and the Law* (3rd edn, 1986) at pp. 705–716.

[263] TULRCA, s. 235A(1) as inserted by TURERA, s. 22.

[264] TULRCA, s. 235A(2).

[265] TULRCA, s. 235A(3). *Cf* the economic delicts where usually some sort of contractual relationship would have to be established. See, for example, *Falconer v. ASLEF and NUR* [1986] IRLR 331 where the individual in that case had bought his ticket in advance.

[266] See, for example, *Barretts & Baird (Wholesale) Ltd v. IPCS* [1987] IRLR 3 and *Lonrho plc v. Fayed* [1989] 2 WLR 631, CA.

[267] TULRCA, s. 235A(4).

[268] TULRCA, s. 235A(5).

11.67 *Commissioner for protection against unlawful industrial action.* The Trade Union Reform and Employment Rights Act 1993 also created a new office, the commissioner for protection against unlawful industrial action. The commissioner can provide assistance to individuals who are the actual or prospective parties in proceedings where it is alleged that a union has called unlawful industrial action which affects the supply of goods or services.[269] Such individuals may apply to the commissioner for assistance and the commissioner, as soon as reasonably practicable after receiving the application, must consider it and decide whether and to what extent it should be granted.[270] In deciding this question the commissioner must have regard to the following matters (1) whether it is unreasonable, having regard to the complexity of the case, to expect the individual to deal with it unaided, and (2) whether, in the commissioner's opinion, the case involves a matter of substantial public interest or concern.[271] The assistance provided may include the making of arrangements for, or for the commissioner to bear the cost of, the giving of advice or assistance by a solicitor or counsel, and the representation of the applicant in court in steps preliminary or incidental to the proceedings, or in arriving at or giving effect to a compromise agreement.[272] There are also provisions which enable the commissioner to recover expenses if the assisted individual's action is successful.[273]

THE LAW OF PICKETING

11.68 It is an obvious tactic for employees who are in dispute with their employer not only to withdraw their labour but also to picket outside his premises in order to turn back other employees and to prevent or disrupt the flow of goods or supplies entering or leaving those premises. It would seem that this activity is not *per se* unlawful.[274] However, it is very easy for pickets to commit civil wrongs such as nuisance or trespass. Moreover, pickets may also be in danger of breaking the criminal law through the common law offence of breach of the peace and the statutory offence of obstruction of a police officer in the execution of his duty, or, in extreme cases, the serious crime of mobbing and rioting.[275] There is also a specific statutory offence relevant to pickets contained in the Trade Union and Labour Relations (Consolidation) Act 1992, s. 241. It is important to consider each of these in turn.

11.69 The immunities
It is lawful for a person in contemplation or furtherance of a trade dispute to attend at or near his own place of work for the purpose only of peacefully obtaining or communicating information, or peacefully persuading any person to work or abstain from working.[276] This provision restricts lawful picketing to an employee's own place of work. Under the original provisions[277] the only restriction on the location of a picket-line was that it could not take place outside a person's home.

---

[269] TULRCA, s. 235B(1) as inserted by TURERA, s. 22.
[270] TULRCA, s. 235B(4) and (5).
[271] TULRCA, s. 235B(3).
[272] TULRCA, s. 235A(6).
[273] See TULRCA, s. 235C as inserted by TURERA, s. 22.
[274] *Hubbard v. Pitt* [1975] ICR 308, CA.
[275] *Sloan v. Macmillan* 1922 JC 1.
[276] TULRCA, s. 220(1)(a).
[277] TULRA, s. 15.

Changes introduced in 1980 sought to eradicate the practice of secondary picketing, and, in particular, render unlawful the activities of ''flying pickets'' i.e. union members who were prepared to picket any factory or business premises in the country in order to further a dispute.[278] Any attempt to argue under the present law that these people are not pickets but merely demonstrators, appears to have been scotched by two recent decisions of the English courts.[279] Although the statutory language seems to create a right to picket since it declares that it shall be lawful etc., the House of Lords has held that such a view is inaccurate. In *Broome v. DPP*[280] it was made clear that statute merely protected the attendance of pickets at the places specified and then only if their attendance was for one of the protected purposes; nothing grants any authority to pickets to require other people to stop or even to listen to them. A picket who attempts to stop vehicles by standing in front of them is guilty of obstruction under English law[281] and could be arrested for a breach of the peace in Scotland.

11.70 *Conditions for immunity.* Before there can by any immunity for picketing under the civil law, three requirements must be satisfied. The first is that the picketing must be undertaken in contemplation or furtherance of a trade dispute.[282] The second requirement is that the picketing must only be carried out by persons attending at or near their own place of work. There is some uncertainty about the exact meaning of ''place of work'' since it is not defined. The Secretary of State's Code of Practice on Picketing considers that the purport of this phrase is to permit attendance at an entrance to, or exit from, the factory, site or office at which the picket works. However, problems still remain where the factory or site is made up of a number of self-contained units. As far as the requirement that the picketing should be ''at or near'' that place of work, it is clear that the word ''near'' is to be interpreted in a realistic and purposive way which takes account of the particular circumstances of the case and the geographical location of the employer's premises. Thus pickets were still near their workplace when they had to picket at the entrance to an industrial estate which was some 1,232 yards from their employer's premises.[283]

11.71 Special rules are created for those employees who have more than one place of work (e.g. mobile workers) or where the location of their workplace makes picketing impracticable there (e.g. oilrig workers). In such cases a person's place of work is any premises of his employer from which he works or from which his work is administered.[284] The effectiveness of this provision for mobile workers is circumscribed by the requirement that the place which is picketed must be

---

[278] This provision was used on a number of occasions during the miners' strike of 1984–85 by small employers concerned that such activity might put them out of business. See, for example, *Richard Read (Transport) Ltd v. NUM (South Wales Area)* [1985] IRLR 67 and the unsuccessful actions raised by three Stirling road haulage firms to obtain interdicts against the Scottish Area of the NUM for secondary picketing — *Glasgow Herald* March 31, 1984. See also Roger Benedictus, ''The Use of the Law of Tort in the Miners' Dispute'' (1985) 14 ILJ 176.

[279] *Thomas v. NUM (South Wales Area)* [1985] ICR 886, HC; *News Groups Newspapers Ltd v. SOGAT 82 (No. 2)* [1987] ICR 181.

[280] [1974] ICR 84, HL.

[281] *Broome*, above.

[282] An issue discussed earlier in this chapter. See paras 11.26–11.33.

[283] *Rayware Ltd v. TGWU* [1989] IRLR 134, CA. Approved in Scotland in *Timex Electronics Corporation v. AEEU* 1994 SLT 438.

[284] TULRCA, s. 220(2).

premises of the employer. Consequently, even where the workers, when working normally, perform many of their activities during the course of their employment at the premises of one major customer, there will be no right to picket at that place since that location does not form part of their own employer's premises.[285] However, a worker not in employment can picket his former place of work so long as his last employment was terminated in connection with a trade dispute or the termination of his employment was one of the circumstances giving rise to a trade dispute.[286] This provision only applies for as long as the picket remains unemployed. It can provide an empty right, particularly where the employer dismisses his employees employed at one factory (plant A) and then transfers all of the business which was formerly conducted there to another of his factories (plant B). In such a case the dismissed workers would be entitled to picket plant A but not plant B where their work is now being performed. Thus they would be restricted to picketing premises which the employer no longer use![287] The third special case applies to union officials. They can picket at any place of work of a member of the union whom they are accompanying and whom they represent so long as it is for the purpose of peacefully obtaining or communicating information, or peacefully persuading any person to work or abstain from working.[288] An official who has been elected or appointed to represent some of the members of the union can only represent those members on the picket line. However, a national official can represent all of the members.[289]

11.72 The third requirement for lawful picketing is that the only purpose of the picketing must be peacefully to obtain or communicate information or peacefully to persuade a person to work or abstain from working. If the picketing is not peaceful there can be no immunity in law.[290] Equally, if the picketing involves some other purpose, such as where pickets walk around in a circle in front of factory gates in order to seal them off from traffic,[291] there can be no immunity since this entails a purpose other then the specific statutory purposes. Picketing which is in breach of any of these requirements loses the statutory protection and also takes the activities of the pickets outwith the immunities provided by the Trade Union and Labour Relations (Consolidation) Act 1992, s. 219. In such circumstances an employer would have a cause of action against the individual pickets,[292] the union officer who organised the picketing and against the union itself for such delicts as inducement of breach of contract, interference with contractual relations and intimidation.[293] Picketing involving large numbers of people is not *per se* illegal: although in such a case it would not be difficult to

---

[285] *Mersey Docks and Harbour Co. v. Verrinder* [1982] IRLR 152.

[286] TULRCA, s. 220(3).

[287] In *News Group Newspapers Ltd v. SOGAT 82 (No. 2)* [1987] ICR 181 it was held that dismissed printers had no right to picket outside the company's new plant at Wapping since this had never been their place of work. They could only picket outside the company's premises in Bouverie St which were no longer in use.

[288] TULRCA, s. 220(1)(b).

[289] TULRCA, s. 220(4). This provision ensures that the members on a picket line cannot be swamped by union officials brought in from other branches or districts of the union.

[290] *Messenger Newspapers Group Ltd v. NGA (1982)* [1984] IRLR 397.

[291] *Tynan v. Balmer* [1967] 1 QB 91. See also *Mersey Docks and Harbour Co. v. Verrinder* [1982] IRLR 152 where the judge considered that the purpose of the picket line was not merely to obtain or communicate information; it was also intended to regulate the flow of container traffic between the pickets' employer and his major customer.

[292] *United Biscuits (UK) Ltd v. Fall* [1979] IRLR 110.

[293] See, generally, *News Group Newspapers Ltd v. SOGAT 82 (No. 2)* [1987] ICR 181.

establish some ulterior purpose.[294] Equally, mass picketing may make it easier to establish that the picket has an intimidating effect so as to amount to unlawful inducement to employees to break their contracts, unlawful interference with the performance of those contracts and unlawful inducement to persons to interfere with such performance.[295] Further, picketing is not necessarily unlawful simply because it may involve the commission of offences under the Trade Union and Labour Relations (Consolidation) Act 1992, s. 241.[296] Nevertheless, the activities can go beyond s. 220 and therefore outwith the immunities conferred by it if they involve the commission of unprotected wrongs such as nuisance or trespass; or the picketing is secondary in nature.[297]

11.73 *Nuisance and trespass.* As far as nuisance is concerned, there has been a conflict of authority in England as to whether picketing *per se* amounts to a nuisance, or whether it is necessary for there also to be some violence, obstruction, annoyance or molestation for the picketing to constitute a nuisance.[298] It is submitted that the correct view and the one supported by the most recent authorities[299] is that picketing along does not constitute a nuisance. There must at the very least be some unreasonable obstruction of the highway[300] or possibly some unreasonable harassment of those wishing to work.[301] Although there is no express authority on the point, it is submitted that picketing would constitute a nuisance under Scots law so long as the picketing caused some annoyance to, or interfered with, the property rights of neighbouring proprietors.[302] A trespass can also be committed by pickets when they stray onto the lands of another without his permission. This is all the more likely where the picket develops into an occupation of the employer's premises. Formerly, there might have been some protection against the consequences of such an occupation since the First Division had held in *Plessey Co. plc v. Wilson*[303] that, where the occupation primarily involved interferences with the trade or business of the employer, there could be a defence by the provision that an interference with the trade, business or employment of some other person would not be actionable in delict if it was done in contemplation or furtherance of a trade dispute.[304] However, as a result of the *Plessey* case, the provision was repealed and is not to be found in the Trade Union and Labour Relations (Consolidation) Act 1992, s. 219.[305] This means that an

---

[294] See the speech of Lord Reid in *Broome v. DPP* [1974] ICR 84, HL.

[295] *Timex Electronics Corporation v. AEEU*, 1994 SLT 438, IH.

[296] *Thomas v. NUM (South Wales Area)* [1985] ICR 886.

[297] Both grounds are discussed in *Thomas*, above and in *News Group Newspapers*, above.

[298] Compare *J. Lyons & Sons v. Wilkins* [1899] 1 Ch 255 and *Ward Lock & Co. v. Operative Printers' Assistants' Society* (1906) 22 TLR 327. See also *Hubbard v. Pitt* [1975] ICR 308, CA and *Mersey Docks and Harbour Co. v. Verrinder* [1982] IRLR 152 and in Scotland *Galt v. Philp* 1983 SCCR 295.

[299] See *Thomas v. NUM (South Wales Area)* [1985] ICR 886 and *News Group Newspapers Ltd v. SOGAT 82 (No. 2)* [1987] ICR 181.

[300] *News Group*, above.

[301] *Per* Scott J in *Thomas*, above at p. 915. Doubted by Stuart Smith J in *News Group*, above at p. 206. Under English law, special damage has to be proved in order to establish a public nuisance.

[302] See Niall R. Whitty, "Nuisance" in *Stair Memorial Encyclopaedia of the Laws of Scotland*, Vol. 14 (1988) at para. 2046.

[303] [1983] IRLR 139. But see also the judgment of Lord Dunpark in *Phestos Shipping Co. Ltd v. Kurmiawan* 388 at p. 391.

[304] TULRA 1974, s. 13(2).

[305] EA 1982, s. 19(1).

employer is now free to obtain interdicts in order to prevent the continued unlawful occupation of his premises.[306]

11.74 *Secondary action by primary pickets.* The activities of pickets, even at their own place of work, could involve unlawful secondary industrial action since their attempts to persuade lorry drivers etc. to turn back might result in them inducing breaches or interfering with contracts between employees and an employer who is not a party to the trade dispute. In order to ensure that immunity is retained in such circumstances, picketing at a worker's own place of work is now the only form of protected secondary action so long as that worker's employer is a party to the dispute; the same rules also apply to union officials if they are accompanying union members whom they represent.[307]

11.75 The Code of Practice

Those responsible for organising pickets should also be aware of the Secretary of State's Code of Practice on Picketing. This Code advises the organiser *inter alia* to seek directions from the police on the number of people who should be present on the picket line. This advice is reinforced by para. 31 which declares that large numbers on a picket line are likely to give rise to fear and resentment amongst those wishing to cross it and recommends that pickets and their organisers should ensure that, in general, the number of pickets does not exceed six at any entrance to a workplace; frequently a smaller number will be appropriate. The Code of Practice is admissible in evidence and can be taken into account by a court[308] and para. 31 has had a significant impact on the conduct of picketing and has been relied upon by the courts in phrasing the terms of the injunction or interdict applicable where there has been mass picketing.[309] The Code has been criticised for being a misuse of the idea of Codes of Practice, particularly in relation to the section on essential supplies and services.[310] The present law and the Code of Practice have also been criticised for the strains they place upon the police who have to control the behaviour of pickets and who may be required to decide where people should picket and in what numbers.[311] As a final point the Trade Union and Labour Relations (Consolidation) Act 1992, s. 64 protects a member against unjustifiable disciplinary action *inter alia* where he has failed to take part in a strike or other industrial action.

11.76 Picketing and the criminal law

Pickets receive no protection as far as the criminal law is concerned. There are a number of crimes which can be committed by pickets. The most obvious are

---

[306] See the decision of Lord Clyde in *Caterpillar Tractors plc v. Brannan, Glasgow Herald* March 26, 1987 and the decision of Lord Cameron of Lochbroom in *Shell UK Ltd v. McGillivray* 1991 SLT 667.

[307] TULRCA, s. 224.

[308] TULRCA, s. 297.

[309] See the terms of the injunction awarded by Scott J in *Thomas v. NUM (South Wales Area)* [1985] ICR 886 and Stuart Smith J in *News Group Newspapers Ltd v. SOGAT 82 (No. 2)* [1987] ICR 181 which specifically restricted the number of pickets at any workplace to six. Attempts in both of these cases to avoid the Code by arguing that the people present were demonstrators and not pickets proved unsuccessful since they often broke ranks and dispersed to join the official picket line. The interim interdict awarded in *Timex Electronics v. AEEU* also restricted the picketing to "numbers [not] exceeding six".

[310] I. T. Smith and J. C. Wood, *Industrial Law* (5th edn, 1993) at p. 574.

[311] Lord Wedderburn, *The Worker and the Law* (3rd edn, 1986) at p. 546.

breach of the peace, obstruction of a police officer in the execution of his duty contrary to the Police (Scotland) Act 1967, s. 41, malicious mischief or vandalism and assault.[312] Even peaceful picketing may involve a breach of the peace since the offence can be committed where there is no actual disturbance if it can be shown that the accused's conduct is likely to lead to a disturbance.[313] In English law there is a specific offence of obstruction of the highway contrary to the Highways Act 1980, s. 137. The width of this offence is illustrated by the decision of the House of Lords in *Broome v. DPP*[314] where it was held that a picket had been rightly convicted of obstruction when he stood in front of a lorry holding a placard and shouting at the driver to stop. There is no equivalent statutory offence in Scotland. However, there can be no doubt that a complaint of breach of the peace would be relevant in such circumstances so long as it can be shown that the picket's conduct might reasonably be expected to cause any person to be alarmed, upset or annoyed.[315]

11.77 Moreover, the criminal law also recognises that the police must be given some discretion as regards their control of picket-line behaviour. Under English law the most appropriate offence which enables the police to regulate the behaviour of pickets is that of resisting or wilfully obstructing a constable in the execution of his duty contrary to s. 51(3) of the Police Act 1964. It is clear that the courts have construed this offence as granting a police officer a reasonable discretion in deciding whether he is being obstructed. For example, in *Piddington v. Bates*[316] a police constable asked a picket to move away because he believed that two pickets were enough outside a factory and not three. One picket pushed gently past the policeman. He was arrested and subsequently convicted of obstruction of a police officer in the execution of his duty. In *Tynan v. Balmer*[317] the divisional court upheld the conviction of a picket organiser for obstruction of a police officer when he refused to obey instructions from the police that the pickets should stop walking around in a circle in front of a factory. In Scotland a complaint of obstruction of a police officer under the Police (Scotland) Act 1967, s. 41 would also be applicable in these circumstances.[318] A charge of breach of the peace would also be relevant since it is clear that under Scots law a refusal to move on when requested to do so by the police could competently be charged as a breach of the peace.[319] The wide nature of this common law crime undoubtedly gives the police

---

[312] This point is borne out by the statistics concerning arrests during the miners' strike of 1984–85. In Scotland, of the 1,015 people prosecuted here, 678 were charged with breach of the peace, 249 with obstructing the police and 30 with vandalism. See, generally, Peter Wallington, "Policing the Miners' Strike" (1985) 14 ILJ 145.

[313] See, for example, *Raffaelli v. Heatly* 1949 JC 101 (peeping Tom); *Young v. Heatly* 1959 JC 66 (improper remarks by teacher to pupils in private).

[314] [1974] ICR 84, HL.

[315] See the statement on breach of peace by Lord Justice General Emslie in *Stewart v. Jessop* 1988 SCCR 492, and *Norris v. McLeod* 1988 SCCR 572.

[316] [1960] 3 All ER 660.

[317] [1967] 1 QB 91.

[318] This provision is discussed by G. H. Gordon in *The Criminal Law of Scotland* (2nd edn, 1978) at para. 29–12.

[319] *Montgomery v. McLeod* 1977 SLT (Notes) 77.

considerable discretion in controlling the behaviour of pickets in Scotland.[320] In very serious cases, where the behaviour of the pickets through sheer force of numbers is intimidatory or disturbs the public peace, a charge of mobbing and rioting might be libelled.[321]

11.78 There is also a specific statutory offence contained in the Trade Union and Labour Relations (Consolidation) Act 1992, s. 241 which is relevant to pickets. There was a time when prosecutions under the predecessor section[322] appeared to have fallen into disuse.[323] However, there have been two fairly recent reported prosecutions in Scotland and it was used widely in England as a means of regulating the behaviour of pickets during the miners' strike of 1984–85. Interestingly, only four such prosecutions were recorded in Scotland during this period.[324] Section 241(1) declares that a person commits an offence who, with a view to compelling any other person to abstain from doing or to do any act which that person has a legal right to do or abstain from doing, wrongfully and without legal authority:

(1) uses violence to or intimidates such other person or his wife or children, or injures his property; or

(2) persistently follows such other person about from place to place[325]; or

(3) hides any tools, clothes or other property owned or used by such other person, or deprives him or hinders him in the use thereof; or

(4) watches or besets the house or other place where such other person resides, or works, or carries on business, or happens to be, or the approach to such house or place; or

(5) follows such other person with two or more other persons in a disorderly manner in or through any street or road.[326]

11.79 It has always been accepted in Scotland that s. 241 creates only one offence. The five heads listed in the section which appear to set out particular categories of crimes are regarded as merely different ways of committing the same offence. In all prosecutions it must be shown that the act complained of was done with a view to compel etc. and that it was done wrongfully and without legal authority. As far as this last point is concerned it appears that s. 241 does not make anything wrongful that was not wrongful before.[327] This means that the act complained of

---

[320] Indeed, it may even be used in order to prevent people joining a picket line so long as the police have a reasonable apprehension that a breach of the peace will be committed. The turning back of people intending to join picket lines by means of road blocks was certainly a tactic that the police adopted in both Scotland and England during the miners' strike. See Peter Wallington, "Policing the Miners' Strike" (1985) 14 ILJ 145.

[321] *Sloan v. Macmillan* 1922 JC 1. The crime was libelled unsuccessfully against a number of pickets who picketed outside the Longannet Power Station during the miners' strike of 1972. See Peter Wallington, "The Case of the Longannet Miners and the Criminal Liability of Pickets" (1972) 1 ILJ 219. No charges of mobbing and rioting were brought during the 1984–85 miners' strike. This was unlike the position in England where unlawful assembly and riot charges were used. See Wallington (1985), above.

[322] See the Conspiracy and Protection of Property Act 1875, s. 7.

[323] See Richard Kidner, "Picketing and the Criminal Law" (1975) Crim LR 256.

[324] These points are discussed by Peter Wallington in "Policing the Miners' Strike" (1985) 14 ILJ 145.

[325] *Elsey v. Smith* 1982 SCCR 218 where it was held that this particular head of offence can be committed by a car following another on the motorway.

[326] This head of offence can also be committed by persons in a car: see *Elsey*, above.

[327] *Ward Lock & Co. Ltd v. Operative Printers' Assistants' Society* (1906) 22 TLR 327.

must attract either criminal or civil liability itself without reference to s. 241. It is not a defence to argue that the act has immunity from actions in delict under the Trade Union and Labour Relations (Consolidation) Act 1992, s. 219. Acts which do attract such immunity still remain wrongful for the purpose of s. 241.[328] Looking to the five heads of offence listed in s. 241 several points can be made. First, as regards head 1, intimidation need not produce actual fear in the other person. It is enough if threats are used which would arouse in a person of common sense a natural alarm of personal violence or of violence to his family.[329] As far as watching or besetting is concerned, it is clear that a besetting can be committed both outside and inside the relevant place so that an occupation of an employer's premises by his employees can be a breach of s. 241.[330]

---

[328] *Galt v. Philp* 1983 SCCR 295.
[329] *Agnew v. Munro* (1891) 2 Wh 611.
[330] *Galt*, above.

SUBJECT INDEX